ECONOMIC DEVELOPMENT MODEL FOR UNIFORM WEALTH CREATION

SIVAGAMINATHAN KANAKASUNDARAM

BLUEROSE PUBISHERS
India | U.K.

Copyright © Sivagaminathan Kanakasundaram 2025

All rights reserved by author. No part of this publication may be reproduced, stored in a retrieval system or transmitted in any form or by any means, electronic, mechanical, photocopying, recording or otherwise, without the prior permission of the author. Although every precaution has been taken to verify the accuracy of the information contained herein, the publisher assume no responsibility for any errors or omissions. No liability is assumed for damages that may result from the use of information contained within.

BlueRose Publishers takes no responsibility for any damages, losses, or liabilities that may arise from the use or misuse of the information, products, or services provided in this publication.

For permissions requests or inquiries regarding this publication,
please contact:

BLUEROSE PUBLISHERS
www.BlueRoseONE.com
info@bluerosepublishers.com
+91 8882 898 898
+4407342408967

ISBN: 978-93-6783-791-7

First Edition: January 2025

Table of Contents

Chapter 1 – Basics of the Economic Development Model	– 2
Chapter 2 – Growth in Production of Cement & Manufacturing of Cement Plant machineries	– 8
Chapter 3 – Growth in Production of Coal	– 14
Chapter 4 – Production of Consumer Products of Basic Needs	– 23
Chapter 5 - Production of Consumer Products of Secondary Needs	– 48
Chapter 6 – Developments in Communication and Information Broadcasting Sectors	– 61
Chapter 7 – Growth in Production of Drugs and Pharmaceuticals	– 76
Chapter 8 – Growth of Engineering & Construction Industries for Industrial Infrastructure	– 86
Chapter 9 – Growth in Fertilizer, Pesticides and Chemicals Production	– 105
Chapter 10 - Growth in Power Generation, Transmission, Distribution and Manufacturing of Power Generation Equipment	– 125
Chapter 11 – Growth in Machine Building Industry	– 162
Chapter 12 – Growth in Production of Petroleum and Petrochemical Products	– 175
Chapter 13 – Development of Science, Electronics, Research and Defence Establishments	– 207
Chapter 14 – Growth in Production of Steel and Metals (Aluminium, Copper, Manganese, Zinc and Lead)	– 229
Chapter 15 – Growth in Transportation Infrastructure and Services	– 258
Chapter 16 – Growth of Service Sectors including Banking, Insurance and Financial Institutions and Information Technology	– 303
Chapter 17 – Social Development – Achievements and Threats	- 344

1: Basics of the Economic Development Model

The Directive Principles of State Policy, in Articles 36 to 51 of the Indian Constitution, state that:
a. the ownership and control of the material resources of the community are so distributed as best to subserve the common good
b. the operation of the economic system does not result in the concentration of wealth and means of production to the common detriment

The Indian governments believed that
i) development should result in a diminution of economic and social inequalities
ii) process of reducing inequalities should be achieved by raising incomes at lowest levels and reducing incomes at the top.
iii) prevention of private monopolies and concentration of economic power in different fields in the hands of small numbers of individuals was required to reduce disparities in income and wealth.
iv) private monopolies were to be prevented and setting up of smaller and medium size private enterprises and Cooperative Organizations to be encouraged.

Assessment of investments required for Economic Development

Planning Commission of India studied investments made by UK, USA, Japan, etc. during their development phases and found
a) Britain made an average net investment of 10 to 15% during 1870-1913.
b) USA made a net investment of 13 to 16% of the national product (gross investment 21- 24%) to increase national income five-fold between 1869 and 1913 (increase in per capita income by over 130%).
c) Japan made new capital formations of 12% of the national income during 1900-1909, which rose to 17% for the period 1909-19 but declined to 12%. in the period 1920-1929.
d) USSR made a net investment of 20% of the national income in the decade 1928-1938 to increase the national product in 1928 by around 130% in 1940.

A somewhat low rate of capital formation might have been adequate for countries like the U.K. and the U.S.A., in which modern industrialism took root early.

The underdeveloped countries which made a late start had to aim at comparable development within a briefer period. In underdeveloped countries with low standards of living and rapidly increasing population, a rate of growth (in production capacity and production in all sectors) commensurate with needs (forecasted demands) could not be achieved until the rate of capital formation of around 20% of the national income is realized.

Based on this study, following algorithms were developed and used for the development model
1) A doubling of per capita income within a generation or so (that is in 25 to 30 years) required a rate of net investment of the order of 12-15% of the national income and capital formation of around 20% of the national income.
2) The First Five Year Plan (I 5YP) was based on Harrod-Domar model.
3) The II 5YP was made using Mahala Nobis model designed to determine optimal allocation of investment between productive sectors in order to maximize long-run economic growth.
4) Five Year Plans were made on the basis of Incremental Capital-Output Ratio, which is the ratio of investment to be done to targeted increase in National Income.

Investment Planning in Five Year Plans

a) In the I, II and III 5YPs, Investments were planned to obtain rise in National Income of Rs. 1890 Cr (1960-61 prices), Rs. 2680 Cr and Rs. 4500 Cr with an ICOR expected of 1.8:1, 2.3:1 and 2.31:1 respectively.

b) For the IV and V 5YPs, the ICOR assumed were 3.4 and 3.7 respectively.

c) The ICOR, which relates the increase in GDP at market prices to the total investment over the Plan period, was expected to be around 5 in VII 5YP. (7.3.21)

d) An expected investment of Rs. 798000 Cr in VIII 5YP implied an investment rate of 23.2 % of GDP. The stipulated ICOR of 4.1 suggested this investment was expected to generate a growth of 5.6 % in GDP. (8.3.2.8; 8.2.8.2)

e) The projected public sector plan outlay for IX 5YP, consistent with the accelerated GDP growth of 7 % per annum envisaged, was placed at Rs.859200 crore at 1996-97 prices. (9.3.1)
Investment Rate planned in IX plan was 28.3% of GDP at market price. IOCR planned was 4.0 (9. Table 2-4)

f) Investment of 28.41% of GDPmp during X plan was expected to yield a GDP growth rate of 7.93% per annum with an assumed IOCR of 3.58. (10. Table 2.7)
Investment requirement forecasted for X plan was Rs 40,81,700 Cr (including Private investment of Rs 24,76,100 Cr, Public sector investment of Rs. 12,12,800 Cr and Additional required of Rs. 392800 Cr (10. Table 2.14)

g) The total public sector outlay in XI 5YP (Centre, States and including their PSEs) was estimated at Rs 3644718 Cr. The public sector outlay was expected to be 13.54% of GDP compared to the average of 9.46% of GDP that was achieved in the X Plan. (11.1.154)
Investment Rate in XI plan planned was 36.7% of GDPmp, ICOR planned was 4.1 and planned GDP Growth Rate – 9% per annum. (11.2.5) (11. Table 2.2)

Achieved GDP Growth, Rates of Investment and ICOR in Indian Economy (1951-2013) (Ref. 8 Table 1.1 and updates in subsequent plans)

S. No	Period	Growth in GDP at Factor Cost	Investment Rate %	ICOR	Investment by Public Sector in Rs. in Cr.	Investment by Private Sector in Rs. Cr.	Total Investment in Rs. in Cr.
1.	1951-56	3.61%	10.66	2.95	1560 (46.4%)	1800	3360
2.	1956--61	4.27%	14.52	3.40	3650 (54.1%)	3100	6750
3.	1961-66	2.84%	15.45	5.44	8576.5 (67.7%)	4100	12676.5
3A	1966-69 (Annual Plans)	4.66%	15.99	3.43	6756.5		
4.	1969-74	3.08%	17.87	5.80	13655 (60.3%)	8980	22635
5.	1974-75 to 1979-80	3.24%	21.47	6.63	36703 (43.3%)	27048	63751
6.	1980-81 to 1985-86	5.06%	20.98	4.15	68354 (47.8%)	74646	143000
7.	1985-86 to 1989-90	5.81%	22.70	3.91	154218 (45.7%)	168148	322366

S. No	Period	Growth in GDP at Factor Cost	Investment Rate %	ICOR	Investment by Public Sector in Rs. in Cr.	Investment by Private Sector in Rs. in Cr.	Total Investment in Rs. in Cr.
7A.	1985-86 to 1991-92*	5.31%	23.17	4.36			
8	1992-97	6.8% in GDPmp	24.4	3.43	391000 (34.7%)	735801	1126801
9	1997-2002	5.7%	24.3	4.53	5,94,500 (29%)	14,55,500 (71%)	20,50,000
10	2002-07	7.6%	32.4	4.3	2,95,513 (22%)	10,47,191 (78%)	13,43,242
11	2007-12	8%	33.7	4.2	15,36,773 (63.4%)	8,87,504 (36.6%)	24,24,277
12	2012-17 (Planned)	9%			28,90,823	26,83,840 (48.14%)	55,74,663

Strategy of public sector investment - After investing 44% and 30% of total outlay of I and II 5YPs for agriculture, irrigation and power projects, government embarked on development of industrial sector in 3 5YP. (3.3.5. Table 2) It felt that all industries of basic and strategic importance, public utility services and other industries (which were essential and required investment on a scale which only the State, in existed circumstances, could provide) should be in the public sector.

A number of basic industries which required large investments and extensive collaboration with foreign firms or governments and which could be undertaken only on the assurance of future prospects, with no immediate gain in sight, could not normally be started if reliance was to be placed entirely on private enterprise. Moreover, in the case of industries where for technological reasons, the plants had to be large, requiring big investments, by organizing them in the public sector, undue concentration of economic and industrial power in private hands could be prevented. (3.16.2)

Heavy Electricals plants at Hyderabad was started with the collaboration of Czechoslovakia and Barauni and Gujarat Koyali Refineries, Bhilai, Bokaro and Visakhapatnam Steel plants were built with the collaboration of USSR governments, Durgapur Steel Plant with the collaboration of UK government, Rourkela Steel Plant with the collaboration of German government, Noonmati Refinery with the collaboration of Rumania government, Haldia Refinery with the collaboration of French / Rumania governments, etc

The book describes the principles and success of Economic Development Model, adopted by Indian governments, with **average net investment of 21.68% of the national income,** jointly by government, public institutions and private sector, by making planned and coordinated investments, through 11 Five Year Plans in various sectors of economy, required to achieve incremental targeted production capacities in all sectors, which themselves were set to meet the forecasted demands in all sectors and make country self-sufficient.

This investment model, with average 47% of total investment for starting public sector units, helped to achieve incremental production targets in each Five-Year Plan, by reinvesting in new projects or for increasing existing production capacities. The model gave sizable income through continuously increasing dividends by public sector units from 1980-81, which started increasing rapidly from 2006-07 onwards.

Corrective actions suggested to achieve constitutional targets –

1) To advocate for continuation of joint (public and private sectors) investment of 20% of the national income for increasing the production capacities according to forecasted increase in demands, for building national assets and achieving targeted growth in GDP. (As, such planned investment has stopped from 2014)

2) To stop closure of companies, which are producing at or near rated capacities with designed per unit consumption of raw materials and consumables, because they were making cumulative losses accruing from startup periods, without considering production losses in respective sectors after closure of these companies and arranging for meeting the demands for these products.

3) To stop disinvestment in Central Public Sector Establishments to prevent reduction of income to governments in the form of dividends, which have very high potential to increase year after year.

4) To stop strategic sale of CPSEs, with high potential for growth and good market share, to prevent creation of corporate house monopoly in critical sectors by transfer of national assets.

5) To stop privatization of Rs. 600,000 Cr worth of national assets under Asset Monetization Plan, which is aimed to sell most national assets, hiving off business of ONGC, privatization of airports and port operations, disinvestment in insurance and banking operations, etc.

Approach

1) Rate of investment done in the past and GDP growth obtained during corresponding periods have been presented as a proof of success.

2) Loss in production on account of shutdown of CPSEs have also been presented

3) Losses in dividends from CPSEs on account of disinvestment and strategic sale have been brought out

Hypothetical Model

The development model referred to in this book is a virtual / hypothetical model and does not refer to models actually used in five-year plans. This book does not give how much investments were made project wise to increase production levels in various sectors to meet forecasted demands. It only gives the increase in installed capacities and actual production achieved in 16 sectors including contribution from public sector units.

Unrestricted growth of private sector illustrated

a) All the 12 Five Year plans were made jointly with private sector investment averaging 53%, contrary to the propaganda that private sector companies were not allowed to start or produce freely prior to liberalization in 1991, as a measure of extending protection to public sector units.

b) List of major private sector companies, which operated in each sector, is given. The lists show that about 457 of total listed 637 private companies were started before 1991, 170 companies were started between 1991 and 2013 and only 10 private companies were started after 2014.

c) In sectors like Cement, Consumer Products for Basic and Secondary Needs, Communication including mobiles and television, Finished and Saleable steel, Aluminium, Copper, (Zinc and Lead after 2002), bulk drugs and formulations, Di-Ammonium Phosphate, complex fertilizer and Bio-Fertilizer, etc., private sector companies played a lead role before liberalization.

d) Actually, around 1967, measures were taken for import liberalization following devaluation, decontrol of certain commodities like steel, coal, paper, fertilizers and commercial vehicles, delicensing of a number of industries, etc.

e) Licensing for production in any particular sector was never a constraint in achieving desired production capacities in any sector and were used to protect smaller private companies.

f) Crucial part played by private sector in the development of economy with participation of several big groups of private sector companies like Tata, Birla, L&T, Bajaj, Murugappa, Kirloskar, Mahindra, Hinduja, Godrej, ITC, Wadia, and others contributing in a big way to economic development up to 2002 and private sector companies playing leading role in several sectors.

Support of public sector for private sector growth

Many big ventures of private companies got investment support from public sector units like LIC, UTI, Financial Institutions, public sector banks, etc. including Reliance Industries Ltd., the largest private sector company in India by market capitalization.

In India, many small private sector banks were rescued from closing down by public sector banks at the initiative of Reserve Bank of India. If such a set up was there in US, banks like Silicon Valley Bank, Signature Bank, First Republic Bank, 29 banks between 2015-20, etc. would not have closed down.

Contribution of public sector to Indian economy

The public sector units' contributions to India's GDP, to government as dividends and to government's capital expenditure.

The book promotes economic development model, which besides helping to achieve production targets, also played a very big role in improving the living standards of the people of Scheduled Tribe, Scheduled Caste and Other Backward Communities by providing reservation for these people in education and employment in CPSEs and government offices.

The fact that no private companies (like Tata group, or Birla group or L& T group, etc.) grew into a monopolistic company controlling any sector dominantly up to 2000 is testimony to success of this model. After selling of public sector units from 2001-02, companies like Reliance Industries, Vedanta, Adani group have become monopolistic companies in some crucial sectors.

Growth in GDP

Nominal GDP in 2019: $2.94 trillion-India GDP (PPP): $10.51 trillion. The services sector accounts for about 61.5%, industrial sector 23 % and agriculture 15.4 % of country's GDP. India has become the fifth-largest economy in 2019, overtaking the United Kingdom and France.

Ref: IMF's World Economic Outlook Database, October 2019. Countries by GDP: The Top 20 Economies in the World (investopedia.com)

With a GDP of roughly $ 3.4 Trillion, India, in January 2024, was the fifth-largest economy in the world, after the US, China, Japan and Germany.

Ref : India set to be world's 3rd largest economy by 2027-28: FM - Times of India (indiatimes.com)

Thus, India, not only remains unchanged in the fifth rank from October 2019, but has also not overtaken Germany's GDP of $ 3.86 Trillion in October 2019 even in January 2024. So where is the growth?

 I dedicate my book to Jawaharlal Nehru, Architect of Modern India, whose approach to meticulous planning of five-year plans inspired me to write this book and I express my gratitude to my wife, who supported me all through these 2 years, I was engaged in writing this book.

This improvement in living standards of Scheduled Tribe, Scheduled Caste, Other Backward Communities people of India can give a hint for improving median wealth of Native Americans, which was only 8.7% of median wealth among all Americans in 2000 (Chang 2010, 14).

Similarly, Australian economists can also take hint for improving the living standards of indigenous Australians or aboriginals.

Abbreviations –

(AA.BB.CC) – Reference, where AA – 5YP number, BB – Chapter and CC – Bullet number
Mt - Million tons
Bt - Billion tons
Lakh – 100,000
Cr – Crore – Ten Million - 10,000,000
MMSCMD - million metric standard cubic meters per day
Dates are given in DD.MM.YYYY format.
Ckms – Circuit kms

Note – Some Tables and Graphs have been removed from the book to limit the number of pages of the book. However, these information can be provided to interested readers against specific request to author.

2: GROWTH IN PRODUCTION OF CEMENT AND MANUFACTURING OF CEMENT PLANT MACHINERIES

Cement is required for all buildings and structures - from houses, office and factory buildings to dams and roads. The demand for the cement in India has been influenced mainly by the housing, infrastructure, irrigation and so on.

India achieved self-sufficiency in 1992-93 and became the second largest cement producer of the world in 2006-07. (11.v3.7.1.166)

Targeted Growth for Cement Production

The cement requirements were forecasted by the government for the last financial year of each 5-year plan and the target cement production capacity for the various 5-year plans were set. The capacity built up and actual production achieved at the end of each 5-year plan and some other periods are given in Table 1.1.

Growth of Cement Production

India's cement production increased from 2.69 Mts in 1950 to 4.3 Mts in 1955-56, 7.97 Mts in 1960-61 and 10.8 Mt in 1965-66, 12.2 Mts in 1968-69

During the period 1969-74, the government decided that the public sector should enter the field of consumer goods industries, particularly in fields in which adequate private investment was not forthcoming. Specific provision was made for public sector role in consumer goods industries like cement. (4.14.37)

Growth during VI 5YP - The scheme of partial decontrol of cement introduced in February 1982 and the liberal policy adopted by the Government in respect of price and distribution and permitting MRTP / FERA companies to set up projects generated enthusiasm among the entrepreneurs to set up additional capacity. 4 Cement plants (Ambuja Cements, L & T Cement, UltraTech Cements and Vasava Datta Cement), were started in 1983 in private sector.

Growth during VII 5YP – Decontrol and delicensing - Consequent on complete decontrol of cement in March, 1989 and subsequent delicensing of the industry in July 1991, the industry made big strides both in production as well as capacity addition. (8.2.8.8)

Status

In 1992-93, the county turned from cement shortage to cement surplus status by 1992-93, when it exported nearly 3 Mts of cement/clinker. (8.5.23.1)

Cement capacity reached 71.19 Mts and production 56 Mts in 1993. India ranked fifth among the cement producing countries after China, Russia, Japan and USA.

In 2001-02 - The cement industry in India became **self-sufficient both in raw material availability and process technology as well as indigenous sources of plant and machinery.** It was comparable to the best in the world in respect of quality standards, fuel and power consumption and environmental norms. It contributed to 6% of the world production. (10.7.1.172)

Installed capacity of Cement industry was 140.53 Mts (129.43 Mts from 120 large plants and 11.1 Mts from 365 mini plants). Of these 365 mini plants, only about 132 plants, were reported to be in operation, producing about 4 Mts of cement. Production of cement was 100.1 Mts in 2000–01 (10.7.1.172 / 12.4.49)

In 2006-07 - India became the second largest cement producer in the world. (11.v3.7.1.166)

In 2008-09 - As of March 2009, Indian cement industry comprised of 148 large cement plants and 365 mini-cement plants, with installed capacities of 219 Mt and 11 Mt respectively. (12.4.65)

In 2010-11 - Production of cement was 228.3 Mts. (12.4.49).

India's cement production increased to 255.83 Mts in 2013-14 to 274 Mts in 2015-16, 291 Mt in 2017-18 and 329 Mt in 2019-20. India: cement production volume 2022 | Statista

In 2022, 210 large cement plants accounted for a cumulative installed capacity of over 410 MT, while over 350 mini cement plants had an estimated production capacity of 11.10 MT. IBEF Presentation

In 2023 - India's cement production reached 374.55 Mts in FY2023. (Ibef.org)

Cement Production by CPSE

Cement Corporation of India Limited was incorporated on 18.01.1965.

The cement plants at Rajban, Neemuch, Akaltara and Yerraguntala with a total capacity of 1.4 Mts were expected to be commissioned during 1979-80. *World Bank Document (P56)

Chunar Cement Factory, Unit of U.P Cement Cooperation, was started in **1982** with capacity of 1.68 Mts. (6.16.70). The factory was stopped in the year 1999 due to some technical problem.

In **1984-85** the public sector provided 14% of cement output (7. Annex 2-3) with 1.99 Mts by CCI with capacity of 2.62 Mts and 2.26 Mts from 8 smaller State Government-owned companies with capacity of 4.96 Mts. World Bank Document

Hira Cement Works, which started producing cement in 1968, was taken over by Industrial Development Corporation of Orissa Ltd. in 1980s. The company discontinued producing Portland Pozzolana cement, reaching a peak production of 0.457 Mts in **1988-89.**

IDCOL Cements Ltd., subsidiary of Industrial Development Corporation of Orissa Ltd., was founded in 1993 to operate Hira Cement Works. This plant produced 0.419 Mt in 1995-96.

Steel Authority of India was setting up a 2 Mts slag cement capacity at Chilhati.

In 1995-96, the public sector accounted for 10% of capacity and production, down from 18% in 1984-85. The capacity of public sector plants increased from 7.6 in 1985 to 9.9 Mts in 1995. World Bank Document

In 1996-97, over 85% of capacity was with private sector, the public sector accounting for 15% of capacity and CCI contributing to less than 5% of production. (9.5.213)

Public Sector Companies

Cement Corporation of India Ltd.

Cement Corporation of India Ltd. - CCI was incorporated on 18-1-1965 to help achieve self-sufficiency in cement production in India. CCI manufactures special grade cement also for manufacture of sleepers for Indian Railways.

Mandhar unit, first CCI plant (capacity 0.38 Mts), **Kurkunta** plant (0.198 Mts), **Bokajan** unit (0.198 Mts), **Rajban** unit (0.198 Mts), **Akaltara** unit (0.4 Mts), **Nayagaon** unit (0.4 Mt), **Yerraguntala** unit (0.4 Mts), **Adilabad** unit (0.4 Mt), **Tandur** unit (1 Mt) and **Delhi** grinding unit (0.5 Mts) were commissioned on 19.07.1970, 1.10.1972, 01.04.1977, 01.04.1980, 01.04.1981, 01.03.1982, April 1982, 01.4.1984, 1.7.1987 and 01.05.1990 respectively.

Sick **Charkhi-Dadri** unit was taken over by Government and vested with CCI in 1981. After rehabilitation, clinker production started on 10.5.1982 with 0.174 Mts. Capacity.

Nayagaon **Neemuch** expansion project for another 1 Mts was undertaken with clinkerisation at Nayagaon and grinding of clinker at Delhi and Bhatinda. They started commercial production on 1.05.1990.

The public sector cement plants' production was 15% of total production in 1979-80, 14% in 1984-85 and 6% in 1989-90 and total installed capacity was 4.216 Mts in 1994.

CCI started a joint venture company Damodhar Cement & Slag Ltd., Madhukunda with West Bengal Industrial Development Corp. on 19.7.1983 for manufacture of slag of 0.3 Mts and cement grinding of 0.27 Mts.

CCI made a net profit of Rs. 831.84 Cr in 2005-06.

The performance of CCI was adversely affected due to severe liquidity crunch and power shortage. 7 units Mandhar (on 6.6.1996), Charkhi Dadri (on 14.8.1996), Akaltara (on 9.12.1996), Nayagaon and Nayagaon Expansion (on 30.6.1997), Kurkunta (on 1.11.1998), Adilabad (on 5.11.1998) and Delhi (on 8.2.1999) were closed and Bhatinda unit was not commissioned.

Yerraguntala plant was sold to India Cements Ltd. on 21.01.1998 for Rs. 200.70 crore.

The rehabilitation scheme sanctioned by BIFR on 3.05.2006 suggested closure of 7 unviable plants located at Mandhar, Kurkunta, Akaltara, Charkhi Dadri, Nayagaon and Adilabad and Delhi / Bhatinda Grinding units, and sale of assets of those plants through Asset Sale Committee.

Total installed capacity of the plants was 4.248 Mts in 2007-08. Installed capacity of 3 operating plants was 1.446 Mts.

Under revival schemes, expansion of Rajban Unit and modernization of Tandur unit were taken up.

Tandur unit produced of 0.7 Mts in 2013-14. Dispatches of cement during 2014-15 were 9.47 Lakhs MT. Overall capacity utilization of CCI Ltd. stood at 66%.

As on 2015, CCI was earning profit from 2007 with its Rajban, Bokajan and Tandur plants.

The installed capacity in 2019-20 was 1.4615 Mts for cement.

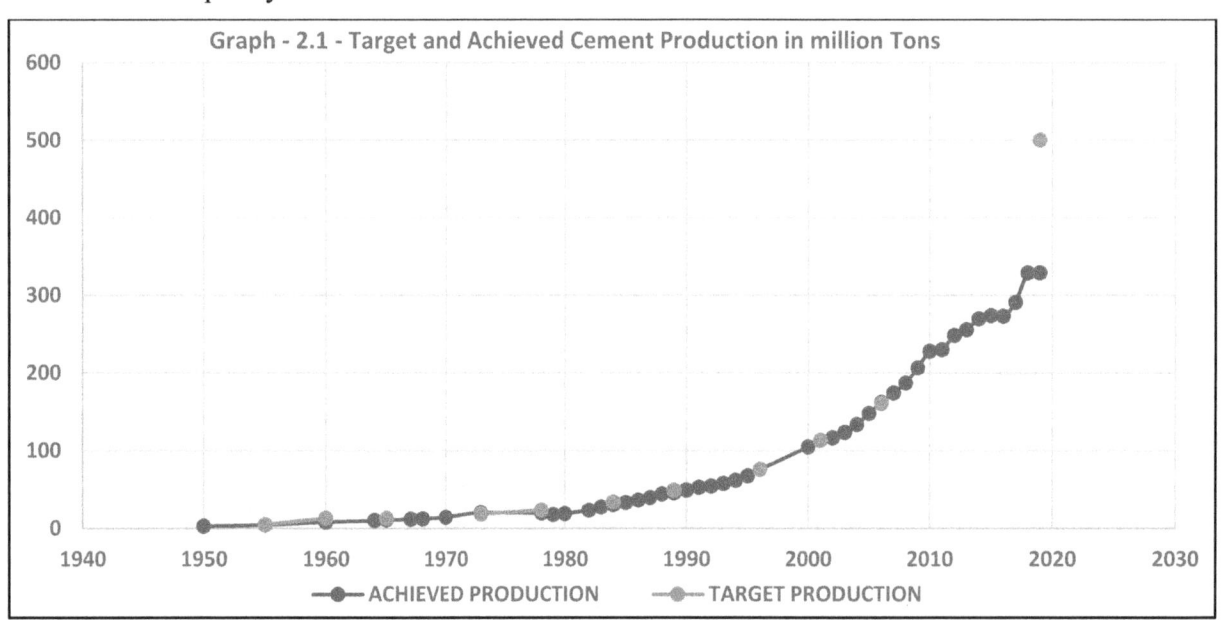

Graph - 2.1 - Target and Achieved Cement Production in million Tons

TABLE 2.1 - Cement production in million Tons

Year	Target Capacity	Target Production	Total Achieved Capacity	Total Achieved Production	CPSE Achieved Capacity	CPSE Achieved Production	CPSE's share in Production
1950-51				2.69			
1955-56		4.8	4.3	4.3			
1960-61	16	13		7.97			
1964-65				9.78			
1965-66		13		10.8			
1967-68				11.46			
1968-69				12.2			
1970-71	26			14.3			
1973-74		18		19.7		2.3	11.68%
1978-79		23.5	22.6	19.42		3.88 (Exp)	
1979-80			24.29	17.6		3.6	20.45%
1980-81				18.6			
1981-82			29				
1982-83				23.3			
1983-84				27.1			
1984-85	43	34	42.62	30.17	7.58	4.25	14.10%
1985-86				33.1			
1986-87				36.5			
1987-88				39.6			
1988-89				44.3			
1989-90	61.8	49	60	45.8		2.766	6.04%
1990-91			63	49		2.86	5.84%
1991-92			65	53		3.161	5.96%
1992-93				54.54		2.964	5.43%
1993-94			69	57.96		0.349	
1994-95				62		0.342	
1995-96			88.2	67.72	9.9	0.419	10%
1996-97	90	76	105	76			
2000-01				105			
2001-02	135	113	140.53				
2002-03			151.17	116.35		0.534	
2003-04			157.74	123.5		0.585	
2004-05			165.39	133.57		0.806	
2005-06			171.34	147.81		0.942	
2006-07	202.64	160.56	174.99	162		1.023	
2007-08				174.3		0.909	
2008-09			230	186.9		0.956	
2009-10				206.6		0.968	
2010-11				228.3		0.9	
2011-12	298			230.4		0.855	
2012-13				248.23		0.708	
2013-14				255.83		0.836	
2014-15				270.04	3.848	0.953	
2015-16				274		0.913	
2016-17				273		0.791	

Year	Target		Total Achieved		CPSE Achieved		CPSE's share in
	Capacity	Production	Capacity	Production	Capacity	Production	Production
2017-18				291		0.753	
2018-19				329		0.634	
2019-20		500		329		0.585	
2020-21				353 (Est)			
2021-22			500	(Est. 381) 298			2%
2022			421.1				

Manufacturing of Cement Machineries

The government set targets for manufacturing of cement machineries required for establishment of new cement plants to meet growing demands for cement. The targets set and achieved manufacturing of cement machineries are given in Table – 1.2.

Machine Building in Private Sector -

Associated Cement-Vickers-Babcock Wilcox plant at Durgapur was to be established during III 5YP for manufacture of cement plant equipment. (3.26.55)

Targets were set production of complete cement plant machineries for 6 to 7 plants, each of 500 tons per day capacity by private sector.

Table – 2.2 Cement Machineries Production in Rs. Crores

Year	Target Production	Total Achieved Production	Year	Target Production	Total Achieved Production
1960	2	0.6	1984		58.2
1964		2.1	1985		95.4
1965		4.9	1986		98
1967		7.9	1987		125
1968		8.18	1988		275.3
1970		4.2	1989		321
1973		8.1	1993		323.7
1975		5.7	1994		295.2
1980		33.6	1995		365.8
1982		45.3	1996		455.34
1983		44.8			

Acquisition is a bad strategy

On May 15, 2022, Adani Group acquired Holcim's stake in Ambuja Cements and ACC for US$10.5 billion.

Adani's Ambuja Cements Ltd acquired Sanghi Industries Ltd, the world's largest single-stream cement plant, located at Sanghipuram in Kutch district, in December 2023 and CK Birla's Orient Cement at of INR 8,100 Crore in October 2024.

Acquisition of existing companies does not increase existing installed capacity or reduce shortfall in supply. (The acquiring company's inventory and operating cost reduce and profit increases additionally due to reduced competition in the market). If the same amount was invested for starting new companies, the installed capacity and production would have increased and shortfall would have reduced. **Thus, acquisition of operating companies for profit is a bad policy and promotes monopoly.**

Summary – The cement production was 374.55 Mts in 2022-23. However, the contributions from public sector were small, as new plants did not come up in public sector after 1990.

Private Sector Players -

ACC (1936 – 17 plants), Dalmia Cements (1939), Hyderabad Industries Ltd (1946), India Cements (1946), Grasim Industries Ltd (1947), Shree Digvijay Cement (1949), Ramco Cements (1961), Chettinad Cements (1962), Kesoram Cement Ltd (1969), Century Textile & Industries Ltd (1974), Mangalam Cements (1976), Rasi Cements (1978), Jaypee Rewa Cement plant (1979), Orient Cement (1979), Ambuja Cements (1983), L & T Cement (1983, 1995 and 2000, was India's largest cement producer with installed capacity of over 14 Mts), UltraTech Cements (1983), Vasava Datta Cement (1983), Dharani Cement (1985), Sanghi Industries (1985)

J K Cements (1994), Binani Cement (1996), Indian Rayon Cement Division (1998), Star Cement (2001)

36 Plants started before 1991, 4 plants started between 1991 and 2013.

3: GROWTH IN PRODUCTION OF COAL

Coal is required for many industries like power plants, railways, cement, sponge iron, pig iron / steel, fertilizer, brick and others. Coal was the mainstay of energy sector accounting for over 50% of primary commercial energy supply from 1950-51. This share was 73.1% in 2022-23. India's power output grows at fastest pace in 33 years, fuelled by coal | Reuters

Targeted Growth for Coal Production

The coal requirements for power, cement, fertilizers, iron and steel, etc. industries were forecasted by the government for the last financial year of each 5-year plan and the target coal production capacities for the various 5-year plans were set. Total projected demand for XII 5YP of 980.50 Mts was set considering coking coal requirement of 67.2 Mt, and non-coking coal requirement for power plants, cement, sponge iron / steel, fertilizer, brick and other industries of 738.44 Mt, 47.31 Mt, 50.33 Mt and 77.22 Mt respectively. (12. Table -14.27)

Exploration of Coal Deposits

Geological Survey of India undertook preliminary exploration to identify potential coal and lignite deposits.

Mineral Exploration Corporation Ltd. was carved out of Geological Survey of India in 1972 for carrying out detailed and systematic exploration of mineral potential deposits.

Central Mine Planning & Design Institute Ltd. provided consultancy for geological exploration and remote sensing to generate geological and geo-engineering data and prepare mining project reports, geophysical survey through multi-probe geophysical logging; high resolution shallow seismic survey; hydro geological investigation and identification of coal bed methane resources.

Neyveli Lignite Corporation, Gujarat Minerals Development Corporation and **Rajasthan State Mines and Minerals Ltd** undertook exploration drilling for establishing lignite resources.

The coal reserves predicted and proven since 1950 are given in Table – 2.1.

India had an estimated 1000 billion cubic meters of Coal Bed Methane (10.7.3.12)

Table – 3.1 - Coal Reserves in Million Tons							
DATE OF PREDICTION	TOTAL RESERVE	PROVED RESERVES	INDICATED RESERVE	COKIING COAL	NON-COKING COAL	LIGNITE	PROVED LIGNITE RESERVES
1950-51	20000			2000			
1955-56	40000						
1960-61	50000			2800		2073	
1979-80	85444	24604			67533		
1984-85	156000	35826				3300	1900
1989-90	186000						
1990-91				8507	60346		
1991-92	196020	67000				6500	
1996-97	204650	72730	89840			27450	
2000-01	220980	84410	98550			34610	
2006-07	255000					38270	
2010-11	285862						
2011-12	293497					41960	

Coal Production in India

In 1950-51, **coal production was with private sector** and the production was 33 Mts (6.15.54).

Of the total estimated consumption of 32.307 Mts, 31.1% was consumed by Railways, 13.6% by Iron, Steel and Brass industries, 9.4% by Brick, Tiles and Refractories industries, 8.5% by Cotton, Woolen, Jute and Paper mills, 6.9% by Steam electric utilities.

Railways (40%) and iron and steel industry (21%) consumed metallurgical grade coal. (1.27.18)

In 1955-56
National Coal Development Corporation was set up in 1956 with the collieries owned by the railways.

Singareni Collieries Company Ltd. was taken over by Government of Andhra Pradesh in 1956. (2.18.8)

Neyveli Lignite Corporation Ltd. was incorporated on 14.11.1956 to produce raw lignite required for a 250 M.W thermal power plant, a 70,000 tons urea fertilizer plant and a briquetting and carbonization plant for producing 0.38 Mts carbonized briquettes. (3.27.37)

In 1960, production from the mines of NCDC, Singareni collieries and **private sector** increased to 13.7 Mts, 2.6 Mts and 45.7 Mts. respectively. (3.27.4)

Nationalization of Coal Mines

i) In 1970, adequate capital investment to meet the burgeoning energy needs of India **was not forthcoming from the private coal mine owners**.

ii) Unscientific mining practices adopted by some of them and poor working conditions of labour in some of the private coal mines became matters of concern for Government.

First, the coking coal mines and the coke oven plants other than those with the Tata Iron & Steel Company Ltd. and Indian Iron & Steel Company Ltd., were nationalized on 5.1.**1972** and brought under Bharat Coking Coal Limited. Coking and non-coking coal mines in 7 States were nationalized on 1.5.**1973**
*The industry was reorganized in **1975** with the creation of **Coal India Ltd.** Singareni Collieries Company Ltd, however, continued to be a jointly owned company of Andhra Pradesh and Central Governments. (8.8.33.1)

Growth during V 5YP - With the introduction of new methods in the development of mines, production was raised by 22 Mts in the first 2 years of V Plan. The 100 Mts level was reached in **1975-76**. (6.15.54)

Growth during VI 5YP - 59 major coal-handling plants and 19 washeries with total capacity of 32.86 Mts were set up during the VI Plan. (7.6.92)
*Sectoral breakup of total consumptions of coal in 1984-85 of 139.23 Mts were: Power – 44.7%, Steel & coke ovens – 17%, Railways – 6.8%, Cement – 5.09%, Fertilizers – 2.8%, Soft coke / LTC – 1.5%, jute, paper, cotton textiles, chemicals, bricks, etc. - 19%.

India became third largest producer of coal (398 Mts) in 2005 after China and USA.

During X 5YP, it was decided to allot Coal blocks / linkage to successful bidders for setting up thermal power stations. (10.10.37)

In 2008-09 - The production capacities of Bharat Cooking Coal Ltd, Eastern Coalfields Ltd, Northern Coalfields Ltd, South Eastern Coalfields Ltd., Neyveli Lignite Corp. Ltd and Coal India Ltd. were 29.138, 29.385, 65.51, 104.55, 24.0 and 412.13 Mts respectively.

23.2 Mts of coking coal was imported in 2010-11 to meet the 40 Mts demand of coking coal for steel plants and coke ovens. (12. Annex. 14.2)

In 2011-12 - The expected production from captive blocks fell short of the projected target of 104 Mts in the terminal year of XI Plan because only 29 captive blocks could start production out of the 195 blocks allocated till then. The main impediments were delays in forest and environmental clearances, problems of land acquisition, etc. (12.14.100)

*Out of the total consumption of 584.78 Mts of non-coking coal, power plants, fertilizer plants, captive power plants, Steel DRI and cement plants consumed 405 Mts, 85 Mt, 40 Mt, 28.8 Mt and 25.98 Mt respectively.

*The import of coal in 2011-12 was 90 Mts and was projected to be 185 Mts in 2016-17 (12.14.129)

*The coal washing capacity at the end of XI Plan was 29.88 Mts. for coking coal and 95.96 Mts. for non-coking coal. (12.14.112)

*Private sector was allowed to do coal mining in Meghalaya, which had private ownership of land and coal.

In 2023 - 24 –

Coal production grew to over 893 Mts in 2022-23 and is expected to top 1 billion Tons by March 2024. Coal Index: Drop in coal index hints at reduced input cost for steel | Delhi News - Times of India (indiatimes.com)

Coal Bed Methane

The government offered 33 blocks, in 4 rounds of bidding (in 2001, 2003, 2005 and 2008), for CBM covering 17,416 sq. km of area. Raniganj coalfield commenced commercial production in 2007. The production of 0.2 MMSCMD was confined mostly to private sector. (12.14.113)

Table – 3.2 - Target, Total achieved, CPSE achieved Coal Production in million Tons

Year	Target Production	Total Achieved Production	CPSE Achieved Production	CPSE's Share in Total Production
1950-51		34.431		
1955-56	38	38.3	4.6	12%
1960-61	60	55.67	10.7	19.22%
1964-65		62.71		
1965-66	97	67.73	13.7	20.22%
1967-68		68.52		
1968-69		71.5		
1970-71		72.95		
1973-74	93.5	78.2	75.6	96.68%
1979-80		103.96		
1980-81		114		
1984-85	165.03	147.5		
1989-90	226	200.89		
1990-91		211.73		
1991-92		229.29		
1992-93		238.11		
1996-97	308	289.29	279.55	96.63%
2000-01		313		96.00%
2001-02	370.6	327.64	312.53	95.39%
2003-04			306	
2004-05			323.58	

Year	Target Production	Total Achieved Production	CPSE Achieved Production	CPSE's Share in Total Production
2006-07	405	430.84	400.41	92.94%
2007-08		457	422.08	92.36%
2008-09		492.76	450.12	91.35%
2009-10		533	484.99	90.99%
2010-11		533.06	484.46	90.88%
2011-12	680	540	488.21	90.19%
2012-13			604	
2013-14			663	
2014-15			779	
2015-16			486	
2016-17	795		600	
2017-18			781	
2019-20			602.14	
2022-23		893		

Table – 3.3 - Target, Total achieved, CPSE achieved Lignite Production in million Tons

Year	Target for Production	Achieved Total Production	CPSE Production	CPSE's Share in Production
1960-61	4.8	0.05		
1968-69		4		
1970-71		3.39		
1973-74	6			
1975-76		3.03		
1976-77		4.02		
1977-78		3.58		
1978-79		3.3		
1979-80		3.12		
1980-81		5.11		
1984-85	8	7.8		
1989-90	15.2	11		
1990-91		14.07		
1991-92		12.12		
2000-01		24.25		
2001-02	45	24.3		
2003-04		20.56		
2004-05		21.57		
2006-07	55.96 / 20.41	31.28		
2011-12	54.96	43.1		
2012-13			26.22	
2013-14			26.61	
2014-15			26.54	
2015-16			25.45	
2016-17	68.6		27.62	
2017-18			25.15	
2018-19			24.25	
2019-20			24.86	

Public Sector Organizations, which contributed for growth in Coal Sector

Indian Bureau of Mines (IBM)

Indian Bureau of Mines was set up on 1-03-**1948** to undertake the inspection of mines and detailed exploration of mineral deposits such as Iron Ore, Limestone, Dolomite, Coal, Copper, Tungsten, etc. Later it undertook technical consultancy and preparation of mineral maps leading to complete inventory of mineral resources.

IBM undertook inspection of 2500 mines for scientific and systematic mining; mineral conservation and mines environment, mineral beneficiation studies, utilization of low-grade ores and analysis of environmental samples, modernization and collection, processing, dissemination of data on mines and minerals through various publications. (11.7.2.40)

National Coal Development Corporation

National Coal Development Corporation - NCDC was set up in October **1956** with 11 collieries owned by railways of capacity 2.9 Mts.

8 New collieries were opened between 1956 and **1961** and scientific techniques of coal mining were introduced and production increased to 8.05 Mts.

By **1966**, contribution of NCDC to nation's coal production of 67.72 Mts increased to 9.6 Mts. NCDC's production increased to 15.55 Mts in **1973-74**.

NCDC's collieries were taken over by Coal Mines Authority Ltd. on 1.5.1973.

Neyveli Lignite Corporation Ltd.

Neyveli Lignite Corp. Ltd. - NLC was incorporated on 14.11.**1956** to meet the electricity demand of southern states of India by excavating lignite required for generation of power.

NLC was engaged in exploration and mining of 30.6 Mts. of lignite in 3 Neyveli mines and 1 Barsingsar mine.

NLC diversified into renewable energy production and installed 1404 MW solar power plant and 51 MW capacity windmills. 230MW solar power plant was commissioned in **2017-18.**

NLC Ltd. was engaged in operating power plants of 4661.06 MW capacity on 31.08.2020 comprising Thermal-3240 MW, Solar-1370.06 MW & Wind-51 MW. Commissioning of 2X500 MW Neyveli TPS Unit-I and 709 MW Solar plant were completed in 2019-20. 2x500 MW Neyveli TPS Unit 2 was commissioned on 3.2.2021.

NLC has 3 joint ventures namely NLC Tamil Nadu Power Ltd. (with Tamil Nadu Electricity Board, for setting up 1000 MW coal-based power project at Tuticorin), MNH Shakti Ltd. (with Mahanadi Coal Fields Ltd.) and 2000 MW Neyveli Uttar Pradesh Power Ltd. (with Uttar Pradesh Rajya Vidyut Utpadan Nigam Ltd)

Mining and Allied Machinery Corporation Ltd.

Mining and Allied Machinery Corporation Ltd. was incorporated in **1964** to manufacture mining equipment. The company was once the conduit for subtle technology transfer across the Iron Curtain - the British technology that it obtained by a collaboration with Dowty Mining of the UK was given to the former USSR in the form of exports of specialized wrenches, winders and haulages, while the Soviet (and Polish) mining drills and other equipment it imported were reverse - engineered and exported to the West. After the war, it was manufacturing scrapper chain conveyors. It was closed on 1.01.2002.

Bharat Coking Coal Ltd.

Bharat Coking Coal Ltd - BCCL was incorporated on 1.1.**1972** to take over the private coal mines in Jharia, Jharkhand and Raniganj, West Bengal.

BCCL is engaged in extraction of coking coal (for supply to steel plants) and non-coking coal (for power houses, fertilizer, cement plants) from 35 underground, 13 open cast and 18 mixed mines in Jharia Coalfield and 64 mines in Raniganj Coalfield. BCCL also runs 6 coking coal washeries, 3 non-coking coal washeries, 1 captive power plant and 5 bye-product coke plants in Jharkhand.

The maximum **installed capacity of BCCL was 46.05 Mts** of raw coal and 6.4 Mts washed coal (coking)in 2019-20.

BCCL was meeting almost 50% of total prime coking coal requirement of integrated steel sector.

Mineral Exploration Corporation Ltd.

Mineral Exploration Corp. Ltd. - MECL was carved out of Geological Survey of India in **1972** and incorporated on 21.10.1972 for undertaking detailed and systematic exploration of mineral potential deposits and to reduce the time lag between the initial discovery of a mineral prospect and its eventual exploitation.

MECL carried out promotional work for coal, lignite and other minerals on behalf of and funded by Government in first phase, and contractual work for exploration of various minerals, CBM, geothermal and geo-technical projects on behalf of public sector, private sector and Central / state governments. During 2004-05 a total of 35 exploratory drilling projects were undertaken by MECL while developmental mining of 7 units were in progress.

The company was having 30% of market share of exploratory drilling in India in 2007-08.

MECL, as contractual agency for Central Mine Planning and Design Institute, undertook detailed exploration drilling activities in Non-Coal India Ltd Blocks and was expected to achieve 8.09 lakh meters in non-CIL blocks during XII 5YP establishing 5.2 Bts of private coal reserves. (12.14.109)

Coal Mines Authority Ltd.

Coal Mines Authority Ltd. - CMAL was established on 1.5.**1973** to manage and develop NCDC collieries and other non-coking coal mines nationalized on 1.5.1973.

CMAL owned 36 collieries in Bihar, Orissa, Madhya Pradesh and Maharashtra besides 4 coal washeries, one by-product coke oven plant and 2 large central workshops.

CMAL was renamed as Coal India Ltd following government's decision to restructure coal industry on 1.11.1975.

Central division of CMAL became Central Coalfields Ltd., a separate public sector company.

Coal India Limited

Coal India Ltd. - CIL was incorporated on 14.6.**1973** under Coal Mines (Nationalization) Act as **Coal Mines Authority Ltd**. This company was merged with Bharat Coking Coal Ltd. in **1975** and renamed as CIL.

Coal India is engaged in coal mining, acquisition of coal mines, exploration, manufacturing and distribution of coke, coal belt methane gas and byproducts through its 3 units (North Eastern Coalfields and marketing offices) and 8 subsidiaries (including Bharat Coking Coal Ltd, Central Coalfields Ltd, Eastern Coalfields Ltd, South Eastern Coalfields Ltd, Mahanadi Coalfields Ltd, Western Coalfields Ltd and Northern Coalfields Ltd., engaged in production of coal and CMPDIL engaged in Research and Development of coal mining).

Coal India Africana Limitada is registered in Republic of Mozambique.

CIL entered into Memorandum of Understanding with SAIL, RINL, NTPC and NMDC for formation of joint venture company International Coal Ventures Pvt Ltd. for acquisition of coal properties abroad. CIL also formed a Joint Venture with NTPC Ltd. namely CIL-NTPC Urja on 27.4.2010.

CIL acquired the assets of Mining and Allied Machinery Corporation (under liquidation) to revive MAMC's operation and to support underground mining activities with indigenous mining equipment for which CIL had entered into agreement with BEML and DVC.

CIL was supplying almost 99% of crushed coal to power sector in 2011-12. (12.14.140)

A total of 212 Coal Handling Plants with 277 Mts capacity were operating in different subsidiary companies of CIL.

The maximum **installed capacity of CIL was 460.44 Mts.**

Western Coalfields Ltd.

Western Coalfields Ltd. - WCL was incorporated on 29.10.**1975**.

It was bifurcated into South Eastern Coalfields L td and WCL w.e.f. 1.1.1986.

WCL is extracting coal from 45 open cast, 2 mixed and 39 underground mines in Nagpur, Chandrapur and Yavatmal districts of Maharashtra and Betul and Chhindwara districts of Madhya Pradesh.

The maximum installed capacity of WCL was 146.403 Mts.

WCL contributes about 8.19% of the national coal production.

Central Mine Planning & Design Institute Ltd. - Consultancy in coal and mineral exploration

Central Mine Planning & Design Institute Ltd. - CMPDIL was incorporated on 1.11.**1975** to provide:
i) Consultancy in coal and mineral exploration, mining and engineering.
ii) Consultancy in geological exploration and remote sensing to generate geological and geo-engineering data and assess in situ coal services for preparation of mining projects report, geophysical survey through multi-probe geophysical logging, high resolution shallow seismic survey, hydro geological investigation and identification of coal bed methane resources.
iii) Design of systems for mines, beneficiation and utilization plants, coal handling plants, coal, power and other units, power supply systems, workshops, etc. and
iv) Feasibility reports etc.

CMPDIL rendered consultancy services to 7 subsidiary companies of Coal India Ltd. and to non-CIL clients like NALCO, Tata Steel, HINDALCO, GMDC, SAIL-ISP, OMC, CEA DGH HPGCL, CSEB, NTPC, MECL, Essar Mineral Resources, UCM Coal Company Ltd, JSPL, Adani Mining Pvt Ltd., Field Mining and Ispat Ltd etc.

CMPDIL, with its contractual agency Mandakini Coal Company Ltd undertook 11.2 lakh meters of exploratory drilling in CIL blocks and 9.01 Bts of coal reserves were proved during XI Plan. (12.14.110).

During the year 2016-17, CMPDIL received 26 non-CIL consultancy jobs from 16 organizations.

Central Coalfields Ltd.

Central Coalfields Ltd. - CCL was incorporated on 1.11.**1975** to manage the coal mines of central division of Coal Mine Authority, now Coal India Ltd.

CCL was engaged in production of raw coal, washed coal, slurry, soft coke etc. through it 24 underground mines and 41 Open Cast Mines at Hazaribagh, Ranchi and Bokaro in Jharkhand in 2010-11. (There were 71 mines in 2004-05).

CCL has 4 coking coal washeries and 3 washeries for washing / beneficiation of non-coking coal.

71 Mts Magadh Open Cast Mine Project and 27 Mts Amrapali Open Cast Mine Project were made operational in 2019-20.

The maximum installed capacity of CCL was 81.09 Mts of raw coal.

Eastern Coalfields Ltd.

Eastern Coalfields Ltd. - ECL was incorporated as a subsidiary of Coal India Ltd. on 1.11.**1975** to reorganize the nationalized coal industry by conversion of Eastern division of erstwhile CMAL. into a company.

ECL is engaged in production of coal for the power sector through 88 under-ground and 24 opencast mines at Burdwan, Bankura and Purulia in **West Bengal** and Dhanbad, Godda, Deoghar and Pakur in Jharkhand.

The maximum installed capacity of ECL was 56.76 Mts.

Northern Coalfields Ltd.

Northern Coalfields Ltd. - NCL was incorporated on 28.11.**1985** to takeover specific coal mining activities carried out in Madhya Pradesh and Uttar Pradesh.

NCL is engaged in Coal extraction from 10 operating mining projects at Jhingurda, Block-B, Jayant, Amlohri, Nigahi in Madhya Pradesh and Bina, Krishnashila, Kakri, Dudhichua, Khadia in Uttar Pradesh.

The maximum installed capacity of NCL was 94.5 Mts.

South Eastern Coalfields Ltd.

South Eastern Coalfields Ltd. - SECL was incorporated on 28.11.**1985** to take over business of Bilaspur division of Western Coalfields and Talcher area of Central Coalfields Ltd. (Talcher area was taken out in 1992 to form Mahanadi Coalfields).

SECL is having 16 operating areas at Korba, Raigarh and Surguja in Chhattisgarh and Sahdol in Madhya Pradesh grouped into 3 coalfields namely Central India Coalfields, Korba Coalfields and Mand-Raigarh Coalfields.

The company had 24.5% of market share for its product in 2004-05.

37 Projects of capacity 120.94 MT were under implementation in **2010-11**.

SECL was operating 64 mines underground, 21 opencast and 1 mixed mine on 31.03.2014

The maximum installed capacity of SECL was 169.4 Mts in 2019-20.

In 2013-14, SECL was contributing 21.97% of total coal production.
SECL was operating a Coal Carbonization plant 'Dancuni Coal Complex' at Dancuni in West Bengal, on lease basis from Coal India Limited.

Mahanadi Coalfields Ltd.

Mahanadi Coalfields Ltd. - MCL was incorporated on 3.4.**1992** to take over business of the coalfields of Orissa region of South Eastern Coalfields Ltd.

MCL is in the mining of coal, with 24 mining projects at Angul, Jharsuguda and Sundargarh district of Orissa. MCL is having coal reserves spread over 2 coalfields viz. Talcher and Ib Valley.

MCL is having 4 subsidiaries namely MNH Shakti Ltd., MJSJ Coal Ltd., Mahanadi Coal Railway Ltd. and Mahanadi Basin Power Ltd and 1 joint venture company Neelachal Power Transmission Company Pvt Ltd.

The maximum installed capacity of MCL was 174.591 Mts. **MCL contributed about 19.35% of coal production in 2013-14.**

MCL took initiative for Solar Power Plant, Paradip Port modernization and setting up of washeries.

Earth Moving & Mining Equipment Sector

Bharat Earth Movers Ltd was the leading manufacturer of earth moving and mining equipment required for mining and construction sectors. Investment in earth moving and mining equipment and construction equipment infrastructure over US$ 1 trillion was planned in the construction industry over the period 2011 to 2020. (12. Annex.13.2.17)

Table – 3.4 CPSEs Share in Domestic Output

Domestic Production of Hard Coal (Non-coking Coal) in million Tons							Total Output by CPSEs / Share of CPSEs to Domestic Output (%)						
1968-69	1998-99	2004-05	2005-06	2008-09	2009-10	2010-11	1968-69	1998-99	2004-05	2005-06	2008-09	2009-10	2010-11
71.4	253.33	382.62	401.515	422.548	487.64	483.54	12.61	223.47	358.88	343.39	353.6	395.51	390.22
							17.66	88.216	93.8	85.52	83.68	81.11	80.7
Coking Coal in million Tons													
	43.843			34.455	34.455	49.533		38.618			27.27	27.27	42.496
								88.082			79.14	79.15	85.8
Lignite in million Tons													
3.98		30.34					3.98		21.57				
							100		71.09				

CPSE's share in production of hard coal in 2007-08 and 2011-12 were 84% and 80% respectively and corresponding share for coking coal in 2007-08 was 79% and for lignite in 2011-12 was 85%.

Contribution to Manufacturing GDP

Coke, petroleum products, and nuclear fuel, rubber and plastics Industries contributed 10.6% to Manufacturing GDP in 2009-10

Planned and Actual Contribution to XI 5YP by Coal sector CPSEs

Against the estimated Internal and Extra Budgetary Resources availability of Rs 69926.77 Cr (Rs 51542.55 Cr from CIL, Rs 3340.30 Cr from SCCL and Rs 15043.92 Cr from NLC), the proposed plan outlay for PSUs was Rs 35774 Cr (at constant price) in XI 5YP. While the resource position of SCCL and NLC was just sufficient to meet the plan outlay, there was a huge surplus in that of CIL. (11.10.189)

Actual expenditure during XI Plan under Ministry of Coal was Rs. 26,337.62 Cr. This comprised Rs. 26,374.20 Cr of IEBR of CIL, SCCL and NLC and balance Rs. 1,500 Cr Gross Budget Support for Ministry of Coal funded schemes. The major shortfalls were in the reported expenditure of CIL and NLC whereas SCCL was expected to spend Rs. 3,707.59 Cr against the approved IEBR of Rs. 3,340 Cr. (12.14.121)

Summary

Coal industry was in the hands of private sector up to 1970 and the production was only about 72 Mts. After nationalization of coal mines in 1972-73, the coal production increased rapidly with Coal India Ltd and its subsidiaries playing leading role. CPSE units were contributing more than 80% from 1973-74 onwards.

Private sector players

Adani Mining Pvt Ltd. (2007)

4: PRODUCTION OF CONSUMER PRODUCTS OF BASIC NEEDS

Consumables, daily need of common people

The cost of living of a large majority of people depends on relatively few commodities like food grains, vegetable oils, sugar, salt, cookware, kerosine, cloth, soap, etc.

Targeted growth for consumer products production

The requirements for cloth, food items, detergents and soaps, foot wear, consumables (like dry batteries, electric bulbs, etc.), bicycles, bicycle tires, sewing machines, typewriters, etc. were forecast by the government for the last financial year of each 5-year plan and the target capacity and production of these items for the various 5-year plans were set.

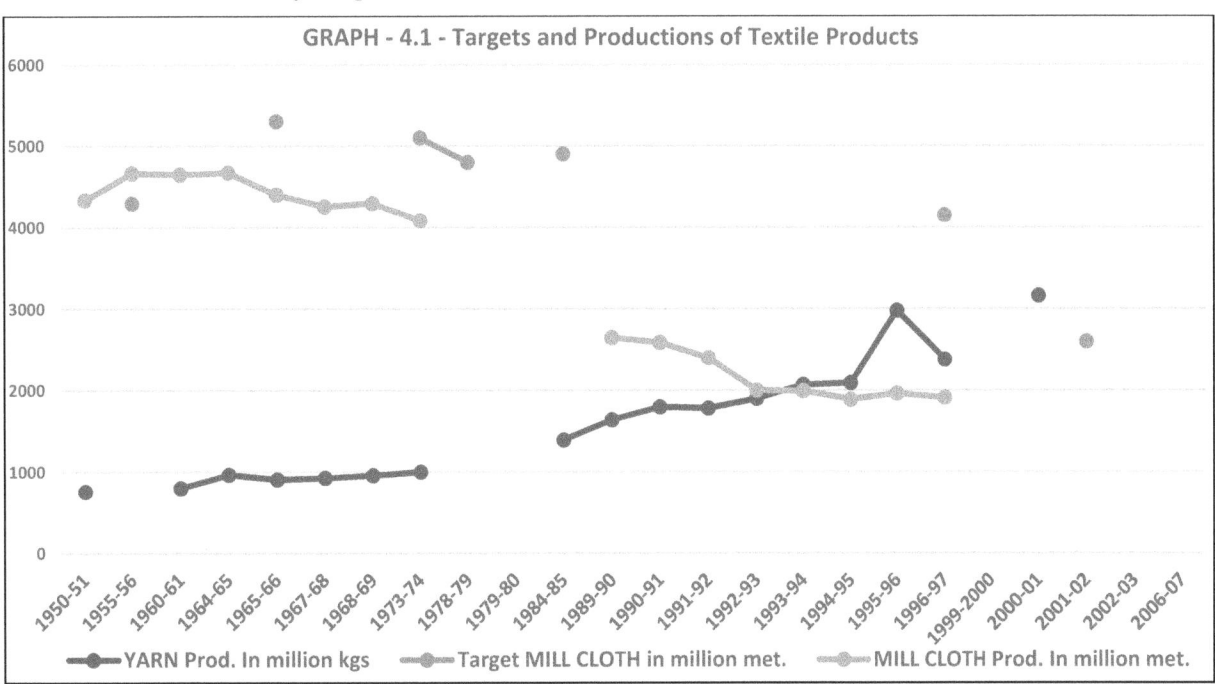

Meeting consumer needs for housing

Hindustan Prefab Ltd. - HPL was established as a government department in **1948**, for meeting the housing needs of people who migrated from Pakistan as refugees. HPL was incorporated as Hindustan Housing Factory Ltd in 1953.

Housing and Urban Development Corporation – HUDCO was created on 25.04.**1970,** against the backdrop of housing deficit in India in 1960s and 1970s, as a private limited company under the ownership of Indian Government for addressing issue of housing finance and urban infrastructure development. HUDCO provided finance for setting up new towns and consultancy services for designing and planning projects relating to Housing and Urban Development programs in India as well as abroad.

Life Insurance Corporation - LIC provided financing for housing. Up to March 1977, LIC had provided Rs. 728.56 Cr in loans for various housing programs. (6.23.23). The contribution of LIC for housing loan increased from Rs.185 Cr. in 1984-85 to Rs.825 Cr. in 1990-91.

National Housing Bank - NHB was set up on 09.07.**1988** for
(i) overall regulation and licensing of housing finance companies

(ii) establishing a contractual deposit scheme linked to guaranteed loan from scheduled banks
(iii) refinancing at less than commercial rates of interest of HUDCO and bank's schemes and
(iv) land development and shelter program of public and private agencies; (8.14.3.10)

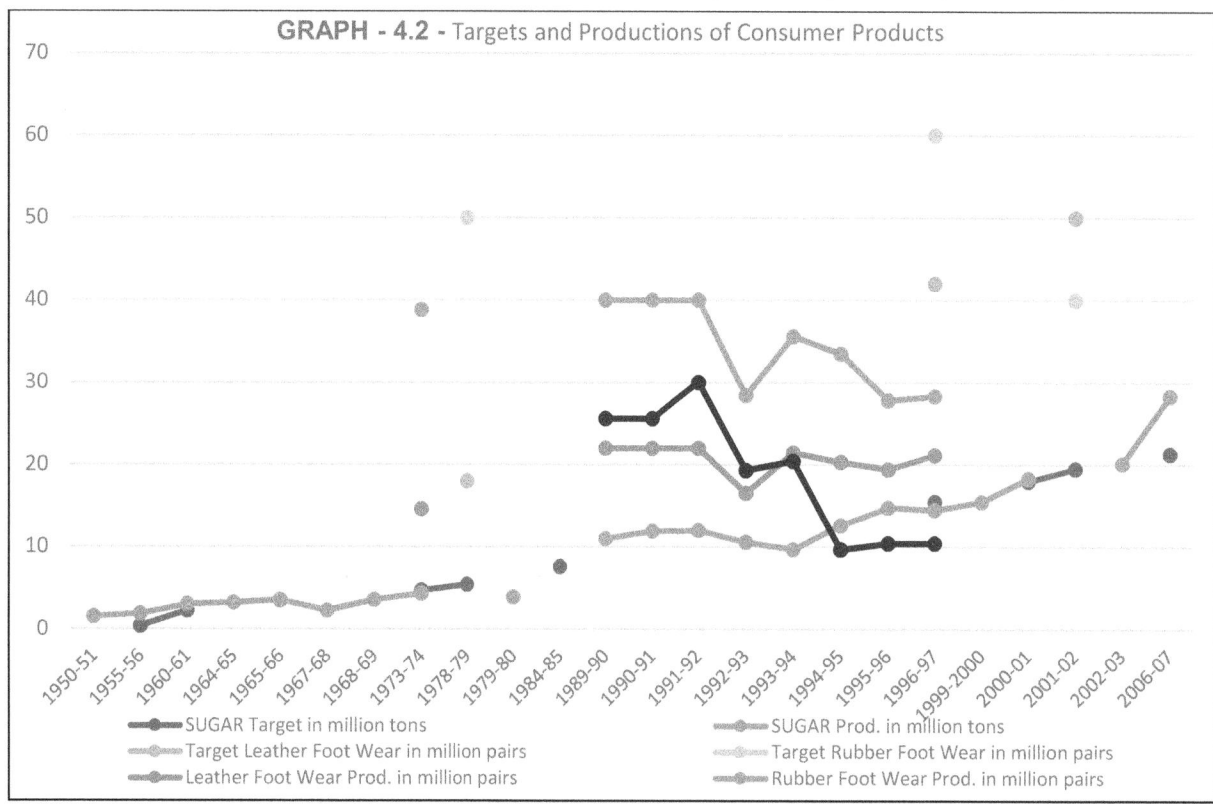

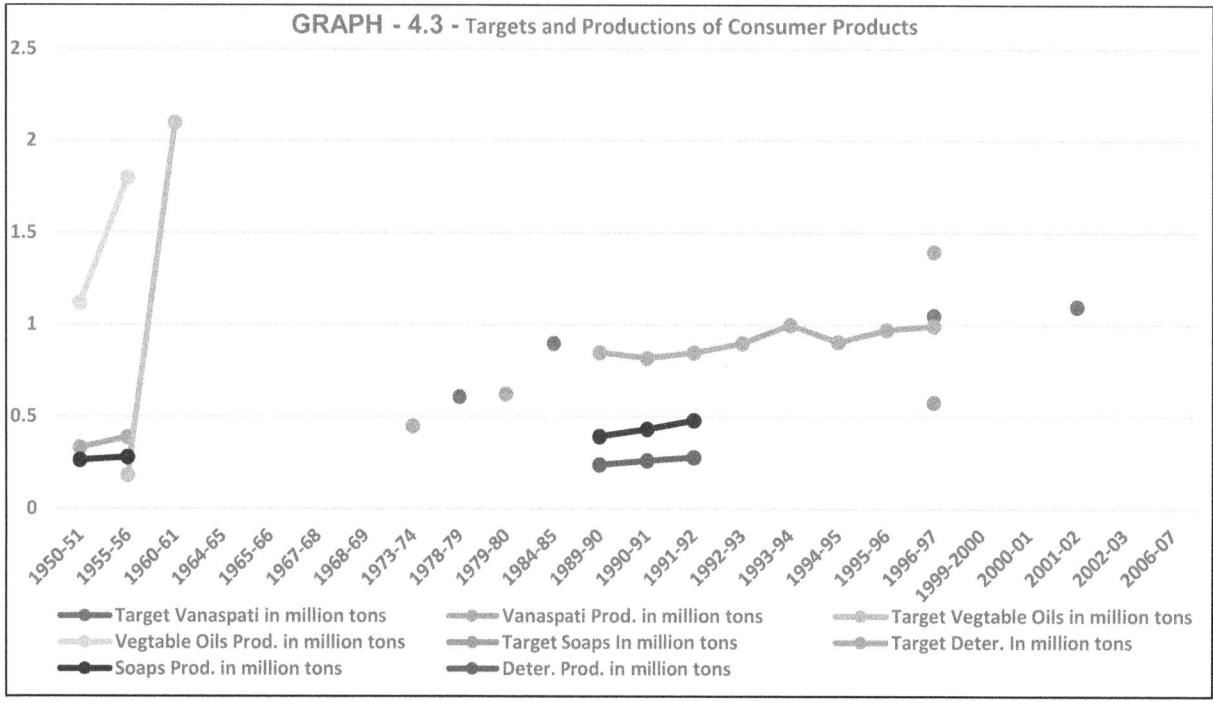

Meeting consumer needs for clothing

Textile Production in 1950-51 -

In 1951, there were 3 million handlooms and about 23,000 power looms (1.25.19) and the production of mill cloth, man-made cloth and yarn were 4338 million meters, 2743 million meters and 757 million kgs respectively.

National Textile Corporation Ltd (NTC) was incorporated in April **1968** for managing the affairs of **sick textile undertakings, in the private sector**, taken over by the Government, which increased from 16 in 1968 to 103 by 1972–73. These units were nationalized under the Sick Textile Undertakings (Nationalization) Act in 1974.

Textile Modernization Fund was introduced in **1986** with a corpus of Rs.750 Cr to promote **modernization of** textile industry, including **private sector mills**, As the response was encouraging, TMF was proposed to continue during VIII Plan. (8.v2.5.26.1 / 2)

Textile Restructuring Asset Trusts were formed for improving efficiency of textile plants.

Textile exports grew from Rs.35,478 Cr in 1996-97 to $ 12.10 billion in 2000-01. (9.5.240) (10.7.1.329)

Textile industry contributed about 14% to national industrial production and export (about 35% to total national export earnings) in 2001-02. (10.7.1.160)

Modernization of textile mills - Rs. 5057 Cr was sanctioned to 1232 proposals till 31.01.2002 under Technology Upgradation Fund Scheme for modernization of textile sector to enable them face competition from China, Taiwan, South Korea, Japan, etc. (10.7.1.165)

The turnover of textile industry in 2006-07 was US$ 47 billion and export US$ 17 billion. (11.7.1.314/317)

In 2011-12, textile sector contributed about 12% of manufacturing output, 11% of merchandise exports and employed about 45 million people. (12. Annex.13.2 – 70)

WOOL

In 2003, India had 61.5 million sheep, about 4.2% of world's sheep population. (11.v2.5.68)

India was **seventh largest producer of raw wool** producing 1.8% of world production in 2006-07.

Export of wool items increased from Rs 3597.31 Cr in 2002–03 to Rs 4969.02 Cr in 2005–06. There were 718 wool units in organized sector and more in small-scale sector. (11.v2.5.71)

During 2002-07, **Central Wool Development Board** implemented Integrated Wool Improvement Program for unorganized wool sector aimed at improvement of wool fibre and breed; product development; provision of quality testing centre and Common Facility Centre for scouring, drying, carding, design development, product diversification, training and development of specialty fibre such as Angora and Pashmina. These programs covered 2.55 million sheep and benefited 55091 families up to 2006-07. (11.v2.5.72)

The size of woolen industry was Rs. 10,000 Cr., divided and scattered between organized and decentralized sectors. India had **third largest sheep population** in the world in 2011-12, 6.40 crore sheep producing 43.30 million kgs of raw wool, of which about 85% was carpet grade wool. (12.Annex.13.2 – 84/85)

It was estimated that raw wool production would increase from 114.2 million kg in 2008–09 to 260.8 million kg by 2019–20.

JUTE

National Jute Manufacturers Corp. Ltd. was incorporated on 3.6.**1980** to take over the six jute mills taken over by the government.

In **1986**, the Government announced a package of Rs.150 Cr Jute Modernization Fund and Rs.100 Cr Special Jute Development Fund, allowed duty free import of identified jute machinery items for modernization and made usage of jute packaging materials by specified end-users mandatory to compete with synthetic packaging material. (8.v2.5.27.1)

As government departments gave order for packing material to jute mills in accordance with Jute Mandatory Packaging Act, jute mills were not forced to undertake modernization or diversification. The jute sector was expected to achieve self-reliance through modernization and diversification. (12. Annex. 13.2 – 78)

COIR

India accounted for 90% of world's coir production (Rs 1300 Cr in 2006-07) and its coir products were exported to about 90 countries across the world. (11.v2.5.90)

Coir Industry is mostly confined to Kerala, Tamil Nadu and Karnataka. Under Gram Sadak Yojana (Bharat Nirman), it was decided to use Coir geo-textiles for construction of rural roads in 9 States and to extend to all 28 States. (12. Annex. 13.2 – 104)

SILK

The production of raw silk increased from 2.5 million Ib to 3.6 million Ib between 1950-51 and 1960-61. (3.3.30)

India was **second largest producer of silk** in the world with 15.5% share in world production. (12. Annex. 13.2 – 80)

Meeting consumer needs for food products

Government departments and public sector enterprises like National Projects Construction Corp. Ltd., Hindustan Steelworks Construction Ltd., Water & Power Consultancy Services (India) Ltd., Engineering Projects (India) Ltd., etc. contributed for **construction of dams and irrigation canals** to supply water required for irrigation.

Fertilizers, pesticides and insecticides required for increasing production and yield of agricultural and horticultural products and protecting the crops were supplied at subsidized rates by fertilizer and chemical industries. (This is described in chapter 9).

Growth in production of some food products

SALT

The production of salt in 1950-51 was 2.642 Mts. This production was expected to be increased by 0.429 Mts with contribution from Mandi Salt Works and others in public sector during I 5YP.

Hindustan Salts Ltd. was incorporated on 12.04.**1958** to take over the departmentally managed salt works at Kharaghoda (Gujarat), Sambhar Lake (Rajasthan) and Mandi (Himachal Pradesh) and make available quality iodized salt to weaker sections through Public Distribution System.

Sambhar Salt Ltd. was formed on 30.09.**1964,** as a subsidiary of HSL, to manage Sambhar Salt source. The installed capacities in 2019-20 were 468 tons for Bromine and 7339 tons for Magnesium Chloride

Distribution of Food Grains and other Food Products

Central and **State Warehousing Corporations** provided for an addition of 2 Mts of storage capacity during 1955-60 for building up buffer stocks of food grains and other strategic commodities to moderate price fluctuations. (2.2.34)

National Agricultural Cooperative Marketing Federation of India was established on 2.10.**1958** to promote co-operative marketing of agricultural produce to benefit the farmers. NAFED undertook price support operations in respect of oilseeds, coarse grains, pulses, potatoes and onions.

National Cooperative Development Corporation was set up on 13.03.**1963** for planning and promoting programs for production, processing, marketing, storage, export and import of agricultural produce, foodstuffs, industrial goods, livestock and certain other notified commodities and services on cooperative principles.

Food Corporation of India was established in **1965** to support the farmers by procuring part production at Minimum Support Price so that farmers get reasonable profit. FCI maintained buffer stock to meet contingencies, stored, transported and distributed to targeted population at subsidized rates. (4.1.57)

Food Corporation of India in some States and **Civil Supplies Corporations** or co-operatives, in other States undertook distribution of sugar.

State Trading Corporation of India undertook the responsibility for importing and distributing edible oils.

Department of Coal and Coal India Ltd handled soft coke distribution.

Indian Oil Corporation. Hindustan Petroleum. Bharat Petroleum, etc. handled distribution of kerosine.

National Textile Corporation controlled production of controlled cloth and distributed them through the National Consumers Cooperative Federation.

National Consumers Cooperative Federation (established on 16.10.**1965** to function as apex body of consumer cooperatives) and **Coffee Board** (established in 1942) procured and distributed tea and coffee respectively.

Supply of match boxes was arranged through **Khadi and Village Industries Commission.**

State Governments received paper at controlled price for conversion into exercise books through their own organizations.

In the absence of any public sector agency, toilet soaps were supplied and distributed by **Indian Soap and Toiletries Manufacturers Association.**

Civil Supplies Corporations of Tamil Nadu, Punjab and Kerala had opened their retail outlets. (6.7.54)

North Eastern Regional Agricultural Marketing Corporation Ltd was incorporated in **1982** for marketing products of Agri-Horti sector of North-Eastern region and support North Eastern farmers for getting remunerative prices for their produce and enhance agricultural, procurement, processing and marketing infrastructure of the region.

MILK

Anand Milk Union Limited is a state government cooperative society, based in Anand, Gujarat. The Kaira District Co-operative Milk Producers Union Ltd was formed on 19.12.**1946** with just 2 village co-operative societies and is today known as Amul Diary.

National Dairy Development Board was set up under Ministry of Fisheries, Animal Husbandry and Dairying. NDDB was founded by Dr Verghese Kurien in **1965** to extend the success of Kaira Cooperative Milk Producers' Union (Amul) to other parts of India.

Under Operation Flood Project, the number of dairy cooperative societies increased from 34,523 in 1984-85 to 64,000 in 1991-92. The peak milk procurement increased from 7.9 to 13.5 million kgs/day, fluid milk from 5 to 11 million liters/day and rural milk processing capacity from 8.8 to 17.8 million liters/day. (8.V2.1.8.6)

Production of milk powder and infant milk increased from 22,000 tons in 1970 to 1,65,000 tons in 1989. Production of cheese was 2,000 tons in 1990. (8.v2.6.13.7)

India's output of liquid milk reached 69 Mts in 1996. Indian dairy industry had a capacity of 20 million liters/ day. (9.5.364)

In 1998, India became the largest milk producer in the world, when its output surpassed that of the United States.

Milk production was expected to touch 81 Mts in 2000-01. (10.7.1.336)

India contributed 24.64% of global milk production. Milk production increased from 146.31 Mts in 2014-15 to 230.58 Mts in 2022-23. Press Information Bureau (pib.gov.in)

Food Processing Industries

Modern Food Industries (India) Ltd. was set up in **1965** at Kozhikundram, Tamil Nadu as first branded bread manufacturer. It launched vitaminized bread in 1968, sweet bread in 1971, fruity bread in 1981 and wheat-min brown in 1991.

Status of Food Processing Industry in 1996-97 contributed 18% to industrial GDP in 1996-97, primarily functioning in informal and un-organized sector. (9.5.354)

In 1996-97, there were about 34,000 **modern rice mills** processing 65% of the paddy production. (9.5.357)

Nearly 12.5 Mts of wheat was being converted into various wheat products annually in 2001-02 and the country had 820 functioning roller flour mills with 19.5 Mt. capacity. (10.7.1.335)

There were about 75,000 **bakery units** in small and cottage sectors producing above 60% of total output with annual turnover of about Rs.15,000 Cr. By 2002, the output of biscuits was expected to reach 4.4 Mt while that of bread 2 Mts. (9.5.359)

The production of bakery products was more than 3.7 Mts in 2001-02, with organized sector producing 65% of breads and biscuits. Soft drinks, beer and alcoholic drinks were also part of the food processing industry.

The installed capacity of **pasta products** was estimated at 34,000 tons/ year/ per shift of eight hours. About 178 units existed in the small-scale sector producing pasta products. (9.5.361)

Fish production increased from 0.78 Mts in 1951 to 4.789 Mts in 1994-95. (9.5.369).

In 2006-07, food processing industry contributed 14% to the manufacturing GDP employing 13 million people directly and 35 million people indirectly. (11.v2.5.99)

Production of Food Processing Industry at current prices in Rs Cr. were 66472.05 in 2002–03, 76264.13 in 2003–04, 86128.19 in 2004–05, 94127.99 in 2005–06 and 104758.54 in 2006–07. (11.v2.5.102)

As a leading producer of food grains, milk, fruits and vegetables, India had the advantage of adequate food at the farm gate to ensure food security for the nation and to even have a surplus for exports. (12. Annex. 13.2 – 88)

FRUITS AND VEGETABLES

India ranked second in the production of fruits and vegetables in 2001-02.

India produced about 50 Mts of fruits, about 9% of the world's fruit production, and 90 Mts of vegetables, accounting for 11% of the world's vegetable production in 2006. Yet, only about 2% of these fruits and vegetables were processed. Lack of processing and storage capacities for fruits and vegetables resulted in 35% waste in the annual production (Rs 54000 Cr). (11.v2.5.98)

SUGAR

During 1969-74, when adequate private investment was not forthcoming, public sector contributed through cooperatives in sugar and textiles, (4.14.37)

India was **world's largest producer of sugar-cane** in 1979-80. (6.16.73)

Sugar industry was second largest Agro-based industry in India. After many years, the country resumed sugar export in 1989-90. (8.v2.5.24.1)

India, as the **largest sugar producing country in the world,** contributed 15% to world's sugar production **in 2001-02**. (10.7.1.139)

On 30.09.2001, there were 506 sugar mills with production capacity of 16.82 Mts (average crushing capacity of a factory was 2355 tons/day). 70 sick public and private sector mills had been referred to the BIFR and were not in operation. (10.7.1.142)

Molasses, produced from sugar cane, was used for the manufacture of alcohol and a host of alcohol-based downstream chemicals. Anhydrous alcohol / ethanol, being an environment friendly auto fuel, was blended with gasoline and used as an auto fuel. (10.7.1.147)

A certain percentage of sugar production in factories was levied by the government on a pre-fixed price for distribution under PDS and the remaining production went for free sale. (11.7.1.303)

Withdrawal of stockholding limits on wholesale dealers of sugar was done with effect from 07.07.2000 and

government issued sugar policy on reduction of levy obligation of domestic sugar producers from 40% gradually to 10% from 1.03.2002. (10.7.1.64)

In **2006-07**, 582 sugar factories with an aggregate capacity of 19.797 Mts. were there (410 in small segment, 64 in the Mid-size segment and only 8 units were large, having crushing capacities of 10000 Tons /day and above.) (11.7.1.300)

Ethanol capacity of 1550 million liters had been established in major sugarcane-producing States, which was sufficient to meet 10% ethanol-doping requirement. (11.7.1.309)

Family Planning Products

Hindustan Latex Ltd. was incorporated on 1.3.**1966** to be a leader in the field of contraceptives and healthcare products and to assist in the National Family Welfare Program.

Leather Products

Bharat Leather Corporation Ltd. was incorporated on 30.03.1976 to undertake manufacture of luggage, handbags, saddlery and harness, tanning and dressing of leather.

During 1985-90, the value of leather goods exports rose from Rs.584 Cr to Rs.2030 Cr. and was expected to reach Rs.3200 Cr in 1991-92. (8.v2.5.25.1)

India ranked **first among major livestock holding countries in 2001-02**, with 19% of bovine, 20% of goat and 4% of sheep / lamb population and accounted for about 10% of global supplies of raw skins and hides. (10.7.1.149)

Leather exports increased from Rs. 3,036 Cr in 1991-92 to Rs. 9,004 Cr in 2000-01. (10.7.1.150)

The turnover of the leather industry was Rs 25000 Cr in 2004–05, of which Rs 10800 Cr was exported. Exports rose to US$ 2.9 billion in 2006–07. (11.7.1.227)

Handicrafts

Exports of handicrafts during the period 1997-2002 were about Rs. 41,470 Cr. (10.7.1.329)

Public Sector Companies Contributing for Increasing Agricultural Yield

National Seeds Corporation Ltd.

National Seeds Corporation Ltd. - NSC was incorporated on 19.3.**1963** to develop seed industry, to supply quality seeds and other Agro-input / services and to enhance agricultural productivity.

Starting with production of 30-40 tons of maize foundation seed, NSC was producing more than 0.15 Mts of certified / quality seeds per year covering 627 varieties of 80 different crops and hybrids of cereals, millets, pulses, oilseeds, fodder, fibre and vegetables and tissue culture plants like banana in **2019-20** at 8 central / state farms (through its registered 12500 seed growers and farms) located at Bangalore, Nandikotkur (Andhra Pradesh) and Kullu, Himachal Pradesh. NSC was marketing quality seeds, planting materials and bio-fertilizers through its 11 Regional Offices, 8 Central / State farms and 83 Area Offices spread all over India.

NSC accounted for 5% of total seeds distributed by the organized sector.

It was imparting training to State Seed Corporations' personnel in the production of seeds. NSC plays key roles in implementation of National Mission on Oil seeds & Oil Palm, National Food Security Mission, Mission for Integrated Development of Horticulture and National Mission on Agricultural Extension and Technology.

State Farms Corporation of India Ltd.

State Farms Corporation of India Ltd. - SFCI was incorporated in **1969** for production and distribution of test stocks, breeder, foundation and certified seeds of different crops through 6 central / state government's agriculture farms in different states

SFCI undertook activities like plantation and maintenance of fruit crops, multiplication of quality seedings of Horticultural crops, production of vegetable seeds, cultivation of bio-fuel & medicinal plants and popularizing new high yielding varieties by distributing seeds of the same among farmers and forestry plantations on wastelands.

The cultivable land under possession at these 6 farms was 19616 ha. Central Government owned 4 Farms namely Suratgarh, Sardargarh and Jaitsar in Rajasthan and one in Raichur, Karnataka. 2 Farms in Hisar, Haryana and Girijapuri, District Bahraich in U.P were on lease from respective State Governments. 6 Farms of SFCI were closed over the years due to poor performance. 4 Farms were handed over to the respective state Governments. Chengam Farm and Raebareli Farm were in the process of being handed over to Tamil Nadu and UP state governments.

Andaman & Nicobar Islands Forest & Plantation Development Corporation

Andaman & Nicobar Islands Forest and Plantation Dev. Corp. Ltd. - ANIFPDC was incorporated on 21.01.**1977** to undertake scientific harvesting, natural re-generation and development of forest resources.

ANIFPDC was engaged in forestry operation, cultivation and marketing of Red Oil Palm and Rubber Plantation.

ANIFPDC owned 1593 hectares of Red Oil Palm estate at Little Andaman and a processing unit with a capacity of 4 MT Fresh Fruit Bunches/ hour. The production capacity of Crude Palm Oil was 1400 MT/annum.

The gross area of Rubber estate at Katchal was 614 hectares.

ANIFPDC was engaged in production of Crude Palm Oil, Kernel / Nut, Raw Rubber Sheet, etc.

ANIFPDC had forestry divisions at Little Andaman and North Andaman, Oil Palm division at Hut Bay, Little Andaman and Rubber Division at Katchal.

ANIFPDC was generating 75% of turnover through harvesting of timber, but became loss making due to ban imposed by Supreme Court of India on timber harvesting. Expansion of rubber projects and red oil palm became constrained by the Natural Forest Policy, 1988 which discouraged conversion of natural forests to man-made plantations.

The Cabinet Committee on Economic Affairs, chaired by the Prime Minister, approved the closure of ANIFPDC on 16.08.2017. ANIFPDC is undergoing process of closure as on 31.03.2023.

Agrinnovate India Ltd.

Agrinnovate India Ltd. was incorporated on 19.10.**2011**, as the commercial arm of Indian Council of Agricultural Research to enhance global agricultural development through partnerships and efficient use of innovations of National Agricultural Research System.

Public Sector Companies Meeting Consumer Needs for Housing & Infrastructure for civil Amenities

Hindustan Prefab Ltd – Refer Chapter 8.

Housing and Urban Development Corporation -

HUDCO was established on 25.04.**1970** under the ownership of Government, against the backdrop of housing deficit in India in 1960s and 70s, for addressing housing finance and urban infrastructure development. HUDCO provides finance for setting up new towns and consultancy services for designing Housing and Urban Development programs in India and abroad.

As on 31.07.**1980**, HUDCO had sanctioned 1274 schemes in 319 towns and cities in 17 States and 4 Union Territories to provide about 6.8 lakh dwelling units, 62,000 developed plots and a number of shops and commercial complexes. About 86% of these plots were for Economically Weaker Sections and Low-Income Groups. HUDCO financed rural housing, apex cooperative housing societies and urban development schemes. (6.23.21)

During **1985-90**, HUDCO sanctioned Rs.2834.18 Cr to facilitate construction of 2 million dwelling units. (8.14.3.11)

HUDCO started financing development of infrastructures including projects of drainage, electricity, water supply, sewerage, solid waste management and roads in the urban areas in **1989**. Later social infrastructure components like primary schools and playgrounds, hostels for working women, healthcare centres, police stations and jails, courts, etc. received funding at low cost.

HUDCO financed 2.15 million houses costing Rs. 1247.80 Cr. till 30.06.**1991.** About 1.6 million units were completed. (8.14.3.4)

HUDCO won UN-Habitat Scroll of Honour Award for contributions to development of housing in **1991**.

HUDCO's financed State and Rural Housing Boards, Slum Clearance boards, Development Authorities, Improvement Trusts, Cooperative Societies etc. with 55% sanctions for EWS and LIG housing projects and balance for MIG, HIG, rental and commercial housing projects during **1992-97**. (8.14.7.7)

HUDCO had sanctioned schemes for construction of about 6 million dwelling units in rural areas till **2001-02.** (10.1.79)

Till 31.3.2005, HUDCO has sanctioned 15437 projects involving total cost of Rs.1,60,601 Cr with a sanctioned loan of Rs.69,345 crore. Financial assistances were made available to Municipal Corporations, Road Development Corporations, Primary Cooperative Societies, NGO's / Private Developers, Joint Sector and individuals.

HUDCO provided term loans for construction of roads and other transportation sectors including construction of airports (Cochin International Airport and Calicut International Airport), railways, ports, metro rails, bridges and flyover, Railway Over-Bridges, subways, bypasses, bus terminal, parking complexes, bus stops / stations, purchase of public transport vehicles, Intelligent Traffic Management system etc. Infrastructure for Kerala State Road Transport Corporation and UPSRTC were also funded by them. HUDCO sanctioned Rs. 100 Cr for KSRTC in 2002 for purchasing 550 buses and 350 mini-buses and 260 crores in 2014 for purchasing 1500 buses.

Of the total 151.77 lakhs dwellings sanctioned by HUDCO, rural dwellings constituted 94.43 lakhs. 84.24% dwellings were sanctioned to Economically Weaker Sections during the year. HUDCO started a new scheme HUDCO Nav Nagar Yojana offering an integrated planning-to-financing solution for new township layout development.

HUDCO's revenue for 2022-23 was Rs. 7049.46 Cr.

Hemisphere Properties India Ltd

Established on 17.01.2005. HPIL was incorporated demerging surplus land demarcated at the time of disinvestment of Videsh Sanchar Nigam now Tata Communications Ltd. The MCA and NCLT approved the demerger among Company and TCL and surplus land of 739.69 acres demerged into Hemisphere Properties India Ltd.

Public Sector Companies Meeting Consumer Needs for Clothing

British India Corporation Ltd.

British India Corp. Ltd. - BIC was incorporated in 1920 in private sector and was nationalized in **1981** to take over the controlling shares from private hands.

BIC was manufacturing **wool / worsted fabrics** through Lal Imli and Dhariwal wool mills.

Its 3 subsidiaries namely Elgin Mills Co. Ltd., Cawnpore Textiles Ltd. and Brushware Ltd. were closed. The implementation of the revival plan was expected to start in 2016-17.

BIC with 2 wool mills and 2 cotton subsidiary companies was making continuous losses due to obsolete machinery. Winding up of the 2 cotton subsidiaries of BIC was ordered. It was under closure / liquidation in 2022-23.

Handicrafts & Handlooms Export Corp. of India Ltd.

Handicrafts & Handlooms Export Corp. of India Ltd. - HHEC was incorporated on 11.04.**1958** to develop, promote and market the products of Indian crafts and skills abroad by providing a marketing channel for Craftsmen and Artisans. It undertook exports of handicrafts, handlooms, khadi products of village industries, readymade garments, hand-knitted carpets, fashion garments, gold and silver jewelry and import of bullion, silk, timber and cotton. Company was also engaged in retail sale of handicrafts and handlooms goods. The company had 21 procurement centres in the country. The Administrative Ministry took the decision for closure of HHEC on 08.03.2018.

HHEC is undergoing process of closure as on 31.03.2023.

National Textile Corporation

National Textile Corp. Ltd. - NTC was incorporated on 1.4.**1968**

NTC was given a provision of Rs. 17.5 crores during 1969-74 primarily for the purpose of reconstruction and modernization of viable mills taken over by Government. (4.14.34)

As a result of the take-over of 14 more mills during the period 1980-85, the number of mills under NTC increased from 111 to 125. NTC was estimated to have spent about Rs. 236 Cr during this period on modernization and renovation. Out of the 125 mills under the control of NTC, 103 mills were nationalized and the remaining 22 mills were under NTC's management. The total installed capacity of the 125 mills was 4.14 million spindles and 60,315 looms. (7.7.145)

NTC managed the affairs of 124 Sick Textile mills taken over by the Government of India in a series of 3 Nationalization Acts (1974, 1986 and 1995) in 1995.

NTC Ltd. was managing 119 mills through its **9 subsidiaries** namely NTC (Delhi, Punjab and Rajasthan) Ltd, NTC (Guj.) Ltd., NTC (Uttar Pradesh) Ltd., NTC (South Maharashtra) Ltd., NTC (Maharashtra North) Ltd., NTC (West Bengal, Assam, Bihar and Orissa) Ltd, NTC (A. Pradesh, Karnataka, Kerala and Mahe) Ltd., NTC (Madhya Pradesh) Ltd. and NTC (Tamil Nadu and Pondicherry) Ltd.

Of the 119 mills, 8 were referred to the BIFR. During the period 1992-97, NTC identified 53 viable mills and 66 unviable mills. The Government proposed to modernize the viable mills and close / privatize the unviable mills. (10.7.1.163) The BIFR scheme envisaged closure of 66 unviable mills and revival of 53 viable mills.

All 9 subsidiary companies were merged with NTC - (Holding Company) making it into a single Company w.e.f. 01.04.2006.

5 Joint Ventures of some NTC mills were running in profit since 2006-07.

The company made operational loss of Rs.50 Cr during 2007-08 mainly due to huge interest burden (Rs.609 crore).

The installed capacity of NTC in 2008-09 for yarn was 1155770 spindles and for Cloth was 1374 looms.

The Company completed modernization of 18 old mills as on 2009-10.

NTC, by 2010-11, closed 78 mills and was in the process of reviving 40 mills. Out of these 40 mills, 18 mills were modernized in first phase by NTC directly and 16 mills were to be revived through joint venture partnership. NTC was manufacturing and selling of wide range of fabrics in cotton / blended/ woolen yarn from its **43 mills in 2010-11.**

4 new Greenfield mills were being set up in 2010-11.

In 2013-14, NTC had 23 working mills in the State of Andhra Pradesh (1), Gujarat (1), Karnataka (1), Kerala (4), Madhya Pradesh (2). Maharashtra (5), Puducherry (1), Tamil Nadu (7) and west Bengal (1) with good infrastructure for the production of a variety of yarns and woven fabrics. Due to positive net worth, BIFR vide its order dated 20.10.2014 discharged NTC from its purview. Setting up a new composite unit at Amravati and utilization of vast available land bank with NTC were part of the revival plan.

In 2019-20, NTC had 23 working mills (as per BIFR / GOI approved strategy) with good infrastructure for the production of a variety of yarns and woven fabrics

NTC had made a turnaround within a short span to emerge as a debt-free company with a highly competitive revival strategy. Apart from re-branding, NTC had developed a new marketing and corporate strategy that included revamping of all NTC stores and setting up of new stores.

NTC has so far closed 77 mills and has transferred 2 mills in the State of Pondicherry to the State Government of Pondicherry.

NTC planned to modernize 24 mills by itself through generation of funds from the sale of its surplus assets and 16 mills were to be revived through Joint Venture route.

NTC had modernized 18 mills and was in the process of setting up 3 composite textile units including one in Special Economic Zone area. NTC would be setting up 1 technical textile unit and modernizing 2 more units taken out from the list of joint ventures apart from going into ginning and garmenting by way of forward and backward integration to have a presence in all components of the value chain.

National Textile Corp. Ltd. (APKK&M) - NTC (APKK&M) was incorporated on 23.10.**1974** under the Sick Textile Undertaking (Nationalization) Act, 1974 as a 100% subsidiary of NTC Ltd. to manage the business of nationalized textile mills situated in Andhra Pradesh, Karnataka, Kerala and Mahe (Pondicherry).

NTC (APKK&M) is manufacturing textile yarn and textile fabric of cotton blends, 100% synthetic etc. in its 10 operating mills at Chittoor, Tadipatri in Andhra Pradesh, Bangalore and Tolahunse in Karnataka, Kollam, Trissur, Kannur in Kerala and Mahe (Pondicherry).

National Textile Corp. (DP&R) Ltd. - NTC (DP&R) was incorporated in **1974** as a 100% subsidiary of NTC Ltd. to rehabilitate and run the nationalized sick textile mills.

NTC (DP&R) was manufacturing cotton / blended / woolen yarn and woolen cloth in its 6 units at Beawar, Bijainagar and Udaipur in Rajasthan and Kharar and Malout in Punjab. The revival scheme envisaged modernization of 5 viable mills and closure of the remaining 4 mills, out of which three have been closed.

National Textile Corp. (Gujarat) Ltd. - NTC (Gujarat) was incorporated in **1974** to take over the assets and liabilities of 11 nationalized textile mills of Gujarat. NTC (Gujarat) was manufacturing cotton and P.V. Yarn in its 11 operating mills at Ahmedabad, Bhavnagar, Rajkot, Palod and Viramgam in Gujarat. The subsequently adopted revival scheme envisaged modernization of 5 viable mills and closure of the remaining 4 mills, out of which 3 have been closed.

National Textile Corp. (MP) - NTC(MP) was incorporated on 1.11.**1974** as a 100% subsidiary of NTC Ltd. to manage the affairs of 7 sick textile mills in Madhya Pradesh which were nationalized under Sick Textile Undertakings (Nationalization) Act, 1974.

NTC (MP) was manufacturing yarn and cotton cloth in its 2 units at Burhanpur and Bhopal in Madhya Pradesh.

National Textile Corp. (MN) Ltd. - NTC (MN) was incorporated in **1974** as a 100% subsidiary of NTC Ltd. to own and manage 11 nationalized textiles mills (7 more mills were entrusted to corporation w.e.f. 1.4.1997). NTC (MN) was manufacturing yarn and fabric in its 8 units at Mumbai and Akola.

National Textile Corporation (South Maharashtra) - NTC (SM) was incorporated on 1.4.**1974** as a 100% subsidiary of NTC Ltd. to manage the affairs of 17 sick textile mills in Maharashtra which were nationalized under Sick Textile Undertakings (Nationalization) Act, 1974.

NTC(SM) was manufacturing cloth and yarn and undertaking job conversion of yarn in its 15 operating units.

National Textile Corp. (TN&P) Ltd. - NTC (TN&P) was incorporated in **1974** as a 100% subsidiary of NTC Ltd. to own and manage 15 sick textile units in Tamil Nadu and Pondicherry. NTC (TN&P) was producing yarn in its 8 units Tamil Nadu after restructuring effected in recent years. Closure of 6 unviable mills and revival of 9 viable mills was recommended by SITRA. 5 of 6 unviable mills had already been closed. Two mills in Pondicherry were transferred to Pondicherry Government with effect from 1.4.2005.

National Textile Corp. (UP) Ltd. - NTC (UP) was incorporated in **1974** as a 100% subsidiary of NTC Ltd. to manage the business of 11 textile mills situated in U.P. The company aimed to produce cheaper cloth and yarns for the weaker sections. NTC (UP) was producing yarn in its 2 units namely Swadeshi Cotton Mill at Allahabad and Bhanjan in U.P. 9 units were selected for closure and 2 units at Bhanjan and Allahabad were to be revived. Accordingly, 9 units have been closed. Production of yarn is going on in only two units.

National Textile Corp. (WBAB&O) Ltd - NTC (WBAB&O) was incorporated in **1974** to take over the assets and liabilities of 16 nationalized mills. NTC (WBAB&O) was producing cotton yarn and cloth in its 6 units in West Bengal. 10 Units were closed. Modernization of 6 revivable mills was under process.

Apollo Design Apparel Parks Ltd., Aurangabad Textiles & Apparel Parks Ltd, Goldmohur Design & Apparel Parks Ltd and **India United Textile Mills Ltd** were established in 2007

The Cotton Corporation of India Ltd.

Cotton Corporation of India Ltd. - CCI was incorporated on 31.07.**1970** to act as a canalizing agency for import of cotton particularly long and extra-long staple varieties and to undertake other developmental activities related to productivity and quality of cotton.

Whenever market prices touch the support prices announced by the govt, CCI procures the entire quantity of cotton offered in Agricultural Produce Market Committee yards at remunerative prices to prevent distress sale by farmers. CCI is providing services through its 19 branch offices and 303 procurement centres across 83 districts in various cotton growing states The corporation introduced a scheme for supply of contamination free cotton to meet growing demand of textile mills at stable prices under Go-down Storage Facility. Revenue from operations in 2021-22 was Rs. 23565.24 Cr.

Jute Corporation of India Ltd.

Jute Corporation of India Ltd. - JCI was incorporated in the year **1971** to ensure reasonable price for jute growers for their produce by undertaking purchase of raw jute at the minimum support price.

JCI conducts purchase operation of raw jute at minimum support price to procure and maintain buffer stock as and when advised by the Government i.e. to serve as stabilizing agency.

JCI undertakes building infrastructure for orderly marketing of raw jute and establishing market linkages, providing market information as a decision support system to the jute growers, ensuring timely supply of raw jute backed by stringent quality control system to the buyer mills.

The company is having its regional offices and 171 departmental purchase centres in 7 jute growing states of Assam, Meghalaya, Tripura, Bihar, Orissa, Andhra Pradesh and West Bengal.

The corporation was importing and exporting of raw jute as and when necessary and trading in jute goods.

It received subsidy in reimbursement of losses on price support account. During 2007-08, the Corporation procured 0.766 million bales of raw jute.

During 2022-23, JCI procured 4.24 lakh quintals under MSP operations and 1.37 lakh quintals of raw jute under Commercial operations. Revenue from operation was Rs. 142.32 Cr.

Central Cottage Industries Corp. of India

Central Cottage Industries Corp. of India - CCICI was incorporated on 4.2.**1976** to promote, develop and assist Cottage Industries by organizing their sale in India and abroad.

CCICI is providing services in the field of retail trading of handicrafts and handlooms, procured from all over the country. Company is also engaged in export activity. The operating units of the corporation are situated at Mumbai, Kolkata, Bangalore, Chennai, Hyderabad, Varanasi, Patna, Delhi and Gurgaon. It also has two franchisee showrooms at Gurgaon and Patna. The corporation entered into a joint venture with Handicraft and Handlooms Exports Corp. of India for sale of 24 carat gold coins.

During 2022-23, Two new Showrooms of Crafts and Hastkala Academy, New Delhi and Salarjung Museum Shop, Hyderabad were opened. Revenue from operations was Rs. 43.77 Cr.

North Eastern Handicrafts & Handloom Development Corp. Ltd.

North Eastern Handicrafts & Handloom Development Corp. Ltd. - NEHHDC was incorporated on 31.3.**1977** to promote and develop handicrafts and handlooms industries in the North-Eastern Region.

NEHHDC is marketing handicrafts and handlooms products made by the weavers and artisans of the North Eastern Region through its regional sales promotion offices situated at Guwahati and Delhi, 5 sales emporia situated in Shillong, Guwahati, Bangalore, New Delhi and Kolkata, one sales promotion office at Chennai and one craft development centre at Silchar and provides necessary assistance to artisans & craftsmen of the region in terms of loan, technology and training etc.

The Corporation also conducts North East craft Fairs and exhibitions to promote sales.

The company has set up a Handicraft Design Bank and a Museum at Guwahati.

NEHHDC was setting up an ERI Silk Spinning Plant at Integrated Textile Park, Mushalpur, Baksa (Assam) with a project cost Rs. 14.92 crores during 2022-23

National Jute Manufacturers Corp. Ltd.

National Jute Manufacturers Corp. Ltd. - NJMC was incorporated on 3.6.**1980** with an objective to take over the six jute mills, the management of which was earlier taken over by the Government of India.

NJMC was producing 0.16 Mts (12.31% of total production) of jute goods in 1984-85. (7.7.155) NJMC was manufacturing of Jute goods through 6 units at North 24 Parganas, Howrah, Kolkata and Katihar (Bihar).

It had one subsidiary namely Birds Jute and Exports Ltd.

Due to disconnection of power supply by CESC / BSEB in all units of NJMC, there was no production for more than 8 years since 2003-04.

Govt decided to revive mills at Khardah, Kinnison in WB and RBHM in Bihar and close remaining 3 mills.

The installed capacity was expected to be 305 TPD after completion of modernization.

Regular production started in Khardah and Kinnison mills in WB and RBHM Mill in Bihar during 2012-13.

The Union Cabinet, at a meeting held on 10.10.2018, chaired by PM Modi, gave the green signal for the closure of NJMC. NJMC is undergoing process of closure as on 31.03.2023.

Brushware Ltd

Brushware Ltd. - BL was incorporated in the year 1893 in private sector and was nationalized in the year **1981**. BL was in the manufacturing of all types of brushes like industrial, domestic, personal and paint brushes catering to the needs of Defence, Railway, HAL, Sugar mills, textile mills, road ways etc. However, production activity of the company is almost closed since 1994-95.

National Handlooms Development Corp.

National Handlooms Development Corp. Ltd. - NHDCL was incorporated on 22.2.**1983** to serve as a agency for development of the Handloom sector.

NHDCL is engaged in ensuring the availability of raw material like yarn, dyes and chemicals to handloom weavers and supply of handloom fabrics.

The Corporation organizes appropriate technology exhibitions, quality dyeing training programs, workshop on awareness and provides marketing support like organization of Expos, Silk Fab, Wool Fab and Establishment of marketing complexes etc.

NHDC supplied 16.79 million kg of yarn during 2000- 01 to the handloom agencies.

During 2001-02, the NHDC supplied 17.581 million kg of hank yarn up to February 2002. (10.7.1.290)

The domestic market share of the company for yarn supply to Handloom Sector during the year 2010-11 was approximately 17.50%.

In 2013-14, Corporation entered into MoU with 13 supplier mills so as to ensure regular supply of yarn from them to handloom weavers in a time bound manner.

In 2019-20, Corporation was operating 46 warehouses for ensuring timely supply to handloom weavers/ agencies.

Birds Jute & Exports Ltd.

Birds Jute & Exports Ltd. - BJEL was incorporated on 30.06.1904 in private sector under the name Lansdowne Jute Company Ltd with the objective of taking over as a going concern, the business of the manufacturing jute goods at Dakhindari from the Arathoon Jute Mills Ltd.

The name of the company was changed to Birds Jute & Export Ltd on 15.12.1971 and started to run as a processing factory for bleaching, blending, dyeing and printing of jute cotton and blended fabrics / curtain, etc.

It became a subsidiary of National Jute Manufacturers Corp. Ltd. on 20.11.1986 after remaining closed for around 7 years due to financial stringency. However, the company became sick and remained closed since October, 2002. The revival plan prepared by IDBI Bank including financial restructuring was approved by BIFR on 2.8.2012.

The Union Cabinet, on 10.10.2018, decided to close Birds Jute and Exports Ltd. BJEL is undergoing process of closure as on 31.03.2023.

Public Sector Companies Meeting Consumer Needs for Food Products

Hindustan Salts Ltd.

Hindustan Salts Ltd. - HSL was incorporated in the year **1958** with an objective to take over and manage the departmentally managed salt works at Kharaghoda (Gujarat), Sambhar Lake (Rajasthan) and Mandi (Himachal Pradesh) and to make available quality iodized salt to weaker sections through Public Distribution System.

Subsequently to manage Sambhar salt source, a separate company Sambhar Salt Ltd. was formed on 30.09.1964 as a subsidiary of HSL.

HSL is engaged in production of industrial and edible salt, Magnesium Chloride and liquid bromine through its 3 operating units at Kharaghoda, Mandi and Ramnagar in Uttaranchal.

It has two sales depots at Gandhinagar and Bharuch in Gujarat and 1 subsidiary namely Sambhar Salts Ltd.

There are proven rock deposits of approximately 116 Mt in Mandi rock mines. Hindustan Salts Ltd. had installed capacity of 900 TPA for Liquid Bromine in 2008-09.

Steps were taken to restart Rock Salt mining and implementation of Solution Mining Project at Mandi. Consultant recommendation for starting 300000 TPA Vacuum Salt Production was under consideration in 2013-14. HSL was installing plant for production of Magnesium Chloride at Kharaghoda. It was planning to expand its production capacity of Magnesium Chloride from 7500 T to 21500 T. HSL was undertaking installation of a Salt Refinery of 0.1 Mt at Kharaghoda in 2019-20.

(i) The production of rock salt during 2021-22 was 286 T against 485 T in the previous year.

(ii) The production of Bromine and Magnesium Chloride during 2021-22 was 437 T and 3553 T against 173 T and 1862 T respectively in the previous year.

Sambhar Salts Ltd.

Sambhar Salts Ltd.- SSL was incorporated on 30.09.**1964** to manage Sambhar Salt source.

SSL is in the production of edible and industrial salt at Sambar Lake works in Rajasthan. The production capacity of Sambhar Salts was 0.18 Mt in 2010-11. Salt Refinery of 0.1 Mt was installed to ensure that the calcium and magnesium ratio of the salt produced conform to the ratio of 2:1 as per the requirement of chlor-alkali plants. The Company set up a Salt Refinery of 0.1 Mt at Gadha / Nawa (Rajasthan) to produce refined salt.

The installed capacity of Sambhar Salts for refined and process salt in 2019-20 was 90783 tons.

Hindustan Vegetable Oils Corp. Ltd.

Hindustan Vegetable Oils Corp. Ltd. - HVOC was incorporated in the year **1984** by merger of two nationalized companies namely M/s Ganesh Flours Mills and M/s Amritsar Oil Works to promote the edible oil supply to the consumers at competitive price. HVOC is one of the taken over enterprises in production of edible oil and ready to-eat extruded food with its operating unit at Delhi.

The breakfast foods unit at Delhi was producing wheat / corn flake.

The other units of the company producing edible oil were closed in 2001.

In 2013-14, as regards breakfast food unit, whose production activities were discontinued in the year 2012, the Government has decided to bring the unit under the purview of liquidation and offer voluntary separation to its employees.

Public Sector Companies Contributing for Distribution of Food Grains

National Agricultural Cooperative Marketing Federation of India Ltd

National Agricultural Cooperative Marketing Federation of India Ltd - NAFED was founded on 2.10.**1958** to promote the trade of agricultural produce and forest resources across the nation. NAFED is now one of the largest procurements as well as marketing agencies for agricultural products in India.

NAFED is the nodal agency to implement price stabilization measures. NAFED, along with FCI and proactive role of state governments, physically procures oilseeds, pulses and copra under the Price Support Scheme.

In 2008, it established, National Spot Exchange, a Commodities exchange, as a joint venture with Financial Technologies (India) Ltd.

The NAFED exported 3,60,220 tons of onions during 1989-90 which helped maintain the price line in domestic market. The NAFED also procured 6,022 tons of copra as price support operation. (8.V2.1.6.3)

NAFED has been undertaking production and distribution of certified seeds.

During 2018-19, NAFED undertook seed business of 11170.74 Tons through its empaneled seed producers, NFSM- Pulses (1780.67 Tons) and NFSM - Oilseeds (1820.64 Tons).

Further, general supplies of 75694.31 Quintals were made to state Governments / Institutions.

National Cooperative Development Corporation

National Cooperative Development Corporation - NCDC was set up on 13.03.**1963** for planning, promoting and financing production, processing, marketing, storage, export and import of agricultural produce, foodstuffs, industrial goods, livestock and certain other notified commodities (like fertilizers, insecticides, agricultural machinery, lac, soap, kerosene oil, textile, rubber etc.) and services (like income generating stream of activities such as poultry, dairy, fishery, sericulture, handloom etc.) on cooperative principles.

NCDC financed projects in the rural industrial cooperative sectors and for certain notified services in rural areas like water conservation, irrigation and micro irrigation, Agri-insurance, Agro-credit, rural sanitation, animal health, etc.

Loans and grants were advanced, through state governments, for financing primary and secondary level cooperative societies and direct to the national level and other societies having projects extending beyond one state.

NCDC is endowed with organizational, financial management, Management Information Systems capabilities in the areas of sugar, oilseeds, textiles, fruits & vegetables, dairy, poultry and livestock, fishery, handlooms, and healthcare infrastructure to help cooperatives to identify / formulate projects and successfully implement them.

NCDC promoted 239 cold storage units with capacity of 0.683 Mt, of which 229 cold storages with 0.635 Mt capacity were installed. NCDC promoted 2442 number of processing units up to 1989-90. (8.V2.1.6.4)

As on October, 2020, NCDC had 18 Regional Directorates for providing financial assistance to cooperatives / societies / federations

Food Corporation of India Ltd.

Food Corporation of India - FCI was set up on 14.01.**1965** to implement the following objectives of the National Food Policy:

1. Effective price support operations for safeguarding the interests of the poor farmers

2. Distribution of food grains throughout the country for Public Distribution System

3. Maintaining a satisfactory level of operational and buffer stocks of food grains to ensure National Food Security

4. Regulate market price to provide food grains to consumers at a reasonable price

Each year, FCI purchases roughly 15 to 20% of India's wheat output and 12 to 15% of its rice output. The purchases are made from the farmers at Minimum Support Price declared by the Government of India. There is no limit for procurement in terms of volume, any quantity can be procured by FCI provided the stock satisfies Fair Average Quality specifications.

FCI procures rice and wheat from farmers through many routes like paddy purchase centres, mill levy, etc., and stores them in depots. FCI maintains many types of depots like food storage depots, buffer storage complexes, private equity go-downs and silo storage facilities.

The stocks are transported throughout India and issued to the state government nominees at the rates declared by the Government of India for further distribution under the Public Distribution System for the consumption of the ration card holders. (FCI itself does not directly distribute any stock under PDS, and its operations end at the exit of the stock from its depots).

The difference between the purchase price and sale price, along with internal costs, are reimbursed by the Union Government in the form of food subsidy. In 2010-11, the annual subsidy was around $10 billion. FCI does not decide anything about the MSP, imports or exports. It just implements the decisions made by the Ministry of Consumer Affairs, Food and Public Distribution and Ministry of Agriculture.

The domestic market share of FCI in procurement of wheat, rice and foodgrains in 2011-12 were 41%, 34% and 30% respectively.

FCI started procurement of pulses in various regions from the crop year 2015–16, and pulses are procured at market rate, which is a sharp deviation from its traditional minimum support price-based procurement system.

One of the reasons for the six-fold increase in food subsidy was the non-revision of the price at which food grains are given to beneficiaries since 2002. For example, rice was given to families under the Antyodaya Anna Yojana at Rs. 3/Kg since 2002, while the cost of providing this had increased from Rs 11/Kg in 2001-02 to Rs 33/Kg in 2017-18.

Table – 4.1 – Food Grain Procurement and Food Subsidy Released

YEAR	RICE Proc. By Centre in Mts	Rice Proc by States in Mts	Wheat Proc. By Centre In Mts	Wheat Proc by States in Mts	Food Subsidy Released Cr	Rice Prod. in Mts[1]	Wheat Prod. in Mts[1]	RICE Proc. In % of Prod.	Wheat Proc. In % of Prod.	Food Subsidy Released Cr to FCI	Food Subsidy Released Cr to States
1949-50						22.5	6.4				
1950-51			6.46			21	6		10.77		
1954-55			9.04								
1959-60			10.32								
1964-65			12.26								
1996-97	12.96		8.157								
1997-98	15.486		9.298		7500						
1999-2000	17.309		14.144		9200						
2004-05	24.683		16.795		25746						
2009-10	32.034		25.382		58242						
2010-11	34.198		22.514		62930	95.98	86.87	35.63	25.92		
2011-12	35.036		28.335		72371	105.31	94.88	33.27	29.86		
2012-13	34.044	27	38.148		84554	105.24	93.5	32.35	40.80		
2014-15	32.165	29.645	28.023	24.489	113171	105.48	86.53	30.49	32.39		
2015-16	34.216	33.404	28.088	24.489	134919	104.41	92.29	32.77	30.43	112000	22919
2018-19	44.399	43.948	35.785	31.534	171127	116.4	102.2	38.14	35.01	140098.7	31029.49
2019-20	24.168	23.951	34.132	30.095	150664					119164	31500

As of 2016-17, the total storage capacity in the country was 78.8 Mt, of which 35.4 Mt was with the Food Corporation of India and 42.4 Mt was with the state agencies.

FCI is engaged in procurement and distribution of food grains through its 171 district offices spread all over the country. Company runs on "no profit no loss" basis. FCI was ensuring steady supplies of food grain to 0.5 million Fair Price Shops under PDS to cover 141 million Above Poverty Line people / 67 million card holders; and ensuring food for all other Welfare Schemes. The Government of India also provides budgetary support to the Corporation for meeting capital expenditure such as construction of storage, go downs, etc.

Gross Turnover of Food Corp. of India in FY 2022-23 was Rs. 225599 Cr (decrease of 4% from turnover in 2021-22).

North Eastern Regional Agricultural Marketing Corporation

North-Eastern Regional Agricultural Marketing Corp. Ltd. - NERAMAC was incorporated on 31.03.**1982** with an objective to contribute for the Agro - horticultural development of the region by purchasing the marketable surplus of fruits and vegetables like ginger, pineapple, cashew, orange, apple, kiwi etc. in the North Eastern Region to the maximum possible extent directly from farmers, through co-operatives or farmer societies, and thus eliminating the middlemen, through a network of NERAMAC centres and to make necessary arrangement for its processing and marketing.

NERAMAC is mainly involved in trading and marketing along with production of Agro-products like fruit juice and cashew nut from its 10 operating units at Nalkata, Agartala and Byrnihat (Meghalaya), 2 sales outlets at Guwahati and Agartala and one franchise outlet at Guwahati.

NERAMAC has 8 procurement and marketing offices in Assam, Tripura, Meghalaya, Nagaland, Mizoram, Manipur, Arunachal Pradesh and Sikkim.

Company also conducts food processing investors meets, awareness and capacity building programs. NERAMAC provides budgetary support in the form of working capital loan at a low interest or zero interest. In 2019-20, NERAMAC was working for export of fresh organic produces to neighboring countries, trading through e-commerce platforms, e-auction of produces and opening stalls at Delhi metro stations and Guwahati Airport.

70 Farmer producers' organizations were registered along with 16 small entrepreneurs for food processing business. Conducted E-Auction of 5.6 Tons of black rice of Manipur.

Public Sector Companies Supplying Milk and Milk Products

Anand Milk Union Limited / Gujarat Co-operative Milk Marketing Federation Ltd.

Anand Milk Union Limited (AMUL) is a **state government cooperative society**, based in Anand, Gujarat. The Kaira District Co-operative Milk Producers Union Ltd was formed on 19.12.**1946** with just 2 village co-operative societies and 247 liters of milk and is today better known as Amul Diary.

Within a short span, 5 more unions were set up in Mehsana, Banaskantha, Baroda, Sabarkantha and Surat.

In **1970**, it spearheaded the "White Revolution" of India, which made the country the world's largest producer of milk and milk products.

To avoid competing against each other, the Gujarat Co-operative Milk Marketing Federation Ltd., an apex marketing body of these district cooperatives, was set up in **1973**. The Kaira Union, which had the brand name Amul with it since 1955, transferred it to GCMMF.

Amul's daily milk procurement is approximately 26.3 million liters per day from 18600 village cooperative societies, 18 member unions covering 33 districts and 3.64 million milk producer members. Its product range comprises milk, milk powder, health beverages, ghee, butter, cheese, pizza cheese, ice-cream, paneer, chocolates, and traditional Indian sweets, etc.

GCMMF is India's largest food product marketing organization with 2021-22 turnover of US $ 6.2 billion.

Aavin

Aavin is a **state government co-operative** under the ownership of Tamil Nadu Cooperative Milk Producers Federation Ltd., Ministry of Cooperation, Government of Tamil Nadu and the trademark of Tamil Nadu Co-operative Milk Producers' Federation Ltd.

The Dairy Development Department was established in Tamil Nadu in the year **1958** to oversee and regulate milk production and commercial distribution in the state. The Dairy Development Department took over control of the milk cooperatives. It was replaced by the Tamil Nadu Cooperative Milk Producers Federation Limited in the year 1981. On 01.02.1981, the commercial activities of the cooperative were handed over to Tamil Nadu Co-operative Milk Producers' Federation Ltd which sold milk and milk products under the trademark "Aavin".

Aavin procures milk, processes and sells milk and milk products including butter, yogurt, ice cream, ghee, milk shake, khoa, tea, coffee, chocolate, etc. Tamil Nadu is one of the leading states in India in milk production with about 14.5 million liters per day and currently has 1 crore daily consumers.

Revenue for 2018-19 was Rs. 5994 Cr (US $ 750 million)

National Dairy Development Board

National Dairy Development Board (NDDB) was founded by Dr Verghese Kurien on 16.07.**1965** to extend the success of the Kaira Cooperative Milk Producers' Union (Amul) to other parts of India It was under the ownership of Ministry of Fisheries, Animal Husbandry and Dairying of the Government of India.

Operation Flood Project was started in 1970 by NDDB (8.v2.1.8.6)

NDDB's subsidiaries include Indian Dairy Machinery Company Ltd, Mother Dairy and Indian Immunologicals Ltd., Hyderabad

In 2012, under the National Dairy Plan, NDDB initiated plans to boost dairy farming by targeting 40,000 villages in 14 major milk producing states including Punjab. The project was aimed at covering about 2.7 million milch animals in these states.

Mother Dairy

Mother Dairy, a wholly owned subsidiary of National Diary Development Board, was founded in **1974** under 'Operation Flood' to produce and market milk, dairy products, edible oil, fruits and vegetables. It currently sells milk, milk products, under Mother Dairy brand and fresh fruits and vegetables through 400 Safal outlets and frozen vegetables, pulses and honey under "Safal" brand and manufactures and markets edible oils under the "Dhara" brand.

Safal, the fruit and vegetable arm of Mother Dairy, has a plant in Bengaluru, which produces around 23,000 Tons of aseptic fruit pulp and concentrates annually. It supplies to food processing companies such as Coca-Cola, Pepsi, Unilever, Nestle, etc. Safal also has a presence across 40 countries viz., USA, Europe, Russia, Middle East, Asia, Africa, etc. and exports fresh fruits & vegetables (Grapes, Banana, Gherkin, Onion, etc.), fruit pulp & concentrate, frozen fruits & vegetables, etc.

Sandwich bread, brown bread, and a first in the category, milk and fruit bread for kids, are the three variants launched by Mother Dairy as its breakfast basket in July 2020.

As of 2020, Mother Dairy had a revenue over Rs. 10,000 Cr (nearly $1.6 Billion). It markets curd, lassi, chach, probiotic milk, flavored milk, paneer, butter, bread, cheese, ghee, fruit yogurt, cream, edible oil, frozen drumsticks, frozen cut okra and frozen Haldi paste cubes, milk shake, sweets, etc.

Indian Dairy Machinery Company Ltd

IDMC Ltd was set up in **1978** to manufacture dairy components and equipment. IDMC was incorporated as a wholly owned subsidiary company of the National Dairy Development Board in 1992.

IDMC is a leading manufacturer and supplier of a complete range of equipment for the dairy industry through 5 modern manufacturing units. IDMC provides a complete process solution together with automation right up to installation and commissioning for milking, cooling milk at the collection point (using bulk milk coolers for maintaining the quality of milk), receiving, processing and storing of milk or finished products (in tanks and silos) before packing or further processing.

IDMC has developed 3 types of milking systems, which are as close to nature as milk extraction by a calf. Because of high sanitation of IDMC's milking machines, the bacterial load in milk is minimum. Moreover, during storage of milk in bulk milk cooler the bacterial multiplication is drastically reduced.

IDMC provides complete support for building milk plants of capacities from a thousand to a million litres of milk per day with as many variants as the market demands.

IDMC provides complete process solutions for producing

(1) butter such as cream pasteurization, cream pre-treatment, cream-ageing and butter washing including butter reworking and texturization.
(2) cheese and by-product systems including culture preparation systems to manufacture cheddar, processed or mozzarella cheese in various forms, cheese spreads and other varieties of soft and hard cheeses in various formats of packaging such as cheese slices, chiplets, tubs and bricks.
(3) paneer
(4) many varieties of ice-cream
(5) curd, butter milk and cultured butter milk.
IDMC provides complete preprocessing and aseptic packaging system and quality sterilizer.

IDMC manufactures road and rail milk tanker barrels in single, two and three compartments in hygienic and aerodynamic design.

IDMC undertakes Industrial refrigeration for plants manufacturing liquid milk, ice-cream, butter, yoghurt, cheese and other milk products, meat processing plants, fruit and vegetables pack houses, brewery, steel and shipyards; air-conditioning for airports, commercial, industrial and residential complexes; supply of heat exchangers for dairy, food, chemical, textile, hydrocarbon, refrigeration, marine, steel, fertilizer, brewery, beverage, petrochemical and power plants.

IDMC set up a fully automated cattle feed plant to manufacture 1000 tons of cattle feed per day in 2012.

IDMC is a key project engineering and process equipment manufacturing company in the pharmaceutical, bio-technology and healthcare sectors.

IDMC is manufacturing equipment for fruit and milk-based beverages, carbonated soft drinks, non-carbonated drinks, fruit / ready-to-serve beverages, raw fruit handling and fruit pulp processing as well as packaging equipment.

IDMC manufactures packaging film for milk and milk products such as curd, butter milk, ghee, laminates for milk, frozen vegetables & liquid products such as edible oil and lube oil, high barrier laminates and stand-up cum zip-lock pouches for milk powder, processed food and health drinks, surface printed pouches for bread and baby diapers, re-usable top gusseted & rope handled bulk weight pouches for seeds, wall putty, distemper, etc. (in its packaging division of capacity 12000 tons of poly films and laminates).

Indian Immunologicals Limited

Indian Immunologicals Ltd - IIL was established in   as a subsidiary of National Dairy Development Board.

It is noted for developing veterinary and human vaccines for foot-and-mouth disease, bacterial vaccines, canine vaccines, measles and MMR.

IIL is a major supplier of DPT, TT and Hepatitis B vaccines to India's large Universal Immunization Program. The Gachibowli-Hyderabad facility is engaged in the production of vaccines, while the Karakapatla-Hyderabad facility produces animal health formulations and human vaccines. IIL's facility in Ooty exclusively produces human anti-rabies vaccine, "Abhayrab".

Pristine Biologicals Ltd is IIL's subsidiary in New Zealand and is involved in the production of serum used in the manufacture of vaccines.

IIL is the third largest animal health player in the Indian market and the market leader in veterinary biologicals in India. IIL also introduced the world's first vaccine against Porcine Cysticercosis –Cysvax. IIL is the only producer of companion animal vaccines in India

The Ooty plant was set up in 1998 in order to phase out use of the older and unsafe sheep brain vaccine (nerve tissue vaccine) with the modern tissue culture vaccine. The plant commenced commercial production in September 2006 and meets most of the requirements of Universal Immunization Program.

IIL exports its products to more than 50 countries across the world with a customer focus in Middle East, Asia, Africa, CISR countries and expanding in Central and Latin America.

It is leading the cross-continental research collaboration in association with the Griffith University of Australia to develop 'live attenuated SARS-CoV-2 Vaccine or COVID-19 vaccine' using the latest codon de-optimization technology.

Public Sector Companies undertaking Food Processing

Modern Food Industries (India) Ltd

Modern Food Industries (India) Ltd - MFIL was set up in 1965 as Modern Bakeries (India) Ltd at Kozhikundram, Tamil Nadu.

Achievements - It was the first branded bread manufacturer. It launched vitaminized bread in 1968, sweet bread in 1971, fruity bread in 1981 and wheat-min brown in 1991. MFIL had bread manufacturing units in 13 cities spread across India.
MFIL marketed fruit juice concentrate *Rasika*, MFIL aerated soft drink Double Seven. MFIL was manufacturing bread, ready-to-serve food / drink, edible oil, wheat products, nutritional diet, etc.
Modern Foods had over 40% of the bread market in India.
MFIL was divested by the Government of India to Hindustan Unilever Ltd. in January 2000 though it had a market share of 40%.

Public Sector Companies supplying Personal Products

Bharat Ophthalmic Glass Ltd.

Bharat Ophthalmic Glass Ltd., set up in **1965** in Durgapur, was India's first ophthalmic glass manufacturing company. BOGL was incorporated in the year 1972 with an objective to take over the Ophthalmic Glass Plant at Durgapur from National Instruments Ltd. which was first conceived in 1957 as part of credit agreement between India and erstwhile USSR.

BOGL was in the manufacturing of bifocal lenses / optical raw glass having its single operating unit at Durgapur, West Bengal. BOGL also manufactured electronic valves, tubes, other electronic components, radio, television and communication equipment and electrical capacitors (fixed and adjustable).

HMT Chinar Watches Ltd

HMT Chinar Watches Ltd - HCWL was incorporated, as 100% subsidiary of HMT Ltd. in 1999 as a part of restructuring plan of HMT Ltd. with an objective to de-merge the units engaged in the watch business from the HMT Ltd. and to boost industrial activity in the State of J&K.

HCWL was manufacturing hand wound mechanical and quartz watches at their 2 watch factories located at Zainakote (Srinagar) and watch assembly unit at Bari Brahmani (Jammu).

New series of quartz watches under the name "GALAXY" were launched in the market.

Product installed capacity of HCWL for Gents watches was 0.5 million in 2008-09.

The decrease in the level of operation of company was also due to lack of availability of manpower. The BRPSE in its recommendations submitted to Department of Heavy Industries proposed handing over of the subsidiary to the Govt. of Jammu and Kashmir as first option. This was under consideration of State govt. Cabinet Committee on Economic Affairs, on 6.01.2016, approved closure of HMT Chinar Watches Ltd.

NCLT Chandigarh Bench passed an order for dissolution of HCWL w.e.f. 10.03.2022.

HMT Watches Ltd.

HMT Watches Ltd. - HWL was incorporated on 9.8.**1999** as a 100% subsidiary of HMT Ltd. with an objective to acquire all the assets, properties and liabilities of HMT Ltd.'s watch business as a part of restructuring plan of the HMT Ltd.

HWL was in the manufacturing / production of all kinds of watches and its components with 4 units at Bangalore, Tumkur and Ranibagh (Nainital).

Product installed capacity of HWL for watches & components was 7.5 million nos. in 2008-09.

CCEA, on 6.01.2016, approved closure of HMT Watches Ltd. HWL is undergoing process of closure as on 31.03.2023.

Public Sector Companies Catering to Family Planning

Hindustan Latex Ltd.

Hindustan Latex Ltd. (subsequently rechristened as **HLL Lifecare Ltd.**) - HLL was incorporated on 1.3.**1966** with an objective to be a leader in the field of contraceptives and healthcare products and to assist in the National Family Welfare Program.

HLL is in manufacturing of contraceptives and healthcare products like Condoms, Cu T, Blood Bags, Surgical Sutures, OCP's etc. through its **6 production units** - two at Thiruvananthapuram, and one each at Kochi, Belgaum, Indore and Manesar through 6 business groups, namely (i) Condoms and FMCG products (ii) Hospital products (iii) Pharmaceutical products and other contraceptives (iv) Procurement and Consultancy services (v) Infrastructure Development Services and (vi) Healthcare Services.

Another unit of the Hindustan Latex Ltd. was to be set up at Farakka to meet the increased demand of Nirodh (5.5.157).

The company was having **17.40% of market share for condoms and 51% market share for Blood Collection Bags in 2004-05.**

During this year the company set up a bulk drug plant at its Kanagala factory.

In 2007-08, the company ventured into the business of pregnancy test kits, diagnostic services and also the business of procuring, installing, operating and maintaining various equipment required by hospitals. Production capacity of HLL Lifecare Ltd. in 2008-09 were - for Condoms - 1316 million pieces, Blood Bags 5 million pieces and Copper T 5.5 million pieces.

HLL has factories in 7 locations across India. 4 Factories were built in Peroorkada, Aakkulam, Kakkanad and Irapuram, Kerala. The other 3 factories are in Belgaum, Manesar and Indore. One of HLL's contraceptive products is Ormeloxifene, branded as Saheli, **the world's first** and only non-hormonal, non-steroidal oral contraceptive, taken as a weekly pill.

HLL has one joint venture namely **Life Spring Hospitals Pvt Ltd in** association with Acumen Fund Inc., USA, established as a cluster model with 12 hospitals functioning in and around Hyderabad.

HLL set up **Hind Labs MRI Scan Centre** in 3 Medical College Hospitals at Thrissur, Kottayam and Alappuzha.

HLL received an order to supply 193 million pieces of Sanitary Napkins at various blocks covering 108 districts across the country.

The Government of India made HLL as Project Management Consultant for the revival of **DPT vaccine manufacturing facility** at Central Research Institute, Kasauli and it was in advanced stage of completion. HLL incorporated a fully owned subsidiary company **HLL Biotech Ltd** in March 2012, to set up a state of art integrated vaccine complex at Chengalpattu for universal immunization program of Government of India and other new generation vaccines against preventable diseases.

In April 2014, HLL formed another 100% subsidiary Company **HLL Infra Tech Services Ltd**. to carry on the business of providing Infrastructure Development, Facilities Management, Procurement Consultancy and allied services.

Goa Antibiotics and Pharmaceuticals Ltd. is the third subsidiary of HLL (a joint venture with EDC Ltd. (State Finance Corporation of Goa)), engaged in pharmaceutical formulations.

HLL Medipark Ltd is the fourth subsidiary of HLL.

The installed capacity of HLL Life Care in 2019-20 were 13 million pieces of blood bags, 1953 million pieces of condoms, 5 million pieces of Copper T, 26 million pieces of Pregnancy test kits, 991 million cycles Steroidal OCP and 6 lakh dozens of Sutures.

HLL Mother & Child Care Hospitals Ltd

HLL Mother & Child Care Hospitals Ltd was incorporated on 01.08.**2017** to establish and operate 100 bedded Mother & Child Hospital wings at 20 district hospitals in Uttar Pradesh. The proposal to merge HMCCHL with HLL was submitted to the Ministry of Health & Family Welfare on 07.08.2019. HMCCHL is undergoing process of closure as on 31.03.2023.

Summary

Public sector organizations mostly provided indirect support to farmers by supply of seeds, saplings, fertilizers, pesticides, etc., procurement of food grains at MSP ensuring reasonable profit to farmers, transport, storage and distribution to targeted population, maintaining buffer stock, etc.

Some public sector organizations took up supply of salt, milk and milk products, vegetable oils, sugar, kerosine, bread, etc. Many sick textile mills were taken over to prevent mill labours losing jobs and then these mills were modernized to make them viable. The public sector organizations played a major and leading role in providing home loan and infrastructure development.

Private Sector Players Dominated Consumer Products Segment

Companies, which manufactured - Agro Equipment - 5, Batteries - 2, Bicycles - 5, Biscuits and Chocolates – 5, Cleaning and Personal Hygiene Products - 7, Cosmetics - 1, Cars – 1, Drip irrigation systems – 1, Electric Fans – 6, Food, Food supplement and Beverages - 6, Foot wear - 1, Home appliances - 11, Equipment used to manufacture hydrogenated oil, biscuits, soaps & glass - 1, Lamps, Light fittings - 5, Milk and milk products - 3, Motorcycles - 3, Radio and Transistor - 3, Rayon - 4, Sewing machine - 1, Shaving blades - 1, Electrical Switches - 3, Tractor and tractor implements – 14, Watches - 1, Water purification device - 1, selling of Imported fruits - 1, Trading Spices and polyester yarn – 1, Sugar mills - 7, Jute mills – 2, Tea companies - 5, Textile mills, Apparel and threads Manufacturers - 38, etc.

Adani Wilmar (1999)

Adani Agri Fresh (2004)

5: PRODUCTION OF CONSUMER PRODUCTS OF SECONDARY NEEDS

Secondary Need Products

Secondary essentials include agriculture machinery like pumps, tractors, motors, diesel engines, paper and paper boards, newsprint, bicycles, cars, silk and artificial silk, etc.

Targeted growth for consumer products production

The requirements for agriculture machinery including pumps, diesel pumps, electric motors, diesel engines, refrigerators, storage batteries, paper and paperboard, newsprint, two wheelers, three wheelers, tractors, cars, multi utility vehicles, commercial vehicles, trucks, Jeeps and Station Wagons, auto tires, etc. were forecasted by the government for the last financial year of each 5-year plan and the target capacity and production of these items for the various 5-year plans were set.

Table 5.1 – Production of Agriculture Pumps, Tractors, Diesel Engines and Pumps

Year	Production of Agriculture Electric Pumps in Million Nos.	Production of Diesel Engines in Million Nos	Production of Diesel Pumps in Million Nos	Target for Production of Tractors in Million Nos	Production of Tractors in Million Nos
1950-51	0.343	0.055			
1960-61	0.109	0.0447		0.003	0.007
1964-65	0.191	0.0746			
1965-66	0.244	0.0931		0.01	
1967-68	0.288	0.114			
1968-69	0.346		0.118		
1973-74					0.242
1978-79				0.055	
1979-80					0.0625
1984-85				0.1	
1989-90					0.1251
1990-91					0.1435
1991-92					0.155
1992-93					0.146
1993-94					0.1386
1994-95					0.1578
1995-96					0.2017
1996-97				0.24	0.2448
2001-02				0.301	

Meeting Consumer Needs for Agriculture Machinery

HMT Tractors commenced operations in **1971** in collaboration with Zetor / Motokov, Czechoslovakia Republic with the manufacture of 25 HP tractors in Pinjore, Haryana.

Meeting Consumer Needs for Paper & Paper Boards, Newsprints, etc.

Paper Corporation of India Ltd was incorporated on 06.01.**1945**.

Nepa Ltd. was incorporated on 26.01.**1947** by Nair Press Syndicate Ltd. under the name of **"National Newsprint and Paper Mills Ltd"** for production of newsprint. The company was taken over in 1949 by the State Government of Central Province and Berar (present Madhya Pradesh).

Commercial production started with an installed capacity of 30000 TPA in **1956**.

NEPA was expected to meet about one-third of the country's requirement of newsprint (1.29.22).

State government undertook **Andhra Paper Mills** expansion during 1955-60. (2.19.39)

Mandya National Paper Mills Ltd. was incorporated in **1957** by the State government.

Hindustan Photo Films Manufacturing Co Ltd. was established in **1960**

Production of a growing number of new industrial items started during II 5YP including newsprint, staple fibres, etc. (3.3.25)

During 1969-74
Hindustan Paper Corporation was established in **1970**.

Nagaland Pulp and Paper Co. Ltd. was incorporated in **1971** as a joint venture between Government of Nagaland and Hindustan Paper Corporation to construct an integrated pulp and paper mill at Tuli in Nagaland.

During 1975-80
Mysore Paper Mill Ltd., which was established in 1936 by the then Maharaja of Mysore in Bhadravati, became a government company in **1977**.

Tamil Nadu Newsprint and Papers Limited was established by the Government of Tamil Nadu to produce newsprint and writing paper using bagasse, a sugarcane residue.

During 1980-85
Nagaland Pulp and Paper Company Ltd. was commissioned in mid-**1982**.

Hindustan Newsprint Ltd. was incorporated in **1983** to take over the assets and liabilities of Kerala Newsprint Project of HPC.

Nagaon and Cachar paper projects of Hindustan Paper Corporation Ltd. were commissioned in **1985** and **1986** respectively with a total capacity of 0.2 Mt of paper and paper board

During 1985-90
3 Large paper mills and a large number of small mills based on imported second-hand machinery were established between 1985-90. (7.7.157)

Hindustan Newsprint Ltd. of capacity 80,000 TPA, Mysore Paper Mills of capacity 75,000 TPA and Tamil Nadu Newsprint Project, the first newsprint project based on bagasse, of capacity 50,000 TPA were commissioned. (7.7.160)

Punjab Agro News Prints Ltd. was incorporated in **1989** by the State Govt to manufacture paper and paper products.

During 1992-97 –
Uttar Pradesh Newsprint project, based on a newsprint furnish of 60% bagasse chemical pulp and 40% chemi-mechanical pulp (eucalypt-plantation grown), of capacity 89,000 TPA, was being put up by NEPA Ltd. in end 1992 at Hempur (Nainital).

Lack of private sector investment - The newsprint manufacture was capital intensive and involved a long gestation period. Even though the prices were not administered, profitability was comparatively low and the private sector was not coming forward to take up manufacture of newsprint. Government encouraged creation of bagasse based additional capacity in tandem with new sugar capacity. (8.v2.5.29.1)

Paper and Newsprint Industry in 2001-02

Total installed capacity of 515 registered pulp and paper mills was 5.1Mt (10.7.1.183)

(Mysore Paper Mills had an annual capacity of 0.075 Mt)

Total installed capacity of 64 newsprint mills (4 in the Central public sector, 2 in State public sector and 58 in the private sector) was 1.204 Mt. (NEPA, Hindustan Newsprint Ltd, Tamil Nadu Newsprint project and Uttar Pradesh Newsprint project had an installed capacity of 0.030 Mt / 0.088 Mt, 0.08 Mt, 0.05 Mt, 0.089 Mt respectively in 2008-09. (10.7.1.187)

The Indian paper industry had a total turnover of more than Rs 10,000 Cr. (10.7.1.182)

Clandestine imports and dumping of paper and paper products from other countries affected the health of the paper industry

The capacity utilization of the paper industry was 60% as about 194 paper mills were sick or lying closed and that of the newsprint industry was 55%. (10.7.1.184)

Paper Industry in 2006-07

The turnover was nearly Rs 17000 Cr per annum in 2006-07. (11.v2.7.1.238)

There were about 666 industrial units with a total installed capacity of 8.50 Mt for paper and paperboard. However, 98 units with a capacity of 1.1 Mt remained closed due to environmental problems. The industry produced 5.80 Mt of paper and paperboard. **The country was almost self-sufficient in most varieties of paper and paperboard**, and imports were taking place only of items such as coated paper, cheque paper, etc. (11.v2.7.1.239)

Newsprint Industry in 2006-07

There were 77 mills including 2 Central and 2 State public sector units, with a total installed capacity of 1.59 Mt. The domestic production was 1.03 Mt in 2006–07. (11.v2.7.1.242)

Paper Industry in 2011-12

The Indian Paper industry produced 10.11 Mt of paper in 2011-12. The annual turnover of the Indian paper industry was nearly Rs. 30,000 Cr. (12. Annex. 13.2 – 65)

30 Large integrated paper mills, which used wood and bamboo-based pulp, accounted for 31% of domestic production. 150 Paper mills, contributing 22% of production, used Agro-based (bagasse and straws) and about 473 mills, contributing 47% of total production, used recycled fibre or waste paper for paper production. (12. Annex. 13.2 – 66)

Meeting Individual Consumer Needs for Transportation, etc.

Production of automobiles, bicycles, motorcycles, scooters, etc. started during II 5YP. (3.3.26)

Between 1956-60, the number of small-scale units engaged in the production of **bicycles** increased from 44 to 150 and electric motors from 6 to 74. (3.25.45)

During 1969-74, the government decided that the public sector should enter consumer goods industries, particularly where adequate private investment was not forthcoming. Provision was made for the public sector role in industries like paper, scooters and watches. (4.14.37)

Scooters India Ltd was incorporated in **1972** for the manufacture of scooters, mopeds, motorcycles and their components.

Production of Crawler tractors in 1973-74 was 278 Nos.

Maruti Udyog Limited was founded by the Government of India in **1981** with Suzuki Motor Corporation as a minor partner. Production commenced in 1983 with the introduction of the Maruti 800. In 1984, the Maruti Van was released and the installed capacity of Gurgaon plant reached 40,000 units.

Automobile Industry in 2004-05 -
The Automobile Manufacturers put up a manufacturing capacity of 9.5 million vehicles from 1993. India was the world's **second largest manufacturer of two wheelers**, **fifth largest manufacturer of commercial vehicles** and manufactured the largest **number of tractors in the world**. ANNUAL REPORT OF DEPT OF PUB ENT 2004-05.pdf (Page 43).

Automobile Industry in 2005-06 -
The turnover of the automobile industry reached Rs 165000 Cr and the passenger car segment crossed the one million mark. (11.v2.7.1.129)

Indian car manufacturers achieved full indigenization in popular makes such as Tata Indica, Tata Indigo, Mahindra Scorpio, Bajaj Pulsar, TVS Victor, etc.

Automobile Components Industry in 2005-06 –
Around 500 manufacturers in the organized sector of the auto components industry and more than 10000 in the small-scale sector had a turnover of about Rs 54000 Cr.

The fact that 9 manufacturers were Deming Prize winners, 4 were Japan Institute of Plant Maintenance award winners, and one was a Japan Quality Medal winner bore testimony to the quality of the auto components produced in India.

Annual exports of auto components crossed Rs 11000 Cr in 2006–07. (11.v2.7.1.133 / 135)

Tire Industry in 2005-06
The installed capacity for tires was 85 million units against which 66 million units were produced. **All types of tires,** barring some specialized ones such as aircraft tires and snow tires, were **manufactured in India**. (11.v2.7.1.134)

Gems and Jewellery

India accounted for nearly 55% of world net exports of cut and polished diamonds in value terms. The industry was importing rough diamonds from Belgium, UK, UAE, Israel, Hong Kong, Switzerland and other mining countries. The polished diamond is exported to countries such as UAE, Hong Kong, USA, Belgium and Israel. (11.v2.7.1.99 / 101)

India is the largest consumer of gold in the world with annual demand for gold of over 800 tons. (11.v2.7.1.100)

Public Sector Companies Contributing for Increasing Agricultural Yield

HMT Tractors Ltd

HMT Tractors was incorporated on 7.2.**1953** in technical collaboration with Zetor / Motokov, Czechoslovakia to manufacture agricultural machinery like Tractors. HMT Tractors Ltd commenced manufacture of 25 HP tractor at the Pinjore plant Haryana in 1971.

The Food Processing Unit manufactured dairy machinery like continuous butter and Milk Pastries making machines, Cream separators etc. from **1980** to 1991 in technical collaboration with Fortschritt Landmaschinen (FLM), East Germany

Over the years, HTL developed tractors ranging from 25 HP to 75 HP in two, three and four-cylinder engine variants successfully meeting the TREM IIIA emission norms. HMT Tractors achieved **market leadership in tractors** by enlarging its range to cover most of the applications. HMT produced and marketed over 400,000 tractors since inception in India and abroad.

HMT was manufacturing tractors and Food Processing Machines through 2 manufacturing and 2 service divisions at Pinjore, Mohali, Hyderabad and Aurangabad.
Installed Capacity of HMT for tractors was 8800 nos. in 2008-09.

Constraints of reduction in farmer-consumers - One reason for low performance of the company was non-availability of finance at the retail level from banks and other financing agencies due to high levels of defaults by the customers, which resulted in banks restricting the finance and exercising greater discretion in disbursement of loans to farmers for purchasing tractors.

Mismanagement and rising competition post liberalization in 1991 in the form of Mahindra & Mahindra, TAFE and Sonalika Tractors hurt HMT the most. The tractor division was closed down in 2016 leaving behind manufacturing of food processing machinery as the main product of the Company.

HMT had six subsidiaries namely HMT Machine Tools, HMT watches, HMT Chinar Watches, HMT (International), HMT Bearing and Praga Tools Ltd.

The company has two financial joint ventures namely SUDMO HMT Process Engineers (I) Ltd. and Nigeria Machine Tools Ltd.

The Company was awarded with "Indywood Built in India Excellence Award" in the Category "Public Sector Units – Precision Engineering" on 4.12.2017.

Public Sector Companies Meeting Consumer Needs for Paper, Paper Boards and Newsprints

Nepa Ltd.

NEPA Limited was incorporated in **1947** as "National Newsprint and Paper Mills" in the private sector and was taken over by the government of Central Province and Berar (now Madhya Pradesh) in 1949. It was inaugurated on 26.04.**1956**. (4.14.52)

The Central Government acquired controlling interest in 1959. The name of the company was changed to **Nepa Limited** in 1989. NL has an operating unit at Nepanagar and a plantation unit at Hempur (Uttaranchal).

NEPA produced 42 GSM newsprint meeting all international parameters of strength, opacity, surface smoothness, brightness etc. for the first time in India.

NEPA manufactured economy newsprint by using old newspapers and over issue newspapers, to cater to the requirement of the lowest segment of the market at minimal cost, yet maintaining all other parameters of quality though in lower brightness.

Financial restructuring of the company was done in March 2000. (10.7.1.191)

The revival and modernization plan, taken up in 2016-17, was expected to enhance the production capacity 3-fold resulting from diversified product portfolio including high brightness newsprint, writing and printing paper.

Andhra Paper Mills-

Andhra Paper Mills - APM was established as Carnatic Paper Mills Ltd. at Rajahmundry in 1921. The mill was shut down due to insolvency within a few years. In 1929, APM was incorporated to take over the assets of Carnatic Paper Mills Ltd. The Andhra Pradesh Government took over APM in 1953. Its capacity at that time was 10 TPD.

The Andhra Pradesh government transferred the assets to a new company Andhra Pradesh Paper Mills Ltd. and incorporated it on 29.06.**1964.**

The ownership of the company changed to West Coast Paper Mills Ltd. in 1966, to Digvijay Investments Ltd. in 1981, to American pulp and paper company International Paper in 2011 and to West Coast Paper Mills Ltd. in 2019

The company was renamed as "International Paper APPM Limited" maintaining the link to the history and positioning of the Andhra Paper Mills brand in 2013 and to Andhra Paper Limited, which not only reflected the business of the Company, but also brought back the old glory to the Company in January 2020.

Pulp Mill had a production capacity of 1,82,500 TPA.

Hindustan Paper Corp. Ltd.

Hindustan Paper Corp. Ltd. - HPC was incorporated on 29.5.**1970** to establish pulp and paper / newsprint mills in the country to make paper available for mass consumption.

HPC manufactures writing and printing paper, caustic and chlorine in Nagaon Paper Mill and Cachar Paper Mill, each of capacity 100000 tons, which started commercial production in 1985 and 1988 respectively.

HPC has **4 subsidiary companies** namely Hindustan Newsprint Ltd in Kottayam (capacity 0.1 Mt), Nagaland Pulp and Paper Co. Ltd. in Mokokchung., Nagaland (capacity 33,000 tons), Mandya National Paper Mills Ltd. (capacity 18200 tons, incorporated by Government of Karnataka on 7.11.1957 for manufacture of writing and printing paper and taken over by HPC in 1974) and Jagdishpur Paper Mills Ltd, Sultanpur, Uttar Pradesh.

The market share of HPC was 12.5% in 2003-04.

HPC was one of the largest manufacturers of paper and newsprint in South East Asia. HPC had built up a capacity of about 0.335 Mt of paper and newsprint.

Hindustan Paper Corp. Ltd. was producing newsprint with capacity utilization of 104.16%, 105.87% and 87.51% in 2006-07, 2007-08 and 2008-09 respectively.

The byproducts of HPC were Liquified Chlorine Gas (capacity 18150 Tons), Caustic Soda (capacity 36300 Tons), Calcium Hypochlorite (capacity 14310 Tons), Hydrochloric Acid (capacity 6600 Tons) and Chlorine Dioxide (capacity 1090 Tons).

The government asked HPC to make MNPM operational using waste paper instead of bagasse by July 2013 to attract a prospective buyer of MNPM. The mill, after reopening, was expected to manufacture craft paper.

The rail and road connectivity for Cachar Paper mills was not good due to meter gauge tracks. The availability of fibre raw material for Cachar Paper Mill was not adequate. The National Company Law Tribunal on 2.5.2019 ordered liquidation of these 2 paper mills.

On behalf of the Government of Assam, Assam Industrial Development Corporation took over the assets of Nagaon and Cachar paper mills on 28.03.2022.

Nagaland Pulp and Paper Co. Ltd.

Nagaland Pulp and Paper Co. Ltd. - NPPC was incorporated on 14.09.**1971** as a joint venture between Government of Nagaland and Hindustan Paper Corporation to construct an integrated pulp and paper mill at Tuli in Nagaland. The commercial production commenced in 1982. NPPC manufactured pulp, writing and printing paper, newspaper and plantations of various cellulosic raw materials.

There was no production since 1992 due to escalation of project cost, non-performance of defectively designed coal-fired boilers, inadequate and erratic grid power, non-availability of feed, deficient infrastructure in transport / telecommunication, shortage of skilled manpower etc.

Revival and restructuring of the NPPC, taken up during 2002-07 on the recommendation of BRPSE, was not successful due to lack of captive power generation at NPPC. (11.v2.7.1.126)

A 30 years tripartite agreement executed on 25.05.2006 between Government of Nagaland, HPC and NPPC proposed handing over bamboo growing 12676 hectares of the Govt of Nagaland purchased land to NPPC for undertaking captive bamboo plantation and giving exemption on payment of royalty on raw material. Revised rehabilitation program (phase-1) was approved on 04.06.2013.

Despite several futile attempts to revive the mill, NPPC was finally put to the hammer for liquidation in 2019.

Mysore Paper Mill Limited

Mysore Paper Mill Limited – MPM was established in 1936 by the then Maharaja of Mysore at Bhadravati. In **1977**, the company became a government company.

MPM closed functioning in 2016.

Hooghly Printing Co. Ltd.

Hooghly Printing Co. Ltd. - HPCL was incorporated on 03.1.1922 to cater to the printing and stationery requirements of the Andrew Yule Group companies and became a government company on 10.05.**1979**. 90% of the order booking of the company was from Central and State Government departments.

Till 1991 HPCL was basically a letterpress printing company and then was upgraded to "Offset" procedure of printing.

In 1998-99 HPCL upgraded the procedure of printing from bi-color to four color offsets using a high-speed computer-controlled Offset Printing Machine along with balancing equipment.

Cabinet Committee on Economic Affairs approved the closure of HPCL and its merger with the holding company, Andrew Yule Company Ltd. on 19.09.2018.

HPCL merged with Anderw Yule & Co. Ltd. w.e.f. 04/06/2021

Tamil Nadu Newsprint and Papers Limited

Tamil Nadu Newsprint and Papers Limited - TNPL was established by the Government of Tamil Nadu to produce newsprint and writing paper using bagasse, a sugarcane residue. The Company commenced production in 1984 with an initial capacity of 90,000 TPA.

TNPL emerged as the **largest bagasse-based paper mill in the world** with a capacity of 0.245 Mt, consuming about 1 Mt of bagasse every year. TNPL installed 300 TPD hardwood pulp line with ECF bleaching & a 500 TPD ECF bleach plant for chemical bagasse pulp line.

During 2004–09, TNPL raised plantations in 37,556 acres involving 8235 farmers in 28 districts of Tamil Nadu under the Farm Forestry scheme and 2,735 acres under the Captive Plantation Scheme. (as on 31.03.2009).

TNPL established a state-of-the-art clonal propagation and research centre to achieve self-sufficiency in planting material and production of quality clonal / seedling plants with a capacity of 15 million plants per annum.

Hindustan Newsprint Ltd.

Hindustan Newsprint Ltd. - HNL was incorporated on 07.06.**1983** as a subsidiary of Hindustan Paper Corp. Ltd. with an objective to take over the assets and liabilities of Kerala Newsprint Project of HPC.

HNL undertook production of Newsprint grades of 45 GSM and 48.8 GSM in from the Kottayam unit.

HNL implemented an expansion cum diversification project to upscale its capacity from 0.11 Mt to 0.28 Mt for producing both newsprint and premium paper grades in 2007-08. (11.v2.7.1.126)

HNL maintains captive plantations in 3625 ha. of forest land leased by Government of Kerala.

HNL was operating with capacity utilization of 113%, 116% and 108% in 2006-07, 2007-08 and 2008-09 respectively.

The company's domestic master share was 14% in 2010-11. (10.7.1.10)

The NCLT Kochi approved the resolution plan for HNL submitted by the Kerala Industrial Infrastructure Development Corporation on 29.01.21 and is under implementation by KINFRA.

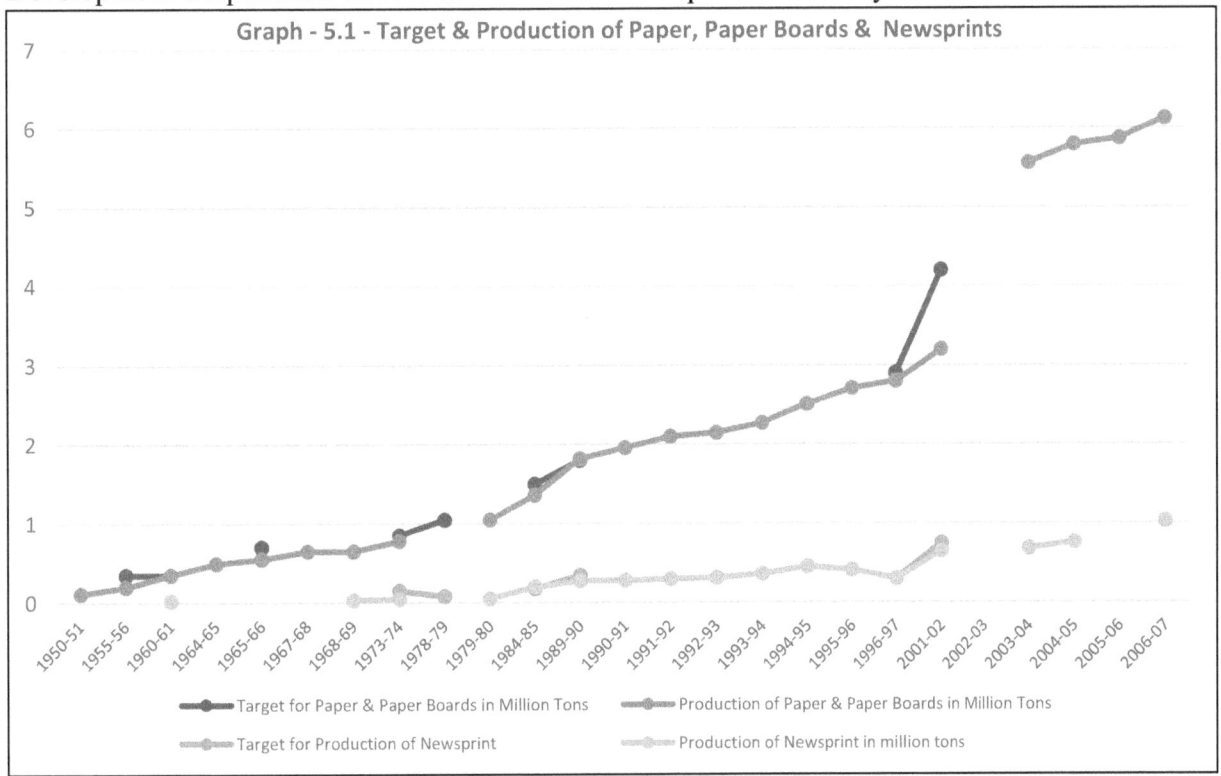

Punjab Agro Newsprints Ltd

Punjab Agro News Prints Ltd. - PANL was incorporated on 27.01.**1989** by the State Government for manufacture of paper and paper products.

A 200 TPD composite newsprint, printing and writing paper project of PANL continued through 1992-97.

The PANL was amalgamated with Punjab Agro Industries Corporation with effect from 27.06.2003.

Jagdishpur Paper Mills Limited

Jagdishpur Paper Mills Limited was incorporated on 8.5.**2008** as a subsidiary of Hindustan Paper Corporation Ltd. The matter of land allotment was being taken up with Uttar Pradesh State Industrial Development Corporation.

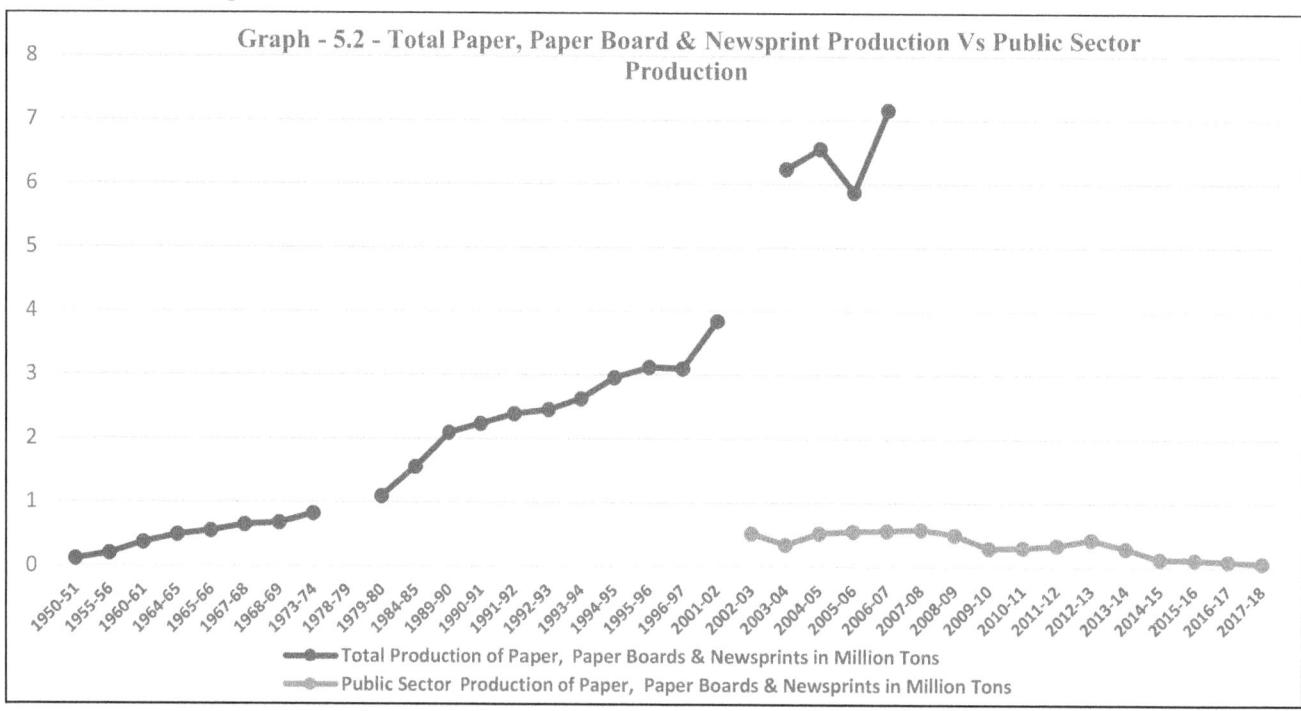

Public Sector Companies Meeting Consumer Needs for Individual Transportation

Scooters India Ltd.

Scooters India Ltd. - SIL was incorporated on 7-9-**1972** to manufacture scooters, mopeds, motorcycles, 3 wheelers and their components to provide economical and safe means of transportation for movement of cargo and people. SIL bought over plant machinery, design, drawing, documentation, copyrights etc. lock stock and barrel from Innocenti of Italy.

In 1975, SIL started its commercial production of scooters under the brand name of Vijai Super for the domestic market and Lambretta for the overseas market in Lucknow. They introduced 3 wheelers under the brand name of Vikram / Lambro.

In 1997, SIL discontinued their two-wheeler production and concentrated on manufacturing 3 wheelers. SIL developed a ten-seater electric trolley bus during 2002-03 and a new starter motor and alternator for Vikram 750-D air cooled three-wheelers for improved lighting and battery charging in 2003-04. The company upgraded its products to meet Bharat Stage II emission norms applicable.

SIL introduced the Vikram CG-1500 model of 3-wheeler in 2006-07 and 1000 cc CNG vehicles in 2008-09.

During 2009-10, SIL continued their **leadership in the passenger carrier (6+1) segment** of vehicles with a **market share of 83.82%.**

The government approved closure of loss-making SIL in January 2021. SIL is undergoing process of closure as on 31.03.2022.

Maruti Udyog Limited

Maruti Technical Services Ltd. was promoted by Sanjay Gandhi to develop an indigenous mass-produced 'people's car' and was granted a license to produce 50,000 cars per year in **1973**. The company had units in Gurgaon. By 1977, the company had manufactured only 100 cars and faced mounting losses. In 1980, the government enacted a law and acquired it.

Maruti Udyog Limited - MUL was founded by Government of India on 24.02.1981 with Suzuki Motor Corporation as a 26% minor partner to manufacture cars for middle-class Indians, when the market size was under 40000 units and 1 in 14000 people owned a car. Production commenced in December 1983 with the introduction of Maruti 800. The first car was affordable back then and was thus incredibly popular. In 1984, the Maruti Van was released and the installed capacity of **Gurgaon** plant reached 40,000 units.

In 1985, Gypsy, a 970 cc 4WD off-road vehicle, was launched.
In 1986, the Maruti 800 was replaced by the 796-cc hatchback Suzuki Alto.
In 1987, MUL started exporting to western markets.
Suzuki increased its equity from 26% to 40% in 1987 / 1989.
By 1988, the capacity of the Gurgaon plant was increased to 100,000 units per annum.
In 1989, Maruti 1000 was introduced as India's first contemporary sedan.
By 1991, 65% of the components, for all vehicles produced, were indigenized. After liberalization of the Indian economy in 1991, Suzuki increased its stake in Maruti to 50% in 1992.

Maruti's second plant was opened in 1995 with annual capacity reaching 200,000 units.

MUL had a 55% market share in the largest selling A & B segments, which accounted for 85% of cars sold in the Indian market in 2003.
MUL manufactured 370,000 cars at its plants in Gurgaon in FY 2002-03.
In 2002-03, the capacity utilization was 102% while capacity was 350000.
MUL Overall Market share in 1999-2000, 2000-01, 2001-02 and 2002-03 were 62%, 58%, 59%, and 57% respectively. Wayback Machine (archive.org)
The annual sale of MUL was 472,122 units in 2003-04.

Maruti Suzuki Automobiles India Ltd. was incorporated on 13.04.**2005**, as a joint venture of Maruti and Suzuki, to manufacture parts of motor vehicles like brakes, gear boxes, axles, road wheels, suspension shock absorbers, radiators, silencers, exhaust pipes, steering wheels, steering columns and steering boxes and other parts and accessories.

The **Manesar** manufacturing plant was inaugurated in **February 2007** with a production capacity of 100,000 vehicles and the capacity was increased to 300,000 vehicles in 2008 and then to 800,000 vehicles.

MUL rolled out its 100,000th vehicle in 1986, 1 millionth vehicle in 1994, 2 millionth vehicle in 1997, 4 millionth vehicle in 2003, 5 millionth car in 2005, 10 millionth vehicle in 2012 and its 15 millionth vehicle in May 2015.

In 2012, the company decided to merge **Suzuki Powertrain India Ltd.,** started as a JV by Suzuki Motor Corp. along with Maruti Suzuki for manufacturing diesel engines and transmissions, with itself.

Suzuki increased its equity further to 56.21% as of 2013.

In July 2014 it had a market share of 45%.

Suzuki Motor Gujarat, wholly owned by Suzuki Motor Corporation, was opened in **Hansalpur**, Ahmedabad, in **2017** with a capacity of 750,000 units.

Maruti Suzuki has two manufacturing facilities in **Gurugram and Manesar**, and one manufacturing complex in Gujarat which supplies its entire production to Maruti Suzuki.

All manufacturing facilities have a combined production capacity of 2,250,000 vehicles annually (1.5 million from Maruti Suzuki's two plants and 750,000 from Suzuki Motor Gujarat. The Gurgaon facilities also manufacture 240,000 K-series engines annually).

As of September 2022, MUL had a market share of 42% in the passenger car segment.

Tyre Corporation of India Ltd.

Tyre Corporation of India Ltd. - TCIL was incorporated on 24.02.**1984** when erstwhile Inchek Tyres Ltd. and National Rubber Manufacturers Ltd. were nationalized to protect the employment of around 4000 employees and to ensure supply of automotive tires to different State Transport Undertakings, government departments and Defence through its Kankinara (West Bengal) unit.

The company showed operating profit, however, **due to high interest payment on Central Government loans** it was incurring net loss. The Company has not manufactured its own brand tires since 1.4.2002. It is doing 100% jobbing work for manufacturing automotive tires for bus / truck for private tire majors like M/s. JK Tyre & Industries Ltd., M/s. Ceat Ltd. & M/s. Birla Tyres Ltd.

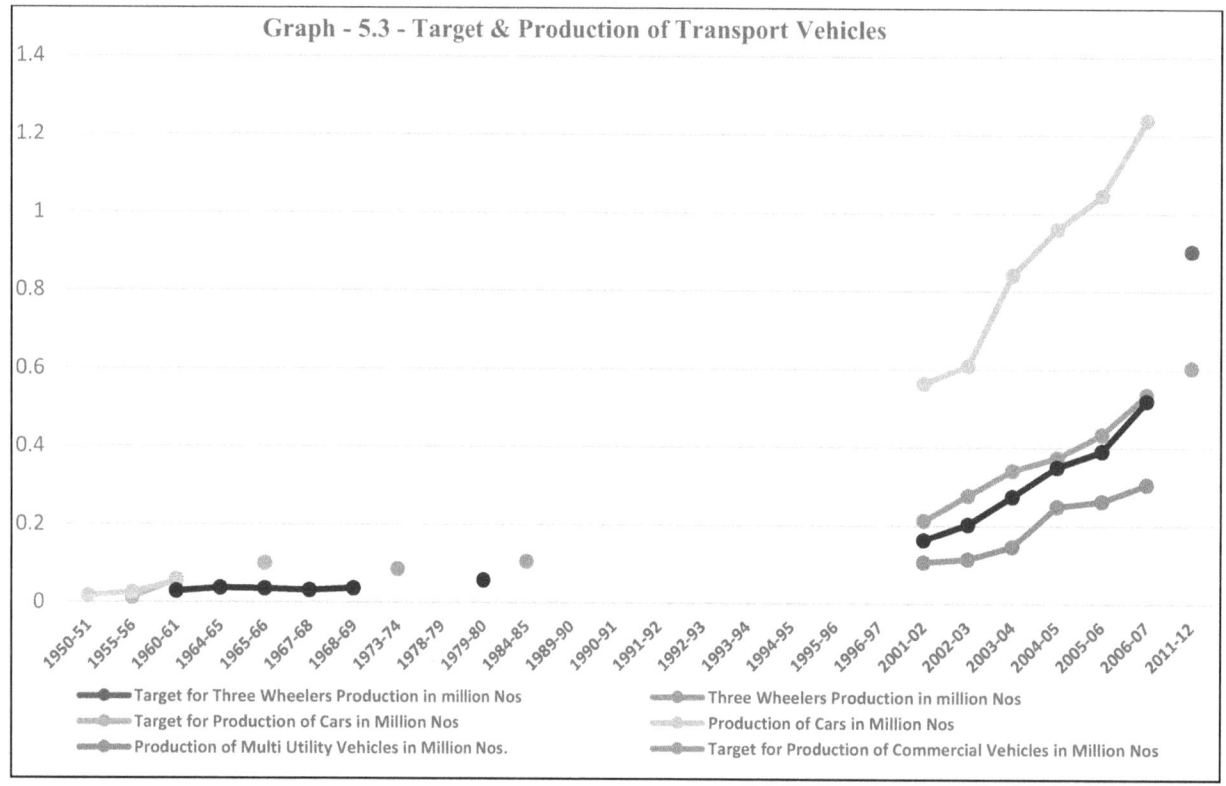

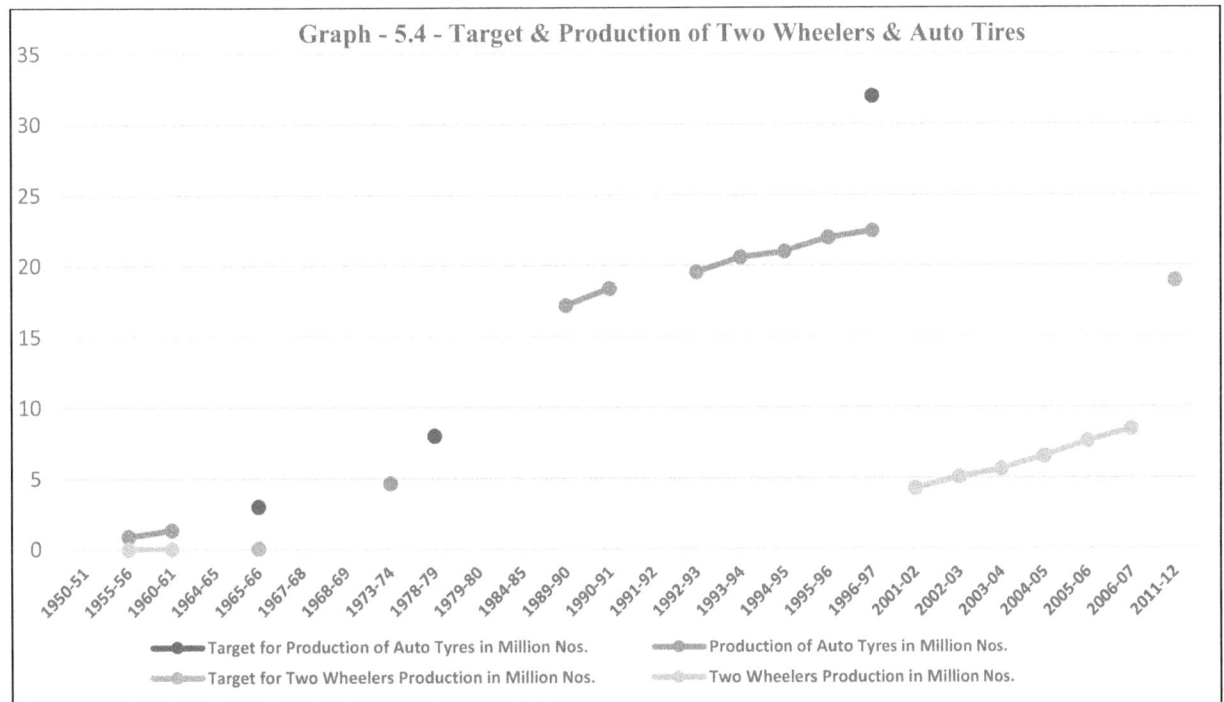

Graph - 5.4 - Target & Production of Two Wheelers & Auto Tires

Public Sector Companies Meeting Consumer Needs for Special Products

Hindustan Photo Films Mfg. Co. Ltd.

Hindustan Photo Films Mfg. Co. Ltd. - HPF was incorporated on 30.11.**1960** to make India self-reliant in the field of photosensitized goods and to cater to health care, education, defense and entertainment needs. HPF commenced its business in 1967.

HPF was engaged in manufacturing polyester-based X-ray (medical and industrial) and graphic arts films, magnetic audio tapes, cine color positive films and chemicals for X-Ray films through its 3 units at Udhagamandalam and 1 unit at Chennai.

HPF had installed capacities to manufacture 5.06 million Sq. M of Cine Products, 12.33 million Sq. M of X-Ray Films and 2.25 million Sq. M of graphic arts films in 2008-09.

Hindustan Photo Films Ltd was declared bankrupt by the BIFR in 1996. High Court of Madras on 29.08.2016 dismissed the petition against implementation of the BIFR order for winding up of HPF. HPF was wound up and was undergoing liquidation.

Summary

The public sector was playing a supporting role to the private sector in paper, paper board and newsprint production. It contributed 8 to 9.5% of total production during the period 2004-2007.

In the automobile sector, Maruti Udyog Ltd. played a very significant leading role and made purchase of cars affordable to middle class people. It had very big market share and continues to do so.

Scooters India contributed to reducing the waiting list for scooters during the 1970s and 1980s.

Hindustan Paper Corporation Ltd., Hindustan Photo Films Manufacturing Co. Ltd. and Nagaland Pulp & Paper Company Ltd. were under closure / liquidation in 2022-23.

Private Sector Players –

2 Alcoholic beverages companies - Shaw Wallace & Company Ltd – 1886, Khasa Distillery Company – 1945.

1 Almirahs, Locks & Keys company – Godrej and Boyce - 1923

19 Auto-component companies - Rane (Madras) Ltd – 1929, Stanes Motors South India Ltd – 1930, India Pistons Ltd – 1949, Bosch Ltd (Started as Motor Industries Company Ltd.) – 1951, Rane Engine Valve Ltd – 1959, Gabriel India Ltd – 1961, Lucas TVS – 1962, Sundaram Clayton – 1962, L.M. Van Moppes Diamond Tools India Private Ltd – 1962, Wheels India – 1962, Sundaram Clayton – 1962, Rane Brake Lining Ltd – 1964, Amalgamations Repco Ltd. – 1967, IP Pins & Liners Ltd – 1988,
IP Rings Ltd – 1991, Tata Auto-Comp Systems – 1995, Amalgamations Valeo Clutch Pvt Ltd – 1997, BBL Daido Private Ltd – 2001, TAFE Gears Division – 2018.

4 Batteries companies – AMCO Batteries – 1932, Exide Industries Ltd – 1947, TAFE Power Source Division - 1993 and Fujikawa Power Ltd -2009,

1 Generator sets, engines, pumps company – Greaves Cotton – 1859

17 Coaches, electric cars, auto rickshaws, motor cycles, scooters and passenger car companies – Simpsons & Co – 1840, Ford India Private Ltd. – 1926, General Motors India Pvt. Ltd. – 1928, Hindustan Motors Ltd. – 1942, Premier Automobiles Ltd. – 1944, Bajaj Auto Ltd, - 1945, Bachraj Trading Company / Bajaj Tempo Motors – 1945, Standard Motor Products of India Ltd – 1948, Enfield India – 1955, Kinetic Engineering Ltd – 1972, Kinetic Motor Company Ltd. – 1984, Lohia Machinery Ltd – 1986, Tata Motors – 1988.
Reva Electric car Company – 1994, Fiat Chrysler Automobiles India / FCA India Automobiles Pvt Ltd – 1997, Yamaha motor India – 2007, Mahindra Two Wheelers Ltd. - 2008

8 Paper companies – Imperial Tobacco Co. of India Ltd – 1910, Orient Paper Mills – 1936, Sirpur Paper Mills – 1938, Orient Paper and Industries Ltd – 1939, J K Papers Ltd – 1962, Khanna Paper Mills – 1965, Grasim Industries Pulp plant – 1963, Century Pulp and Paper Ltd – 1984,

2 Plywood and Veneer companies - Century Plyboards India Ltd – 1986 and Sharon Veneers Private Ltd.- 1987.

11 Tires and 1 tire retreading companies – TVS Tyres – 1911, Dunlop India Ltd. - 1936, Alliance Tyre Company – 1950, J K Tyre & Industries Ltd. – 1951, MRF - 1952, Ceat Tyres of India – 1958, Goodyear India Ltd - 1961, Apollo Tyres Ltd.– 1972,
Birla Tyres – 1991, Continental Tyres India Pvt Ltd. – 1992, Bridgestone TVS India Pvt Ltd – 2000 and Stanes Tyre & Rubber Products Ltd – 1962.

6: DEVELOPMENTS IN COMMUNICATION AND INFORMATION BROADCASTING SECTORS

Communication, A Basic Need

Postal service was the main communication medium at the time of independence and telegram was used for urgent communication. Money order, Postal order and cheques were used for money transfer. Telephones helped with voice communications. Radio was the media for information broadcast.

Targeted Growth in Communication

Targets were set by the government for the number of post and telegraph offices, telephone exchanges, radio-broadcasting studios, television studios, radio transmitters, High, Low and Very Low Power Transmitters, village community radio centres, to be set up, Coaxial cabling system, microwave system, UHF system and optical fibre cabling system to be made ready during each five-year plan, to provide targeted telephone, mobile, internet and broadband connections to achieve the targeted radio and television coverage of the population.

Growth in Postal Services

The number of post offices increased from 22,116 in 1947 to 1.55 lakh in 2005-06, with more than 1.39 lakh Post Offices in rural areas, offering services for delivery of mails, parcel, money transfer, Money Order, sale of Postal Order, etc. (8.10.2.1)

In 1991-92, India had the **largest number of post offices** in the world. (8.v2.10.1.2)

The Indian postal system had a network of 1,29,322 Extra Departmental Branch Offices, 2371 Postal Sanchar Seva Kendras, 290 postal finance marts (which served as a front end for the tie-ups with mutual funds, other financial instruments and banks for vending their retail services) and 5405 Panchayat Sanchar Sewa Kendras (where agents appointed by Gram Panchayat provided postal services) in the rural areas as on 31.03.2007.

Period 1992-97
Speed Post was introduced to provide a faster and assured service competing with the private courier service.

Period 2002-07
Automatic sorting was introduced in association with the Computer Maintenance Corporation. (10.2.7) (12.3.4)

Period 2007-12
With the introduction of 'One India One Rate' scheme, speed Post was expanded to cover more than 1,200 towns.

Period 2012-17
Under the National Address Database Management Project, GIS maps for the entire country and address database for 300 million households was proposed to be developed between 2012 and 2017. (12.16.56)

Banking Services Provided by Post Offices

Postal savings accounted for 43.7% of gross domestic savings and 53% of household savings in 1989-90. As a part of resource mobilization, post office savings increased from Rs. 21,430 Cr in 1985-86 to Rs. 91,795 Cr in 160.5 million accounts on 31.03.1996 and **Rs. 2,18,695 Cr** on 31.03.2001. (10.8.5.1)

Instant money-order service was initiated during the period 2002-07. (12.3.20)

With a customer base of 175 million, a branch network, double the size of all the banks in the country put together, and a diverse product range, the Post Office Savings Bank was **the largest retail banking network** in the country. (12.3.18)

Insurance Services Provided by Post Offices

Postal Life Insurance (PLI), initially meant only for the Postal employees, catered to employees of the Civil and Military Personnel of the Central and State Governments, local bodies, government aided educational institutions and so on from 2011-12. (12.16.45)

As on 31.03.2012, PLI had 5.6 million policies and Rural PLI had 19.63 million policies with a total sum assured of Rs. 79,183.44 Cr and Rs. 82,540.86 Cr respectively. (12.16.47)

Growth in Tele-Communication Services

The telephone network consisted of 84000 connections in 1947. (11.12.1.2)

The telephone exchanges in the country were 11,000 (rural) in 1989-90, 23400 on 31.3.98 (providing telephone facilities to 0.301 million of the total 0.6 million villages and STD / ISD facility to more than 90% of the subscribers), 35023 (including 26953 rural) in 2001-02 and 38338 in 2007. (9.7.2.10/24) (10.8.5.35)

The telephone connections increased to 17.8 million Direct Exchange Lines by **31.03.98,**

The telecom network expanded to 71.39 million Public tele-com connections and 135.44 million Private tele-com connections as of March 2007. Thus, India's telephone network, including mobile phones, became the second largest among the emerging economies. Rural phones (Fixed + CDMA) were 2,26,55,691 in 2007. (11.12.1.2)

Tele-density increased from 18.31% in March 2007 to 26.2% in 2008 and 78.7% in 2012. (11.12.1.6)

Indian Telephone Industries was founded in **1948** as a departmental factory for manufacturing telephones and other articles.

Hindustan Cables Ltd was founded at Rupnarayanpur in **1952** to make India self-reliant in manufacturing telecommunications cables.

Wireless Planning and Coordination Wing was set up in **1952** to ensure orderly utilization of radio frequency spectrum and Geostationary Orbit. (9.7.2.18).

Wireless Monitoring Organization was set up in **1952** for monitoring all wireless transmissions and providing technical data logistic support to the WPC Wing in the enforcement of the National and International Radio Regulatory and statutory provisions for efficient management of Radio Frequency Spectrum and Geo-Stationary Orbit.

Centre for Development of Telematics was set up in **1984** to develop digital switching systems, suitable for the Indian environment and with a capability for introduction of Integrated Services Digital Network in the future.

Mahanagar Telephone Nigam Ltd. was incorporated in **1986** to take over the management, control and operation of telecom networks in Mumbai and Delhi.

Of the 447 district-headquarters in the country, 380 were put on the subscriber trunk dialing network by 1989-90 (10.6.3/5)

Value added services, including **cellular phone services**, were **thrown open to the private sector** in **1992.** (10.8.5.29)

Jobs done during 1992-97

(i) Licenses were issued to 36 companies for operation of Public Mobile Radio Trunked Services in 80 cities.
(ii) 16 Licenses were issued for the operation of E-Mail service using the INSAT satellite system.
(iii) Cellular Mobile Telephone Services started in 4 metropolitan cities with 2 operators in each city. In other telecom circles, 22 operators started their services in more than 50 cities.
(iv) Internet services were being provided in about 20 cities by DOT and VSNL.
(v) The public data network "INET" was extended to 95 cities. HV-NET started to provide 64 Kbps data and voice communication capability from any point in the country.
(vi) Integrated Services Digital Network started in 9 cities. (9.7.2.1.9)

During 1997-2002

Telecom Regulatory Authority of India was set up in **1997** to ensure quality services like billing, fault repair and redressal of grievances and value for money to the consumers. (9.7.2.19)

In 1998, Internet Service Providers were allowed to set up submarine cable landing stations for international gateways for internet services.

Migration from the regime of fixed license fee to a new regime of revenue sharing was permitted in **1999.**

Bharat Sanchar Nigam Ltd. was set up to take over the operational network of the Department of telecommunication from 1.10.**2000.**

MTNL launched its mobile services in Delhi and Mumbai as the third operator.

Status in 2001-02

National long-distance service was opened to operators w.e.f. 13.08.2002.
National Internet Backbone covering all States was commissioned.

In 2006-07

In those areas where there were no other existing telecom service providers, BSNL towers were being used to provide wireless broadband connectivity in 2006-07. (11.10.54)

In 2011-12

Number of mobile subscribers reached 919.17 million in March 2012 with the increase in the number of rural subscribers powered by low tariffs. More than 5,55,000 villages out of more than 6,00,000 villages in the country had the benefit of mobile coverage. (12.16.3).

The telephone connections increased to 620.52 million urban and 330.82 million rural connections in March 2012. Share of wireless phones increased from 80.19% in March 2007 to 96.62% (919.17 million) in March 2012. (12.16.7/9)

The expansion during 2008-12 in mobile services was led by private sector service providers whose market share increased from 73.5% to 86.3%. (12.1.79)

Overseas Communications Service –

Before 1947, private companies provided external communications services to and from India. The government nationalized the Indian Radio and Cable Communication Company in 1947 and Overseas Communications Service OCS was established in the Department of Telecommunications in 1947.

In **1950**, countries with which India was connected by direct radio telegraph, telephone and photo services numbered 7, 2 and 2 respectively. To contact the rest of the world, India was dependent on the communication system of Cable and Wireless Ltd., London. (3.27.80)

In **1955-56**, the Overseas Service provided multi-address broadcasts for the Indian embassies and consular bodies abroad and news-cast services for the press. (12.2.22.14)

In **1960-61**, countries with which India was connected by direct radio telegraph, telephone and photo services numbered 23, 23 and 9 respectively. (3.27.80)

By **1984-85**, the Indo-USSR Tropo Project was completed. (7.9.7)

Videsh Sanchar Nigam Ltd. was established in **1986** to offer telephony, telex, telegraph, Internet access, packet switched data transmission, video conferencing, television relay and other value-added services. VSNL functioned as the sole provider of international telecommunication services and linked the country's telecommunications system to many countries around the world.

Against 6 countries available on the international subscriber dialling network in 1985, 178 countries were added by 31.03.**1990**. (8.10.6.5)

VSNL expanded International Trunk Dialling Services to most of the countries by 31.03.1990. VSNL ventured to offer mobile international telecom services to the customers on land, on the high seas and in the air. (10.8.5)

VSNL had a monopoly position till **2004** for international connectivity (9.7.2.20)

Table – 6.1

YEAR	TARGET OF POST OFFICES IN NOS.	POST OFFICES IN OPERATION IN NOS	YEAR	TARGET FOR TELEPHONE CONNECTIONS IN NOS	TELEPHONES IN OPERATION IN NOS	MOBILES IN OPERATION IN NOS	BSNL + MTNL MOBILES IN OPERATION IN NOS	PRIVATE Cos MOBILES IN OPERATION IN NOS.
1947-48		22116	1950-51		1,68,000			
1950-51		36000	1955-56		2,80,000			
1955-56	55000	54900	1960-61	4,50,000	4,60,000			
1960-61	75000	71000	1965-66	6,60,000				
1965-66	94000		1973-74	760000				
1979-80		136999	1984-85	1400000	8,80,000			
1984-85		143751	1989-90	38,00,000	25,78,000			
1989-90		147236	1996-97		1,45,33,000	3,40,000		
1996-97		153000	1997-98		1,78,00,000			
2000-01		154919	2001-02	3,82,33,000	3,85,95,000	64,31,000	2,14,000	58,77,000
2001-02	155750		2006-07	8,28,00,000	4,07,80,000	16,60,50,000		
2005-06		155000	2009-10	60,00,00,000				
2006-07	157895		2011-12		3,21,70,000	91,91,70,000		
			2016-17	1,20,00,00,000				

Growth in Radio Broadcast Services

Radio Broadcasting in 1947

In **1947**, 6 broadcasting stations operated 6 medium wave and 4 shortwave transmitters, excluding the high-power shortwave transmitters in Delhi. The broadcast coverage provided by the medium wave transmitters extended over 114,000 square kms serving a population of about 32.6 million.

In **1950-51**, the broadcasting system consisted of 21 stations, operating 30 medium wave transmitters and 14 shortwave transmitters, covering about 303029 square kms and about 80 million of the population. (1.31.96)

Jobs Done During 1951-56

Six 50 KW MW transmitters were commissioned at Bombay, Bangalore, Ahmedabad, Lucknow, Jullundur and Calcutta; 20 KW MW transmitters were installed at Indore, Madras, Ajmer, Patna, Cuttack, Vijayawada, Trichur and Delhi

Medium wave transmitters were installed at Nagpur, Guwahati, Poona, Rajkot and Jaipur.

Each language area was provided with at least one transmitting station bringing the total number of stations to 26.

During 1960-61

The number of broadcasting stations increased to 28, covering 37% of the total area and 55% of the population with 59 transmitters. (3.3.33) (3.27.85)

The number of transmitters increased to 110 in **1965-66** and 127 in **1968-69.** (4.15.1)

Commercial broadcasting was introduced on the Vividh Bharati channel in **1967** to mobilize resources for the network.

Status of Broadcasting in 1979-80

With a network of 84 broadcasting centres, including 66 full-fledged stations, 14 auxiliary centres, 2 exclusive Vividh Bharati Commercial Centres and 2 relaying centres, the All India Radio provided coverage to 90% of the population and 78% of the area of the country. (6.18.23)

In 1984-85

Coverage by AIR increased to 95 % of the population and 86 % by area. (7.9.44)

Significant support work relating to radio and TV broadcasting was carried out by ISRO (satellite launching), Bharat Electronics Ltd (manufacturing equipment needed by Akash Vani and Door Darshan), NPL (propagation studies) etc. under their own charters and programs. (7.9.56)

In 1989-90

The coverage of AIR increased to 93% of the population. The number of broadcasting centres (including auxiliary centres) rose to 134 and the number of transmitters to 226.

The major achievements of AIR during 1985-90 included the introduction of hourly news bulletins from six in the morning till midnight and introduction of FM broadcast. (8.v2.10.10.2)

In 1989-90, 29 centres carried commercial broadcast service. (8.v2.10.11.5)

Jobs Done During 1992-97

AIR set up 73 Broadcasting Centres and 167 Transmitters. extending coverage to 97 % of the population in 1996-97.

During 1997-2002 -

AIR's medium wave coverage was extended to 98% of the population while FM services covered 30% of the population (10.8.4.11)

Status of Broadcasting in 2006-07

Radio broadcasting infrastructure consisted of 229 AIR analogue terrestrial radio medium wave and short-wave stations, 264 analogue private terrestrial stations, and one private satellite radio (World Space). (11.12.4.6)

Number of radio sets was 132 million. Total radio coverage of the population reached 99.13%. There were 42 private FM stations. (11.12.4.7)

In 2011-12

AIR commissioned satellite earth stations at Leh (J&K) and Rohtak (Haryana), enabling these areas to distribute news and other important programs to other AIR stations in the regions.

From 6 radio stations in 1947, the network grew to 279 stations with 436 transmitters providing coverage to 99.18% of the population and 91.85% area of the country.

Growth in TV Broadcasting Services

Television, introduced in Delhi in **1959**, covered an area of 0.2 million sq. kms and a population of over 83.2 million with 7 full-fledged centres, 3 program production centres, 7 SITE-on-going centres and 4 relay centres in **1979-80**. (6.18.23)

In 1984-85

TV coverage increased to 33 % of population and 17 % of the area. (7.9.44)

In 1989-90

The Door Darshan coverage increased to 53% of the population, supported by 31 studios and 535 transmitters (including transposers). (8.v2.10.10.3)

There were 50032 Community TV sets in 566148 villages as on 1-1-1990.

In 1992-97

Door Darshan had set up 41 studios and 950 transmitters and covered 87 % of the population in 1996-97.

Jobs Done During 1997-2002

Door Darshan had nearly 400 million viewers. During 1997-2002, Door Darshan added a number of new satellite channels. (10.8.4.10)

Status of TV Broadcasting in 2006-07

The television broadcasting system consisted of 1398 analogue terrestrial transmitters and 4 digital transmitters in the public sector, 6000 Multi-System Operators, and 65000 Local Cable Operators in private sector, 3 digital DTH satellite television operators in public and private sectors.

Entertainment Industry in 2006-07

Turnover of entertainment and media industry in 2007 was Rs. 50080 Cr.

Status of TV Broadcasting in 2010

The Door Darshan network had 1,415 analog transmitters and 67 studio centres. (12.16.76)

In 2011-12

India's broadcasting sector comprised 800 plus satellite TV channels, 100 Multi System Operators, 6,000 Independent Cable operators, around 60,000 Local Cable Operators, 7 DTH operators and several IPTV service providers.

In 2012, out of a total of 138 million TV homes, about 30 million were dependent on Doordarshan's terrestrial broadcast services and 74 million were covered by cable services and the rest by Direct to Home and Internet Protocol Television services.

Door Darshan was the world's largest terrestrial broadcaster with over 1,400 terrestrial TV transmitters, covering 88% of India's geographical areas and about 92% population of the country. (12.16.70)

Entertainment Industry in 2015

The Media and Entertainment Industry evolved as the fastest growing sectors of the economy, and it was expected to reach Rs. 1.19 trillion in 2015.

Table – 6.2 Communication Network

YEAR	COAXIAL SYSTEM IN ROUTE KMS	MICROWAVE SYSTEM IN ROUTE KMS	UHF SYSTEM IN ROUTE KMS	OPTICAL FIBRE SYSTEM IN ROUTE KMS
1973-74	T 7000	T 12000		
1989-90	5953	10478	9980	2323
1991-92	27420	36786	21157	8810
1996-97	T 30420	T 56786	T 171157	40000
1997-98				46000
2001-02				T 1,40,000
2006-07		64,506.64		5,19,155

T - Target

Indian Telephone Industries Ltd.

Indian Telephone Industries was founded in **1948** as a departmental factory.

Indian Telephone Industries Limited - ITI was incorporated on 25.10.**1950** for manufacturing telephones and to tap the opportunities of convergence of communication, internet and entertainment business.

Achievements during 1955-60 - The capacity of the factory increased to 35,000 exchange lines and 50,000 telephone instruments per annum in **1955-56.**

ITI started assembling telephone instruments from imported parts but was in a position to produce 520 out of the 539 parts of a telephone instrument in 1955-56. 12 of the remaining items were manufactured by other Indian firms, only 2 were being imported from abroad.

ITI aimed to manufacture 85% of the components required for exchange line equipment during 1956-60. (2.22.12)

The production of exchange lines increased from 30,000 in 1955-56 to 78,000 in 1960-61 and that of telephone instruments from about 50,000 to 120,000.

ITI produced Rs. 6.4 million worth of transmission equipment in 1960-61.

ITI established units in Srinagar in **1969, Naini** in **1971, Raebareli** in **1973** and **Palghat** in **1976.**

Achievement during 1980-85 - ITI established a crossbar equipment plant of 0.2 million lines capacity at Rae Bareli, expanded the Palghat Unit for the manufacture of new types of electronic exchanges and set up 2 electronic switching factories of 0.5 million lines capacity each (6.18.17).

Mankapur factory was started in Gonda, UP in **1983.** (7.9.5)

ITI's Capacity in 1989-90 -

ITI had capacities of 0.161 million lines for the Switching system, 2.914 million lines for the switching equipment and 0.914 million numbers for telephone instruments. (8. V2 .10. Annex. 2).

In 1992-97 - ITI aimed to produce 4.934 million lines of electronic switching equipment at its Bangalore complex, 1.728 million lines at Rae Bareli unit, 3.27 million lines at Mankapur unit, 0.282 million lines of digital trunk auto exchange equipment at Palghat unit and cordless telephones and transmission equipment including the fibre optic systems. (8.v2.10.8.4)

ITI's Financial Performance in 2000-01

After suffering losses during 1994-99, as a result of DOT and MTNL resorting to global competitive bidding, ITI staged a turnaround during 1999-2001.

ITI manufactured telecom equipment covering whole spectrum of switching (large, medium and small switches), transmission (digital, microwave, fibre optics and satcom products like GSM (BTS), C-DoT, TRU expansion, SMPS, STM, etc.), access products and subscriber premises equipment, CDMA & GSM equipment etc. in its units at Bangalore, Mankapur, Naini, Rae Bareli, Palakkad and Srinagar.

Mankapur & Rae Bareli plants were modernized for manufacturing of GSM mobile equipment. These 2 facilities supplied more than 9 million lines per annum to both domestic and export markets. The Palakkad unit was undertaking data handling with assembly and personalization of smart cards and electronic manufacturing facilities for PCB's, HDPE Pipe, Smart Energy Meters, Micro PC under Smart city mission etc. It also produced Information and Communication Technology equipment like network management systems, encryption and networking for internet connectivity, and secure communications networks and equipment for India's military.

ITI took up turnkey projects like GSM / WLL CDMA infra, MLLN and SSTP, projects related to National Population Register, Solar Panel, LED based products, National Optical Fibre Network for providing Broad Band services to rural Panchayats, National Network for Spectrum for Defence, Banking Products etc.

ITI implemented GSM Network for BSNL West (Gujarat, Maharashtra, Chhattisgarh and Madhya Pradesh) and South Zones and MTNL (Mumbai).

ITI deployed the G-PoN technology in BSNL Network with the collaboration of M/s Alphion Corp., USA and also setup Data Centre facility at Bangalore.

ITI entered the security and surveillance market to provide digital security services like CCTV surveillance, GPS tracking, Cloud surveillance systems, Smart School Program and IOT services.

ITI's **financial joint ventures** include India Satcom Ltd., ITI Communications Pte Ltd. (Singapore) and Fibcom India Ltd.

Wireless Planning and Coordination Wing

Wireless Planning and Coordination (WPC) Wing was set up in **1952**, as the national radio regulatory authority to ensure orderly utilization of radio frequency spectrum and Geo Stationary Orbit (GSO). It was supported by the Wireless Monitoring Organization (WMO) in this activity. Besides allocation of frequency spectrum, WPC / WMO undertake removal of interference problems, radio noise measurements etc. (9.7.2.18). WPC is also responsible for grant of licenses for various telecom services like Unified Access Service Internet and VSAT service.

Wireless Monitoring Organization

Wireless Monitoring Organization - WMO was set up in **1952** for monitoring wireless transmissions across the entire radio frequency spectrum and provide technical data logistic support to the WPC Wing in the enforcement of the National and International Radio Regulatory and statutory provisions for efficient management of Radio Frequency Spectrum and Geo-Stationary Orbit.

There are 28 Wireless (including 5 International) Monitoring Stations and 1 International Satellite Monitoring Earth Station (at Jalna, Maharashtra) strategically located all over the country.

Hindustan Cables Ltd.

Hindustan Cables Ltd. - HCL was incorporated on 04.08.**1952** to make the country self-reliant3 in the manufacturing and supply of various types of telecommunication wires and cables. The **Rupnarayanpur unit** was set up in collaboration with STC of UK, for production of Paper Insulated Dry Core Cables. The installed capacity was expanded to 63 LCKM for manufacture of Polythene Insulated Jelly Filled Cables and Aerial Cables. It also had facilities for manufacturing 1 million pairs of telephone coiled cords and 1.5 million pieces of computer cords.

HCL set up its **first Hyderabad Unit** in **1972** for production of Paper Insulated Dry Core, Polythene Insulated Jelly Filled, PCM and Aerial Cables and **second Hyderabad unit** in **1982** for manufacture of

30 LCKM PIJF Cables of range up to 3600 pairs. The installed capacity of the unit was increased to 44 LCKM.

The units of HCL are at Burdwan, Narendrapur, Allahabad, and Hyderabad. HCL's R&D Centre was set up in Hyderabad in 1981 to develop microprocessor-based cable testing instruments and special application cables.

In **1984,** HCL acquired Machine Tool Works in Narendrapur, Calcutta (which was manufacturing cable making equipment and a wide range of special purpose machine tools) from Cycle Corporation of India. This unit supplied materials for production of telecom cables to other units of HCL.

In **1987**, a pilot plant was set up at Hyderabad for production of fibre optic cables.

R&D Centres at Hyderabad and Naini developed Gas Alert System for the use of ONGC and coal mines **and** indigenous off line fibre coloring unit and 6 fibre central loose tube design cable respectively.

Modern plant - HCL was one of the largest factories in South Asia with computerized Robotic Reel Handling system, Tandem Insulating Lines, High Speed Horizontal Twiners, Drum Twisters and pioneer in induction of Computerized Automatic Cable Test set for meeting stringent specification.

HCL's Turn Key Projects division undertook designing network systems, connecting cable network through exchanges and interfacing with major trunk routes, satellites, microwaves and other telecommunication channels.

Fall in demand for communication cables - Due to introduction of various wireless services, there was a drastic reduction in laying of Jelly Filled & Optical Fibre Cables in external plant network of BSNL / MTNL. There was total stoppage of production and no internal generation of fund in HCL since 2004 due to complete obsolescence of its products arising out of advent of wireless technology.

HCL was **profitable until 1994**, but began incurring losses in 1995.

HCL was referred to BIFR in 2002 for revival / reconstruction.

The Union Cabinet in its meeting held on 28.09.2016, inter alia, approved closure of the company. HCL is undergoing process of closure as on 31.03.2023.

Hindustan Teleprinters Ltd.

Hindustan Teleprinters Ltd. - HTL was constituted under the Ministry of Communications to manufacture teleprinters with Italian collaboration in December, **1960** with initial production capacity of 170 teleprinters.

HTL was producing 5010 units in 1968-69. (4.15.32)

Jobs done during 1980-85 -
HTL was modernized to start manufacturing Electric Typewriter and the Electronic Teleprinter. (7.9.6)

Achievements during 1992-97
HTL manufactured 0.125 million electro mechanical teleprinters of Olivetti technology till 1987 and thereafter 60000 electronic teleprinters based on Sagem's know-how up to 1994

Diversification planned in 1992-97
HTL planned to diversify into manufacture of Roman and bilingual electronic teleprinters. Electronic key hoards, FAX machines, payphones, chip cards, voice cards and C-DOT switching exchanges (up to 1400 lines). (8.v2.10.8.6)

Diversification on teleprinters becoming obsolete - With changes in market and customer preferences, HTL diversified into digital switching, transmission, data and access products. Forte areas included telephone exchanges with indigenous C-DOT technology, large switching exchange with Siemen's know-how, Main Distribution Frames and Line Jack Units.

Diverse manufacturing facilities - HTL set up a modern plant for Optical Fibre Cable manufacturing in Chennai with a capacity of 4 million km of cables. HTL also had manufacturing facility for Fibre Reinforced Plastic Rod, Impregnated Glass Fibre Reinforcement and Aramid / Kevlar Rods at Hosur in Tamil Nadu.

Himachal Futuristic Communications Ltd acquired 74% equity stake in HTL Ltd. under divestment policy of Govt of India in 2000 and Govt of India still retains 26% equity stake in the Company.

Instrumentation Ltd. – Telecom Equipment

Instrumentation Ltd. - IL was incorporated on 21.3.**1964** for providing instrumentation and control systems to sectors such as power, steel, fertilizer, refineries & other process industries, nuclear application, service sectors of offshore projects like Oil & Natural Gas and Defence.

IL diversified into the manufacturing of Telecom Exchanges (based on C-DOT technology), Railway Signalling systems, special products for Defence, Power Electronics (UPS etc.,) and Photo Identity jobs of Election Commissions.

The Kota unit was manufacturing Telecom equipment, Instruments and Automation products, Panels/Cabinets, Gas analysers, etc. and was undertaking large turnkey projects.

National Film Development Corp. Ltd.

National Film Development Corp. Ltd. - NFDC was incorporated on 11-05-**1975** to promote and develop film industry in accordance with the National economic policy.

NFDC was restructured in 1980 by the merger of erstwhile Indian Motion Picture Export Corporation and Film Finance Corporation.

NFDC is in financing, production, distribution, export and import of quality films with socially relevant themes, creative and artistic excellence.

NFDC also ensured the welfare of the Cine Artistes through the Cine Artistes Welfare Fund of India set up by the company.

Revenue from operation in 2022-23 was Rs. 115.4 Cr

Telecommunications Consultants India Ltd.

Telecommunications Consultants India Ltd. - TCIL was incorporated on 10.3.1978 **for extending the telecom expertise available with DOT to friendly developing countries**.

TCIL is providing services related to network projects, software support, switching and transmission systems, cellular services, rural telecommunication, optical fibre-based backbone network, e-Governance, civil and architectural consultancy for Cyber Cities, Telecom Complexes, etc.

It aims in upgrading Broadband Multimedia Convergent Service Networks, working as systems integrator in Telecom billing, customer care, value added services, e-governance networks, developing IT training infrastructure and participating in SWAN projects in various States.
TCIL has also diversified into road construction.

TCIL has **7 financial joint ventures** including Bharti Hexacom Ltd., United Telecom Ltd., Nepal, TCIL BellSouth Ltd., USA, TCIL Saudi Ltd., Telecommunication Consultants Nigeria Ltd. and **5 subsidiaries** - Intelligent Communication System India Ltd., TCIL Oman LLC, Tamil Nadu Telecommunications Ltd, TCIL Bina Toll Road Ltd. and TCIL Lakhnadon Toll Road Ltd.

TCIL caters to the local needs of countries mainly in developing world. TCIL diversified into WLL, Fibre to the Home, Cyber cities, Cyber Park, solar, Disaster Management domains, E medicine and e-education.

Centre for Development of Telematics

Centre for Development of Telematics - C-DOT was set up in August, **1984** to develop digital switching system, suitable for Indian environment and with a capability for introduction of Integrated Services Digital Network in future. C-DOT successfully produced 128 port Electronic Private Automatic Exchange and Rural Automatic Exchange. The production of the same by a large number of licensees started immediately.

Jobs done during 1992-1997 - C-DOT developed digital switching systems ranging from 1500 to 40,000 lines for urban and semi-urban applications, low-capacity digital radio technologies for interconnecting rural and urban exchanges, satellite system for digital multiplexers and optical communication systems. (9.7.2.34)

During 2002-07 - Development of products for broad-band fixed and mobile subscribers' access system, and high band width backbone systems were part of the strategy for this period. (10.8.3.65)

Mahanagar Telephone Nigam Ltd.

Mahanagar Telephone Nigam Ltd. - MTNL was incorporated on 28.02.**1986** for providing basic telephone services, cellular (GSM and CDMA) mobile services, internet and value-added services in Delhi and Mumbai through its 558 exchanges and other network of capacity 10.72 million.

MTNL has **2** wholly owned **subsidiaries** namely Millennium Telecom Ltd and Mahanagar Telephone Mauritius Ltd., (which provides mobile services in Mauritius)

MTNL has **2 financial joint ventures** namely (a) United Telecom Ltd. along with VSNL, TCIL and NVPL (local partner in Nepal) to provide CDMA based basic service in Nepal and (b) MTNL STPI IT Services Ltd. with Software Technology Parks of India.

MTNL started 3G services including video calling, mobile TV and mobile broadband with high-speed data connectivity up to 3.6 Mbit/s from 11.12.2008. MTNL was the first 3G Mobile service provider in India.

MTNL provided Tri Band Internet services including games on demand, video on demand, and IPTV services.

MTNL began offering (FTTH) triple play high speed broadband service in Delhi in 2011 and IPTV, HDTV, 3DTV, video on demand, bandwidth on demand, instant video conferencing, interactive gaming, etc.

On 23.10.2019, MTNL merged with Bharat Sanchar Nigam Ltd.

As of June 2021, it had 3.28 million subscribers. MTNL's revenue for FY2021 was Rs. 1798.41 Cr.

Videsh Sanchar Nigam Ltd

Videsh Sanchar Nigam Ltd - VSNL was established on 19.03.**1986** to offer telephony, telex, telegraph, internet access, packet switched data transmission, video conferencing, television relay and other value-added services. VSNL linked India's telecommunications system to 236 countries around the world.

Achievements during 1994-97 - VSNL increased its international circuits capacity from 3,331 circuits in 1992 to 14,535 circuits in 1997, traffic from 487 million telephone paid minutes in 1992-93 to 1,385 million telephone paid minutes in 1996-97 and decreasing the ratio of domestic lines to international lines from 2500:1 in 1991 to about 700:1. This enabled VSNL to handle the explosion in telecom traffic to and from India.

VSNL was a profit-making company – Refer Ch. 17

VSNL's Communication network – (i) VSNL handled telecom traffic through gateways in Delhi, Mumbai, Chennai and Calcutta, using terrestrial and submarine cables (one linked Chennai and Penang, the second linked Mumbai and Fujairah (UAE) and the third SEA-ME-WE-2 fibre optic digital cable system running from France to Singapore, a network of satellite earth stations across the country and the DoT's telecom network. The earth stations receive telecom signals from satellites of INTELSAT and INMARSAT.

(ii) VSNL was a joint contributor for FLAG submarine cable project of capacity 5 Gbit/s, which runs from the United Kingdom to Japan.

(iii) VSNL planned to contribute for the SEA-ME-WE-3 fibre optic cables project (of capacity 10 Gbit/s each), which connected 12 countries from the United Kingdom to Singapore. (In India, the cable system landed at Mumbai and Kochi).

(iv) VSNL was establishing 6 more gateways - at Jalandhar, Kanpur, Gandhinagar, Hyderabad, Bangalore and Kochi.

(v) VSNL operated the Indian gateway of the Iridium Mobile Satellite Project and the SAN of the ICO's mobile phone project (for marketing digital voice, data, fax and a range of messaging services in India and some South Asian and Central Asian countries).

Competitiveness of VSNL – Refer Ch. 17

WTO's pressure on VSNL – Refer Ch. 17

VSNL's expansion plans – Refer Ch. 17

Disinvestment of VSNL - Instead of offering (financial) support to VSNL, government chose to divest its holding in VSNL. After 2 rounds of divestment since 1992 (including a $526 million Global Depository Receipts issue in 1996-97), the Government's holdings came down to 65%.

Millennium Telecom Ltd.

Millennium Telecom Ltd. - MTL was incorporated on 28.02.2000 by MTNL as a wholly owned subsidiary to provide internet, intranet and ITES in India and abroad.

MTL was providing Internet and related value-added services (ISDN, Multimedia, paging etc.), application development and rolling out services.

MTL was converted in to a 50:50 joint venture of MTNL and Bharat Sanchar Nigam Ltd.

MTL executed video surveillance contract on behalf of MTNL, Disaster Management Service for governments of Maharashtra and Gujarat, leasing data centre of MTNL, BSNL, ITI, etc., remote monitoring of customer network and undertook Infrastructure Leasing Business of MTNL Mumbai, etc.

Bharat Sanchar Nigam Ltd.

Bharat Sanchar Nigam Ltd. - BSNL was incorporated on 15.9.**2000** to take over the business of providing telecom services and network of erstwhile Department of Telecommunications along with all assets and liabilities, contractual rights and obligations.

BSNL's Cell One network (GSM / GPRS) was launched in 2002.

Constraint for BSNL / MTNL for mobile services

The five-year tax holiday under section 80 IA of Income Tax Act available to private operators was not extended to MTNL and BSNL and level playing field was not ensured to them. (10.8.5.48)

BSNL was subjected to additional financial liabilities like corporate tax, license fees, payment of dividend etc. which were not applicable to erstwhile DOT. (10.8.5.55)

Achievements of BSNL - BSNL was providing all types of telecommunication services in 48-telecom circles spread all over India other than Delhi and Mumbai. BSNL had a network of 38158 telephone exchanges and over 45 million lines covering 5000 towns with over 35 million telephone subscribers in 2004-05.

BSNL had 80.05% market share in basic telephone connections, 18.82% in mobile connections and 6.699% in WLL connections in 2007-08.

Out of 0.593 million villages in the country, 0.519 million villages were provided with telephone facility by 31.03.2008.

On 27.02.2010, BSNL Mobile launched 3G services on Pan India.

Airtel launched the first 4G mobile network in 2014.

BSNL's Bharat Fibre (FTTH) was launched in 2019. It offered IPTV, Video on Demand, VoIP, Audio On-Demand, Bandwidth on Demand, remote education, video conferencing services, interactive gaming, Virtual Private LAN services, etc.

BSNL's optic fibre network provided fixed access to deliver high-speed Internet up to 300 Mbps.

BSNL was the fourth largest ISP in India and also had the largest fibre-based telecom network of 0.75 million kms, among the four operators in the country as on 18.04.2019.

BSNL's broadband provided telecom services to enterprise customers including MPLS, P2P and Internet leased lines.

On 24.10.2019, the Government of India decided to merge MTNL with BSNL.

BSNL had over 121.82 million customers across India as on 30.11.2019.

Undersea cable laying - BSNL laid undersea cable (designed to deliver 4G mobile services at 400 Gbit/s speed in Port Blair and 200 Gbit/s on nearby islands) from Chennai to Andaman & Nicobar Islands in a record time of less than 24 months and commissioned in August 2020.

BSNL Landline was the largest fixed-line telephony in India with over 9.55 million customers and 47.2% market share in the country as of 28.02.2021.

On 27.07.2022, the Government announced merger of **Bharat Broadband Network Ltd** with BSNL. This gave BSNL additional 0.567 million kms of optical fibre, laid across 0.185 million village panchayats, using the Universal Service Obligation Fund.

Manufacturing activities of BSNL - BSNL has 7 in-house manufacturing units / telecom factories located at Kolkata, Gopalpur, Kharagpur, Jabalpur, Richhai, Bhilai & Mumbai engaged in production of GSM Tower, SIM card, Pay phones, Mini Pillar, MPJ Box etc. During 2007-08, BSNL's Telecom factories supplied 4099 nos. of GSM Towers and 5.697 million SIM Cards.

Cause for BSNL Making Losses - BSNL's 4G roll out (along with Reliance Jio and Airtel) faced delays because of government's decision to implement indigenous technology for BSNL's 4G network (indirectly preventing 4G roll out with its competitors, who were allowed to use imported 4G network equipment, thus making BSNL uncompetitive in providing 4G services for about 9 years till indigenous technology was developed by Tata Consultancy Services, thus leading to BSNL losing mobile customers and BSNL becoming a loss making company).

BSNL started 4G service in some parts of India such as Bihar, Jharkhand and Uttar Pradesh, since January 2019, but was limited to a few cities or towns in these states. Most of 4G services were available in Southern India. BSNL was trying to launch pan India 4G services by September 2022.

BSNL's Late Entry for Providing 4G and 5G Services – BSNL placed an order of Rs. 15000 Cr with TCS in May 2023 for purchase of 4G equipment. With this ordered equipment BSNL hoped to cover entire India with its 4G network by end of 2023.

After deploying 4G network, BSNL hoped to quickly upgrade to 5G network by end of 2023 as BSNL's 4G stack was upgradable to 5G with just a few software upgrades. By November / December 2023, BSNL hoped to start deploying 5G network all over the country.

Gross Turnover of Bharat Sanchar Nigam Ltd. in FY 2022-23 was Rs. 19128 Cr (increase of 14% over turnover in 2021-22).

RailTel Corporation of India Ltd.

RailTel Corporation of India Ltd. - RTCL was incorporated on 26.9.**2000** for modernizing Railways' train control and operational safety systems and creating nationwide broadband telecom and multimedia network to supplement national telecom infrastructure and to spur growth of telecom, internet and IT enabled value-added services by laying optical fibre cable network on the side of the railway track for leasing of bandwidth, co-location services, VPN, ISP and other services.

Achievements - RailTel, as a service provider, had provided 28 Gbit/s capacity OFC backbone to facilitate reach of telecom in rural and remote areas up to 2007, cyber-café at 26 Railway stations and Wi-Fi internet services at 27 Railway stations by 2007-08

RailTel had signed an MOU with all Telcos for using RailTel's OFC infrastructure at Railway stations for providing rural telephony and continuous coverage of Cell One mobile phones along the railway tracks.

Indian Infrastructure Finance Company Ltd. (IIFCL)

Indian Infrastructure Finance Company Ltd. - IIFCL was created in **2006** to provide access to funds at competitive rates to facilitate the funding needs of the Telecom sector.

IIFCL provides long-term finance to viable infrastructure projects in transportation, energy, water, sanitation, communication sectors and social and commercial infrastructure.

Bharat Broadband Network Ltd

Bharat Broadband Network Ltd - BBNL was incorporated on 25.02.**2012** to set up National Optical Fibre Network required for provision of at least 100 Mbps bandwidth on sharing basis in about 2,50,000 Gram Panchayats, enabling B2B, G2C, B2C and P2P broadband services, internet service and various types of e-services to villagers as well as to government and other institutions located in the villages.

Bharat Net is a part of the infrastructure for construction of National Level Broadband Highway for Digital India Program.

Achievements - 100,000 Gram Panchayat were made service ready by December 2017, remaining 150,000 Gram Panchayat's were to be connected by March 2021.

Contribution of Post and Telegraph for IV 5YP

Posts and Telegraphs was expected to contribute Rs. 225 crores at 1968-69 rates of postal charges for IV 5YP. (4.4.17)

For V 5YP

The total contribution of posts and telegraphs at 1973-74 rates of postal and telecommunication charges for the V Plan was Rs. 380 Cr. The aggregate contribution to the Plan, taking the additional revenue raised by the Posts and Telegraphs through revision of postal and telecommunication rates into account, worked out to Rs. 1114 crores. (5.4.11).

For VI 5YP

The gross surplus was estimated at Rs. 1,729 Cr comprising Rs. 2,482 Cr from the tele-communication wing and (-) Rs. 753 Cr from the postal wing, based on the anticipated growth of tele-communication and posts and telegraphs services during the plan. (7.4.31)

Contribution by Telecom Public Sector for VIII 5YP –

Internal resources of telecom public sector contributed about 80% of the anticipated Plan expenditure of Rs.27,480 Cr. (9.7.2.6)

For XI 5YP

The public sector investment in the telecommunication sector (through BSNL and MTNL) was to be mainly funded through IEBR of Rs 89581.56 Cr at current price (including Rs 337.47 crore by C-DOT as internal resources) over the XI Plan period. (12.1.25)

Summary

The postal services were provided completely by public sector till private courier services started around 1990 and emails became popular.

The Indian postal system also played a crucial role in resource mobilization and contributed for 5-year plans.

Development in landline telephone services was entirely powered by DOT / BSNL till mobiles became affordable to the common man.

Though constraints imposed by government and the restraints faced by BSNL restricted its share in mobile customer base, its contribution for infrastructure developments like installations of towers, laying of fibre optic cables, etc. was very high and rural customers were served largely by BSNL.

Table – 5.3 - CPSEs Share in Domestic Telecommunication Services

Total Wired Lines in the country – Nos. in Cr.							Serviced by CPSEs / Share of CPSEs to Total Domestic Service (%)						
1968-69	1998-99	2004-05	2005-06	2008-09	2009-10	2010-11	1968-69	1998-99	2004-05	2005-06	2008-09	2009-10	2010-11
	1.78			3.38	3.7	3.47		1.78			3.3	3.13	2.87
								100			86.84	84.59	82.7
Total Wireless Lines in the country – Nos. in Cr.													
	0.09			39.18	58.43	81.16		0.09			6	7.45	9.73
								100			15.31	12.75	11.99
Total Lines in the country – Nos. in Cr.													
	1.87			42.56	62.13	84.63		1.87			9.3	10.58	12.6
								100			21.64		14.89

Radio broadcasting was solely developed by All India Radio. FM broadcasting was largely in the hands of private sector.

TV broadcasting was initially developed by Door Darshan independently till private channels, cable TV operators and then private DTH operators became dominant.

Private Sector Players

Companies manufacturing - Electronic surveillance systems – 1, Microwave Transmission Equipment – 1, Push button and Cordless phones, Fax machines and mobile network operation company – 1, Mobile network operation companies – 9, Overseas communication services – 1. AMG Media Networks (2022)

7: GROWTH IN PRODUCTION OF DRUGS AND PHARMACEUTICALS

Drugs & Pharmaceuticals, A basic need for health

Drugs are a basic need for living healthy, protecting from diseases, curing diseases and giving longevity.

Targeted Growth for Drugs and Pharmaceuticals Production

The requirements for bulk drugs, basic drugs and formulations etc. were forecasted by the government for the last financial year of each 5-year plan and the target capacity and production of these items for the various 5-year plans were set.

Drugs & Pharmaceuticals Production in India

Achievements in I 5YP –
The setting up of the **Penicillin factory** at Pimpri, Pune in the early 50's and the construction of **Indian Drugs and Pharmaceuticals Ltd.** plants at Rishikesh and Hyderabad in the 60's were milestones in the history of the pharmaceutical industry and building blocks on which the structure of the pharmaceutical industry was built. (9.5.185)

Government's **Penicillin Factory** of capacity 4.8 million mega units was set up in **1954**.

Hindustan Anti-Biotics Ltd was set up in **1954,** in cooperation with the WHO and UNICEF, to provide affordable drugs.

Expansions in private sector were taken up to achieve a production target of 500 tons of Benzene hexa-chloride, 50 tons of Calcium lactate, 48 tons of Para-amino salicylic acid, 0.4 million lbs. of Sulpha drugs, etc. in 1955-56.

Achievements during 1955-60
Development of pharmaceuticals, plastics and dye-stuffs industries required primary organic chemicals like benzene, toluene, xylene, naphthalene, phenol and anthracene. Provision was made for the recovery of crude benzol from coke-oven gases at the steel plants, the South Arcot Lignite project and the Durgapur Coke-oven project. (2.19.41)
Production of sulpha, antibiotic drugs and D.D.T. started during II 5YP. (3.3.25)

Achievements during 1961-66
National Industrial Development Corporation set up the **Indian Drugs and Pharmaceuticals Ltd.** on 5.04.1961 for managing **Synthetic Drugs project** at Sanat Nagar, **Antibiotics plant** near Rishikesh, **Surgical Instruments Project** at Madras and **Phytochemical project in Kerala**.

Rishikesh Antibiotics plant of capacity 300 tons was commissioned in October, **1965.**

Synthetic Drugs Hyderabad plant of capacity 851 tons of main drugs and 4560 tons of intermediates (vitamins, sulpha drugs. Anthelmintics, Analgesics, Antipyretics, Diuretics, Antitubercular drugs, etc.) was commissioned in October, **1965**.

Madras Surgical Instruments project of capacity 2.5. million pieces of 166 types of instruments was commissioned on the 31.07.**1965** (Tool Room was commissioned in 1964.)

Phyto-chemical plant, started at Neriamangalam in Kerala, for producing caffeine from tea pruning and drugs like Ephedrine Pepion etc. was abandoned due to finding the project unviable.

IDPL was set up as pharmaceutical, bulk drug manufacturing and drug discovery company with branches in Hyderabad, Gurgaon and Rishikesh.

The initial installed capacities of Rishikesh Antibiotics Project were - a) Potassium Salt of Penicillin Tons to be converted into Sodium Salt – 30 Ton and Procaine Salt – 55 Ton; b) Streptomycin Sulphate – 70 Ton; c). Dihydro streptomycin Sulphate – 15 Ton; d) Chloro-tetracycline – 70 Ton; e) Oxytetracycline base – 25 Ton; f) Tetracycline base + Tetracycline hydrochloride – Total 25 Ton; g) Nystatin – 10 Ton.

Lack of private sector investment - During 1969-74, the government decided that the public sector should enter pharmaceuticals field as adequate private investment was not forthcoming. (4.14.37)

During 1975-80

The management of Bengal Chemical and Pharmaceutical Works Ltd. was taken over by the Government on 15.12.**1977**, nationalized on 15.12.1980, named **Bengal Chemicals & Pharmaceuticals Ltd.**, and launched on 27.03.1981 for manufacturing industrial chemicals, pharmaceuticals like antibiotic injectables, tablets and capsules and household products.

Smith Stanistreet Pharmaceuticals Ltd. was incorporated on 19.07.**1978** to manufacturer of homeopathic or biochemic pharmaceutical preparations.

Status in 1979-80

The contributions of the public sector were 26% and 6.3% in the case of bulk drugs and formulations respectively.

During 1980-85 -

The government acquired **Bengal Immunity Company Ltd,** engaged in the production of drugs and pharmaceuticals essential to the general public, in 1984.

Status in 1989-90

After introduction of Drug Price Control Order 1986, the pharmaceuticals industry witnessed good growth for the subsequent 3 years and India became **net exporter of drugs in 1989-90.** (8.v2.5.21.3)

Indian Vaccine Corporation Ltd. was set up in **1989** with French collaboration in Gurgaon to produce vaccines for measles; Vero rabies, killed polio vaccine and quadruple vaccine (DPTP).

Bharat Immunologicals and Biologicals Corporation Ltd. was established in **1989** in Bulandshahr in collaboration with the Soviet Technology Consultancy Corp. to manufacture 100 million doses of oral polio vaccine and other immunizers. (8.18.4.6)

Status in 1991-92

Indian drug industry with about 14000 units manufactured a wide range of basic drugs and pharmaceuticals covering almost all therapeutic regimes including antibiotics, bacterial, steroids and hormones, vaccines, psychotropic preparations and a wide variety of synthetic drugs, including herbal preparations. (8.v2.5.21.1)

More than 30% production of bulk drugs came from the small-scale units. (9.5.186)

Status in 1996-97 –

The Indian drugs and pharmaceuticals industry became **one of the largest and most advanced among the developing countries.** (9.5.184)

The drug industry was able **to meet 70% of the country's requirements of bulk drugs and almost the entire demand for formulations.** The **public sector investment** was **the engine of growth for the pharmaceutical industry in the last 3 decades.** (9.5.185)

Status in 2000-01

The Indian drugs and pharmaceuticals industry ranked fourth in world accounting for 8% of world production by volume and 1.5% by value.

The production of bulk drugs and dosage forms by 250 odd large-scale units and about 8,000 small-scale units increased from Rs. 700 Cr and Rs. 3840 Cr. in 1990-91 to Rs. 4,533 Cr and Rs. 15000 Cr. in 2000-01 respectively. (10.7.1.128)

The Indian pharmaceutical industry achieved global recognition as a low-cost producer. India ranked 17th in terms of export value of bulk actives and doses drugs. It **exported drugs to nearly 200 countries** including the highly regulated markets of **Europe, United States, Japan and Australia**. (10.7.1.129)

The **Central Drug Standards Control Organization** monitored drug quality through nearly 35,000 samples/year. (10.7.1.132)

Public sector pharmaceutical units became sick due to the government policy of allowing small formulators to take on a large part of production, late revision of prices and infrastructure problems. Some of the units, earlier in the private sector. were taken over by the Government after they became sick. Still, PSUs served as an indirect way of price stabilization after prices were fully decontrolled. (10.7.1.137)

Status in 2006-07

Production increased from Rs. 30500 Cr in 2002-03 to Rs. 71942 Cr. In 2006-07. India **held fourth** and thirteenth positions **in terms of volume** and value of production respectively. Exports grew to Rs 24942 Cr. in 2006–07. (11.v2.7.1.192)

The number of drug manufacturing licenses issued up to 2003 were as follow: bulk drugs (1333), formulations (4534), large volume parenteral (134), and vaccines (56) making the total of 6057 manufacturing units. About 300 of these were large units. (11.v2.7.1.193)

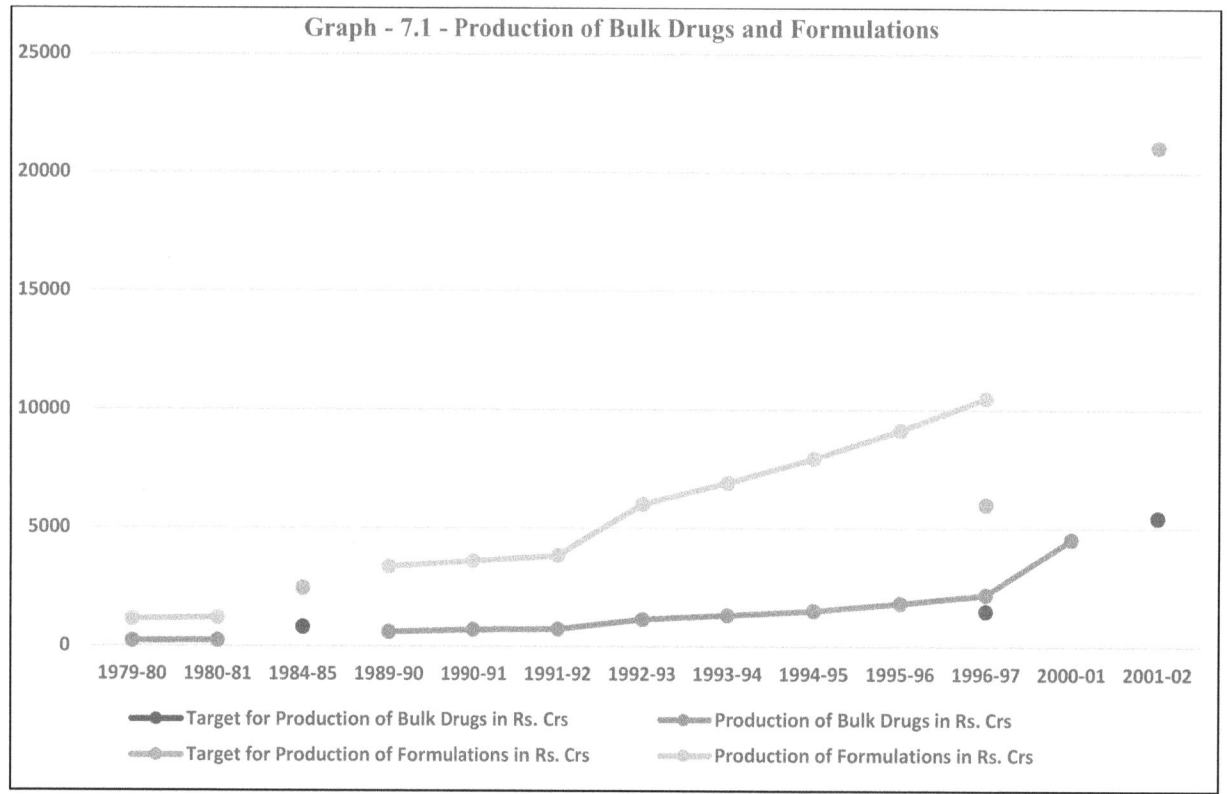

Graph - 7.1 - Production of Bulk Drugs and Formulations

Foreign recognition - India had the **largest USFDA approved plants outside the US.** India accounted for almost **half of Drug Master File filings and one-fourth of Abbreviated New Drug Applications in the US in 2006.** (11.v2.7.1.194)

Astra-Zeneca, Altan Pharma, Eisai and Ethypharm had set up R&D centres and wholly owned subsidiaries and Eli Lily had entered into collaboration with Jubilant.
Pfizer, Johnson & Johnson, GSK, Merck, Eli Lily, Novartis, and Novo Nordisk were using India as a base for running their phase II and phase III clinical trials.

Schedule M Compliance – XI Plan provided interest subsidy to support Schedule M compliance by SMEs in drugs and pharmaceutical sector and another scheme to assist the Pharma CPSEs to meet WHO pre-qualification. (11.v2.7.1.209)
Since the GMP norms were made mandatory w.e.f. 1.07.2005, 370 units, not in a position to comply with the GMP norms, were closed. (11.v2. 7.1.203)

Status in 2011-12
The soft patent regime prior to 2005 provided opportunity for this industry to consolidate its position and witness significant growth in generic production and exports. (12. Annex. 13.2.57)

Status in 2023
Indian pharmaceutical industry included a network of 3000 drug companies and about 10500 manufacturing units. India is the largest provider of generic drugs, supplying over 50% of the global demand for vaccines, about 40% of generic demand in US, and about 25% of all medicines in the UK. **India ranked third in pharmaceutical production by volume** and 14th by value. (Indian Express dated 24.05.23)

Public Sector Organizations which contributed for Growth in Production of Drugs and Pharmaceuticals

Central Drugs Standard Control Organization

Central Drugs Standard Control Organization - CDSCO is a regulatory body for cosmetics, pharmaceuticals and medical devices. Drug Controller General of India (of CDSCO), assisted by Drug Technical Advisory Board and the Drug Consultative Committee, regulates pharmaceutical and medical devices. Zonal offices carry out pre and post-licensing inspections, post market surveillance, and drug recalls (where necessary).

Bengal Chemicals and Pharmaceuticals Ltd.

Bengal Chemicals and Pharmaceuticals Ltd. - BCPL was established in **1901**, as Bengal Chemicals & Pharmaceutical Works Ltd., by Acharya Prafulla Chandra Ray, renowned scientist, for production of quality drugs and pharmaceuticals, chemicals and home products with indigenous technology.

BCPW expanded and diversified into industrial chemicals, Bulk Drugs, Perfumeries, Cosmetics, Toiletries, Hospital & Surgical Equipment, Fire Extinguisher etc.
BCPW maintained leadership in technology up to 1950, declined in 60's and became sick in 1970.
It was taken over by government on 15.12.1977 and nationalized on 15.12.1980 to save the company from closure, to support the health programs of the government, to bridge the gap between demand and supply of life saving drugs and vaccines and to set up multi-disciplinary Research and Development Centre for inventing new molecules, processes and home products.
BCPL was incorporated on 27-03-1981.

BCPL was involved in manufacturing of Ferric Alum, Sulphate, bleaching powder under Chemical division, life-saving injectables like snake venom antiserum, spirituous & non-spirituous preparations, analgesic, antibiotic, anti-microbial and non-steroid anti-inflammatory drugs, tablets, capsules, ointments, systemic alkalizer, enzymes etc. under pharmaceutical formulations division, Cantharidin hair oil, phenol (disinfectant fluid), toilet disinfectant fluid, bleaching powder and naphthalene balls under cosmetics & home products Division at 4 manufacturing units at Maniktala (Kolkata), Panihati (24 Parganas), Mumbai and Kanpur.

Reconstruction – As BCPL became sick in 1993, a revival package was approved by the BIFR on 4.04.1995. In 2006, Government approved another rehabilitation scheme for revival of the company.

BCPL had installed capacity of 150 million for tablets, 50 million for Capsules, 60 MT for Ointment, 3000 KL for Phenol, 800 KL for Hair Oil and 144 MT for Naphthalene in 2008-09.

Following decades of losses, BCPL returned to profitability in the financial year 2016–17.

BCPL launched its Hand Sanitizer in August 2020, during COVID-19 pandemic. BCPL manufactured 60,680 bottles of Phenol 450ml. in a single day in September, 2020 as against an average daily production of 30,000 bottles.

BCPL became loan free company from 31.03.2022.

Hindustan Anti-Biotics Ltd.

Hindustan Antibiotics Ltd. - HAL was incorporated in **1954** to manufacture life-saving drugs for distribution through government hospitals.

3 Subsidiaries of HAL are Karnataka Antibiotic and Pharmaceuticals Ltd., Maharashtra Antibiotic and Pharmaceuticals Ltd. and Manipur State Drugs and Pharmaceuticals Ltd.
The company had 1 financial joint venture namely Hindustan Max-G.B. Ltd.
The total number of products manufactured by the company was 78 in 2007-08.
HAL had installed capacity of 48 million for Vials, 240 million for Tablets and 204 million for Capsules, 12 million bags for I.V. Fluids and 4.8 million Ton for Agro-chem in 2008-09.
Maharashtra Antibiotics & Pharmaceuticals Ltd (MAPL) is under liquidation.
Pimpri plant produced bulk drugs (capacity 60 MMU) and formulations in various dosage forms – injectables (132 million vials), capsules (250 million), tablets (120 million), large volume parenteral (12 million bottles annually), liquid orals, etc.

HAL developed health care products like Hamycin, Ampicillin Sodium, Benzyl Penicillin Potassium, Benzyl Penicillin Sodium, Benzathine Penicillin (Longacillin), Cefuroxime Sodium, Amoxycillin Trihydrate (Delamin), Cefotaxime Sodium (Haltax), Ceftriaxone Sodium (Haxone), Meropenem (Halpen), etc.
The company diversified into the agricultural and veterinary areas and developed Aureofungin (anti-fungal used in preservation of the fruits and vegetables), Humaur (bio-organic foliar spray), Streptocycline (antibacterial for effective control of diseases in plants), Azotomeal, Phosphomeal, etc.

The installed capacity for formulations and bulk drugs in 2019-20 was 777 million.
The bulk plant, which was producing fermentation based bulk drugs like Penicillin-G, Streptomycin Sulphate, Gentamycin etc., was idle in 2023.
HAL has re-started manufacturing IVF products.

HAL established 12000 Cloud Clinics by 2023 to measure 45 health parameters in 5 minutes, from which one can identify their physical fitness & take corrective action accordingly. The data of the people on its cloud storage and can be very useful to Health Institutions, Govt. Hospitals, CPSEs etc.

Indian Drugs and Pharmaceuticals Ltd.

Indian Drugs and Pharmaceuticals Ltd. - IDPL was incorporated on 5.4.**1961** to create self-sufficiency in respect of essential life-saving medicines / formulations through its units at Rishikesh, Hyderabad and Gurgaon.

It had two joint ventures, namely IDPL (TN) Ltd., Chennai and Bihar Drugs & Organic Chemicals Ltd., Muzaffarpur.
The company had three subsidiaries - Rajasthan Drugs & Pharmaceuticals Ltd., Uttar Pradesh and Orissa Drugs & Chemicals Ltd. in collaboration with the respective State Government Industrial Development Corporations.
IDPL had installed capacity of 1641 million nos. for Tablets, 430 million nos. for Capsules, 600 Kilo liters for Liquid Orals and 2 million bottles for Dry Syrup in 2008-09.
IDPL was involved in patent development through National Institute of Pharmaceutical Education and Research to provide affordable drugs.
A new formulation unit was inaugurated in Hyderabad in February 2017.

The manufacturing activities were closed for want of funds.

On the 9.02.2021, the Government of India announced the liquidation of IDPL. IDPL is under process of closure as on 31.03.2023.

Indian Medicines & Pharmaceutical Corp. Ltd.

Indian Medicines & Pharmaceutical Corp. Ltd. - IMPCL was incorporated on 12.7.**1978** to manufacture **Ayurvedic, Unani and Siddha Medicines** on the basis of classical principles and approved formula both in domestic and international market, enhance capacity portfolio covering nutraceuticals, health supplements and cosmetics based on herbals and supply to CGHS, CCRAS, CCRUM, ESIC, Central / State government institutions, etc. as per their requirements.

IMPCL is engaged in the production of 327 Ayurvedic and 321 Unani Medicines in its Mohan (Almora), Uttarakhand unit.
IMPCL started a financial joint venture with KMVN Ltd. to supply Central Government / CGHS Hospitals at cost plus pricing system.
During 2013-14, IMPCL undertook production of 185 Ayurvedic and 100 Unani medicines.
The installed capacity of IMPCL in 2016-17 was 179 nos. of Ayurvedic and 79nos of Unani Medicines. Total products of Ayurvedic and Unani medicines were around 296. IMPCL is a profit-making organization since its inception till date.

Rajasthan Drugs and Pharmaceuticals Ltd.

Rajasthan Drugs and Pharmaceuticals Ltd. - RDPL was incorporated on 2.11.**1978** as a joint venture of Rajasthan State Industrial Development and Investment Corp. Ltd. and IDPL to supply life-saving and other essential drugs to the State Government departments and institutes, Central government Institutes, viz ESIC, Defence, Railways, other PSUs, etc.

RDPL was manufacturing various pharmaceutical medicines in its Jaipur unit.
RDPL was a prime partner in the implementation of "Jana Aushadhi" program, which supplied generic medicines to the public at affordable price.

In 2013-14, the company was diversifying into pharma prescription markets, veterinary markets, marketing of Ayurvedic and other Indian system of medicines.

The production in RDPL stopped since October, 2016.

The government decided to close RDPL in February 2021. The Committee of Ministers recommended transfer the shares of RDPL to the State Government of Rajasthan in June 2022. RDPL is under process of closure as on 31.03.2023.

Orissa Drugs & Chemicals Ltd.

Orissa Drugs & Chemicals Ltd. - ODCL was incorporated on 01.05.**1979** as a joint venture of IDPL with Industrial Promotion and Investment Corporation of Orissa Ltd. to manufacture life-saving drugs to the State Government of Orissa at low price. UDCL started commercial production in 1983.

ODCL was manufacturing 247 pharmaceutical formulations in the form of Tablets, Capsules, Injections, Powder and Liquid orals in Bhubaneswar unit.

As ODCL made huge loss, it was referred to BIFR in 1992, which declared it a sick unit and ordered for liquidation in 2003. The then management moved the court and after IDPL submitted revival proposal, Orissa High Court stayed the liquidation.

ODCL continued to incur loss up to 2010. Good Manufacturing Practice certified ODCL was constantly making profits for 5 years consecutively from 2011-12 and was ready to pay back the principal amount to its financiers. Hence Orissa High Court stayed liquidation of ODCL in June 2018. There has been no production activity since January, 2021. ODCL is under liquidation as on 31.03.2023.

Maharashtra Antibiotics & Pharmaceuticals Ltd

Maharashtra Antibiotics & Pharmaceuticals Ltd – MAPL was incorporated on 16.11.**1979** for manufacturing lifesaving drugs.

MAPL had WHO compliant facilities to manufacture tablets, capsules, dry and liquid injectables, syrup, etc.

The unit became sick due to financial losses and was shut down in 2003. The cabinet in its meeting held on 28.12.2016 approved the Department of Pharmaceutical's proposal to close the CPSE.

Goa Antibiotics and Pharmaceuticals Ltd

Goa Antibiotics and Pharmaceuticals Ltd – GAPL was incorporated on 09.12.**1980**, as a joint venture between Hindustan Antibiotics Ltd., Pune and Economic Development Corp. Ltd, a Govt of Goa undertaking, as a subsidiary of HLL Lifecare Ltd.

GAPL is engaged in manufacturing and supply of Allopathic medicine at its unit at Tuem, Pernem, Goa. The product range of the company comprises of 338 products of Allopathic Formulation through its unit at Tuem.

Besides company is having lease facility at Ajmer and Jaipur for manufacturing of Ayurvedic and Homeopathic medicine respectively.

The company also runs a chain of 24 X 7 Retail Pharmacy Outlets in the State of Goa at Goa medical college, Bambolim and Hospicio Hospital, Margao.

The installed capacity and capacity utilization in 2022-23 were – Vials – 15 million Nos. and 7.35%; Tablets – 240 million Nos. and 26.38%; Capsules – 190 million Nos. and 13.65% and Syrups – 1.8 million Liters and 22.85%. Revenue from operations was Rs. 51.68 Cr, down from Rs. 70.75 Cr in 2021-22.

Karnataka Antibiotics and Pharmaceuticals Ltd.

Karnataka Antibiotics and Pharmaceuticals Ltd. - KAPL was incorporated on 13.3.**1981** as a joint venture of Hindustan Antibiotics Ltd. and Karnataka State Industrial Investment and Development Corp. Ltd. to supply life-saving drugs and health care products at reasonable price.

KAPL is manufacturing 98 products comprising allopathic formulations, injections, capsules, tablets, syrups and suspensions in Bangalore unit, with WHO-GMP Certified manufacturing facilities. At Kotur, Dharwad unit, Ayurvedic products are being manufactured.

KAPL had installed capacity of 37.8 million nos. for capsules, 16.9 million for liquids / parenteral, 135 million nos. for tablets, 61.8 million vials of dry powder and 3 million bottles of dry syrup & suspension in 2008-09.
KAPL set up a Cephalosporin injectable manufacturing facility. KAPL started production of Oxytocin injection in July 2018. The value Oxytocin production during 2019-20 was Rs 31.82 Cr.
The capacity utilization in 2022-23 were – Vials – 77%; Tablets – 144%; Capsules – 292% and Liquid Parenteral – 99%. Revenue from operations was Rs. 527.57 Cr, up from Rs. 473.87 Cr in 2021-22.

Indian Vaccine Corporation Ltd.

Indian Vaccine Corporation Ltd. - IVCOL was incorporated in March **1989**, as a joint venture of Indian Petrochemicals Corporation Ltd., Pasteur Merieux Serums and Vaccines (PMSV), France and Department of Biotechnology, to manufacture Injectable Polio Vaccines, based on Vero cell Technology to be supplied by PMSV, for the mass immunizations program of Govt. of India.

However, IPV was not approved by W.H.O. As a result, the project was put on hold in February 1992. PMSV subsequently got disinterested and expressed its desire to exit the joint venture. Efforts were made to rope in 'Strategic partner' as part of the restructuring exercise. This status continued till 2007-08. To utilize the infrastructure already created at project site, the promoters decided to give the balance 69.40 acres of land available with IVCOL to Reliance Life Sciences Private Ltd. on a commercial lease for forty years for setting up a Super Specialty Hospital and to develop an Integrated Life Science Centre.

IVCL was not carrying out any manufacturing activity. The disinvestment of IVCOL did not materialize.

Bharat Immunological and Biologicals Corp. Ltd.

Bharat Immunological and Biologicals Corp. Ltd.- BIBCOL was incorporated on 10.3.**1989**, in collaboration with the Soviet Technology Consultancy Corp., to manufacture 100 million doses of Oral Polio Vaccine and other immunizers to eradicate Poliomyelitis. BIBCOL is manufacturing Oral Polio Vaccine and zinc dispersible tablet in Bulandshahr unit. (8.18.4.6)

BIBCOL had **60% market share** in polio vaccines. BIBCOL achieved a turnover of Rs.30.53 crores in 2005-06. BIBCOL formulated over 12.5 Cr doses of OPV in 2006 and became debt-free.
BIBCOL is one among the top 20 biotech companies with WHO-cGMP certified infrastructure.
BIBCOL developed monovalent OPV type 1, 2 & 3 and bio-valent OPV (type 1& 3) in 2010-11.
BIBCOL also started the development of Mineral Vitamin Mix powder for management of severely malnourished children in collaboration with AIIMS, New Delhi.
Further BIBCOL added Diarrhea Management Kit for management of diarrhea among young children.
In 2016-17, BIBCOL was aiming to get the license for manufacturing of Ready to Use Therapeutic Food and diversify into Plasma derived medicines.
Production of Oral Cholera Vaccine and Plasma Derived Medicine were taken up in 2022-23.

During the year 2021-22 BIBCOL supplied Oral Polio Vaccine of net sale value Rs. 78.39 Cr.

Manipur State Drugs & Pharmaceuticals Limited

Manipur State Drugs & Pharmaceuticals Ltd – MSDPL was incorporated on 18.7.**1989** for manufacturing lifesaving drugs.

The union cabinet approved the Department of Pharmaceutical's proposal to close MSDPL on 28.12.2016.

IDPL (Tamil Nadu) Ltd.

IDPL (Tamil Nadu) Ltd. - The company was established in **1994** as a subsidiary of the Indian Drugs & Pharmaceuticals Ltd. to **manufacture surgical Instruments, drugs, hospital equipment and aids and appliances for handicapped**.

The company was involved in production of 50 types of products including formulations such as tablets, capsules, vials and ampoules and liquid orals and surgical instruments, fabrication and general engineering of hospital equipment.

The company diversified into manufacturing of tricycles, wheel chair and aids & appliances for the differently abled persons.

After Surgical Instruments Division was shut down in 2001, only Human Formulations were being produced.

IDPL (Tamil Nadu) was a Schedule-M compliant plant and was engaged in manufacture of pharmaceuticals formulations up to September'2018. There is no production activity in this unit since October' 2018.

Bihar Drugs & Organic Chemicals Limited

Bihar Drugs & Organic Chemicals Ltd - BDOC was set up in **1994**, as a wholly owned subsidiary of the Indian Drugs & Pharmaceuticals Ltd, to manufacture Acetic Acid and other related products.

The Company became sick and remains closed since November 1996.

HLL Biotech Limited

HLL Biotech Limited – HBL, a state-of-the-art integrated vaccine complex, was incorporated on 12.03.**2012,** as a subsidiary of HLL Lifecare Ltd, to manufacture all biological preparations including prophylactic and therapeutic vaccines, Anti-Sera, Plasma and Hormonal products and other new generation vaccines against preventable diseases to implement universal immunization program of Government of India.

HBL commenced production on 30.01.2015.

HBL received the test manufacturing licenses for liquid pentavalent vaccine (RTF). The project made significant progress in 2019-20 but yet to reach commercial operations due to certain intricate factors associated with this Industry. HBL had submitted proposal to government for infusion of additional funds.

Biotechnology Industry Research Assistance Council

Biotechnology Industry Research Assistance Council – BIRAC was set up in March **2012** by Department of Biotechnology, Government of India as an interface agency to strengthen and empower the emerging biotech enterprises to undertake strategic research and innovation, addressing nationally relevant product development needs.

Bihar Drugs and Organic Chemicals Ltd, IDPL (Tamil Nadu) Ltd, Indian Vaccine Corp Ltd, Maharashtra Antibiotics & Pharmaceuticals Ltd, Manipur State Drugs & Pharmaceuticals Ltd, Hindustan Fluorocarbons Ltd, Indian Drugs & Pharmaceuticals Ltd, Rajasthan Drugs & Pharmaceuticals Ltd, Orissa Drugs & Chemicals Ltd were under closure / liquidation in 2022-23.

Summary

Public sector pharmaceutical units provided considerable support in the growth of the industry by putting up modern plants for the manufacture of bulk drugs at a reasonable cost. Most public sector companies operated with the motive of supplying larger supplies of anti-malarial medicines, polio vaccines, antibiotics, etc. to government hospitals, aided institutions and common people at affordable price or free of cost, assist the campaign against disease and protect health of the people.

BIBCOL captured 60% of polio vaccines market share in India.

Some public sector companies were formed to take over sick private companies.

The contribution of the public sector amounted to 26% in the case of bulk drugs and 6.3% in the case of formulations in 1979-80. The contribution of public sector to total drug production could not be given as comparable quantitative total production figures could not be found for Indian drug industry.

Reference - copu_03_22_1966.pdf (eparlib.nic.in) – For details about Anti-Biotics plant, Synthetic Drugs plant, Surgical Instruments plant and Phyto-chemical plants.

Private Sector Players

Medicine manufacturers – Glaxo Laboratories – 1924, GlaxoSmithKline Consumer Health Care Ltd. – 1924, Cipla Ltd. / Chemical, Industrial & Pharmaceutical Laboratories Ltd. – 1935, IPCA Laboratories Ltd – 1949, Pfizer India – 1950, Zydus Life Sciences Ltd / formerly Cedilla Healthcare Ltd. - 1952, Torrent Pharmaceuticals Ltd. / Trinity Laboratories Ltd – 1959, E. Merck (India) Pvt Ltd. – 1967, Lupin Ltd – 1968, Alkem Laboratories Ltd. – 1973, Glenmark Pharmaceuticals Ltd – 1977, Biocon Ltd. – 1978, Sun Pharmaceutical Industries Ltd – 1983, Dr. Reddy's Laboratories Ltd – 1984, Aurobindo Pharma Ltd. – 1986, Century Pharmaceuticals Ltd – 1989, Mankind Pharma – 1991

Health care products and medical devices company - Johnson & Johnson – 1947

Medical equipment company - L&T Medical Equipment & Systems – 1987

8: GROWTH OF ENGINEERING AND CONSTRUCTION INDUSTRIES FOR INDUSTRIAL INFRASTRUCTURE

After starting production of basic and secondary need products, next stage was manufacturing machineries required for setting up factories for production of these products. Third stage was starting companies to undertake consultancy, engineering and construction of new factories with these indigenous machineries.

Construction Sector

This sector contributes to construction of industrial factories and mining infrastructure, highways, roads, railways, ports, airports, power systems, irrigation and agriculture systems, telecommunication systems, hospitals, schools, townships, offices, houses and other buildings; urban infrastructure, including water supply, sewerage, and drainage, and rural infrastructure.

Contribution of Construction Sector to GDP

The share of construction sector in GDP was 5.4% in 1970-71, 4.4% in 1990-91, 5.1% in 1999-2000, 6.9% in 2006-07, 8% in 2006–07 and 7.9% in 2010–11 (10.7.7.6) (12.19.3)

Growth of Construction Industry

Central Machine Tool Institute

CMTI was established in **1965** in collaboration with Institute for Machine Tools and Production Engineering (VUOSO), Czechoslovakia, including supply of 40 types of machine tools, for harnessing know-how in the manufacturing technology sector to practical purposes and assisting technological growth in India.
CMTI changed its name to Central Manufacturing Technology Institute in 1992.

Need Felt for Engineering, Consultancy & Construction Services in 1979-80

Government realized the need for
(i) developing project consultancy and design engineering organizations for projects where such consultancy organizations did not exist in the country
(ii) financing these consultancy organizations in the initial stages
(iii) drawing requisite expertise from amongst highly experienced and motivated Indians abroad, if not available in India, and
(iv) encouraging such Indians, who were abroad and capable of setting up consultancy organizations, by way of financial incentive and other measures. (6.8.3)

Building Materials and Technology Promotion Council

Building Materials and Technology Promotion Council - BMTPC was established in **1980** to promote cost-effective, environment friendly, energy-efficient, and disaster-resistant technologies and building materials for sustainable habitat development. Around 39 technologies were developed and licensed to private entrepreneurs for commercial production. (11.11.102)

BMTPC prepared Vulnerability Atlas of India for formulating disaster mitigation plans and establishing techno-legal raging in disaster-prone areas, revised it in digitized format with latest data and then brought out the Landslide Hazard Zonation Atlas of India. BMTPC also formulated guidelines for construction of safer and durable houses to withstand earthquake / cyclone. (11.11.104)

Construction Industry Development Council – Training of Construction Personnel

Construction Industry Development Council - CIDC was established in **1996,** by the Planning Commission and the constituents of Indian construction industry, to professionalize and improve the functioning of the industry.

Its functions included training, testing, and certification of construction workers by upgrading their skills in 47 designated trades through programs spread over 19 states and supported by State Governments. CIDC conducts programs in 29 Industrial Training Institutes across Madhya Pradesh, Rajasthan, Haryana, and Bihar. Till date, over 250,000 workers have been trained, tested and certified under CIOC and have found gainful employment with construction companies.

Status in 2005

The construction industry employed 31.46 million personnel in 2005 in around 27770 enterprises. (The employment figures were 14.5 million in 1995). (11.8.1.4)

Status in 2011

The construction industry employed 41 million personnel in 2011 in around 31000 enterprises. (12.19.4)

Public Sector Enterprises engaged in manufacturing of machineries for Steel Plants, Fertilizer Plants, Petrochemical Plants, Refineries, Sugar Mills, Tea & Jute Industries

HMT Ltd

HMT Tractors Ltd. – Refer Chapter 5.

HMT Ltd. was incorporated in 1953. HMT has 6 subsidiaries namely HMT Machine Tools, HMT watches, HMT Chinar Watches, HMT (International), HMT Bearing and Praga Tools Ltd.

The company has 2 financial joint ventures namely SUDMO HMT Process Engineers (I) Ltd. and Nigeria Machine Tools Ltd.
HMT was awarded with "Indy Wood Built in India Excellence Award" in the Category "Public Sector Units – Precision Engineering" in 2017.
The gross turnover of HMT Ltd. was Rs. 51.59 Cr and sales of HMT (International) Ltd reached Rs, 14.15 Cr in 2022-23.

Heavy Engineering Corp. Ltd. – Refer Ch. 11

Bharat Heavy Plate & Vessels Ltd. – Refer Ch. 11

Richardson and Cruddas (1972) Ltd. – Refer Ch. 11

Braithwaite and Co. Ltd. - Refer Ch. 11

Bharat Wagon & Engineering Co. Ltd. – Refer Ch. 11

Lagan Jute Machinery Company – Refer Ch. 11

Andrew Yule & Company Ltd. - Refer Ch. 11

Public Sector Enterprises Engaged in Production of Heavy Engineering Equipment

Bharat Yantra Nigam Ltd.

BYNL was incorporated on 9.7.**1986** to integrate, monitor and coordinate the activities of 6 subsidiary companies, Bharat Heavy Plate & Vessels Ltd., Bharat Pumps and Compressors Ltd., Bridge and Roof Co. (India) Ltd., Richardson and Cruddas Ltd., Triveni Structurals Ltd. and Tungabhadra Steel Products Ltd.

BYNL was primarily a corporate policy formulation and monitoring organization for ensuring effective functioning of subsidiary companies in the area of investment, production rationalization, capacity utilization, human resource development etc. The company was not engaged in any manufacturing activity.

The government decided to shutdown BYNL on 12.10.2007 and the six subsidiaries of BYNL became independent public sector enterprises.

Bharat Bhari Udyog Nigam Ltd.

Bharat Bhari Udyog Nigam Ltd. - BBUNL was incorporated in September, **1986**. BBUNL did not have any manufacturing units of its own other than 4 subsidiaries namely Burn Standard Co. Ltd., Braithwaite and Co. Ltd., Bharat Wagon and Engineering Co. Ltd. and Braithwaite Burn and Jessop Construction Co. Ltd.

BBUNL's group products were wagons, cranes, steel castings like bogies, couplers for wagons, various refractory items mainly for steel plants, fabrication and erection of steel bridges, civil and marine construction, structural fabrication, ash handling plants, other capital goods items, turnkey project jobs etc.

BBUNL was executing domestic / export orders in wagons, civil structure/ construction etc. after getting the same manufactured through subsidiary companies and others.

Four more subsidiary companies had closed namely Bharat Process and Mechanical Engineers Ltd., Weighbird India Ltd., Bharat Brakes and Valves Ltd. and RBL Ltd. (last 2 subsidiaries of Burn Standard Company Ltd).

Two more subsidiaries namely Lagan Jute Machinery Co. Ltd. and Jessop and Co. Ltd. ceased to be CPSEs w.e.f. 4.7.2000 and 29.8.2003 respectively on transfer of shares of LJMC to M/s Murlidhar Ratanlal Exports Ltd. and shares of JCL to M/s Indo Wagon Engineering Ltd.

In 2013-14, BBUNL group comprised of only one subsidiary company namely Braithwaite Burn and Jessop Construction Co. Ltd and 2 joint ventures namely Lagon Engineering Co. Ltd. and Jessop and Co. Ltd.

The gross turnover of Braithwaite Burn and Jessop Construction Co. Ltd in 2022-23 was Rs. 301.79 Cr.

Public Sector Enterprises Engaged in Contract and Construction Services

Hindustan Prefab Ltd. - Mass Housing, Infrastructure Development

Hindustan Prefab Ltd. – HPL was set up in **1948** as 'Govt. Housing Factory' / Hindustan Housing Factory Ltd. for solving the housing problem created due to influx of refugees from West Pakistan. HPL was incorporated on 27.01.1953 to pioneer prefabrication technology for ensuring optimum quality and effortless construction techniques, to undertake mass housing and development of urban infrastructure and to carry on manufacturing of PCC and RCC components, construction and maintenance work etc. HPL began its business on 16.08.1955.

On 9.03.1978, the name was changed to Hindustan Prefab Ltd. (11.11.105)
HPL introduced PRC railway sleepers, as substitute to wood and steel railway sleepers, and produced precast prestressed concrete railway bridge girders. HPL built a large number of residential, industrial, and institutional structures including Ashoka Hotel, Palam Airport Terminal Building, East and West Block in R.K. Puram, Vikas Bhawan in IP Estate, Hotel Oberoi Intercontinental using pre-cast concrete and prefabrication techniques.
Production of PRC Railway sleepers and PC Poles stopped in mid-2004.

From 2004, HPL focused on securing project management contracts for mass housing projects under various Govt. schemes, construction of Economically Weaker Section / Low Income Group housing with infrastructure, sewerage treatment plant, sports complexes, campus development, reality advisory, disaster rehabilitation projects, educational, hospitals and other institutional buildings of Central & State Governments in North Eastern States, border and tribal areas and 14 other States. It undertook projects under Jawaharlal Nehru National Urban Renewal Mission, National Rural Health Mission, etc.

Government approved financial restructuring of HPL and converted Government loan and interest as on 31.03.2008 amounting to Rs. 128 Cr into equity. Consequent to the restructuring, HPL didn't avail any budgetary support from the Government and maintained a positive net worth.

HPL signed memorandum of understanding with SAIL on 19.01.2011 to carry out techno-economic feasibility study on production of prefabricated structure in steel and concrete.

HPL was poised to play a major role in Government's agenda of "Housing for all by 2022" by promoting prefab technology.

Prime Minister's Office directed the Ministry of Housing and Urban Affairs to initiate closure of the company in September 2019.

National Projects Construction Corp. Ltd. - Irrigation, Power, Steel, Transportation Projects

National Projects Construction Corp. Ltd. - NPCC was incorporated on 09.01.**1957** as a premier construction company to create necessary infrastructure for economic development of the country.

NPCC undertook construction of irrigation, river valley projects, dams, barrages, canals, flood control, hydel power, thermal power, steel and coal plants, rural and urban transportation, railways, townships and other residential buildings, institutional buildings, office complexes, roads, bridges, flyovers, hospitals and health sector projects, industrial structures, surface transport projects, environmental projects, tunnels and underground projects, real estate works, etc.

Over the last 57 years, NPCC has completed more than **254 projects of national importance** (up to 2016-17) across the country including remote and hazardous locations where private sector was reluctant to work (including River Valley Projects, dams like Pench & Totladoh in Maharashtra, Singda in Manipur, Rajghat in U.P., Bakreshwar Dam in West Bengal, etc.

NPCC constructed major canal systems in Iraq and executed projects in the Middle-east, Nepal and Bhutan.

NPCC executed Indian Institute of Crop Processing Technology, Thanjavur Complex Phase – I; Indian Agricultural Research Institute Campus at Pusa New Delhi

On going projects were 1. Indo - Bangla Border Fencing & Roads in Tripura, Meghalaya, Mizoram & Assam for MHA · 2. Road works under Bharat Nirman Yojna, etc.

NPCC was acquired by WAPCOS at a consideration of Rs. 79.80 crores in 2018-19

The following sites could not be opened.
https://npcc.gov.in › html › more_introduction, *https://npcc.gov.in › ExecutedProjects* , *https://npcc.gov.in › OngoingProject* , *https://npcc.gov.in › html › ongoing_projects* , https://npcc.gov.in › InterProjects

The gross turnover of NPCC in 2022-23 was Rs. 1614.12 Cr.

Jessop and Company

The management of Jessop and company was taken over by Government in **1958** and subsequently in 1973, it was wholly taken over by Government.

Achievements - Jessop and Co. Ltd. manufactured 475 diesel road rollers up to February 1952. (1.31.80) In 1956 Jessop supplied radial gate for Nagarjuna Sagar Dam in 1956, manufactured the first Electrical Multiple Unit coach for Indian Railways in 1959 and Caisson gates for Haldia Dock Project in 1976. Braithwaite, Burn & Jessop, partnership company of Jessop and Co, started construction of Vidyasagar Sethu, the first cable-stayed bridge in India, in 1972 and completed in 1993.
In 1986, with the formation of Bharat Bhari Udyog Nigam Ltd., Jessop became a subsidiary of BBUNL.

Disinvestment – Refer Ch. 17

New cars used by the tram system of Kolkata were delivered by Jessop in **2012.**
Today, Jessop manufactures railway coaches and wagons, cranes, road rollers and hydraulic equipment.

Tungabhadra Steel Products Ltd. - For Hydro-Mechanical Equipment for Irrigation, etc.

Tungabhadra Steel Products Ltd. - TSPL was incorporated on 20.02.**1960** as a joint venture project of Governments of Karnataka and Andhra Pradesh to manufacture gates and hoists required for spillways, sluices and canal gates of Tungabhadra Dam.

The company became a central PSE in 1967.
TSPL was manufacturing hydro mechanical equipment like radial gates, stop-log gates, penstock pipes, EOT cranes, dome walls, skid assembly, diffuser assembly, etc. for irrigation, power and other core sectors.

In pursuance of the Cabinet Committee on Economic Affairs' decisions on 29.12.2014 and 22.12.2015. TSPL is undergoing process of closure as on 31.03.2023.

National Buildings Construction Corp. Ltd. - Institutional & Residential Buildings, Hospitals

National Buildings Construction Corp. Ltd. - NBCC was incorporated on 15.11.**1960** to undertake engineering, consultancy and construction services for quality execution of projects.

NBCC was made executing agency for
(i) construction of rural roads in Bihar and Tripura under Pradhan Mantri Gram Sadak Yojana
(ii) establishing world class infrastructure in urban conglomeration in Haryana, Tripura, Meghalaya, Bihar, Jammu & Kashmir, Sikkim and Assam under Jawaharlal Nehru National Urban Renewal Mission.

Some of the iconic **projects completed** by NBCC include:
(i) Mysore Airport, Bangalore
(ii) Border fencing along Indo-Bangladesh and Indo-Pak Border
(iii) Rural roads under "Pradhan Mantri Gram Sadak Yojana" in Bihar, Jharkhand and West Bengal
(iv) 235m High TV Tower in New Delhi
(v) 30 Km. long, 270 cusec, pre-stressed pipe line with horizontal slipform system, from Murad Nagar to Sonia Vihar (Delhi)
(vi) ESIC Medical Colleges, Mandi (Himachal Pradesh) and Coimbatore, Medical College & Hospitals, Guwahati and Patna
(vii) Central Bureau of Investigation Headquarter, New Delhi, Indian Institute of Corporate Affairs Building, Manesar, National Institute of Food Technology Entrepreneurship Management, Sonepat, Civil Services Officers Institute, New Delhi, Administrative and Academic Building of Rani Lakshmi Bai Central Agricultural University, Jhansi, Garvi Gujarat Bhavan, New Delhi
(viii) Seelampur Metro Station and Delhi Metro's Elevated Via-Duct from Connaught Place to Kirti Nagar stretch.

NBCC undertook re-development of Sarojini Nagar, Netaji Nagar, New Moti Bagh, Nauroji Nagar, Kidwai Nagar (East), Ayurvigyan Nagar at AIIMS, AIIMS Western Campus, Ansari Nagar and WHO Building, IP Estate, New Delhi government colonies on self-sustaining model (without seeking any government funding)

Some of the iconic **ongoing projects** included:
(i) Indo-Bangla Border Fencing in Assam, Mizoram, Tripura and Meghalaya
(ii) Pradhan Mantri Gram Sadak Yojana Works, Tripura and Odisha
(iii) All India Institute of Medical Sciences at Kothipura and Deoghar
(iv) Gosikhurd Irrigation, Nagpur
(v) Indian Institutes of Technology, Mandi, Kharagpur and Bhubaneshwar.
(vi) Indian Institute of Management, Ranchi
(vii) Integrated Exhibition Cum Convention Centre, Pragati Maidan, New Delhi
(viii) ISPAT Post-Graduate Medical Institute and Super Specialty Hospital at Rourkela
(ix) Amrapali Works at Noida and Greater Noida, Uttar Pradesh
(x) Redevelopment of Gomti Nagar Railway Station, Lucknow
(xi) Utkal University, Bhubaneshwar

In 2019-20, NBCC completed Gujarat Bhawan in New Delhi.

Joint ventures of NBCC are Jamal – NBCC International (Proprietary) Ltd. in Botswana, NBCC-MHG, IJM-NBCC-VRM in Delhi, AMC-NBCC in Agartala and NBCC-R.K. Millen & Co., Howrah and Real Estate Development & Construction Corporation of Rajasthan Limited

Subsidiary companies - (i) NBCC Services Ltd.
(ii) NBCC Engineering & Consultancy Ltd.
(iii) NBCC Gulf LLC to carry out construction of buildings, roads, airports, harbor, water sewerage and electricity network in Oman and its neighboring countries.
(iv) NBCC International Ltd.
(v) NBCC Environment Engineering Ltd.
(vi) Hindustan Steelworks Construction Ltd. (became a subsidiary of NBCC(I) Ltd. in 2017).

Overseas operations – Starting from 1977, NBCC executed many projects in Libya, Iraq, Yemen, Nepal, Maldives, Mauritius, Turkey, Botswana.
(i)) Construction of Indo Maldives Friendship Faculty of Hospitality and Tourism Studies, Indira Gandhi Memorial Hospital and Renovation work of Indira Gandhi Memorial Hospital, at Male, and Institute for Security & Law Enforcement Studies at Addu, Republic of Maldives.
(ii) Indira Gandhi Centre for Indian Culture, Phoenix, New Supreme Court Building at Port Louis and Social Housing Projects at Mare Tabac & Dagotiere, Mauritius
(iii) Meer Housing Project (3600 Dwelling Units), Turkey

NBCC entered into a MoU with AI Naba Services LLC, Oman and JSV Belzarubezhstroy for jointly executing projects in Sultanate of Oman & Republic of Belarus respectively.

Presently, NBCC has its presence in Oman, Mauritius, Maldives, Seychelles & Dubai implementing various projects and future plan includes Burundi, Malawi, Sierra Leone, Eswatini (erstwhile Swaziland).

The gross turnover of NBCC (India) in 2022-23 was Rs. 6736.31 Cr.

NBCC Environment Engineering Ltd and NBCC International Ltd are undergoing process of closure as on 31.03.2023.

Hindustan Steelworks Construction Ltd. – Construction of Steel Plants

Hindustan Steelworks Construction Ltd. - HSCL was incorporated on 23.06.**1964** to create an organization capable of undertaking complete construction of modern integrated Steel plants.

HSCL was involved in construction of steel plants (Bokaro, Bhilai, Rourkela, Vizag, Durgapur etc.), power, oil and gas plants, mining projects, oil refineries, railways and airports buildings, commercial complexes, roads/ highways, flyovers, bridges, dams, industrial and township complexes etc. and carried out expansion programs of SAIL and RINL between 2010-14 along with regular operation and maintenance of these plants.

HSCL has one joint venture namely HSCL-Sricon Infrastructure Pvt Ltd. for construction of Nagpur-Hyderabad Section of NH 7.

The company showed operating profit in 2010-11. Interest on Govt. of India loan was one of the main contributors to net loss.

HSCL became a subsidiary of National Buildings Construction Corp Ltd with effect from 01.04.2017. HSCL undertook projects of Vizag, Bokaro, Durgapur, Bhilai, Rourkela townships, irrigation work of Bagmati, fishery harbor at Yanam, bridges of Kolkata Port Trust, 2x5000 Tons capacity food grain go-down for FCI in Dimapur, construction of residential and non-residential buildings, barracks and quarters for Indo-Tibetan Border Police, Assam Rifles and other armed forces at Sitamarhi, Patna, Yupia (Itanagar), Haflong (Assam), etc., construction of workshops at NMDC steel plant at Jagdalpur and new plate mill of Rourkela Steel plant, etc.
In April 2017, HSCL's board allotted 51% of HSCL's post issued share capital to NBCC.

The gross turnover of HSCL in 2022-23 was Rs. 759.84 Cr.

Triveni Structurals Ltd. - Towers, Rocket Launching Platforms, Dam Gates

Triveni Structurals Ltd. - TSL was incorporated on 2.7.**1965** as a joint venture with Voestalpine of Austria to meet the demand of fabricated structures and infrastructure requirement of core sectors e.g., Power Plants, Steel Plants, Nuclear, Defence, Fertilizers, Petrochemicals & Chemical Industries.

TSL was engaged in design, fabrication and erection of hydraulic gates, pressure vessels, pipes & penstocks, building structures, T.V. towers, M.W. towers and transmission towers, satellite launching platforms, VLF antenna system for Indian Navy, Defence projects, Skylark, passenger ropeways at Nainital & Joshimath, railway wagons and parts for diesel engines for Diesel Loco Works, Varanasi, miscellaneous jobs of BHEL and fabrication erection of Gas Holders, etc.
The joint venture with Voestalpine came to an end in 1990.
Dam Gates of Ramganga River project, Srisailam Dam, Indira Sagar dam, Chandil Dam, Ranjeet Sagar Dam, etc. were made by TSL.
TSL played a major role in TISCO renovation.
Triveni Structural Ltd. had an **installed capacity** for building 13600 Tons of structures in 2008-09.

TSL is under liquidation subsequent to High Court of Allahabad order dated 08.10.2013.

Bridge & Roof Co. (India) Ltd.- Construction of Refineries, Power, Fertilizer Plants

Bridge & Roof Co. (India) Ltd. - B&R was incorporated on 16.01.1920 as a wholly owned subsidiary of Balmer Lawrie and Co. Ltd. On 30.09.**1972**, it became a public sector company.

B&R undertook fabrication and construction of refineries, power, hydrocarbon, fertilizer, ferrous and non-ferrous metals plants, housing and urban development, cross country pipelines, environmental projects, sports complex, roads and highways, etc. and production of bailey bridge, railway wagon, bunk house, Porta-cabins, freight container, pot shell etc.

The Company diversified into projects in Educational Institutions, Healthcare Units, Fire Protection and fire extinguishing system, Bailey Suspension Bridges etc.

Refinery projects executed - Cryogenic LPG storage tanks, terminal's storage tanks, 60000 KL Crude Oil Storage tanks, floating roof storage tanks, SS Silos, 42850 KL Oil Terminal, Foreshore terminal, dispatch terminal, Integrated refinery expansion project at Kochi Refineries, offsites works for MRPL; TGTU, RTF, LLDPE, GGS II units; CDU, VDU, Crude and Vacuum Furnaces; Flare Stack structure; non-IFP Heaters.

Power projects executed for - B-unit of Bokaro TPS, Sagardighi STPP of WBPDC, Darlipali STPP, Durgapur Steel Plant, Hinduja National Power Corp., Vizag, Bakreshwar Power Development Corp. Ltd., Simhadri TPS, Kakrapar Atomic Power Project, etc.

Bridges built - Girder bridges, Bailey type bridges at Doyang Hydro Electric Plant Nagaland, on Shyok river and at Kullu, installation of open web through girders, re-girdering of railway bridges, etc.

Wagons - Manufacture of BOBYN, BOXN and BTPN type wagons,

Steel Plant projects - Blast Furnace for Bokaro Steel Plant; LD Convertors for Rashtriya Ispat Nigam Ltd.; BOF Gas holder for IISCO steel plant; Main Distillation column of oxygen plant for TISCO.

Fertilizer projects - Urea Storage silo for FCI, Talcher; Urea Prilling tower at NFL, Guna; NPK Prilling tower of HFC Haldia.

Buildings - Govt. of WB Hospitals at Chhatna, Onda, Purulia and Falakata; construction of 98 cyclone proof shelters at Sundarbans; 120000 capacity Salt Lake Stadium; Terminal building of Kolkata airport. B&R executed several projects in Iraq, Abu Dhabi, Nepal & Maldives.

The gross turnover of Bridge & Roof Company was Rs. 3315.38 Cr and had an order book of Rs. 8836.91 Cr. in 2022-23.

Projects and Development India Ltd. – Execution of Fertilizer, Refinery and Chemical Plants

Projects and Development India Ltd.- PDIL was incorporated on 7.3.**1978** to develop self-sufficiency in providing engineering and consultancy services for fertilizer and allied chemical industry. PDIL is engaged in engineering, consultancy, construction and commissioning of fertilizer plants and production of catalyst.

PDIL diversified into oil and gas, refinery, City Gas Distribution, pipeline, coal, power, petrochemical and infrastructure development.

PDIL was referred to BIFR in 1996-97. After implementation of reconstruction package, PDIL recorded substantial improvement in its operating and financial performance. (9.5.162)
PDIL had installed capacity of 1260 Tons of catalyst in 2008-09.

Fertilizer Projects – (i) PDIL completed world's largest single stream gas based 2200 Tons SPD ammonia plant for M/s Burrup Fertilizer Pvt Ltd. in Karratha, Australia.

(ii) PDIL provided engineering services for revamp / modernization / energy saving schemes for National Fertilizers Ltd., Tata Chemicals Ltd., Nagarjuna Fertilizers and Chemicals Ltd., Gujarat Narmada Valley Fertilizers & Chemicals Ltd., IFFCO, Chambal Fertilizer, Rashtriya Chemicals & Fertilizers Ltd., etc.

Oil & Gas and Refinery Projects - PDIL bagged orders for executing hydrogen plants for refinery expansion project at Vadinar and IOCL, Barauni and Skid Mounted Mini Refinery-II of ONGC at Tatipaka.

Chemical Projects - PDIL undertook Methanol Plant, Hydrogen Plant, Methyl Amines, Sulphuric Acid, Phosphoric Acid, Nitric Acid, Sodium Nitrite / Nitrate, Ammonium Nitrate, Ammonium Bi-Carbonate projects etc.

PDIL provided consultancy services to GAIL for GSU and GPU modification job at Pata Petrochemical Plant. In 2010-11,
PDIL was providing PMC Services for Algeria Oman Fertilizer Project at Arzew, Algeria and executing the job of Health Study of Natural Gas Let Down station in Ammonia Plant at Oman for OMIFCO.

PDIL Commissioned Hindustan Urvarak & Rasayan Ltd plants and the gross turnover in 2022-23 was Rs. 98.6 Cr.

BBJ Construction Co. Ltd. – Construction of Steel Bridges

Braithwaite Burn and Jessop Construction Company Ltd - BBJCC, setup in 1935, was incorporated as CPSE on 13.08.**1987** after it was taken over from the private sector to continue design, fabrication and erection of steel bridges.

BBJCC was undertaking construction of steel bridges, rehabilitation / replacement of early steel bridges, construction of PSC Girder Bridges, fabrication of Steel Structure, civil construction including heavy foundations and piling work through Heavy Plant Yard and Angus Works, located at Kolkata and Hooghly respectively.
BBJCC had **40% of market share for erection of steel bridges.**
As the traditional bridge building gradually shrank, BBJCC diversified into concrete bridges, bridge substructure work and civil work relating to Metro Rail projects in different cities.
BBJ Construction Co. Ltd stands amalgamated with Bharat Bhari Udyog Nigam Ltd w.e.f. 10.07.2015.

The gross turnover of Braithwaite Burn and Jessop Construction Co. Ltd in 2022-23 was Rs. 301.79 Cr.

High Speed Rail Corporation of India Ltd.

High Speed Rail Corporation of India Ltd. - HSRC was incorporated on 25.07.**2012** for conducting pre-feasibility studies of dedicated high-speed corridors for diamond quadrilateral, which connects New Delhi-Mumbai-Chennai-Kolkata-New Delhi and pre-feasibility studies of dedicated high speed rail corridor between Delhi-Chandigarh-Amritsar.

Final Report of Feasibility Study of Mumbai - Ahmedabad corridor, Interim pre-feasibility Report-II for Delhi-Chandigarh-Amritsar corridor and Interim Report for Chennai – Bengaluru – Mysore corridor were submitted by JICA in July 2015, Systra of France in Sep 2015 and China Railway Eryuan Engineering Group in June 2015 respectively.
Planning study report for Delhi - Chennai High Speed Rail Corridor by China Railway SIYUAN Survey and Design Group Co. Ltd has been completed.

HSRC's name was changed to HSRC Infra Services Ltd. The gross turnover of HSRCIS in 2022-23 was Rs. 16.57 Cr.

Operating at a speed of 320 kmph, the High-Speed Rail was expected to traverse 508.17 km between Mumbai and Ahmedabad in just two hours,

The National High-Speed Rail Corporation Limited completed 160-meter-long bridge over the Mohar River as part of construction of the Mumbai-Ahmedabad High-Speed Rail corridor in March 2024.

Public Sector Enterprises Engaged in Production of Medium and Light Engineering Equipment

Weighbird India Ltd – Refer Ch. 11

Vignyan Industries Ltd. – Refer Ch. 11

RBL Ltd.

RBL Ltd. was incorporated on 08.11.**1963**.

RBL Ltd was manufacturing metals, chemicals, and products for last 60 years.

Currently, company operations are under liquidation.

Bharat Earth Movers Ltd.

Bharat Earth Movers Ltd. - BEML was incorporated on 11-05-**1964** to provide total engineering solutions for defence, earth moving and infrastructure sectors.

BEML is manufacturing a wide range of construction, mining and earth moving equipment, railway & metro coaches, and defence vehicles for mining, steel, cement, power, irrigation, construction, road building, defence, railway and metro transportation system and aerospace through its 9 manufacturing units at Bangalore, Kolar Gold fields, Palakkad and Mysore.

Achievements – BEML developed (i) Hydraulic Excavator, Front End Loader, indigenous engine for Boat for PMP Bridge during 2007-08.
(ii) new models Bulldozer, Dump Truck, Excavator, Dozer, 140 series electronic engine, Back-Hoe loader & Motor Grader BS III Compliant.
(iii) CAN based single 7LCD display instrumentation in class Bulldozers during 2013-14.
(iv) Two Arjun armoured repair & recovery vehicles for CVRDE in 2017-18.
(v) 750 HP Bulldozer for Coal India Ltd. in 2019-20.
(vi) Unmanned Train Operation in January 2021. Bogie Run Test Machine was developed indigenously.

BEML has 3 **subsidiary companies**, including Vignyan Industries Ltd. and BEML Brazil Industrial Ltd. BEML has a **joint venture company**, namely BEML Midwest Ltd with M/s Midwest Granites Ltd., Hyderabad and M/s Sumber Mitra Jaya, Indonesia.
In 2010, BEML acquired Mining and Allied Machinery Corporation, which was engaged in manufacturing of underground mining equipment.
Government holds 54.03%. Balance 46% is held by public, financial institutions, foreign institutional investors, banks and employees.
BEML has undertaken development of 550hp motor grader, 8 Ton Tyre Handler, Snow Cutter, 1500 hp Engine for Main Battle Tanks. Self-propelled Mine Burier, Vande Bharat Sleeper Coaches, etc.
The gross turnover of BEML in 2022-23 was Rs. 3898.95 Cr.

Bharat Pumps & Compressors Ltd. – Refer Ch. 11

BIECCO Lawrie Ltd. - Switchgear, Sub-stations, Switchyards, Small Hydel Projects

BIECCO Lawrie Ltd. - BLL was incorporated on 23.12.1919 as British India Electric Construction Co. Ltd. In 1972 BIECC was taken over by Balmer Lawrie Co., a PSE. It was renamed as BLL and in **1979** it became an independent government company.

BLL was manufacturing of medium voltage switchgear & spares, executed Electrical Turnkey projects like, 33/66 KV sub-stations and switchyards, undertook repair of motors / alternators and Lube Oil Blending and filling in 2 units at Kolkata and 4 branches at Delhi, Lucknow, Mumbai and Chennai.

BLL was executing various projects under the Accelerated Power Distribution and Reform Program and Rajiv Gandhi Grameen Vidyutikaran Yojana.

BLL was executing greenfield as well as renovation & modernization of various mini & micro hydel projects in Arunachal Pradesh.

Installed capacity of BLL. was 1375 Nos. of Control & Switchgear, 10000 KL of Lube oil blending in 2008-09.

BLL entered in to Un-manned Substations projects in different states, in collaboration with Entech, a South Korea based company in 2013-14.

BLL provided security solutions through Wi-Max-based Wireless Video Surveillance System.

The government decided to shut down Biecco Lawrie Ltd in October 2018.

Bharat Process and Mechanical Engineers Ltd

Bharat Process and Mechanical Engineers Ltd was incorporated on 14.10.**1980**.
It was manufacturing general-purpose machinery and equipment for 43 years.

Currently, company operations are under liquidation.

CPSE Engaged in Industrial Development and Technical Consultancy Services

National Small Industries Corp. Ltd. – Promotion of Small-Scale Industries – Refer Chapter 15.

Engineers India Ltd. – Setting Up Hydrocarbon Industries, Fertilizer Plants, etc.

Engineers India Ltd. - EIL was set up on 15.03.**1965**, following the memorandum of agreement dated 27.06.1964 between the Government of India and Bechtel International Corporation, for providing indigenous technology solutions across the hydrocarbon projects and becoming a globally competitive Engineering, Procurement, Construction and consultancy organization for setting up hydrocarbon, mining, metallurgy, fertilizers and processing industry plants and infrastructure sectors in the country.

In May 1967, EIL became a wholly-owned Government of India enterprise.

EIL has emerged as **Asia's leading project design engineering and turnkey contracting company** in the field of Petroleum Refining, Petrochemicals, Fertilizers, Pipelines, Offshore and Onshore Oil Gas, Terminals Storages, Mining and Metallurgy infrastructure.

EIL has an engineering office in Abu Dhabi, which is the hub for its activities in the Middle East, a marketing office in Shanghai, inspection offices in London and Milan and a wholly owned subsidiary, EIL Asia Pacific SDN BHD in Malaysia.

EIL has set up 3 **joint venture** companies – (i) TEIL Projects Ltd. (for pursuing projects oil & gas, fertilizer, steel, railways, power and infrastructure sectors),
(ii) Jabal Eiliot Company for providing projects engineering and consultancy services in Saudi Arabia
(iii) Ramagundam Fertilizers and Chemicals Ltd.

EIL diversified to gas-based fertilizer, urban infrastructure, water and waste management, nuclear, solar and wind power and city gas distribution.

It has a subsidiary namely Certification Engineers International Ltd for undertaking independent certification and third-party inspection assignments.

EIL developed FGH and CFC technologies.

EIL provided PMC services for underground crude oil storages at Vishakhapatnam, Mangalore and Padur in 2013-14.

EIL secured Guru Gobind Singh Polymer Addition project of HMEL and the brown field expansion projects of ONGC in 2017-18.

EIL secured Project Management Consulting assignment for setting up a grass root refinery in Mongolia in 2019-20.

Projects executed - EIL has executed over 7000 assignments including 500 major projects valued over US$200 Billion. EIL's project portfolio consists of 89 refinery projects including 10 greenfield refineries, 12 mega petrochemical complexes, 11 fertilizer plants, 44 oil and gas processing projects, 213 offshore platforms including 40 process platforms, 50 Pipeline projects, 33 mining & metallurgy projects, 14 ports, storage & terminals projects, over 40 infrastructure projects including airports, highways, flyovers, bridges, water and sewer management, as well as energy-efficient intelligent buildings and 24 turnkey projects.

The gross turnover of EIL in 2022-23 was Rs. 3283.76 Cr.

Water & Power Consultancy Services (India) Ltd. – River and Water Management Projects

Water & Power Consultancy Services (India) Ltd. - WAPCOS was incorporated on 26.6.**1969** to become a leading consultancy organization in water, power, infrastructure development and allied sectors covering concept to commissioning and operation and maintenance of projects.

WAPCOS specializes in irrigation and drainage, flood control and land reclamation, river management, dams, reservoir engineering and barrages, integrated agriculture development, watershed management, hydropower and thermal power generation, power transmission and distribution, rural electrification, ground water exploration, minor irrigation, water supply and sanitation (rural and urban), environmental engineering including environmental impact assessment and environmental audit, ports and harbors and inland waterways, rain water harvesting, survey & investigations, etc.

WAPCOS diversified in to roads, bridges and rural development.

WAPCOS has ventured into software development, City Development Plans, Financial Management System, technical education, quality control and construction supervision.

WAPCOS has successfully completed (or executing) consultancy assignments in 40 countries. WAPCOS is currently engaged in providing consultancy services in 32 countries including Afghanistan, Bhutan, Cambodia, Ethiopia, Eritrea, Laos, Lesotho, Mozambique, Rwanda, Sudan, Swaziland, Uganda, Zambia and Zimbabwe. In 2019-20, the Company secured new business in Asia, Africa, Middle East, South America, Pacific Islands for providing consultancy services in 47 countries.

WAPCOS is involved in National Rural Drinking Water Program, Sarva Shiksha Abhiyan, Pradhan Manti Gram Sadak Yojna, National Livelihood Mission, Swachh Bharat Abhiyan etc.

The gross turnover of WAPCOS in 2022-23 was Rs, 1419.61 Cr.

Engineering Projects (India) Ltd.

Engineering Projects (India) Ltd. - EPI was incorporated on 16.4.**1970** as Indian Consortium of Industrial Projects Ltd, to undertake turnkey projects in metallurgy, mining, fertilizers, oil and petrochemicals, process plants, coal & material handling systems, transmission lines / sub stations, civil and structural projects including housing, townships, hospitals & institutional buildings, sports stadia, airports, irrigation projects, dams & canal works, shore protection works, water supply and environmental engineering, roads & highways, Defence, etc. The name was changed to EPI on 14.12.1970.

EPI signed 4 nos. of Memorandum of Understandings for executing monorail projects and infrastructure development projects in India, Sri Lanka, Bangladesh, Maldives, Oman, other Gulf and African countries. EPI commissioned New Blast Furnace of capacity of 8000 Tons/day at Bhilai Steel Plant on 02.02.2018 and provided its raw material handling and fuel & flux crushing system.

The Govt. Medical College (Ph-1 work) for 100 MBBS admissions & hospital project at Barmer, was completed by EPI on 29.08.2019.

The gross turnover of EPI in 2022-23 was Rs. 1131.96 Cr.

Metallurgical & Engineering Consultants (India) - Steel Plants, Refineries, Chemical Plants

MECON Ltd. / Metallurgical & Engineering Consultants (India) - MECON was incorporated on 31.3.**1973** to build indigenous capability for design and consultancy of steel and other plants.

MECON provided design, engineering and consultancy services for the iron and steel industries including setting up of integrated steel plants. It diversified into coal and chemicals, refineries, petrochemicals and power plants, roads & highways, railways, water management, ports & harbors, gas & oil, pipelines, non-ferrous, mining, general engineering, environmental engineering and other related areas.

MECON completed over 2800 engineering consultancy and 120 EPC / turnkey assignments worth more than Rs. 300 billion up to 2007-08. MECON provided quality design, engineering & consultancy services for about 130 projects in different countries.

MECON has worked for various clients in Qatar, Saudi Arabia, Oman, UAE, Vietnam, USA, Indonesia, etc.

The company formed **4 financial joint ventures** namely Kudremukh Iron Ore Company Ltd., Neelanchal Ispat Nigam Ltd., Global Procurement Consultant Ltd. and Metallurgical & Engineering Consultants (Nigeria) Ltd.

MECON achieved highest ever gross turnover of Rs. 889.46 Cr and bagged order for providing EPMC services for Small-Scale NG Liquefaction project in 2022-23.

Educational Consultants (India) Ltd. - Establishment of Educational Institutions

Educational Consultants (India) Ltd. – EdCIL was incorporated in **1981** to promote Indian education abroad, provide technical assistance, undertake institutional development, supply educational aids and work as testing agency.

EdCIL is providing consultancy services in all areas of education ranging from feasibility studies to detailed project reports for establishment of educational institutes with ancillaries on a turnkey basis.

EdCIL is engaged in promotion of Indian education abroad by placement of international students in Indian institutions and deputation of Indian teachers / experts abroad, conducting education fairs, seminars-cum-counselling sessions, improving liaison with Indian Missions abroad etc.

The gross turnover of EdCIL in 2022-23 was Rs. 439.10 Cr.

Hospital Services Consultancy Corporation Ltd. - Setting Up Hospitals & Medical Institutes

HSCC (India) Ltd. - HSCC was incorporated on 30.3.**1983** to provide specialized consultancy services in the health care and other social sector.

It undertook architectural planning, design, project management, procurement, supply, installation and commissioning of medical equipment, information technology / recruitment / training for setting up hospitals and medical related institutes and laboratories projects, which were assigned to it by Ministry of Health & Family Welfare, Ministry of External Affairs, private & public sector organizations as well as various State Governments.

The company also diversified into hospital waste management, hospital computerization, health related management studies and training & recruitment.

HSCC was continuously making profit for 20 years.

During 2007-08
i) HSCC was awarded 22 projects relating to project management services, 15 projects relating to procurement management services and 5 projects relating to studies and training services.
ii) HSCC made alliance with Manpower Corporation Ltd. for deputation of medical / paramedical manpower abroad and with Educational Consultants India Ltd. for placement of international students in Indian Medical Institutions, design and implementation of projects for establishment of medical institutions within country and abroad.

HSCC successfully completed major healthcare projects comprising hospital, medical colleges, laboratories etc. not only in India but also in many countries.

The Government received Rs. 49.55 Cr. through buyback transaction in December 2017.
HSCC was acquired by NBCC India for Rs. 285 Cr during 2018-19.

HSCC was executing following projects in 2022-23: 1. AIIMS at Guntur. 2. AIIMS at Rajkot. 3. Govt. Medical College at Chandrapur. 4. Advanced Neurosciences Centre at PGIMER, Chandigarh. 5. New Medical Colleges at various Locations in Rajasthan. 6. Regional Cancer Centre at NEIGRIHMS, Shillong & Imphal 7. Hospital Block at RML Hospital, New Delhi. 8. RIIMS, Imphal. 9. Construction of Teaching Hospital at Flacq, Mauritius. 10. MedClinics at 4 Locations, Mauritius. (Ref. www.hsccltd.co,in)

The gross turnover of HSCC in 2022-23 was Rs. 1102.86 Cr.

Certification Engineers International Ltd. - Safety Studies for Oil & Gas Facilities

Certification Engineers International Ltd. - CEI was carved out of Engineers India Certification Agenda, which had been carrying out certification activities as a division of EIL since 1984, and incorporated on 26.10.**1994** to undertake activities related to certification, re-certification, safety audit and safety management systems for offshore and onshore oil and gas facilities and third-party inspection of equipment and installations in the hydrocarbon and other quality sensitive sectors of the industry.

CEI is also providing services in the field of risk analysis, health, safety and environment audits, energy audit, quality audit and vender assessment.

The gross turnover of CEI in 2022-23 was Rs. 47.85 Cr.

Broadcast Engineering Consultants India Ltd. - Consultancy in Broadcast Engineering

Broadcast Engineering Consultants India Ltd. - BECIL was incorporated on 24.3.**1995** to provide consultancy in broadcast engineering and share the expertise of All India Radio and Door Darshan with Indian companies.

BECIL is providing consultancy services and executing turnkey jobs related to terrestrial & satellite broadcasting, FM broadcasting, establishment of TV channels, installation of teleports, design of Digital Newsrooms, Direct to Home system, Cable Head-End systems, distance education systems, Multichannel Multipoint Distribution System, CATV network, data broadcasting, studios including audio-video systems, acoustics, stage lighting, sound reinforcement system, establishment of electronic facilities for coverage of major sporting events, supply of electronic equipment to various defence organizations and security agencies etc.

BECIL also undertakes operation and maintenance of broadcast systems of all types in India and abroad. BECIL diversified into supply of communication and security equipment, setting up of TV Studios for distance education and content monitoring etc.

Jobs completed – i) BECIL rendered services for design to system integration for several private TV channels. ii) BECIL created Common Transmission Infrastructure for 248 private FM Channels in 87 cities. iii) BECIL commissioned 4 FM towers at Jaipur, Delhi, Chennai and Hyderabad by 2007-08. iv) BECIL completed setting up Multi Media Studio in Rashtrapati Bhawan, TV Studio for EDUSET Networking program at Delhi College of Engineering, etc.

BECIL executed various projects including revamping of information set up in Afghanistan and augmentation of Television Hardware in Jalalabad and Nangarhar provinces of Afghanistan.

The gross turnover of BECIL in 2022-23 was Rs. 1068.35 Cr.

Indian Oil Technologies Ltd.- Oil Exploration and Extraction

Indian OIL Technologies Limited was incorporated on 20.06.**2003**. It was involved in service activities incidental to oil and gas extraction, including directional drilling, spudding in, derrick building, repairing and dismantling, cementing oil and gas well casings, pumping wells, and other service activities, excluding surveying.

IOTL works as the technology - marketing arm for the entire range of technologies developed at Indian Oil's R&D centre at Faridabad to oil companies in India and aboard.

The R&D centre of IOC has developed several technologies and technical expertise both in refining and lubricant sector. IOTL also offers i) state-of-the-art sludge disposal technology for hydro carbon sector, ii) consultancy services for revamp of petrochemical units, iii) assistance in production of modified asphalt, bitumen emulsion, iv) evaluation of performance of refinery units, v) providing training in refining processes, lubricant and fuel technology, etc.

IOTL is majorly in Mining & Quarrying business from last 21 years and currently, company operations are dissolved.

HLL Infra Tech Services Limited - Hospitals, Medical Institutions

HLL Infra Tech Services Limited - HITES was incorporated on 03.04.**2014** as a wholly owned subsidiary of HLL Lifecare Ltd to carry on infrastructure development, facilities management, procurement consultancy and allied services in setting up and maintaining world class healthcare facilities.

HITES set up AIIMS at Guwahati and upgraded Government Medical Colleges at Agra, Kanpur and Cuttack during 2017-18. OPD Services in AYUSH Block of AIIMS Gorakhpur was inaugurated on 24.02.2019. 200 Bedded Hospital at Chitrakoot was completed on 13.09.2019.

Medical Colleges at Kozhikode and Alappuzha were completed and foundation stone for construction of Government Medical College Hospital at Sirsa, Haryana project was laid in 2022-23. The gross turnover of HITES in 2022-23 was Rs. 359.15 Cr.

NBCC Engineering & Consultancy Ltd

NBCC Engineering & Consultancy Limited - NECL was incorporated on 15.12.**2015** as a subsidiary of NBCC (India) Ltd to provide engineering & consultancy services regarding projects undertaken by holding company & other parties.

NBCC Engineering and Consultancy Ltd. has been dissolved w.e.f. 16.03.2023.

Public Sector Enterprises Engaged in Marketing Services

RITES Ltd. - Supply & Operation of Railway Rolling Stock in Other Countries

RITES Ltd. - RITES was incorporated on 26.04.**1974** to supply, operate and maintain railway rolling stock and other transport equipment and offer related services including export of consultancy.

RITES is providing consultancy, engineering and project management services for railways, highways, urban transport, airports, ports and harbors, inland waterways, ropeways etc. in India and over 62 countries abroad.

RITES provided export packages for supply of locomotives, coaches, spare parts and modernization of workshops including to Sri Lanka and Senegal.

RITES secured consultancy contracts from Saudi Arabia, Indonesia, Nepal, Botswana, Afghanistan and UAE (Sharjah). RITES operates in all countries (except in Pakistan) of SAARC region and Maldives besides 40 other countries.

The company formed **6 subsidiaries** namely – i) RITES (AFRIKA) Proprietary Ltd in Botswana (specializing in development and management of airports, roads, buildings and water supply infrastructure),
ii) RITES Mohawarean Arabia Co. Ltd in Saudi Arabia (liquidated in 2020-21),
iii) RITES Infrastructure Services Ltd. (liquidated in 2022-23)
iv) Railway Energy Management Company Ltd. in India,
v) Tanzania Railways Ltd in Tanzania and
vi) RITES Colombia Ltd.

Tanzania Railways Ltd was incorporated on 25.05.2007 by equity participation between RITES and Govt of Tanzania for building railway network of 2700 km spread in Tanzania for carrying both passengers and freight traffic. RITES was given a leasing contract by Tanzania Railways Ltd. for operating passenger coaches in addition to the existing operation of diesel locomotives in Tanzania and Mozambique.

RITES diversified into renewable energy projects including installation of windmills and solar plants through Railway Energy Management Company Ltd.

RITES formed 6 financial joint ventures namely
i) Companhia Dos Caminhos De Ferro da Beira S.A.R.L, Beira (CCFB) in Mozambique for concessioning of Rail Network,
ii) SAIL RITES Bengal Wagon Industry Pvt Ltd.
iii) BNV Gujarat Rail Pvt Ltd.
iv) Geoconsult - RITES (India) Ltd.
v) RICON (joint venture with IRCON)
vi) Ganga Expressway Consultants Pvt Ltd (for development of eight lane access control expressway).

The company formed 3 more financial joint ventures for establishment of Rail Network at Colombia, Austria and Mozambique.
RITES formed financial joint venture namely Geoconsult – RITES NRT 1 in Austria.
RITES was given new rail projects in Malaysia.
RITES set up wagon factory, SAIL RITES Bengal Wagon Industry Pvt Ltd. at Kulti, with an assured off–take agreement for 1200 wagons / annum and rehabilitation of a minimum of 300 wagons / annum.
RITES undertook development of Cape Gauge DMU Train sets and Self-Propelled Accident Relief Train for Angola.

The gross turnover of RITES in 2022-23 was Rs. 2519.62 Cr.

Antrix Corporation Ltd. - Marketing Services of Indian Space Research Organization

Antrix Corporation Ltd. - ACL was incorporated on 28.9.**1992** to work as commercial marketing arm of Indian Space Research Organization (ISRO).

The business portfolio consists of (i) Remote Sensing Services; (ii) Trading of Satellites and Spacecraft Systems; (iii) Transponder Leasing Services; (iv) Launch Services; (v) Mission Support Services; (vi) Ground System Services (vii) Spacecraft Testing Facilities like in-orbit test; and (viii) hosting for other satellite companies.

ACL gets the space products manufactured at various ISRO centres and undertakes leasing of INSAT satellite transponders for television broadcasting, Digital News gathering, DTH, VAST and other applications.

The gross turnover of ACL in 2022-23 was Rs. 38.16 Cr.

NBCC Services Limited - Maintenance and Renovation Services

NBCC Services Limited - NSL was incorporated on 16.10.**2014** as a subsidiary of NBCC (India) Limited to undertake maintenance work and to act as an execution agency for Corporate Social Responsibility projects on behalf of institutions and NGOs.

The operation- cum –maintenance of buildings includes civil and plumbing works, electrical, HVAC works, firefighting works, operation of DG sets, pumps, lifts etc. NSL completed renovation work of NCLAT at MTNL building in 2019-20.

Graph – 8.1 Construction, Consultancy and Marketing Jobs Executed by CPSEs

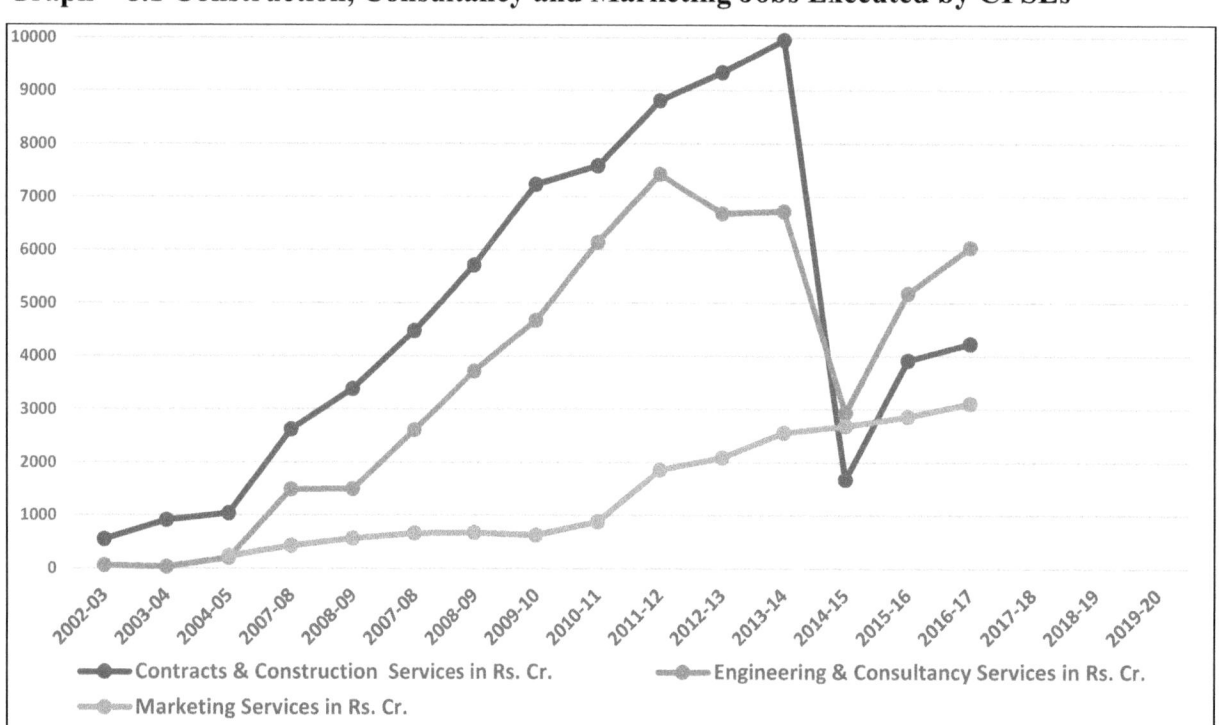

Newspace India Ltd.

Established on 06.03.2019 to undertake Building Operational Launch Vehicles of ISRO through Industry, Providing Launch Services & Providing INSAT/ GSAT satellites transponder capacities for meeting various applications needs like Direct to Home, VSAT, TV, DSNG and Inflight and Maritime Connectivity, Providing transponder capacity form foreign satellites to Indian Users on back to back basis, Owning and operating the satellites on Demand Driven model, Satellite building as per customer requirements, Mission Support Services for Satellites and launch vehicle tracking, Technology Transfer/ spin off of technologies emanating from R and D activities of ISRO.

Private Sector Players

Companies manufacturing - Engineering products

Engineering products companies –

Power station and industrial boiler companies - ACC-Vickers-Babcock Ltd. – 1959, Texmaco Rail & Engineering Ltd. – 1998, **Chiller and Cooling system companies** - Paharpur Cooling Towers – 1948 and Kirloskar Chillers Pvt Ltd. – 1995, **Engineering Co.** - Lloyds Steels Industries Ltd – 1974, **Forging Equipment Company** - L&T Special Steels & Heavy Forgings Pvt Ltd. – 2009, **Generating sets, Diesel engines company** – Kirloskar Oil Engines Ltd. – 2009, **Machine tool company** - Mysore Kirloskar Ltd. – 1941, **Manufacturing partner for ISRO in 1970, for DRDO in 1985** – Larsen & Toubro Ltd – 1970, **Motors, transformers, drives manufacturers** – Kirloskar Electric Co. Ltd. – 1946, Bharat Bijlee Ltd – 1946, **Water treatment plant manufacturer** – Ion Exchange Ltd. – 1964

Light Engineering companies –

Air compressors, air-conditioning and refrigeration company - Kirloskar Pneumatic Co. Ltd – 1974, **Bearing** companies – National Bearings Company Ltd – 1946, SKF India Ltd – 1961, Bimetal Bearings Ltd – 1961, FAG Bearings India Ltd – 1962, NRB Bearings Ltd – 1965, Tata Timken Ltd / Timken India Ltd – 1987, **Transmission chains** companies - L. G. Balakrishnan Brothers Ltd – 1960, TI Diamond Chains Ltd.- 1960, **Compressors, vacuum solutions** companies - Chicago Pneumatic Ltd – 1957, Atlas Capco India – 1960, **Control valves** company - Audco India Limited / L&T Valves Ltd – 1961, **Diesel Engines, industrial and marine gear boxes, concreting equipment, Transit mixer, Power train** Company - Greaves Cotton – 1859, TAFE Motors & Tractors Ltd – 1960, **Drives for motors** companies - Siemens India – 1957, Larsen & Toubro Ltd - Control and Automation – 1977, NELCO Ltd. – 1978, Rockwell Automation / Allen Bradley India Ltd.- 1983, **Forgings** company - Shardlow India Ltd – 1960, **Gear boxes, gears** companies - Gajra Gears Pvt Ltd.- 1962, Shanti Gear Products Pvt Ltd.- 1972, Shanti Gears Ltd – 1972, **Diesel Generator** companies - Kirloskar Cummins Ltd- 1961, Mahindra Powerol – 2002, **Grinding wheels, abrasives** company - Carborundum Universal Ltd – 1954, **Lamps, Lighting equipment** companies - Philips Electrical Co. (India) Pvt Ltd. / Philips India Ltd – 1948, TI Miller – 1960, Crompton Greaves Ltd, - 1966, **Lifts and Elevator manufacturing companies** – OTIS Elevator Company (I) Ltd (1953), ECE Industries (1945 / 1961), Johnson Lifts Pvt. Ltd. (1963), **Machine tools** company - Praga Tools Corp. – 1943, **Synthetic yarn manufacturing machines** Company - Lohia Machines Private Ltd – 1972, **Materials handling equipment** Company - Hercules Hoists Ltd – 1982, **Metals & chemicals parts** Company - United Motors (India) Ltd – 1920, **Motors, MV Switchgear, transformers** company - Hindustan Electric Co Ltd / Asea Brown Boveri Ltd / ABB Ltd – 1949, **Nuts and fasteners, electrical, automotive and textile industries stampings** company - Guest Keen Williams – 1920, **Office automation equipment** company - Latham India Ltd – 1977, Gestetner, **Plastic injection moulding tools** company - Nypro Forbes Moulds Ltd – 2002, **Power tools** company - Black & Decker Bajaj Private Limited – 1993, **Pumps** company - Kirloskar Brothers – 1888, **Switchgear** companies - Siemens India – 1957, Jyoti Ltd.- 1957, Anchor Electricals Pvt. Ltd – 1963, Southern Switchgear Ltd – 1963, Bhartiya Cuttler Hammer Electric Ltd – 1965, Larsen & Toubro Ltd - Control and Automation – 1977, Havells India – 1983, L & T Switchgear & Automation Products – 1989, Schneider Electric India Pvt Ltd – 1995, **Tools** companies - Addison & Co Ltd   1873, TAFE Engineering Plastics & Tools

Division – 1964, **Welding electrodes and welding equipment** companies - Union Carbide India Ltd.- 1934, L & T Eutectic Welding Alloys – 1962, Eutectic Welding Alloys Ltd – 1972, **Wire Phosphating and Wire Drawing** company - Kuduma Fasteners Ltd – 1987

Construction companies – Shapoorji Pallonji & Company Pvt Ltd – 1865, Gammon India Ltd – 1922, Simplex Infrastructures Ltd – 1924, Hindustan Construction Co Ltd – 1926, Engineering Construction Corporation – 1944, L&T Construction Buildings & Factories business – 1944, KEC International Ltd – 1945, L&T's Heavy Civil Infrastructure business – 1946, Coromandel Engineering Company Ltd – 1947, GMR Group – 1978, Tata Projects Ltd – 1979, L & T Infrastructure Engineering Ltd. – 1990, Mahindra Life Space Developers – 1994, L&T Infrastructure Development Projects Ltd – 1995, L & T Transportation Infrastructure – 1997 and L&T's Power Transmission and Distribution – Reliance Infrastructure - 2008

Construction, mining and earth moving equipment companies - Larsen & Toubro Ltd – 1945 and L & T Construction Equipment Ltd./ L & T Poclain Division – 1975, Mahindra Construction Equipment - 2011

9: GROWTH IN FERTILIZER, PESTICIDES AND CHEMICALS PRODUCTION

Importance of Fertilizers and Chemicals

The Indian fertilizer industry plays an important role in ensuring the food security by increasing agricultural productivity by easing availability of adequate quantity of quality fertilizers.

Pesticides including insecticides, fungicides, weedicides, etc., are used extensively in agriculture for protecting plants.

The chemical industry provides basic inputs to pharmaceuticals, petrochemicals, fertilizers and a large number of other allied chemical and consumer industries.

Targeted Growth for Fertilizer, Pesticides and Chemicals Production

The fertilizer requirements for targeted food production and demand for acids for fertilizer production, by-products recovery, pickling operations in steel plants, petroleum refining, manufacture of organic intermediates and drugs, and uranium extraction from the ores were forecasted by the government for the last financial year of each 5-year plan and the target fertilizers and chemicals production capacity to be created and production to be made in the various 5-year plans were set.

Fertilizer Production in India

In 1947, **Fertilizers and Chemicals Travancore Ltd.** started production of ammonium sulphate with an installed capacity of 50,000 TPA at Udyogamandal.

In 1950-51, the consumption of nitrogenous fertilizers (in terms of N) was 55,000 tons and that of phosphatic fertilizers (in terms of P_2O_5) was 7000 tons. (3.3.13)

Achievements in I 5YP –
Sindri Fertilizers and Chemicals Ltd was established in 1951 with a capacity of 350,000 tons of ammonium sulphate. It commenced production in October 1951. (1.4.26)

Hindustan Chemicals and Fertilizers Ltd. was established in 1956

Private Sector in 1955-56 - Ammonium sulphate production capacity of private sector units increased from 78670 tons in 1951 to 131270 tons in 1955-56 and that of Super Phosphate from 123460 tons to 192855 tons.

Growth during II 5YP -
Bihar **Government Superphosphate Factory** started production in 1958 with a capacity of 16,500 tons.

3 New fertilizer plants in the public sector at Nangal, Neyveli and Rourkela were started during II 5YP. Nangal and Rourkela fertilizer plants were set up to produce nitro-limestone corresponding to 70,000 and 80,000 TPA of fixed nitrogen respectively. The Nangal plant came into partial production in January 1961. (3.26.3)

Neyveli fertilizer plant was set up to produce urea and sulphate / nitrate corresponding to 70,000 tons of fixed nitrogen using lignite. (2.3.33)

The expansion of Sindri fertilizer factory to increase its output from 66,000 to 117,000 tons of nitrogen started.

Fertilizer Corporation of India was started in 1961 by consolidating Sindri Fertilizers and Chemicals Ltd. and Hindustan Fertilizer and Chemicals Ltd.

During III 5YP

The government gave approval to private sector for setting up fertilizer plants of total capacity 3,66,250 tons in Ennore, Madhya Pradesh, Vishakhapatnam, Kothagudem, Rajasthan and Durgapur (joint venture with WB govt) besides expansion of Sahu Chemicals, Varanasi. (3.26.75)

FACT undertook III stage expansion project for additional production of ammonium phosphate, sulphate and chloride.

Madras Fertilizers Ltd was incorporated in 1966 to manufacture ammonia, urea and complex fertilizers at Manali, Chennai.

Indian Farmers Fertilizer Cooperative Ltd was incorporated in 1967, as a multi-unit cooperative society to produce fertilizers.

Gorakhpur Fertilizers was started in 1968.

Namrup Fertilizers - Namrup-I plant was commissioned in 1969,

Achievements in IV 5YP (1969-74) -
During 1969-74, 8 projects of 1.31 Mts capacity were approved in the private sector.
FACT Cochin Division was set up in the 1970's at Udyogamandal.
Kanpur Fertilizers and Cements Ltd was set up in 1970 by Imperial Chemical Industries, as Duncans Fertilizers for production of urea. Expansion of Trombay Fertilizers unit was taken up during IV 5YP. (5.5.7)

Achievements in V 5YP
Between 1961 and 1977, FCI created 17 fertilizer units. 7 Started operating while the remaining 10 were at various stages of implementation in 1977.

FCI and National Fertilizers Ltd., were split into 5 entities in 1978 to reorganize fertilizer industry
i) **Hindustan Fertilizer Corporation Ltd.** was given the Namrup, Haldia, Barauni and Durgapur units,
ii) **FCI** was assigned Sindri, Gorakhpur, Ramagundam, Talcher and Korba units and Jodhpur Mining Organization.
iii) Trombay and Thal units were allocated to **Rashtriya Chemicals and Fertilizers Ltd.** and
iv) Bathinda and Panipat units were given to **National Fertilizers Ltd.**
v) The fifth entity was planning and development company, **Project and Development (India) Ltd**.

Talcher and Ramagundam plants achieved commercial production by 1979-80. (6.16.39)

During 1980-85
i) Execution of phosphatic fertilizer plants at Haldia, Mangalore, and Paradeep-1 and expansion of Goa plant were under progress. (7.7.128)
ii) Gas-based fertilizer plants were set up at Thal - Vaishet and Hazira tor manufacture of nitrogenous fertilizers. The first phase of these plants was completed during 1984-85. (7.6.55)
iii) Work on plants at NFL Vijaipur, Guna, Sawai Madhopur (Rajasthan), IFFCO at Aonia, KRIBHCO at Jagdishpur and Shahjahanpur and Tata Chemicals at Babrala (U.P.) were under progress.
iv) In the public sector, 7 New phosphatic fertilizer projects were started (using rock phosphate and pyrites from Rajasthan) and expansion of Tuticorin and Cochin plants were completed. (7.7.128)

During 1985-90
4 Gas-based nitrogenous fertilizer plants at Aonia, Vijaipur, Jagdishpur and Namrup Expansion III and DAP project at Paradeep were commissioned.

4 Gas-based projects were under implementation at Babrala, Shahjahanpur, Kota and Kakinada. (8.V2.1.4.2)

Fertilizer Companies' losses –

The prices of fertilizers were controlled by govt. As retail prices were considerably lower than the fair cost of production plus freight, the manufacturers were compensated for the difference under the production-cum-transfer subsidy system. Calculation of fair prices was based on reasonable norms of production level, energy consumption, working capital margin etc.

The subsidy burden was steadily increasing due to (i) escalations in the costs of inputs which were not compensated by corresponding increases in the retail prices of fertilizers; (ii) increase in the volume of production of fertilizers and (iii) high capital costs of new fertilizer plants.

The fertilizer industry was complaining that, though it was assured of a 12% post-tax return on net worth, in actual practice, a number of items were excluded and hence enough subsidy was not given to industry. (8.v2.5.19.4)

Complete de-control of prices could adversely affect the consumption of fertilizers by small and marginal farmers in the initial years. Hence, phasing out subsidy was to be done gradually, giving time to farmers to adjust. (8.v2.5.19.5)

During IX 5YP - The total investment in the fertilizer sector during IX 5YP was estimated at Rs.13,300 Cr, of which Rs.9,300 Cr was to be in public sector and balance in the private sector. (9.5.168)

Installed capacities of the fertilizer industry in 2001-02 were – 12.058 Mt of nitrogen and 5.387 Mt of P_2O_5 (phosphate). (11.v2.7.1.212)

The country achieved self-sufficiency in 2001-02 of nearly 100% for urea and 85% for Di-ammonium Phosphate (DAP).

Price control and fertilizer subsidy – The Retention Price cum Subsidy scheme price arrangement, however, encouraged the urea manufacturers to focus more on claiming costs rather than controlling costs by enhancing production efficiency.

Only urea was under retention pricing scheme whereas phosphatic and potassic fertilizers were covered under a concession scheme. Government notified the maximum retail price of urea under the concession scheme and the indicative MRP for decontrolled fertilizers, namely DAP, Muriate of Potash (MOP), and complexes. The MRP of single super phosphate (SSP) was left to be notified by the states. (10.7.1.121)

The development of the Indian fertilizer industry, even while remaining under the regime of industrial licensing till 1991, had been phenomenal due to the favorable price environment, in which industry was able to meet its increasing cost of production with reasonable assured return on investment through a controlled price mechanism. The farm gate price of fertilizers was kept low through fertilizer control order and industry was insulated from the external competition. A balance was struck between the interest of the industry and that of the farmers by the Central budget absorbing the subsidy burden. (10.7.1.122)

The move by the government to decontrol phosphatic and potassic fertilizer in 1992 did not succeed, as it was a partial decontrol and resulted in over-dose of controlled nitrogen nutrient (low priced) against lower dose of market (high) priced phosphatic and potassic nutrients. The long-term adverse effect on the soil made it essential to provide incentive to the farmers by way of subsidy on phosphatic and potassic fertilizers again. (10.7.1.123)

Achievements in X 5YP

The turnover of fertilizer industry from 2001-02 to 2005-06 in Rs. Cr. were 7249, 8280, 8017, 8999 and 9364 respectively. (Annexure – 11.v3.7.1.4)

Production of urea in 2005–06 from 28 functional units was 20.098 Mts. (11.v2.7.1.212)

Capacity additions such as Brahmaputra Valley Fertilizer Corporation Ltd. revamp project and Oman India Fertilizer Company materialized during 2002-07.

India became the **fourth largest producer of fertilizer (21.352 Mts of urea) in 2006-07**. It met the bulk needs for nitrogenous and phosphatic fertilizers, but potassic fertilizers' needs were met through imports. (11.7.1.210)

Many urea units were producing urea using uneconomic feedstock such as naphtha and diesel oil. (11.v2.7.1.56)

Non-natural gas-based urea production units were given 3 years to convert into NG/LNG units. Pipeline connectivity already existed for 22 units. The units at Goa, Mangalore, and Tuticorin were expected to be serviced by the Reliance Gas Transportation Infrastructure's Tuticorin-Chennai–Mangalore pipelines. (11.7.1.215)

Achievements in XI 5YP - Production of NPK and organic manures in 2010-11 were 26.5 Mts and 4 Mts respectively. (12.12.163)

India became the second largest consumer of fertilizers in the world, after China, consuming about 26.5 Mts of NPK in 2012. (12.12.163)

Fertilizer Industry in 2011-12

With rising demand for urea and DAP and no major investment for domestic capacity addition during 2009-12, the industry was exposed to volatility of world markets. Investment for revival of closed units of FCI and HFCL was expected to bridge the demand–supply gap of urea. (12. Annex. 13.2 – 38 / 42)

Government felt necessity to ensure long-term supply of natural gas by pipeline connectivity to attract fresh investment (from private sector) and to incentivize use of alternative feedstock like coal, CBM, etc. (12. Annex. 13.2 – 43)

Joint Ventures Abroad

It was realized that long-term supplies of raw materials and intermediates can be ensured to fertilizer sector by investing and setting up JVs for mining in countries with rich reserves of natural gas, rock phosphate and potash with appropriate buy-back or long term off-take arrangements. (12. Annex.13.2 - 45)

Soil Health Improvement

Imbalanced nutrient use coupled with neglect of organic matter resulted in multi-nutrient deficiencies in Indian soils - hardly 35% for N, 15–20% for P and only 3–5% for micronutrients like zinc. As nutrient additions did not keep pace with nutrient removal by crops, the fertility status of Indian soils was declining rapidly under intensive agriculture and was showing signs of fatigue, especially in the Indo-Gangetic plain in 2011-12.

Soil Testing - By 2010–11, there were 1,049 soil tests labs with a soil analysis capacity of 10.6 million soil samples/ annum. The State Governments had issued 40.8 million soil health cards to the farmers by October 2011. State Governments were advised to utilize resources from Rashtriya Krishi Vikas Yojana, State Agricultural Universities, APMC, KVKs, NGO, etc. to increase testing capacity.

Substantial addition of soil organic matter by use of biological sources of nutrients like bio-fertilizers, organic manure and bio-compost was felt necessary for sustained soil health and fertility. (12.12. 164/165)

Government introduced Nutrient Based Subsidy for Phosphatic and Potassic fertilizers w.e.f. 1.04.2010 to ensure balanced use of nutrients. (12. Annex. 13.2 – 39)

Production of bio-fertilizers in 2019-20

39 units had been set up for manufacture of 7,975 Tons of biofertilizer per year

Status in 2020

In 2020, production of ammonium sulphate, DAP, NPK fertilizers and urea were 0.8479 Mt, 3.7738 Mts, 2.098 Mts and 24.6031 Mts respectively.

Fertilizer Industry in 2022
There were 34 gas based urea manufacturing units with installed capacity of **25.834 Mts** approx. (Urea Policy(Pricing and Administration) | Department of Fertilizers)
The ammonia capacity was **239.41 Mt** per annum in 2022.

Status in 2022-23 –
Production of total fertilizer products was 48.68 Mts, urea was 28.49 Mt, DAP was 4.35 Mts, NP/NPK complex fertilizers was 9.30 Mts and SSP was 5.64 Mt during 2022-23. FAI-AR-2022-23.pdf (faidelhi.org)

Production of Pesticides in India

During I 5YP
Construction of 2 D.D.T. plants of capacity 700 tons started. (1.4.36)

Hindustan Insecticides Ltd. was established in 1954.

During II 5YP
Second D.D.T. plant was established in Travancore-Cochin. (2.3.34)

Status in 1979-80
Installed capacity for technical grade pesticides was 70,425 tons and Production of pesticides were 50,041 tons. (6.16.43)

Status in 1984-85
Out of 126 pesticides cleared for use by the Registration Committee, 57 were being manufactured.
Installed capacity for pesticides was 99,000 tons.
Production of major technical grade pesticides was 65,000 tons. (7.7.134)

During 1985-90
A number of new pesticides including Bu-tackler, Isoproturon, Monocrotophos and Pyrethroids were taken up for manufacture. (8.v2.5.22.2)

Institute of Pesticide Formulation technology, set up by the Government with the assistance of UNDP / UNIDO in May 1991, was actively engaged in development of new, safer and environment-friendly pesticides and formulations. It was participating in the proficiency tests conducted by the Organization for Prohibition of Chemical Weapons worldwide to assess the capabilities of laboratories. (10.7.1.200)

Status in 1991-92
Out of the 137 pesticides approved for use, DDT and BHC were high volume pesticides. The others were largely used by farmers for fighting pests of a variety of crops such as fruits, vegetables, cotton, groundnut, sugarcane, rice, wheat, etc.
Installed capacities for other pesticides were 34500 tons, 39590 tons and 44550 tons in 1989-90, 1990-91 and 1991-92 respectively.
Production of other pesticides were 27050 tons, 28000 tons and 27000 tons in 1989-90, 1990-91 and 1991-92 respectively. (8. State. 5.5)

The country was largely self-sufficient in the manufacture of pesticides but some of the intermediates and new varieties of insecticides were being imported. (8.v2.5.22.1)

Status in 1996-97
More than 60 technical grade pesticides were being manufactured in India by more than 125 units. Over 500 units were making pesticide formulations. (9.5.202)

Installed capacity for technical grade pesticides was 139,300 tons and production of technical grade pesticides was 98,000 tons (9.5.203)

Status in 2001-02
India ranked 12th in Agro-pesticides globally and second in Asia alone.

Pesticide industry was able to meet 95% of the country's demand. (10.7.1.197)

Insecticides accounted for 76% of the total Pesticide domestic market. (10.7.1.198)
The industry was composed of 67 large units in the organized sector (10 were multinational companies) manufacturing technical grade, and over 400 SSI units, engaged in formulations. The only PSU in the sector was Hindustan Insecticide Ltd. (10.7.1.199)
Demand for technical grade pesticides was 43,380 tons
Installed capacity of pesticide industry was – 128900 tons

Monitoring pesticide use in 2011-12
Central and State insecticide inspectors from 68 State Pesticide Testing Laboratories in 23 States and 1 Union Territory drew samples (up to 68,110 samples/ annum) of insecticides from the market for analysis and monitored the quality of pesticides to ensure safe, efficacious, and judicious use of pesticides. Department of Agriculture and Cooperation monitored pesticide residues and advised States to take necessary action. (12.12.166)

Production of Chemicals in India

Travancore Titanium Products Ltd. was incorporated in 1946 to manufacture anatase grade titanium dioxide (required for paint pigment, welding rod fluxes, optical coating, printing ink, glass, etc.).

Status in 1951 and 1956
The production capacities of private sector for Sulphuric Acid, Caustic Soda and Soda Ash in 1951 were 150000 tons, 19000 tons and 54000 tons respectively. These capacities increased to 213000 tons, 37000 tons and 86000 tons respectively in 1955-56.

Achievements in II 5YP
Hindustan Organic Chemicals Ltd was established in 1960 to manufacture basic chemicals and Benzene Hexachloride to reduce country's dependence on import of vital organic chemicals. (6.16.43)
Production of Dyestuffs in 1960-61 was 11.5 million lbs. (3.26.82)
Durgapur Industries Board undertook organic chemicals project for the manufacture of caustic soda, phenol, phthalic anhydride and some other organic chemicals. (3.26.30)
The overall demand for the acid in 1960-61, for fertilizer production, by-products recovery, pickling operations at the steel plants, petroleum refining, manufacture of organic intermediates and drugs, and uranium extraction from the ores was 0.36 Mt. (3.26.79)

Achievements in VIII 5YP
Total installed capacity of around 50 units in the organized sector for dyes and dye stuff in 1996-97 was 49,000 tons and the production of dyes and dye stuff was 30,160 tons. Dyes and dyestuffs sector became capable of meeting most of the domestic demands in 1996-97. (9.5.201)

Status in 2001-02
Production of alkali, organic chemicals, inorganic chemicals, dyestuffs and dye intermediates and total chemicals were 4.342 Mts, 1.166 Mts, 0.374 Mts, 0.0248 Mts and 5.990 Mts respectively.
The Indian chemical industry **ranked 12th by volume in the world production of chemicals.** (10.7.1.207)

The turnover of Chemical and Pharmaceutical industry from 2001-02 to 2005-06 in Rs. Cr. were 810, 981, 1005, 1298 and 976 respectively. (Annexure – 11.v3.7.1.4)

Status in 2006-07

Installed capacities for Alkali, Organic Chemicals, Inorganic Chemicals, Dyestuffs and dye intermediates and Total Chemicals were 7.072 Mts, 1.889 Mts, 0.748 Mts, 0.052 Mts and 9.908 Mts respectively. Production of Alkali, Organic Chemicals, Inorganic Chemicals, Dyestuffs and dye intermediates and Total Chemicals were 5.269 Mts, 1.545 Mts, 0.602 Mts, 0.0325 Mts and 7.534 Mts respectively. (11.7.1.183)

Status in 2011-12

The turnover of India's chemical industry manufacturing organic and inorganic chemicals, petrochemicals, dyes, paints, pesticides, and specialty chemicals in the small and large units (including MNCs) was $108 billion. (12. Annex. 13.2 - 63)

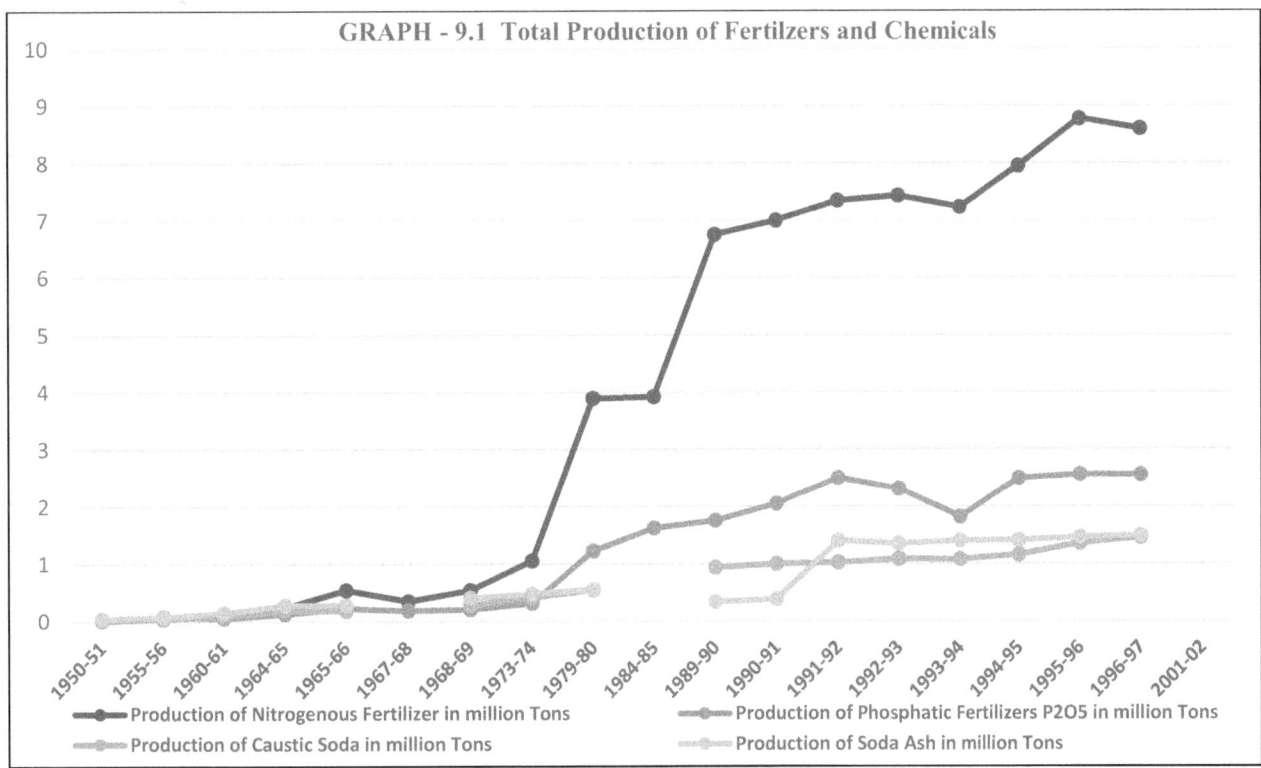

GRAPH - 9.1 Total Production of Fertilzers and Chemicals

Public Sector Enterprises Engaged in Production of Fertilizers

Fertilizers and Chemicals (Travancore) Ltd.

Fertilizers and Chemicals (Travancore) Ltd. - FACT was incorporated in 1943 in private sector promoted by Seshasayee Brothers. In 1947, FACT started production of ammonium sulphate with an installed capacity of 50,000 TPA at Udyogamandal. FACT expanded to produce a wide range of fertilizers for all crops and soil types.

It became an enterprise of Kerala State government in **1960** and Central Government in 1962. FACT diversified into full-fledged engineering services in fertilizer field and petrochemicals.
FACT Cochin Division was set up in the 1970's at Ambalamedu for manufacture of 0.485 Mt of Complex Fertilizer (FACTAMFOS), 0.33 Mt of Sulphuric Acid and 0.1152 Mt of Phosphoric Acid.
The Caprolactam plant in Udyogamandal was commissioned in 1990.

FACT manufactured Ammonia, Sulphuric Acid, Ammonium Phosphate-Sulphate (FACTAMFOS), Ammonium Sulphate, Zincate Ammonium Phosphate, Caprolactam, complex fertilizers, Gypsum, Nitric Acid, Soda Ash and coloured Ammonium Sulphate.

FACT provided engineering and consultancy services and fabricated and erected equipment through 2 Consultancy / Engineering / Fabrication units at Udyogamandal and Kochi.
FACT formed a joint venture company, 'FACT-RCF Building Products Ltd on 2.5.2008 for the manufacture of load bearing panels and other value-added products using phosphor gypsum.
Installed capacity of FACT was 0.6335 Mt for Factamfos 20:20, 0.225 Mt for Ammonium Sulphate and 50000 Tons for Caprolactam in 2008-09.
Installed capacities of FACT in 2019-20 were 0.22546 Mts for Ammonium Sulphate and 0.635141 Mts for FACTAMFOS.
The gross turnover of FACT in 2022-23 was Rs. 6198.14 Cr. and made a net profit of Rs. 612.99 Cr.

Sindri Fertilizers and Chemicals Ltd

Sindri Fertilizers and Chemicals Ltd., established in **1951** with a capacity of 0.35 Mt of ammonium sulphate, commenced production in October 1951. (1.4.26)

The expansion of Sindri Fertilizer Factory to increase its output from 66,000 tons to 117,000 tons of nitrogen could not yield target capacity during II 5YP, due to teething problems.
It was modernized in 1974. All old plants were stopped on 16.03.2002.
After a series of CCEA decisions in August 2011and May 2013 regarding revival of FCIL, the cabinet decided on 21.5.2015 to revive Sindri Unit through 'bidding route' by setting up a 1.3 Mt Urea plant on 500-600 acres of land.

The plant, with a capacity for manufacturing 2200 TPD Ammonia and 3850 TPD neem coated urea, revived by Hindustan Urvarak and Rasayan Ltd, with NTPC, IOCL and CIL contributing 29.67% equity each and FCIL contributing 11%, commenced urea production on 5.11.2022. PM Modi to dedicate revived Sindri fertilizer plant in Jharkhand | India News - Times of India (indiatimes.com)

Pyrites, Phosphates and Chemicals Limited

Pyrites, Phosphates and Chemicals Limited - PPCL was set up on 27.3.**1960**, as a subsidiary of National Industrial Development Corporation Ltd., for exploring and mining of pyrites and rock phosphate deposits.

PPCL identified huge deposits of Iron Pyrites at Amjhore, Bihar and Saladipura, Rajasthan. It mined Rock Phosphate in Mussoorie hills and Doon Valley in Uttar Pradesh (Maldeota and Durmala underground mines, taken over from FCI in 1969) and developed Mussoorie Phos as a natural and eco-friendly phosphatic fertilizer for direct application from this Rock Phosphate,

PPCL was engaged in manufacture of Single Superphosphate (SSP) fertilizer at Amjhore and Saladipura The rock phosphate mined from Mussoorie deposits is powdered and supplied for direct application as a source of phosphatic fertilizer P_2O_5 in acidic soils in the North East and Southern regions. As Sulphur and rock phosphate are imported, the activities of PPCL help in saving of foreign exchange.
Pyrites is used as a substitute of Sulphur in the manufacture of Sulphuric acid and for soil amendment.

Installed capacities of PPCL's production units were – (i) Dehradun – 0.12 Mt for M Phos
(ii) Rajasthan State Mines and Minerals Ltd, Jhamarkotra – 0.15 Mt for Raj Phos
(iii) Rajasthan State Mineral Development Corp., Udaipur – 60000 Tons for Uday Phos
(iv) West Bengal Mineral Development and Trading Corp. Ltd., Purulia – 12000 Tons for Purulia Phos.

Annual productions of phosphatic fertilizers during 1993-94 to 1997-98 were 118150 Tons, 120512 Tons, 120046 Tons, 125006 Tons and 110101 Tons respectively.

PPCL's production of SSP and Sulphuric Acid were 171,171 Tons and 65,005 Tons in 1994-95 and 230,000 Tons and 79,000 Tons in 1996-97 respectively.

Mining operations In Dehradun Unit were suspended from 1.09.1998 as withdrawal of import substitution incentive resulted in mounting losses.

Government of India approved closure of all 3 units situated at Amjhore, Dehradun and Saladipura with effect from 2002-2003.

Hindustan Chemicals and Fertilizer Ltd.

Hindustan Chemicals and Fertilizer Limited - HCFL was set up in 1956 for fertilizer production to ensure food security.

HCFL operated Haldia & Durgapur units in West Bengal, Barauni unit in Bihar and Namrup unit in Dibrugarh, Assam.

HCFL **merged with Fertilizer Corporation of India on 1.01.1961.** Commercial production commenced from 1.01.1969 with a capacity of 55,000 MT of urea and 1,00,000 MT of Ammonium Sulphate.

Fertilizer Corporation of India Ltd.

Fertilizer Corporation of India Ltd. - FCIL was incorporated on 01-01-**1961** by merging Sindri Fertilizer & Chemicals Ltd. with Hindustan Chemicals & Fertilizer Ltd. to manufacture fertilizers, heavy chemicals etc.

Between 1961 and 1977, FCI created 17 fertilizer units. 7 Started operating (Gorakhpur factory was started on 20.04.1968) while the remaining 10 were at various stages of implementation in 1977.

FCI and National Fertilizers Ltd., were split into 5 entities in 1978 to reorganize fertilizer industry
i) **Hindustan Fertilizer Corporation Ltd.** was given the Namrup, Haldia, Barauni and Durgapur units,
ii) **FCI** was assigned Sindri, Gorakhpur, Ramagundam, Talcher and Korba units and Jodhpur Mining Organization.
Iii) Trombay and Thal units were allocated to **Rashtriya Chemicals and Fertilizers Ltd.** and
iv) Bathinda and Panipat units were given to **National Fertilizers Ltd.**
v) The fifth entity was planning and development company, **Project and Development (India) Ltd**.

Talcher and Ramagundam plants achieved commercial production by 1979-80. (6.16.39)
FCIL was manufacturing urea and Ammonium Nitrate in Sindri, Gorakhpur, Ramagundam and Talcher units.
On 10.06.1990, there was a sudden leak of ammonia gas in Gorakhpur factory. It was closed instead of being secured.

Due to continuous losses, FCIL became sick and government decided to close down FCIL. Accordingly, all the 6 plants were closed and there were no production activities during 2006-08.

The loss of the company rose during 2007-08 due to charging of interest of Rs. 1506.06 Cr including penal interest on Government of India loans amounting to Rs. 15028.13 Cr.

NFL expressed its willingness for revival of Ramagundam Unit. Likewise, M/s KRIBHCO showed keen interest in revival of Gorakhpur Unit and M/s RCF showed interest in Talcher Unit.

A Joint Venture company named Hindustan Urvarak & Rasayan Ltd. was incorporated on 15.06.2016 with equity participation of 29.67% each by NTPC, IOCL and CIL and 11% by FCIL and Hindustan

Fertilizer Corporation for setting up gas-based Ammonia urea plant of 1.27 Mt capacity each at Gorakhpur, Sindri and Barauni.

HURL set up Gorakhpur Fertilizer Factory with a capacity of 3,850 TPD of neem coated urea. It was commissioned on 7.12.2021.

Barauni plant started urea production on 18.10.2022.

Ramagundam Fertilizers and Chemicals Ltd was incorporated on 17.02.2015 to set up natural gas-based ammonia urea complex with a capacity of 2200 TPD Ammonia and 3,850 TPD Urea as a joint venture of NFL, Engineers India Ltd. and FCIL.

RFCL started production on 22.03.2021 and produced 8,40,436 Tons of neem coated urea in 2022–23.

A Joint Venture named Talcher Fertilizers Ltd. was incorporated on 13.11.2015 with 31.85% equity each of GAIL, RCF & CIL and 4.45% equity of FCIL for setting up coal-gasification technology-based Ammonia urea plant of 1.27 Mt capacity. The plant is expected to be commissioned in September 2024.

Gujarat State Fertilizer Company

Gujarat State Fertilizer Company - GSFC was incorporated in **1962** and its plants were commissioned in 1967. It manufactured Ammonia through Steam Naphtha Reforming process.

GSFC set up DAP fertilizer complex in Sikka, Jamnagar, Caprolactam plant in 1974 (as Caprolactam was needed for the manufacturing of downstream products like nylon yarn, tire cord, etc.) and India's first Melamine plant.

GSFC expanded into Nylon-6 production.

GSFC started production of Argon gas, which is largely used in welding, in 1981.

Financial constraints - The Ammonia plant had technical snags which stabilized only by the end of 2003. The expansion of DAP plant at Sikka during 1999-2003 caused liquidity problems. The drought during this period further depressed prices and demand for all products. There was also shortage of gas that led to use of costly LSHS and Naphtha. The margins in Melamine and Caprolactam were low in this period due to depressed industrial demand internationally.

Increased availability of natural gas from GAIL, GSPC and Gujarat Gas made GSFC financially strong.

GSFC started production trial of complex Water-Soluble Fertilizer 19-19-19 grade in 2006.

GSFC acquired a strategic stake in Karnalyte Resources Inc., Canada and started a joint venture with Tunisian Indian Fertilizers S.A to ensure consistent supply of Potash and 0.180 Mtpa of Phosphoric Acid respectively.

GSFC formed a subsidiary, namely GSFC Agrotech Ltd for production of liquid bio-fertilizers, plant growth promoters - Sardar Amin granules, tissue culture and seeds.

GSFC diversified into manufacturing MEK-Oxime, Phosphoric Acid, Potassic Acid, etc.

45 TPD Nylon-6-II plant started production in July 2016. The capacity of the two Nylon-6 plants became 23,000 TPA.

A new plant for the production of eco-safe bio-degradable products, 5,000 TPA of Sardar Amin Granules and 40,000 TPA of Sardar Amin Liquid, was commissioned in October 2018.

A new Melamine-III plant of 40,000 TPA, with integrated Molten Urea producing unit of 50,000 TPA was commissioned in March 2019.

Its fertilizer manufacturing capacity in 2023 was 1.7 Mt.

The production in 2022-23 was 1,3895 Mt of fertilizers including 0.5 Mt of Ammonium Sulphate, 0.3 Mt of Ammonium Sulphate Phosphate, 0.194 Mt of DAP, 0.021 Mt of NPK, 0.371 Mt of Urea, 0.0872 Mt of Mt of Caprolactam, 0.0268 Mt of Nylon-6, 0.0478 Mt of Melamine, etc.

Madras Fertilizers Limited

Madras Fertilizers Ltd. - MFL was incorporated on 08.12.**1966** as a joint venture between Government of India and AMOCO India Inc., a subsidiary of Standard Oil Company of USA, with GOI holding 51% equity. MFL commenced commercial production on 1.11.1971. In 1972, National Iranian Oil Company (NIOC) joined in MFL. AMOCO disinvested its shares in MFL in 1985, which were acquired by GOI and NIOC.

MFL is manufacturing Ammonia, Urea, NPK, complex fertilizers, bio-fertilizers and eco-friendly agrochemicals through its **Bio-Fertilizer plants** at Chennai, Jigani (Karnataka) and Krishna (AP).
The company has 2 financial **joint ventures,** one with M/s Fortune Biotech Ltd. for manufacturing Neem based pesticides and another with M/s Indian Potash Ltd.

MFL incurred losses because of high investments made between 1993 and 1998 for revamp of Ammonia and Urea Plants and policy changes in pricing of Urea and complex fertilizers. Ammonia Plant was revamped in 1997, with capabilities to become gas compatible by doing minor modifications in the front end in the future.

Company's market share in complex fertilizer was 23% in 2003-04.

The installed capacities of MFL in 2019-20 were 400 tons for bio-fertilizers, 0.4867 Mts for neem urea and 0.8442 Mts for NPK.
Feed stock for Ammonia was converted from Naphtha to Re-gasified LNG during 2019-20.

MFL produced 519800 Tons of Neem coated urea and 7507 Tons of NPK complex (20-20-0) in 2022-23. The capacity utilization of plants was 106.8% and 2.7% for Urea and NPK Plants respectively.

Indian Farmers Fertilizer Cooperative Ltd

Indian Farmers Fertilizer Cooperative Limited - IFFCO was started in **1967** with 57 member cooperatives, it is today the **biggest co-op in the world** by turnover on GDP per capita (as per World Cooperative Monitor 2021), with around 35,000 member cooperatives reaching over 50 million Indian farmers.

With market share in urea and complex fertilizers (P2O5 terms) being around 19% and 31% respectively, IFFCO is India's largest fertilizer manufacturer. **Revenue in 2022-23 was Rs. 62990 Cr (US $ 7.9 Billion).**

In 1964, the Cooperative League of USA proposed to the Government of India that the American Cooperatives were interested to collaborate with Indian Cooperatives in setting up fertilizer production capacity. IFFCO was registered on 3.11.1967, the U.S. Cooperatives, through Cooperative Fertilizer International, provided financial aid and technical know-how and proposals submitted for Ammonia, Urea and NPK plants at Kalol and Kandla.

Kandla Unit was commissioned in **1974**, expanded in 1981 and 1999, to produce 0.5154 Mt of NPK (10:26:26), 0.7 Mt of NPK (12:32:16), 1.2 Mt of DAP (18:46:0) and 0.9166 Mt of P2O5 and water-soluble fertilizers.
Kalol unit was commissioned in 1975 and expanded in 1997 to produce ammonia (0.363 Mt) and urea (0.5445 Mt).

Phulpur plant was commissioned in 1981 and expanded in 1997 to produce ammonia (0.974 Mt) and urea (1.698 Mt)

IFFCO took over Paradeep plant in 2005, which now produces phosphoric acid (0.875 Mt), Sulphuric acid (2.31 Mt) and 1.92 Mt fertilizers of grades NPK (10:26:26), NPK (12:32:16), NP (20:20:0:13) and DAP (18:46:0).

IFFCO produced 4.88 Mt of urea and 4.68 Mt of NPK / DAP across its 5 plants during 2022-23.

National Fertilizers Ltd.

National Fertilizers Ltd. - NFL was incorporated on 23.8.**1974** for implementation of fertilizer plants at Bathinda and Panipat with an installed capacity of 0.511 Mt of Urea each.

Nangal plants of FCIL were transferred to NFL upon reorganization of NFL-FCI in April 1978.

NFL executed Guna gas-based fertilizer project of 0.726 Mts Urea capacity in 1984.
The Vijaipur plant was commissioned on 1.7.1988.
NFL revamped its 3 plants for change-over of feedstock from furnace oil / LSHS to natural gas / Re-gasified LNG and undertook capacity enhancement of urea units at Vijaipur-I & II plants including a carbon dioxide recovery plant in 2007-08.

National Fertilizers Ltd. had installed capacity of 3.231 Mt for urea in 2008-09.

NFL is manufacturing Urea, solid and liquid Bio-Fertilizers, Bentonite Sulphur, Ammonia, Methanol, Nitric Acid, Ammonium Nitrate, Sodium Nitrite, Sodium Nitrate, Argon, Liquid Oxygen, Liquid Nitrogen, Carbon Di-Oxide etc. in its Nangal, Bhatinda, Panipat. Vijaipur – I and Vijaipur – II units.

NFL makes Complex fertilizers like DAP/ NPK/ SSP, Mycorrhiza, Agro-inputs like certified quality seeds (under Seed Multiplication Program), compost / vermin compost manure, agrochemicals like insecticides / herbicides, Bentonite Sulphur etc.

NFL is offering project commissioning, plant operation and maintenance services to various chemicals and petrochemical industries in India and abroad.

NFL operates mobile Soil Treatment Vans for soil testing and analysis to advice the farming community on balanced use of fertilizers.
NFL is involved in trading of imported fertilizers like DAP, Muriate of Potash, APS, etc.

NFL has 2 joint ventures namely Urvarak Videsh Ltd. (with RCF and KRIBHCO to explore investment opportunities and to render consultancy services for setting up projects in nitrogenous, phosphatic & potassic sectors) and Ramagundam Fertilizers and Chemicals.

Urea installed capacity of NFL was 3.568 Mts and the share in urea production was 16% during 2013-14.

Ramagundam Fertilizers and Chemicals Ltd was incorporated on 17.02.2015 as a joint venture of NFL, Engineers India Ltd. and FCIL. RFCL started production on 22.03.2021 and produced 8,40,436 Tons of neem coated urea in 2022–23.

In 2022-23, NFL achieved highest cumulative urea production of 3.935 Mt, highest sale of all fertilizers of 6.672 Mts and agrochemical of 2481.10 KLIMT. Vijaipur-2 Unit achieved highest Ammonia and Urea production of 0.693845 Mt and 1.186918 Mt respectively.

Gross Turnover of National Fertilizers Ltd. in FY 2022-23 was Rs. 29617 Cr (increase of 87% over turnover in 2021-22).

Southern Petro-Chemical Industries Corporation

Southern Petrochemical Industries Corporation Ltd. - SPIC was incorporated on 18.12.1969 and became a joint venture between the M.A. Chidambaram Group and Tamil Nadu Industrial Development Corporation in **1975**.

SPIC promoted **Tamil Nadu Petroproducts Ltd** in the joint sector along with TIDCO.

In 1997, SPIC set up a wholly owned subsidiary SPIC Fertilizers & Chemicals Ltd., with a capacity of 1,200 TPA of urea and 6.85 TPA of ammonia at Jebel Ali free trade zone in UAE in 1997.
SPIC Fertilizers and Chemicals FZE, subsidiary of SPIC. signed an agreement in 1997 with M. W. Kellogg, U.K. for its fertilizer complex in Dubai.
Government of Tamil Nadu and SPIC entered into an agreement to set up a plant for production of 1.27 Mt of Urea in Tuticorin.

During 2022-23, SPIC produced 0.7592 Mt of neem coated Urea.

Rashtriya Chemicals and Fertilizers Ltd.

Rashtriya Chemicals and Fertilizers Ltd. - RCF was incorporated on 6.3.**1978**, as part of re-organization of FCIL to carry on business of Trombay and Thal units.

RCF is manufacturing nitrogenous, phosphatic and potassic fertilizers and industrial chemicals including Urea, NPK, Bio-fertilizer, Methanol, Methylamines, Ammonium bicarbonate, Ammonium Nitrate, Ammonia, ANP, Nitric Acid, Sulphuric Acid, micronutrients, 100% water soluble fertilizers, etc. The Ujjwala urea and Suphala complex fertilizer brands of fertilizers are in great demand.

Thal III expansion of RCF for capacity 1.155 M could not be taken up during X 5YP due to lack of availability of natural gas / LNG.

The **market share of RCF** was about **12% for Urea** and **75% for complex fertilizer** in 2007-08. The **overall market share** was about **9% of the total fertilizer**.
The installed capacities of Thal unit were 1.707 Mt for Urea and 0.99 Mt for Ammonia and that of Trombay unit were 49,000 Tons for Methanol, 0.3 Mt for Suphala and 0.297 Mt for Ammonia in 2008-09.

RCF took up Thal revamp project to increase Urea capacity by approximately 0.3 Mt.

RCF incorporated a joint venture company Talcher Fertilizers Ltd. with GAIL, CIL and FCIL for production of 1.27 Mt of Ammonia urea.
RCF formed another joint venture company FACT-RCF Building Products Ltd with FACT for manufacturing Gypsum based glass fibre reinforced (GFRG) wall panel with an installed capacity of 1.4 million square meters. Product range included wall plaster and wall putty also.
The company has one **subsidiary** namely Rajasthan Rashtriya Chemicals and Fertilizers Ltd.

The installed capacities of RCF in 2019-20 were 22963 tons for Ammonium bi-carbonate, 32931 tons for concentrated nitric acid, 98561 tons for Sulphuric acid, 0.4198 Mt for Suphala, 2.001931 Mts for urea Thal and 0.3292 Mts for urea Trombay.

RCF was fourth largest producer of fertilizers in India after IFFCO, NFL and KRIBHCO in 2020-21.

RCF was setting up AN Melt plant of 425 TPD and liquid Nano Urea plant of 75 KL per day at RCF Trombay unit during 2022-23.

The gross turnover of RCF in 2022-23 was Rs. 21451.54 Cr and productions were 1.88 Mt of Urea at Thal unit, 0.316 Mt of Urea & 0.643 Mt of Suphala 15:15:15 at Trombay unit.

Hindustan Fertilizer Corporation Ltd.

Hindustan Fertilizer Corporation Ltd. - HFCL was incorporated on 14.03.1978 as part of re-organization of FCIL and NFL to carry on business of Namrup, Haldia, Barauni and Durgapur units

Namrup-II unit was commissioned on 1.10.1976 with an annual capacity of 0.33 Mt of urea.
Urea-I plant was closed in August, 1986.
Namrup-III plant, which was the first to use totally indigenous Urea process, developed by Project Development India Ltd, started production in 1.10.1987 with capacity of 0.385 Mt urea.
Ammonium Sulphate production was discontinued since June, 1992 as the condition of the plant had deteriorated and the civil structure had become unsafe.

During HFCL's operation till 1993-94, the highest capacity utilization was 57.53% in 1987-88 due to inherent design deficiencies, unproven equipment selection and interruptions in gas (feed stock) and power supply.
Due to under performance of all the plants, HFCL made huge losses, was declared sick and referred to BIFR. Subsequently, all the units of HFCL except Namrup were closed down.
The Sulphuric Acid Plant of capacity 82000 tons was also closed down in September, 2000.
Ammonia Plant of Namrup-I was also not in operation since 2002 and it was disposed-off.

The Namrup fertilizer complex was bifurcated from HFCL and renamed as Brahmaputra Valley Fertilizer Corporation Ltd on 5.04.2002.

Besides the units at Durgapur, Haldia and Barauni (Begusarai), HFCL also had one Fertilizer Promotion & Agriculture Research Division.

As the operations of all 3 units became techno-economically non-viable, Government decided to close HFCL in 2002.

Profit making fertilizer PSU's such as NFL, RCF, KRIBHCO and Feedstock PSU like GAIL and NFL showed interest for revival of Barauni and Durgapur units.

Hindustan Urvarak & Rasayan Ltd., incorporated with equity participation of NTPC, IOCL, CIL, FCIL and HFCL set up gas-based Ammonia urea plant of 1.27 Mt capacity each at Barauni. This plant started urea production on 18.10.2022.

HFCL, at present has 2 closed plants at Durgapur and Haldia. Hindustan Fertilizer Corporation Limited (HFCL) | Department of Fertilizers. Hindustan Fertilizer Corp. Ltd was under closure / liquidation in 2022-23.

Krishak Bharati Cooperative Limited

Krishak Bharati Cooperative Limited - KRIBHCO is a Central government cooperative under the ownership of Ministry of Cooperation, Government of India.

KRIBHCO was incorporated on 17.04.**1980** as a national level Multi State Cooperative Society by Government of India to implement first gas based (natural gas from Bombay High / South Bassein) Fertilizer Complex consisting of 2 x 1350 TPD Ammonia plants and 4 x 1100 TPD Urea plants each at Hazira. This plant was commissioned in 1985 in record time.

Bio-Fertilizer Plant at Hazira was commissioned for production of Semi Solid Bio-Fertilizer in 1995.

Capacities of ammonia & urea plants were reassessed to 2x1520 TPD Ammonia and 4x 1310 TPD Urea in 2000.

KRIBHCO established a gas-based (Natural Gas supplied through the Hazira-Vijaipur-Jagdishpur pipeline as feedstock) fertilizer complex Kribhco Shyam Fertilizer Ltd at Shahjahanpur, U.P. in 2005 with 1520 TPD Ammonia Plant and 2620 TPD Urea Plant. Later Kribhco Shyam Fertilizer Ltd. became Kribhco Fertilizer Ltd.

After revamp in 2013, the rated capacity of Hazira Complex was enhanced to 2x3325 TPD Urea and 2 x 1890 TPD Ammonia to become the largest single location urea plant in India.

KRIBHCO has three units to manufacture bio-fertilizers at Hazira, Varanasi and Lanjha (Maharashtra). KRIBHCO markets Liquid Bio Fertilizers and high yielding hybrid seeds of various crops like Bt. Cotton.

KRIBHCO's joint venture project OMIFCO with Oman Oil Company came on stream in Sultanate of Oman in 2005.

KRIBHCO diversified into power sector by investing in Gujarat State Energy Generation.

KRIBHCO incorporated Kribhco Infrastructure Ltd. to undertake logistics business.

KRIBHCO produced 1.324 Mt of Ammonia and 2.221 Mt of Urea in 2022-23 with a capacity utilization of 106.16% for Ammonia and 101.21 % for Urea. Government of India gave Rs. 16925.45 Cr as concession / remuneration in 2022-23.

Paradeep Phosphates Ltd.

Paradeep Phosphates Ltd - PPL was incorporated in **1981** as a joint venture between the Govt of India and the Republic of Nauru to set up phosphatic fertilizers manufacturing unit at Paradeep, Orissa.

In August 1986, PPL commissioned Di-Ammonium Phosphate (DAP) plant with an annual capacity of 0.72 Mts along with off-site facilities, 3.4 km closed conveyor from port to plant site, railway siding raw material storage yards and a 3.1 km long pipe rake.

0.66 Mt Sulphuric acid plant and 0.225 Mt Phosphoric Acid plant were commissioned in June 1992. PPL also commissioned two 16 MW captive power plants designed to run on excess steam generated by the Sulphuric Acid Plant.

With the divestment of RN's stake, PPL became a public sector enterprise in 1993.

Production in 1993-94 to 1997-98 were 118150 MT, 120512 MT, 120046 MT, 125006 MT and 110101 MT respectively.

Government divested 74% stake in PPL in favor of Zuari Maroc Phosphates Pvt Ltd in February 2002.

During the year 2003-04, the same plant executed an export order to Nepal of around 5000 MT of DAP. PPL bagged an award from Fertilizer Association of India during 2003-04 for their turnaround performance.

In March 2007, ZMPPL. was holding 80.45% stake in PPL and the Government of India remaining 19.55%.

Government exited PPL on 27.05.2022.

No capacity addition or expansion was done in Paradeep plant after privatization. Paradeep and Goa plants of Zuari have an NPK / DAP production capacity of 1.8 Mt and 0.8 Mt respectively. The installed capacity of Goa plant for total fertilizers is 1.2 Mt. The installed capacity for Phosphoric acid is 0.3 Mt. The production in 2022-23 was 2.032 Mt. History of Paradeep Phosphate Limited (paradeepphosphates.com)

ppl-ar-2022-23-cover-to-cover-sgaads-v7-interactive-compressed.pdf (paradeepphosphates.com)

Brahmaputra Valley Fertilizer Corp. Ltd.

Brahmaputra Valley Fertilizer Corp. Ltd. - BVFCL was incorporated on 5.4.**2002** to de-merge the Namrup I, II & III plants from Hindustan Fertilizer Corp. Ltd.

BVFCL largely met the Urea requirement of North East India and some parts of north Bengal & eastern Bihar.

Namrup-II and Namrup-III Units were revamped. But even after revamp, the energy consumption remained very high. Due to non-availability of natural Gas beyond the contracted quantity, Namrup-II plants were being run at 50% load with one stream of Urea Plant during the post revamp period w.e.f. Nov-2005. Performance of Namrup-III plants hampered due to repeated failure of Urea Reactor liner leakage.

BVFCL had installed capacity for urea of 0.24 Mt in Namrup-II plant and 0.27 Mt in Namrup-III plant in 2008-09.

BVFCL proposed setting up Namrup-IV brown field ammonia urea plant of capacity 0.8646 Mt consuming available 1.72 MMSCMD of Natural Gas in the XII 5YP. The proposed capacity of Namrup-IV project was to be enhanced to 1.27 Mt to have a standard size plant, on receipt of confirmation for additional 0.627 MMSCMD of Natural Gas for the proposed project.

The installed capacity of BVFCL in 2019-20 for neem coated urea was 0.509944 Mt.

BVFCL was producing Neem Coated Urea, Liquid Bio Fertilizer and Vermi Compost. It is also doing trading of other fertilizers like SSP, MoP, DAP, Rock Phosphate, City Compost etc.

A 3000 Tons Water Soluble NPK production facility, established by utilizing in-house funding only, is expected to commence production shortly.

The production in 2021-22 were 0.17028 Mt of urea, 53.805 Tons Bio-Fertilizers and 107.169 Tons of Vermi Compost. Brahmaputra Valley Fertilizer Corporation Limited (BVFCL) | Department of Fertilizers

The gross turnover of BVFCL in 2022-23 was Rs. 1146.5 Cr.

Talcher Fertilizers Limited

Talcher Fertilizers Ltd., a joint venture of GAIL (India) Ltd., Rashtriya Chemicals and Fertilizers Ltd., Coal India Ltd. and Fertilizer Corp. of India Ltd was formed in **2015** for setting up a Coal Gasification based fertilizer plant of capacity 1.27 Mt of urea at the site of the closed FCIL plant unit at Talcher, Angul district, Odisha. The plant is scheduled to be commissioned by September 2024.

Public Sector Enterprises Engaged in Production of Insecticides

Hindustan Insecticides Ltd.

Hindustan Insecticides Ltd. - HIL was incorporated in **1954** to manufacture DDT and its formulation to meet the demand of National Malaria Eradication (National Vector Borne Disease Control) Program, and to supply insecticides and pesticides at reasonable prices for public health and agricultural purposes. This plant came as a gift from WHO and went into production in April, 1955.

In 1957, HIL set up second factory at Udyogamandal for the manufacture of DDT to fight dreaded diseases like Malaria, Dengue, Kala Azar, Japanese Encephalitis, etc.

HIL set up a plant for the manufacture of Malathion, an insecticide used in public health, at Rasayani, Maharashtra in 1977.

Another DDT plant was set up at Rasayani in 1983.

HIL was manufacturing Agro-pesticides formulations like Endosulfan, Dicofol, Malathion, Butachlor, DDVP etc. and 44 Agro-formulations. Its product range comprised of 10 products.

HIL started incurring losses from 1997- 98. (10.7.1.199)

HIL had a **subsidiary company** namely Southern Pesticides Corp. Ltd., which was closed w.e.f. 2.4.2002.

HIL obtained export orders of DDT 75% from Govt. of Mozambique and Govt. of Namibia against global competition. HIL also exported Malathion Technical, Endosulfan Technical and formulation to various countries in Europe, Africa and Latin America.

HIL was the largest producer of DDT in the world and the only other producer was in China.

HIL set up a manufacturing facility for Buprofezin, a new generation insecticide, used for the control of brown plant hopper on paddy crop, potatoes, citrus, cotton and vegetables. The total demand of Buprofezin technical was 750 Tons.

HIL was in process of doubling the capacity for Mancozeb, a fungicide.

HIL, in line with the Govt. initiative of organic farming, was planning to manufacture eco-friendly pesticides like Neem formulation. HIL set up a manufacturing unit of Long-Lasting Insecticides Net with the support of United National Industrial Development Organization in December 2020.

The revenue from operations of HIL in 2021-22 was Rs. 353.98 Cr. Hindustan Insecticides Limited | Department of Chemicals and Petrochemicals

Public Sector Enterprises Engaged in Production of Chemicals

Hindustan Organic Chemicals Limited

Hindustan Organic Chemicals Limited - HOCL was incorporated on 12.12.**1960** for setting up chemical manufacturing units for production of organic chemicals and chemical intermediaries.

HOCL was manufacturing basic organic chemicals, which are important intermediates in the manufacture of drugs and pharmaceuticals, dyes, dye intermediates, plastics, rubber chemicals, pesticides, Resins, Paints, Textile Auxiliaries & Explosives and laminates in 1979-80. (6.16.56)
Its products were Phenol, Acetone, Nitrobenzene, Aniline, Nitrotoluenes, Chlorobenzenes & Nitro chlorobenzenes.

The company took up 2 major projects of diversification, namely, 40,000 TPA phenol plant along with 24,000 TPA acetone project at Cochin and a polytetrafluorethylene project and a caustic soda / chlorine project at Medak. Both these projects were expected to be completed in 1985-86. (7.7.139)
The production of HOCL during 1984-85 was about 0.1 Mt.
HOCL was engaged in the production of 20 products including Phenol, Acetone, Formaldehyde, Nitrobenzene, Aniline, Conc. Nitric Acid. N2O4, etc. in its Rasayani and Cochin units.

HOCL has one subsidiary, namely, Hindustan Fluorocarbons Ltd. and one joint venture namely HOC - Chematur Ltd.

Government attempted disinvestment of HOCL in 2001-02. (10.7.1.213)

HOCL was having **47% market share for Phenol and 42% share in Acetone in 2007-08.**

As per the restructuring plan approved by the Cabinet Committee on Economic Affairs, Rasayani unit was closed down in 2017 as the operations of the unit was found unviable.

The installed capacity was 24640 tons for Acetone, 10454 tons for H2O2 and 39979 tons for Phenol in 2022-23 and the actual productions were 23306 tons for Acetone, 10323 tons for H2O2 and 37350 tons for Phenol. HOCL 62nd Annual Report 2022-23 bilingual.pdf (hoclindia.com)

The gross turnover of HOCL in 2022-23 was Rs. 631.43 Cr.

Gujarat Aromatics Ltd.

Gujarat Aromatics Ltd. - Gujarat Aromatics Ltd was incorporated on 11.12.**1975** at Ahmedabad. It was originally promoted by Gujarat Industrial Investment Corporation Ltd.

The company manufactured synthetic cresol and its by-products viz., Sodium Sulphite, sodium sulphate, gypsum and soda ash, dyestuff, chemicals, drugs and pharmaceuticals etc.

The company became Atul Products Ltd. in 1988.

It is manufacturing para cresol, para Anisic aldehyde and para Anisic alcohol for the first time in India. With a portfolio of 29 products, Aromatics serves about 400 customers in 37 countries. The products are majorly used by customers belonging to Chemical Additive, Flavor and Fragrance, Personal Care, Pharmaceutical and Paper industries. About Aromatics | Atul

Hindustan Fluorocarbons Ltd.

Hindustan Fluorocarbons Ltd. - HFCL was incorporated on 14.7.**1983** as a joint venture of Hindustan Organic Chemicals Ltd. and Andhra Pradesh Industrial Development Corp. to manufacture various grades of Poly-tetra Fluoroethylene (PTFE) with know-how from ATOCHEM, France as import substitute. The company commenced its business in 1987.

HFCL is engaged in the production / marketing of PTFE, TFE and (Chloro Fluoro Methane Gas) CFM-22 in Medak unit. PTFE is a versatile engineering plastic and CFM-22 (R-22) is mainly used as refrigerant gas.
HFCL developed specialty fluorochemical TFE-ETHER and commercialized it in 2010-11.
Efforts were taken to increase the capacity of the monomer plant by de-bottlenecking and improving the conversion factors.

The installed capacity for Chloro-Di-Fluoro Methane was 1262 tons in 2019-20.

Cabinet Committee on Economic Affairs decided to close HFL on 29.01.2020. HFL is under process of closure as on 31.03.2023.

Balmer Lawrie & Co. Ltd.

Balmer Lawrie & Co. Ltd. - BL which was incorporated in 1867, as a partnership firm, became a Private Ltd. Co. in 1924, converted to Public Ltd. Co. in 1936 and thereafter became a subsidiary of IBP Co. Ltd. in 1972. However, in view of arrangement made between IBP and Balmer Lawrie Investment Ltd (BLIL), BL became a subsidiary of BLIL on 15.10.**2001**.

The company is engaged in manufacturing of barrels and drums, greases and lubricants and leather chemicals and providing services in the areas of travel and tours, logistics services, logistics infrastructure services, engineering & technology services etc. through its **54 plants** spread all over India.

It has a **subsidiary** Visakhapatnam Port Logistics Park Ltd. and two overseas subsidiaries namely Balmer Lawrie (UK) Ltd. and Balmer Lawrie (Tea) Ltd.

The company has 6 financial **joint venture companies** (in the field of industrial purchasing, container and suction, blending and packaging of special tea) including Balmer Lawrie (UAE) LLC, Balmer Lawrie Van Leer Ltd, Transafe Services Ltd., Balmer Lawrie Hind Terminals Ltd. and Avi-Oil India Pvt Ltd. Balmer Lawrie UK has a joint venture in Indonesia viz. PT Balmer Lawrie Indonesia.

The company was having **33% market share in greases** and approximately **50% share of Barrels & Drums market in 2004-05.**

Installed Capacity of Balmer Lawrie & Co. Ltd. was 5.5 million Nos of Barrels & Drums, 0.1 Mt of Greases & Lubricants, 4260 Tons of Leather Chemicals in 2019-20 (up from 3.909 million Nos of Barrels & Drums, 73200 Tons of Greases & Lubricants, 3350 Tons of Leather Chemicals in 2008-09).

The gross turnover of BL in 2022-23 was Rs. 2309.98 Cr.

Projects and Development (India) Ltd.

Projects and Development India Ltd – PDIL was incorporated on 07.03.1978 for undertaking contract, construction and technical consultancy services for chemical and fertilizer industries. It was actively involved in the setting up gas-based fertilizer plants as prime consultant.

PDIL undertook Commissioning of Hindustan Urvarak & Rasayan Limited plants, revival of closed Ammonia-Urea Plants and implementation of energy saving projects in Green Ammonia besides diversification in Oil & Gas Sectors.

The gross turnover of PDIL in 2022-23 was Rs. 98.6 Cr.

Contribution to Manufacturing GDP

Chemicals products Industry contributed 12.2% to Manufacturing GDP in 2009-10.

Graph – 9.2 Production of Fertilizers in Public Sector Units (Not including KRIBHCO, SPIC and IFFCO)

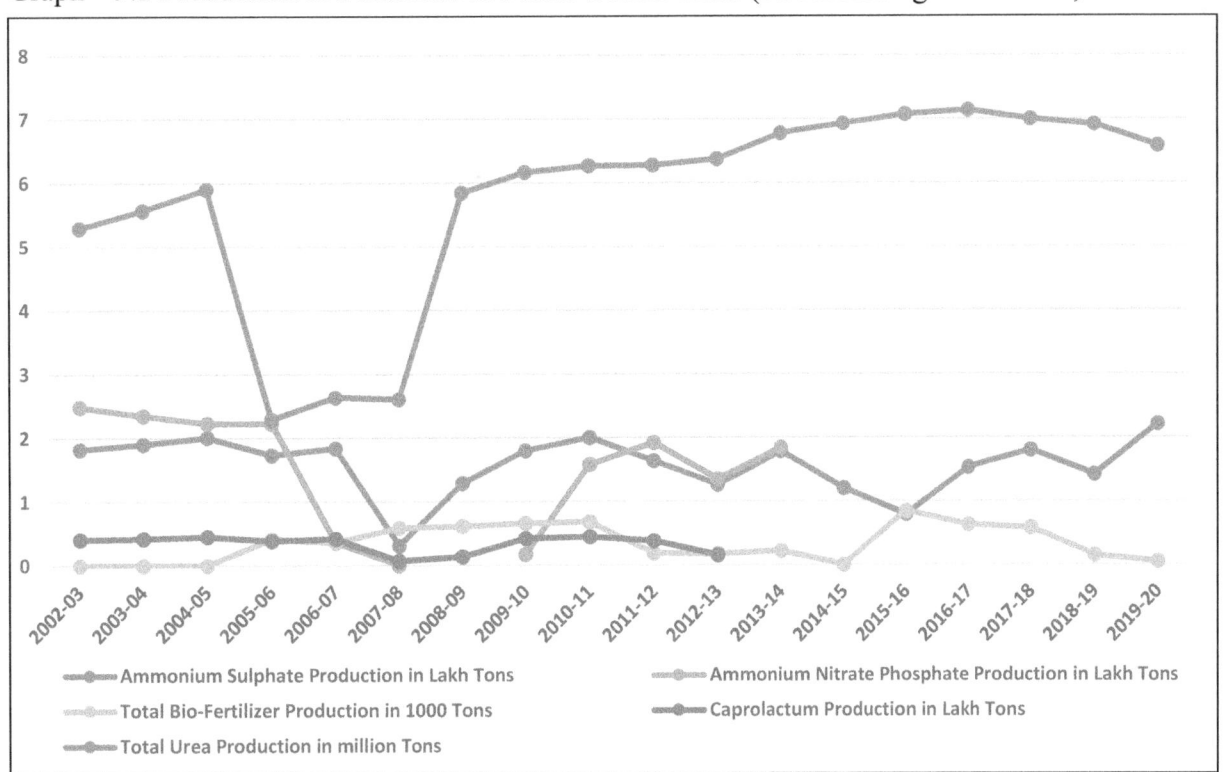

Table – 9.1 CPSEs Share in Domestic Fertilizer Production

Total domestic production of Nitrogenous Fertilizers in Lakh Metric Tons							Production by CPSEs in Lakh metric tons / Share of CPSEs to Total Domestic Production (%)						
1968-69	1998-99	2004-05	2005-06	2008-09	2009-10	2010-11	1968-69	1998-99	2004-05	2005-06	2008-09	2009-10	2010-11
5.63	100.86	113.39	113.54	109	119	121.57	4.01	31.76	30.54	29.58	28.87	31.18	31.49
							71.23	31.49	26.93	26.05	26.4	26.2	26.05
Phosphatic Fertilizer in Lakh Metric Tons													
2.13	29.76	40.67	42.21	38.07	43.21	43.23	0.53	7.26	2.66	2.95	1.61	2.27	2.44
							24.88	24.4	6.54	6.99	4.2	5.25	5.37

Item	Units	Domestic Production		Total CPSE Production		Share of CPSEs %	
		1997-98	2007-08	1997-98	2007-08	1997-98	2007-08
Nitrogenous Fert.	Lakh MT	100.86	109.00	31.76	28.87	31.49	26.4
Phosphatic Fert.	Lakh MT	29.76	38.07	7.26	1.61	24.4	4.2

Summary

The installed capacities of public sector units for production of Ammonia 6.0329 Mts ((0.3465 (MFL) + 1.452 (RCF) + 1.749 (KRIBCO) + 2.4854 (IFFCO)), Ammonium Sulphate 0.67546 Mts ((0.22546 (FACT) + 0.1 (HFCL) + 0.35 (Sindri)), Bio-Fertilizer 1060 MT ((400 (MFL) + 660 (NFL)), Caprolactam 0.05 Mts (FACT), Complex Fertilizer 1.0535 Mts ((0.6335 (FACT) + 0.42 (RCF)), Di-Ammonium Phosphate 1.92 Mts (IFFCO), Urea 17.326594 Mts ((0.055 (HFCL) + 0.48675 (MFL) + 1.27 (SPIC) + 0.715 (HFC) + 3.568 (NFL) + 2.660544 (RCF) + 1.27 (BVFCL) + 4.2423 (IFFCO)) + 3.059 (KRIBHCO)), Sulphuric Acid 2.722 Mts ((0.33 (FACT) + 0.082 (HFC) + 2.31 (PPL)), Phosphoric Acid 0.9902 Mts ((0.1152 (FACT) + 0.875 (PPL) and P_2O_5 0.9166 Mts (IFFCO).

*The above installed capacities of urea, Di-Ammonium Phosphate, complex fertilizer and Bio-Fertilizer were 67.1%, 26.3%, 20.1% and 13,3% of total installed capacities respectively.

Private Sector Players –

Fertilizer companies - East India Distilleries Parry India Ltd. – 1842, T. Stanes & Co – 1861, Union Carbide India Ltd. – 1934, Coromandel International Ltd / Coromandel Fertilizers Ltd – 1961, Grasim Industries – 1972, Deepak Fertilizers and Petrochemicals Ltd – 1979, Indo-Gulf Fertilizer – 1985, Chambal Fertilizers Ltd.- 1985, Nagarjuna Fertilizers and Chemicals Ltd - 1985

Adhesives - Pidilite Industries Ltd.- 1959,

Carbon products - Birla Carbon – 1988, Indian Rayon's Hi-Tech Carbon plant – 2004,

Chemicals – Union Carbide India Ltd. - 1934, Tata Chemicals – 1938, Kanoria Chemicals & Industries – 1960, Jayshree Chemicals Ltd – 1962, Indo Gulf Company – 1964, Zuari Agro Chemicals Ltd. – 1967, Gujarat Alkalies & Chemicals Ltd -1973, Punjab Alkalies & Chemicals – 1975, Bihar Caustic and Chemicals Ltd / Aditya Birla Chemicals Ltd – 1976, Gujarat Heavy Chemicals Ltd. – 1983, Chemfab Alkalies Ltd – 1985, Digvijay Chemicals Ltd – 1987, Vishnu Chemicals Ltd – 1989, Solaris Chemtech Industries – 2001,

Explosives - Indo Gulf Industries – 1981,

Paints - Nerolac Paints – 1920, Jenson Nicholson Paints - 1922, Asian Paints - 1942, Addisons Pants & Chemicals Ltd – 1948, Tata Pigments Ltd. – 1983.

10: GROWTH IN POWER GENERATION, TRANSMISSION, DISTRIBUTION AND MANUFACTURING OF POWER GENERATION EQUIPMENT

Essentiality of Power Generation

Modern life depends so largely on the use of electricity that the quantity of electricity used per capita in a country is an index of its material development and of the standard of living attained in it.

Percentage share in energy consumption in 1994-95 were: Industry – 42.1%, Transport – 20.8%, House hold – 12.3%, Agriculture – 9.3%, Feedstock – 10.3%. (9.6.20)

Targeted Growth in Power Plant Installation, Power Generation and Distribution

Electricity required for residential areas, offices, public places, industries, railways, agriculture etc. were forecasted by the government for the last financial year of each 5-year plan and the target for (hydel, thermal, nuclear, renewable resources) power generation capacity, peak demand, fuel requirement for forecasted power generation, manufacturing of power generation equipment like boilers, turbines, generators, etc., power transmission and distribution systems like transformers, transmission lines, ACSR conductors, pump sets to be energized, villages to be electrified, etc. for the various 5-year plans were set.

Hydro-Power Potential of the Country

The total hydro-power potential of India was assessed to be 40000 MW in 1950-51 (1.26.19), 35000 MW in 1955-56 (2.17.29), 41000 MW in 1960-61 (3.24.40), 75400 MW at 60% load factor in 1976 (6.15.8), 89,830 MW at 60% load factor in 1984-85 (7.6.10) and 149 GW (including the plants of less than 25 MW capacity) in 2011-12. (12.14.53)

Only 14.29% of the potential water resources available had been harnessed for electricity in 1968-69. (4.12.1)

Hydro-Electric Potential assessment

In 1992, About 40 % of the total hydel electric potential of 84000 MW (at 60% load factor) lied in North-Eastern region. (8.2.7.4)

Wind energy potential was assessed as 20,000 MW and potential of mini / micro hydel resources as 5000 MW.

63 Sites for pumped storage schemes were identified with a potential of 94,000 MW in 1996-97.

Potential of the North-East region was assessed as 50,000 MW in 2011-12. (12.14.66)

Nuclear Power Potential of the Country

Assessment in 1979-80

The assured uranium resources were placed at 34000 tons of Ug in 1979-80. Of which about 15000 tons were considered economically exploitable. The established uranium resources were considered capable of supporting natural uranium reactors of about 8000 MW of installed capacity. (6.15.9)

Assessment in 1984-85

The uranium resources in India were estimated to be 70,000 tons, the thermal reactor equivalent of about 1,900 million tons of coal. These resources alone were expected to be equivalent to 120 billion tons of coal if used in breeder reactors. (7.6.14)

Thorium oxide deposits assessed in **1991-92** were 363,000 tons. Thorium resources, when used through breeder reactors, were expected to produce 900,000 billion kwh of electricity. (8.v2.8.9.1)

Estimates in 1997

The potential deposits were placed at 850 billion cubic meters of coal bed methane, 6156 trillion cubic meters of gas hydrates and 600 million tons of oil shale.

Renewable Power Potential of the Country

In the early 80s, India was estimated to have renewable energy potential of about 85 GW from commercially exploitable sources, viz. (i) Wind: 50 GW (at 50 m mast height) (ii) Small Hydro:15 GW (iii) Bio-energy: 20 GW and (iv) solar radiation sufficient to generate 50 MW/sq. km using solar photovoltaic and solar thermal energy.

Wind power potential

Wind energy potential, assessed in 1991-92 and 2006-07 were 10,000 MW and 45195 MW respectively. (8.v2.8.10.1) (11.10.219)

Centre for Wind Energy Technology estimated wind energy potential at 80m height (with 2% land availability) as 100 GW. Some studies estimated even higher potential ranges up to 300 GW. (12.14.187)

Biomass potential

As per study sponsored by Ministry of New and Renewable Energy, the availability of biomass in India was estimated at about 750 Mt per year.

Ample potential was expected for setting up biogas plants considering the livestock population of 512.06 million, which included about 299.98 million total population of bovines (comprising of cattle, buffalo, Mithun and yak).

Bagasse potential

About 14 GW power could be generated through bagasse-based cogeneration in the country's 550 sugar mills, if these sugar mills were to adopt technically and economically optimal levels of cogeneration for extracting power from the bagasse produced by them.

Growth in Power Generation in India

Four multi-purpose projects, Damodar Valley, Bhakra-Nangal, Tungabhadra and Hirakud began before I 5YP.

Power Generation in 1950-51

The installed electricity generating capacity in 1950-51 stood at 2300 MW with 630 MW in State-owned public utilities, 1080 MW in private companies-owned public utilities, and 590 MW in industrial establishments having their own power stations and total electricity generated was 5100 million kWh. (1.26.20) (9.6.13)

The average per capita consumption of electricity was only 14 kWh per year in 1950-51 (as compared with 2207 kWh in the United States of America) (1.26.30).

Power Generation by Private Sector in 1950-51

Ahmedabad Electric Co., Calcutta Electric Supply Corporation and Tata's Power Installations were major power generating companies in 1950-51. (1.26.48)

Power Plants Started during 1950-55

Kosi (Stage I) – 40 MW, Koyna (Stage I) – 240 MW, Chambal (Stage I) – 80 MW, Rihand – 240 MW and Krishna - (Capacity not confirmed). (1.26.45)
Bhakra Nangal - 96 MW, Damodar Valley – 194 MW and Hirakud Dam – 48 MW. (1.26.49)

The Machkund hydro-electric station was being developed by Madras jointly with Orissa.
Bokaro thermal station was being constructed by Bihar and Bengal through Damodar Valley Corporation. (1.26.54)
Tungabhadra project.
Kakrapar project on the Tapti. (1.26.8)

Power schemes completed during 1950-55:
Nangal – 48 MW, Bokaro – 150 MW, Chola (Kalyan) – 54 MW, Khaperkheda – 30 MW, Moyar (Madras) – 36 MW, Madras City Plant Extensions – 30 MW, Machkund (Andhra and Orissa) – 34 MW, Pathri (Uttar Pradesh) – 13.6 MW, Sarda (Uttar Pradesh) – 27.6 MW, Sengulam (Travancore) – 48 MW, Joe (Mysore) – 72 MW. (2.17.33)

Considerable progress was made in Bhakra, Hirakud, Koyna, Chambal, and Rihand power stations. (2.17.33)

Power Generation in 1955-56
The installed electricity generating capacity in March, 1956 increased to 3420 MW with 1400 MW in State-owned public utilities, 1300 MW in private companies-owned public utilities and 700 MW in industrial establishments having their own power stations and total electricity generated was 12 billion kWh. (2.17.40)
Additions by the public and private sectors during I 5YP were 800 MW and 200 MW respectively. (2.17.32)

Achievements in II 5YP
Neyveli Lignite Corporation was inaugurated in 1956.
Chambal, Rihand, Koyna and Nagarjuna Sagar river valley projects started during this period.
Hydro Power generation in 1960-61 was 7.84 billion kWh. (9.6.13)

Achievements in IV 5YP - The ninth thermal unit of 100 MW at Neyveli went into operation in 1969-70 and the station had a total capacity of 600 MW.
Hydro-electric Power stations generated 25.25 billion kWh in 1970-71. (9.6.13)

Achievements in V 5YP
National Thermal Power Corporation Ltd. was founded on 7.11.1975 to undertake construction, operation and maintenance of thermal and hydro-electric projects in the Central Sector. First, it started work on NTPC Singrauli (Uttar Pradesh) thermal power project in 1976.

National Hydroelectric Power Corporation was incorporated in 1975 to plan, promote and develop hydroelectric power projects.
North Eastern Electric Power Corporation Ltd. was formed on 2.04.1976 to plan, design, construct, operate and maintain power stations in the North Eastern Region.
The hydro-electric potential developed till the end of 1978 was 39.4 billion kWh or about 10% of the total available potential. (6.15.8)

Generation Schemes, which were in Operation in 1979-80

Northern Region – 5172 Mw (major - Singrauli Super Thermal Station Phase I – 630 MW, Anpara Thermal Station (UP)- 630 MW, Tanda Thermal Station (UP) – 440 MW, Singrauli Super Thermal Station

Phase II – 420 MW, Obra Thermal Station Extension II and III (UP) – 400 MW, Beas H.E. Scheme extension Unit I (Debar) (Punjab, Haryana, Rajasthan) – 330 MW, etc. - total 26 Power plants)

Western Region – 5937 MW (major - Wanakbori Thermal Station (Gujarat) – 630 MW, Korba Super Thermal Station – 630 MW, Trombay Thermal Station – 500 MW, Ukai Left Bank Canal H.E. Power House, Korba West Thermal Station – 420 MW, Korba West Thermal Station Extension – 420 MW, Satpura Thermal Station Extension II – 420 MW, Koradi Thermal Station Stage III – 420 MW, Chandrapur Thermal Station – 420 MW, etc. – total 23 Power plants)

Southern Region – 4565 MW (Major - Kalinadi H.E. Scheme (Karnataka) – 775 MW, Ramagundam Super Thermal Station – 630 MW, Madras Atomic Power Project – 470 MW, Srisailam H.E. Project – 440 MW, Raichur Thermal Station – 420 MW, Neyveli Thermal Station – 420 MW, Kadamparai Pumped Storage Schemes (Tamil Nadu) – 400 MW, etc. - Total 16 Power plants)

Eastern Region – 3323 MW (Major - Kolaghat Thermal Station (West Bengal) – 630 MW, etc. - total 18 Power plants)

North Eastern Region – 669 MW (total 11 Power plants)

Total – 19666 MW (Total 94 Power plants)

Achievements in VI 5YP –
Hydro Power generation in 1980-81 was – 46.54 billion kWh. (9.6.13)
The production of commercial energy in 1984-85 was almost entirely in the public sector and investments in this sector absorbed about 30 % of VII plan outlays. (7.1.7)

RM&LE Programs
Phase-I of the Renovation, Modernization & Life Extension program, taken up in September 1984, covered 163 thermal units with a total capacity of 13,570 MW. (10.8.2.30)
Phase-II of the RM&LE program was taken up in 1990-91 for 198 thermal units with a total capacity of 20,870 MW. (10.8.2.31)

Achievements in VII 5YP –
Hydro power generation in 1990-91 was 71.66 billion kWh.

Achievements in VIII 5YP –
The Hydro Power generation in 1996-97 was 68.63 billion kWh.
In 1996-97, the peak deficit was 18.0 % and energy deficit was 11.5 %. (9.6.56)

Achievements in IX 5YP –
Renovation, Modernization & Uprating works were completed on 18 hydro schemes with an aggregate installed capacity of 4,860 MW during the IX plan. (10.8.2.35).
Installed power generation capacity (on 31.03.2002) included central govt generation of 31605.51 MW + state govts generation of 62245.47 MW = 93850.98 MW (89.45% of total installed power) (private was 10.7%)

India **ranked sixth in the world in** terms of **energy demand** accounting for 3.5% of world commercial energy demand in 2001. (10.7.3.1)
Hydroelectricity accounted for only 24 % of total power generation in 2001-02. (10.1.88)

Better Performance of Central Power Plants
The Plant Load Factor of the Central thermal Power plants was better during the period 1998-99 to 2000-01 (71.1, 72.5 and 74.3) than PLF of private sector power plants (68.3, 68.9 and 73.1) (10.8.2.27).

Lack of Private Investment During IX 5YP

Significant volumes of private investment could not be attracted as power producer was expected to sell power to a public sector distributor who may not be in a position to pay for the power purchased. The inflow of private investment was much below the targeted level. Since the financial problems of the SEBs worsened over the IX 5YP period, even this volume of investment was not expected to continue. (10.1.86)

Achievements in X 5YP

India became **world's fifth largest energy consumer**, accounting for about 3.45% of the world's total annual energy consumption in 2004. (11.10.2)

India **ranked world's seventh largest energy producer in 2006-07,** accounting for about 2.49% of the world's total annual energy production.

Projects taken up during the period 2002-07

Teesta Low Dam-III and IV, Sewa-II, Omkareshwar, Subansiri Lower, Parbati-III, Purulia PSP (Pump Storage Project), Chamera Hydro Electric Project III, Uri-II, Kishanganga, Tipaimukh, Turial HEP, Tuivai HEP (Mizoram), Lower Kopili HEP, Ranganadi Stage II, Kameng HEP, Tripura Gas, etc.

The installed capacity of captive power plants increased from 588 MW in 1950 to 24680 MW in March 2007. (11.10.69)

Private sector contribution –

Hydro, Thermal and Nuclear power generations in 2006-07 were 34653.77 MW (including 1306.15 MW in private sector), 86014.84 MW (including 9021.52 MW in private sector) and 3900 MW respectively.

Execution of Ultra-Mega Power Projects

Government permitted the private sector to set up coal, gas or liquid-based thermal, hydel, wind or solar projects with foreign equity participation up to 100% under the automatic route. The government also launched 9 coal based Ultra Mega Power Projects with an initial capacity of 4,000 MW each.

i) Development of coal-based Sasan and Mundra Ultra Mega Power Projects with a capacity of 4000 MW were allotted to Reliance Energy and Tata Power, respectively through tariff-based competitive bidding on Build Own and Operate basis. The projects included development of power projects as well as associated coal mines in respect of pithead sites and imported coal sourcing in respect of coastal sites. (11.10.39)

ii) During X plan, capacity addition target in private sector was 7121 MW, but actual capacity addition was 2670.6 MW (37.5% of target), whereas achievement ratio for Central and State sectors were 55.47% and 51.79% respectively. **Private investment was inadequate** both in generation and in distribution during X plan, due to problems anticipated about the capacity of unviable public sector distribution companies to pay for power.

National Grid

The total inter-regional transmission capacity of national power grid at 220 kV and above was 14100 MW (at the end of X Plan). (11.10.75)

Achievements in XI 5YP -

Of the total hydro-electric potential of about 145320 MW, power plants of 34506 MW had already been developed by 2011-12 and plants of capacity 11951 MW were under development and 98863 MW capacity remained yet to developed. (Ref. Table 12.14.18)

Power Plants Capacity Addition during XI 5YP

Actual installed capacity addition in XI 5YP was 54,964 MW. About 90,000 MW of generation capacity was under construction at the end of XI 5YP, which was expected to start commercial production during XII 5YP. (12.14.21)

Public Sector Contribution to Power Generation in 2011-12
The installed generating capacity of public sector on 31.3.212 was 93.52% of the total hydro-electric generation capacity of 38990.4 MW, 76.63% of the total thermal power generation capacity of 131603.18 MW and 14.34% of the total Renewable Energy Source generation capacity of 24503.45 MW and 100% of the total nuclear power generation capacity of 4780 MW. (12. Table 14.8)

Construction of Super Critical Projects
During XI 5YP, 11 supercritical units (based on supercritical technology with higher stream parameters of 565/593°C, design efficiency of over 40% and lower CO_2 emissions by about 5% as compared to a typical 500 MW subcritical unit) with a total capacity of 7,400 MW were installed. (12.14.28)

During XI 5YP, power purchase agreements were signed for 4 UMPPs in Sasan, Mundra, Krishnapatnam and Tilaiya (Jharkhand) with private investors. Out of these, one unit of 800 MW of Mundra by Tata Power was commissioned in March 2012.

National Grid

The power system in the country was demarcated into 5 regions. 5 Regional grids have been operating in synchronous mode as a single system from 31.12.2013. This is the **largest single system in the world**, both in terms of the grid size and system capacity of around 200,000 MW. (12.14.64).

The capacity for transfer of power across regions at the end of the XI Plan was 27,750 MW. (12.14.64).
BIMSTEC Energy Centre was established on 22.01.2011 by India, Bangladesh, Bhutan, Nepal, Sri Lanka, Myanmar and Thailand for trading of energy among member countries.
Bangladesh is connected with the Eastern and North Eastern Regions of India with a power transfer capacity of 1160 MW from India to Bangladesh.
Presently, about 2070 MW power from the existing hydro projects in Bhutan is being imported to India. India is providing about 2-3 MW of power (Since 5th April 2016) from Manipur to Myanmar.

Private Sector's Inability
29 Hydel projects of total capacity 30000 MW entailing an investment of Rs. 2.7 lakh Cr, awarded to private companies by 6 North Eastern states, were languishing as these companies were unable to complete these projects due to lack of funding and expertise. The government was asking public sector PSUs to take over the projects as they have requisite money and expertise. (TOI dated 9.11.22)

Power generation status in 2022-23
Installed Electricity Generating Capacity, as on 31.03.2023 is 416058.89 MW comprising of Thermal 237268.91 MW, Hydro 46850.17 MW, Nuclear 6780.00 MW and 125159.81 MW from Renewable Energy Sources.

Installed Electricity Generating Capacity in private sector, as on 31.03.2023 was 210277.53 MW (50.54%) comprising of Thermal 85311.14 MW (35.96%), Hydro 3931 MW (8.39%), Nuclear 0 MW and 121035.39 MW (96.7%) from Renewable Energy Sources.

The cumulative energy generation in 2022-23 was 1624.47 billion units (1206.21 BU by thermal, 162.1 BU by hydro, 102.01 BU by Solar, 71.81 BU by Wind, 45.86 BU by nuclear, 11.17 by small hydro and 2.24 BU by biomass / bagasse) Renewable energy generation share during the year 2022-23 was about 22.92 % of total energy generation in the country.

57% Of Power generation was by using fossil fuels in 2022-23.

The national average PLF for thermal stations was 64.15% (PLFs of public sector generation companies were higher than private sector companies)

National Grid in 2022-23

Interregional transmission capacity by the end of the 9th plan was 5,750 MW which increased to 13,450 MW by the end of the 10th plan and to 27,150 MW and 75,050 MW by the end of the 11th and 12th plan respectively.
As on 31.03.2023, inter-regional transmission capacity in the country was 1,12,250 MW.

Hydro-electric potential

Central Electricity Authority assessed the economically exploitable hydro power potential as 133410 MW from schemes having capacity above 25 MW. As on 31.03.2023, the hydroelectric schemes in operation account for only 31.56% (42104.55 MW) and those under execution for 11.26% (15023.5 MW) of the total potential.

In addition, 105 sites for development of Pumped Storage Schemes with probable capacity of 111060.6 MW have been identified. 8 Nos. Pumped Storage Projects of capacity 4745.60 MW are in operation and 4 Pumped Storage project (2780 MW) are under construction.
Approved_CEA_Annual_Report_2022_23.pdf

Development of Atomic Energy

Tata Institute of Fundamental Research, founded in **1945**, trained a team of scientists in nuclear physics. The Atomic Energy Commission setup in **1948** laid the foundation for atomic energy development in India.

Indian Rare Earths Ltd. was established in **1950**
The **Monazite Processing Plant** at Alwaye began production in **1952.**

Bhabha Atomic Research Centre - The Government of India created the Atomic Energy Establishment, Trombay on 3.01.**1954** to consolidate all the research and development activities for nuclear reactors under the Atomic Energy Commission. (The centre was renamed as Bhabha Atomic Research Centre on 22.01.1967).

Department of Atomic Energy was set up in **1954** to take charge of development work in this field.

The Thorium / Uranium Plant at Trombay began production of thorium nitrate and uranium in **1955.**

Trombay Uranium Purification Plant, set up to process the impure uranium extracted from monazite into uranium metal of atomic purity for use in a reactor, was expected to be completed in **1957.**

A high-power, high-flux reactor, received under the Colombo Plan from Canada, was expected to go into operation in **1958**. (2.24.6)

A Pilot Plant at Ghatsila, for extracting Uranium Ore from the tailings of Indian Copper Corporation and for beneficiation of other low grade uranium ores, was expected to be completed by **1960**. (2.24.8)

Three experimental nuclear reactors were built; the last one Zerlina attained criticality in **1961.**

Heavy Water Plant - Department of Atomic Energy commissioned the first heavy water plant of India at Nangal plant of National Fertilizers Ltd. in **1962**.

Heavy Water Plant at Baroda is the first plant set up in India for the production of heavy water.

Power Reactor Fuel Reprocessing Plant-

India's first spent fuel reprocessing plant was commissioned in **1965** at Trombay to reprocess spent fuel arising from research reactors. The recovered plutonium was utilized to feed various programs of the department.

In seventies, the country commissioned a reprocessing plant at Tarapur (PREFRE) and subsequently one more reprocessing plant was commissioned at Kalpakkam (KARP). Spent fuel from KAPS and MAPS were reprocessed at PREFRE and KARP respectively and fuel from Dhruva and CIRUS were reprocessed at Plutonium Plant, Trombay.

Uranium Thorium Separation Facility was commissioned at BARC, Trombay for separation of uranium from thorium rod irradiated in a research reactor. The recovered uranium was used for various programs of the department.

Uranium Corporation of India was founded in **1967** for mining uranium at Jaduguda, Bhatin, Narwapahar, Turamdih and Banduhurang and milling of uranium ore.

The first of the nuclear power stations, of 380 MW capacity, constructed by DAE, was commissioned at Tarapur in **1969**. TAPS-II was also commissioned in October 1969.

The **Nuclear Fuel Complex** was established in **1971** for manufacturing natural and enriched uranium fuel, zirconium alloy cladding and reactor core components under one roof.

Rajasthan APS -1 was put into service on 16.12.**1973**.

Achievements in VI 5YP –

Rajasthan APS -2 was put into service on 1.04.**1981.**
Madras APS-1 and APS-2, designed and fabricated indigenously, using indigenous fuel, heavy water, instrumentation and control systems, was commissioned on 27.01.**1984** and 21.03.**1986** respectively.

Achievements in VII 5YP –

A 100-MW heavy water reactor, DHRUVA, was commissioned on 11.11.**1985**. (7.17.13)
Thal heavy water project was commissioned in **1986**.
The Orissa Sands Complex Project of Indian Rare Earths Ltd. was commissioned in October, **1987**. (8.v2.5.30.8)
The first unit of the Narora Atomic Power Station was commissioned on 1.1.**1991**.
The Manuguru Heavy Water project, the largest heavy water production facility in India, commenced production in March, **1991** along with the heavy water plant at Hazira. (8.5.30.2)
The neutron source reactor KAMINI at Kalpakkam was completed and zero energy reactor PURNIMA III at Trombay attained criticality in **1991**. (8.18.4.5)

Achievements in VIII 5YP –

(i) **UCIL** completed uranium mining and milling project at Narwapahar, Bihar. The **Nuclear Fuel Complex** took up 5 new projects during VIII 5YP for meeting fuel requirement of the new nuclear power reactors. (9.5.269)
(ii) NFC took up New Zircaloy Fabrication Plant, New Uranium Oxide Plant and New Fuel Assembly Plant during this period. (9.5.270)
(iii) Narora APS-1 and APS-2 of capacity 220 MWe each were commissioned on 1.01.**1991** and 1.07.**1992** respectively.
(iv) Kakrapar APS-1 and APS-2 of capacity 220 MWe each were commissioned on 6.05.**1993** and 1.09.**1995** respectively.

Achievements in IX 5YP –

i) Development of Fast Breeder Technology with MOX fuel and advanced heavy water reactors on U-233 were taken up to overcome the problem of limited availability of natural uranium in India. (10.7.1.229)

ii) NPCIL completed refurbishment and upgradation of Rajasthan Atomic Power Station (RAPS)-2 (200MWe), and commissioned Kaiga 1 & 2 (2x220MWe) and RAPS 3 and 4 (2x220 MWe) in **2000.** (10.8.2.66)

iii) 2x1,000 MWe Light Water Reactors were set up at Kudankulam, with the co-operation of Russian Federation. A 40 MWe Fast Breeder Test Reactor was set up at Kalpakkam. (10.8.2.68)

The PLF of NPCIL stations increased from 60% in 1995–96 to 82% in 2000–01. (11.10.64)

In 2001-02, nuclear energy accounted for 2.4 % of total electricity generated. (10.1.89)

Achievements in X 5YP -

i) The Kudankulam project (2 × 1000 MWe) construction started.

ii) NPCIL initiated expansion activities for another 2 units of 1000 MWe. Further, the design of 700 MWe indigenous PHWRs was also undertaken by NPCIL. (11.10.65)

iii) Indira Gandhi Centre for Atomic Research undertook the design, development, construction, and operation of the country's first 500 MWe liquid-sodium-cooled FBR.

iv) The government set up **Bharatiya Nabhikiya Vidyut Nigam Ltd.,** in September 2003 to implement the first 500 MWe prototype FBR project.

(v) Tarapur APS – IV and Tarapur APS – III of capacity 540 Mwe each were commissioned on 12.9.**2005** and 18.8.**2006** respectively.

In 2006, nuclear energy installed capacity was 3900 Mwe. (11.10.10)

Achievements in XI 5YP -

Kaiga Generating Stations 3 and 4 were commissioned on 6.05.**2007** and 20.01.**2011** respectively.

Rajasthan APS – 5 and AFS - 6 of capacity 220 MWe each were put into service in **2010.**

Kudankulam Nuclear Power Stations 1 and 2 were commissioned on 31.12.**2014** and 31.03.**2017** respectively.

Kakrapar APS-3 of capacity 700 MWe was commissioned on 30.06.**2023**

Development of Renewable Energy

Wind Power - CSIR set up a wind power division in the National Aeronautical Laboratory in Bangalore for the purpose of making wind surveys and conducting pilot studies on a few windmills and wind behaviour. (3.24.43)

The **Indian Renewable Energy Development Agency** was established on 11.03.**1987** for operating a revolving fund for development, promotion and commercialization of technologies relating to new and renewable sources of energy by providing soft term finances. IREDA receives funds from Government of Netherlands, Line of credit from World Bank and assistance in the pipeline from DANIDA, ADB etc. (9.6.290)

The achievement during VIII 5YP was 860 MW in the wind power program, (9.6.287), 115 MW in the biomass-based co-generation / combustion program, (9.6.288) and 93 MW in small hydro power (9.6.289)

India achieved capacity addition of 1,367 MW through wind farms during IX 5YP and **ranked fifth in the world in 2001-02**. (10.7.3.18)

As on 31.03.**2007**, power generation from renewables was 10406.69 MW (8.1% of total installed generating capacity). Of this, wind power accounted for 7092 MW followed by small hydro at 1975.60 MW and biomass (including co-generation) at 1158.63 MW

Achievements in IX 5YP

SPV systems of standalone power projects aggregating to 46.64 MWp capacity were installed under Jawaharlal Nehru National Solar Mission. (12.14.194)

The grid interactive renewable power as on 31.03.2012 were Wind - 10,260 MW, Small Hydro - 1,419.17 MW, Biomass Power - 626 MW, Waste to Energy - 46.2 MW, Bagasse Cogeneration - 1,369.7 MW and Solar Power - 939.74 MW and Total 14,660.81 MW. (12.14.189)

National Action Plan on Climate Change

Jawaharlal Nehru National Solar Mission was launched with the aim to install 20GW solar power, 2 GW of off-grid Solar, 20 million sq. meter of solar thermal collector area and to provide solar lighting to 20 million rural households by 2022. (12.14.194)

Ministry of New and Renewable Energy

The MNRE Ministry has been implementing biomass power / co-generation program since mid-nineties.

Over 800 biomass power and bagasse / non-bagasse cogeneration projects aggregating to 10205.61 MW capacity were installed in the country for feeding power to the grid till 31.10.2022. (Biomass IPP – 1871.11 MW, Bagasse Cogeneration – 7562.45 MW, Non-Bagasse Cogeneration - 772.05 MW). As on 31.03.2023, the installed capacity of Renewable Energy (including Large Hydro) generation projects was 171.99 GW, comprising of 42.63 GW of Wind Power, 66.78 GW of Solar Power, 10.80 GW of Bio Power, 4.94 GW of Small Hydro and 46.85 GW of Large Hydro.

Energization of Agricultural Pumps and Electrification of Villages

Rural Electrification – Out of the total 561107 villages, as per 1951 censes, the number of electrified villages increased from 3687 in 1951 to 7400 in 1955-56.

Achievement in IV 5YP –

Rural Electrification Corporation was set up in 1969 to help State Electricity Boards energize pump-sets to boost agriculture and to provide loans to a number of Rural Electric Cooperatives.

Additional funds for rural electrification were provided by **Agricultural Refinance Corporation**, Land Development Banks and commercial banks.

Achievements in V 5YP

Nearly 4 million electrical pump sets were in operation in 1980. (6.15.46)

Achievement in VI 5YP

64 % of villages were electrified by 1985. (7.1.12)

Achievement in VIII 5YP

About 85% of the total 5,87,288 villages had been electrified and 11.5 million pump sets had been energized till March, 1996. About 13 States had completed 100% village electrification. (9.6.123) (9.6.124)

During 2005-09

The Government of India launched Rajiv Gandhi Grameen Vidyutikaran Yojana in April 2005 to provide electricity access to all rural households and extend free connections to all BPL households (estimated at 2.3 Cr) by 2009.

Electricity access was provided to 731527 households (including 672588 BPL households). (11.10.83)

Losses of State Electricity Boards -

Many electricity undertakings were facing liquidity problems as a result of their inability to recover dues from consumers. In turn, these undertakings also defaulted on payments to be made to Central undertakings like CIL, NTPC, NHPC, BHEL etc., from whom they purchased coal, electricity and power equipment. (8.8.65.19)

Losses to Power Generation Companies due to subsidy –
State Electricity Boards were making continuous losses as they were not recovering the full cost of power supplied. SEBs starved of resources to fund expansion and typically ended up even neglecting essential maintenance. The annual losses of SEBs in 2001-02 were estimated at Rs. 24,000 Cr, and this led to outstanding dues of Rs. 35000 Cr to Central Public Sector Undertakings. (10.1.83)
Power tariffs did not cover costs because some segments, especially agriculture and household consumers, were charged very low tariffs. (10.1.84)
The average Aggregate Technical & Commercial loss was 40% including losses from billing to collection. (11.10.47) More than 75%–80% of the total technical loss and almost the entire commercial loss occurred at the distribution stage. Theft and pilferage losses were estimated at about Rs 20000 Cr.

Efforts for Loss Reduction
i) 14 States restructured their power sector and made transmission, distribution, and generation into separate entities.
ii) Distribution was privatized in Orissa and Delhi.
iii) 25 States constituted State Electricity Regulatory Commissions and 21 SERCs issued tariff orders.
iv) Central Government notified the National Electricity Policy in 2005, National Tariff Policy in 2006 and the Rural Electrification Policy on 28.08.2006.
v) 9 States showed a reduction in cash loss of Rs 5254.60 Cr from their loss levels of 2001-02 through Accelerated Power Development and Reforms Program. However, AT&C losses continued to remained high in most States. (11.10.36)
Franchising in Bhiwandi, Maharashtra brought down network losses from 63% to 19% and service levels improved. The Franchise model was being expanded to Nagpur, Aurangabad, Jalgaon and Agra. (12.14.77)

Tables – 10.1 A and 10.1 B - CPSEs Share in Power Generation

Item	Units	Domestic Production		Total CPSE Production		Share of CPSEs %	
		1968-69	2005-06	1968-69	2005-06	1968-69	2005-06
Power	Million Units	47439	599846	NA	258391	NA	43.08

Item	Units	Domestic Production		Total CPSE Production		Share of CPSEs %	
		1998-99	2008-09	1998-99	2008-09	1998-99	2008-09
Thermal Power Generation	GWh	353662	590101	135423	245961	38	42
Hydro Power Generation	GWh	82690	113081	25339	43359	31	38
Nuclear Power Generation	GWh	12015	14713	12015	14713	100	100

Power Generation Equipment Manufacturing

Diwan of Mysore set up **Government Electric Factory** in 1933 at Bangalore for manufacturing electric appliances. GEF continued to make distribution transformers and other electrical products for power distribution.

Light and Heavy Electrical Equipment Production in I 5YP

Hindustan Cables Ltd. was established in 1952.

For the manufacture of heavy electrical equipment, a Consultant's Agreement was reached with Associated Electrical Industries Ltd., of U.K. (2.19.32)

Achievement in II 5YP –
Bharat Heavy Electricals Ltd was set up in **1956** with technological help from the Soviet Union for manufacturing a wide range of products for power, transmission, transportation sectors, etc.
The **Heavy Electrical Project** at Bhopal entered the stage of initial production. (3.3.22)

Achievements in III 5YP
Three heavy electrical equipment projects were set up at Hardwar and Ramachandrapuram to manufacture heavy motors, rectifiers and control equipment, etc. required for increasing power generation at an annual rate of 2000 MW per year from 1971 onwards. (4.14.9)
A heavy engineering project for the manufacture of high-pressure boilers for thermal power plants of capacity 28,000 tons (2500 tons of steam per hour) was tied up with assistance from Czechoslovakia. (3.26.59)

Achievements in IV 5YP –
Production facilities were set up for electric generation equipment and supporting facilities in Bharat Heavy Electricals Ltd (5.5.46)
Plant and equipment of about 4.859 million kW capacity were taken up for manufacture by the indigenous public sector manufacturers, out of total 9.264 million kW generating capacity planned to be added during the IV Plan period.
Manufacture of 3.37 million kW capacity plant and equipment was also taken up for supply to spillover State projects. Plant and equipment for new generation schemes which were yet to be identified were also taken up. There was adequate capacity in the country for manufacture of other heavy electrical equipment and no import of such equipment was envisaged. (4.12.16)
The installed capacity was expected to increase to 3.58 million KW for steam turbines and generators, 1.7 million KW for hydro-turbines, generators and power boilers, 1.63 million HP for electric motors above 200 HP and 14.94 million KVA for transformers. (4.14.42)

Achievement in V 5YP –
In 1976, Government Electric Factory changed its name to KAVIKA (Karnataka Vidyut Karkhane Ltd) and was a leading distribution transformer maker in Mysore state.

Achievements in X 5YP
Production of Heavy Electrical Equipment Capital Goods in 2004 and 2005 were Rs 16500 Cr. and Rs. 21000 Cr respectively. (11.v2.7.1.152)

Power Generation Equipment Manufacturing by Private sector
Government took initiative for developing indigenous capability for manufacturing of supercritical boilers and turbine generators to support large-scale induction of supercritical units. (12.14.29)
a) L&T-MHPS Boilers Pvt Ltd. was formed on 16.04.2007 as a joint venture between Larsen & Toubro Ltd. and Mitsubishi Heavy Industries Ltd., for manufacturing Supercritical Boilers and Pulverizers with capacities of 4000 MW each for boilers and Turbine Generators.
b) Toshiba JSW Power Systems Pvt Ltd., incorporated in September 2008 for manufacturing super critical steam turbines and generators, started commercial operation in January 2011.

c) Alstom Bharat Forge Power Pvt Ltd., incorporated on 08.01.2010 in Sanand, Gujarat, to manufacture 300 – 800 MW subcritical and super critical equipment of capacity 4000 MW, started production in May 2015.

d) Thermax Babcock Wilcox Energy Solutions Ltd. was founded on 26.06.2010 to manufacture Subcritical Boilers of capacity 1000 TPH (300 MW) and above and the full range of Supercritical Boilers with an annual capacity of 3,000 MW with provisions for an expansion up to 5000 MW.

e) Hitachi Power Europe GmbH, Germany, and BGR Energy Systems Ltd., India established a joint venture Co. BGR Boilers Pvt Ltd. on 06.08.2010 for manufacturing of **Super critical steam generators 660 – 1100 MW** and **Sub Critical steam generators up to 500 MW.**

f) Hitachi Ltd., Japan and BGR Energy Systems Ltd., India established a joint venture Co. BGR Turbines Co. Pvt Ltd. on 06.08.2010 for manufacturing **Super critical Steam Turbines & Generators of capacity 660 – 1000 MW.**

g) A joint venture of Ansaldo Caldaie Boilers India Pvt Ltd. and GB Engineering Enterprises was planning to build a boiler manufacturing plant in Tamil Nadu. The capacity of the plant was to become 2,000 MW and 4000 MW per annum after completion of first and second phases.

h) Doosan Heavy Industries & Construction acquired AE & E Chennai Works Pvt Ltd. in 2011 to set up a boiler manufacturing company 'Doosan Chennai Works' to manufacture Boiler pressure parts. 'Doosan Power Systems India' merged with 'Doosan Chennai Works' in 2012 and integrated company was named as 'Doosan Power Systems India' Pvt Ltd.

Wind Power Generation Equipment Manufacturing

India became the second largest wind turbine manufacturer next to China. The installed manufacturing capacity was 6,000 MW. 16 Companies were manufacturing 43 models of wind turbines and its components of varying technologies and capacities. Till the year 2000, most of the machines were of 500 kW or lower capacity. In 2011-12, there were about 14 models from 5 different manufacturers of capacity 2 MW and above, the largest capacity being 2.5 MW. (12.14.211)

Material requirement for manufacture of Power generation equipment

Government arranged to manufacture Cold Rolled Grain Oriented Steel, Cold Rolled Non-Grain Oriented Steel, thicker boiler water plates, etc. and augment indigenous capacity for tubes and pipes, produce gas-insulated substations and create short circuit testing facilities for transformers etc. to ensure that there was no shortage of key material for meeting the capacity addition requirement of the power industry (12.14.89)

Growth of Distribution Systems - Transmission Lines

Achievements in I 5YP
About 30578 kms of sub-transmission and transmission lines of 11 kV and above, were added, representing an increase of 100% over that of 1951. (2.17.34)

Achievements in II 5YP
Transmission lines in circuit kms in 1960-61 were 157888 (500V to 11/15 kV – 102027; 11/15 kV to 66/78 kV – 41960; 110 kV and above – 13901)

Achievements in III 5YP
For the formation of grids, the country was divided into five regions, each with a Regional Electricity Board. (4.12.5)
Inter-State lines between Mysore and Maharashtra as well as between Madhya Pradesh and Maharashtra were established early in 1961.

States grid systems were interconnected enabling inter-State transfer of power. The Riband power system in Uttar Pradesh was connected with the Bihar DVC-West Bengal grid. Mysore grid was connected with Tamil Nadu, Andhra Pradesh and Kerala grids. (4.12.4)

Transmission lines in circuit kms in 1965-66 = 290818 (500V to 11/15 kV – 185969; 11/15 kV to 66/78 kV – 76358; 110 kV and above – 28491)

Achievements in V 5YP
By March 1980, the total length of 400 and 220 KV lines in transmission and distribution networks was 33000 circuit kms, while that of 132 and 110 KV lines was 58000 circuit kms.

National Grid - Southern Region Load Dispatch Centre become fully operational. (6.15.43)

Achievements in VIII Plan
11340 circuit kms of 400 kV Transmission lines and 15152 circuit kms of 220 kV Transmission lines were completed. (9.6.60)

Achievements of IX, X and XI Plans (12. Table 14.10)
200 kV to 765 kV Transmission lines in 2001-02, 2006-07 and 2011-12 were 150642 CKms, 187555 CKms and 257481 CKms respectively.
200 kV to 765 kV substations capacity in 2001-02, 2006-07 and 2011-12 were 1176743 MVA, 249439 MVA and 399801 MVA respectively.
HVDC Link capacity in 2001-02, 2006-07 and 2011-12 were 5200 MW, 8000 MW and 9750 MW respectively.

Private Investment and Participation in Distribution

To create Transmission Super Highways, the government allowed private sector participation in the transmission sector. A PPP project at Jhajjar in Haryana for transmission of electricity was awarded under the PPP mode. (12.3.95)

Public Sector Enterprises Engaged in Generation of Power

Damodar Valley Corporation

Damodar Valley Corporation was established on 07.07.1948 as the first multi-purpose river valley project of independent India for achieving flood control and irrigation (by construction of dams and reservoirs of capacity 1.850 million cu. M), power generation and navigation in the Damodar valley.

DVC commissioned the first dam at Tilaiya and first pulverized fuel power plant in Asia at Bokaro in 1953, the first underground hydel station at Maithon in 1957 and the first reheat unit of India at Chandrapura Thermal Power Station in 1963.
DVC started a joint venture with SAIL - Bokaro Power Supply Company Ltd in 2001 and a joint venture with TATA Power (first PPP in the Indian power sector) Maithon Power Ltd. in 2007.
DVC undertook green field projects at Koderma, Durgapur and Raghunathpur in between 2011 to 2016. Bulk order for 11 × 660 MW supercritical units for NTPC and DVC was being implemented during XII 5YP. (Ref.12.14.29)

DVC power stations – Tilaiya Hydel Station, Hazaribagh, Jharkhand (4 MW, February – July 1953). Maithon Hydel Station, Burdwan, West Bengal (63.2 MW, October 1957 – December 1958), Panchet Hydel Station, Dhanbad, Jharkhand (80 MW, December 1959 – March 1991), Mejia Thermal Power Station in Bankura, West Bengal (capacity 2340 MW, commissioned from December 1997 – August 2012), Chandrapura Thermal Power Station, Bokaro (500 MW, July – November 2011), Durgapur Steel

Thermal Power Station (1000 MW, May 2012 – March 2013), Koderma Thermal Power Station, Jharkhand (1000 MW, July 2013 – June 2014), Raghunathpur Thermal Power Station, Purulia, West Bengal (1200 MW, March 2016), Bokaro Thermal Power Station A (500 MW, February 2017) – Total 6687.2 MW

Solar PV Projects of DVC – MTPS Solar PV Project, Mejia, (1.061 MWp, October 2018- February 2022), KTPS Solar PV Project, Koderma (1.162 MWp, March 2021 – February 2022), DSTPS Solar PV Project, Andal, Burdwan, West Bengal (0.428 MWp, February 2022), RTPS Solar PV Project, Raghunathpura (1.117 MWp, February 2022), Maithon Solar PV Project (0.102 MWp, February 2022) and DVC HQ, Kolkata (0.053 MWp, December 2016). Total = 3.923 MWp.

DVC has transmission lines of 33 KV – 1527 CKms, 132 KV – 3639 CKms, 220 KV – 2957 CKms and 400 KV – 478 CKms.
Total interconnecting tie lines with other utilities like PGCIL, WBSEB, GRIDCO, JSEB was 1236.6 Ckms in 2022.

DVC's thermal power plants of capacity 3036.88 MW generated 43084.76 MU with PLF of 73.43% and hydel plants of capacity 186.2 MW generated 236.61 MU during 2022-23.

Neyveli Lignite Corporation Ltd.

Neyveli Lignite Corp. Ltd. - NLC was incorporated on 14.11.1956 to meet the electricity demand of southern states of India by excavating lignite required for generation of power.

NLC is engaged in mining of lignite in 3 mines in Neyveli and 1 mine in Barsingsar of a total capacity of 30.1 Mts and coal mining of 20 Mts.
Installed Capacity in 2008-09 was 2490 MW
NLC has diversified into renewable energy production and installed 1404 MW solar power plants and 51 MW windmills. 230MW solar Power Plant was commissioned in 2017-18.

NLC India Ltd was engaged operating power plants with installed capacity of 4661.06 MW as on 31.08.2020 comprising Thermal-3240 MW, Solar-1370.06 MW & Wind-51 MW. Commissioning of Unit-I (500 MW) of Neyveli New TPS (2X500 MW) and Solar 709 MW were completed in 2019-20. Unit 2 of Neyveli New TPS (2x500 MW) was commissioned on 3.2.2021.

NLC has 3 Joint Ventures namely NLC Tamil Nadu Power Ltd. (with Tamil Nadu Electricity Board, for setting up 1000 MW coal-based power project at Tuticorin), MNH Shakti Ltd. (with Mahanadi Coal Fields Ltd.) and Neyveli Uttar Pradesh Power Ltd (of capacity 2000 MW, formed with Uttar Pradesh Rajya Vidyut Utpadan Nigam Ltd).

The installed capacity was 6061.06 MW (including 1000 MW coal based thermal power plant of NTPL subsidiary) as on 31.03.2023 comprising Thermal-4640 MW, Solar-1370.06 MW Wind-51 MW.

NLC's thermal power plants generated 21959 MU with PLF of 68.87% during 2022-23.

National Hydroelectric Power Corporation Ltd.

National Hydroelectric Power Corporation Ltd. - NHPC was incorporated on 7.11.1975 to plan, promote and develop hydroelectric power projects. NHPC later expanded to Solar, Geothermal, Tidal, Wind energy projects.

NHPC was having 10 operating power stations in 2004-05.
Installed Capacity in 2008-09 was 3614.2 MW

The Subansiri Lower project of 2000 MW was at standstill from 16.12.2011 to October, 2019 due to agitation launched by various activists against construction. Works restarted from 15.10.2019 after clearance from NGT. (The project was in advance stage of construction. 4 Units were likely to be to be commissioned in 2023-24 and remaining 4 units in 2024-25).

URI Hydro Electric Power project Stage-II of 240 MW was inaugurated on 4.07.2014.

In 2014-15, NHPC was operating 20 power stations (including units of subsidiary companies).

NHPC has 3 joint ventures namely Narmada Hydroelectric Development Corp. Ltd., Loktak Hydroelectric Development Corporation Ltd. and Bundelkhand Saur Urja Ltd.

In 2015–16 NHPC made a profit after tax of Rs. 24.40 billion.

In late 2016, NHPC commissioned a 50 MW wind Power Project in Jaisalmer, Rajasthan.

In 2016-17, NHPC had 22 operating power stations with an installed capacity of 6717 MW (including units of subsidiary Companies) namely Baira Siul PS, Chamera Power Stations I, II and III, Parbati III PS in Himachal Pradesh, Loktak PS in Manipur, Salal PS, Uri PS, Dulhasti PS, Sewa II PS, Chutak PS, Nimmo Bazgo PS and Uri II PS in Jammu and Kashmir, Tanakpur PS and Dhauliganga PS in Uttarakhand, Rangit PS and Teesta V PS in Sikkim and TLDV III PS and TLDP IV PS in West Bengal, Jaisalmer Wind Power Station in Rajasthan and Indra Sagar PS and Omkareshwar PS in Madhya Pradesh.

During 2017-18, NHPC successfully commissioned all the 3 units of Kishanganga H.E. Project and commenced the commercial operation of the 50 MW Solar Power Project in Tamil Nadu.

NHPC's major strategic projects include world's longest inclined pressure shafts (1546M) in Parbati-II H.E. Project, (Parbati – II project of 4x200 MW, is likely miss the target date for commissioning of 2023-24 - as assessed by CEA), India's largest reservoir at Indira Sagar Power station and India's first concrete faced rockfill dam in Dhauliganga Project.

NHPC achieved highest annual generation of 26121 million Units in 2019.

NHPC had 24 operating power stations (including those of subsidiary companies) with a generation capacity of 31329 million units in 2019-20.

In 2022-23, NHPC generated 24450.81 million units (of the total hydro power generation of 162098.77 million units). NHPC was engaged in the construction of 9 projects of total capacity of 5999 MW. In addition, 15 Projects with aggregate capacity of 10787.10 MW are under clearance stage. Dibang Multipurpose Project (12 x 240 MW), which will be the largest hydropower project in the Country, is expected to be commissioned in 2031-32.

National Thermal Power Corp. Ltd.- Development of Thermal Power Stations

National Thermal Power Corp. Ltd. - NTPC was incorporated on 7.11.1975 to augment the power supplied primarily by State Electricity Boards and to provide power and power related products.

It started work on thermal power project in 1976 at NTPC Singrauli, UP. NTPC's core function is the generation and distribution of electricity to State Electricity Boards in India. NTPC also undertakes consultancy, turnkey projects, engineering, construction, operation and management of power plants.

By the end of 1994, its installed capacity crossed 15,000 MW.

In 2002, it incorporated 3 subsidiary companies: "NTPC Electric Supply Co. Ltd.", "NTPC Vidyut Vyapar Nigam Ltd." and "NTPC Hydro Ltd." to undertake small and medium hydropower projects.

In 2002, its installed capacity crossed 20,000 MW.

3 Subsidiaries namely Pipavav Power Development Co., Kanti Bijlee Utpadan Nigam Ltd. and Bhartiya Rail Bijlee Co. Ltd. were added after 2002.

During the year 2004-05, 4 units of 500 MW each were commissioned ahead of schedule.
During 2007-08, 1740 MW of capacity was added including 500 MW at Sipat II, 500 MW at Kahalgaon II and 740 MW at Block III of Ratnagiri Gas and Power Pvt Ltd.
By the end of 2010, its installed capacity crossed 31,000 MW.

Over the time, NTPC diversified into hydro power, coal mining, power trading, power distribution, oil & gas exploration, nuclear, wind and solar power; equipment manufacturing, and providing R&M services of power stations. etc.

NTPC was the first independent power producer in Asia and second in the world by Platt's in 2010.
2 Bulk orders for 11 × 660 MW supercritical units for NTPC and DVC and 9 × 800 MW supercritical units for NTPC—were approved and being implemented. (Ref. 12.14.29)

NTPC was ranked as the number one independent power producer in the world by Platts in 2011.

NTPC had **22 joint ventures in 2014-15.** Patratu Vidyut Utpadan Nigam Ltd was incorporated on 15.10.2015 as a joint venture of NTPC with Jharkhand Bijlee Vitran Nigam Ltd. to build 4000 MW power plant.

Power projects of 3,478 MW (including 910 MW through JV and Subsidiary Companies) were commissioned in 2017-18.
The generation capacity of NTPC Ltd. in 2019-20 was 381 billion units.

It was the largest power Co. in India with an electric power generating capacity of 67,907 MW. Although the Co. had approx. 16% of the total national capacity, it contributed to over 25% of total power generation due to its higher operating efficiency. (approx. 80.2% against the national average PLF of 64.5%). NTPC currently produces 25 billion units of electricity per month.

Government of India now holds 51.1% of its equity shares (after divestment of its stake in 2004, 2010, 2013, 2014, 2016, & 2017)

NTPC acquired Jhabua Power's 600 MW Seoni plant in September 2022 as part of plan to buy stranded assets and was set to buy KSK Mahanadi (which came under insolvency resolution process in April 2022) power plant project of capacity 3600 MW on 1-2-2024. (TOI)

Table 10.2

Period	Coal	Gas / Liquid	Hydro	Small Hydro	Solar	Wind	Total No. plants	NTPC Capacity	Joint Venture Capacity
2004-05	13	7							
30.9.2008	18*	8*					26	27850 MW	2044
2010-11	15+4	7+1							
2014-15	17+4	7+1	1		8				
2016-17	18 "	7 "	1		10				
31.3.2020	24	7 "	1	1	11	1			

* Includes joint venture units; " Does not include joint venture units

NTPC currently operates 55 power stations (24 Coal, 7 combined cycle gas / liquid fuel, 2 Hydro, 1 Wind, and 11 solar projects). Further, it has 9 coal and 1 gas station, owned by joint ventures or subsidiaries.

NTPC generated 321059.43 million units of thermal power in 2022-23 with a PLF of 75.74 (of the total 1206210.67 million units) and 3132.81 million units of hydro power.

Total revenue of NTPC in 2010-11, 2014-15, 2019-20 and 2022-23 were over Rs 57,000 Cr, Rs. 75000 Cr, Rs. 100000 Cr and Rs. 163770 Cr respectively.

North Eastern Electric Power Corporation Ltd.

North Eastern Electric Power Corp. Ltd. - NEEPCO was incorporated on 02.04.1976 to construct, operate and maintain hydro, thermal and gas power stations utilizing the power potential of North Eastern Region.

Installed Capacity in 2008-09 was 1130 MW

NEEPCO was having 9 plants at Umrangso HEP (275 MW) and Assam Gas Based Power Station (291 MW) in Bokuloni, Agarthala Gas Based Power Station (135 MW) in Ramchandra Nagar & Tripura Gas Based Power Station (101 MW) in Monarchak in Tripura, Doyang HEP (75 MW) in Nagaland and Yazali HEP (Lower Subansiri) (405 MW) and Pare HEP (110 MW) in Arunachal Pradesh, Tuirial HEP (60 MW) in Mizoram. Synchronization of units I and II of 150 MW each of Kameng HE Project (600 MW) were done in January 2020.

NEEPCO was executing 5 hydro, thermal and solar power projects including Lungreng HEP (815 MW), Chhimtuipui HEP (635 MW) and Mat HEP (76 MW) in Mizoram.
The Co. set up a 5 MW Monarchak Solar Power Project in Tripura.

The installed capacity of NEEPCO from 2019-20 is 2057 MW (8 hydro power plants of total 1,525MW and 3 gas-based plants of 527MW and a solar plant of 5 MW) for generating 7854 million units.

Government sold 100% equities to NTPC for Rs. 4000 Cr. in March 2020.

600 MW Kameng Hydro Power Station was dedicated to the Nation on 19.11.2022.

NEEPCO generated 3282.66 million units of thermal power 5202.44 million units of hydro power in 2022-23. The gross turnover was Rs. 4556.55 Cr.

Satluj Jal Vidyut Nigam Ltd.

Satluj Jal Vidyut Nigam Ltd. – SJVNL, formally Nathpa Jhakri Power Corporation Ltd., was incorporated on 24.5.1988 to develop hydro-electric power projects in river Satluj Basin. SJVNL is in the generation of hydro power and rendering technical consultancy services from concept to commissioning for hydro-electric projects, tunnels for railway projects, major civil works, etc. for public and private sector organizations.

1500 MW Nathpa Jhakri Hydro Electric Project, the first project of SJVNL and the largest underground hydro project, was commissioned by 18.05.2004 with its all 6 units.
Installed Capacity in 2008-09 was 1500 MW

412 MW Rampur HE Project and 47.6 MW Khirvire Wind Power Project were commissioned in 2014.

SJVNL ventured into ultra-mega hybrid renewable energy parks with a power generation capacity of 4000 to 5000 MW in Gujarat, 5 MW Solar PV Project in Gujarat, 1320 MW Thermal project in Bihar.
SJVNL diversified into Power Transmission business and formed a joint venture namely Cross Border Power Transmission Co. Ltd. with PGCIL and IL&FS.
SJVNL has 2 subsidiary companies namely SJVN Thermal Pvt Ltd. and SJVN Arun-3 Power Development Co. Pvt Ltd and formed 2 joint venture companies namely Bengal Birbhum Coalfields Ltd. and Kholongchhu Hydro Energy Ltd.

Satluj Wangchu Power Plant was commissioned in 2019-20. The generation capacity of SJVN Ltd. in 2019-20 was 9187 million units.

Memorandum of Understandings were signed with Government of Himachal Pradesh for Luhri-I, Luhri-II, Sunni Dam, Dhaulasidh, Jangi Thopan Powari, Purthi, Bardang & Reoli Dugli Hydro Electric Power Plants.

The installed capacity of SJVNL in 2022-23 was 2227 MW including 1,972 MW hydro, 97.6 MW wind and 156.9 MW solar plants. It has 123 km transmission lines.

75 MW Parasan Solar Power Plant was commissioned and SJVNL generated 9130.48 million units of hydro power in 2022-23.

Tehri Hydro Development Corporation Ltd.

Tehri Hydro Development Corporation Ltd. - THDC was incorporated on 12.07.**1988** to promote, execute, operate and maintain hydro power projects in Bhagirathi - Bhilangna Valley, as a joint venture of Government of India and Government of Uttar Pradesh.

4 x 250 MW Tehri Power Station is in operation since **2006-07** and 400 MW Koteshwar HEP started generation from **2011-12**.
THDC commissioned 50 MW and 63 MW wind power projects in Patan and Dhwarka on 29.06.**2016** and 31.03.**2017** respectively. Total installed capacity of THDCIL was 1513 MW.

24 MW Dhukwan Small Hydro Project, on Betwa river in UP, was commissioned on 13.01.**2020**.

Diversification - THDCIL signed MoU with Solar Energy Corporation of India on 13.02.**2015** for setting up grid connected Solar Power Project up to 250 MW capacity.
THDC signed an agreement with SECI and Kerala State Electricity Board on 31.03.**2015** for development of 50MW Solar Project in Kasaragod. It was commissioned in December 2020.
Patan and Dwarika wind power projects started generation since 2017-18.
THDC, in **2019-20**, was executing 14 projects of capacity 5719 MW.

The installed capacity of THDC in 2019-20 was 5596 million units.

The government sold its 74.49% stake in THDC India Ltd for Rs 7,500 Cr to NTPC in March 2020.

As on 2022-23, THDC Is implementing projects of capacity of 1444 MW comprising 1,000 MW Tehri Pumped Storage Plant, (expected to be commissioned from October 2023 to February 2024) and 444 MW Vishnugad Pipalkoti Hydroelectric Project.
THDC signed MoU with UP Government for implementation of 1320 MW Thermal Power Plant at Khurja.

THDC is developing 2000 MW UMREPPs through SPV/JVC in UP and 10000 MW in Rajasthan in 2022-23. Ministry of Power allotted 1200 Kalai-II and 1750 MW Demwe Lower Hydro-Electric Projects in Lohit Basin of Arunachal Pradesh to THDCIL.

The installed capacity was 1587 MW. THDC generated 4539.97 million units of hydro power in 2022-23.

Narmada Hydroelectric Development Corp. Ltd.

Narmada Hydroelectric Development Corp. Ltd. - NHDC was incorporated on 1.8.**2000,** to plan and integrate development of hydro power potential of Narmada River and its tributaries in M.P., as a joint venture of NHPC Ltd. and MP Government. The name of the company changed to NHDC Ltd. w.e.f. 24.06.2009.

NHDC completed 8x125 MW Indira Sagar Hydroelectric Project and 8x65 MW Omkareshwar Hydroelectric Project in MP in May **2005** and November **2007** respectively.

Installed Capacity in **2008-09** was 1520 MW.

NHDC signed MoU with MP Govt. on 29.06.**2009** for supercritical 2 x 660 MW Reva Thermal Power Station in Khandwa. However, as of November 2017, the project did not receive environmental clearance, and plans appear to be deferred or abandoned.

Installed Capacity in **2019-20** was 4357 million units.

NHDC generated 5443.49 million units of hydro power in 2022-23.

NTPC Hydro Ltd.

NTPC Hydro Ltd. was set up as a subsidiary of NTPC Ltd., in **2002** to undertake development of small and medium sized hydro-electric projects up to 250 MW capacities.

The company's maiden project namely Lata - Tapovan Hydro Electric Project (171 MW Capacity), located in Chamoli District of Uttarakhand State was suspended by the order of Supreme Court of India since 2014 and the matter is still pending in the court.

The other project undertaken is Rammam Stage-III Hydro Electric Power Project (120 MW capacity) located in Darjeeling District, West Bengal. On 19.03.2015, Bharat Heavy Electricals Ltd secured the supply contract. Physical progress made as on 20.12.2023 was 43.7%.

Pipavav Power Development Co. Ltd.

MOU was signed between NTPC, Gujarat Power Corporation Ltd. and Gujarat Electricity Board on 20.02.**2004** for development of 1000 MW thermal power project at Pipavav as joint venture with GPCL. Pursuant to the decision of the Gujarat Government, NTPC Ltd. has dissociated itself from this company. PPDCL is under winding up. https://power.industry-report.net

Ratnagiri Gas and Power Pvt Ltd.

Established in 08.07.2005. Combined cycle gas-based power plant using LNG/ RLNG as a fuel.

NLC Tamil Nadu Power Ltd.

NLC Tamil Nadu Power Ltd. is a coal based 2 × 500 MW Power Project at Tuticorin, set up as a joint venture of Neyveli Lignite Corporation Ltd. and TANGEDCO (Tamil Nadu Generation and Distribution Company) in **2006**.

Units 1 and 2 were commissioned on 18.06.2015 and 29.08.2015 respectively. Power evacuation from this project is being carried out by M/s Power Grid Corporation of India.

During the year 2021-22, NLC TNPL generated 4182.457 million units with a PLF of 47.75%. NTPL-21-22.pdf (nlcindia.in)

Coastal Karnataka Power Ltd.

Coastal Karnataka Power Ltd. - CKPL was incorporated on 10.02.2006 as a subsidiary of Power Finance Corporation Ltd for the development of Tadri Ultra Mega Power Project in Karnataka. Although, identification of land and water resources were finalized, due to agitation by the local people further progress could not be made.

Ministry of Power was requested on 25.05.2016 to seek confirmation from the State Government for closure of the CKPL UMPP.

Coastal Maharashtra Mega Power Ltd.

Coastal Maharashtra Mega Power Ltd. - CMMPL, a subsidiary of Power Finance Corporation Ltd., was established in **2006** to facilitate the development of Ultra Mega Power Project in Maharashtra. The site for the development of UMPP in Maharashtra is, however, yet to be finalized by Government of Maharashtra.

Orissa Integrated Power Ltd.

Orissa Integrated Power Ltd. - OIPL was set up in **2006** as a subsidiary of Power Finance Corporation Ltd. Central Electricity Authority selected Sundergarh in Orissa as site for setting up of UMPP. As the Government of India could not accept Orissa Government's demand for 50% allocation of power (as the entire power of the project had been already allocated to various states long back) the consent of Orissa govt is still awaited. Further the allocation of 150 cusecs of water for the project is also awaited from the Government of Orissa.

Jharkhand Integrated Power Ltd.

Jharkhand Integrated Power Ltd. – JIPL was incorporated on 2.01.**2007** as a subsidiary of Power Finance Corp for the development of 4000 MW Tilaiya UMPP in Hazaribagh.

Reliance Power was selected as developer for the implementation of the project in 2009 through tariff based international competitive bidding process, as Reliance Power had committed to provide power at Rs 1.77 a unit for over 25 years.
Reliance Power pulled out of the project on 28.04.2015 on the ground that the state had failed to make adequate land available. Out of 1,700 acres of land required for the project, the state had acquired only 417 acres though the ministry of environment and forest had given its nod for 1,220 acres of forest land in November 2010.

Bhartiya Rail Bijlee Co. Ltd.

Bhartiya Rail Bijlee Co. Ltd. - BRBCL was incorporated on 22.11.**2007** as a joint venture of NTPC Ltd. and Ministry of Railways, to set up, operate and maintain 4x250 MW Coal Based Thermal Power Project at Nabinagar in Bihar for meeting traction and non-traction requirement of electricity for Railways and other consumers.

BRBCL started its operation in FY 2016-17.
With the addition of 250 MW in FY 2021-22, capacity became 1000 MW w.e.f. 1.12.2021.
The gross turnover of BRBCL for 2022-23 was Rs. 3424.74 Cr and generation was 6926.8 million units with PLF of 79.07.

Sakhigopal Integrated Power Co. Ltd

Sakhigopal Integrated Power Co. Ltd was incorporated by PFC Consulting Ltd. on 21.5.**2008** to undertake execution of 4000 MW integrated power project at a coastal location in Odisha using desalination technology.

After selection of Bijoy Patna in Bhadrak district as site of UMPP in May 2012, the officials of Ministry of Power, PFC / PFCCL and CEA had been requesting Government of Odisha during various meetings across different forums for according 'in principle' approval for the second additional UMPP in Odisha. However, the same was still awaited. AR_Sakhigopal Integrated Power Company Limited.pdf (pfcindia.com)

Ghogarpalli Integrated Power Co. Ltd

Ghogarpalli Integrated Power Co. Ltd was incorporated by PFC Consulting Ltd. on 21.5.**2008** to undertake execution of 4000 MW integrated power project in Odisha.

After selecting Kalahandi as site for the UMPP in May 2012, the officials of Ministry of Power, PFC / PFCCL and CEA requested Government of Odisha during various meetings across different forums for according 'in principle' approval for the second additional UMPP in Odisha.

As the activities of the UMPP were not progressing for a considerable time, on 25.05.2016, Ministry of Power was requested to seek confirmation from the state government for closure of the UMPP.

Ministry of Power vide letter dated 2.6.2023 requested PFCCL to take necessary action for the closure of Odisha's II additional UMPP. Annual Report_GIPCL.pdf (pfcindia.com)

Akaltara Power Ltd.

Akaltara Power Ltd. - APL, a subsidiary of Power Finance Co. Ltd., was established to develop an Ultra Mega Power Project in the state of Chhattisgarh.

Statutory clearances for land and water availability were being obtained.

IIT Roorkee was asked to ascertain availability of water and to prepare the project report.

Coastal Tamil Nadu Power Ltd.

Coastal Tamil Nadu Power Ltd. - CTNPL, a subsidiary of Power Finance Corporation Ltd., was established for setting up an integrated coastal Ultra Mega Power Project of 4000 MW capacity in Cheyyur, (Kancheepuram) in Tamil Nadu. Tamil Nadu Minister of Electricity conveyed the approval of Cheyyur site for development of the UMPP to the Union Minister of Power on 5.9.2007.

CTNPL has initiated the action for appointment of Technical Consultant for preparation of Detailed Project Report and other related works. ultra_mega_project.pdf (grist.org)

Kanti Bijlee Utpadan Nigam Ltd.

Kanti Bijlee Utpadan Nigam Ltd. - Kanti Power Plant was started in Muzaffarpur in **1985** with an initial capacity of 2x110 MW. KBUNL was incorporated as Vaishali Power Generating Co. Ltd., a joint venture of NTPC and Bihar State Electricity Board, on 06.09.**2006** to take over Muzaffarpur Thermal Power Station. (VPGCL was renamed as KBUNL on 10.04.2008).

Company test synchronized unit # 2 of 2x110 MW of MTPS on 17.10.**2007**.

KBUNL completed renovation & modernization of both the units of Stage-I, first unit started commercial operation on 01.11.2013 and the second on 15.11.2014.

KBUNL implemented expansion of MTPS by adding 2 x 195 MW units, started on 18.03.**2017** and 01.07.2017 respectively.

KBUNL took up expansion of MTPS for addition of 2x250 MW units for which the Board had approved the Feasibility Report.

KBUNL became a wholly owned subsidiary of NTPC in June 2018.

Operation of stage-1 220 MW units were discontinued in September 2021 on expiry of Power Purchase Agreement with Bihar SEB.

Stage-II units operated with a plant availability factor of 88%, 88% and 93% in 2019, 2020 and 2021 respectively.

Nabinagar Power Generating Co. Ltd.

Nabinagar Power Generating Co. Ltd. was started as a joint venture between NTPC and Bihar State Power Holding Co. Ltd.

The project's capacity was increased from originally proposed 3960 MW to 4380 MW in 2016. Nabinagar Super Thermal Power Project was expected to be the third biggest power project in India in 2016.

Bihar govt handed over the thermal plant to NTPC on 33 years lease. Unit 1- Commercial Operation started on 06.09.**2019**. Unit 2- was commissioned on 30.07.**2021**. Unit 3 started operation on 01.06.**2022**.

Kanti Bijlee Utpadan Nigam Ltd. and Nabinagar Power Generating Company Ltd. are no longer subsidiaries of NTPC as the same have been amalgamated with NTPC effective from 1.04.2022.

Tungabhadra Steel Products Ltd.

Tungabhadra Steel Products Ltd. - TSPL was incorporated on 20.02.**1960** as a joint venture of Governments of Karnataka and Andhra Pradesh. TSPL became a central PSE in 1967

TSPL is generating power at Malaprabha Mini Hydel Plant. Hydel Power generation capacity in 2008-09 was 5.009 million units.

Subsequent to decisions made on 29.12.2014, CCEA approved closure of TSPL on 22.12.2015.

Patratu Vidyut Utpadan Nigam Ltd.

Patratu Vidyut Utpadan Nigam Ltd. - PVUNL was incorporated on 15.10.**2015** as a subsidiary of NTPC jointly with Jharkhand Bijlee Vitran Nigam Ltd. to acquire, establish, revive, renovate, modernize, operate and maintain the performing existing units (of existing capacity 840 MW) and further expand capacity in Phase-I by 3x800 MW and Phase-II by 2x800 MW.

PVUNL started its operation in FY 2016-17.

In 2022-23, PVUNL was pursuing setting up of Ph-I 3 x 800 MW power project at Patratu.

Closure of Companies

Dingchang Transmission Ltd. was struck from Registrar of Companies on 17.08.2021.

NMDC Power Ltd. was dissolved w.e.f. 14.10.2021.

Tatiya Andhra Mega Power Ltd., Coastal Maharashtra Mega Power Ltd., Shongtong Karcham Wangtoo Transmission Ltd., Tanda Transmission Company Ltd and Bijawar-Vidarbha Transmission Ltd. had been approved for closure by the Government (as on 31.03.2022). The first 4 companies were struck off with ROC/MCA during 2022-23.

Chhattisgarh Surguja Power Ltd, was also struck off with ROC / MCA during 2022-23.

Bihar Infrapower Ltd., Bihar Mega Power Ltd., Bijawar – Vidarbha Transmission Ltd., Coastal Tamil Nadu Power Ltd., Deoghar Mega Power Ltd., Ghogarpalli Integrated Power Company Ltd, Orissa Integrated Power Ltd., Sakhigopal Integrated Power Company Ltd. remained approved for closure as on 31.03.2023

Kishtwar Transmission Ltd. and MP Power Transmission Package-I Ltd. were removed from list of CPSEs during 2022-23.

Transfer of Companies

MP Power Transmission Package-II Ltd., Koppal-Narendra Transmission Ltd., Kallam Transmission Ltd., Karur Transmission Ltd., Gadag Transmission Ltd. and Rajgarh Transmission Ltd were transferred to Adani Transmission Ltd (w.e.f. 01.11.2021), ReNew Transmission Ventures Pvt Ltd (13.12.2021), Consortium of IndiGrid 1 Ltd and IndiGrid 2 Ltd (28.12.2021), Adani Transmission Ltd (18.01.2022), Renew Transmission Ventures Pvt Ltd. (17.03.2022) and G R Infraprojects Ltd (30.05.2022) respectively.

Kishtwar Transmission Ltd. and MP Power Transmission Package-I Ltd. were transferred to Sterlite Grid 24 Ltd and Megha Engineering and Infrastructures Ltd.

Public Sector Enterprises Which Contributed for Nuclear Power Generation

Uranium Corporation of India Ltd.

Uranium Corporation of India Ltd. - UCIL was incorporated on 04.10.**1967** to mine and refine uranium ore to produce concentrate and recover by-products to meet the requirement of Nuclear Power Program.

UCIL is mining and processing Uranium Ore in Jaduguda, Bhatin, Narwapahar, Bagjata, Banduhurang and Turamdih and upcoming mining projects at Mohuldih in East Singhbhum, Tummalapalle in Andhra Pradesh, Gogi at Karnataka and 2 mills at Jaduguda and Turamdih in Jharkhand.
UCIL is working under monopolistic conditions with 100% market share. UCIL contributes about 100% of the national Tri uranium octoxide (U_3O_8) production.

Revenue from operations during 2022-23 was Rs. 2192.12 Cr.

Nuclear Fuel Complex

Nuclear Fuel Complex - NFC was established in **1971** for manufacturing natural and enriched uranium fuel, zirconium alloy cladding and reactor core components.

Natural uranium, mined at Jaduguda Uranium mine in Singhbhum, is converted into nuclear fuel assemblies. NFC supplies zircaloy clad uranium oxide fuel assemblies and zirconium alloy structural components for all 14 operating atomic power reactors in India. The Hyderabad plant has a capacity of 250 tons of UO_2 and is expected to expanded to 600 tons capacity.

NFC products are supplied to the Department of Atomic Energy, the Indian Navy, Hindustan Aeronautics Ltd. and other defence organizations, as well as chemical, fertilizer, and ball bearing industries.
NFC was planning to establish 2 major fuel fabrication facilities to meet the expected jump in nuclear power production.

Two numbers of He-Back Filling Chambers with automatic door closing system were manufactured in NFC-Hyderabad and handed over to NFC-Kota on 22.08.2023.

Nuclear Power Corporation of India Ltd.

Nuclear Power Corp. of India Ltd. - NPCIL was incorporated on 03.09.**1987** to develop nuclear power technology and to produce nuclear power as a safe and viable source of energy. NPCIL is engaged in design, construction, commissioning and operation of nuclear power plants.

NPCIL in 2004-05 owned and operated 13 nuclear power reactors of total capacity 2670 Mwe.
In 2007-08, NPCIL was generating nuclear energy through 2 Boiling Water Reactors and 15 Pressurized Heavy Water Reactors of total capacity 4120 MW.
The first memorandum of understanding for the setting up 6x1650 MWe Jaitapur nuclear project was inked in 2009 with French nuclear supplier Areva.

In 2010-11, NPCIL generated electricity through 19 Nuclear Power Reactors of total capacity 4680 MW. NPCIL was constructing Kudankulam NPP Units-1&2 (2x1000MW Light Water Reactors), Kakarapar APP-3&4 (2x700 MW PHWRs) and Rajasthan APP–7&8 (2x700 MW PHWRs), of aggregate capacity 4800 MW,

NPCIL was also generating electricity from wind mill of capacity 10 MWe at Kudankulam site.

New green projects were initiated – 5 inland projects at Gorakhpur, Chutka (MP), Mahi Banswara, (Rajasthan), Bhimpur, (MP) and Kaiga-5&6 (Karnataka) for setting up indigenously designed 700 MW PHWRs and 3 coastal projects at Mithi Virdi (Gujarat), Kovvada (AP) and Haripur (WB) for setting up LWRs of 1000 MW or higher unit sizes.

In 2014-15, NPCIL operated 20 Nuclear Power Reactors of capacity 5680 MW. 12 Nuclear Power Plants were under International Atomic Energy Agency safeguards.

In 2016, French power company EDF and NPCIL signed a revised MOU to carry forward Jaitapur NPP project.

In 2016-17, NPCIL operated 21 Nuclear Power Reactors of capacity 6780 MW. 14 Of these reactors were under IAEA safeguards and 7 under DAE safeguards.
Expansion of Kudankulam for 6X1000 MW started. (construction of units 3 & 4 started on 29.06.2017 and 5 & 6 started on 14.11.2018).

In Feb 2017, NALCO Board advised for winding up of NPCIL - NALCO Power Company Ltd.

NPCIL has **3 subsidiaries** – Anushakti Vidhyut Nigam Ltd, NPCIL – Indian Oil Nuclear Energy Corporation Ltd, NPCIL - NALCO Power Co Ltd and **1 joint venture** L&T Special Steels and Heavy Forgings Pvt Ltd.

In 2019-20, installed capacity was **6780 MW with 22 reactors.**
In 2020, EDF submitted its techno-commercial offer for Jaitapur NPP project, with EDF supplying European Pressurized Reactors.
NPCIL generated 46472 million units against installed capacity of 56673 million units in 2019-20.

Government of India approved setting up of 10 units of 700 MW PHWRs (in fleet mode) and KKNPP Units-5&6 of 1000 MW LWRs.

KAPS3 achieved criticality on 22/07/2020.

NPCIL generated 46982 MUs with both PAF and PLF at 87% in 2022-23. Construction works are in progress at KAPP-4, RAPP-7 8 and KKNPP-3 to 6.

Bharatiya Nabhikiya Vidyut Nigam Ltd.

Bhartiya Nabhikiya Vidyut Nigam Ltd. - BHAVINI was incorporated on 22.10.**2003** for construction, commissioning and operation of 500 MWe Prototype Fast Breeder Reactor at Kalpakkam as well as the other FBRs that may come up in future.
The Prototype Fast Breeder Reactor was developed by BHAVINI. **Fuel loading at the 500 MWe PFBR started at Kalpakkam in March 2024.**

Public Sector Enterprises Engaged in Renewable Sources Power Generation

Indian Renewable Energy Development Agency Ltd.

Indian Renewable Energy Development Agency Ltd. - IREDA was incorporated on 11.3.1987 to finance and promote investment in renewable energy sources.

IREDA is promoting self-sustaining investment in energy generation from renewable sources, improvement of energy efficiency, conservation and environmental technologies.
Till 31.3.2008, IREDA had **sanctioned loan of Rs. 8865.65 Cr for 1845 projects** and disbursed an amount of Rs. 4983.10 Cr.

IREDA has one financial joint venture namely MP Wind Farms Ltd.

IREDA also set up a 50 MW Solar Power Project at Kasaragod, Kerala.

As per National Energy Policy, approximately Rs. 21 Lakh Cr will be required over FY22 to FY30 to meet the target of 500 GW energy from non-fossil sources. During FY 2022-23, IREDA introduced new schemes and modified existing schemes to sustain growth of IREDAs market share in renewable Energy.

Gross turnover in 2022-23 was Rs. 3481.97 Cr.

Solar Energy Corporation of India Ltd.

Solar Energy Corporation of India Ltd. - SECI was set up on 09.09.**2011** to harness solar energy and develop large scale solar installations, solar plants, and solar parks, to promote and commercialize the use of solar energy and implement 750 MW SPV grid connected projects to achieve grid connected total solar power capacity of 20,000 MW by 2022 under Jawaharlal Nehru National Solar Mission.

SECI is responsible for solar park scheme, grid-connected solar rooftop scheme, defence scheme, solar canals, and Indo-Pak border scheme.
SECI is active in trading of solar power from projects set up by it.
SECI's mandate was broadened to cover all segments of renewable energy namely, geo-thermal, off-shore wind, tidal etc. apart from solar energy and the Co. was renamed to Renewable Energy Corporation of India.

Traded 14819 million units of solar and wind power during 2022-23.

Rewa Ultra Mega Solar Ltd.

Rewa Ultra Mega Solar Ltd., a joint venture between Madhya Pradesh Urja Vikas Nigam Ltd. and Solar Energy Corporation of India was established in **2015**.
It started producing power in 2018 and reached its full capacity of 750MW in January 2020.

It is one of the largest single-site solar power plants in the world.

Power Grid Corporation of India has developed the 220/400 KV inter-state transmission system under green corridor to facilitate evacuation of power from the project site to consumers.

The project generated 1,120,000MWh electricity in 2023.

Public Sector Enterprises Engaged in Transmission & Distribution of Power

NTPC Electric Supply Co. Ltd.

NTPC Electric Supply Co. Ltd. - NESCL, a subsidiary of NTPC, was incorporated on 21.08.**2002** to acquire, establish & operate electricity distribution network in various circles / cities across India.

NESCL is providing consultancy in implementation of turnkey projects under Rajiv Gandhi Grameen Vidyutikaran Yojana, projects of sub-stations for utilities, supply of electricity in 5 Km area around NTPC power stations and retail distribution of power in various industrial parks developed by Kerala Industrial Infrastructure Development Corporation, SEZs and other industrial areas by forming joint venture company KINESCO Power & Utility Pvt Ltd.

NESCL implemented RGGVY in 31 districts in MP, Chhattisgarh, Orissa, Jharkhand and WB.

As on 31.03.11, 14433 Un-electrified / De-electrified villages, 11279 partially electrified villages and 2.323 million Below Poverty Line rural house hold connections were electrified.

All business operations were transferred to NTPC Ltd. w.e.f. 01.04.2015.

NESL is under liquidation as on 2022-23.

REC Power Distribution Co. Ltd.

REC Power Distribution Co. Ltd. - RECPDCL was incorporated on 12.07.**2007** as a subsidiary of REC Ltd. to promote, develop, construct, own and maintain the 66 KV and below voltage class distribution electric supply lines, manage Decentralized Distributed Generation & associated distribution system and to take up consultancy / execution of works in the above areas for Govt. bodies / other agencies.

RECPDCL undertakes third party quality inspection of works executed under Rajiv Gandhi Gramin Vidut Yojana, Feeder Renovation Program and High Voltage Distribution System projects.

During 2010-11, RECPDCL completed third party inspection of 1617 feeders under Feeder Renovation Program.

RECPDFL carried out the material inspection of more than 17500 distribution transformers in 13 DISCOMS under RGGVY and High Voltage Distribution System projects of Uttar Haryana Bijli Vidyut Nigam Ltd.

After amalgamation of RECPDCL with REC Transmission Projects Co Ltd., the company's name changed to 'REC Power Development and Consultancy Ltd' from 16.07.2021.

The gross turnover of RECPDCL in 2022-23 was Rs. 284.84 Cr.

Byrnihat Transmission Co. Ltd.

Byrnihat Transmission Co. Ltd. - BTCL was incorporated on 23.03.**2006** as a 'Shell Co.' to take up the implementation of Misa - Byrnihat Transmission Project as a joint venture of PowerGrid and Meghalaya State Electricity Board.

BTCL was closed by the holding company Power Grid Corporation of India Ltd.

REC Transmission Projects Co. Ltd.

REC Transmission Projects Co. Ltd. - Government of India in 2006-07 invited private sector investment in 14 major transmission projects on "Build, Own and Operate" basis. RECTPL, a subsidiary company of REC was set up on 8.01.2007, as Bid Process Coordinator for North Karanpura Transmission System and Talcher Augmentation Transmission System.

RECTPCL formed subsidiaries North Karanpura Transmission Co. Ltd., Talcher II Transmission Co. Ltd. & Raichur Sholapur Transmission Co. Ltd. for development of the projects. After selection process, the first two projects were transferred to Reliance Power Transmission Ltd. on 20.05.2010 & 27.04.2010 respectively and third project was transferred to a Consortium of Patel Engineering Ltd., Simplex Infrastructures Ltd. & BS Transcomm Ltd. on 07.01.2011.

RECTPCL was made Bid Process Coordinator for Transmission Systems associated with Independent Power Producers of Vemagiri Area: Packages A, B & C. Vemagiri Transmission System Ltd. for Package-A was incorporated on 21.4.2011. During 2017-18, RECTPCL made **3 subsidiaries** namely, Mandar Transmission Ltd, Chandil Transmission Ltd. and Dumka Transmission Ltd.

After amalgamation of RECPDCL with RECTPCL, the company's name changed to 'REC Power Development and Consultancy Limited' from 16.07.2021.

Bokaro Kodarma Maithon Transmission Co. Ltd.

BKMTCL was incorporated on 31.01.**2007** to undertake preliminary survey work, identification of route, preparation of survey report, conduct the bidding process for selection of Transmission Service Provider for developing "Evacuation System for 1000 MW Maithon RB, 1000 MW Koderma and 500 MW Bokaro extension.

East-North Interconnection Co. Ltd.

East North Interconnection Co. Ltd. was incorporated on 1.02.**2007** as a subsidiary of Power Finance Corporation Ltd. for the development of Transmission system for enabling import of NER / ER surplus power to NR. ENICL entered into a transmission services agreement with PGCIL on 6.8.2009 and 28.1.2013.

The ENICL project was awarded by Ministry of Power on 7.1.**2010** for a 25 years period on a BOOM basis.

466 Ckm Purnia – Biharsharif transmission line was commissioned on 16.09.**2013** and 443 Ckm transmission line from Bongaigaon to Siliguri was commissioned on 12.11.**2014**.

India Grid Trust acquired ENICL from the Sterlite Sponsor in May 2020.

North Karanpura Transmission Co. Ltd.

North Karanpura Transmission Co. Ltd - NKTCL was set up on 23.04.**2007** as a subsidiary of REC Transmission Projects Co. Ltd. to establish transmission system for evacuation of North Karanpura 3 x 660 MW project of NTPC.
After selection process, NKTCL was transferred to Reliance Power Transmission Ltd on 20.05.2010. Reliance Power could not complete the project.
Hence, NKTCL was awarded to Adani Transmission Ltd. on 24.05.**2016** for 35 years period on Build, Own, Operate and Maintain basis.

Talcher-II Transmission Co. Ltd.

Talcher-II Transmission Co. Ltd. - TTCL was incorporated in **2007**.
After the selection process, TTCL was transferred to Reliance Power Transmission Ltd on 27.04.2010. The Co. was yet to commence its business operations.

Raichur Sholapur Transmission Co. Ltd

Raichur Sholapur Transmission Co. Ltd - RSTCL was transferred to the consortium of Patel Engineering Ltd., Simplex Infrastructures Ltd. and BS Transcomm Ltd. on 07.01.2011.

Power Grid Corporation of India Ltd.

Power Grid Corp. of India Ltd. - National Power Transmission Corp. Ltd. was incorporated on 23.10.**1989** by taking over the transmission assets and manpower from the power sector undertakings namely NTPC, NHPC, NEEPCO, NLC, NPC, THDC and CEA to provide services for transmission of electric power across the country through inter-state transmission system by way of construction, operation and maintenance of National Grid comprising extra High Voltage AC and High Voltage DC transmission lines, sub-stations, load dispatch centres and communication facilities. The company's name was changed to Power Grid Corporation of India Ltd. on 23.10.1992.

PGCIL planned for establishment of an integrated National Power Grid, in a phased manner, for strengthening the regional grids (five grids structured on geographical contiguity basis) and to support the generation capacity addition program of about 1,00,000 MW during 2002-2012.

The first 500 kV HVDC line in Asia was commissioned in **1990** between Rihand and Dadri.

PGCIL's transmission system extended to 22,220 Ckms and 42 substations with transformation capacity of 12,200 MVA, when commercial business started in **1992-93**.

In **2003-04**, a shell Co. "Bina Dehgam Transmission Co. Ltd.", was formed to facilitate private investment in transmission sector.

During **2004-05**, PowerGrid commissioned about 3000 Ckms of transmission lines and 3 new substations with transformation capacity of 3000 MVA.
Inter-regional capacity was enhanced to 9500 MW by 2004-05.
PGCIL's transmission system extended to 66,800 CKms and transformation capacity of 73,000 MVA with 111 substations by **2007-08**.
Inter-regional power transfer capacity was expected to be enhanced to 30,000 MW by **2012**.

PGCIL, during XII 5YP, planned to enhance the inter-regional power transfer capacity to above 72,250 MW.

Growth of National Grid –

PGCIL took over management (of Southern Regional Load Dispatch Centre in 1994, ERDC and NERLDC in 1995, NRLDC and WRLDC in 1996),

Connected Western and Southern regions in 1997, Eastern and Southern regions in 1999, J&K and Punjab in 2001,

2000 MW Talcher – Kolar bipolar HVDC link was commissioned in 2002, 220 kV transmission line from Pul-e-Khurmi to Kabul transmission system in Afghanistan was completed in 2008, One Nation – One Grid – One Frequency dream accomplished and Bangladesh was also connected to national grid to strengthen SAARC grid in 2013, 100 MW power supply from Palatana in Tripura to Bangladesh was inaugurated and transmission lines to Nepal were inaugurated in 2016, Ladakh region was connected to national grid in 2019, commissioned 11 renewable energy management centres in 2020 and 250th 765 / 400 kV substation was completed in 2021.

PowerGrid was implementing Aurangabad Wardha 1200kV transmission line. PowerGrid designed the transmission line tower in-house.

PowerGrid was **one of the largest transmission utilities in the World.** PowerGrid's transmission system wheeled about 50% of country's total power generation in 2016-17 and 2019-20 with **transmission system availability being consistently maintained at more than 99%.** PGCIL was playing active role in development of SAARC Grid.

Diversification - In addition, PGCIL diversified into telecom business to utilize spare telecommunication capacity inherent with ULDC schemes leveraging its Right of Way along countrywide transmission infrastructure use. PowerGrid laid optical fibre network of over 16,000 Km on its transmission lines for leasing out telecom network bandwidth.

PowerGrid is providing services to domestic and international clients with global footprints in 20 countries.

PGCIL formed **subsidiary companies** viz. PowerGrid Kala Amb Transmission Ltd., PowerGrid Jabalpur Transmission Ltd., PowerGrid Warora Transmission Ltd., PowerGrid Parli Transmission Ltd., PowerGrid Southern Interconnector Transmission System Ltd., Grid Conductors Ltd., Byrnihat Transmission Co. Ltd. and Parbati Koldam Transmission Co. Ltd.

PGCIL formed **joint ventures** Torrent PowerGrid Ltd. (for 1100 MW generating project at Surat) and Jaypee PowerGrid Ltd. (for 1000MW Karcham-Wangtoo Hydro Project)

PGCIL formed financial joint venture Power links Transmission Ltd. with Tata Power.

PowerGrid had 13 operating Joint Ventures in 2016-17.

Joint Venture PowerGrid IL&FS Transmission Co. Pvt Ltd. was formed with IL&FS to undertake projects of intra-state transmission and sub-transmission works for State power utilities.

PGCIL managed 177699 Ckms transmission lines and 278 substations with a transformation capacity of 527446 MVA and maintained system availability of 99.86% as on 31.3.2024. It has 48 subsidiaries, 12 Joint ventures, owns / operates 100000 km telecom network. Company Overview | POWERGRID

Power System Operation Corporation Ltd.

Power System Operation Corporation Ltd - POSOCO was incorporated as a subsidiary of Power Grid Corporation of India Ltd. on 20.03.**2009** to ensure integrated operation of regional and national power system to facilitate transfer of electric power within and across the regions and trans-national exchange of power.

It manages operational and manpower requirements of the Regional Load Dispatch Centres and National Load Dispatch Centres. POSOCO was made the designated entity to operate RLDC / NLDC with effect from 1.10.2010. (12.14.65)

The company was renamed as Grid Controller of India Ltd. in 2022-23.

As on 31.03.2023, 55.37 GW Solar and 42.12 GW Wind energy was integrated and monitored at Renewable Energy Management Centres set up by Govt. of India under Green Energy Corridor Scheme. In FY 2022-23, the total cleared volume in Real Time Market was 24,186 MU. Energy facilitated through inter-regional exchange was 236 BU.

All India energy consumption reached 1510 BU, Maximum Demand Met 211.9 GW, Thermal generation 1131 BU, Hydro generation 174 BU, Solar Generation 102 BU and wind generation 71.8 BU during 2022-23.

PowerGrid NM Transmission Ltd.

PNTL was incorporated on 20.05.**2011** to establish transmission system (of 765 kV D/C and 765 kV S/C lines traversing Tamil Nadu and Karnataka) associated with Nagapattinam Cuddalore Area Package A. All the project elements had been progressively commissioned by January 2019.

PowerGrid Unchahar Transmission Ltd.

PUTL was incorporated on 17.12.**2012** to establish transmission system (of 400kV D/C line traversing UP) associated with Unchahar Thermal Power Station. PUTL started its operation in FY 2016-17.

PowerGrid Kala Amb Transmission Ltd. was incorporated on 29.07.**2013**. Project was commissioned in July 2017.

PowerGrid Vizag Transmission Ltd.

PVTL was acquired by PowerGrid on 30.08.**2013** under tariff based competitive bidding for establishing and strengthening transmission system (Srikakulam Vemagiri 765kV DC Line and Khammam Nagarjuna Sagar 400kV DC Line traversing AP and Telangana) in Southern Region for import of power from Eastern Region. PVTL started its operation in FY 2015-16.

PowerGrid Warora Transmission Ltd.

PWTL was acquired by PowerGrid on 24.04.2015 under tariff based competitive bidding from REC Transmission Projects Co. Ltd. for establishment of Transmission system. PWTL was commissioned on 10.07.2018

PowerGrid Parli Transmission Ltd. - The entire project was commissioned on 04.06.**2018.**

Power Grid Kala AMB Transmission Ltd., Power Grid Vizag Transmission Ltd., Power Grid Warora Transmission Ltd., Power Grid Parli Transmission Ltd. and PowerGrid Jabalpur Transmission Ltd. have been monetized through PowerGrid infrastructure Investment Trust in May 2021 and these companies ceased to be PowerGrid subsidiaries w.e.f. 13.05.2021.

Public Sector Enterprises Engaged in Trading of Power

NTPC Vidyut Vyapar Nigam Ltd.

NTPC Vidyut Vyapar Nigam Ltd. - NVVN was incorporated on 1.11.**2002** to develop wholesale power market, **to trade surplus power** and to effectively utilize installed capacity and thus reduce cost of power. NVVN purchases all forms of electrical power from any source including import and sells such power to any consumer including export.

NVVN served over 28 Power Utilities in 5 electricity regions of the country.
It crossed the trading volume of 1000 million units in October, **2004**.
During **2005-06**, NVVN diversified into the business of fly ash trading.

In **2016-17**, the customer base of NVVN increased to more than 100 including state government and private power utilities, IPPs, and captive power generators in all 5 power regions of India. NVVN was supplying power to Bangladesh and Nepal also.

NVVN commissioned a total solar capacity of 733 MW as a nodal agency for Jawaharlal Nehru National Solar Mission by **31.03.2017**.

Supply of additional 60MW power to Bangladesh from Tripura commenced during **2018-19**.
NVVN is exporting 710 MW power to Bangladesh and 350 MW to Nepal.

NVVN played a key role in meeting the power demand of A&N by supplying 15 MW DG power. Approx. 40% of total A&N power requirement is being fulfilled by NVVN.

Public Sector Enterprises Which Provide Financial Assistance and Consultancy Services for Generation, Transmission & Distribution of Power

Rural Electrification Corp. Ltd.

Rural Electrification Corp. Ltd. - REC was incorporated on 25.7.**1969** to extend financial assistance for rural electrification schemes, to projects of power generation, transmission, distribution, energy conservation, systems improvement, renovation and modernization of power plants in both public and private sectors.

REC also offered appraising, consultancy, technical support and monitoring (of projects) services to State Electricity Boards / Power Utilities, Rural Electric Cooperatives, etc. (6.5.38)

It acted as Nodal Agency for operationalization of the National Electricity Fund, which provided interest subsidy on loans disbursed to Central and State Power Utilities, State Electricity Boards, Rural Electric Cooperatives, NGOs, Distribution Companies both in public and private sector, to improve the infrastructure in distribution sector.

REC is engaged in implementation of Rajiv Gandhi Grameen Vidyutikaran Yojana (Scheme for rural electricity infrastructure and household electrification).

REC tied up a line of credit for €100M with KfW, under Indo-German Development Cooperation, for financing renewable energy power projects (solar, wind, small hydro, biomass power, and cogeneration power & hybrid projects) at concessional rates of interest.

REC incorporated REC Transmission Projects Co. Ltd. and REC Power Distribution Co. Ltd. as subsidiary companies.

RGGVY was subsumed as 'Deendayal Upadhyaya Gram Jyoti Yojana' in 2014; It is the Nodal Agency for (i) Implementation DDUGJY scheme, (ii) Pradhan Mantri Sahaj Bijli Har Ghar Yojana (iii) Village Electrification and (iv) Ujwal Discom Assurance Yojana (Uday).

Government disinvested 5% equity capital out of 65.64% shareholding through OFS transaction on 8.04.2015.

On 20.03.2019, Power Finance Corp. acquired 52.63% controlling stake in REC for Rs. 14,500 Cr. REC merged with PFC in 2020.

Gross Turnover of REC Ltd. in FY 2022-23 was Rs. 39208 Cr.

Power Finance Corporation Ltd.

Power Finance Corporation Ltd. - PFC was incorporated on 16.7.**1986** to provide financial resources for the creation and development of an economically sustainable Indian Power sector by extending financial assistance to power projects in generation, transmission, distribution, renovation / modernization, energy conservation etc.

The assistances included Rupee Term Loan, Foreign Currency Term Loan, Line of Credit, Suppliers Credit, Working Capital Loan, Bridge Loan, Bill discounting, Lease Finance, Debt Re-financing, take out Financing, Guarantees and Consultancy Services, Financial Assistance to Equipment Manufacturers, etc.

PFC has **18 subsidiary companies** namely - Chhattisgarh Surguja Power Ltd (previously Akaltara Power Ltd) at Akaltara, Coastal Karnataka Power Ltd at Tadri, Coastal Maharashtra Mega Power Ltd at Girye, Coastal Tamil Nadu Power Ltd, Deoghar Mega Power Ltd., Ghogarpalli Integrated Power Co. Ltd., Jharkhand Integrated Power Ltd in Taliya, Orissa Integrated Power Ltd, Sakhigopal Integrated Power Co. Ltd., Tatiya Andhra Mega Power Ltd. Darbhanga Motihari Transmission Co. Ltd., DGEN & Uttarakhand Transmission Co. Ltd., Patran Transmission Co. Ltd., Purulia & Kharagpur Transmission Co. Ltd., RAPP Transmission Co. Ltd., PFC Consulting Ltd., PFC Green Energy Ltd, PFC Capital Advisory Services Ltd., Power Equity Capital Advisors Pvt Ltd.

Two shell companies namely Bokaro–Kodarma-Maithon Transmission Co. Ltd. and East-North Interconnection Co. Ltd. were also formed for transmission projects.

PFC had 2 **Joint Ventures** namely Energy Efficiency Services Ltd. (created with REC, NTPC and PGCIL to promote energy efficiency and energy conservation projects) and National Power Exchange Ltd. (which was dissolved on 31.03.2017).

PFC formed 9 more Subsidiaries with 100% shareholding in each (including PFC Consulting Ltd.).

During 2022-23, based on PFC's net worth, it was the largest NBFC (revenue from operations of Rs. 39651.75 Cr.) operating in India. According to Forbes 2023 rankings, PFC ranked 378th in terms of assets size.

PFC Consulting Ltd.

PFC Consulting Ltd was incorporated on 25.3.**2008**, by converting PFC's Consultancy Services Group into a subsidiary company. CSG was providing consultancy services to Power Sector since October 1999 as a part of PFC.

PFCCL was nominated as 'Bid Process Coordinator' by Ministry of Power, for the development of Independent Transmission Projects. PFC, as the Nodal Agency for development of Ultra Mega Power Projects, entrusted all the work related to UMPPs to PFCCL.

PFCCL completed (i) Assisting Uttar Pradesh Rajya Vidyut Utpadan Nigam Ltd. for development of "Saharpur- Jamarpani" Coal Block, (ii) selection of JV Partner for Kaiga 3 & 4 Atomic Power Project (iii) Selection of JV Partner for Power Project linked to Banhardih Coal Block in Jharkhand (iv) Advisory services for JV formation between Govt. of Jharkhand and NTPC Ltd. for Patratu Thermal Power Station.

UMPPs Awarded - Sasan Power Ltd., MP; Coastal Gujarat Power Ltd.; Mundra UMPP; Coastal Andhra Power Ltd.; Krishnapatnam UMPP; Jharkhand Integrated Power Ltd.; Tilaiya UMPP.
30 Independent transmission projects were awarded.

The services offered by PFCCL include **efficiency improvement projects** for both State-owned utilities and Independent Power Producers. PFCCL handled consultancy assignments relating to procurement of power for Govt. of Punjab, Rajasthan & Jharkhand.

The gross turnover in 2022-23 was Rs. 133.03 Cr.

PFC Green Energy Ltd.

PFC Green Energy Ltd. - PFC GEL was incorporated on 30.03.**2011** to provide financial assistance to projects for generating green energy through renewable and non-conventional sources.

PFC Capital Advisory Services Ltd.

PFC Capital Advisory Services Ltd. - PFCCAS was incorporated as a subsidiary of Power Finance Corporation Ltd. on 18.07.**2011** to meet power sector requirements for financial advisory services including syndication services.
PFCCAS carries out down selling of project loans under written by PFC. PFCCAS was successful in arranging sanction of loans of Rs. 1060 Cr out of loans underwritten by PFC.

Public Sector Enterprises Engaged in Manufacture of Power Generation Equipment

Bharat Heavy Electricals Ltd.

Heavy Electricals Ltd. was established in **1956**. The Government of India signed an agreement on 17.11.1955, with Associated Electrical Industries, UK, for the establishment of a factory at Bhopal for the manufacture of heavy electrical equipment in India. The Company was registered as Heavy Electricals (India) Ltd. on 29.08.1956.

One unit was started at Tiruchirappalli to manufacture high pressure boilers and another unit at Hyderabad to manufacture steam turbo generators, high-pressure pumps and compressors with collaboration from Czechoslovakia and the third plant at Haridwar with erstwhile USSR collaboration for large steam turbo generating sets, motors and hydro generating sets including turbines and generators.

Bharat Heavy Electricals Ltd. was incorporated on 13.11.1964 to manage these 3 units. These 3 plants went into production in the latter half of the sixties.
Bhopal plant was manufacturing thermal and hydro generator plants for orders from Electricity Boards.

HE(I)L and BHEL formally merged in January 1974.

BHEL upgraded its facilities to manufacture thermal generating sets of capacities 30 MW to 210 MW, hydro generating plants of various ratings and transmission products up to 400 kV ratings.

BHEL contributed 910 MW of power generating equipment to India's capacity of 4,579 MW by end of IV Plan.

BHEL enhanced its power generating equipment manufacturing capacity from 6,000 MW to 10,000 MW per annum by December, 2007.

BHEL became the only Co. in the world to have integrated facilities to manufacture power project equipment. BHEL supplied nearly **64%** of India's total installed power generating capacity in the utility sector in 2007-08.

Installed Capacities in 2008-09 were Turbines - 10000 MW, Generators - 10000 MW, Boilers, Valves & Boilers Auxiliaries - 417014 MT, Power Transformers - 20500 MVA and Electrical Machines - 1340 Nos.

Units were set up at Jagdishpur for manufacture of stampings for electrical machines and transformers and at Tirumayam for power plant piping systems.

BHEL achieved the capability to deliver 15,000 MW capacity power equipment in 2011.

BHEL entered into collaboration with Alstom, Siemens and General Electric (USA.) for supercritical technology for boilers, turbine generators and Advance-class Gas Turbines respectively. BHEL augmented its manufacturing capacity to 20,000 MW by March 2012. (Ref. 12.14.29)

BHEL entered into **7** strategic **joint ventures** in supercritical coal fired power plants - "BHEL GE Gas Turbine Services Ltd." with GE Pacific (Mauritius) Ltd., "Power Plant Performance Improvement Ltd." with Siemens AG of Germany, "NTPC BHEL Power Projects Pvt Ltd." with NTPC, Udangudi Power Corporation Ltd. with Tamil Nadu Electricity Board, Barak Power Pvt Ltd. with PTC India Ltd., Raichur Power Corporation Ltd. with Karnataka Power Corporation Ltd., Latur Power Co. Ltd with Maharashtra State Power Generation Co Ltd and Dada Dhuniwale Khandwa Power Ltd with MP Power Generating Co. Ltd.

BHEL has one **subsidiary** namely BHEL Electrical Machines Ltd.

Bharat Heavy Plates and Vessels at Visakhapatnam merged with BHEL on 30.08.**2013** to become the 17th manufacturing unit (Heavy Plates and Vessels Plant) of BHEL.

BHEL has 17 manufacturing units – 1 unit each at Bhopal, Rudrapur, Ranipet, Hyderabad, Goindwal and Jhansi, 2 units each at Haridwar, Tiruchirappalli and Jagdishpur, 3 units at Bangalore and 2 repair units, 8 service centres and 8 overseas offices.

BHEL retained its market leadership position during 2013-14 with **72% market share in the power sector.**

BHEL was engaged in engineering and manufacturing of 180 products under 30 product groups catering to Power Generation, Transmission, Transportation, Renewable Energy, Oil, Gas, Defence sectors in 2013-14.

In 2017, equipment supplied by BHEL constituted **55%** of the total installed power generation capacity in India.

BHEL had infrastructure to execute more than 150 project sites across India and abroad.

BHEL expanded its portfolio by adding Flue Gas Desulphurization, water management system, Air Cooled Condenser and other Balance of Plant Systems.

BHEL undertook various development projects with focus on low-carbon emission technologies, Advanced Ultra Super Critical Technology, Solar PV, 765/1200 kV Transmission System, ±800 kV HVDC system, IGBT based Propulsion Systems for higher rating Locos & EMU, Metro coaches, e-mobility, Energy storage systems, etc.

Installed Capacities in 2019-20 were Turbines / Generators - 19767 MW, Boilers, Valves & Boilers Aux. - 833805 MT, Power Transformers - 44901 MVA, Traction machines – 3206 numbers and Electrical Machines - 2248 numbers. The worldwide installed base of BHEL power generating equipment exceeded 190GW.

BHEL executed 463 coal sets, 424 hydro sets, 103 gas sets, 12 nuclear sets and 60 numbers MW scale grid-connected solar PV plants in India till 2022-23. Supplied 75 nos. of 6000 HP WAG-9H Electric Locomotives to Indian Railways.

BHEL Electrical Machines Ltd.

BHEL Electrical Machines Ltd. - BHEL-EM was incorporated on 19-01-**2011** as a subsidiary of BHEL under a joint venture agreement with Government of Kerala to take over the Kasaragod unit of Kerala Electrical & Allied Engineering Co. Ltd.

BHEL-EM is engaged in production of Brushless alternator, Train Lighting Alternators, DG Sets for Railway Power Car and Traction alternators etc.

BHEL - EM was transferred to Government of Kerala on 11.08.2021.

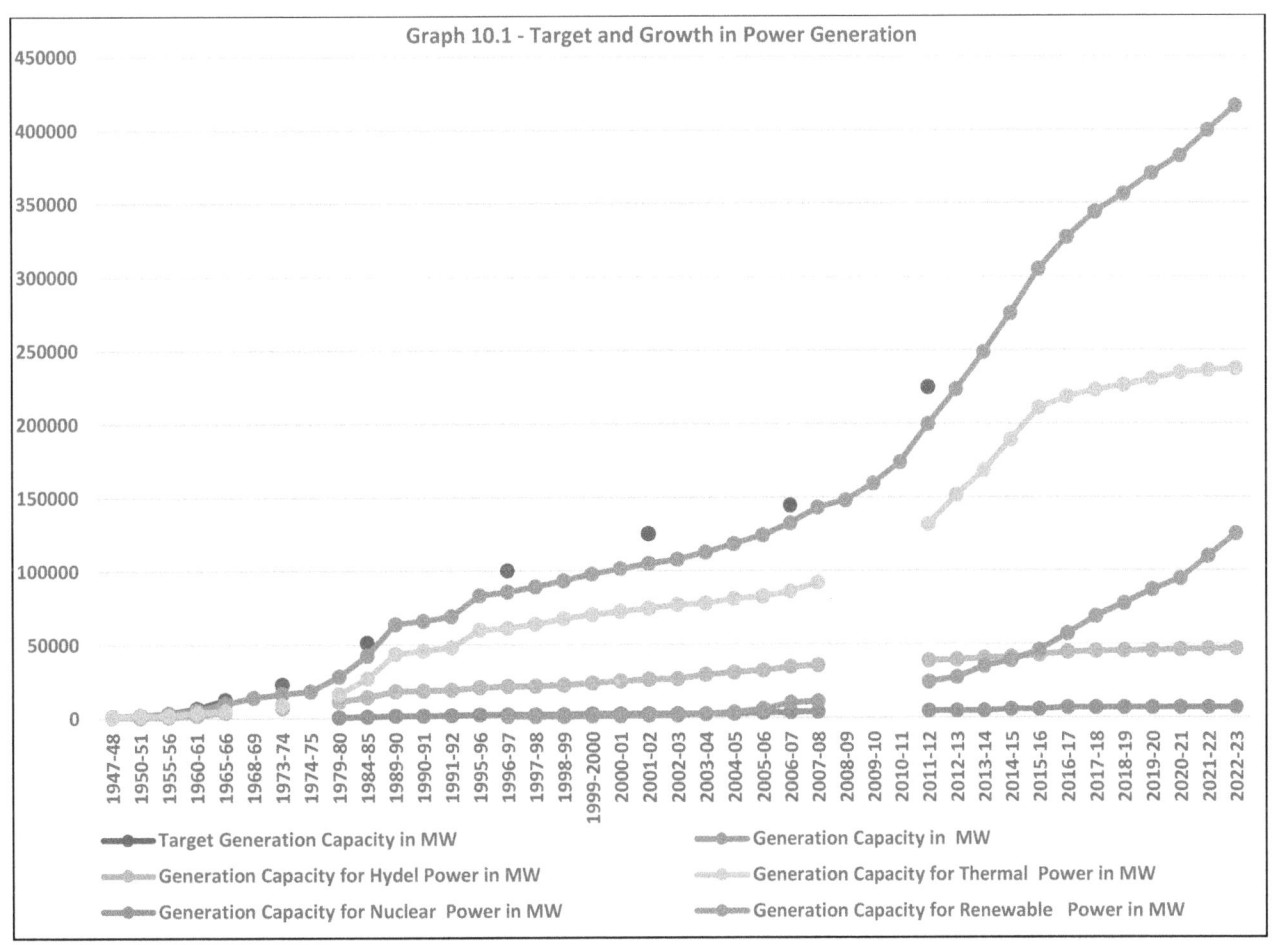

Table – 10.3 CPSEs Share in Domestic Power Generation

Domestic Thermal Power Generation in GWh							Total Generation by CPSEs / Share of CPSEs to Total Domestic Generation (%)						
1968-69	1998-99	2004-05	2005-06	2008-09	2009-10	2010-11	1968-69	1998-99	2004-05	2005-06	2008-09	2009-10	2010-11
	353662			590101	640876	665008		135423			245961	264761	273775
								38			42	41.3	41.2
Hydro Power Generation in GWh													
	82690			113081	106680	114257		25339			43359	40887	46049
								31			38	38.3	40.3
Nuclear Power Generation in GWh													
	12015			14713	18636	26266		12015			14713	18636	26266
								100			100	100	100
Power Generation in million Units													
47439			599846							258391			
										43.08			

Adani Power Ltd

APL set up Mundra Power Plant between 2009 and 2012, Kawai thermal power generation project from 2008-10 and 40 MW solar power project in Bitta, Kutch in 2013 and Tiroda Thermal Power Station in Maharashtra from 2012-14.

APL acquired Udupi Power Corporation Ltd from Lanco Infratech in 2014, Raikheda Thermal Power Station from GMR Chhattisgarh Energy Ltd. In 2019, took over Avantha Korba West Power Station from Korba West Power Company Ltd, with approval of NCLT in 2019 and Lanco Amarkantak Power Plant, located at Pathadi village in Korba from Lanco Infratech in 2024.

Adani Green Energy Ltd

Kamuthi Solar Power Project, Wind power project in Lahori (MP) and Khavda renewable energy project were set up by AGEL.

AGEL acquired Kodangal Solar Parks Pvt Ltd between 2018 and 2019, Essel Group's solar power portfolio of 205MW located in Punjab, Karnataka and Uttar Pradesh in 2019 for US$185 million, SoftBank Group Corp backed SB Energy Holdings Ltd for $3.5 billion in 2021 and Inox Wind's 50 MW wind power project at Dayapar village in Kutch in October 2022.

Adani Transmission Ltd / Adani Energy Solutions

ATL constructed more than 3800 circuit kms of transmission lines originating from Mundra Thermal Power Station, connecting Mundra-Dehgam, Mundra-Mohindergarh and Tirora-Warora.

ATL acquired 3 wholly owned subsidiaries of PFC Consulting (CPSE) – the Chhattisgarh -WR transmission line, Sipat transmission line and Raipur-Rajnandgaon-Warora transmission line in 2015, GMR Group's transmission assets in Rajasthan— the Maru Transmission Services Ltd, Aaravalli Transmission Services Ltd and Reliance Infrastructure's transmission assets of the Western Region System Strengthening Scheme in 2016, Mumbai Generation Transmission & Distribution business from Reliance Infrastructure for Rs. 18,800 Cr in 2017, KEC International's Bikaner-Sikar transmission asset and PFC Consulting's Bikaner-Khetri transmission project in Rajasthan in 2019 and Alipurduar Transmission from Kalpataru Power Transmission Ltd adding 650 circuit kilometres of network in Bihar and West Bengal in 2020.

Adani Transmission Step Two acquired Essar's Mahan-Sipat transmission with operating assets of 3373 ckt. km in Central India.

Acquisition is a bad strategy

Acquisition of existing companies does not increase existing installed capacity or reduce shortfall in supply. (The acquiring company's inventory and operating cost reduce and profit increases additionally due to reduced competition in the market). If the same amount was invested for starting new companies, the installed capacity and generation would have increased and shortfall would have reduced. **Thus, acquisition of operating companies for profit is a bad policy and promotes monopoly.**

Contribution To Manufacturing GDP

Machinery, equipment and others contributed 11.1% and Electrical machinery & apparatus, telecom and others contributed 6.0% to manufacturing GDP in 2009-10. (12. Table 13.8)

Summary

The production of commercial energy in 1984-85 was almost entirely in the public sector. (7.1.7) The public sector contribution to total Hydro, Thermal and Nuclear power generation in 2006-07 were 96.2%, 89.5% and 100% respectively.

The installed generation capacity of public sector on 31.3.2012 was 93.52% of the total hydro-electric power, 76.63% of the total thermal power, and 14.34% of the total Renewable Energy Source power and 100% of the total nuclear power.

The Plant Load Factor of the Central Thermal Power plants was better during the period 1998-99 to 2000-01 (71.1, 72.5 and 74.3) than PLF of private sector power plants (68.3, 68.9 and 73.1) (10.8.2.27).

Private Sector Players –

Power generation companies - Calcutta Electric Supply Corp. – 1899, Tata Hydroelectric power supply Co. - Tata Power Co. Ltd – 1910, Bombay Suburban Electric Supply Co – 1929, Renusagar power plant – 1967, Gujarat Industries Power Co. Ltd. – 1985,
Essar Power – 1991, Jaiprakash Power Ventures Ltd.- 1994, JSW Energy Ltd – 1994, Indowind Energy Pvt Ltd – 1995, Reliance Power Ltd. / Bawana Power Pvt Ltd. – 1995, Adani Power Ltd (1996), Suzlon Energy Ltd.- 1995, Indraprastha Power Generation Co. – 2001, Essel Mining's Wind Farms – 2004, Orient Green Power Co. Ltd – 2006, Reliance Infrastructure Ltd. – 2008, Aditya Birla Renewables Ltd – 2011, Aditya Birla Group – 2013, Adani Green Energy Ltd.- 2015, Adani Solar - 2015

Transmission companies - CESC Transmission & Distribution Division – 1899, Jaypee Powergrid Ltd – 2006, Adani Transmission Ltd.- 2013.

Power generation equipment manufacturers - Texmaco – 1943, English Electric Company of India / GE T&D India Ltd. / Areva T & D – 1957, Larsen & Toubro Ltd – 1965,
Bajaj Electricals - 1999, L&T MHPS Boilers Pvt Ltd – 2007, L&T MHPS Turbines Pvt Ltd – 2007.

11: GROWTH IN MACHINE BUILDING INDUSTRY

Importance of Machine Building

Production of high precision machine tools formed the basis for the subsequent expansion of heavy and light engineering industries. Machine building covers metallurgical, textile, cement and other process plants / machineries, power plant and other industrial machinery and engineering sectors.

Targeted Growth for Machine Building Capabilities

After forecasting targets for production of Cement, Steel, Coal, Electricity, Food, Cloth, Consumer Products of Basic and Secondary Needs, Fertilizer, Pesticides, Chemicals, Drugs and Pharmaceutical Products, Housing Needs, Petroleum and Petrochemical Products, Transportation Needs, etc., forecasting was done to assess the **manufacturing plants' capacities**, required to produce the targeted quantity of all these products. The machineries needed for setting up the assessed manufacturing plants were forecasted by the government for the last financial year of each 5-year plan and the target machine building capacity for the various 5-year plans were set. The capacity built up and actual production achieved at the end of each 5-year plan and some other periods are given Graphs – 11.1 to 11.3.

Machine Building Capacity in 1950-51

Machine Tools production in 1950-51 of 1100 Nos was totally in the private sector, though they had a production capacity of 3000. (1.4.12)

Achievements in I 5YP –

i) Nahan Foundry Ltd. was established in 1952.
ii) Prototype Machine Tool Factory, Ambernath was established in 1953 under Defence Ministry.
iii) **Hindustan Machine Tools** was incorporated in **1953**.
iv) Construction of the **machine tool factory** (of capacity 1600 machine tools) commenced **at Jalahalli** in Mysore State. (1.29.21)
v) The structural steel fabrication capacity in 1955-56 was 1.8 Lakh Tons.
vi) Machine Tools production increased to 3000 in 1955-56 by capacity utilization.
vii) New types of machine tools were also developed. (2.19.9)

National Industrial Development Corp. - NIDC was incorporated on 20.10.**1954** to achieve a balanced development of industries in the public and private sectors, to establish new units in the Aluminium industry and manufacture of heavy equipment for earth moving, mining etc. and rolls and rolling mill equipment required in ferrous and non-ferrous industries.

The number of small-scale units manufacturing machine tools were 344 in 1956. (3.25.45)

Machine building Capacities in 1956 – Production capacity (in terms of value in Rs. Lakhs) for the manufacture of cotton and Jute textile machinery - 412, Sugar machinery - 28, cement machinery - 56, Electric motors below 200 HP - 2.4 lakhs HP and Electric Transformers below 33KV – 5.4 Lakh KVA.

Achievements in II 5YP –

i) The number of small-scale units manufacturing machine tools increased to well over 500. (3.25.45)
ii) In 1960-61, India was producing progressively increasing quantities of machine tools and machinery for use in agriculture, transport, chemicals and pharmaceuticals, textiles, jute, cement, tea, sugar, flour and oil mills, paper, mining etc. Indigenous manufacturing capacity was existing for most of the machinery and equipment needed by the railways, except diesel and electric locomotives. The value of graded machine tools produced in the country increased from Rs. 34 lakhs in 1950-51 to Rs. 550 lakhs in 1960-61. (3.3.22)

iii) Steps were taken for establishment of **coal mining machinery plant** at Durgapur. The aggregate production value of industrial machinery and capital goods in 1961 was 11 times the value at the beginning of the decade. (3.3.22)

Heavy Engineering Corporation Ltd. was established in 1958.

iv) The bulk of the machinery required for the modernization of the jute industry in the preparatory and spinning departments were being manufactured within the country. (3.3.24)

v) Production of a growing number of new industrial items like milling machines and other types of machine tools, tractors, industrial explosives, etc. started during II 5YP. (3.3.25)

vi) The value of ungraded machine tools produced by small units rose from Rs 1.3 Cr in 1956 to Rs. 4.0 Cr in 1960. (3.25.45)

Achievements in III 5YP
Mining and Allied Machinery Corporation Ltd was set up in Durgapur in **1964** to manufacture mining equipment.
HMT Bearings Ltd was incorporated in **1964 in Hyderabad** to produce ball and roller bearings.
The **Central Manufacturing Technology Institute** was established in **1965** with support from the then Czechoslovakian government to develop advance manufacturing technologies for the Indian industry.
Bharat Heavy Plate and Vessels Ltd. was incorporated on 25.06.**1966** for manufacturing various types of pressure vessels, columns, heat exchangers, storage vessels, spheres etc. for processing industries in core sectors like fertilizers, petrochemicals, refineries, chemical, Nuclear, Space and other industries.

Machine Building in Private Sector -
A.V.B. (Associated Cement-Vickers-Babcock Wilcox) plant was established at Durgapur for the manufacture of equipment for the cement industry and high-pressure boilers. (3.26.55)

Achievements in IV 5YP
HMT—printing machines unit was established in **1972** in Kalamassery.

Achievements in V 5YP
By mid 1970s, the **share of indigenously produced capital equipment** in the total supply of machinery went above **80%.** (9.5.129)
Hindustan Machine Tools diversified to manufacture lamp machinery, printing machinery, tractors and watches.
Indian Dairy Machinery Company Ltd - IDMC Ltd. was set up in **1978** to manufacture dairy components and equipment and to reduce the dependence of the domestic dairy industry on the import of a large number of diverse dairy equipment.

Status in 2000-01
The share of HMT in the machine tools sector was **35%.** (10.7.1.99)

Machine Building Industry in 2001-02
Indian industrial machinery manufacturers had the capability to manufacture a variety of equipment of stringent specifications required for the chemical industry, ferrous, non-ferrous metal manufacturing industries, etc. (10.7.1.96)

With the abolition of quantitative restrictions on import of capital goods since 1991, the tendency to import in segments like textiles, electrical machinery, automobile, auto-ancillary and leather products became very high. The share of imported capital goods in these segments varied in the range of 20-50%. (10.7.1.95)

The **textile machinery** manufacturing industries were **exporting 15%** of the annual production to over 50 countries. (10.7.1.162)

Machine Building Industry in 2005-06

The industry consisted of 450 manufacturing units including 33% in the organized sector. (11.7.1.153)

Production of Mining & construction equipment in 2003-04, 2004-05 and 2005-06 in value terms were Rs. 4150 Cr, Rs. 4750 Cr and Rs. 6300 Cr. respectively.

Production of Process plant equipment in 2003-04, 2004-05 and 2005-06 in value terms were Rs. 2850 Cr, Rs. 3560 Cr and Rs. 5000 Cr. respectively.

Textile Machinery Industry in 2005-06

The textile machinery industry had an installed capacity of Rs 3800 Cr. The industry was unable to cope with the demand of domestic textile and clothing units. In 2007, 80% of the requirement was being imported. The liberal policy of import of second-hand textile machinery had affected the indigenous industry. (11.7.1.155)

Mining and Construction Equipment Sector

The mining and construction equipment industry was dominated by a few large manufacturers in each product segment. **Bharat Earth Movers Ltd** supplied to nearly **half of the total market.** The domestic demand increased from Rs 6300 crore in 2004–05 to Rs 8400 crore in 2006–07. (11.7.1.157)

Machine Tools Industry in 2011-12

There were 8–10 large companies (turnover above Rs. 100 Cr), 10–15 medium companies (50–100 Cr) and rest were small. HEC, HMT, Bharat Pumps and Compressors Ltd were 3 CPSEs in the machine building sector. **New investments were few, due to low returns on investments.** (12. Annex. 13.2. 13)

About 70% of India's requirement of machine tools was met through imports in 2011-12. The capacity utilization of public sector units' manufacturing plant machineries was about 68% in 2011-12.

Capacities in PSUs such as HMT and HEC were not optimally utilized. It was required to create modern state of the art capacities and realize full potential of PSUs' capacities. (12. Annex. 13.2-14)

Building high class modern capacities in the private sector and revisiting the existing policies to protect and promote selected capital goods industries were considered essential. (12. Annex. 13.2-9)

Need for acquiring technology by tier-2 suppliers of priority sectors (like HAL) and adopting 'offset policy' as one of the means to boost domestic content in the total equipment imported (like Rafale) were emphasized. A review of the current FDI policy from the point of view of transfer of technology as well as considerations of national security were also recommended. This was proposed to be achieved by giving preference to joint ventures instead of 100% foreign-owned companies. (12. Annex. 13.2-10)

Earth Moving & Mining Equipment Sector in 2011-12

Planned investment of more than US$1 trillion in earth moving and mining equipment as well as the construction equipment infrastructure was expected to drive the construction industry to grow at 16–17% CAGR over the next 10 years. (12. Annex. 13.2-17)

Products manufactured in India, by assembly plants of the MNC's, were meeting the global standards. The domestic content was nearly 35% in standard equipment whereas the same was about 78% in high technology equipment (12. Annex. 13.2-18)

The capability of Bharat Earth Movers Ltd. needed to be, inter alia, strengthened by providing support for transfer of technology. (12. Annex. 13.2-19)

Graph - 11.1 Target and Production of Plant Machineries

Graph - 11.2 Target and Production of Plant Machineries

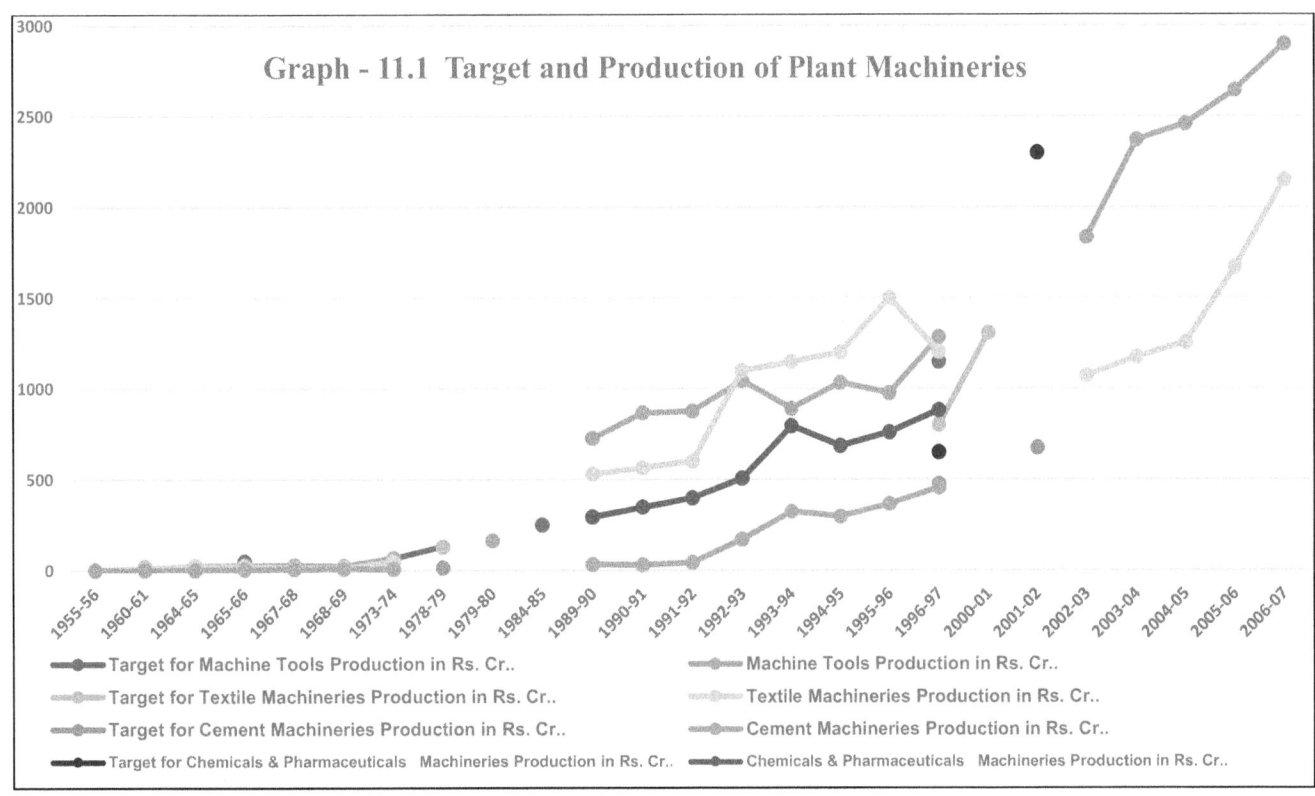

Contribution To Manufacturing GDP

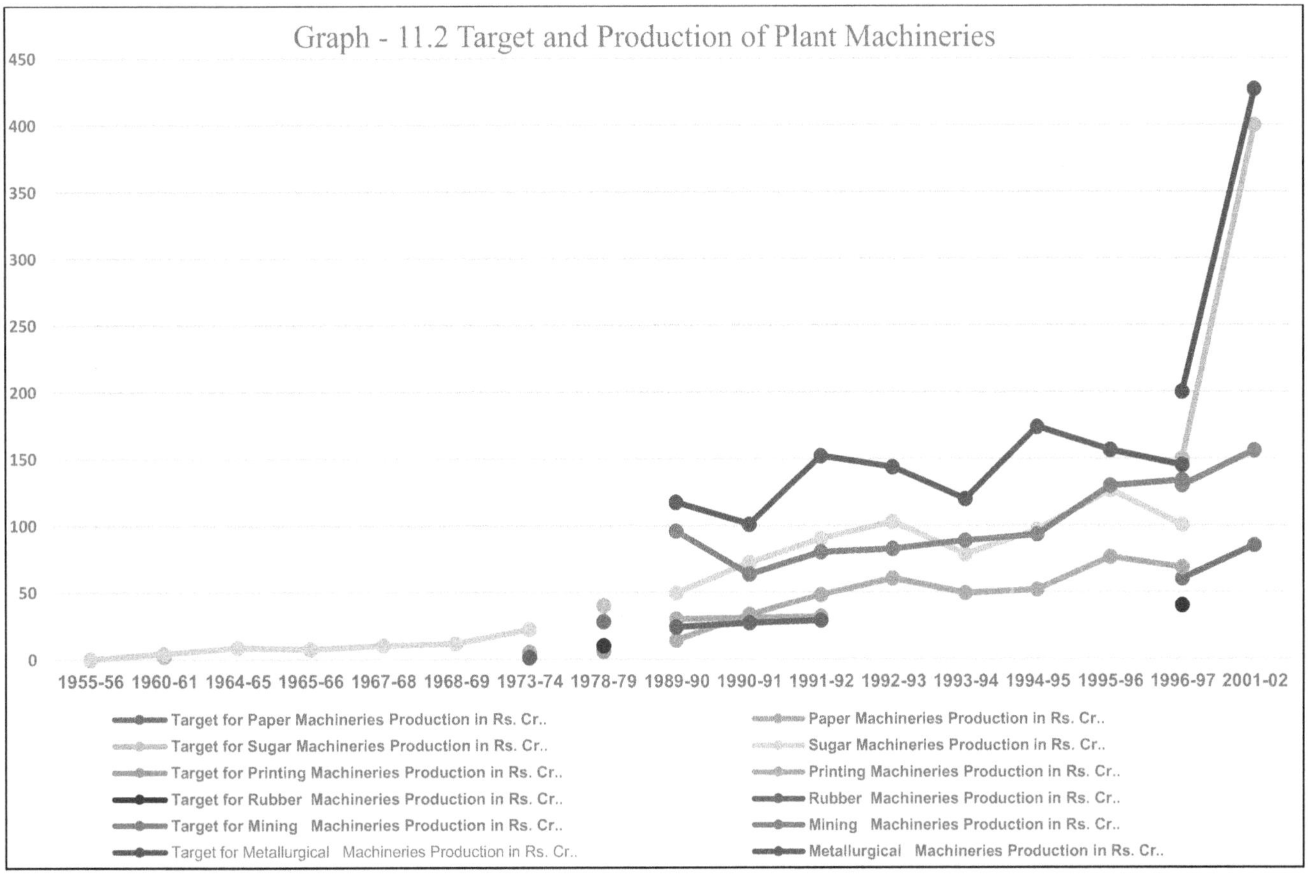

Machinery and equipment Industry contributed 11.1% to manufacturing GDP in 2009-10. (12. Table 13.8)

Public Sector Enterprises Engaged in Production of Machineries for Steel Plants, Fertilizer Plants, Petrochemical Plants, Refineries, Sugar Mills, Tea & Jute Industries

Praga Tools Ltd.

Praga Tools Ltd. - PTL was incorporated on 28.05.1943 in the private sector. Government of India acquired controlling interest in PTL in **1959** to manufacture machine tools of international quality at reasonable cost.

PTL was manufacturing of machine tools / accessories and CNC machining centres in Secunderabad and Hyderabad units.

HMT Ltd. took over PTL as one of its subsidiaries in 1986. PTL has gained immense expertise in supplying & trading of Machine tools, thread rolling machinery, surface grinding machine etc.

HMT Ltd.- Food Processing Machineries, Machine Tools

HMT was incorporated on 7.2.**1953** to manufacture agricultural machineries like Tractors. HMT Tractors Ltd commenced operations in 1971 in technical collaboration with Zetor / Motokov, Czechoslovakia Republic.

HMT had 6 Machine Tools divisions started in 1953 in Bengaluru, 1961 in Bengaluru, 1963 in Pinjore, 1965 in Kalamassery, 1967 in Hyderabad and 1975 in Ajmer; 1 Precision Machinery Division in Bengaluru and 1 CNC Systems Division started in 1986 in Bengaluru; 1 Die Casting Division started in 1971 in Bengaluru; 1 Printing machinery Division started in 1972 in Kalamassery; 5 Watch Factories started in 1962 in Bengaluru, 1972 in Bengaluru, 1975 in Srinagar, 1978 in Tumkur and 1982 in Ranibagh; 1 Quartz Analog Watches unit started in 1981 in Bengaluru and 1 specialized Watchcase division in Bengaluru; 1 HMT Bearings division started in 1981 in Hyderabad; 1 Stepper Motor division started in Tumkur in 1983; 1 Ball Screw division started in Bengaluru in 1985 and 1 Central Re-conditioning division started in Bengaluru in 1991.

Food Processing Unit at Aurangabad Maharashtra had technical collaboration with Fortschritte Land Machinen, East Germany for various dairy machineries from 1980 to 1991.

The product ranges are Continuous Butter Making Machines, Milk Pasteurizers, Cream Separators, Ghee Clarifier, Centrifugal Pumps, Homogenizers, Plant heat exchangers for dairy and non-dairy applications, oil purification and clarification system and chillers. The installed capacity for food processing machineries was 296 machines. Auxiliary Business Division at Bengaluru caters to a range of activities like assembly of watches.

HMT was in the manufacturing and selling of tractors, Food Processing Machines through (2 manufacturing and 2 service divisions at) Pinjore, Mohali, Hyderabad and Aurangabad units.

HMT had 6 **subsidiaries** namely HMT Machine Tools, HMT watches, HMT Chinar Watches, HMT (International), HMT Bearing and Praga Tools Ltd.

HMT had 2 financial **joint ventures** namely SUDMO HMT Process Engineers (I) Ltd. and Nigeria Machine Tools Ltd.

HMT was awarded with "Indy wood Built in India Excellence Award" in the Category "Public Sector Units – Precision Engineering" on 4.12.2017.

The gross turnover of HMT Ltd. in 2022-23 was Rs. 51.59 Cr. HMT undertook product upgradation, manufacturing collaborations and turnkey projects of dairy machineries.

During 2022-23, HMT introduced Surface Wheel Lathe, Twin Head CNC grinding machine (developed by Ajmer Unit), 3 Piece manipulator, Spent Fuel Chopper (to dispose the spent fuel of nuclear plant) etc. HMT supplied a 3 Piece Robo Manipulator to BARC for use in nuclear plants. HMT also launched a Mini Homogenizer and Series of Watches.

National Industrial Development Corp.

National Industrial Development Corp. - NIDC was incorporated on 20.10.**1954** to achieve a balanced development of industries in the private and public sectors, to establish a new Aluminium plant and manufacture of heavy equipment for earth moving, mining etc. and rolls and rolling mill equipment required in ferrous and non-ferrous industries.

It built up industrial schemes of its own or collaborated with the private industry. It established a consultancy for private and public sectors. It also rendered assistance for the modernization of industries. NIDC provided assistance to cotton, jute, and sugar industries for modernization.

Since 1963, the NIDC ceased to be a financing institution for private industry.
In 1970 it rendered consultancy services worth Rs. 69 lakhs for meeting the country's industrialization requirements.

NIDC formulated projects for setting up new Industries and developing new lines of production, which according to central government would contribute to industrial development of the country.
NIDC was phenomenal in the establishment of primary producing units in the public sector in India.
NIDC also rendered services to global organizations such as UNICEF, World Bank, USAID, etc.

Heavy Engineering Corp. Ltd. - Machinery for Iron & Steel Industry

Heavy Engineering Corp. Ltd. - HEC was incorporated on 13.12.**1958** to achieve self-reliance in manufacturing of machinery for Iron and Steel Industry and other core sector industries and supply spares & services for Steel, Mining, Coal, Railways and other strategic sectors.

HEC, Ranchi is manufacturing
(i) medium heavy castings, forgings, forged rolls and crankshafts (at Foundry Forge Plant),
(ii) equipment like Coke Oven, Rolling Mills, Sintering Plants, Blast Furnaces, Converters, EOT Cranes, Excavators, Draglines, OB Drills and Crushers (at Heavy Machine Building Plant),
(iii) conventional and CNC heavy machine tools and Rail Machine Tools (at Heavy Machine Tools Plant), and undertaking
(iv) consultancy and turnkey projects in steel and mining sectors (at Heavy Machine Building Plant),
(v) Turnkey jobs in Bulk Material Handling, low temperature Carbonization plants, Coal handling plants, Coal Washeries, sintering plants, Continuous Casting Plants and Raw Material handling system, etc. (by Turnkey Project Division).

HEC was having **80% share** in **Crushing and Grinding Machines** market.

Installed Capacities - HEC had installed capacities of 29088 Tons, 3200 Tons, 9831.17 Tons, 2000 Tons, 2000 Tons and 6946.9 Tons for steel castings, forgings, rolls, mining spares, steel plant spares and EOT cranes respectively in 2008-09.

R&D wing of Machine Tools Division developed Heavy Duty Centre Lathe, CNC Deep Hole Boring Machine and CNC Double Column Vertical Turning and Boring machine.
R&D wing of Heavy Machine Building Plant developed Basic Oxygen Furnace Shop for Neelachal Ispat Nigam Ltd., 120 Ton Hot Metal Charging Ladle, 110T Steel teeming Ladle, 20M3 fabricated Scrap Box, 6000T Wagon Pusher machine for handling 58 loaded railway wagons, Cranes of various capacity, etc.

HEC also developed special forgings for Nuclear Sector.

HEC entered into collaboration with Hegenscheidt of Germany and Schenck Process for manufacture of new generation railway machine tools and Coal Washeries respectively.

The **installed capacity** of HEC in 2019-20 was 1950 ton for 24/96 dragline, 4067 ton for 5/10 cu. M. rope shovel, 6947 ton for EOT cranes, 9831 ton for forging and forged rolls, 1335 ton for machine tools and accessories, 16384 tons for medium and heavy steel casting, 2000 tons for mining spares and 2000 tons for steel plant components.

The modernization cum revival plan of HEC was sent to Ministry of Heavy Industries for approval on 17.10.2017 and 06.05.2020.

HEC installed a new Coal Handling plant in Bhilai Steel Plant and executed Coal Handling Plants for SECL and NCL and Madhuband Coal Washery project for BCCL during 2022-23.

The gross turnover in 2022-23 was Rs. 92.44 Cr.

Weighbird India Ltd

Weighbird India Ltd was incorporated on 01.06.**1962**. It was manufacturing (general purpose machinery & equipment) from last 61 years and currently, company operations are under liquidation.

Vignyan Industries Ltd. - – Ferrous, Steel and Stainless-Steel Castings, Tools

Vignyan Industries Ltd. - VIL was incorporated on 25.09.**1963** as private limited company with Polish collaboration to manufacture steel casting for railway, rolling mills, heavy engineering, construction, infrastructure industries and steel sectors.

The company became 'sick' in 1974. Government of Karnataka took over its management and handed over to Bharat Earth Movers Ltd. VIL was rehabilitated with the assistance of financial institutions and became a subsidiary of BEML in October 1984 and deemed government company in 1975.

VIL was producing all kind of **tools,** ferrous and stainless steel castings for mining and construction, rail and metro, Defence, aerospace, engineering and infrastructure industries in Tarikere (Karnataka) unit.
The installed capacity increased to 10000 MT during 2009-10 from 4000 MT in 2008-09.
VIL supplied 100 Tons of Ballast Castings of U-2 grade to Mishra Dhatu Nigam Ltd during 2016-17.

VIL is under liquidation as on 31.03.2023.

Mining and Allied Machinery Corporation Ltd

Mining and Allied Machinery Corporation Ltd – MAMC was set up in Durgapur, West Bengal, in 1964 to manufacture mining equipment.

MAMC manufactured specialized wrenches, winders and haulages in collaboration with Dowty Mining of the UK and exported them to the former USSR. It also manufactured mining drills and other equipment in collaboration with Poland. MAMC was a major supplier of mining equipment including scrapper-chain conveyors. MAMC was manufacturing heavy industrial materials required for coal mining, defence materials, submarine equipment, etc.

MAMC ceased to be a major supplier of mining equipment by 1998-99, with only a hundredth of its installed capacity of scrapper-chain conveyors, the company's product of pride, was operational. In 1998, the Government offered a voluntary separation scheme. The assembly line was closed on 1.1.2002.

In 2010, BEML acquired MAMC.

Central Manufacturing Technology Institute

Central Manufacturing Technology Institute - CMTI was established in **1965** with support from the then Czechoslovakian government to develop and advance manufacturing technologies for the Indian industry by leveraging its advanced facilities.

CMTI over the last 5 decades developed special purpose machines, inspection systems, test rigs for testing of products, tooling, complex machined parts for public and private sectors, etc.

CMTI has supported and served the manufacturing sector by focusing on Nanotechnology, Precision engineering, Metrology (Micro and Nano), Additive Manufacturing, Mechatronics, Vision and Image processing, Digital Design and Human Resource Development (creating 'Industry Ready' engineers).

Bharat Heavy Plate & Vessels Ltd. – Equipment for Fertilizers, Petrochemicals, Refineries

Bharat Heavy Plate & Vessels Ltd. - BHPV was incorporated in **1966** to fabricate equipment required for processing industries in fertilizers, petrochemicals, refineries, chemical, Nuclear, Space and other sectors.

BHPV is manufacturing process plants, cryogenics and combustion systems in Visakhapatnam unit. BHPV diversified into Bubbling Fluidized Bed Combustion & Heat Recovery Steam Generating Boilers.

BHPV had an **installed capacity** of 23210 Tons for manufacture of process plant equipment, cryogenics and combustion systems.
HPVP Vizag achieved highest ever order booking in 2022-23 for legacy products, since BHEL's taking over the plant in 2013.

Bharat Pumps & Compressors Ltd. – For Oil & Natural Gas, Petrochemicals, Refineries, etc.

Bharat Pumps & Compressors Ltd. - BPCL was incorporated on 1.1.**1970** to provide quality products and services to core sectors like Oil and Natural Gas, Petrochemicals, Refineries, Nuclear and Thermal Power Plants, Fertilizers, other process downstream industries and public transport services.

BPCL was manufacturing centrifugal pumps, reciprocating pumps and compressors, sucker rod pumps, cementing units and their spares for oil exploration companies, and varieties of industrial, high pressure seamless gas cylinders including CNG cylinders and cascades in Allahabad unit.

Installed capacity was 283 Pumps, 23 Compressors and 48000 Gas Cylinders in 2008-09.
During 2010-11, BPCL signed an agreement with GE Oil & Gas, Italy for manufacturing higher range of Centrifugal Pumps.
BPCL had a **market share of 90% for centrifugal pumps** in 2011-12.

BPCL had invested nearly Rs. 100 crores in purchase of new machines and had projected business of Rs. 1600 crores but this target was never achieved and as a result, company incurred loss.

Government announced the liquidation of BPCL on 14.01.2021. BPCL was undergoing process of closure on 31.03.2023.

Richardson and Cruddas (1972) Ltd. – Sugar Plant Machineries, Rubber Machineries

Richardson and Cruddas (1972) Ltd. - R&C was incorporated on 15.03.**1973** to take over the assets and liabilities of the old engineering company R&C (originally set up in 1858). R&C took up manufacture of capital infrastructure engineering products for steel, oil and natural gas, fertilizer, infrastructure, power, transportation sectors, sugar plant machineries, etc.

R&C is manufacturing medium and heavy structural including Switch Expansion Joints, Railway Points & Crossings, Structure for War Ships like Hull, Seats, boiler drums, Sub Sea templates and Submarine parts, Sugar Plants Equipment & Rubber Machineries, Offshore Platforms & On shore drilling rigs, etc. in Mumbai in Mulund (West) and Byculla, Nagpur and Chennai units.

Despite increase in turnover due to higher production of fabrications, the company incurred heavy loss during 2007-08 mainly due to high input cost, interest burden and prior period adjustments.

Installed Capacity of R&C was 28300 Tons of fabrications, 2960 Tons of plant equipment and 20000 Nos. of Hand Pump in 2008-09.

BIFR order of 23.06.11 for change of management was expected to hand over assets of more than Rs 10000 Cr. to highest private bidder Oberoi Construction Ltd for Rs 1098 Cr.

The gross turnover of R&C in 2022-23 was Rs. 14.8 Cr.

Braithwaite and Co. Ltd. – Wagons, Bogies, LPG Bullets, Jute Machines, etc.

Braithwaite and Co. Ltd. - BCL was incorporated on 1.12.**1976** by acquisition of Braithwaite and Company (India) Ltd. BCL became a subsidiary of Bharat Bhari Udyog Nigam Ltd. in 1986.

BCL is manufacturing railway engineering items viz. freight Wagons, Bogies, etc. for Indian Railways in Clive Works and Victoria Works in Kolkata and Angus Works at Bhadreswar, WB.
Angus Works is manufacturing wagons for Railway and Non-Railway Sectors, Steel Castings like Couplers, Bogies, Cranes (erection, revamping, maintenance, supply of spares), Dished end, Barrel, LPG Bullets, Jute Carding Machines etc.,
Clive and Victoria Works' are manufacturing Wagons for Railway and Non-Railway sectors, Structural and LPG Bullets.

BCL had an installed capacity of 1200 wagons, 1800 bogies, 1000 couplers and 3500 Tons of steel castings in 2008-09.

All the units are engaged in refurbishing and repairing wagons for Indian Railways starting from 2015-16.

BCL developed 25 Tons Axle Load BOXNS wagon for dedicated freight corridor system and Milk Tank Van conforming to upgraded design of RITES.

During 2022-23, Braithwaite ventured into redevelopment of railway stations and installation of solar power projects. BCL developed container flat wagon (Spine car) and self-contained unloading system of EUR rakes. Gross turnover was Rs. 1043.3 Cr.

Indian Dairy Machinery Company Limited – Refer Ch. 4

Bharat Brakes & Valves Ltd. – Locomotives for Railways

Bharat Brakes & Valves Ltd. - BBVL was incorporated on 22.07.**1978.**

BBVL was manufacturing rail locomotives powered from an external source of electricity or by electric accumulators or by compression ignition engines or other means (like gas turbine, steam engines etc.), diesel-electric locomotives, etc. from last 45 years.
BBVL was making vacuum brakes, slack adjusters for wagons and coaches and vacuum exhausters for locomotives.

Vajpayee cabinet decided to close BBVL in April 2003. Currently, company operations are under liquidation.

Bharat Wagon & Engineering Co. Ltd. – Wagons, Sugar Mill Machinery, LPG Cylinders

Bharat Wagon & Engineering Co. Ltd. - BWEL was incorporated on 04.12.**1978** to take over the assets and interests of the erstwhile Arthur Butter & Co. Muzaffarpur and Britannica Engineering Works, Mokama.

BWEL was manufacturing rolling stock - open / covered wagons of all types and special purpose wagons for Railways, sugar mill machinery, fuel storage tanks, miscellaneous project equipment, turnkey projects and steel fabrication in Mokama and Muzaffarpur units.

The Muzaffarpur unit stopped production of LPG cylinder, fuel storage tanks.

BWEL had a product installed capacity of 880 vehicle units for wagons in 2008-09.

BWEL contributed about 5% of the national wagon production.

The Cabinet Committee on Economic Affairs approved the closure of the BWEL on 23-08-2017. BWEL stands dissolved w.e.f. 05.07.2022.

Lagan Jute Machinery Company

Lagan Jute Machinery Company - LJMC was set up in **1955** by James Mackie & Sons, Belfast, Northern Ireland for manufacturing jute machinery. It was taken over by Government of India in 1978.

In 1987, LJMC became a subsidiary of Bharat Bhari Udyog Nigam Ltd.

High quality and complex machines supplied by LJMC are running satisfactorily in the industry for over 60 years in India, Bangladesh, Ethiopia, Vietnam, Cuba, Kenya, Egypt, Myanmar, Republic of Mali and Nepal.

LJMC was sold off by Vajpayee government in June 2000 for Rs. 2.53 Cr.

Andrew Yule & Company Ltd. – Transformers, Switch Gears, Blowers, Tea Machinery

Andrew Yule & Company Ltd. - AYCL was incorporated on 26.05.1919 in the private sector. With the abolition of managing agency system, AYCL lost its traditional business and GOI acquired AYCL in **1979**.

Engineering division in Kalyani, WB, produces industrial fans and blowers, air pollution control equipment, water treatment plants, heavy machinery, and undertakes engineering turnkey contracts for installation / commissioning of electrical equipment.

The electrical division produces power and distribution transformers, high voltage switching gear, low voltage control gear, flame proof switch gear, voltage regulators and rectifiers, plant communication, and fire alarm and detection systems. The switchgear and electrical systems group is located in Kolkata, while the transformer and switchgear unit is located in Chennai.

AYCL is manufacturing tea machinery, water pollution control equipment, electro-magnetic contactors, moulded case circuit breakers, pole mounted sectionalizer / capacitor switch, etc.

AYCL has 3 subsidiary companies Hooghly Printing Co. Ltd., Yule Engineering Co. Ltd. and Yule Electrical Co. Ltd and one financial joint venture namely Phoenix Yule Ltd. at West Bengal.

Tea division of the company has 15 Tea Estates. Of which 10 are located in Assam, 4 in Dooars and 1 in Darjeeling.

R & D Electrical division developed VCBs of different voltage and current grades.

Gross turnover of AYCL in 2022-23 was Rs. 374.04 Cr.

Bharat Process and Mechanical Engineers Ltd – Refer Ch. 8.

HMT Machine Tools Ltd. – Machine Tools

HMT Machine Tools Ltd. - HMTL was incorporated on 9.8.**1999** as a subsidiary of HMT Ltd. as a part of restructuring plan of HMT, to provide manufacturing solutions and to manufacture machine tools.

HMTL is manufacturing machine tools, Industrial machinery, peripherals etc., providing services in reconditioning and refurbishing of machines, project consultancy etc. and servicing of machines, through its 9 units at Bangalore, Pinjore, Kalamassery, Hyderabad and Ajmer.

The market share of HMTL products fell from 35% in 2002-03 to 19% in 2004-05.
Product installed capacity of HMTL were 1297 Nos. of Machine tools & Printing machines and 301 CNC systems in 2008-09.
Developed 4-Guideway Lathe M/C in 2019-20.
Developed CNC Heavy duty Cylindrical Grinding Machine and CNC Double Column Vertical Turning Lathe.
HMT Machine Tools Ltd. developed several import substitutions at almost half the price of imported machines and achieved sales of Rs. 142.24 Cr in 2022-23.

HMT Bearings Ltd.

HMT Bearings Ltd. - HBL was set up on 24.10.**1964** as Indo Nippon Precision Bearings Ltd to produce Taper Roller, Cylindrical Roller and Ball Bearings. As the project could not take off. Andhra Pradesh Industrial Development Corporation implemented the project in 1970 in collaboration with M/s Koyo Seiko Co Ltd, Japan.

The production started in 1971 with an installed capacity of 1.1 million nos. in Hyderabad unit.
These bearings are manufactured with inner diameter from 20mm to outer diameter of 240mm for use in tractors, automobiles etc.
The company was taken over by HMT Ltd. in the year 1981.
Installed Capacity of HBL was 3.1 million bearings in 2008-09.

The cabinet committee an Economic Affairs proposed for closure of HBL on 29.12.2014 and 05.01.2016. HBL was dissolved on 29.06.2022.

Public Sector Enterprises Engaged in Production of Heavy Engineering Equipment

Burn Standard Co. Ltd. - Largest Wagon Builder

Burn Standard Co. Ltd. - BSCL was incorporated on 1.12.**1976** to take over the assets of nationalized private company Burn and Co. Ltd and Indian Standard Wagon Ltd.

BSCL was manufacturing basic Magnesia Carbon Bricks and Bulk Refractories for steel plant convertor operations at Salem Refractory.
The Howrah works was manufacturing railway freight wagons, couplers, bogies, knuckles, yokes and special alloy cast iron casting.
Burnpur works was manufacturing railway freight wagons, bottom discharge wagons, etc.
The Central Project Division was undertaking turnkey projects for Material and Ash Handling equipment of power plants.

BSCL had 2 subsidiaries namely Bharat Brakes and Valves Ltd. and RBL Ltd. which remained closed since 31.7.2003. The loss was mainly on account of high interest burden of about Rs. 161.87 Cr.

BSCL had installed capacity of 2100 vehicle units of wagons, 2400 bogies, 2400 couplers and 61292 Tons of refractories in 2008-09.

Salem Refractory unit was transferred to SAIL with effect from 15.9.2010.

Bulk production of stainless-steel wagon started in 2010-11.
During 2013-14, BSCL was the **largest wagons builder in India**.

On 4.04.2018, Cabinet approved closure of loss-making BSCL. BSCL stands dissolved w.e.f. 26.09.2022.

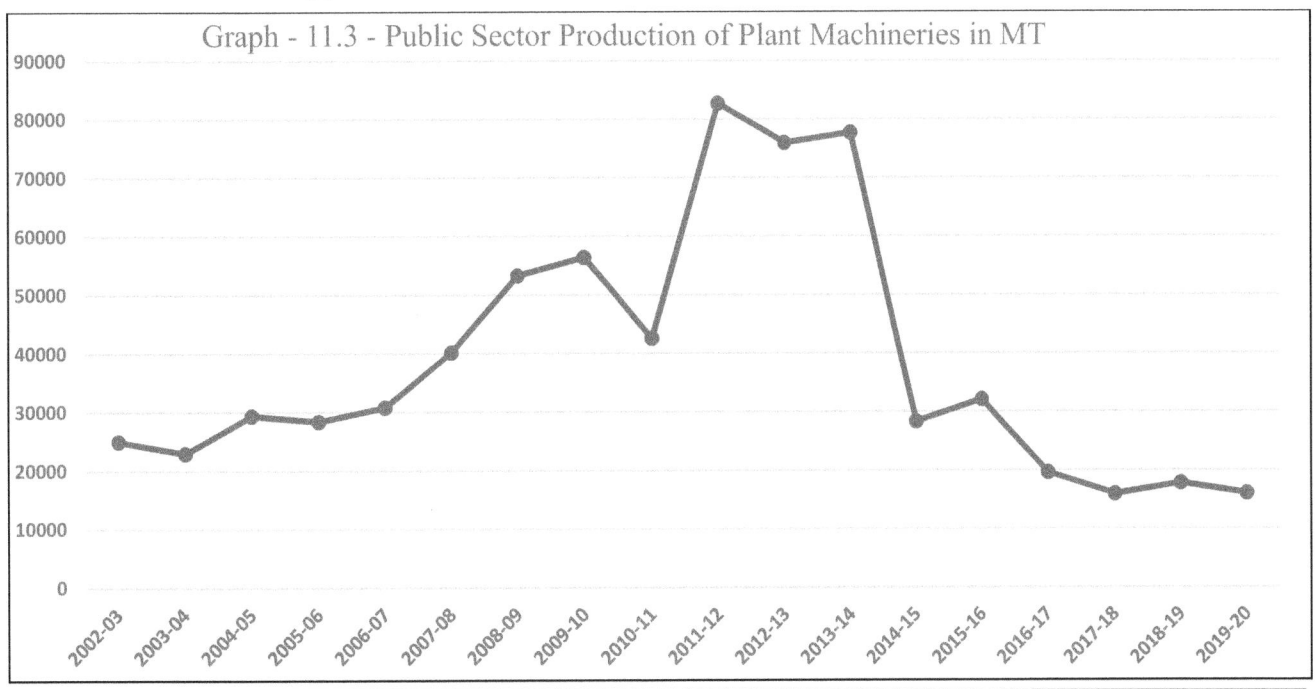

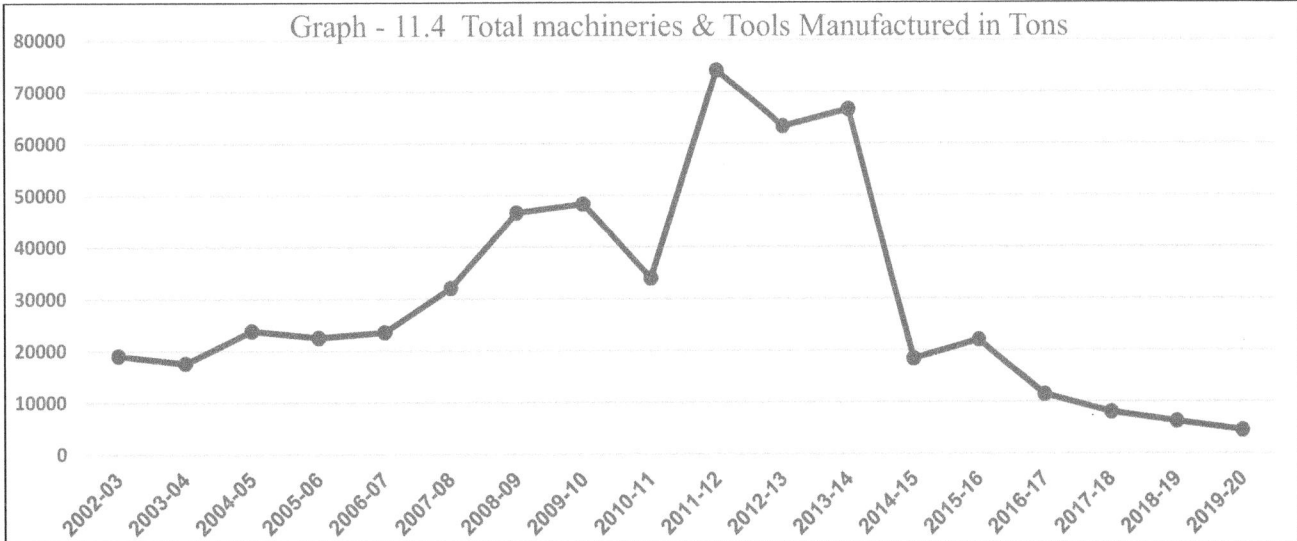

Production of BHPV not included for 2005-06, 2006-07, 2007-08 and 2014-15 onwards. HEC EOT Crane Production not included in 2005-06. Richardson Cruddas Production not included for 2010-11 and Braithwaite Production not included in 2014-15 and drastically reduced thereafter. The fall in production curve is due to these missing production figures.

Summary

Indian industrial machinery manufacturers attained the capability to manufacture a variety of equipment of stringent specifications required for the chemical industry, ferrous, non-ferrous metal manufacturing industries, etc. in 2001-02.

The production of all plant machineries has been given in terms of value in Rs. Cr., whereas the production of plant machineries by public sector units have been given in Tons or number of machines. Hence share of public sector units to total production could not be given.

However, the steady rise in production of plant machineries can be seen up to 2013-14.

Private Sector Participants

Machine building companies

Forbes and Company Ltd. 1767, Indian Sugar and General Engineering Corp. / ISGEC Heavy Engineering Ltd. – 1946, Bosch Ltd (Motor Industries Company Ltd.) – 1951, ELECON Engineering Co Ltd – 1951, ELGI Equipments Ltd – 1960, UTMAL Utkal Machinery Ltd / Larsen & Toubro Heavy Engineering Works – 1960, Bharat Forge – 1961, Cummins India Ltd – 1962, Lakshmi Machine Works Ltd – 1962, Schaeffler India / FAG Bearings India Ltd – 1962, Dynamatic Technologies Ltd. – 1973, Polymechplast Machines Ltd – 1978, BMD Foundry Machinery / DISA India Ltd. – 1984, Honda India Power Products Ltd. – 1985,

Birmingham Thermotech Ltd – 1995, Texmaco Rail & Engineering Ltd - 1998.

12: GROWTH IN PRODUCTION OF PETROLEUM AND PETROCHEMICALS PRODUCTS

Petroleum as Vital Raw Material

Furnace Oil, Low Sulphur Heavy Stock and Light Diesel Oil are required for power, fertilizer, and general trade. Initially the natural gas was used as feedstock in the production of fertilizers, but gas was then used for power generation, industrial applications and later in the transport sector. Naphtha and fuel oil were required for the manufacture of nitrogenous fertilizers, high-speed diesel oil for road transport and LDO for agricultural development programs.

Petrochemicals is an 'enabler' industry playing a vital role in agriculture, infrastructure, healthcare, textile, consumer goods and packaging. The Indian petrochemical industry consisted of building blocks, commodity polymers, performance plastics, synthetic fibre, synthetic rubber, surfactants, and downstream plastic processing industry. (12. Annex.13.2 - 64)

Targeted Growth for Production of Petroleum and Petrochemical Products

Petroleum products required for many industries like power, fertilizer, petrochemical industries, refineries, sponge iron, steel plants, transport sector, domestic cooking gas, etc., were forecasted by the government for the last financial year of each 5-year plan and the target petroleum and petrochemical products production required, refining capacity required to be developed, etc. for the various 5-year plans were set.

Production targets were set considering contribution from private sector and joint ventures

The target set, capacity built up and actual production achieved at the end of each 5-year plan and some other periods are given in Tables – 11.1A, 1B and 11.2 and Graph – 11.1

Exploration of Petroleum Deposits

Geological Survey of India started geophysical surveys in Cambay area in 1948.

During II 5YP
Valuable oil and natural gas resources were found in Naharkatia in Assam and Cambay-Ankleshwar area in Gujarat. Exploration started in Jaisalmer, Rajasthan during I 5YP. (3.3.29, 3.24.38 and 3.27.8)
Government contributed one-fourth of the expenditure incurred on Standard Vacuum Oil Company's exploration in West Bengal basin. (3.27.9)
Moran oil field was discovered by Assam Oil Company in **1956**.

Oil and Natural Gas Commission was set up on 14.08.**1956**. It undertook geological surveys, geophysical investigations and exploratory drilling for oil in Punjab, Cambay and Brahmaputra and Ganga valleys. During exploration in Cambay and Ankleshwar, Oil and/or gas was struck in many of the wells. (3.27.10)

Oil India Ltd. - OIL was formed in **1959** to undertake intensive exploration in Upper Assam. ONGC was given the responsibility of covering the rest of the country.
Oil struck at Ankleshwar in Gujarat and Rudrasagar in Assam in **1960**.
India's first deviated well NHK122 was drilled by OIL in **1963** and ONGC started offshore seismic surveys in Gulf of Cambay.

Estimates made in 1965-66
Initial recoverable petroleum reserves of about 172 Mts were established.

Oil discovered in Geleki by ONGC in **1968**.

During IV 5YP (1969-74)
India's first offshore well spudded in Gulf of Cambay in **1970**.
ONGC started offshore drilling at Aliabet and in Bombay offshore area. Drillship Sagar Samrat struck oil in Bombay High in **1974**. Oil and gas fields like North Bassein, South Bassein, South Tapti, B-37, B-38, etc. were discovered.

During V 5YP (1975-80)
Oil India discovered oil at Kharasin in Arunachal Pradesh.
Detailed offshore seismic surveys were conducted over a large part of the continental shelf. Exploratory drilling was done by ONGC in the Bombay offshore area, off the Godavari basin, Kerala coast and Mangalore coast. Oil and gas were discovered in the Godavari basin, Ratnagiri-9 and 12 structures.

Estimates made in 1977-78
By 1-1-1978, the total initial recoverable reserves had increased to 452 Mts. (6.15.71)
Oil India conducted offshore exploration in Mahanadi delta.
By 1979-80, ONGC and OIL had together drilled over 3100 wells totaling 4.9 million meters and the inventory of geological reserves of oil reached over 2.3 billion tons. (6.15.72)

Estimates made in January 1980 -
As on 1.01.1980, the definite balance net recoverable reserves of oil were 360 Mts and reserves of gas was 352 billion cu-meters. (6.15.7)

Assessment made in 1984
The prognosticated geological resources of hydrocarbons were estimated at about 17 Bts, with 63 % offshore, 37 % on land and 50% of prognosticated resources in the form of natural gas. The established geological reserves were only 4 Bts. of hydrocarbons and about 1 Bt of natural gas. (7.6.12)

During VI Plan
First well spudded in Godavari offshore in **1981**.
ONGC struck Gas at Razole in AP and Ghotaru in Rajasthan in **1983-84**.
Oil struck in Kutch offshore, Godavari offshore and Changmai in Assam in **1984-85**.

During VII 5YP
ONGC struck oil in Tapti offshore area and Namti structure (Assam) in **1986-87**.
Commercial gas was found in Rajasthan (by OIL) and Nada in Gujarat in **1988-89**.
South Heera field discovered in Mumbai offshore in 1989-90.

Assessment in 1991-92
Geological reserves of hydrocarbons established were 5.32 Bts. (8.v2.8.8.1)

During VIII 5YP
2D and 3D Seismic surveys were done over (145604 Seismic Line Km on shore and 109682 SLK off shore) and (4788 Seismic Square kms on shore and 79846 SSK off shore) respectively. (9.6.244)
Exploratory and development drilling of 2883 and 2718 thousand meters respectively were done. (9.6.246)

Assessment in 1996-97
The prognosticated and established geological resources of hydrocarbons were 21.31 Bts and 5.32 Bts respectively. (9.6.6)

Assessment in 2006
The reserve accretion during X Plan was 1652.92 Mts, excluding private / joint venture share. (11.10.122)

Coal India Ltd and ONGC were already implementing 2 Coal Bed Methane projects. (11.10.9)
The oil shale reserves were estimated at 100 billion barrels. (11.10.111)

During XI 5YP

The balance recoverable reserve position of Oil + Oil Equivalent Gas increased from 1,847 Mts on 1.04.2007 to 2015 Mts on 1.04.2011. (12.14.151)
The prognosticated and established CBM resources were 92 trillion Cubic Feet and 8.92 TCF respectively in 2011-12. (12.14.175)

New Exploration Licensing Policy (NELP) Program

In 9 rounds of bidding, a total investment of US$ 15.88 billion was made by various operators in Exploration & Production sector till 2010–11. (12.14.153)
302 Exploration blocks were offered in 9 rounds from 1998-2012. (Blocks awarded were – 24 in round I in January 1999, 23 in round II in December 2000, 23 in III, 20 in IV, 20 in V, 52 in VI, 41 in VII, 32 in VIII and 18 in IX rounds).
Under 6 rounds of NELP, 162 exploration blocks (including 115 during X Plan) were awarded covering an area of about 40% of the Indian sedimentary basins. 37 Discoveries were made up to 2007.
In addition, 26 blocks were awarded for exploitation of CBM and 6 trillion Cubic Feet of gas reserves were established till 2007. (11.10.97)
73 Production Sharing Contracts were signed during the XI Plan period.

Open Acreage Licensing Program

In 8 rounds from 2017, 144 exploration blocks comprising 242055 sq. Kms have been awarded. OALP guarantees marketing and pricing freedom with revenue sharing model, apart from offering reduced royalty rates.
Why ONGC, GAIL or OIL can alone not handle this exploration keeping entire benefit to government? Are these CPSEs not capable of handling this area?

Underground Coal Gasification (UCG)

ONGC signed an agreement of collaboration with Skochinsky Institute of Mining, Russia on 25.11.2004 for implementation of Underground Coal Gasification project in India. The Vastan Mine block in Surat district was selected for UCG pilot project. (12.14.178)

Coal Bed Methane (CBM)

Government awarded 33 CBM exploration blocks in 4 rounds of bidding held between 2001 and 2008. Contracts with PSUs / private companies for 23 blocks in 3 rounds of bidding were signed. In addition, two blocks to ONGC–CIL consortium and one block to Great Eastern Energy Corporation Ltd were awarded on nomination basis. (11.10.100)
Commercial production of CBM commenced in Raniganj (South) in West Bengal in July 2007. (12.14.175)

Shale Gas Exploration

MoU was signed between Ministry of Petroleum & Natural Gas and Department of State, USA on 6.12.2010 for cooperation in resource assessment, regulatory framework, training and so on. A multi-organization team was constituted involving Directorate General of Hydrocarbons, ONGC, OIL and GAIL for collection of required geochemical and Petro-physical data for assessment of shale oil and shale gas prospects in Indian on land sedimentary basins. (12.14.177)

National Gas Hydrate Program

A MoU was signed on 30.08.2010 in the area of marine gas hydrate research and technology development between the Leibniz Institute of Marine Sciences, Germany and Directorate General of Hydrocarbons for research on methane production from gas hydrate by carbon dioxide sequestration. (12.14.179)

NGHP-02 operations in 2015 confirmed the presence of extensive sand-rich depositional systems throughout the deep-water portions of the Krishna-Godavari and Mahanadi Basins. Areas B and C of the Krishna-Godavari Basin, were expected to contain substantial gas hydrate accumulations in sand-rich systems. Results of the India National Gas Hydrate Program Expedition 02 | U.S. Geological Survey (usgs.gov)

Petroleum Production in India

Liquid Petroleum production in 1950-51 was 60 million gallons. Digboi Refinery, started by Assam Oil Company in 1901 with installed capacity of 0.5 Mts, was the only source of petroleum in 1950-51. Its yield met about 7% of India's requirements. (1.27.7)
Petroleum Refining (in terms of input of crude oil) was 0.25 Mts in 1950-51. Petroleum refining required imports of crude petroleum of 1.7 Mts. (1.30.23)
Power alcohol production in 1950-51 was 5 million gallons. (1.26.17)

Achievements in I 5YP
Port facilities were provided at Trombay for upcoming Standard Vacuum Oil Co. and Burmah-Shell Oil Co. petroleum refineries. (1.31.51)
StanVac and Caltex were invited to set up refineries in the country by Government of India.
In 1951, **Burmah Shell** began to build a **refinery in Trombay (Mahul)** under an agreement with the Govt.
Standard Vacuum Refining Company of India (StanVac) incorporated an Indian company in 1952 to set up India's first modern refinery of capacity 1.25 MTS. Construction of StanVac refinery started in 1952 at Trombay. It started operation in July 1954, six months ahead of schedule. It was the largest single foreign investment of $ 35 million in India after 1947. NEW OIL REFINERY IS OPENED IN IDIA; $35,000,000 Plant on Island Near Bombay Started in '52 by Standard Vacuum Co. NEW OIL REFINERY IS OPENED IN INDIA - The New York Times (nytimes.com)
On Assam Oil Company agreeing to government participation, AOC was granted prospecting licenses over areas adjacent to **Naharkatia,** where oil was struck in **1953**. (2.18.26)
Construction of the **Caltex Refinery at Visakhapatnam** began in **1955.** (2.4.36)
Government signed an agreement with StanVac for joint exploration for petroleum in WB basin. Departmental exploration for oil was initiated in **1955-56** in Jaisalmer. (2.18.9)
Oil and Natural Gas Division was established by the Ministry of Natural Resources and Scientific Research for undertaking exploration. (2.18.9)

Achievements in II 5YP - 3
Coastal refineries were set up in the private sector adding 6.2 MTPA crude throughput capacity. (6.15.75)
1) Visakhapatnam Refinery - Caltex Oil Refining (l) Ltd refinery of capacity 0.65 MTS, was commissioned in **1957-58**.
2) Construction of two refineries at Noonmati (first public sector refinery of capacity 0,57 MTPA, built with Rumanian collaboration) and Barauni (with a capacity of 2 Mts) were taken up in the public sector. (3.27.38)
3) **Oil and Natural Gas Commission** was established in **1956** for undertaking geological surveys, geophysical investigations and exploratory drilling for oil. (3.3.29). ONGC discovered oil and gas in Cambay-Ankleshwar (Gujarat) and Sibsagar (Assam). (3.27.40)
4) **Indian Refineries Ltd.** was established in **1958.**

5) The **Indian Oil Company** was set up in **1959** to undertake the distribution and marketing of oil products (by importing 1.9 Mts kerosene, high-speed diesel oil, etc. from U.S.S.R. Export Organization). (3.27.41)
6) Oil refineries were being located at Cambay in Gujarat in addition to those existing at Digboi (Assam Oil Company), Vishakhapatnam (Caltex Refinery) and Bombay (Burmah Shell & StanVac Refineries). (3.24.38)
7) **Oil India Ltd**. was founded in February 1959 as a privately held oil exploration company with Burmah Oil Company holding two-thirds of the stock and Government holding the rest. Government raised its share to 50% in 1961.

Consumption of petroleum products in 1960 -
Household requirements (kerosene for lighting) represented 25% of the total consumption of 7.5 Mts in 1960. The demand of the transport sector (diesel oil and gasoline) was more than 30%. The share of industry was about 20% mainly in the form of furnace oil. (3.12.27)

Achievements in III 5YP –
1) Soviet and Indian governments signed a contract (under Indo-Soviet Treaty of Friendship and Cooperation) in October 1961 for the construction of Koyali, Vadodara refinery.
2) The Noonmati refinery was commissioned on 1.01.1962.
3) World's first crude oil conditioning plant was commissioned at Naharkatia in 1963.
4) The crude throughput capacity was raised to 10.2 MTPA in III 5YP. (6.15.75)
5) In 1962, the StanVac exited the Lube Oil project and the company's operations in India came to Esso Standard Refining Company of India.
6) In the early 1960s, the Public Sector Indian Oil Refineries Ltd and Indian Oil Marketing Ltd merged to form **Indian Oil Corporation Ltd.**
7) The Government encouraged Indian Oil Corporation to tie up with Mobil to form the joint venture company **Indian Oil Blending Ltd** for manufacturing lubricants.
8) **Koyali Refinery** began production in October 1965.
9) **Lube India Ltd,** was incorporated with equal stakes of Esso and the Government of India to manufacture lubricant oil base stocks for use by Indian Oil Blending Ltd. The plant, of capacity 165 TPA, was commissioned in **1968-69**.
10) **Cochin Refinery** - Government of India, Phillips Petroleum Company of USA and Duncan Brothers & Company Ltd of Calcutta signed an agreement for the construction of Cochin refinery, registered on 6.09.**1963**, Construction started in March 1964 and the first unit came on stream on 23.9. **1966**.
11) **Madras Refinery** - Chennai Petroleum Corporation Ltd was formed in **1965** as a joint venture between the Government of India, AMOCO and National Iranian Oil Company.

Achievements in IV 5YP -
OIL commissioned the 1158 km oil pipeline to Guwahati and Barauni refineries in 1968.
Madras Refinery of capacity 2.5 Mts went on stream in 1969-70
In IV Plan, the total refining capacity reached 24 MTPA. (6.15.75)

Achievements in V 5YP –
1) **Haldia Refinery** of 2.5 MTPA capacity for processing Middle East crude was commissioned in January, 1975 for producing fuel products and lube base stocks.
2) Domestic crude production went up to 11.77 Mts by **1979-80.**
3) Bombay High offshore field attained a production potential of 5.0 MTPA of oil after the completion of the Phase III-A development in **December, 1978.** (6.15.73)
4) 3.0 MTPA expansion of Koyali refinery was completed in October, **1978**.

5) **Bongaigaon Refinery and Petrochemicals Ltd.,** the first indigenous grass root refinery integrated with a Petrochemical complex, was incorporated on 20.02.1974 and the Crude Distillation Unit was commissioned in February, **1979**.

6) The completion of **Mathura Refinery** of 6 Mts installed capacity 1979, slipped the target of 1979 due to power shortage and other problems. (6.15.75)

Achievements in VI 5YP –

Oil India was setting up an LPG extraction plant at Duliajan. (6.15.87)
Consumption of petroleum products - 38.8 Mts. (8.8.18.1) (8.8.18.3)
Manali Petrochemical Ltd (unit 1) was started by SPIC, a joint venture of Tamil Nadu government, in 1986.

Achievements in VII 5YP

A geological reserve accretion of 1536 Mts of oil and oil equivalent of natural gas was achieved through exploration of ONGC and OIL during VII plan. Significant discoveries were made in Dahej and Gandhar in Cambay basin and Neelam field in Bombay offshore basin. (8.8.19.2)

Western offshore production reached a peak of 21.72 Mts in 1989-90.

Cumulative production of crude oil and natural gas during VII Plan were 157.13 Mts and 59.65 billion M^3 respectively. (8.v2.8.20.2)

The relative shares of HSD, SKO, Petrol, LPG and LDO in the total consumption of petroleum products in 1990-91 were 38.6%, 15.4%, 6.5% and 2.7% respectively. (8.12.15)

Financial Constraints of Petroleum Industries –

The tariff structure did not provide adequate returns to the producing agencies so as to enable them to expand their operations in tune with the growing demand for energy. (8.14.1)

Achievements of VIII 5YP –

i) The new grassroot refineries at Mangalore (3 Mts) and Panangudi (0.5 Mts) were commissioned.
ii) Although a number of private sector promoters were issued Letters of Intent for setting up refineries, only 15 MTPA Reliance and 9 MTPA Essar refineries were expected to come up by the year 2001. (9.6.252)
iii) The total crude oil production during 1992-97 was 154.28 (ONGC – 138.32, OIL – 13.97 and JVC / Pvt – 1.99) Mts. (9.6.247) (10.7.3.35). Public sector contribution was 98.7% of total production.
iv) Total Gas production during 1992-97 was 101.71 (ONGC – 93.4, OIL – 7.47 and JVC / Pvt – 0.84) BCM. (9.6.248) (10.7.3.35). Public sector contribution was 99.2% of total production.

Achievement in IX 5YP –

i) **Petronet India Ltd.** was incorporated on 26.05.**1997** as joint venture by IOCL, HPCL, BPCL and IBP for the implementation of petroleum product pipeline projects. (9.6.268)
ii) **Petronet LNG Ltd.** was formed in 02.04.**1998** as a joint venture by GAIL, ONGC, IOCL and BPCL to import LNG and set up LNG terminals.
iii) Equity oil was secured by participating in the oil and gas projects in Vietnam and Sakhalin (Russia) and an agreement was signed with Iraq for oil exploration. (10.7.3.49)
iv) **Around 34,050,000 LPG enrolments were made, liquidating the entire waiting list.** (10.7.3.49)
v) **The country achieved self-sufficiency in refining capacity at the end of IX plan**. The country was able to meet the demand with the available domestic production till 2001-02. (10.7.3.42)
vi) Total crude oil and gas production during 1997-2002 were 162.99 Mts and 140.92 BCM **(10.7.3.35).**

Achievements in X 5YP

The refining capacity increased from 118.37 to 148.97 MTPA during the plan. (11.10.97)

LNG supply in 2007-08 was 8.7 Mts (30.45 MMSCMD) with contribution of Dahej – 5 Mts, Hazira – 2.5 Mts, Dabhol – 1.2 Mts (11.10.125)

The 2006 level of production barely catered to 26% of the petroleum products demand. (11.10.8)

Exploration in overseas fields

ONGC Videsh Ltd., OIL, Indian Oil Corporation and GAIL acquired overseas exploration and production assets. OVL acquired 22.24 Mts of oil and oil equivalent of gas during X 5YP from its overseas activities. (11.10.97)

Strategic Crude Oil Storage

The government decided to construct 15 Mts of strategic storage in various phases, over and above the existing storage capacity for crude oil and petroleum products at the various refineries for use in emergency in case of short-term supply disruption. (11.10.105)

Achievements in XI 5YP

Refinery projects like MRPL expansion and Paradip refinery projects slipped into the XII Plan due to delays in providing captive power equipment by BHEL to these refineries. (12.14.152)

The cumulative crude oil and natural gas production during XI Plan were 177 MMT and 212.54 BCM. (The public sector crude oil productions were 85.1%, 86.1%, 84.4%, 74.3% and 72.4% and natural gas productions were 76.1%, 75.4%, 53.7%, 48.74% and 54.6% of total production during 2007-08 to 2011-12 respectively). (12.14.151)

The actual demand for Petroleum Products in Mts in 2011-12 were LPG – 15.358, MS – 14.993, Naphtha – 11.105, ATF – 5.536, SKO – 8.229, HSDO – 64.742, LDO – 0.415, Lubes – 2.745, FO / LSHS – 9.232, Bitumen – 4.628, Pet Coke – 6.145, others – 4.869 and total Petroleum Products – 147.997

The consumption of natural gas in 2011-12 was 194 MMSCMD with 91 MMSCMD for power sector, City Gas – 13, Industrial (Petrochemical) – 16, Refineries Internal consumption – 25, Sponge Iron and Steel - 6 and 43 MMSCMD for fertilizer sector. (12. Table 14.37)

LPG consumption increased from 10.85 Mts in 2006–07 to 15.36 Mts in 2011–12. (12.14.150)

Oil, Gas from Overseas Assets

OVL, OIL, GAIL, IOCL, BPCL and HPCL invested Rs. 59,108 Cr (US$ 13 billion) up to 31.03.2011 on acquisition oil producing assets. There were 9 major production assets in Russia, Sudan, Brazil, Syria, Vietnam, Venezuela and Colombia. Overseas production of OVL were 8.8 MMTOE, 8.78 MMTOE, 8.87 MMTOE, 9.43 MMTOE and 8.75 MMTOE in the years 2007-08 to 2011-12 respectively. Production from overseas oil and gas blocks was about 10.22% of India's domestic production in 2011-12. (12.14.154)

Refining capacities of public sector units

With grass-roots refineries at Bhatinda (9 MTS), Paradip (15 MTS) and expansion of some of the refineries in operation, the total refining capacity was projected to be around 218.37 MTS by the year 2012–13.

Promoting Bio-Fuels

Blending of 5% ethanol with petrol was in practice from November 2006 in 14 States and 3 UTs to get cleaner emission. It was proposed to increase the percentage of blend to 10%. Oil Marketing Companies were able to contract 55.87 Cr litres of ethanol against the requirement of 105 Cr litres of ethanol for 5% blending in the entire notified area. (12.14.160)

Flaring of Natural Gas

The total volume of gas flared was 3.5– 4.0 MMSCMD. Need was felt to stop such flaring through use of this gas by the local industry and/or gathering it either through compression or by liquefaction mode and then re-injecting the gas into pipeline. (12.14.180)

Oil Companies' Losses

The total under-recoveries by the Government and oil PSUs during XI Plan **in Rs. Cr** were 19891 for petrol, 212629 for diesel, 99149 for domestic LPG, 111527 for PDS Kerosene) (12.14.162)

Petroleum production from 2013-14

i) The production of crude oil during 2013-14, 2014-15, 2015-16, 2016-17, 2017-18, 2018-19 and 2022-23 were 37.79, 37.46, 36.94, 36.01, 35.68 Mts, 34.20 Mts and 29.18 Mts.
ii) The refinery production (crude throughput) during 2013-14, 2014-15, 2015-16, 2016-17, 2017-18, 2018-19, 2021-22 and 2022-23 were 222.5, 223.28, 232.87 Mts, 245.37 Mts, 251.94 Mts, 257.21 Mts, 241 Mts and 255.2 Mts (BPCL report)
iii) The overall natural gas production in million M³ during 2013-14, 2014-15, 2015-16, 2016-17, 2017-18, 2018-19 and 2022-23 were 35407, 33656, 32249, 31897, 32649, 32,873 and 34450 respectively.

During 2022-23

Consumption of Oil Based Petroleum Products and Natural Gas was 223.01 Mts and 160.83 MMSCMD respectively. Country's Crude Oil imports was 232.7 Mts and Natural Gas 26.3 BCM.

Annual_Report_2019-2020_English.pdf (mospi.gov.in)   mospi_Annual_Report_2017-18.pdf
mospi_annual_report_2015-16.pdf   State-wise Production of Crude Oil and Natural Gas 2022-23 - Energy Portal

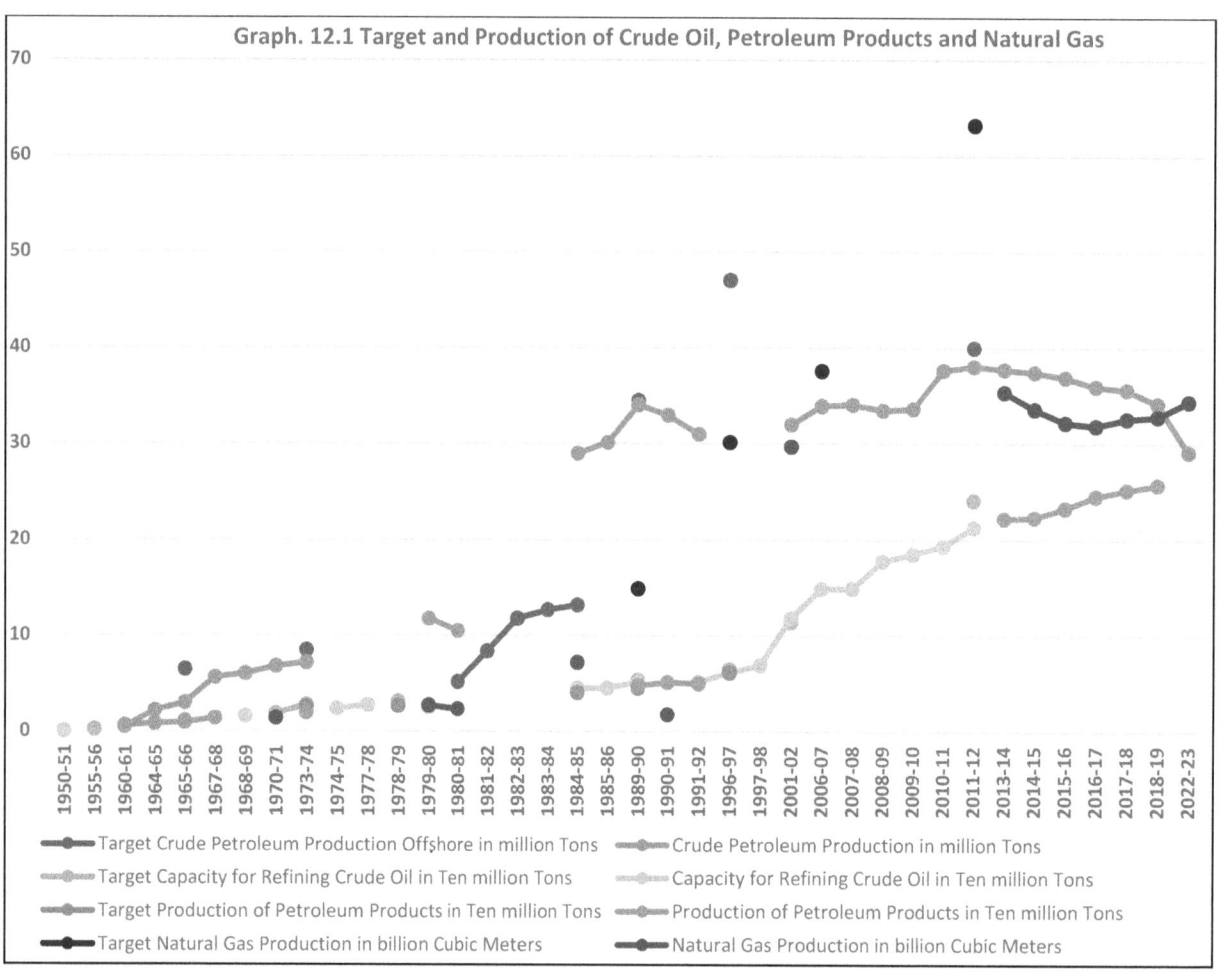

CPSEs Share in Domestic Output in 2011-12

The shares of ONGC, GAIL, Indian Oil Corporation and BPCL were 74% in crude oil, 82% in natural gas transmission, 46% and 23% in supply of petrol and diesel respectively.

Table – 12.1A and 1B - CPSEs Share in Domestic Output of select items

Item	Units	Domestic Production		Total CPSE Production		Share of CPSEs %	
		1968-69	2005-06	1968-69	2005-06	1968-69	2005-06
Crude Oil	Mts	6.06	32.19	3.08	27.64	50.83	85.87
Refinery Crude	Mts	16.55	130.11	8.09	96.95	48.88	74.51

Item	Units	Domestic Production		Total CPSE Production		Share of CPSEs %	
		1998-99	2008-09	1998-99	2008-09	1998-99	2008-09
Crude Oil	MMT	32.7	33.5	29.7	28.8	90.8	86.0
Natural Gas	BCM	27.4	32.8	24.5	24.7	89.4	75.3
Refineries Throughput	MMT	68.5	160.8	68.5	112.2	100	69.8

Petrochemicals Production in India

During I Plan
Facility for production of polystyrene using imported monomer was set up. It was expected to be commissioned in 1956-57.
The capacity for moulding powders achieved by 1955-56 was 1180 tons. (2.19.57)

During II Plan
Schemes were approved for the manufacture of cellulose acetate, polyethylene, polyvinyl chloride and urea-formaldehyde.

During III Plan
The petrochemicals industry in India made beginning in the 1960's with the commissioning of integrated petrochemicals complex of 60,000 tons capacity by **National Organic Chemicals (India) Ltd.**, followed by a small cracker and an LDPE plant by **Union Carbide (India) Ltd.**, a PSF plant by **Imperial Chemical Industries** and a synthetic rubber plant by **Synthetics and Chemicals**. All these plants were set up in the private sector.

Achievements in IV 5YP –
Indian Petrochemical Corporation Ltd. - IPCL was established on 22.03.1969, as a Government of India undertaking, to promote development of petrochemical industry. Construction of petrochemicals complex at Vadodara began in 1970 and production commenced in 1973.
Production of Polyester Filament and Staple in 1973-74 was 11,300 tons (5. Annex. 6)

Achievements in V 5YP
The industry saw a phenomenal growth with the commissioning of 1,30,000 tons capacity IPCL cracker at Baroda in 1978-79 and several other plants in the private sector during the 1980's. (6.16.44) (9.5.171)
Bongaigaon Refinery & Petrochemicals Ltd. was incorporated on 28.2.1974 and commissioned in 1979. Gujarat Aromatics Ltd, was incorporated by Gujarat Industrial Investment Corporation Ltd., on 11.12.1975 at Ahmedabad.
Construction of polyester filament yarn project **Petrofils Cooperative Ltd.,** a joint venture of the Government of India and Weaver's Cooperative Societies, started. (5.5.59)

Liberalization in 1980s

Keeping in view of the increase in demand for petrochemicals, 9 letters of intent / industrial licenses were issued for setting up crackers involving an investment of Rs. 40,000 Cr. (9.5.173)

The industry was delicensed except for hazardous products like ethylene, propylene, butadiene, xylenes, toluene, polycarbonate, mono ethylene glycol, etc. (9.5.174)

Achievements in VII 5YP -

(i) **Maharashtra Gas Cracker Complex** Nagothane, of capacity 300,000 TPA of Ethylene, taken up by IPCL, was commissioned in the last quarter of 1991-92. (8.v2.5.20.2)

(ii) Aromatics plants of Bharat Petroleum Corporation Ltd., Bombay and Cochin Refineries Ltd. and a number of downstream units were commissioned.

(iii) Letters of Intent were issued for setting up crackers at Hazira, Auraiya, Gandhar, Vizag and Haldia and for expansion of NOCIL cracker. (8.v2.5.20.3)

Achievements in VIII 5YP -

Self-sufficiency in Petrochemical Products - With the installation of 7.5 Mt mega cracker at Hazira, the country almost reached the stage of self- sufficiency in petrochemical building blocks. The new capacity additions in PVC (at Gandhar Cracker of IPCL and Hazira Cracker of Reliance Industries Ltd.), in Polypropylene (at Baroda Complex of IPCL and Hazira Complex of RIL) and in synthetic rubber (at Baroda Complex of IPCL), bridged the gap between domestic production and consumption. **India become net exporter of PFY, PSF, PVC, PS and LAB.** (9.4.178)

IPCL, commissioned Phase-I of Gandhar petrochemical complex.

IPCL and Hindustan Organic Chemicals took up expansion / diversification schemes, the Petrofils Cooperative Ltd. turned sick due to surplus capacity, cheaper imports, lower demand, steep price hike of raw materials and intermediate inputs, severe liquidity crunch, working capital shortage, etc. (9.5.177)

Achievement in IX 5YP –

Creation of additional production capacities of 3.61 Mts of major petrochemical reduced import dependency of petrochemicals considerably. (10.7.1.217)

Auraiya (UP) cracker complex of GAIL with an ethylene capacity of 0.3 Mts and cracker complex of Haldia Petrochemicals Ltd with an ethylene capacity of 0.42 Mts and other downstream polymer products were commissioned. (10.7.1.218)

Reliance Group's 1.4 Mts p-xylene and 0.6 Mts polypropylene plants at Jamnagar were also commissioned.

Petrochemical industry in 2001-02

Installed capacity, Production and Consumption of commodity polymers in Mts were 4.252, 3.974 and 3.826 respectively. The corresponding factors for Synthetic Fibre in Mts were 2.071, 1.669 and 1.718 respectively.

India's export of plastic goods was worth US$ 1 billion

IPCL was disinvested and liquidation of the Petrofils Cooperatives Ltd was under progress. (10.7.1.222)

Petrochemical Sector's Contribution to Manufacturing Sector

The petrochemical sector's yearly output was approximately Rs 1,20,000 Cr, which was 15% of the manufacturing sector's output. Its export of about Rs 16,000 Cr was 16% of the manufactured products' exports and it contributed about 20% of the national revenue. (10.7.1.216)

Achievements in X Plan –
Petrochemical Industry in 2006-07

Installed capacity, Production and 2005-06 Consumption of commodity polymers in Mts were 5.187, 5.183 and 4.795 respectively. The corresponding factors for Synthetic Fibre in Mts were – 3.246, 2.244 and 1.893 respectively.

Brahmaputra Cracker and Polymer Ltd was incorporated in January 2007 for implementation of Assam Gas Cracker project. (11.v2.7.1.264)

Petrochemical Industry in 2013-14

Total production of the Indian chemicals industry was 19.308 Mts in 2013-14 and the production of polymers was 9 Mts with imports of around 2.8 Mts.

Petrochemical Industry in 2022-23

Production of Total basic major chemicals and petrochemicals from FY 2015 to FY 2023 (up to Sept 2022) in Mts were 23.108, 24.788, 25.744, 26.739, 27.858, 30.984, 29.181, 32.115 and 26.57 Mts respectively. India: basic major chemicals and petrochemicals production volume 2022 | Statista

India's total ethylene capacity and production were 8.677 Mts and 7.595 Mts respectively in FY2023-24.

Contribution to Manufacturing GDP

Coke, petroleum products, and nuclear fuel, rubber and plastics Industry contributed 10.6% to Manufacturing GDP in 2009-10.

Public Sector Enterprises Engaged in Exploration of Crude Oil and Natural Gas

Oil India Ltd.

Oil India Ltd. - OIL was incorporated on 18.2.1959 as a joint venture of Government of India and Burmah Oil Company to manage oil fields of Naharkatia in Assam. It became a CPSE in 1981.

OIL undertakes exploration and production of crude oil and natural gas, extraction and bottling of LPG and transportation of crude oil through Dibrugarh, Kamrup, Bhubaneshwar, Noida, Jodhpur and Tripoli units.

It has offices for Rajasthan Project at Jodhpur, Bay Exploration Project at Bhubaneswar and Kakinada and Ganga Valley Project at Noida, and Branch Offices at Kolkata, Tripoli and Libreville (Gabon).

QIL has **43** Production Sharing Contracts in Arunachal Pradesh, Rajasthan, Gujarat, Orissa, Andhra Pradesh, Libya, Sudan and Iran.

OIL produced 3.20 Mts crude oil, 49500 Tons of LPG and 2.01 BCM of natural gas during 2004-05.

It was contributing about **9.14% of domestic crude oil production** (27.43% of onshore production) in 2007-08.

Achievements in 2007-08 - (i) Made small and medium size discoveries 8 in Assam and 1 in Rajasthan; (ii) Struck gas in one joint venture in Assam; (iii) Discovered gas at Farsi offshore block, Iran; (iv) carried out 33912 LKM of Aero-Magnetic survey in Gabon; (v) completed 2D acquisition in Libya.

OIL has 5 overseas subsidiaries namely Oil India Sweden AB, Oil India Cyprus Ltd, Oil India (USA) Inc, Oil India International Ltd, Oil India International B.V. and Oil India International PTE Ltd.

Farmed in Niobrara Shale oil & gas asset in USA in 2013.

The installed capacity of OIL for crude oil and natural gas in 2019-20 was 6.9 MMTOE.

OIL is in the business of transportation of finish products of NRL Refinery.

OIL also has 174.1 MW Wind Energy and 14 MW Solar Energy generation plants.

OIL also holds 10% stake in Brahmaputra Cracker and Polymer Ltd and 23% stake in Duliajan Numaligarh Pipeline Ltd.

OIL is carrying out domestic EP activities in 63 nos. of operated acreages of area 62,934 sq. km. OIL holds non-operating participating interests in 2 Pre - NELP blocks - Kharsang (Arunachal Pradesh) and Dirok (Assam), 2 NELP blocks in West Bengal onshore and Gujarat-Kutch shallow offshore, and 1 DSF block in Arunachal Pradesh.

During 2022-23 - The productions were 3.18 BCM of natural gas, 3.18 Mts of Crude oil, 32,100 tons of LPG, pipeline throughput was 6.79 Mts of crude oil and transported 1.42 MMT of petroleum products through Numaligarh Siliguri product pipeline.

OIL carried out 1333 LKM of 2D and 680 Sq.M of 3D seismic survey and drilled 16 exploratory wells and 29 development wells. Annual_Report_2022_23.pdf (oil-india.com)

ONGC Videsh Ltd

ONGC Videsh Ltd. - OVL was incorporated as Hydro Carbon India (Pvt) Ltd. on 5.3.1965 to takeover assets and liabilities of ONGC under the joint venture agreement which was operating in Iran. When the JV agreement was declared null and void by Iran Government, HCI started marketing the expertise of ONGC abroad. The name of the company was changed to OVL on 15.6.1989.

OVL is engaged in exploring, drilling, extracting and producing crude oils, asphalt, bitumen, natural gas, chemicals etc. and exporting abroad.
It has **overseas offices** at Dubai, Iran, Iraq, Netherlands, Russia, Sudan, and Vietnam.
Its **subsidiaries** include ONGC Amazon Alaknanda Ltd. in Bermuda, ONGC Do Brazil Exploracao Petrolifera Ltda. and ONGC Campos Ltda. in Brazil, ONGC Nile Ganga (Cyprus) Ltd., Jarpeno Ltd., joint venture ONGC Mittal Energy Ltd. in Cyprus, ONGC Nile Ganga B.V. and ONGC Nile Ganga (San Cristobal) B.V. in Netherlands, ONGC Narmada Ltd. in Nigeria and Carabobo One AB.

The productions of gas and condensate by OVL were 1349038 M and 39104 MT during 2004-05.
OVL, in 2007-08, had **17** un-incorporated **joint ventures** in Colombia, Congo, Cuba, Egypt, Iran, Libya, Myanmar, Russia, Sudan, Syria and Vietnam.
During 2007-08, OVL and its group companies acquired stakes in 11 oil and gas projects in Egypt, Colombia, Myanmar, Brazil, Congo and Turkmenistan.

OVL had participating interest in 37 E&P projects in 17 countries including Vietnam, Russia, Iraq, Iran, Libya, Syria, Sudan, Qatar, Cuba and Nigeria.
During 2008-09, OVL acquired San Cristobal Project in Venezuela, Blocks in Brazil, Myanmar and Colombia and UK listed Imperial Energy Corporation Plc., which was undertaking upstream oil exploration and production in the Tomsk region of Western Siberia, Russia.
In 2010-11, OVL was executing 37 projects in 17 countries, as operator in 18 projects and joint operator in 2 projects.

In 2010-11

OVL's consolidated production of Oil plus Oil-Equivalent Gas increased from 8.870 MTOE in 2009-10 to 9.448 MMT in 2010-11.
OVL had oil and gas production from 9 projects in 7 countries. OVL signed agreements with KazMunaiGas (KMG), the national oil company of Kazakhstan, for acquisition of 25% participating interest in Satpayev exploration block on 16.04.2011.

OVL was producing oil and gas from 2 blocks (including Greater Nile Oil Project) in Sudan, one Block in Vietnam, Al Furat Project in Syria, Sakhalin-I Project in Russia and Man Sarovar Energy Project in Colombia.

As on 31.03.2014

OVL had participation in 42 E&P projects in 18 countries.

OVL maintained a combination of 13 producing, 4 discovered, 14 exploration projects and 2 pipeline projects, as operator in 11 projects and joint operator in 7 projects.

OVL had 26 subsidiaries comprising 9 direct subsidiaries and 17 indirect subsidiaries outside India, besides 1 incorporated joint venture and 31 Un-incorporated Joint Ventures.

Of the 33 projects in 2014, 10 projects got completed - Brazil (4), Colombia (1), Cuba (2), Nigeria (2) and Sudan (1).

OVL acquired 15% equity from Rosneft Oil Company on 31.05.2016 and 11% equity on 28.10.2016 in JSC Vankorneft.

As on 31.03.2017, OVL had participation in 38 oil & gas projects (14 producing, 4 discovered, 16 exploration and 4 pipeline projects) in 17 countries

In 2022-23, OVL had participating Interests in 32 oil and gas assets in 15 countries. It produced 6.349 Mts of Oil & 10.171 Mts of Oil Equivalent of Oil & Gas, which is 21.7% and 16.0% of India's domestic production respectively.

GAIL (India) Ltd.

GAIL (India) Ltd. - GAIL was incorporated on 16.8.1984 to undertake exploration, production, processing, transmission, distribution and marketing of natural gas and its fractions. GAIL is supplying natural gas to industrial consumers producing LPG, Propane, Pentane, SBP and Polymers, transporting LPG, LNG to Regassification Terminals.

GAIL has **5 operating units** at Vijaipur, Vaghodia, Pata, Raigad and Godhra.

GAIL produced 1.094 Mts of LPG during 2004-05. Propane was produced at 78% and Ethylene at 92% capacities.

Product installed capacity in 2008-09 of GAIL for LPG was 1.110844 Mts, Liq. Hydro-carbon was 1.505126 Mts and for Polymers was 0.41 Mts.

GAIL held around 50% market share in gas marketing in India. GAIL's share of gas transmission business was 74% in 2010-11.

The company has laid down and maintains HBJ gas pipeline to supply natural gas in Gujarat, MP, Rajasthan, UP and Haryana.

The 5 **subsidiaries** of GAIL are GAIL Global (Singapore) Pte Ltd, GAIL Global (USA) Inc., GAIL Global (USA) LNG LLC, Brahmaputra Cracker and Polymer Ltd and GAIL Gas Ltd.

The **joint ventures** include Aavantika Gas Ltd., Green Gas Ltd., Mahanagar Gas Ltd., Maharashtra Natural Gas Ltd., ONGC Petro-Additions Ltd., Petronet LNG Ltd., Ratnagiri Gas and Power Pvt Ltd., Indraprastha Gas Ltd., Bhagyanagar Gas Ltd., Central UP Gas Ltd., Tripura Natural Gas Co. Ltd., GAIL-China Gas Global Energy Holdings Ltd (for pursuing gas sector opportunities in China) and South East Asia Gas Pipeline Co Ltd (for transportation of gas to be produced from blocks in Myanmar to China).

Product network of GAIL included

(i) **11000 km of natural gas** high pressure trunk pipeline (of capacity 206 MMSCMD), **2038 km of LPG** transmission pipeline (of capacity 3.8 MTS)

(ii) **7 LPG gas processing units** (at Usar, Gandhar, Vaghodia, 2 in Vijaipur, Lakwa and Pata to produce 1.4 MTS of LPG and other liquid hydrocarbons),

(iii) **27 oil and gas exploration blocks** (including 7 in east coast, 2 in Myanmar and 1 on-shore block in Oman), **3 coal bed methane blocks** and

(iv) **13000 KM of optical fibre cable network** offering highly dependable bandwidth for telecom service providers.

GAIL is an equity partner in 3 retail gas companies in Egypt and one retail gas company involved in city gas and CNG business in China. GAL had acquired 20% stake in shale asset in USA.

GAIL has a **5 MW solar plant** and **118 MW wind power plants** across India.

In 2016-17, GAIL had stakes in 12 E&P blocks including 2 overseas blocks (Myanmar). GAIL had 15 JV's.

The capacity of petrochemical complex at Pata, U.P. was increased from 410,000 TPA of polymers to 810,000 TPA during 2018-19.

GAIL was entrusted to execute 2655 km long Jagdishpur-Haldia-Bokaro-Dhamra pipeline as part of the 'Urja Ganga' project in 2019-20.

GAIL is running a pilot project for hydrogen blending in city gas network and is setting up a 10MW Green Hydrogen plant at Vijaipur.

GAIL's renewable energy portfolio stands at 132 MW.

The gross turnover of GAIL in 2022-23 was Rs. 144301.61 Cr. GAIL's LPG transmission in 2022-23 was 4.335 Mt (107 MMSCMD)

Oil and Natural Gas Corporation Ltd.

Oil and Natural Gas Corporation Ltd. - ONGC was incorporated on 23.6.1993 after transforming Oil and Natural Gas Commission into a Public Ltd. company to take over the business of Oil and Natural Gas Commission w.e.f. 1.2.94.

ONGC is engaged in Hydrocarbon exploration and production of crude oil and natural gas in India and overseas.

ONGC conducts **exploration through 7 Basins** (located at Mumbai, Vadodara, Chennai, Kolkata, Jorhat and Dehradun) and oil and gas **production** activities **through 13 Assets** (Offshore Assets - Mumbai High, Neelam-Heera and Bassein & Satellite based at Mumbai and Kakinada, Onshore Assets located at Ankleshwar, Mehsana, Ahmedabad Cambay, Karaikal, Rajahmundry, Agartala, Nazira and Bokaro.

ONGC also produces **value added products** like C2, C3, LPG, Naphtha, SKO, HSD, ATF etc. at Hazira, Uran and Ankleshwar plants and Mini refinery at Tatipaka.

It has **2 subsidiaries** namely ONGC Videsh Ltd. and Mangalore Refinery and Petrochemicals Ltd.

ONGC incorporated **9 joint ventures** namely Petronet LNG Ltd., Petronet MHB Ltd., ONGC Tripura Power Company Pvt Ltd., Pawan Hans Helicopters Ltd., Dahej SEZ Ltd., Mangalore SEZ Ltd., ONGC Petro-additions Ltd., ONGC Mangalore Petrochemicals Ltd. and ONGC TERI Biotech Ltd. Further, there were unincorporated JVs operating on **44 production sharing / exploration contracts** in 2004-05.

The crude oil and natural gas production by ONGC (including JVs) during 2004-05 were 28.13 Mts. and 25.23 BCM respectively.

ONGC's exploration resulted in 6 hydrocarbon findings in on-land, 5 in offshore shallow water and 2 in deepwater offshore. During 2007-08, ONGC achieved **In-place Reserve Accretion** of 182.3 MMTOE.

The first **Coal Bed Methane** development well was spudded in Parbatpur pilot area on 1.12.2007 near Bokaro Steel City.

ONGC was listed in Fortune's 'Most admired group of companies' list-2007. The 'Fortune Global 500', 2008 list has ranked ONGC at 335. ONGC was also ranked as Numero Uno E&P Company in Asia and **the third largest E&P Company in the world in Platts Energy Business Technology Survey 2007-08** based on assets, revenues, profits, EPS and return on invested capital.

The productions of ONGC were 27.94, 27.93 and 27.13 Mts of crude oil and 24.88, 25.12 and 25.44 BCM of natural gas in 2006-07, 2007-08 and 2008-09 respectively.

ONGC contributed 69% of the national production of crude oil and 70% of natural gas in 2013-14.

ONGC was working in 15 oil fields for oil recovery.

ONGC Petro Additions Ltd. was commissioned on 07.03.2017 with production capacity of 1.4 Mts of polymers & 0.5 Mts of chemical.
The installed capacities of ONGC in 2019-20 were 23.3526 Mts for crude oil and 24896 MMSCM for natural gas.
The production assets increased to 17 in 2019-20.
ONGC made 12 new discoveries including 7 new Prospects and 5 new Pool discoveries in 2019-20.
Forbes ranked ONGC 5th largest in India and 269 worldwide in the Global 2000 list of the world's biggest public companies for 2020.

ONGC made 8 new hydrocarbon discoveries including 3 New Prospects and 5 New Pool discoveries in 2022-23. (1 each in OALP and NELP blocks and 6 in nomination blocks).
The gross turnover of ONGC was Rs, 155517.32 Cr in 2022-23. ONGC's standalone crude oil production, standalone gas production and ONGC's overall oil and gas production, including joint ventures for FY 2023 were 19.584 Mts, 20.628 BCM and 42.836 MMTOE respectively. Annual Report 2022-23 - en - ongcindia.com

Prize Petroleum Company Ltd - Exploration and Production of Crude Oil and Gas

Prize Petroleum Company Ltd was incorporated on 28.10.1998 as joint venture by HPCL (with 50% equity by ICICI group / HDFC) to undertake exploration and production of hydrocarbons in India and abroad. It became a 100% subsidiary of HPCL in Dec 2011.
The installed capacity of Prize Petroleum in 2019-20 was 14101 barrels for crude oil.
The gross turnover in 2022-23 was Rs. 3.84 Cr.

Bharat Petro Resources Limited – Exploration and Production of Crude Oil and Gas

Bharat Petro Resources Limited - BPRL was incorporated on 17.10.2006 as a subsidiary of BPCL to implement BPCL's projects in Exploration and Production sector. BPCL transferred all E&P Assets, liabilities and investments along with the commitments & expenditures and also assignment of BPCL's participating interest in Production Sharing contracts to BPRL.

Acquisition for 3D seismic data, covering an area of 2140 sq.km., was carried out in 2008.
BPRL acquired exploration acreages in 2007-08. BPRL consolidated and streamlined operations in Brazil, and ventured into unexplored / virgin basin in Mozambique during 2008-09. BPRL was awarded 'Joint operatorship' with Hindustan Oil Exploration Corporation Ltd. in the Rajasthan block during the NELP VII bid round.
As on 31.3.2009, BPRL had participating interest in **26 exploration blocks** in 6 countries including India. (12 Blocks in India, 6 in Brazil, 4 in Russia, 1 each in Mozambique, Indonesia, Australia and East Timor).

BPRL, in 2010-11, had participating interests in 27 Blocks spread across the globe. (9 Blocks in India acquired under NELP and balance 17 blocks were in 6 overseas Countries).
During 2010-11, BPRL had total 6 discoveries, including 3 in Mozambique, 2 in Brazil and 1 in Indonesia. BPRL has subsidiaries Bharat Petro Resources JPDA Ltd in India and BPRL International BV, in Netherlands (which in turn has 3 subsidiaries BPRL Ventures Indonesia B V, BPRL Ventures Mozambique BV and BPRL Ventures BV).
17 Discoveries were made in Brazil, Mozambique, Indonesia, Australia and in India in 2013-14.

In 2019-20, BPRL was participating in 27 blocks (15 in India & 5 in Brazil, 2 in UAE and 1 each in Mozambique, Indonesia, Australia, Israel, Timor Leste) and had equity stake in 2 Russian entities. Gas was discovered in Mozambique. Production commenced from Madanam Block in Cauvery basin in 2019-20.

The refining capacity in 2022-23 was 250 Mts
BPRL has participating interest in 17 blocks (8 in India, 5 in Brazil, 2 in UAE and 1 each in Mozambique & Indonesia) and equity stake in 2 Russian entities.

Bharat Petro Resources JPDA – Exploration in Area Between East Timor and Australia

Bharat Petro Resources JPDA - BPRL-JDPA was incorporated on 28.10.2006 as a Special Purpose Vehicle. Bharat Petro Resources Ltd. joined the Consortium of OILEX (Operator), Videocon Industries Ltd. and Gujarat State Petroleum Corporation Ltd. to participate in joint petroleum development in the area between East Timor and Australia through BPCL-JDPA, which is a wholly owned subsidiary of Bharat Petroleum Corporation Ltd.

Gail Gas Limited – City Gas Distribution

Gail Gas Ltd. - GGL was incorporated on 27.5.2008 with the objective of taking up distribution and marketing of CNG and Auto LPG as fuel for transport vehicles, Piped Natural Gas for domestic / commercial / industrial purposes

GGL caters to CNG / Auto LPG retail outlets within the cities and along the highways by taking up CNG Corridor Project for setting up CNG stations along the highways. GGL identified 243 cities contiguous to existing and proposed pipelines for City Gas Distribution in phased manner. In the first round of first phase, GGL was assigned the implementation of CGD project in Sonepat, Kota, Dewas, Meerut, Agra and Firozabad.
Gas supply commenced to industrial units in Dewas, Sonepat and Kota and to domestic customers in Dewas. GGL has already laid 365 Km steel pipeline and 554 Km MDPE pipeline in these cities and supplying natural gas to 435 industrial, 13 commercial and 5606 domestic customers.
2 CNG stations were commissioned in Vadodara and one each in Panvel, Vijaipur and Dibiyapur.

GGL incorporated 4 joint venture companies.

GGL was developing CGD network in North Goa and Haridwar through JV.
During 2017-18, GGL was developing CGD projects in Bengaluru, Sonipat, Meerut, Dewas, Firozabad including TTZ area, Vadodara, Kota, East & West Godavari, Haridwar and North Goa through its JVs.

As in 2022-23, GGL has been authorized by Petroleum and Natural Gas Regulatory Board for implementing CGD Projects in MP, Haryana, UP, Karnataka, Uttarakhand, Odisha, Jharkhand.

Public Sector Enterprises Engaged in Refining and Production of Petroleum Products

Indian Oil Corporation Ltd.

Indian Oil Corporation Ltd. - IOC was incorporated on 1.9.1964 by merging Indian Oil Company (established in 1959) with Indian Refineries Ltd. (established in 1958). In 1981 Assam Oil Co. Ltd. was also merged with IOC.

(i) Guwahati Refinery

First public sector Guwahati Refinery of capacity 1 Mt was set up at Noonmati in Guwahati on 1.01.**1962** with Romanian collaboration to processes crude oil from Upper Assam Oil Fields.

Noonmati refinery produces LPG, Motor Spirit (Petrol), Aviation Turbine Fuel, Kerosene, High Speed Diesel, Light Diesel Oil and Raw Petroleum Coke.
Noonmati Refinery ventured into ecologically friendly fuel and subsequently installed 3 new units:
i) The ISOSIV unit produces Lead Free Petrol
ii) The Hydrotreater Unit produces HSD (of very low Sulphur and cetane number conforming to BIS specifications) ATF, Superior Kerosene Oil (with high smoke point and low Sulphur).
iii) The Indane Maximization unit (with technology developed by R&D Centre of IOCL) achieves high LPG yield of 44% (through Fluidized Catalytic Cracking of Reduced Crude Oil, Coker Fuel Oil and Coker Gasoline) and enables the refinery to upgrade all its residual products to high value distillate products and makes it a zero-residue refinery.

INDAdeptG unit of capacity of 35 kTA was commissioned for BS-IV gasoline production in 2022-23.

(ii) Barauni Refinery -

Barauni Refinery was built in collaboration with the Soviet Union and went on stream in July **1964.** The initial capacity of 1 Mts was expanded to 3 Mts by 1969.

Barauni Refinery fully switched over to production of BS-III diesel w.e.f. 1.06.2010.
New units like NHDT and ISOM for Motor Spirit Quality up-gradation were added in 2010.
Barauni Refinery is primarily producing diesel with over 54% of its product mix as HSD. Other products include kerosene, petrol, LPG, Naphtha, Raw Petroleum Coke, Sulphur and bitumen.
Nepal Oil Corporation sources its fuel including, LPG from Barauni Refinery.

Baruni refinery is undergoing expansion from 6 to 9 Mts in 2022-23.

(iii) Gujarat Koyali Refinery

Following agreement signed by USSR and India in October 1961, Gujarat refinery of 2 Mts capacity was set up in Koyali, Vadodara.

The first crude distillation unit (CDU-1) of capacity 1 Mts was commissioned on 11.10.1965 and it achieved rated capacity of 2 Mts on 6.12.1965. CDU-2 and Catalytic Reforming Unit were installed in 1966, CDU-3 of 1.0 Mts capacity was commissioned in 1967 to process Ankleshwar & North Gujarat crudes.
In December 1968, Udex plant was commissioned for production of benzene & toluene.
By 1974-75, the capacity of the refinery was further increased to 4.2 Mts.
CDU-4 of 3 Mts capacity and downstream processing units like Vacuum Distillation, Visbreaker and Bitumen Blowing Units were added during 1978-79 to expand the refinery to process imported crude.
Secondary processing facilities consisting of Fluidized Catalytic Cracking Unit were commissioned in 1982 and the crude processing capacity of the refinery was further increased to 9.5 Mts.
In 1993-94, Gujarat Refinery commissioned country's first Hydrocracker Unit for conversion of heavier ends of crude oil to high value superior products. Country's first Diesel Hydro-de-Sulphurization Unit

(DHDS) to reduce Sulphur content in diesel was commissioned in 1999. MTBE Unit was commissioned in 1999 to eliminate lead in Motor Spirit.

CDU–5 was commissioned in 1999 augmenting capacity of the refinery to **13.7 Mts.**

In 2004, the **World's largest single train Linear Alkyl Benzene Plant** of capacity 1,20,000 tons was set up marking IOCL's entry into Petrochemicals.

DHDS, Hydrotreating (DHDT) and VGO Hydrotreating (VGO-HDT) units were revamped in 2019 to produce BS-IV / BS VI compliant fuel.

A new DHDT Unit of 2.0 Mts, Prime G Unit of 0.7 Mt, Hydrogen Unit and Amine Regeneration Unit were commissioned in 2021 to upgrade quality of fuel.

Major products: LPG, Motor spirit (BS-VI), Superior Kerosene Oil, High Speed Diesel (BS-VI), Naphtha, VG bitumen, RPC Sulphur, Furnace Oil, Marpol FO

Specialty Products: Food Grade hexane, Polymer Grade Hexane, MTBE, LAB, HAB, MARPOL FO, HFHSD, AVGAS (100LL)

Gujarat Refinery expansion (LUPECH) from 13.7 to 18.0 Mts, integration with LOBS and Petrochemicals and establishment of acrylics/oxo alcohol project were in progress in 2022-23 at the Gujarat Refinery,

(iv) Haldia Refinery

The Haldia Refinery for processing 2.5 Mts of Middle East crude per year was commissioned in January, **1975** with two sectors - one for producing fuel products and the other for Lube base stocks.

The fuel sector was built with French collaboration and the Lube sector with Romanian collaboration. The refining capacity of the Refinery was increased to 2.75 Mts in April 1989 through debottlenecking measures.

In 1997, CDU-2 was added to increase the refinery capacity to 4.6 Mts.

The Catalytic Iso-Dewaxing Unit, commissioned in 2003, produced superior quality API Group II **L**ube **O**il **B**ase **S**tocks having lower pour point, very low Sulphur content, and higher viscosity Index as compared to the conventional API Group-I Lube Base Stocks.

With the commissioning of VDU-2 and secondary processing facilities, the refinery capacity increased to 6.0 Mts.

Capacity expansion from 6.0 to 7.5 Mts along with addition of (1.7 Mts) Once-Through Hydro cracking Unit, Hydrogen Generation Unit, Sulphur Recovery Units and Revamp of CDU-II and related Utilities and Offsite facilities were done in 2010.

Project to produce Euro-III / IV quality HSD was completed in 2010.

Capacity expansion of refinery was done from 7.5 to 8.0 Mts along with implementation of new Coker and Coker Gas Oil treater in February 2020.

India's first Wet Sulfuric Acid plant of 380 TPD was commissioned in 2022.

Haldia Refinery introduced API Gr-III LOBS and Low Sulphur Bunker Fuel (Marpol) in line with the IMO specifications.

The products of the refinery are LPG, Naphtha, Motor Spirit, Mineral Turpentine Oil, Superior Kerosene (SKO), Aviation Turbine Fuel, High Speed Diesel (BS-VI quality), Jute Batching Oil, API Group I/II/III Lube Oil Base Stocks, Bottoms - Furnace Oil, Marpol FO, eco-friendly Bitumen emulsion, pet coke, Sulphur and sulfuric acid.

New technologies were implemented for improving lube oil quality, reduction of SO2 emissions and fuel quality upgradation during 2022-23.

(v) Digboi Refinery

Digboi Refinery was set up in 1901 by Assam Oil Company Ltd. The Indian Oil Corp. Ltd. took over the refinery and marketing management of AOCL w.e.f. 1981.

The Digboi refinery had an installed capacity 0.50 Mts. The refining capacity was increased to 0.65 Mts by modernization in July, 1996.
A new delayed Coking Unit of 170,000 tons capacity was commissioned in 1999.
The refinery installed Hydrotreater-UOP in 2002 to improve the quality of diesel.
A Solvent Dewaxing Unit for maximizing production of microcrystalline wax was commissioned in 2003.
The MSQ Upgradation unit was commissioned.

Major Products: LPG, Motor spirit, SKO, HSD, FO, Raw petroleum coke. Specialty Products were MTO and Paraffin Wax.

Digboi refinery was undergoing expansion from 0.65 to 1 Mts in 2023. New technology was implemented for hydro finishing of paraffin wax.

(vi) Mathura Refinery –

Construction of Mathura refinery began in 1972 and refinery (of refining capacity 6 Mts) was commissioned on 19.01.**1982.**

The FCCU and Sulphur Recovery Units were commissioned in 1983. The refining capacity was expanded to 7.5 Mts in 1989 by debottlenecking and revamping.
DHDS Unit was commissioned in 1989 for production of HSD with low Sulphur content (0.25% wt. max.).
The refinery processes low Sulphur crude from Bombay High and Nigeria, and high Sulphur crude from the Middle East.
For production of unleaded Gasoline, **C**ontinuous **C**atalytic **R**eforming **U**nit was commissioned in 1998. With the commissioning of Once Through Hydrocracker Unit in 2000, capacity of Mathura Refinery increased from 6.0 to 8.0 Mts.
Diesel **H**ydro-**t**reating unit & **MS Q**uality **U**p-gradation Unit were installed in 2005 for production of Euro-III grade HSD & MS.
FCC Gasoline Desulphurization and Selective Hydrogenation Units were commissioned in 2010 and supply of Euro-IV grade MS and HSD started from 2010.
FCCU Revamp was undertaken in 2014 to increase the processing capacity of the unit from 1.3 to 1.5 MTS.

Mathura refinery started to produce BS VI grade fuels from 2018.

Major products: LPG, Motor spirit (BS-VI), Superior Kerosene Oil, High Speed Diesel (BS-VI), Naphtha, PNCP grade propylene, Bitumen VG -10/30 Sulphur.

Commercial trial in FCC unit for improvement in propylene yield was successfully completed using INDMAX base catalyst.

(vii) Panipat Refinery

Panipat Refinery was set up in 1998. It commenced with a capacity of 6 Mts and has been recently augmented to 12 Mts.

Diesel Hydro Desulphurization Unit was commissioned in 1999 enabling production of low Sulphur diesel.

Panipat Refinery capacity was increased from 6 to 12 Mts during 2004-05.

PX-PTA units were commissioned in 2006 to produce paraxylene and PTA (an useful raw material for producing other commercial polymers). Benzene is one of the byproducts.

Naphtha Cracker Complex produces ethylene and propylene, which are used to produce polypropylene, low / high-density polyethylene and mono-ethylene glycol.

Panipat Refinery was further expanded taking the total capacity to 15 Mts.

Panipat Refinery is a large contributor of ultra-low Sulphur diesel.

Panipat refinery is undergoing expansion from 15 to 25 MTS in 2023.

(viii) Paradip Refinery

Final approval for the Paradip Refinery project was given by IOC board in February 2009 and the refinery of 15 Mts capacity was commissioned in **2016** to process 100% heavy, high-Sulphur cheaper crude.

Paradip Refinery incorporates Flue Gas Desulphurization facilities for firing high Sulphur Vacuum Residue and Vapor Recovery system from jetty loading to meet the stringent emission norms of SOx and volatile organic emissions despite processing heavy high Sulphur Crude.

The refinery is designed to produce octane-rich low-benzene MS blend component, high yield of LPG and propylene and total premium quality gasoline variants for export. Polypropylene unit in the refinery produces various PP grades.

Major products: LPG, Propylene, Polypropylene, High Speed Diesel (BS-VI), Motor spirit (BS-VI), ATF, Reformate, Superior Kerosene Oil, Sulphur, LCO, Pet Coke, etc.

During 2022-23 - Adding to petrochemical capacity, Mono Ethylene Glycol unit was commissioned in February 2023. IOCL made significant investments for constructing the grassroot Para Xylene and Purified Terephthalic Acid Plant.

(ix) Bongaigaon Refinery and Petrochemicals Ltd.

Bongaigaon Refinery & Petrochemicals Ltd. - BRPL was incorporated on 28.2.1974 and commissioned in 1979. BRPL was the first indigenous grass root refinery integrated with a Petrochemical complex at one location.

CDU-1 of capacity 1.0 Mt was commissioned in 1979. It was de-bottlenecked in 1986 increasing the capacity to 1.35 Mts.

Government of India sold 25.54% shareholding to the public during 1991-92 to 1993-94.

Refinery Expansion Project increasing the overall capacity to 2.35 Mts was completed in 1995.

The remaining 74.46% equity was divested in favour of IOCL on 29.03.2001.

An LPG bottling plant of capacity 22000 Tons was commissioned in 2003.

The crude throughput for the BRPL during 2004-05 was 2.18 Mt. (93%).

Amalgamation of BRPL with IOCL happened in 2009 and the refinery became a part of Indian Oil and is known as Bongaigaon Refinery.

INDMAX project along with increase in crude processing from 2.35 to 2.7 Mts was completed in 2020. The major products of the refinery are LPG, Unleaded MS, Ethanol Blended Motor Spirit, Naphtha, ATF, SKO, HSD, LDO, LSHS, LVFO, RPC and CPC including needle coke.

BRPL is also engaged in production of value-added petrochemicals and polyester staple fibre products.

Indian Oil Corporation

The combined throughput by the 7 refineries of the Indian Oil Corp. Ltd. during 2004-05 was 36.63 Mts. with overall capacity utilization of 88.59%. (Barauni 85%, Gujarat 85%, Guwahati 100%, Haldia 90%, Mathura 80%, Panipat 106%, Digboi 100%)
IOCL exported 3.33 MT petroleum products.

Indian Oil Blending merged with IOCL and Indian Strategic Petroleum Reserve Ltd. ceased to be a subsidiary of IOC in May 2006, consequent upon transfer of IOCL's entire equity holding to Oil Industry Development Board.
During 2007-08, IOC had 8 projects under execution including setting up new refinery at Paradip and expansion of Panipat Refinery from 12 to 15 Mts.
The R & D centre developed 186 lubricant formulations.
Product Installed Capacity in 2008-09 of IOCL for Crude Oil was 49.7 Mts
IOCL entered in other energy fields such as biofuels, gas, wind power, solar and nuclear.
Indian oil commenced supply of greener BS-IV fuels on 1.4.2010.
During 2010-11, Indian Oil's Bio-remediation Technology- Oilivorous-S was utilized for treating oil spills at marine locations caused by collision of ships off Mumbai coast.

IOC had **9 refineries** at Barauni, Koyali, Digboi, Guwahati, Bongaigaon, Haldia, Mathura, Panipat and Paradeep with a combined capacity of 69.2 Mts on 31.03.2017 (which was 54.2 Mts on 31.03.2014).
IOC had a pipeline network of 12848 KM with a capacity of 75.2 Mts. in 2016-17.
IOCL had a market share of 45.5% for Xtra premium petrol and 58% for Xtra mile diesel.

Overseas operations - IOC had 8 oil & gas blocks overseas including Libya and Iran. Indian Oil and Oil India Limited have incorporated a special purpose vehicle Ind-OIL Overseas Ltd in Mauritius to jointly undertake activities related to the acquisition of overseas E&P assets.
Indian Oil (Mauritius) Ltd. and Lanka IOC Ltd., undertake distribution of petroleum products in Mauritius and Sri Lanka respectively. IOC Middle East FZE, Dubai, is engaged in marketing of lubricants and other petroleum products in the Middle East, Africa and CIS regions.

The installed capacity of Indian Oil Corporation Ltd. was 69 Mts for petroleum and petrochemical products in 2019-20.
IOC owns a third of India's 249.9 Mts refining capacity and 29,831 petrol pumps out of 71,046 retail outlets in the country.
The company is already the second-largest player in petrochemicals in the country.

IOCL has **9 subsidiary units** namely Chennai Petroleum Corp. Ltd, IOC Global Capital Management IFSC Ltd., Indian Oil Mauritius Ltd., Lanka IOC PLC, IOC Middle East FZE, Dubai, IOC Sweden AB, IOCL (USA) Inc, IndOil Global B.V., Netherlands, IOCL Singapore Pte Ltd.
IOCL has **28 financial joint ventures**.

IOCL production of petroleum products, gas, petrochemicals and explosives in 2022-23 were 83.966 Mts, 4.145 Mts, 2.202 Mts and 0.342 Mts and refineries and pipelines throughput were 72.408 Mt and 97.382 Mt respectively. The refining capacity was 70.05 Mts.
The Crude throughput of IOCL group refineries, including Chennai Petroleum Corp. Ltd, was 83.72 MMT during 2022-23, with capacity utilization of 103.9%.
IOCL commissioned 2,454 km of pipelines during 2022-23, taking the total length of pipeline network to 17,564 km with a capacity of 119.20 Mts (crude & product pipelines) and 48.73 MMSCMD (gas pipelines) as on 31.03.2023.

Chennai Petroleum Corporation Limited

Chennai Petroleum Corporation Limited - CPCL, a subsidiary of Indian Oil Corporation, was formed as a joint venture company Madras Refineries Ltd. on 30.12.1965 between the government of India, AMOCO and National Iranian Oil Company, holding shares in the ratio 74:13:13 respectively. CPCL grassroot refinery was set up with an installed capacity of **2.5 Mts** in 27 months.

In 1985, AMOCO disinvested in favor of GOI. After a series of disinvestments to public sector institutions in 1992, public issue of CPCL shares in 1994 and restructuring in 2000-01, IOC's holding became 51.88% while NIOC continued its holding at wax and petrochemical feedstocks production facilities.

During 2004-05, 3 Mts Manali Refinery cum modernization project was completed and Lanka IOC Ltd commissioned Lube Blending plant in Sri Lanka.
CPCL processed 8.923 Mts crude during the year 2004-05.
CPCL was executing following projects in 2007-08: (i) 5.8 MGD Sea Water Desalination Plant; (ii) 20 MW Gas Turbine; (iii) Euro-IV Preparedness on Auto Fuels in Manali Refinery; (iv) Refinery-III capacity expansion by 1.0 Mts at Manali Refinery.
During 2007-08, CPCL commissioned 22 Windmills with an installed capacity of 17.6 MW. It also planned to undertake 15 Mts new Grassroot Refinery-cum-Petrochemical Complex at Ennore.
Product Installed Capacity in 2008-09 of Chennai Petroleum Corp Ltd. for Crude was 9.5 Mts and CBR – Crude was 1.0 Mts.
CPCL has 2 refineries, at Manali and Nagapattinam, with a combined refining capacity of **11.5 Mts**.

Manali Refinery had a capacity of **10.5 Mts**.

Nagapattinam Refinery was set up with a capacity of 0.5 Mts in 1993 at Pannangudi, Nagapattinam in Cauvery basin. The capacity was later enhanced to **1.0 Mts**. Project to **increase its capacity to 9.0 Mts**. was expected to be completed by June 2025.

Wax plant at CPCL of installed **capacity of 30,000 tons** was designed to produce paraffin wax, candle wax, waterproof formulations and match wax.

Propylene plant of capacity 17,000 tons was commissioned in 1988. The unit was revamped to enhance the propylene production capacity to 30,000 tons in 2004. CPCL also supplies LABFS to downstream units for the manufacture of liner alkyl benzene.

The main products of CPCL are LPG, Motor Spirit, superior kerosene, ATF, HSD, naphtha, bitumen, lube base stocks, paraffin wax, fuel oil, hexane, propylene, Sulphur and petrochemical feed stocks.
The crude throughput for 2016-17 and 2017-18 were 10.256 and 10.789 M respectively.

CPCL has set up a wind farm, sea water desalination plants and sewage reclamation.

Chennai Petroleum Corp. Ltd. has **two joint ventures** namely Indian Additives Ltd. and National Aromatics and Petrochemicals Corp. Ltd. with M/s. Chevron Oronite of USA and Southern Petrochemical Industries Corp. Ltd.

The installed capacities of CPCL in 2019-20 were 0.5 Mt for Asphalt, 0.78 Mt for ATF, 0.2 Mt for Furnace Oil, 0.95 Mt for Gasoline, 4.5 Mt for HSD, 0.2 Mt for LOBS, 0.38 Mt for LPG, 0.85 Mt for Naphtha, 0.65 Mt for Pet coke and 0.35 Mt for SKO.
CPCL was expanding Manali and upcoming Cauvery Basin (Nagapattinam) refineries capacity from 10.5 to 19.5 Mts in 2023.

Indian Oil Corp. Ltd. refining capacity was 70.05 Mts.

Indian Oil Blending Ltd. – Production of Blending Lube Oils and Grease

Indian Oil Blending Ltd. - IOBL was incorporated in 1963 as 50:50 joint venture of Indian Oil Corp. and Mobil Petroleum Corp. Inc. to indigenize blending of Lube Oil. The agreement with MOBIL ended in 1974 and IOBL became a subsidiary of IOC.

IOBL is undertaking production of blending lube oils in Kolkata and Trombay units and grease in Vashi. IOBL produced 0.198 million KL of lubricating oil and 12959 Tons of grease during 2004-05 at 88% and 93% capacity utilization respectively.

IOBL merged with IOCL in May 2006.

IBP Co. Ltd. – Production of Petroleum, Explosives and Cryogenics

IBP was incorporated as the Indo-Burma Petroleum Company Ltd in Rangoon in 1909 and in 1942 the corporate office was shifted to India. IBP became a government company in 1971 when IOC purchased the majority shares. In 1972, GOI acquired IOC's share-holding in IBP.

IBP dealt with petroleum, industrial explosives, and cryogenics. IBP was manufacturing bulk slurry emulsion explosives like Cartridge and Site Mixed, Cast Boosters, and Detonating Fuse.
The engineering business group of IBP was manufacturing small cryogenic containers for transporting and storing liquid Nitrogen, Oxygen and Argon.

IBP is marketing diverse portfolio ranging from transportation fuels like motor spirit (MS), high-speed diesel to lubricants, LPG and naphtha through 2,524 retail outlets, 378 Superior kerosene Oil and Light Diesel Oil and 69 LPG distributorships. It also had 18% market share in industrial explosives and cryogenic business.

IBP is manufacturing cryo-containers at Nasik, Industrial Explosives at Korba and Site mixed slurry explosives at Singaravli, Kudremukh, Ramagundam, Dhanbad, Rampur, Agucha, Kusmunda, Talcher, Rajmahat etc.
IBP produced 51204 Tons of industrial explosives and 10381 cryo-containers during 2004-05.
IBP has one financial joint venture Petronet India Ltd.

The government was holding 59.58% in IBP, employees 0.70%, financial institutions 23.41% and others 16.31%.
Govt disinvested 33.38% shares for Rs. 1153.68 Cr **to Indian Oil Corporation** in February 2002. After the divestment, the government stake in IBP came down to 26%. As per SEBI guidelines, IOC was to make an open offer for an additional 20% stake at the price they have bid for the stake.

Hindustan Petroleum Corporation Ltd

HPCL was incorporated on 05-07-1952 as Standard Vacuum Refinery Co. of India Ltd. (Stan Vac) and renamed as ESSO Standard Refining Co. of India Ltd. in 1962. After amalgamation of Lube India and ESSO Standard Refining Co, the new company was taken over by GOI in 1974 and renamed as HPCL. Caltex in 1976 and Kosan Gas Co. Ltd. in 1979 were merged with HPCL. HPCL is a subsidiary of Oil and Natural Gas Corporation.

(i) Mumbai Refinery

Construction of Standard Vacuum Oil Company's refinery was started in 1952 at Trombay. The refinery was commissioned in 1954 with a refining capacity of 1.25 Mts.

Capacity of Mumbai refinery was increased to 5.5 Mts in 1985 and then to **9.5 Mts**, in phases.
Mumbai refinery processed 6.12 Mts of crude oil during 2004-05 (111%) as compared to 6.11 Mts during the previous year.

The products currently manufactured by Mumbai Refinery are LPG, Naphtha, Motor Spirit, Food Grade Hexane, ATF, SKO, HSD, LDO, Low Sulphur Heavy Stock, Industrial Furnace Oil, Rubber Processing Oil, Lube Oil Base Stocks, Bitumen, Sulphur, etc.

Mumbai Refinery achieved crude throughput of 9.8 Mts in 2022-23.

(ii) Visakhapatnam Refinery

Vizag Refinery was commissioned in 1957 by Caltex Oil Refining India Ltd. with a crude processing capacity of 0.675 Mts. Caltex Refinery, along with its marketing facilities were nationalized in 1976 and amalgamated with HPCL in 1978.

Capacity of Vizag refinery increased to 7.5 Mts in 1999 and then expanded to **8.3 Mts.**
Offshore Tanker Terminal was commissioned by Visakhapatnam Port Trust for unloading crude. Vizag Refinery constructed Single Point Mooring for discharging of Very Large Crude Carrier.
Vizag refinery processed 7.82 Mts of crude oil during 2004-05 (104%) as compared to 7.59 Mts during the previous year.
Vizag refinery manufactures LPG, Propylene, Naphtha, MS, ATF, SKO, HSD, LDO, LSHS, IFO, Bitumen, Sulphur, VLSFO etc.

Vizag Refinery Modernization Project is under progress to modernize and enhance the capacity of the Vizag Refinery from 8.3 Mts to 15.0 Mts.

(iii) Mangalore Refinery and Petrochemicals Ltd.

Mangalore Refinery and Petrochemicals Ltd. - MRPL was incorporated on 7.3.1988, as a joint venture of HPCL and Indian Rayon and Industries Ltd., for setting up a Refinery & Petrochemical project of capacity 3.69 Mts. MRPL was commissioned in 1996. MRPL became a subsidiary of ONGC on 30.3.2003.

MRPL undertakes refining of crude oil in Phase I and Phase II refinery units at Mangalore. MRPL produces Motor Spirit, HSD, Naphtha, Bitumen, CRMB, VGO, LPG, ATF, Furnace Oil, SKO, LSHS, Mixed Xylene, Pet Coke, Polypropylene & Hydrogen, etc. MRPL Refinery operated at 122% capacity in 2004-05.

MRPL retained market leader position in sale of Bitumen. MRPL is designed to maximize middle distillate Motor spirit and Gas Oil. Installed Capacity in 2008-09 of MRPL for Crude was 9.69 Mts.
MRPL completed Refinery upgradation and expansion project to increase the refining capacity from 9.69 Mts to 11.82 Mts in November 2009.
With commissioning of 3 Mts Crude and Vacuum Distillation unit 3 on 25.3.2012, the capacity of the refinery was increased to **15 Mts** enabling it to process high TAN and heavy crude, to increase distillate yield, to produce value added products like Propylene and upgrade diesel to Euro III / IV grade.

MRPL has 2 joint ventures namely Mangalam Retail Services Ltd and Shell MRPL Aviation Fuel Services Pvt Ltd.
MRPL has one subsidiary ONGC Mangalore Petrochemicals Ltd., which has set up an Aromatic Complex to produce 0.914 Mt of Para-xylene and 0.283 Mt of Benzene in Mangalore SEZ.

As of June 2020, 71.63% shares were held by ONGC, 16.95% shares by HPCL and the remaining shares were held by financial institutions and the general public.

(iv) Mumbai Lubes Refinery

Government of India requested Esso to set up a plant to manufacture lubricant oil base stocks during 1960s for use by Indian Oil Blending. A joint sector company, **Lube India Ltd,** was incorporated with equal stakes of Esso and the Government of India. Lube India plant was commissioned in 1969 for producing of 0.165 Mts of Lubricating Oil Base Stocks.

Lube India was taken over by Government of India and merged with HPCL in 1974.

Further de-bottlenecking and expansion increased the capacity to **0.428 Mts**.
Lube India accounted for over 40% of country's Lube Base Oil production in 2004-05.

(v) HPCL-Mittal Energy Ltd.

HMEL is a joint venture between HPCL and Mittal Energy Investments Pte. Ltd with equity holding of 48.99% each. HMEL's green field Guru Gobind Singh Refinery of 9 Mts capacity was commissioned at Bathinda in March 2012.

HMEL operates a crude oil refinery of 11.3 Mts capacity producing Motor Spirit, HSD, SKO, LPG, ATF etc., HMEL is also operating a Polypropylene unit of capacity 0.5 Mts to produce PP-Homo Polymer Grades.

(vi) HPCL Rajasthan Refinery Ltd.

HPCL Rajasthan Refinery Ltd. - HRRL is a Joint Venture of HPCL and the Government of Rajasthan with equity participation of 74% and 26% respectively.

Setting up of **9 MTS** Greenfield Refinery cum Petrochemical Complex at Pachpadra in Barmer district, to process local and imported crudes, started in 2018 and refinery is expected to operate at 75% of rated capacity in 2025 and at full capacity by 2027.

Hindustan Petroleum Corporation Ltd.

The refining capacity of HPCL increased from 5.5 Mts in 1984–85 to 14.80 Mts in March 2013.
HPCL enjoyed market share of 19.46% among PSU Oil Companies and 17.38% on total industry basis as in 2007-08.
HPCL's 3 refineries have total capacity of 32.8 Mts.

In addition, HPCL has **a Lube refinery** with a capacity of 0.428 Mts, **7 Lube Blending Plants.**

Starting with an ATF pipeline in the early 1980s from Mumbai Refinery to Santa-Cruz Airport, the Pipelines group set up 8 multi-product cross country pipelines and 2 LPG pipelines.

HPCL has **13 joint ventures** in the field of exploration & production, refining and marketing.
It has **4 subsidiaries** including Guru Govind Singh Refineries Ltd, HPCL Rajasthan Refinery Ltd., CREDA HPCL Biofuel Ltd. and Prize Petroleum Company Ltd.

The product range of HPCL comprises of 300+ products like Motor Spirit, HSD, LPG, Naphtha, FO, Auto LPG, CNG & Bitumen etc.

Company also planned to set up a 5 Mts LNG Regassification Terminal in Gujarat under JV. New products were developed for BS VI engines, electric and hybrid vehicles in 2019-20.
The installed capacity of HPCL for petroleum products in 2019-20 was 15.761 Mts.

Disinvestment - HPCL was the first PSE to be listed in BSE in 1992. Government of India's equity holding in the Corporation fell to 51.06%.

HPCL became a Navaratna company in 1997. It is one of the four Indian companies listed in the fortune 500 Global list of companies.

HPCL has 43 Terminals / TOPs, 72 Depots, 54 ASFs, 55 LPG Bottling Plants and 21186 Retail outlets.

The **gross turnover** of HPCL in 2022-23 was Rs. 466192.35 Cr.

HPCL's crude and pipeline throughputs in 2022-23 were 19.09 Mts and 23.25 Mts respectively. The operating cross-country pipeline network increased to 5,132 km. HPCL achieved ethanol blending of 10.59% by blending 129 crore litres of ethanol in MS in 2022-23.

Production in 2022-23 – LPG – 0.856 Mt, Naphtha – 0.497 Mt, MS – 3.587 Mt, ATF – 0.439 Mt, SKO – 0.184 Mt, HSD – 7.502 Mt, LDO – 0.249, FO – 2.191, LSHS – 0.05 Mt, Bitumen – 1.199 Mt, Propylene – 0.045 Mt and total petroleum products – 17.633 Mts HPCL_Annual_Report_2022-23.pdf (hindustanpetroleum.com)

Bharat Petroleum Corporation Limited

Bharat Petroleum Corporation Limited - Bharat Refineries Limited was formed on 24.1.1976 to undertake refining and marketing of Petroleum products by taking over Burmah-Shell Oil Storage & Distribution Company of India Ltd. (which was formed in 1928). It was renamed Bharat Petroleum Corporation Ltd on 1.08.1977.

Government then handed over operations of Burma-Shell Refineries Ltd, which was incorporated on 3.11.1952, to BPCL.

BPCL producing petroleum products and petrochemical feedstocks through its refineries at Mumbai and Ernakulam and Lube blending / filling plants at Mumbai, Kolkata, Delhi and Chennai.

(i) Bombay Refinery

In 1951, Burmah Shell Refineries Ltd. began to build Bombay refinery in Trombay under an agreement with Government of India with original installed capacity of 2 Mts.

The refinery was commissioned in January 1955. Following Government's acquisition of Burmah-Shell, name of the Refinery was changed to Bharat Refineries Ltd. on 1976. In August 1977, the Company was renamed Bharat Petroleum Corporation Ltd.

The installed capacity was increased from 5.25 Mts to 6 Mts in 1985 and further to 6.9 Mts in next stage and to 12 Mts through a modernization project. The project added CDU/VDU, HCU, LOBS, HGU units in additions to the required utilities such as DG, Salt Water Systems etc. The installed capacity was expanded to 14.5 Mts.

Revamp of LOBS production capacity from 300 TMTPA to 450 TMTPA and installation of new Kerosene hydrotreater of 1.5 Mt capacity (to produce ATF and Kerosene meeting Sulphur specification of max 10 PPMW and to increase HSD (diesel) production were completed during 2022-23.

(ii) Kochi Refineries Ltd.

Kochi Refineries Ltd. - Government of India, Phillips Petroleum Company of USA and Duncan Brothers & Company Ltd of Calcutta signed an agreement for the construction of a petroleum refinery in Kochi. KRL was incorporated on 06.09.1963 as Cochin Refineries,

Construction work started in March 1964 and the first unit came on stream in September 1966.

The original capacity of 2.5 Mts was increased to 3.3 Mts in 1973. Production of LPG and ATF commenced after this expansion.

Refining capacity was enhanced to 4.5 Mts in 1984 when a fluidized catalytic cracking unit of 1 Mts capacity was added.

KRL entered into petrochemical sector in 1989 when aromatic production facilities (of capacity 87,200 tons of benzene and 12,000 tons of toluene) were commissioned.

A captive power plant of 26.3 MW was commissioned in 1991.

In Dec 1994, refining capacity was increased to 7.5 Mts with revamp of FCCU to 1.4 Mts capacity. A fuel gas de-Sulphurisation unit was installed to minimize Sulphur-dioxide emission.

An additional captive power plant of 17.8 MW was commissioned in 1998 thus making the refinery self-sufficient in power.

In 2000, a 2 Mts Diesel Hydro De-Sulphurisation plant was added to reduce the Sulphur content in diesel.

A 44,000 tons LPG bottling plant and a 10000 Tons Bitumen Emulsion plant were commissioned in 2003.and 2004 respectively.

KRL processed 7.924 Mts of crude oil during 2004- 05 with capacity utilization of 105.65%.

BPCL acquired the Government's shares in KRL in March 2001. KRL amalgamated with Bharat Petroleum Corporation w.e.f. 18.08.2006 and was rechristened as BPCL-Kochi Refinery.

Capacity expansion cum modernization Phase II was implemented in 2007-08.

A 378000 Tons Biturox Bitumen Oxidation unit was successfully commissioned in 2008.

In August 2010, the refining capacity was further increased to **9.5 Mts** per year.

The capacity of KRL increased to 15.5 Mts through a capacity expansion program in 2018-19.

Refining capacity increased from 50,000 barrels/day (7,900 m^3/d) in 1966 to 310,000 barrels/day (49,000 m^3/d).

KRL produces LPG, naphtha, petrol, diesel, kerosene, ATF, gas oil, fuel oil (both 180 cst and 380 cst) and bitumen.

Specialty Products - Benzene, Toluene, White Spirit, Poly Iso Butene & Sulphur, bitumen products like Natural Rubber Modified Bitumen, Bitumen Emulsion, Low Aromatic Naphthene (High Paraffinic)

The company has one financial joint venture for putting a product pipeline connecting Kochi, Coimbatore and Kurnool.

(iii) Bina Refinery

The BPCL Bina Refinery was incorporated as a joint venture between Bharat Petroleum Corporation Ltd. and OQ SAOC (formerly known as Oman Oil Company SAOC) in 1994.

6 Mts Grassroots petroleum refinery was commissioned in May 2011 to produce fuels of BS-VI grade.

During 2013-14, Bharat Oman Refineries processed 5.45 Mts of crude oil.

Crude oil import facilities consisting of Single Point Mooring system and crude oil storage terminal have been set up at Vadinar. A 935 km cross-country crude oil pipeline from Vadinar to Bina was built for moving crude oil to the refinery.

The refinery expanded its capacity to 7.8 Mts in 2018-19.

In 2021, Bina refinery became wholly owned subsidiary of BPCL.

Bina Refinery was planning in 2023 to increase its capacity to 11 Mts and petrochemical plant production capacity to 2.2 Mt.

Bharat Petroleum Corporation Ltd

BPCL processed 9.14 and 20.95 Mts of crude during 2004-05 (with capacity utilization of 132%) and 2007-08 respectively. (12.13.4.5)

In 2007-08, BPCL had market share of 26.4% in LPG (Bulk and Packed), 29.8% in Motor Spirit, 21.1% in ATF, 24.7% in HSD, 20.8% in Naphtha, 20.5% in lubricants and 21.6% in furnace oil.

Product Installed Capacity in 2008-09 of BPCL for Crude was 19.5 Mts

Metal cutting gas entered foreign markets with a tie up with 'Bahrain Gas'.

BPCL has **3 subsidiary companies** namely Kochi Refineries Ltd., Petronet CCK Ltd. and Bharat Petro Resources Ltd. (Numaligarh Refinery Ltd. till 2023)

BPCL formed **22 joint venture companies** covering refining, city gas distribution, renewable energy, pipelines, gas, into-plane servicing etc.

A new joint venture company **Delhi Aviation Fuel Facility Pvt Ltd** was promoted by BPCL, IOCL and Delhi International Airport Ltd for implementing aviation fuel facility for T3 terminal at Delhi.

In 2019-20, BPCLs crude processing capacity has got enhanced from 21.5 MTS to 27.5MTS with commissioning of Integrated Refinery Expansion Project at Kochi Refinery.

Bharat Oman Refineries Ltd was merged with BPCL on 1.07.2022, followed by the merger of **Bharat Gas Resources Ltd** on 16.08.2022.

BPCL ranked 295 in Fortune Global 500 list for 2022.

The gross turnover of BPCL in 2022-23 was Rs. 533467.55 Cr.

Refineries throughput was 38.53 Mts (Mumbai Refinery 14.66 Mt, Kochi Refinery 16.12 Mt and Bina refinery 7.75 Mt), at a capacity utilization of 109% and pipe lines throughput was 19.06 Mt in 2022-23. Production in 2022-23 – LPG – 1.786 Mt, Naphtha – 1.533 Mt, MS – 7.824 Mt, ATF – 1.796 Mt, SKO – 0.175 Mt, HSD – 18.195 Mt, LDO – 0.127, FO – 1.127, LSHS – 0.108 Mt, Bitumen – 0.808 Mt, Propylene – 0.199 Mt, Petcoke – 1.309 Mt and total petroleum products – 35.941 Mts. Complete-BPCL-AR-2022-23---English-Final-9fc811.pdf (bharatpetroleum.in)

BPCL-KIAL Fuel Farm Ltd

BKFFPL was incorporated in May 2015 with an equity participation of 74% by BPCL and 26% by Kannur International Airport Ltd. to design, construct, commission, and operate the fuel farm at Kannur International Airport for the supply of ATF. It started operating from December 2018.

Numaligarh Refinery Ltd.

Numaligarh Refinery Ltd. - NRL was incorporated on 22.4.1993 for providing a fillip to the industrial and economic development of Assam. NRL with initial installed capacity of 3 Mts was commissioned in 1999. The commercial production commenced from 1.10.2000.

NRL is producing LPG, MS, ATF, SKO, Euro-III and Euro-IV HSD, naphtha, Sulphur and wax.

The company is having **2 joint ventures** namely Brahmaputra Cracker and Polymer Ltd. and Duliajan Numaligarh Pipeline Ltd. (joint venture with Assam Gas Company Ltd. to implement the Duliajan - Numaligarh Gas Pipeline project).

NRL's crude throughput was 3.091 Mts in FY 2022-23 with capacity utilization of 103%. The NRL has commissioned a 130 km long and 1 Mt capacity product pipeline from Siliguri in West Bengal to Parbatipur in Bangladesh on 18th March, 2023.

OIL acquired NRL refinery with shareholding of 69.63% as on 31.03.2023.

NRL has embarked on an integrated refinery expansion project to augment its capacity from 3 Mts to 9 Mts.

Numaligarh Refinery Ltd. is pursuing a Bio Refinery project for production of ethanol from bamboo. Annual_Report_2022_23.pdf (oil-india.com)

Petronet LNG Ltd. – Import of LNG

Petronet LNG Ltd. - PLL was formed on 02.04.1998 as a Joint Venture of GAIL, ONGC, IOCL. and BPCL to import LNG and set up LNG terminals with facilities like jetty, storage, regasification etc. to supply Natural Gas to various industries in the country

PLL entered into agreement with Ras Laffan Liquefied Natural Gas Company, for supply of LNG and set up first and largest LNG supply terminal at Dahej.

In 2011– Petronet received approval for expanding Kochi LNG Terminal capacity up to 5 Mts.

PLL recorded consolidated revenue from operations of Rs. 59,899.35 Cr during 2022-23

Petronet CCK Limited – Execution of Pipe Line Projects

Petronet CCK Limited - PCCKL was incorporated on 18.06.1998 as a joint venture of Petronet India Ltd, Cochin Refineries Ltd. and BPCL for implementation and operation of Cochin-Coimbatore (Irugur)-Karur pipeline.

PCCKL laid the CCK pipeline during 1999-2002 and commissioned in March 2002 for transporting Petrol, Diesel, Kerosene, etc.

PCCK merged with BPCL w.e.f. 1.06.2018.

Indian Strategic Petroleum Reserve Ltd. (ISPRL) – Reserve Oil Storage

Indian Strategic Petroleum Reserves Ltd. - ISPRL was incorporated as a subsidiary of Indian Oil Corporation Ltd. on 16.6.2004 to undertake construction, commissioning, storage, handling, treatment, carriage transport, dispatch, supply of crude oil and petroleum products as strategic reserves for meeting supply disruptions during emergency. ISPRL created strategic crude oil storage capacity for 15 days at Vishakhapatnam (1.33 Mts), Mangalore (1.50 Mts) and Padur (2.5 Mts) in June 2015, October 2016 and December 2018 respectively.

Creda-HPCL Biofuel Ltd – Development of Biodiesel

Creda-HPCL Biofuel Limited - To promote alternate fuels, CREDA-HPCL Biofuel Ltd was incorporated on 14.10.2008 as a subsidiary of Hindustan Petroleum Corp. Ltd. with equity shareholding of 74% by HPCL and 26% by Chhattisgarh State Renewable Energy Development Agency (CREDA).

CHBL planned to undertake cultivation of jatropha plants on 15,000 hectares of land leased by Chhattisgarh government for 30 years. HPCL was given exclusive rights on the entire produce of jatropha seeds for producing biodiesel. Up to 31.03.2014, CHBL leased 7451 hectares of land from Chhattisgarh government and completed plantation on 2340 Ha. Seed yield was found to be very low and Jatropha plant had substantially high cultivation and maintenance costs.

All business activities were suspended w.e.f. 16.07.2015 and approval for closure obtained from Governments of India and Chhattisgarh. CREDA-HPCL Biofuels Ltd and Indian Oil-CREDA Biofuels Ltd had to be closed during 2017-18

Indian Oil CREDA Biofuels Ltd. - Development of Biodiesel

Indian Oil CREDA Biofuels Ltd. - IOCBL was incorporated on 06-02-2009 as a joint venture of Indian Oil Corp. Ltd and Chhattisgarh State Renewable Energy Development Agency (CREDA) formed to produce biodiesel from variety of tree borne oil seed crops.

IOCBL was engaged in plantation activities for Jatropha plants over 5889 hectares in Chhattisgarh.

In line with advice from Niti Aayog, Govt. of India, the Company initiated action for closure in 2017-18.

HPCL Biofuels Ltd. – Production of Ethanol

HPCL Biofuels Ltd. - HBL was incorporated on 16-10-2009 as a subsidiary of Hindustan Petroleum Corp. Ltd. to set up integrated sugar, ethanol & co-gen power plants at Sugauli in East Champaran district and Lauriya in West Champaran district of Bihar.

Company is engaged in producing Ethanol directly from Sugarcane juice for blending in petrol thereby resulting in substantial savings.

HBL plants have crushing capacity of 3500 TPCD, distillery capacity of 60 KLPD and Co-gen capacity of 20 MW.

50% juice was to be converted to Sugar and 50% juice to be converted to Ethanol.

Oil Industry was blending 5% Ethanol with Motor Spirit and marketing in 20 States and 4 Union Territories.

The gross turnover in 2022-23 was Rs. 298.13 Cr.

Konkan LNG Ltd – Regasification of Natural Gas

Konkan LNG Ltd was incorporated on 04.12.2015 for regasification of liquefied natural gas in regasification plant at village Anjanwel, Maharashtra with a regasification capacity of 5 Mts. The company became operational in 2019-20.

Konkan LNG terminal receives and stores liquified natural gas from LNG carriers ranging from 135000 m^3 to 160000 m^3 capacities. The LNG is vaporized and exported as natural gas to GAIL terminal.

The terminal is currently operating only during non-monsoon months due to non-availability of breakwater facilities. Construction work for breakwater has started. After commissioning, the terminal shall be able to operate throughout the year utilizing full capacity.

Public Sector Enterprises Engaged in Production of Petrochemicals

Indian Petrochemical Corporation Limited (IPCL)

IPCL was established on 22.03.1969, as a Government of India undertaking, for promoting the development of the petrochemical industry in India. Construction of its first petrochemicals complex at Vadodara started in 1970. Commercial production commenced in 1973.

IPCL implemented rehabilitation / expansion of Polypropylene plant, revamping of its naphtha cracker, additional Xylenes production, Bicomponent Acrylic Fibres, etc. during VII Plan.

IPCL's second and third petrochemicals complexes were commissioned in 1992 and 1996 at Nagothane and Gandhar respectively.

IPCL completed revamping and expansion program of its Vadodara cracker complex and expansion program of its Maharashtra Gas Cracker Complex, Nagothane during VIII Plan.

Expansion of IPCL's cracker capacity from 0.3 to 0.4 Mts and HDPE/ LLDPE swing plant capacity from 0.16 to 0.22 Mts and IPCL's II phase of Gandhar complex with an ethylene capacity of 0.3 Mts and mono ethylene glycol of 0.10 Mts were completed during IX Plan.

Large Production Matrix - Vadodara Complex, comprising a Naphtha Cracker of 0.13 Mt capacity, Xylene Plant, Propylene Separation Plant and 15 Downstream Plants, produced LDPE, PPCP, PP, PVC, PBR, Acrylic Fibre, Dry Spun Acrylic Fibre & Mono-ethylene Glycol, Linear Alkyl Benzene, Ethylene Oxide, & Acrylates.

Nagothane complex, comprising Ethane / Propane Cracker of 0.4 Mt capacity and Downstream Plants, produced LLDPE, LDPE, HDPE, PP, Wire & Cable, Mono-ethylene Glycol, Ethylene Oxide, etc.

Gandhar complex, comprising a Gas Cracker of 0.3 Mt capacity and Downstream Plants, produced PVC, HDPE, Mono-ethylene Glycol, Caustic Soda, Ethylene Oxide, etc.

Captive Power Plants – Refer Ch. 17

High-Capacity Utilization – Refer Ch. 17

Special / Monopolistic Production – Refer Ch. 17

Infrastructure, Expansion Plans, Market Leader, Financial Strength – Refer Ch. 17

In June 2002, the Government of India. as a part of its disinvestment program divested 26% of its equity shares in favor of Reliance Petro Investments Ltd.

Southern Petro-Chemical Industries Corporation (SPIC)

Southern Petrochemical Industries Corp. Ltd. – SPIC was incorporated on 18.12.1969 and became a joint venture between M.A. Chidambaram Group and Tamil Nadu Industrial Development Corp. in 1975.

SPIC promoted Tamil Nadu Petroproducts Ltd in the joint sector along with TIDCO.
Manali Petrochemical Ltd Plant-II (originally a joint venture of UB and TIDCO) was merged with Manali Petrochemical Ltd (unit 1 started by SPIC in 1986).
SPIC was the Co-promoter for the Aromatics Project being setup in the joint sector by Madras Refineries Ltd.

Brahmaputra Crackers and Polymer Ltd. – Production of HDPE, LLDPE, etc.

Brahmaputra Crackers and Polymer Ltd. - BCPL was incorporated on 08.01.2007 as a subsidiary of GAIL with equity participation from GAIL, OIL, Govt. of Assam and NRL, for setting up 0.28 Mt Gas Cracker Project at Lepetkata, Assam.
BCPL is manufacturing 0.22 Mts of High-Density Polyethylene and Linear Low-Density polyethylene, 60,000 Tons of Polypropylene, Hydrogenated Pyrolysis Gasoline and Fuel oil with natural gas and naphtha as feed stock.

The installed capacity for LLDPE / HDPE / PP was 270695 tons in 2019-20.

ONGC Mangalore Petrochemicals Ltd

ONGC Mangalore Petrochemicals Ltd. – OMPL, a green field petrochemicals project, was promoted by ONGC and Mangalore Refinery and Petrochemicals Ltd. OMPL became a direct subsidiary of MRPL w.e.f. 28.02.2015.

An aromatic complex, set up by OMPL in Mangalore SEZ, sources its feedstock from MRPL. The complex, in 2017-18, was the largest single stream unit in Asia to produce 0.914 Mt of Para-xylene and 0.283 Mt of Benzene.

ONGC Mangalore Petrochemicals Ltd merged with MRPL w.e.f. 15/05/2022.

Summary –

The share of the Government in the domestic refining capacity was about 47% of the total by 1965-66.
Public sector contribution was 98.7% of total crude oil production and 99.2% of total gas production during 1992-97.
The country achieved self-sufficiency in refining capacity by 2001-02.
The public sector contributions were 85.1%, 86.1%, 84.4%, 74.3% and 72.4% of the total crude oil productions and 76.1%, 75.4%, 53.7%, 48.74% and 54.6% of the total natural gas productions during 2007-08 to 2011-12 respectively.
The country was expected to have surplus refining capacity by almost 108 Mts in 2011-12.
CPSE's share in Refinery throughput in 2007-08 was 72%.

Crude oil production of ONGC, OIL and OVL in 2022-23 were 19.584 Mts, 3.18 Mts and 6.349 Mts respectively. These CPSEs contributed 99.77% to the total production of 29.18 Mts

Natural gas production of ONGC and OIL were 20.628 BCM and 3.18 BCM respectively. These CPSEs contributed 69.11% to the overall natural gas production during 2022-23 of 34.450 BCM. (OVL production of 10.171 Mts of Oil Equivalent of Oil & Gas, which is 16.0% of India's domestic production, has not been considered).

IOCL (including CPCL), HPCL. BPCL and NRL refineries crude throughput were 83.72 Mt, 19.09 Mts, 38.53 Mts and 3.091 Mts respectively. These CPSEs contributed 56.6% to the total refinery production (crude throughput) during 2022-23 of 255.2 Mts.

Production of petroleum products by IOCL, HPCL and BPCL were 83.966 Mts, 17.633 Mts and 35.941 Mts respectively. These CPSEs contributed 51.61% to the total production of petroleum products of 266.5 Mts.

Table – 12.2 – CPSEs Share in Domestic Output

Domestic Production of Crude Oil in million metric Tons							Total Output by CPSEs / Share of CPSEs to Domestic Output (%)						
1968-69	1998-99	2004-05	2005-06	2008-09	2009-10	2010-11	1968-69	1998-99	2004-05	2005-06	2008-09	2009-10	2010-11
6.06	32.7	33.98	32.19	33.5	33.5	37.68	3.08	29.7	29.68	27.64	28.8	28.8	27.9
							50.83	90.8	87.34	85.57	86	86	74
Natural Gas in BCM													
NA	27.4	31.76		32.8	32.8	52.22	NA	24.5	24.98		24.7	24.7	25.45
							NA	89.4	78.65		75.3	75.3	48.7
Refineries Throughput in Million metric Tons													
	68.5			160.8	160.8	196.5		68.5			112.2	112.2	115.1
								100			69.8	69.8	58.5
Refinery crude in Mts													
16.55		127.12	130.11				8.09		92.81	96.95			
							48.88		73.01	74.51			

Private Sector Players –

Petrochemical companies
Garware Polyester Ltd – 1933, Dharangadhra Chemical Works / DCW Ltd – 1939, Garware Motors & Engineers Pvt Ltd / Garware Hi-Tech Films Ltd – 1957, Finolex Industries Ltd – 1958, National Organic Chemical Industry Ltd – 1961, Garware Technical Fibres – 1976, Andhra Petrochemicals Ltd – 1984, Manali Petrochemical Ltd – 1986, IG Petrochemicals Ltd - 1988

Reliance Hazira Petrochemicals Plant – 1991, Haldia Petrochemicals Ltd – 1994, Grasim's Chlorinated polyvinyl Chloride plant – 2020

Petroleum companies
Indrol Lubricants and Specialities Pvt Ltd / Castrol India Ltd. - 1979, Mangalore Refineries & Petrochemicals Ltd - 1988, Essar Oil Ltd – 1989, Essar Oil and Gas Exploration and Production Ltd - 1990
Tata Petronet – 1993, Cairn India – 1999, Reliance Industries Ltd / Reliance Petroleum Ltd – 1999, L&T Hydrocarbon Engineering Ltd. – 2009. Adani Welspun Exploration (2005), Adani Total Gas Limited (2005)

13: DEVELOPMENT OF SCIENCE, ELECTRONICS, RESEARCH AND DEFENCE ESTABLISHMENTS

Targeted Growth for Production of Electronic Products

Electronic products required for many industries like defence, communication, nuclear, industrial process control, data acquisition, monitoring, processing, research etc. were forecasted by the government for the last year of each 5-year plan and the targets for manufacturing professional equipment, electronics equipment, consumer electronics, industrial electronics, strategic electronics, communication and broadcasting equipment required during the various 5-year plans were set.

Growth of Scientific and Research Institutions

Establishment of Research Institutions and Laboratories

About 130 specialized research laboratories and institutes were established under the aegis of Indian Council of Agricultural Research, Council of Scientific and Industrial Research, Indian Council of Medical Research, Departments of Atomic Energy, Science and Technology, Space, and Defence Research and Development Organization, etc. (6.19.1)

Department of Atomic Energy

Achievements in VIII 5YP - (9.10.73)
(i) Conceptual design of the Prototype Fast Breeder Reactor and related R and D studies.
(ii) Assembly of 450 MeV Synchrotron Radiation Source.
(iii) Desalination plants on Multi Stage flash, Reverse Osmosis and Low Temperature Vacuum Evaporation process.

Achievements in IX Plan (10.10.35): -
Pressurized Heavy Water Reactors were already in the commercial domain. India was mastering all aspects of this technology and the power reactors and fuel cycle facilities were operating satisfactorily.
Fast Breeder Test Reactor was operating satisfactorily with advanced plutonium-uranium carbide fuel, far exceeding its originally stipulated performance standards. (10.10.34)
Bhabha Atomic Research Centre made good progress in the design and development of Advanced Heavy Water Reactor, utilizing country's vast thorium reserves. (10.10.35)

Dept of Science & Technology

Achievements in VIII 5YP – Treatment of tuberculosis and other diseases using lasers.
Demonstration-cum sale of PARAM super computer.
Integration of seismographs for use by Indian Meteorological Department.

Department of Scientific and Industrial Research

Achievements in VIII Plan - Commercialization of products and processes for CNC tools and Cutter Grinder, Fuel efficient diesel LCV engines, 25 KW solar photo voltaic power plant, licensing of technologies related to Heart Valve, Fly Ash bricks, Glycol based automobile coolant and Special blister packaging machines, etc. (9.10.93)

Department of Bio-Technology

Achievements in VIII Plan - Diagnostic and therapeutic instruments for cancer therapy, diagnostic kits for tuberculosis, hepatitis A and C, Amoebiasis, Leishmaniasis, Streptococcal infection in children and

HIV-I and II; High frequency reproducible regeneration of wheat plants; Transfer of technology for monoclonal M-13 bacteriophage; Cloning of gene coding and expression in E. coli; Biological control of pests and Aquaculture; Establishment of Centre for DNA Fingerprinting and Diagnostics at Hyderabad. (9.10.101)

Dept of Ocean Development

Achievements in VIII Plan - Six expeditions to Antarctica; Survey of entire pioneer area of 1,50,000 sq. km. for Polymetallic Nodules using hydro sweep; Prototype of remotely operated collector unit operating up to 200m depth; Bucket-in-pipe lifting system for transporting nodules from collector system. **(9.10.106)**

Achievements in IX Plan: A Remotely Operated Vehicle system was made ready for inspecting underwater structures, pipelines, sampling etc. up to 250 meters depth. (10.10.72)

India Meteorological Department

India Meteorological Department was established on 15.01.1875 for forecasting the annual monsoon, tracking the progress of the monsoon across India every season, forecasting, naming and distribution of warnings for tropical cyclones in Northern Indian Ocean, Malacca Straits, Bay of Bengal, Arabian Sea and Persian Gulf with the installation (during VIII plan) of CYBER-2000 computer to make forecasting more efficient. IMD operates hundreds of observation stations across India and Antarctica.

Achievements during IX Plan – Design and development of Cyclone Warning Radar and MST Radar which was the third of its kind in the world.

Growth of Research Institutions & Laboratories

Indian Council of Agricultural Research

Indian Council of Agricultural Research was established on 16.07.1929 for coordinating agricultural education and research. It is the largest network of agricultural research and education institutes in the world.
High Security Animal Disease Laboratory (Bhopal) of ICAR developed a vaccine against bird flu in 2006.
ICAR scientists were the first in the world to sequence the pigeon pea genome in 2011.
ICAR published an Integrated Mobile App called Krishi Integrated Solution for Agri Apps Navigation for Farmers of country in 2019.
As of January 2020, ICAR had 4 Deemed Universities, 65 ICAR Institutions, 14 National Research Centres, 6 National Bureaus and 13 (Project) Directorates.

Council of Scientific and Industrial Research

CSIR was established on 26.09.1942 to promote research and development in as many sectors as needed for scientific development of the country. The national laboratories under CSIR undertook turn-key projects and provided basic designs for processes to various industries. Up to 1979-80, more than 1200 processes were released to industries of which over 500 were taken up for commercial production. (6.19.82)

CSIR undertook R and D work related to exploration of oil in the off-shore areas, on alignment of pipelines, location of terminal points of pipelines onshore, discharge of effluents from the terminal pumping stations and from possible spills along the pipelines. (7.17.25)
CSIR built up over the years a network of 40 specialized national laboratories with 80 field extension centres having expertise and knowledge-base in diverse scientific disciplines and serving practically all the socio-economic sectors.

Achievements in VII plan - Some production processes were licensed to other countries - Gugu lipid to France for $ 50,000; pentacle zeolite catalyst to Holland for $ 3,00,000 plus $ 6,50,000 as royalty; membranes for desalination plants to Thailand for $ 1,60,000; azidothymidine and etoposide drugs to the Philippines for $ 50,000. Consultancy for setting up of a Polymer Research Institute in China for $ 1,30,000. Industrial production, based on CSIR knowhow / technologies, worked out to over Rs.4500 Cr during 1985-91. (8.18.4.11)

Achievements in VIII plan:
(i) The country's first all-composite aircraft was designed and fabricated.
(ii) New catalysts were developed for refineries, petrochemical and chemical industry.
(iii) A cost-effective novel process for NMP (a solvent used in refinery processes) was developed.
(iv) New drugs for antifertility, bioenhancer and memory enhancer were developed and novel cost-effective processes for over 30 drugs and 4 drug intermediates were licensed (as anti-AIDS, anti-viral, anti-cancer, anti-bacterial, anti-malarial, analgesics, anti-inflammatory, anti-allergic, etc.)
(v) Technologies were developed for beneficiation of coking and non-coking coal for reduction of ash content, coal carbonization, solvent refining, conversion of synthetic gas/coal to middle distillates etc.
(vi) Development of oil palm processing technologies including a screw press of 5 tons FFB/hour capacity; mechanized pulse mill of 100 kg/hour capacity and hand-operated Daal mill of 40-50 kg/hour capacity in Food Processing Sector

The CSIR's expertise and capabilities were gainfully utilized in USA (Abbot Laboratories, Parke-Davis, Smith-Kline Beecham, FMC, GE, Du Pont etc.), UK, Switzerland, Canada, Finland, China, Brazil, Indonesia and Oman. **(9.10.100)**

Highlights
(i) During VIII 5YP, the industrial production based on CSIR know-how increased to Rs. 10,000 Cr, with a productivity saving worth Rs. 800 Cr.
(ii) 250 New technologies were made available for licensing and 800 technology license agreements were executed.
(iii) A total of 920 patents were filed in India and another 120 patents abroad.
(iv) Technical assistance was rendered to about 4000 entrepreneurs and an external cashflow of Rs. 700 Cr was generated through contract R and D work and consultancy (9.10.101)

Achievements in IX plan:
(i) Total external cash-flow for 1997-2001 crossed Rs. 1,000 Cr, catalyzing industrial production to over Rs. 17,000 Cr;
(ii) Filing of nearly 1,400 Indian patents and 650 foreign patents and increasing the impact factor per research paper from 1.26 to 1.552.
(iii) Design, fabrication and air worthiness testing of 9–14-seater light transport aircraft; certification of the two-seater trainer aircraft; HANSA-3 designed and built by **National Aerospace Laboratory** and commencement of commercial production. (10.10.67)
(iv) Development of mini refineries, self-contained, skid mounted, low cost and low maintenance units congenial for installation in any location, of capacities varying from 0.5 to 2.0 Mts. (10.10.67)
(v) Retrofit technology for conversion of two-stroke engines of petrol/diesel to CNG-operable engines.

Research Papers & Patents - CSIR has published 16,664 research papers in SCI journals of national and international repute during 2007–10. CSIR has 3,250 foreign and 2,350 Indian patents in force and 222 patents licensed as on date. The percentage utilization of patents is 8.67%, which is much above the world average of 3–5%.

Achievements in XI plan:
(i) Technology for Head Up Display for Light Combat Aircraft was transferred to Bharat Electronics Ltd.
(ii) CSIR licensed worldwide commercialization of new generation thrombolytic molecules to Nostrum Pharmaceuticals, USA for $ 150 million.
(iii) A new-generation clot-specific protein that displays plasminogen activation property was transferred to Nostrum Pharmaceuticals at Rs. 19.60 Cr plus 5% royalty.
(iv) Technology for Caerulomycin A, and its proprietary derivatives and analogues for their novel indication of immuno-suppression—a discovery of importance in tissue transplantation like in kidney and heart—was licensed to M/s Nostrum Pharmaceuticals, USA at Rs. 14.70 Cr plus 2% royalty.
(v) A new anti-ulcer drug - a natural agent for treatment of symptoms associated with gastrointestinal toxicity and ulcer—was licensed to M/s IPCA Laboratories Ltd., at Rs. 2.5 Cr plus royalty.
(vi) CSIR developed a low cost 10hp 'Krishi Shakti' tractor suitable for small farmers.
(vii) CSIR developed a catalytic process for the manufacture of epichlorohydrin from allyl chloride and sold to Aditya Birla Group for setting up a plant in Ryong, Thailand.
(viii) Process technology for sugarcane bagasse for the recovery of cellulose, hemi-cellulose and lignin was licensed to Godavari Sugars at Rs. 6.5 Cr plus 3% royalty.

As of April 2022, CSIR runs 38 laboratories, 39 outreach centres, 3 Innovation Centres and 5 units in India. CSIR has 2971 patents in force internationally and 1592 patents in India. CSIR was granted more than 14000 patents worldwide since its inception.

Indian Institute of Chemical Technology

Indian Institute of Chemical Technology was established in 1944 to conduct research in basic and applied chemistry, biochemistry, bioinformatics, chemical engineering for development of pesticides, drugs, organic intermediates, fine chemicals, catalysts, polymers, organic coatings, etc.. IICT is engaged in designing control measures for vector-borne diseases like malaria, filaria, Japanese encephalitis, dengue fever, etc.

Tata Institute of Fundamental Research

Tata Institute of Fundamental Research, a public deemed university, works under the umbrella of the Department of Atomic Energy of Government of India. Dr. Homi J. Bhabha established TIFR with financial support from J.R.D. Tata on 1.06.1945.

Since 1949, the CSIR designated TIFR to be the centre for all large-scale projects in nuclear research. In the 1950s, TIFR gained prominence in the field of cosmic ray physics, with the setting up of research facilities in Ooty and Kolar gold mines.
In 1957, India's first digital computer, TIFRAC was built in TIFR.
In 1970, TIFR started research in radio astronomy with the setting up of the **O**oty **R**adio **T**elescope. Encouraged by the success of ORT, J.R.D. Tata was persuaded to help set up the Giant Metrewave Radio Telescope near Pune.
TIFR attained the official deemed university status in June 2002.
TIFR was involved in building India's first gravity wave detector.
Nuclear Magnetic Resonance spectrometer was developed for solid state studies.

National Physical Laboratory

National Physical Laboratory was set up on 4.01.1947 to establish National Standards of Measurements and to realize the Units based on International System, to conduct research in physics and to assist industries in their developmental tasks by precision measurements, calibration, development of devices, processes, etc.

The indelible ink used to mark the fingernail of a voter during general elections was developed in 1952. NPL established an atmospheric monitoring station in the Institute of Himalayan Bioresource Technology at Palampur (H.P.) at an altitude of 1391 m for generating the base data for atmospheric trace species & properties to serve as reference for comparison of polluted atmosphere in India.

Central Building Research Institute

Central Building Research Institute was established in 1947 for generating, cultivating and promoting building science and technology in India.

Physical Research Laboratory

The Physical Research Laboratory was founded on 11.11.1947 by Dr. Vikram Sarabhai beginning the laboratory at his residence, with research on cosmic rays. Research areas were expanded from cosmic rays and the properties of the upper atmosphere, to include theoretical and radio physics later with grants from the United States Atomic Energy Commission.
PRL also manages the Udaipur Solar Observatory and Mount Abu Infrared Observatory.
The ozone observing station was set up at Mount Abu in 1951. On 12.10.1951, the first measurement of ozone was performed.

PRL developed Meson Telescopes, Photometers, Geiger-Muller Counters, Ionosonde, Dobson Spectrometers, etc.
A research station at Gulmarg in Kashmir was established in 1955 by PRL for observation of airglow during night time, ozone concentration in the atmosphere, the intensity of cosmic rays, etc. As this station was giving fruitful results, a complete **High Altitude Research Laboratory** was set up at Gulmarg in 1963.
In the 1960s, many of rocket payloads were manufactured at PRL.
Research on lunar meteorites and rocks and Earth sciences was started in 1972. Astronomy and Plasma Physics branches were launched in 1970s to provide support to research on space and ionosphere and to commence research on the plasma of high temperature, which was crucial for the development of fusion research. Subsequently **Institute for Plasma Research** was set up in Gandhi Nagar.
3 Radio telescopes were developed at Rajkot, Surat and Thatlej to measure the speed of solar wind.
Solar activity and its effects on space weather were studied by Astronomy and Astrophysics divisions.
Planetary Sciences division undertakes studies to understand the origin and evolution of the solar system with a special focus on inner planets.

Central Leather Research Institute

Central Leather Research Institute was founded on 24.04.1948 to establish adapted preservation methods for new hides and skins, improvement of leather with respect to shrinkage and colour fastness, tanning and finishing techniques, control of product design and development of garments, shoes and other articles. In 2003, the institute came up with a biological dressing for burn patients that helps in healing second and third degree burns faster and more effectively.

Central Electro-Chemical Research Institute

Central Electro Chemical Research Institute was founded on 25.07.1948.

The average power saving by using titanium substrate insoluble anodes in place of graphite anodes in the chloro-alkali industry was about 700 kWh/ ton of caustic soda. it was estimated that over 200 million kWh of power could be saved annually through the use of anodes developed by the CECRI.

National Chemical Laboratory

National Chemical Laboratory was established in 1950 to undertake research in polymer science, organic chemistry, catalysis, materials chemistry, chemical engineering, biochemical sciences and process development.

Based on processes developed at NCL, Pune, Indian Petro-Chemicals Corporation Ltd. put up a 10,000 TPA plant at Vadodara for production of acrylates.

A solvent extraction process for the production of benzene was released to Bharat Petroleum Corporation for processing 1,70,000 tons of feed per annum; the process was also under consideration of Cochin Refinery and the Salempur Aromatics Complex.

Central Food Technological Research Institute

Central Food Technological Research Institute - CFTRI was established on 21.10.1950, to undertake research in the production and handling of grains, pulses, oilseeds, spices, fruits, vegetables, meat, fish and poultry. It has 16 R & D departments, including laboratories focusing on food engineering, food biotechnology, microbiology, grain sciences, sensory science, biochemistry, molecular nutrition and food safety. The institute has developed over 300 products, processes, and equipment designs, and most of these technologies have been released to over 4000 licensees for commercial application. The institute develops technologies to increase efficiency and reduce post-harvest losses, etc.

Central Drug Research Institute

Central Drug Research Institute was established on 17.02.1951 to undertake drug research. It conducts research in Biochemistry, Botany, Clinical and Experimental Medicine, Cancer Biology, Endocrinology, Fermentation Technology, Medicinal and Process Chemistry, Microbiology, Neuroscience and Aging Biology, Parasitology, Pharmaceutics, Pharmacokinetics and Metabolism, Pharmacology, Toxicology, etc.

Central Road Research Institute

Central Road Research Institute - CRRI was established in 1952 to conduct research and development in design, construction, maintenance and management of roads and airport runways. It also works in area of traffic and surface transportation planning of mega and medium cities, management of roads in different terrains, utilization of industrial waste in road construction, landslide control, environmental pollution, road traffic safety analysis, wind, fatigue, corrosion studies, performance monitoring/ evaluation, service life assessment and rehabilitation of highway and railway bridges.

Central Electronics Engineering Research Institute

Central Electronics Engineering Research Institute, Pilani, a constituent laboratory of CSIR, was established in 1953 for advanced research and development in the field of Electronics.

CEERI developed 500-KW and 1-MW fixed-frequency S-band Magnetrons and 6-GHz, 20-W travelling wave tubes.

The Chennai Centre focuses on process control instrumentation and automation as well as machine vision technologies.

National Research Development Corp.

National Research Development Corp. - NRDC was incorporated on 31.12.1953 to promote, develop and commercialize the technologies / knowhow / inventions / patents / processes developed by various national R&D institutions. NRDC is providing technical, commercial and financial measures needed for converting an idea, invention or process into a product in the market and licensing them to entrepreneurs.

During 2004-05, 2006-07 and 2007-08, 42, 39 and 59 new processes respectively were assigned to NRDC for commercialization from various R&D laboratories and universities. It signed 5 major agreements with African nations for technology transfer in 2004-05.
NRDC obtained a foothold in Africa by establishing demonstration centre at Ivory Coast and executing Fuel briquette plant at Nigeria and a Cashew Processing Plant at Cote d' Ivoire.
NRDC was assigned more than 270 technologies by various R&D institutions, and it signed more than 175 license agreements with industry for commercialization during XI 5YP period. (12.8.85).
Over the years since its inception in 1953, the corporation has transferred 2500 technologies and approximately 4800 license agreements executed / technologies licensed **to over 4800 entrepreneurs.**
Successfully completed pilot research project on tomato production in Ghana during 2017-18.
Several agencies and Govt. Departments have started their own Technology Transfer cells in India thereby posing competition for NRDC.

During 2022-23, 40 new technologies were assigned to NRDC for commercialization. It licensed 20 technologies, provided value-addition to 57 technologies, IP assistance provided for 70 technologies.

Central Salt and Marine Chemicals Research Institute

Central Salt and Marine Chemicals Research Institute (formerly Central Salt Research Institute) was inaugurated on 10.04.1954. CSMCRI developed nutrient-rich salt of plant origins, Electrodialysis domestic desalination system, etc.

Indian Space Research Organization

In 1954, the Aryabhatta Research Institute of Observational Sciences (ARIES) was established in the foothills of the Himalayas. The Rangpur Observatory was set up in 1957 at Osmania University, Hyderabad.
The Indian National Committee for Space Research was established in 1962. (It grew and became ISRO on 15.08.1969.)
Thumba Equatorial Rocket Launching Station was established on 21.11.1963

ISRO built India's first satellite **Aryabhata**, which was launched by the Interkosmos (Soviet Union) in 1975.
IOFS officers were drawn from the Indian Ordinance Factories to harness their knowledge of propellants and advanced light materials used to build rockets. An indigenous series of Rohini rockets was developed and launched from 1967 onwards from Thumba with propellant for rockets developed by an IOFS officer. The SLV's first launch in 1979 carried a Rohini technology payload but could not inject the satellite into its desired orbit.

Bhaskara-I, launched on 7.06.1979 from Kapustin Yar aboard Interkosmos launch vehicle, collected data on hydrology, forestry and geology and studied ocean-state, liquid water content in atmosphere, etc.
SLV-3 was successfully launched on 18.07.1980 from Sriharikota carrying a **Rohini Series-1** satellite, making India the seventh country to reach Earth's orbit after USSR, US, France, UK, China and Japan.

India's first indigenously developed communication spacecraft, **APPLE**, was launched in June, 1981 on the European Ariane launcher, and it successfully completed its mission in October, 1983. (7.17.15)

Bhaskara-ll, a remote sensing satellite launched in November, 1981 by a USSR launcher successfully completed its 2-year earth observation mission.

The SLV-3-D-2 launched in April, 1983 from Sriharikota put a 42-kg. indigenous Rohini satellite, carrying a smart-sensor payload, into the desired near-earth orbit.

The basic concepts and complex satellite system of Indian National Satellite **INSAT-1B** were worked out by ISRO, the satellite was built in USA and launched by the US on a space shuttle mission on 30.08.1983. ISRO's Liquid Propulsion Systems Centre was set up in 1985 and started working on a more powerful Vikas engine. Two years later, facilities to test liquid fueled rocket engines were established.

Augmented Satellite Launch Vehicle developed for launching satellites into geostationary orbit had limited success and multiple launch failures; it was soon discontinued.

The PSLV project entered the hardware realization phase in 1986.

2 ASLV Developmental flights were launched in 1987 and 1988, with SROSS-1 and -2 satellites onboard.

IRS-1A, INSAT-1C, INSAT- ID, IRS-1B, INSAT-2A and 2B, IRS-P2, INSAT-2C and IRS-1C and IRS-P3 were launched on 17.03.1988 (from Russia) (8.18.4.13), in July 1988 by the European Launch Vehicle ARI-ANE-4, on 12.07.1990 onboard a US Delta Rocket, on 29.08.1991 from Russia, in July 1992 and July 1993, in 1994, in December 1995. (9.10.83) and 1996 respectively.

With the exception of its first flight in 1994 and two partial failures later, **P**olar **S**atellite **L**aunch **V**ehicle had a streak of more than 50 successful flights. PSLV enabled India to launch all of its low Earth orbit satellites and hundreds of foreign satellites to Geostationary Transfer Orbit.

PSLV-C1 was launched on 29.09.1997 carrying the **I**ndian **R**emote **S**ensing Satellite, IRS-1D, into orbit; PSLV-C2 on 26.05.1999 placed 3 satellites — Indian IRS-P4 (Oceansat) and 2 auxiliary foreign satellites TUBSAT (German) and KITSAT (South Korea);

and PSLV-C3 on 22.10.2001 carried the **T**echnology **E**xperiment **S**atellite in addition to 2 foreign piggyback satellites, BIRD of Germany and PROBA of Belgium. (10.10.24)

After USA refused to help India with Global Positioning System technology following Kargil war, ISRO was prompted to develop its own 'Indian Regional Navigation Satellite System' IRNSS.

Airports Authority of India and ISRO jointly developed GPS and Differential Global Positioning System and other airport modernization equipment from Future Air Navigation System (FANS) program.

Achievements in X 5YP - An Electric Stationary Plasma Thruster (18 milli newton), required for future inter-planetary missions, was developed and tested.

Multi-wavelength astronomy mission ASTROSAT, Indo-French joint climatic mission Megha-Tropiques, microwave remote sensing mission RISAT and oceanography mission OCEANSAT2 were undertaken during X Plan.

The design, development, characterization and realization of the supersonic combustor module, required for future Reusable Launch Vehicles, were completed (11.8.49)

ANTRIX Corporation won contracts for 2 dedicated launches of PSLV and supply of a sophisticated communication satellite in consortium with a leading European manufacturer EADS ASTRIUM. (11.8.49)

India became **one among the 6 countries in the world** to develop Geosynchronous Transfer Orbit launch capability. The technological capability to recover a satellite from orbit through a space capsule recovery experiment was demonstrated, laying the foundation for future reusable launch vehicle systems. (11.8.49)

Liquid Propulsion Systems Centre developed indigenous cryogenic upper stage for GSLV which was successfully test fired by ISRO on 4.08.2007.

ISRO launched **Chandrayaan1** using modified PSLV on 22.10.2008 from S. It entered lunar orbit on 8.11.2008, carrying high-resolution remote sensing equipment. During 312-day operation, it surveyed the lunar surface to produce a complete map of its chemical characteristics and three-dimensional topography.

In 2008, India launched as many as 11 satellites, including 9 from other countries, and went on to become the first nation to launch 10 satellites on one rocket. ISRO put into operation INSAT for communication services, and IRS satellites for management of natural resources.

The **M**ars **O**rbiter **M**ission, informally known as *Mangalyaan,* was launched into Earth orbit on 5.11.2013 by ISRO and it entered Mars orbit on 24.09.2014. India thus became the first country to have a space probe enter Mars orbit on its first attempt.

Subsequently, the cryogenic upper stage for GSLV rocket became operational, making India **the sixth country to have full launch capabilities**. A new heavier-lift launcher GSLV Mk III was introduced in 2014 for heavier satellites and future human space missions.

Launched in 2015, Astrosat is India's first dedicated multi-wavelength Space Observatory.

ISRO's PSLV-C37 successfully launched the 714 kg **Cartosat-2 Series Satellite along with 103 co-passenger satellites** on 15.02.2017 from Satish Dhawan Space Centre, Sriharikota.

Chandrayaan-2 was launched on a GSLV-MkIII on 22.07.2019, consisting of a lunar orbiter, the Vikram lander, and the Pragyan lunar rover, all developed in India. The Vikram lander made a crash-landing due to a software glitch.

ISRO has the world's largest constellation of remote-sensing satellites and operates the GAGAN and NAVIC satellite navigation systems.

ISROs Chandrayaan-3 mission succeeded in making high precision and smooth landing of Vikram lander in the South polar region of moon on 23.08.2023 and started investigation of moon surface through a rover.

National Atmospheric Research Laboratory carries out fundamental and applied research in atmospheric and space sciences.

ISRO Telemetry, Tracking and Command Network provides software development, ground operations, Tracking Telemetry and command and support using tracking stations throughout the country and in Port Louis (Mauritius), Bears Lake (Russia), Biak (Indonesia) and Brunei.

Central Mechanical Engineering Research Institute

Central Mechanical Engineering Research Institute – CMERI was founded in February 1958 to help import substitution efforts of Indian industries. CMERI undertakes research in Robotics, Cybernetics, Embedded system, Biomimetics, Mechatronics, etc.

26 CMERI developed products and processes have been awarded prestigious national awards. CMERI has filed more than 100 patents. 120 Licensees have received products and processes from CMERI for commercial exploitation. Recently, the institute developed Solar electric rickshaw under the CSIR-800 community project program.
CMERI developed Automatic submerged arc welding machine, Portable oxy-gas cutting machine, TIG cutting machine, Swaraj 35 HP Tractor, Sonalika Tractor, Deep Sea-bed Mining System, Single Spindle

Automatic Turret Lathe, Friction Welding Machine, Vision Guided Robotic System, Process Development for manufacture of ADI crankshaft for cars and single cylinder agricultural pump engines, **A**utonomous **U**nderwater **V**ehicle -150, Sub-Terrain Robot, All Terrain Robot, Five Axis µ-CNC Milling Machine, 600 Liter/Day Capacity Semi Continuous Type Biodiesel Plant, Mechanization Project at Durgapur Steel Plant, Remotely Operated Vehicle: 500 m Depth Qualification, Autonomous Mobile Robot, Autonomous Intelligent Robotic Wheel Chair, Outdoor Mobile Robot, Teleoperated Rotary-Wing Aerial Robot, Krishi Shakti 10 HP Tractor, etc.

Central Public Health Engineering Research Institute.

Central Public Health Engineering Research Institute – CPHERI was established on 8.04.1958 to deal with problems of water and air pollution in urban settlements. CPHERI was renamed as National Environmental Engineering Research Institute NEERI in 1974.

Defence Research and Development Organization

Defence Research and Development Organization - DRDO was formed in 1958 by the merger of the Technical Development Establishment and the Directorate of Technical Development and Production of the Indian Ordinance Factories with the Defence Science Organization.

DRDO comprises a network of 52 laboratories engaged in developing defence technologies covering aeronautics, armaments, electronics, land combat engineering, life sciences, materials, missiles, and naval systems.

DRDO started its first major project in surface-to-air missiles in 1960s. Prithvi missile was developed under the **I**ntegrated **G**uided **M**issile **D**evelopment **P**rogram in 1980s. A comprehensive range of missiles, including the Agni missile, Prithvi ballistic missile, Akash missile, Trishul missile and Nag missile were developed between the early 1980s and 2007 under IGMDP.

Since its establishment, DRDO has created major systems and critical technologies like aircraft avionics, UAVs, small arms, artillery systems, Early Warning Systems, tanks and armoured vehicles, sonar systems, command and control systems and missile systems.

DRDO was engaged in the design and development of aircraft, missiles, tanks, armaments and a variety of electronic systems. (7.17.126)

Research on Missiles & Strategic systems and Ballistics are handled by Advanced Systems Laboratory, Defence Research and Development Laboratory, Integrated Test Range, Program Air Defence, Research Centre Imarat and Terminal Ballistics Research Laboratory.

Research on Aeronautics, Unmanned and Manned Aircraft, Air-Borne Systems, Avionics, Parachutes and Aerial systems are undertaken by Aeronautical Development Establishment, Aeronautical Test Range, Centre for Airborne Systems, Defence Avionics Research Establishment and Aerial Delivery Research & Development Establishment respectively.

Research on Armaments, High Energy Weapons, Electronic Warfare, Chemical and Biological warfare, under water weapons, Armaments Testing, Engineering Systems & weapon platforms are done by Armaments Research & Development Establishment, Centre for High Energy Systems and Sciences, Defence Electronics Research Laboratory, Defence Research and Development Establishment, Naval Science & Technological Laboratory, Proof and Experimental Establishment and Research & Development Establishment (Engineers)   -

Research on Explosives and High Energy Materials are carried out by Centre for Fire, Explosives & Environment Safety and High Energy Materials Research Laboratory respectively.

Research on Radars, Artificial Intelligence & Robotics, Combat Vehicles, Electronics Optical systems, Laser Technology, Microwave Devices, Sonar Systems and Wheeled Vehicles are undertaken by Electronics & Radar Development Establishment, Centre for Artificial Intelligence & Robotics, Combat Vehicles Research & Development Establishment, Instruments Research & Development Establishment, Microwave Tube Research & Development Centre, Naval Physical & Oceanographic Laboratory, Vehicles Research & Development Establishment respectively.

National Aerospace Laboratory

National Aeronautical Research Laboratory was set up in Delhi on 1.06.1959 by CSIR. In March 1960, it set up an office in Bangalore, as the National Aeronautical Laboratory. National Aeronautical Laboratory was renamed as National Aerospace Laboratories in April 1993. The company closely operates with HAL, DRDO and ISRO and has the primary responsibility of developing civilian aircraft in India.

Flo Solver was a series of Indian Supercomputers designed and assembled by the NAL.

The maiden flight of two–seater, all composite trainer aircraft Hansa, developed by NAL, took place on 17.11.1993. The aircraft was certified by **D**irector **G**eneral **C**ivil **A**viation for day and night flying in 2000. It was being manufactured along with a private partner. DGCA promoted the use of Hansa-3 by various flying clubs; a total of 14 aircraft are in operation.

Saras, India's first indigenously developed, multi-role civilian aircraft, had its maiden flight on 29.05.2004 and inaugural test flight on 22.08.2004. Till March 2007, prototype-1 had made more than 110 test flights.

The III prototype aircraft (production standard) was under production at CSIR-NAL. SARAS was capable of operation from short runways and flying up to 30,000ft. SARAS was suitable for many roles including executive transport, light package carrier, remote sensing, air ambulance, etc. After successful completion of the test flights and DGCA license, the aircraft was to go in for commercialization by HAL. (11.8.74)

Commercial production of SARAS Mk II is expected to start in 2025 as it is undergoing design changes.

NAL/ADE Black Kite, Golden Hawk and Pushpak, unmanned Micro Air Vehicles developed jointly by Aeronautical Development Establishment of DRDO and NAL, carry miniature daylight video cameras as payload which can take video from an altitude of 80–100 m and relay the imagery of ground zero to the Ground control station during its flight. The prototypes are currently under the user trials as on 2012.

C-NM5, designed & developed jointly by CSIR-NAL & Mahindra Aerospace Pvt Ltd., powered by a 300 HP piston engine driving a 3-blade propeller cruising at a speed of 160 knots with a maximum All Up Weight of 1525 kg, successfully undertook its first flight in Australia. It is an ideal aircraft for air taxis, air ambulances, training, tourism, and cargo.

The HAL/NAL Regional Transport Aircraft or Indian Regional Jet is a regional airliner being designed by NAL and to be manufactured by Hindustan Aeronautics Ltd. The aircraft is planned to be a turboprop or a jet with a capacity of 80–100 passengers. Its basic version of 70–90 seats (RTA-70) is being designed as of 2021 and is expected to enter service in 2026.

Central Institute of Medicinal and Aromatic Plants,

Central Indian Medicinal Plants Organization was established in 1959 for steering multidisciplinary research in biological and chemical sciences and extending technologies and services to the farmers and entrepreneurs of **M**edicinal and **A**romatic **P**lants. Its name was changed to Central Institute of Medicinal and Aromatic Plants.

CIMAP has released several varieties of the MAPs, with agro-technology and post-harvest packages which have revolutionized MAPs cultivation and business scenario of the country.

Indian Institute of Petroleum

Indian Institute of Petroleum was established in 1959, through an act of parliament, for dedicating to research and development in hydrocarbon sector.

IIP develops processes and products for petroleum refining and petrochemical industries, training of personnel in oil and petrochemical industries, and assisting in formulation of standards for petroleum products.

Central Scientific Instruments Organization

Central Scientific Instruments Organization – CSIO was established in October 1959 as a laboratory to undertake design and development of scientific and industrial instruments.

Indo-Swiss Training Centre was started in December 1963 with the cooperation of the Swiss Foundation for Technical Assistance, Zurich.

A large number of instruments were developed by the institute and their knowhow has been passed on to the industry for commercial exploitation.

North East Institute of Science and Technology

North East Institute of Science and Technology, formerly Regional Research Laboratory, Jorhat, was established in 1961 to develop indigenous technologies by utilizing the immense natural resources of North-Eastern India like Petroleum, coal, Natural Gas, Minerals, Tea, Microbes, Aromatic and Medicinal plants.

Over the years, the laboratory has produced more than 117 technologies in the areas of Agrotechnology, Biological and Oil Field Chemicals.

The RRL, Jorhat, developed a flow improver, SWAT-106, for the transportation of Bombay High crude.

National Geophysical Research Institute

National Geophysical Research Institute was established in 1961.

It is engaged in hydrocarbon, coal and mineral exploration, deep seismic sounding studies, exploration and management of groundwater resources, earthquake hazard assessment, structure of earth's interior and its evolution, geophysical instrument development and geothermal exploration.

Institute of Minerals and Materials Technology

Institute of Minerals and Materials Technology, formerly Regional Research Laboratory, Bhubaneswar was established in 1964 to undertake research in mining and mineral / bio-mineral processing, metal extraction and materials characterization, process engineering, marine and forest products development, colloids and Materials Chemistry and environmental sustainability.

Structural Engineering Research Centre

Structural Engineering Research Centre, established in 1965, is involved in designing, construction and rehabilitation of structures. The institute provides services including design consultancy and proof checking to various public and private sector organizations.

National Institute of Oceanography –

National Institute of Oceanography was founded on 1.1.1966 to conduct scientific research and studies on the oceanographic features of the Northern Indian Ocean.

NIO recovered polymetallic nodules from a depth of 4,800 meters in the western Indian Ocean on 26.01.1981, using its first research vessel. Four scientific expeditions to Antarctica were organized in 1981, 1982, 1983 and 1984, and a permanent research station was established there at Dakshin Gangotri. **Department of Ocean Development** further pursued this area and completed the first phase of a project for identification of a mining site, through extensive regional surveys covering an area of 3.8 million sq. kms and over ten thousand locations. (7.17.21)

NIO possesses about 50 patents, most of which are related to marine biotechnology research. Organisms in the marine environment carry molecules that could be useful in the development of new drugs and other healthcare products.

Indira Gandhi Centre for Atomic Research

Indira Gandhi Centre for Atomic Research was established in 1971 as Reactor Research Centre for dedicating to the pursuit of fast reactor science and technology. It was renamed as Indira Gandhi Centre for Atomic Research in December 1985.
The centre houses a Fast Breeder Test Reactor, which attained its first criticality in October 1985.

In 1996, KAMINI reactor reached criticality. State-of-the-art Neutronic Channels were commissioned for FBTR in 1999.
A Boron-Enrichment Plant was commissioned in April 2001.
In 2009, FBTR was operated at a maximum power level of 18.6 MWe with 55 sub-assemblies for 1732 hours. IGCAR also built a 100 MWe reactor for India's first nuclear Arihant class submarine project and operated it on land for testing purposes since it attained criticality in December 2004. The submarine launched on 26.07.2009 had this reactor.

The reprocessing of irradiated thorium rods, which was carried out during the period 1989 to 1992 in the concrete shielded cells, was the first major radioactive operation. The U-233 recovered during the operation was used in fabricating the fuel for the Kalpakkam MINI reactor (KAMINI).

(i) BARC and IGCAR developed indigenous Time Domain Electromagnetic TDEM systems for airborne survey to locate deep-seated uranium deposits.
(ii) Development of BARC Containment Model of 540 Mwe, **the largest nuclear containment model in the world** for ultimate load capacity assessment, for Pressurized Heavy Water Reactor at Tarapur,
(iii) Installation and commissioning of thermal denitration pilot plant;
(iv) Development of prototype magnetic crawler robot for in-service inspection of boiler tubes at thermal power plants; and
(iv) Establishment of country-wide Indian Environmental Radiation Monitoring Network Stations at 115 new locations to provide online information about the radiation levels.

National Remote Sensing Agency

The National Remote Sensing Agency was established in 1974 to conduct aeromagnetic surveys for data collection from satellites and interpretation. The use of microwaves in remote sensing and the development of expertise for modelling in areas like agricultural yield prediction and hydrology was planned to be taken on experimental basis. (6.19.98)
The NRS Centre applies remote sensing to manage natural resources and study aerial surveying.

National Institute for Interdisciplinary Science and Technology

National Institute for Interdisciplinary Science and Technology, formerly Regional Research Laboratory, Trivandrum, was established in 1975 as a CSIR Complex, then named as the Regional Research Laboratory in 1978 and later renamed as NIIST in 2007.

NIIST is engaged in R and D activities in Agro-processing, microbial processes, chemical sciences, material sciences, process engineering and environmental technology.

Centre for Cellular and Molecular Biology

Centre for Cellular and Molecular Biology was set up on 1.04.1977, with the Biochemistry Division of the then Regional Research Laboratory (presently, Indian Institute of Chemical Technology) in Hyderabad forming its nucleus, to carry out research in life sciences.

The Laboratory for Conservation of Endangered Species, an annex of CCMB, attempts to conserve the Indian wildlife by using modern biological techniques and assisted reproductive technologies. They host the National Wildlife Genetic Resource Bank with currently 250 genetic samples of animals, collected from zoos across the country.

CCMB carries out molecular diagnostic tests for 30 genetic disorders and wildlife forensics in its medical biotechnology complex.

Institute of Genomics and Integrative Biology

Institute of Genomics and Integrative Biology was established in 1977 as the Centre for Biochemical Technology. The Functional Genomics Unit was established in 1998 with the focus shifting from chemical to genomics research. The institute was renamed "Institute of Genomics and Integrative Biology" in 2002.

In 2009, a team at the institute sequenced the genome of the wild-type zebrafish, with about 1.7 billion base pairs. Previously Indian scientists had only sequenced bacteria and plant genomes. In December 2009, scientists at IGIB performed the first re-sequencing of a human genome in India and collaborated on decoding the Sri Lankan and Malaysian genomes.

Regional Research Laboratory / Advanced Materials and Processes Research Institute

Advanced Materials and Processes Research Institute, Bhopal, formerly known as the Regional Research Laboratory, was established in May 1981.

A totally indigenous 900-TPD plant for low-temperature carbonization of coal, based on technology developed at Regional Research Laboratory, Hyderabad, went into production in Andhra Pradesh.

Institute of Himalayan Bioresource Technology

Institute of Himalayan Bioresource Technology was established in 1983 to undertake advanced research in Himalayan Bio-resources and modern biology. For socio-economic upliftment, regular training programs and advisory services are rendered to farmers, floriculturists, tea planters and small entrepreneurs involved in food processing sector.

Institute of Microbial Technology

Institute of Microbial Technology - IMTECH was established in 1984 to undertake research in modern biological sciences, and microbe - related biotechnology, immunity and infectious diseases, Protein design and engineering, fermentation science, microbial physiology and genetics, bioinformatics, microbial systematics, yeast biology, etc.

Developed and patented natural, recombinant and clot specific Streptokinase as a vital lifesaving drug.

CSIR-Fourth Paradigm Institute

(Formerly CSIR Centre for Mathematical Modelling and Computer Simulation), established in 1988, is involved in developing modelling approaches for illuminating the structure and evolution of complex systems.

National Centre for Biological Sciences

National Centre for Biological Sciences, established in 1992, is a research centre specializing in biological research ranging from the study of single molecules to systems biology. NCBS focusses on biochemistry, biophysics, bioinformatics, neurobiology, cellular organization and signaling, genetics and development, theory and modeling of biological systems, ecology and evolution, etc.

Central Institute of Mining and Fuel Research

Central Institute of Mining and Fuel Research - CIMFR previously known as Central Mining Research Institute and Central Fuel Research Institute was established in 2007 to provide R&D inputs for the entire coal-energy chain from mining to consumption through integration of the core competencies of the two premier coal institutions of the country.

Open - Source Drug Discovery

Open - Source Drug Discovery is a CSIR-led Team India Consortium with global participation offering a collaborative drug discovery platform for neglected tropical diseases like leishmaniasis, which draw limited attention of research-based pharmaceutical enterprises.

OSDD was launched in September 2008 for making use of open-source philosophy, crowd–sourcing concepts and a collaborative research model, capitalizing on web-based tools to discover novel therapies. All the data and resources generated by the community are openly shared through a web-based portal called SysBorg 2.0.

The project blends together the policies of patenting and open-source research, aiming to make novel drugs available as generic drugs, without Intellectual Property restrictions, and thus ensure affordability and accessibility.

Biotechnology Industry Research Assistance Council

Biotechnology Industry Research Assistance Council - BIRAC was established on 20.03.2012 to strengthen and empower the biotech enterprise to undertake strategic research addressing product development needs through academia-industry collaboration and international linkage, to set up pre-clinical toxicology and phase I clinical trial facilities. In 2019-20, BIRAC launched COVID-19 Research Consortium and Innovation clean technologies for waste management.
Gross turnover in 2022-23 was Rs. 538.97 Cr

National Institute of Science Communication and Policy Research

National Institute of Science Communication and Policy Research was established on 14.01.2021 with merger of National Institute of Science Communication and Information Resources and National Institute of Science, Technology and Development Studies.

Indian Scientific Documentation Centre, which came into being in 1952, was merged with NISCOM in 2002,

Central Glass and Ceramic Research Institute, established in 1950, focuses on the area of glass, ceramics, mica, refractories, etc.

Central Electro Chemical Research Institute came into existence in January 1953.

National Botanical Research Institute established as the National Botanic Gardens was taken over by the CSIR in 1953. It is engaged in research work in the fields of taxonomy, modern biology, classical botanical disciplines and plant sciences. To fight against whiteflies, NBRI developed a pest resistant variety of cotton.

Indian Institute of Toxicology Research (previously the **Industrial Toxicology Research Centre**) was established in 1965.

Public Sector Units, Which Contribute for Production of Electronic Equipment

Bharat Electronics Ltd.

Bharat Electronics Ltd. - BEL was established on 21-04-1954 to manufacture Trans-receivers in technical collaboration with CSF, France, for use by the Indian Army for radio communication.

Subsequently, BEL widened its range of products to defence electronics products like radars and telecommunication equipment in its **9 units** at Bangalore, Ghaziabad, Pune, Machilipatnam, Panchkula, Kotdwara, Navi Mumbai, Chennai and Hyderabad.

It has **2 subsidiaries** namely BEL Optronic Devices Ltd. and BEL-Thales Systems Ltd.
The Company has **2 financial joint ventures** namely GE-BE Ltd. and BEL Multitone Ltd. These JVs were formed in 1996-97 for manufacturing of X-Ray tubes for medical diagnostic imaging equipment and for supply of private paging system.

BEL has a product range of more than 350 products, which are broadly classified into 8 core business groups including Radars, Sonars and Missile Systems; Communication & Network Centric Systems; Electronic Warfare Systems, Gun upgrades; Avionics, Electro Optics; Tank electronics; Telecommunication and Broadcasting; Electronic Voting Machines; Tablet PC; Integrated Traffic Management systems, Components and Turnkey Solutions.

About 60% of its turnover is from indigenous technology developed inhouse or provided by DRDO laboratories. BEL is engaged in the manufacture of multiple products ranging from single products like Passive Night Vision devices etc., to large systems like Battlefield Surveillance Radar, Coastal Surveillance System etc.

BEL formed joint ventures with Thales, France and Rolta India Ltd for manufacture of select defence radars and Battlefield Management System respectively.
BEL's market share in Electronic Defence Systems was 64% in 2011-12.

Revenue from operations in 2022-23 was Rs. 17646.2 Cr.

National Instruments Ltd.

National Instruments Ltd. - NIL was incorporated in 1830 as Mathematical Instruments office associated with Survey of India Department and became a public sector establishment in 1957 to manufacture import substitution surveying instruments. NIL is manufacturing surveying equipment and devices in Kolkata unit.

Instrumentation Ltd.

Instrumentation Ltd. - IL was incorporated on 21.3.1964 for providing instrumentation and control systems to thermal, power, steel and fertilizer sectors, refineries, other process industries, nuclear application, offshore projects like Oil & Natural Gas and Defence.

Diversification - IL diversified into the manufacturing of Telecom Exchanges (based on C-DOT technology), Railway Signalling systems, special products for Defence, Power Electronics (UPS etc.,) and Photo Identity jobs of Election Commissions.

The Kota unit was manufacturing Telecom equipment, Instruments and Automation products, Panels/Cabinets, Gas analysers, etc. and also undertaking large turnkey projects.
The Palakkad unit manufactures Control valves, Butterfly valves, Safety Relief Valves, Bellow Sealed Valves, Pneumatic / Electric Actuators, Custom-built special products like Valve stand etc.

IL has **4 subsidiaries** namely Rajasthan Electronics and Instruments Ltd., Jaipur (established as joint venture with RIICO), IL Power Electronics Ltd. Jaipur, Instrumentation Digital controls Ltd., Kota and Instrumentation Controls Valves Ltd., Palakkad.

Union cabinet on 30.11.2016 decided to close Kota unit and in principle approval was given for transfer of Palakkad unit to Government of Kerala in a time bound manner.

IL Palakkad supplied Passive Air Damper, HSAR and Sodium non return Valve to IGCAR Kalpakkam for their fast breeder reactor in 2019-20.

Market share of IL was 20% in 2022-23. IL introduced Multi Stack Multi path, Rubber lined Butterfly Valves, OSY, Desuperheater, etc. IL valves were used in Chandrayan-3 mission for testing Upper stage - Cryogenic Engines of LVM-3 rocket at ISRO-IPRC.

Electronics Corporation of India Limited

Electronics Corporation of India Ltd. - ECIL was established on 11.04.1967 to meet the electronic, control and instrumentation requirements of strategic sectors such as Defence, Indian Ordnance Factories, Defence Research and Development Organization, nuclear energy, Department of Space, Civil Aviation, Information and Broadcasting, Telecommunications, Insurance, Banking, Police and Para-military Forces, Oil and Gas, Power, Education, Health, Agriculture, Steel, Coal, etc. ECIL also has a strong presence in Electronic Security, Networking and e-governance domains.

ECIL is credited with producing the first indigenous digital computers, TDC 312 and TDC 316, solid state TV, control and instrumentation for nuclear power plants and first earth station antenna of India.
ECIL commissioned 32 m antenna system for lunar mission, established satellite earth station at Antarctica and Digital Radiology centre and handed over Brahmos system to army during 2007-08.

ECIL has a financial joint venture namely ECIL-Rapiscan Ltd.

Present product range of ECIL includes:
i) Control and instrumentation products for nuclear power plants, integrated security systems for nuclear installations, Radiation monitoring instruments;
ii) Defence Sector – V/UHF Radio communication equipment, Electronics Warfare systems and Derivatives, special components for missile systems, Precision servo components like gyros, Control and command systems for Missiles, Training simulators, Stabilized antenna and tracking system for light combat aircrafts, Detection and Pre-detonation of explosive devices, jammers with direction finding abilities, etc.
iii) Commercial Sector: Electronic voting machines; Voter-verified paper audit trail; Totalizer, Wireless local loop (WLL) systems; antenna products; electronic energy meters; X-ray baggage inspection system for airports; computer hardware, software and services; computer education services.

Revenue from operations in 2022-23 was Rs. 2383.11 Cr.

Bharat Dynamics Ltd.

Bharat Dynamics Ltd. - BDL was incorporated on 16-07-1970 to develop Guided Missile and Underwater Guided Weapon Technology and to provide total solutions to the security system needs of the Nation.

BDL is manufacturing sophisticated State of art weapon systems for Armed Forces through Hyderabad, Bhanur, Medak and Visakhapatnam units. The products include Anti-Tank Missiles, Air Defence Missiles, Strategic Missiles, Torpedoes, Mines, Deception Device, etc.
BDL is undertaking the design and development of avionics systems such as Counter Measures Dispensing System for Indian Air Force.

Warhead Manufacturing Facility at Bhanur and Seeker Manufacturing Facility at Kanchanbagh were inaugurated in 2022-23.

Central Electronics Limited

Central Electronics Ltd. - CEL was incorporated on 26.6.1974 to manufacture solar energy systems and strategic electronic goods and to specialize in the field of Solar Photovoltaic Energy sources, particularly for rural applications, Railway Safety and Signaling Electronics, Microwave Phase Control Modules, etc. based on the know how developed on a laboratory scale in CSIR, DRDO and other National Laboratories.

CEL undertakes production of Solar Photovoltaic Products, Railway Electronics including axle counters, Cathodic Protection Systems, Microwave Electronics and PZT Alumina through its unit at Sahibabad.
CEL improved solar cell efficiency from 10.4% to 13.5%, established plants for manufacture of Solar Cells of 17% efficiency, New SPV surface centrifugal pumps, High Efficiency invertors and ferrites.
CEL exported Solar Cells and Modules to Germany, Sudan, Mali, Afghanistan, Nepal, Sri Lanka, Spain and USA. Installed Capacity for Solar PV Modules in 2008-09 was 10000 kW.

The installed capacity of CEL in 2019-20 was 601 numbers for axle counters, 40000 numbers for phase shifters and 27997 kW for Solar PV modules.

Revenue from operations in 2022-23 was Rs. 262.3 Cr.

Computer Maintenance Corporation –

CMC was incorporated on 26.12.1975, as the 'Computer Management Corp. Pvt Ltd' with Government of India holding 100% of the equity share capital.
CMC was renamed CMC Ltd (**C**omputer **M**aintenance **C**orporation) in August 1984.

Achievements, Software package clients, international contracts, Packages developed and **Privatization** – Refer Ch. 17.

Semi-Conductor Complex Ltd.

Semi-Conductor Complex Ltd. - SCCL was incorporated in 1978 to design and manufacture very large-scale integrated circuits to fulfill strategic needs of the country in the area of microelectronics.

SCCL is in Research & Development, manufacturing VLSI, providing ASCI / Micro Electro Mechanical Systems / IT services and development of VLSI based systems, Energy Meters through its unit at S.A.S. Nagar, Punjab.

Rajasthan Electronics & Instruments Ltd.

Rajasthan Electronics & Instruments Ltd. - REIL was incorporated in 1981 as a joint venture of Instrumentation Ltd. and Rajasthan Industries Development and Investment Corp. Ltd. to serve rural electronic, non-conventional energy systems and power generation through wind energy.

REIL is manufacturing Agro Dairy Electronic Items (Electronic Milk Tester, Analyzer, Milk Collection Systems, solar photo voltaic modules, Power Plants, Cathodic Protection System and Electronic Energy meters in Jaipur unit.

REIL took up projects including SPV Home Lighting, Smart Cities of Rajasthan (as Nodal Agency) Grid Connected Rooftop Solar Projects, SPV Water Pumping solutions for Agriculture & Drinking Water, GPRS technology for error free dairying, law enforcement for food safety security by FSSAI through Electronic Milk Adulteration Tester, PMC for Energy Efficiency projects, Development of Solar Electric Hybrid charging stations to charge electric vehicles, etc.

REIL developed Information technology products for business and banking applications, e-governance, electoral process, etc.

The installed capacity of REIL was 10013 numbers for electronic milk analyzer and 19185 kW for SPV module systems in 2019-20.

REIL was executing Export order worth Rs. 68.51 Cr from Guyana Energy Agency for supply of SPV Home Energy Systems in rural households during 2022-23.

BEL Optronic Devices Ltd.

BEL Optronic Devices Ltd. - BELOP was incorporated on 10.11.1990 as a joint venture of Bharat Electronics Ltd. and Delft Instruments International of Netherlands. BEL acquired the shares of DII on 30.7.2002 and it became a government company.

BELOP is manufacturing Image Intensifier Tubes (used in optical instruments for night vision capability and sold only to defence and para military forces) and associated Power Supply Units in Pune. Since inception, BELOP has supplied more than 1,50,000 numbers of Image Intensifier tubes to Indian MOD, MHA and Police forces.

BELOP entered into agreements with Photonics, France in May 2011 for transfer of technology for manufacture of higher specification tubes to cater to the requirements of the Indian Army.

The implementation of the XR-5 project was completed during 2022-23. As a part of diversification, BELOP signed offset contract with Rosoboronexport, Russia for manufacture of aviation hoses.

Antrix Corporation Ltd. – Refer Ch. 8

Instrumentation Digital Controls Ltd

Instrumentation Digital Controls Ltd - IDCL was incorporated on 12.09.2000 with the object to take over the business of PDDC Unit of Instrumentation Ltd., Kota.

Since no expression of interest was received for the P-DDC Unit, the manufacturing facilities of P-DDC Unit was integrated with the main Unit at Kota during 2002-03, as per the directives of Department of Heavy Industry. No commercial activity has been carried out by the Company till date. The Company is to be wound up on receipt of GOI approval.

IL Power Electronics Limited

IL Power Electronics Ltd. - ILPEL was incorporated on 12.09.2000 to take over the business of Jaipur unit of Instrumentation Ltd., Kota. Jaipur Unit was integrated with main unit at Kota during 2002-03. The Company till date has carried out no commercial activity. ILPEL is to be wound up on receipt of Government of India (GOI) approval. GOI has been requested for permission for winding up of the Company.

Instrumentation Control Valves Limited

Instrumentation Control Valves Limited - ICVL was incorporated on 16.11.2000 with the object to take over the business of Palakkad Unit of Instrumentation Ltd., Kota. The Company till date has carried out no commercial activity. As per modified revival scheme of the Holding Company namely, Instrumentation Limited, the ICVL is to be wound up on receipt of GOI approval.

BEL –Thales Systems Limited

BEL –Thales Systems Ltd - BTSL was incorporated on 28.08.2014 as a joint venture company of Bharat Electronics Ltd, Thales India Pvt Ltd and Thales Air System SAS, France to undertake design and development of selected defense and civilian radars. The company started commercial operations during 2016-17. Revenue from operations in 2022-23 was Rs, 78.19 Cr.

Indian Ordnance Factories

Ordnance Factory Board was established on 2.04.1979. OFB, world's largest government-operated production organization, was 37th-largest defence equipment manufacturer in world, 2nd-largest in Asia.

Ordnance factories are divided into 5 divisions (depending upon the type of the main products/technologies employed) - Ammunition and Explosives, Weapons, Vehicles & Equipment, Materials and Components, Armoured Vehicles, Ordnance Equipment Group of Factories, parachutes and opto-electronics.

The ordnance material produced include various small arms to missiles, rockets, bombs, grenades, military vehicles, armoured vehicles, chemicals, optical devices, parachutes, mortars, artillery pieces plus all associated ammunition, propellants, explosives and fuses, revolvers, pistols and rifles for civilian use. IOF products were exported to more than 30 countries worldwide.

The 41 Indian Ordnance Factories were converted into 7 Defence Public Sector Undertakings on 15.10.2021. Of the 2 Gun Powder Factories in Ishapore, second one became a rifle factory.

Advanced Weapons and Equipment India Ltd. - AWE was formed by combining **Field Gun Factory, Kanpur** (started in 1979, manufacturing various types of field guns), **Gun Carriage Factory, Jabalpur** (manufacturing Truck-mounted Self-Propelled Gun Systems, Towed Gun, Dhanush howitzer and its tractor), **Gun and Shell Factory, Cossipore**, Kolkata, **Ordnance Factory Kanpur, Ordnance Factory, Korwa**, UP, **Ordnance Factory, Tiruchirappalli** (started in 1966, manufacturing 9 mm carbines, arms ranging from 5.56 mm rifles to rocket launchers, shell and grenade launchers, aviation, naval and tank armaments, anti-aircraft guns, autocannons, automatic and sniper rifles), **Rifle Factory, Ishapore** (manufacturing Kalantak, Ghatak and Sniper Rifles and Auto Pistols for military and revolvers and sporting rifles for civilian customers) and **Small Arms Factory, Kanpur – 8 Factories** of AWE primarily manufacturing small arms and artillery guns.

Armoured Vehicles Nigam Ltd. – AVANI was formed by combining **Engine Factory, Avadi** (started in 1987, manufacturing Diesel engines for various tanks like infantry combat vehicles, Ajeya and Bhishma Tanks), **Heavy Vehicles Factory, Chennai** (started in 1961, manufacturing Main Battle Tanks including Vijayanta, Arjun, T-60 Bhishma, Ajeya Tanks, etc., self-propelled guns), **Machine Tool Prototype Factory, Ambernath** (started in 1953, manufacturing vehicle gear boxes, gear boxes for Arty equipment & Tanks, multi barrel rocket Chaff Decoy System, Wheel Carriage Assembly for 155mm Dhanush Gun), **Ordnance Factory Project, Medak** (started in 1984, manufacturing amphibious infantry fighting vehicles, surface-to-air and surface-to-surface missile launchers, armoured ambulances, self-propelled howitzers, armoured cars, unmanned ground vehicles, armoured light recovery vehicles, NBC recce vehicles, mine protected vehicles, armoured amphibious dozers, armoured radars, naval armaments), **Vehicle Factory, Jabalpur** (started in 1969, manufacturing bullet-proof vehicles, mine protected vehicles, water bowsers, fuel tankers, field ambulances, tippers, battery command posts, generator sets, light recovery vehicles, field artillery tractors, Stallion truck platform for various military and logistics vehicles) – **5 Factories**

Gliders India Ltd. – **Ordnance Parachute Factory, Kanpur** (Drop Parachutes, personnel parachutes, floats for KM Bridge and inflatable boats) was renamed as Gliders India Ltd.

India Optel Ltd. was formed by combining **Ordnance Factory, Chandigarh** (started in 1963, manufacturing Field Telephone Cable, Carrier Quad Cable, 20 Conductor Cable, 3KV Air Field Lighting Cable, Beta Light Devices, Optoelectronic Sight), **Ordnance Factory, Dehradun** (started in 1943, manufacturing Sighting & Fire Control Instruments for Tanks, Fire Control Instruments for Guns & Mortars, Range Finder, Binoculars, Compasses, Air Field Lighting Equipment, Night Vision Instruments), and **Opto-Electronics Factory, Dehradun** (started in 1988, manufacturing Precision Opto-Mechanical / Electronic Instruments for Sighting and Fire Control of T-72 & Infantry Combat Vehicles, Laser Range Finder) – **3.**

Munitions India Ltd. was formed by combining **Ammunition Factory, Khadki** (started in 1869, manufacturing 5.56 mm Ammunition, Bombs, Grenades, Cartridges for Small Arms, Medium Caliber Ammunition), **Cordite Factory, Aruvankadu** (started in 1903, manufacturing Propellants and Chemicals), **Heavy Alloy Penetrator Project, Tiruchirappalli** (started in 1980, manufacturing empty shots for Kinetic Energy Ammunition of calibers - 120mm, 125mm, Anti-Submarine Rocket hardware, Tungsten Spheres for Pinaka Rocket), **High Explosives Factory, Pune** (started in 1940, manufacturing TNT, HNS, Tetryl (CE), IPN, RFNA, 'G' Fuel, 'O' Fuel, Initiatory Explosives, Acids and Chemicals etc.), **Ordnance Factory, Bhandara** (manufacturing Acids to High Explosives, Single and Double Base Propellant (Ballistite), Double Base Propellant (Rocket)) **Ordnance Factory, Bolangir, Odisha** (started in 1989, manufacturing Tank and Artillery Ammunition), **Ordnance Factory, Chandrapur** (started in 1970, manufacturing Tank Gun and Mortar Ammunition, Anti-Tank and Anti-Personnel Mines, Rockets, Missiles War-Heads etc.), **Ordnance Factory, Dehu Road** (started in 1984, manufacturing Pyrotechnic Compositions & Ammunition), **Ordnance Factory, Itarsi** (started in 1979, manufacturing Propellants and Chemicals), **Ordnance Factory, Khamaria** (started in 1943, manufacturing Small Arms Ammunition, Anti-Aircraft and Anti-Tank Ammunition, Ammunition for Air Force and Navy), **Ordnance Factory Project, Nalanda** (started in 2001, manufacturing Bi-modular Charge System), **Ordnance Factory Varangaon** (started in 1964, manufacturing Cartridges, viz, 7.62 mm Nato Ball M-80 Tracer M-62, 5.56 mm Ammunition) – **12 Factories.**

Troop Comforts Ltd. was formed by combining **Ordnance Clothing Factory, Avadi** (started in 1961, manufacturing all Combat Clothing & Parade Garments, Parachutes, Tents, DLD Covers, Vest etc.) **Ordnance Clothing Factory, Shahjahanpur** (started in 1879, manufacturing All Combat Clothing, Mountaineering Extreme Cold Clothing, Textile &Tentage Items), **Ordnance Equipment Factory, Kanpur** (started in 1859, manufacturing Leather Items, Textile Items, Engineering Equipment including Mountaineering Items), **Ordnance Equipment Factory, Hazratpur** (started in 1983, manufacturing Tents, Mosquito Nets & other Clothing Items) - **4 Factories.**

Yantra India Ltd. – **Grey Iron Foundry, Jabalpur** (started in 1972, manufacturing Automobile Casting of Grey & Malleable Iron for Vehicles & other applications) **Metal and Steel Factory, Ishapore, WB,** (started in 1872, manufacturing Ferrous and Non-ferrous castings & extrusion, component & other stores including Cartridge Cases and shell forgings, Light / Medium / Heavy Steel Forgings including Gun Barrel Forgings), **Ordnance Factory, Ambernath** (started in 1944, manufacturing Cartridge Case, Brass Cup of various sizes, Brass coils, Low and High Tensile Al. Alloy, Extruded sections), **Ordnance Factory,**

Ambajhari, Nagpur (started in 1966, manufacturing Ammunition Hardware viz Shells, Cartridge cases, Fuses, Rockets & Primers, Castings & Extrusion of Special Al. Alloys and Fabrication of Floating & Manually Launched Assault Bridges), **Ordnance Factory, Bhusawal** (started in 1949, manufacturing Drums, Barrels, Ammunition Boxes, Cylinders & Tin Containers, Fuel tanks), **Ordnance Factory, Dumdum** (started in 1846, manufacturing Ammunition Hardware / Components), **Ordnance Factory, Katni** (started in 1942, manufacturing Non-Ferrous Rolled & Extruded Sections, Cups for Small Arms Ammunitions, Diecast components, Heavy Caliber Cartridge Cases), **Ordnance Factory, Muradnagar** (started in 1943, manufacturing Plain carbon and alloy steel castings for Tanks, Empty Bodies of various ammunition Hot Die Tool, Steel forgings. Track Link for Tanks) – **8 Factories.**

Indian Ordnance Factories' total sales were at US$3 billion (Rs. 22,389.22 crores) in the year 2020–21.

A joint venture between Ordnance Factory Board (50.5%), Kalashnikov Concern (42%) and Rosoboronexport (7.5%), namely Indo-Russia Rifles Pvt Ltd was established in Amethi to produce AK-203 (7.62×39mm) assault rifles for Indian Security Forces

Summary

Research institutions and laboratories were set up and operated **almost entirely by public sector units** and these institutions performed exceedingly well at par with best institutions in other countries. As the production details of electronic public sector units are not disclosed for national security considerations, their contribution could not be assessed quantitatively.

Private Sector Players –

Adani Defence & Aerospace (2015)

ADA set up manufacturing facilities for drones, small arms, unmanned aerial vehicles and ammunition and missile manufacturing facilities

Adani Defence Systems and Technologies acquired Alpha Design Technologies Pvt Ltd and PLR Systems Private Ltd in 2020 and General Aeronautics in 2022.

Automation & control instruments companies

ABB India Ltd – 1949, Elico Ltd. – 1960, Emerson Process Management India Pvt Ltd – 1981, Honeywell Automation India Ltd – 1984, Krohne Marshall Pvt Ltd. – 1984, Forbes Marshall Pvt Ltd – 1985, Yokogawa India Ltd. – 1987, Pepperl + Fuchs (India) Pvt Ltd.- 1990
Endress+Hauser India Pvt Ltd – 1994, Schneider Electric India Pvt Ltd – 1995, Wika Instruments India Pvt Ltd – 1997, Danfoss Industries Pvt Ltd – 1999

Computer and peripheral companies

PSI Data Systems - 1976, Larsen & Toubro - 1986

Defence equipment manufacturer

Mahindra Defence Systems Ltd – 2012.

14 - GROWTH IN PRODUCTION OF STEEL AND METALS

Steel as Vital Raw Material

Indian iron and steel industry, with its strong forward and backward linkages, contributes significantly to the overall growth and development of the economy.

Targeted Growth for Steel Production

The steel and other metals requirements for various applications were forecasted by the government for the final year of each 5-year plan and the target mild steel, finished steel, tool, alloy and stainless steel, spring and free cutting steel, electrical steel sheets, steel castings, steel forgings, pig iron, sponge iron, aluminium, ACSR and AA conductors, copper, electrolytic copper, lead, zinc production capacities for the various 5-year plans were set.

The iron ore, coking coal and natural gas required for steel production were assessed and targets set.

Exploration for Metal Ore Deposits

Reserves of good quality iron ore (containing over 60% iron) were estimated to be over 10,000 Mts in 1950-51. (1.27.28)

Total iron ore and manganese estimated reserves in 1960-61 were 21870 Mts and 180 Mt respectively. (3.12.30)

Drilling and exploratory mining work proved existence of about 28 Mts of copper ore (average copper content 0.8%) in Khetri area and about 0.35 Mt of ore containing on an average 6.24% of copper, lead and zinc in Sikkim. (3.27.13).

Mineral Reserves in 1961 -

Bauxite (aluminium ore) - 260 Mts, Copper ore - 32.9 Mts, ilmenite (titanium ore) - 350 Mts, Lead ore - 10.7 Mts, Limestone - 15740 Mts, Magnesite - 100 Mts, Pyrites - 386 Mts. (3.27.14)

Mineral Reserves as on 1.04.2005 –

i) The iron ore resources Hematite ore - 14630 Mts and magnetite ores - 10619 Mts. (11.7.2.30)

ii) Bauxite - 3306 Mts. Out of the leasehold resources of 1079 Mts, 41.94% were in the public sector and 49.06% in the private sector. (11.7.2.33)

iii) Chromite - 232.12 Mts. Out of the 161 Mts of resources in leasehold, 33.67% were in the public sector and 66.33% in the private sector. (11.7.2.32)

iv) Copper ore - 1394 Mts. (11.7.2.34) HCL was only undertaking mining copper ore in India. (11.7.2.35)

v) Lead–zinc ore - 522 Mts with 7.2 Mts of lead metal and 24.25 Mts of zinc metal. (11.7.2.36)

vi) Manganese ore - 380 Mts. (11.7.2.31)

Proven Balance Resources as on 1.04.2007

Bauxite – 2184.311 Mts, Copper Ore – 650.458 Mts, Iron Ore (Hematite and magnetite) – 15432 Mts, Lead-Zinc Ore – 304.372 Mts (11.v2.7.2.27)

Proven Balance Resources as on 1.04.2012

Bauxite – 2091.585 Mts and Chromite – 106.932 Mts

Iron and Steel Production in India

Status in 1951

Production and consumption of Iron Ore in 1951 were 3.657 Mts and 2.672 Mts.

Most of the ores were utilized by the 3 iron and steel plants of Tata Iron and Steel Co, Tata Nagar, Indian Iron and Steel Co, Asansol and Mysore Iron & Steel Works, Bhadravati. (1.29.29)

Private Sector Jobs Planned in I 5YP -

The plan included 850,000 tons of pig iron expansion projects and 0.575 Mts finished steel expansion projects in the private sector and 60,000 tons finished steel expansion projects of Mysore Iron and Steel. (1.29.20)

Achievements in I 5YP
Hindustan Steel Ltd. was established in 1953.

Steel Production in Private Sector –
The combined capacity of Tata Iron and steel Company and Indian Iron and Steel Company was 1.25 Mts.

Planning for starting Steel Plants (II 5YP)

Raw Material Requirements for 3 steel Plants - The annual requirements of mineral raw materials for capacity production of 3 steel plants were estimated to be as follows: Coal – 5.220 Mts, iron ore 5.58 Mts, manganese ore 0.409 Mts, limestone 1.691 Mts, Dolomite – 0.379 Mts.

Arranging Rs. 128+110+115 = 353 Cr investment (in 1953-54), foreign assistance by way of participation in capital, deferred payments for plant and machinery and other forms of credit amounting to about Rs. 75 crores., foreign exchange and supply infrastructure for raw materials of this magnitude **could not have been done by private sector.** Management of Private sector companies like TISCO, IISCO and (Mysore Iron and Steel) etc. would have thought of profiteering from expansion of the existing units with smaller investment and shorter incubation time rather than investing in starting new companies with longer gestation period to earn profit. (2.19.28)

Steel production planned in private sector –
Kalinga Tubes Ltd, and the Indian Tube Company were expected to develop the production of tubes and pipes including E.R.W. tubes and seamless tubes. (2.19.47)

Government Assistance to Private Sector
The Central Government arranged for representation on the IISCO's Board of Directors in view of the of the loan of Rs. 7.9 crores sanctioned by it. (2.19.48)

Achievement in II 5YP –
3 New steel plants were established in the public sector and 2 units expanded in the private sector. The output of steel ingots increased from 1.4 Mts in 1950-51 to 3.5 Mts in 1960-61 and of pig iron from 3.5 lakh tons to 9 lakh tons. (3.3.21)

Rourkela plant's designed capacity was 720,000 tons of flat products of steel, hot and cold rolled. (2.19.22)

Agreement was signed with USSR in March 1955 for construction of **Bhilai steel plant**, which was commissioned in Feb 1959 starting with production of Rails. Bhilai plants designed capacity was 770,000 tons of saleable steel, including 140,000 tons of billets for the re-rolling industry.

Durgapur plant was designed to produce light and medium sections of steel and billets amounting to 790,000 tons per annum.

The combined output of 3 steel plants was only 0.6 Mts in 1960-61 as against the target of 2 Mts. TISCO production fell short of the target set for II Plan period, the actual output of saleable steel for the five-year period was 4.5 Mts as against 5.2 Mts predicted in the 1955 forecasts of the Tariff Commission.

Tungabhadra Steel Products Ltd. was established in **1960,** to undertake manufacture of Gates & Hoists required for spillways, Sluices & Canal Gates of Tungabhadra Dam.

National Mineral Development Corporation, established in November 1958, Orissa Mining Corporation, and Board of Mineral Development, Mysore undertook iron ore projects. (3.27.46)

Finished steel capacity in 1960-61 was - 4.76 Mts. The existed installed capacity of TISCO and IISCO was 3.0 Mts. (3.26.37)

Achievements in III 5YP -
Hindustan Steel Ltd started establishing Durgapur alloy and tool steels plant of 48,000 tons capacity (Including tool steels, constructional steel, stainless steel, die and other alloy steels) and new integrated steel works at Bokaro (3.16.11)

Ordinance Factories - The combined output of constructional steels and spring steels of the Ishapur and Kanpur ordnance factories was estimated at 50,000 tons. (3.26.49)

Iron Ore Production in 1968-69
Iron ore - 28 Mts. The captive mines of the steel plants at Bailadila, Barajamda (Orissa and Bihar), Daitari (0rissa), Beliary-Hospet (Mysore) and Goa. were expected to produce around 20 Mts of iron ore.

The installed capacity for production of ingots was 9 Mts in 1968-69.

Steel Production in Private Sector -
The share of the private sector in the III plan steel target was 3.2 Mts of ingots (mainly for augmenting the supplies of billets to re-rollers). About 200,000 tons of pig iron was also expected to be produced by the private sector on a decentralized basis. (3.26.38)

Achievements (Jobs Planned) in IV 5YP (1969-74)
a) Addition of 8 Mts capacity from the expansion of Bokaro and Bhilai steel plants and from new steel plants at Hospet, Visakhapatnam and Salem,
b) Utilization of surplus extrusion facilities available at the Nuclear Fuel Complex, Hyderabad for the manufacture of seamless tubes of stainless and high alloy steel. (4.14.51)
c) Commissioning of Bailadila 5 and Bellary mines of National Mineral Development Corporation. Production of iron ores from NMDC mines was 14 Mts (Out of envisaged production of 51 Mts). (4.14.49)
d) In 1968-69, palletisation plant of capacity 0.6 Mts existed only in Goa.

The production capacity of ingots in 1973-74 was estimated at 12 Mts.

In the Private Sector
Increasing the capacity of IISCO from 1 to 1.3 Mts of ingots by 1971-72. (4.14.40)
The outputs from alloy steel plants at Durgapur, Mysore Iron and Steel Company and private sector projects were expected to meet the demand for alloy and special steels estimated at 294,000 tons in 1973-74.

Achievements in V 5YP (1975-80)
Kudremukh Iron Ore Company was founded in 1976.
Though a few special categories of steel were still needed to be imported, on the whole the country was expected to emerge as a net exporter of steel. (5.5.39).
The exportable surplus of steel in 1978-79 was estimated at about 1.5 Mts. (5.3.13)
Production of saleable steel from the integrated steel plants in 1976-77 was 6.92 Mts. (6.16.19)

Achievements in VI 5YP (1980-85)
i) The first phase of the Bokaro and Bhilai plants expansion was scheduled to be completed in 1985-86. (7.7.76)
ii) TISCO completed phase-l of their modernization program. (7.7.83)

iii) Coal-based sponge iron pilot plant was commissioned at Kothagudem. (7.7.89)

Achievements in VII 5YP (1985-90)
During VII Plan and 1990-92, the expansions of Bokaro and Bhilai steel plants to 4 Mts each, the II phase expansion of TISCO and the I phase facilities of Visakhapatnam Steel Plant were completed. The II phase of Visakhapatnam Steel Plant was expected to be completed in August, 1992. (8.V2.5.8.1)

Production in 1989-90 (8.Stat. 5.5)
Capacities for Steel Ingots, Alloy and special steels and Sponge Iron were 14.7, 01.49 and 0.57 Mts respectively.
Integrated steel Plants' capacity of saleable steel – 11.57 Mts of Total capacity of 15.07 Mts
Integrated steel Plants' Production of saleable steel – 9.03 Mts of total production of 12.61 Mts

Production in 1991-92 (8. Stat. 5.5)
Capacities for Steel Ingots, Alloy and special steels and Sponge Iron were 16.35, 1.65 and 1.4 Mts respectively.
Integrated steel Plants' capacity of saleable steel – 13.00 Mts of Total capacity of 20.12 Mts
Integrated steel Plants' Production of saleable steel – 10.58 Mts (Total Production 14.26 Mts)

Capacity creation in Private Sector as in 1992-93
Private sector contributed for 41% of the total crude steel output and 54% of the total finished steel output during 1992-93. (11.v2.7.1.289)

Achievements in VIII 5YP (1992-97)
(i) Bhilai and Bokaro Plants achieved the production targets, but Durgapur and Rourkela Plants could not achieve the targets due to delays in completion of modernization projects (9.5.108)
(ii) SAIL raised US $ 125 million through **G**lobal **D**epository **R**eceipts for financing its Plan programs.
(iii) The Vizag Steel Plant (VSP) of Rashtriya Ispat Nigam Limited (RINL) was commissioned fully and the entire production comprised of long products. (9.5.112)

Production in 1996-97
Hot Metal Integrated Steel - 19.89 Mts, Pig Iron - 3.20 Mts, Crude Steel - 16.67 Mts, Saleable Steel - 14.59 Mts and Finished steel - 22.72 Mts. (9.5.105)

Achievements in IX 5YP (1997-2002)
Production in 2002-03 - Capacity for steel Production - 40.41 Mts, Capacity utilization - 86% and Consumption of finished steel – 28.7 Mts. (10.7.1.0)

Achievements in X 5YP (2002-07)
Due to general slowdown in the major steel consuming sectors and restrictions imposed by major steel importing countries, **there was excess capacity in the domestic steel manufacturing sector.** Therefore, no additional capacity was planned for creation in the Tenth Plan, particularly in the hot rolled products (10.7.1.91)
Turnover of Steel Industry and Minerals & non-ferrous metals industry in 2005-06 were Rs. 41742 Cr. and Rs. 12384 Cr. respectively.

Performance of CPSEs during X 5YP (Rs Crore) (Annexure – 11.v3.7.1.4)

Item	Units	Domestic Production		Total CPSE Production		Share of CPSEs %	
		1968-69	2005-06	1968-69	2005-06	1968-69	2005-06
Finished Steel	Mts	4.58	46.82	2.55	12.59	55.68	26.89

Production in 2004-05

i) SAIL plants produced 12.10 Mts of crude steel and 11.03 Mts of saleable steel with a capacity utilization of 101% and 104% respectively.
ii) Alloy Steel plant at Durgapur and Salem Steel Plant together produced 0.379 Mts of saleable steel.
iii) Indian Iron and Steel Co. Ltd. produced 0.357 Mts of crude steel and 0.274 Mts of saleable steel.
(Public Enterprises Survey 2004-05: Vol.-I)

Capacity creation in Private Sector as on 2006-07
Private sector contribution was 67% of the total crude steel output and 74% of the total finished steel output. (11.v2.7.1.289)

Opening up of economy was a challenge to domestic private sector companies also
The Indian steel industry withstood international competition despite the reduction of basic customs duty on steel from 25%–30% in 2002–03 to 5% in 2006–07. By the end of X 5YP, the industry was fully geared to operate in an open economy. (11.7.1.293)

Production in 2006-07
Capacity for steel production - 56.84 Mts, Capacity utilization - 89% and Export of finished steel – 4.75 Mts.
The production value of 4 fuel minerals was Rs 63938.76 Cr, 10 metallic minerals was Rs 12858.71 Cr, and 50 non-metallic minerals and 23 minor minerals was Rs 11068.88 Cr. (11.7.2.26)
India produced 53 Mts of steel in 2007, an increase of over 10% per year since 2000. India became the fifth largest producer of steel in the world. (Ref. 12.4.59)

Steel Production in 2011-12
India became world's fourth largest producer of crude steel in 2011-12, preceded only by China, Japan and USA. (12. Annex.13.2 – 21 / 27)

Steel Production in 2018
As per World Steel, India's crude steel production in 2018 was at 106.5 Mts and **India overtook Japan as the world's second largest steel production country.** Japan produced 104.3 Mts in 2018. Indian industry produced 82.68 Mts of finished steel and 9.7 Mts of raw iron.

Steel Production in 2021
The steel production capacity in 2021 was 143.91 Mts (25.932 million – 18% - in public sector and 117.982 million in private sector). As per Indian Mineral Yearbook, 2019 published by Indian Bureau of Mines, there were 254 reporting mines in 2018-19, out of which 35 mines (13.8%) were in the Public Sector and 219 in Private Sector.

Steel Production in 2023
India, the second largest global steel producer, increased production in 2023 to 140.2 Mts. Global crude steel production remains flat in 2023 | S&P Global Commodity Insights (spglobal.com)

Aluminium Production in India

Aluminium production in 1950-51
Private Sector Companies like Hindustan Aluminium Corp. Ltd., Hirakud were manufacturing aluminium in 1950-51. (1.29.29)

Achievements in I 5YP
The capacity for aluminium production in 1955-56 production was 7500 tons. (2.4.35)

Achievements in III 5YP
Bharat Aluminium Company Ltd. was incorporated in 1965 as the first public sector enterprise in India which started producing aluminium in 1974.

Koyna Aluminium project - The Ratnagiri project was finalized as early as 1966 by the Planning Commission which allocated Rs 135 Cr. for 2 aluminium plants - at Korba and Ratnagiri - to be constructed by the BALCO and to be completed towards the end of V Plan.

Achievements in IV 5YP
The production of aluminium was 125,000 tons in 1968-69.
2 Public sector projects (Koyna and Korba) with a total rated capacity of 150,000 tons were under construction. 70,000 Tons Aluminium was expected to be obtained from the expansion programs of various private sector plants in progress. (4.2.27)

Achievements in V 5YP
With BALCO plant achieving its full capacity of 0.1 Mt of aluminium and the capacity, which existed in the private sector, the total capacity was expected to reach **325,000 tons, adequate to meet the domestic requirements.** (5.5.42)

Achievements in VI Plan
i) **National Aluminium Company Ltd.**, Koraput, the largest aluminium plant of the country, was established in 1981 and started commercial operation in 1987 with an installed capacity of 1.6 Mts of ingots.
ii) Construction of aluminium smelter of 0.218 Mts capacity at Angul and 0.8 Mt capacity alumina plant at Daman Jodi were taken up. (7.7.95)
Installed capacity for aluminium (including addition of 41,000 tons in the private sector) became 362,000 tons in 1984-85. (7.7.96)

Achievements in VII 5YP
Completion Aluminium complex of NALCO, setting up of a captive power plant for BALCO, thereby raising capacities for aluminium as targeted.
In the private sector, expansion of alumina calciner of HINDALCO was taken up. (7.7.97)
Capacity for Aluminium in 1989-90 was 0.61 Mts and remained the same up to 1991-92. (8.Stat. 5.5)
India emerged as a net exporter of aluminium. (8.V2.5.9.1)

During VIII 5YP
Reduction in consumption growth of aluminium during 1992-97 - The consumption of aluminium grew at 5%, much less than average annual compound growth rate of 8.5% envisaged during VIII Plan period due slow-down of the economy during first 2 years of the plan, slow off-take of aluminium by the State Electricity Boards due to paucity of resources, lower investment in the aluminium consuming sectors because of liquidity crunch in the economy, etc. (9.5.117)

Planned expansions didn't materialize during 1992-97
The production target set for the terminal year of VIII Plan was not realized, mainly due to anticipated addition to the capacity not coming through.
i) A new smelter of 150,000 TPA capacity, planned to be set up by **private sector** HINDALCO in Andhra Pradesh was dropped on commercial considerations.
ii) **private sector** Indian Aluminium Co. could not achieve rated production capacity as envisaged.
iii) MALCO could not produce aluminium during 1992-93 to 1994-95 due to non-availability of power.

iv) The public sector National Aluminium Company did not complete its debottlenecking program due to some technical reasons. (9.5.118)

The installed capacity for aluminium in 1996-97 was 0.67 Mts. NALCO's existed capacity was 0.218 Mt. (9.5.119)

Achievements in IX 5YP

(i) INDAL's Belgaum Smelter of 65000 Tons was not expected to be re-energized and a marginal expansion program of its Hirakud smelter was also not expected to materialize, as was anticipated. Besides, INDAL's Alwaye smelter capacity also declined by 7,000 tons due to some technical reasons. (10. Annex. 7.2.5)

(ii) 30,000 Tons by Hindalco and 12,000 tons by NALCO were added to the primary aluminium capacity with the expansion of their smelters. (10.7.2.16)

(iii) NALCO's de-bottlenecking project of its alumina refinery and expansion projects of bauxite mines from 2.4 million TPA to 4.8 million TPA and alumina refinery from 0.8 million TPA to 1.575 million TPA were completed. (10.7.2.17)

(iv) INDAL was taken over by Hindalco from Canadian firm, Alcan. (10.7.2.18)

Good capacity utilization by aluminium producers

The production of aluminium by primary producers in 1999-2000 and 2000-01 were 0.618 Mts and 0.641 Mts respectively. (Capacity utilization of 83% and 86% considering 2002-03 capacity)

Production in 2001-02 -

Installed capacity for alumina - 2.72 Mts. (11.7.2.12)

Production of aluminium, Secondary aluminium (by the unorganized sector) and Bauxite – 0.634661 Mts, 50,000 Tons and 8.6 Mts respectively. (10.7.2.11 / 57)

Consumption of / Demand for Aluminium – 0.7 Mts (11.v2.7.2.29)

Export of aluminium – 0.191537 Mts.

Indigenous aluminium smelting capacity – 0.714 Mts (10.7.2.55)

The installed capacities of BALCO, NALCO, Hindalco, MALCO and INDAL were 0.1 Mt, 0.23 Mt, 0.275 Mt., 0.025 Mts. and 0.117 Mts respectively, making total installed capacity 0.747 Mts in February 2003.

Achievements in X 5YP –

NALCO produced 0.3385 Mts of aluminium metal during 2004-05. The production of calcined alumina and bauxite were 1.5667 Mts and 4.852 Mts with capacity utilization at 100% and 101% respectively. (PES 2004-05: Vol.-I)

Aluminium Industry in 2006-07

Panchpatmali bauxite mine of NALCO, with a capacity of 4.8 Mts, accounted for 40% of the country's bauxite production in 2006-07. (7.2.11)

NALCO had a 35% share in total production. (11.v2.7.2.14)

Total installed capacity for alumina and aluminium were - 4.24 Mts. and 1.183 Mts. respectively. (11.7.2.13)

Export of aluminium – 0.23014 Mts (2005-06)

Consumption / Demand of / for Aluminium – in Mts – 0.92 (11.v2.7.2.29)

The development of special aluminium alloys for "Intermediate Range Ballistic Missile" – Agni and "Surface Missile" – Prithvi were significant achievements of BALCO. BALCO was the first in the Indian Aluminium Industry to produce the Alloy Rods, which is a Feedstock for all Aluminium Alloy Conductors, very much needed for today's power transmission lines.

Aluminium Industry in 2019-20

The aluminium industry of India produced the second-highest volume of aluminium and its products in the world. The aluminium production of the Indian companies contributed nearly 2% of India's GDP.

The top 10 aluminium companies in India were HINDALCO (39% of market share), Vedanta Aluminium Ltd., India Foils Ltd, Sacheta Metals, Jindal Aluminium, NALCO, BALCO, MALCO, INDAL, and Century Extrusions Ltd. Vedanta Ltd was the largest aluminium producing company of India.

The combined aluminium production in India stood at 3.6 Mt in FY20.

Aluminium Industry in 2022-23

Vedanta (which took over BALCO and MALCO), HINDALCO and NALCO produced 1,1714 Mts, 1.021 Mts and 0.3445 Mts of Aluminium respectively in 2022-23.

Copper Production in India

In 1950-51

Indian Copper Corporation, a private sector company established by a British Co. in Ghatsila, was producing copper. (1.29.29)

In 1960-61

Domestic production of copper was 8000 tons against demand of 70,000 tons. (3.27.48)

Planned jobs in III 5YP -

The smelter and the electrolytic refinery associated with the Khetri and Daribo copper mines, for an annual production of 11,500 tons of electrolytic copper, were likely to be established by the middle of 1964. (3.26.52)

The copper reserves estimated to be available at Rangpo were to be exploited by the Sikkim Mining Corporation, a joint venture of the Sikkim Durbar and the Government of India. (3.27.49)

Achievements in III 5YP

Hindustan Copper Ltd. - Development of Khetri Mine was started by National Mineral Development Corporation and the project was handed over to Hindustan Copper Ltd in 1967, when HCL was formed. Subsequently, smelting and refining facilities were added. HCL undertook mechanized mining in 'Khetri' and 'Kolihan' (of capacity 1.0 Mts of ore). The capacity of beneficiation and process plants were 1.81 Mts and 31,000 TPA of refined copper respectively.

Ore reserves were 83.76 Mts in various concentrations in Khetri, Kolihan, Banwas and Chandmari – Kolihan Intervening blocks.

Achievements in IV 5YP

With the commissioning of the Hindustan Copper Ltd, Khetri, the smelting capacity became 57,000 TPA.

Achievements of VI 5YP

The Malanjkhand project was completed. Implementation of Mosabani mine expansion from 50,000 to 80,000 tons/ month was expected to be completed by December, 1985. (7.7.100)

Installed Capacity for refined copper in 1984-85 was 39,400 tons (7.7.102)

Achievements in VII 5YP

De-bottle necking and modernization of the existing smelters of HCL were completed. (8.V2.5.11.1)

Capacity for refined Copper in 1989-90 was 47,500 tons and remained the same up to 1996-97. (9.5.123)

Fall in demand for Copper (Zinc and lead) during VIII Plan (1992-97)

The liberalization of the economy affected non-ferrous metals industry rather severely during 1992-97. There was a sharp decline in the London Metal Exchange prices of non-ferrous metals, particularly copper, lead and zinc and a fall in demand of these metals due to slow-down of the economy during 1992-94. A substantial reduction in import duties made under the new policy dispensation, made imported copper, lead and zinc cheaper than indigenously produced metals. **All domestic companies** had to resort to cutbacks in production, particularly of lead and zinc by Hindustan Zinc Ltd., a major producer of these metals in the public sector. (9.5.115)

Private Sector Investments in VIII plan –
i) Sterlite Industries Ltd. completed implementation a smelter of 0.1 Mt capacity.
ii) Birla Copper Ltd. started implementation of one smelter of 0.1 Mt capacity and one copper rod plant of 80,000 TPA capacity.
iii) SWIL Ltd. started implementation of a scrap-based smelter of 50,000 TPA capacity.
Both smelters of Birla Copper Ltd. and SWIL Ltd. were expected to be commissioned in 1998. (9.5.123)

Achievements in IX 5YP
Anticipated additions to the indigenous copper smelting capacity to the tune of 1,52,500 TPA - 52,500 TPA from the expansion of HCL's Khetri smelter and 1,00,000 TPA from a new smelter of METDIST Ltd. did not materialize.

Production in 2001-02
Total installed Copper smelting capacity – 0.3475 Mts (11.7.2.15)
Production of Copper – 0.39 Mts (Including production from the private sector companies Sterlite Industries Ltd., Indo Gulf Copper Ltd. (Birla Copper) and the public sector Hindustan Copper Ltd. (11.v2.7.2.29)
Consumption of / Demand for Copper – in Mts – 0.374 (11.v2.7.2.29)
Export of Copper – in Mts – 0.061 (11.v2.7.2.29)

Achievements in X 5YP –
Production in 2006-07
India's smelting capacity for copper grew almost three-fold and the production by about 60% during X 5YP. (11.v3.7.2.16)
Production of copper concentrates in 2005-06 - 0.022984 Mts (11.v3.7.2.15)
Production of Copper Ore – 3.293 Mts (11.v2.7.2.27) (11. V3. Annex. 7.2.2)
Installed capacity for copper in 2006-07 – 0.9475 Mts (11. v3. Fig. 7.2.3)
Consumption of / Demand for Copper – 0.44 Mts.
Production of copper – 0.4599 Mt (up to December 2006)

In 2018
The installed capacities for copper cathode in HCL, HINDALCO and Sterlite Industries Ltd were 0.0495 Mt, 0.5 Mt and 0.45 Mt respectively. HCL's installed capacity for copper wire rods was 0.06 Mt.
Sterlite copper smelting plant in Tuticorin of capacity 0.4 Mt has been closed from 2018.
According to government data, India produced 364,000 tons of refined copper in 2020-2021, which was a decrease from 799,000 tons in 2016-2017.

Production in 2022-23
The production of copper cathode by HCL, HINDALCO (Unit Birla Copper) and Sesa Sterlite Ltd. (SSL) during FY 2022-23 and the month of April, 2023 were 7.3 Tons (capacity 0.0685 Mt), 0.407 Mt (0.5 Mt) and 0.148 Mt (0.216 Mt).
India's refined copper production and copper consumption in 2022–2023 were 0.555 Mt, (making it the 10th largest in the world) and 0.986 Mt respectively.

The production of copper metal (cathode) by HCL during April, 2023 was Nil because HCL was selling Metal-In-Concentrate (MIC) in the market directly. The MIC production of HCL during April 2023 was 1972 tons (copper ore 294000 Tons) and it was 1,919 tons (copper ore 224000 Tons) during the corresponding period in the previous year. _for_the_Month_of_April_2023_(1)_1688531962.pdf (mines.gov.in)

Zinc Production in India

Achievements in III 5YP / 1966

Hindustan Zinc Ltd. was incorporated from the erstwhile Metal Corporation of India on 10.01.1966. Udaipur smelter was producing 18,000 tons of zinc per annum using 2000 tons/ day of Zinc ore output of Zawar mines. (4.14.41)

The capacity of the Zinc plant, producing zinc from imported concentrates, by private sector Binani Zinc at Alwaye was 20,000 TPA. (4.14.41)

Achievements in V 5YP

Installed capacity for zinc increased to 92,000 tons against the target of 95,000 tons with the completion of the expansion of Debari smelter (45,000 tons) and installation of a new smelter at Vizag (30,000 tons). (5.5.44) (7.7.105)

Achievements of VI 5YP

i) Installed capacity for zinc in 1984-85 was 96,000 tons. Capacity utilization of zinc smelters was about 60 %. (7.7.104 / 105)

ii) Installation of Leach Residue Treatment Plant at Debar and Smelter of HZL. were completed. (7.7.105)

iii) The preparatory work for setting up the integrated zinc-lead mine / smelter complex (of 70,000 TPA of zinc and 35,000 TPA of lead, based upon the deposits of Rampura-Agucha was completed. (7.7.107)

Achievements in VII 5YP (1989-90)

At Vizag Zinc Smelter, the overall metal recovery was improved from 81.5% to 93% by switching over from pyrometallurgical to hydrometallurgical process following the results achieved by the latter process at Debari (7.7.107)

Expansions of Vizag Zinc smelters of HZL and Binani Zinc Plant in private sector raised capacities for zinc as targeted for the Plan. From a position of dependence on imports, the share of imports in the consumption of zinc registered some decline. (8.V2.5.9.1)

Capacity for zinc ingots in 1989-90 was 99,000 tons and remained the same in 1990-91 also. (8.Stat. 5.5)

Production in 1991-92 (8.Stat. 5.5)

Capacity for zinc ingots – 1,69,000 tons.

With the commissioning of Rampura - Agucha - Chanderiya integrated project of Hindustan Zinc Ltd. **in 1991-92, the country achieved near self-sufficiency in zinc.** (8.v2.5.12.1)

Fall in demand for zinc during 1992-97

The liberalization of the economy affected non-ferrous metals industry rather severely during 1992-97. There was a sharp decline in the London Metal Exchange **prices of** non-ferrous metals, particularly zinc and a **fall in demand** for zinc due to slow-down of the economy during 1992-94. A substantial reduction in import duties made under the new policy dispensation, made **imported zinc cheaper** than indigenously produced metals. **All domestic companies** had to resort to cut-backs in production, particularly of lead and zinc by Hindustan Zinc Ltd., a major producer of these metals in the public sector. (9.5.115)

This led to uneconomical operation of the company, irrespective of productivity of the company and quality of the product.

Achievement of target set for VIII Plan

The zinc capacity creation target of 0.179 Mts was achieved with private sector Binani Zinc Ltd. completing expansion of Alwaye smelter.

Hindustan Zinc Ltd. deferred major investments planned to be taken up in the VIII Plan on commercial considerations. (9.5.125)

Achievements in IX 5YP (1997-2002)

HZL completed expansion of the capacities of its Vizag and Debari smelters in Andhra Pradesh and Rajasthan each by 10,000 TPA (10.7.2.25)

Production in 2001-02

The total installed capacity, production and Consumption of / Demand for Zinc were 0.199 Mts, 0.226Mts. and 0.297 Mts. respectively. (11.v3.7.2.17 / 29)

After privatization, Hindustan Zinc Ltd (HZL) expanded its zinc mining and used the mineral from its captive Rampura Agucha mines to expand smelting. (11.7.2.18)

Achievements in X 5YP

The total installed capacity and Consumption / Demand for Zinc in 2006-07 were 0.449 Mts and 0.455 Mts respectively. (11.7.2.17).

Production in 2022-23

In 2022–2023, India produced an estimated 1.59 Mts of zinc concentrate and the production of mined metal was 1.062 Mts.

Capacity and production of HZL during FY 2022-23 were 0.843 Mts and 0.821 Mts respectively.

Production of Lead in India

Achievements in V 5YP

Installed capacity for lead in 1979-80 was 18,000 tons. (6.2.31)

Achievements in VI 5YP

The expansion of lead smelter at Vizag was completed. (7.7.105).

Rajpura - Dariba lead–zinc mine of 3000 TPD capacity, Sargipalli lead mine and leach residue treatment plant for recovery of zinc, Sulphur and cadmium from the stockpile / current neutral residue at Debari were completed. (7.7.106)

Installed capacity for lead in 1984-85 was 30,000 tons. (7.7.105)

Achievements in VII 5YP

Capacities for lead ingots in 1989-90, 1990-91 and 1991-92 were 30,000 tons, 54,500 tons and 89,500 tons respectively. (8. Stat. 5.5)

Achievements in VIII 5YP

Target for 1996-97 (8. Statement 5.5)

Capacity for zinc ingots – 1,79,000 tons		Capacity for lead ingots – 1,04,000 Tons
Production of zinc ingots – 1,67,000 tons (**9.5.50**)		Production of lead ingots – 96,000 Tons

Production in 1996-97

Zinc ingots   - 140100 Tons   Lead ingots   - 43780 Tons

The capacity for production of lead by HZL and private sector Indian Lead Ltd. were 65000 TPA and 25000 TPA respectively. (9.5.128)

Reduced Production of Lead in 1996-97 after Liberalization

The capacity creation for lead 90000 Tons fell short of 1.04 lakh tons, though marginally, because of the delay in completing the expansion program by private sector - Indian Lead Private Ltd. The lead production target of 96000 Tons set for 1996-97 was not realized primarily because HZL had to resort to cut back in production on commercial considerations as liberalization made imported lead cheaper. Production of lead was 43780 Tons. (9.5.127)

Expansions Planned in IX Plan (1997-2002)
The private sector Indian Lead Ltd. was planning to expand its capacity from 25,000 to 40,000 TPA. No addition to the existing lead capacity of 65,000 TPA of HZL was anticipated. HZL, however, included expansion of the existing Rampura-Agucha lead-zinc mine and concentrator. (9.5.128)

Production in 2001-02 – Refer to data under HZL.

Achievements in IX 5YP
Vizag Lead smelter of HZL remained closed in 2001-02 and secondary capacity with India Lead Ltd. was utilized for producing only 357 ton of lead during April 2001 – February 2002 and both HZL smelters located at Thane and Kolkata remained closed as the company was before the BIFR. (10. Annex. 7.2.5) Secondary lead output of the private sector India Lead Ltd. declined to 50% of its annual capacity due to restrictions in importing lead scrap. (10.7.2.24)

Production of Lead – zinc concentrate, installed capacity for Lead, production of Lead and Consumption of / Demand for Lead in 2001-02 were 0.450438 Mt, 0.043 Mts, 0.071 Mts and 0.132 Mts. respectively. (11.v3.7.2.18 / 29)

Achievements in X 5YP
Production of Lead – zinc concentrate in 2005-06 – 0.984745 Mts.
Production of Lead-Zinc Ore, total installed capacity and Consumption of / Demand for Lead in 2006-07 were 4.414 Mts, 0.085 Mts and 0.275 Mts respectively. (11.v2.7.2.18 / 27)

India's primary lead production was 181,365 tons, 214,399 tons and 216,000 tons in 2019-20, 2020-21 and 2021-22 respectively.

In 2021-22, India's production volume of lead concentrate amounted to 388,040 metric tons. This figure is estimated to have decreased to 242,016 metric tons during financial year 2023.

Ministry of Mines, Government of India, Home

Manganese Production in India

Achievement in I 5YP –
Production of manganese ore increased from 0.88 million ton in 1950 to 1.9 Mts in 1953. (3.27.11)

Achievements in III 5YP
Manganese Ore India Ltd. - In 1962, the Government of India took over the mining activities from Central Provinces Manganese Ore Co. Ltd. Then, Manganese Ore (India) Ltd. was formed jointly by Government of India, State governments Maharashtra and Madhya Pradesh and CPMO.

Capacity Utilization in 2004-05
MOIL produced 0.943 Mts of manganese ore during 2004-05 (100%) (PES 2004-05: Vol.-I)

Production in 2022-23
India's manganese ore production in 2022 was 2.7 Mts, but in 2023 it was 1.65 Mts. MOIL produced 1.302 Mts of manganese ore in 2022-23, which was the second highest production since inception. This was also 10% higher than the previous record sales of 1.392 Mts in 2007-08.

Contribution to X 5YP by Steel CPSEs

The outlay of the Ministry of Steel was Rs 8477 Cr., mainly financed by Internal and Extra Budgetary Resources, except for Rs 65 crore. (11.7.1.125)

Contribution to XI 5YP by Steel and Metals CPSEs

Out of total allocation of Rs 37318.18 Cr for steel sector in XI 5YP, SAIL and RINL accounted for Rs 27409 Cr and Rs 9569.18 Cr respectively. The budgetary support was for restructuring of CPSEs in steel sector and for some of the ongoing and new R&D schemes. (11. 7.1.299)

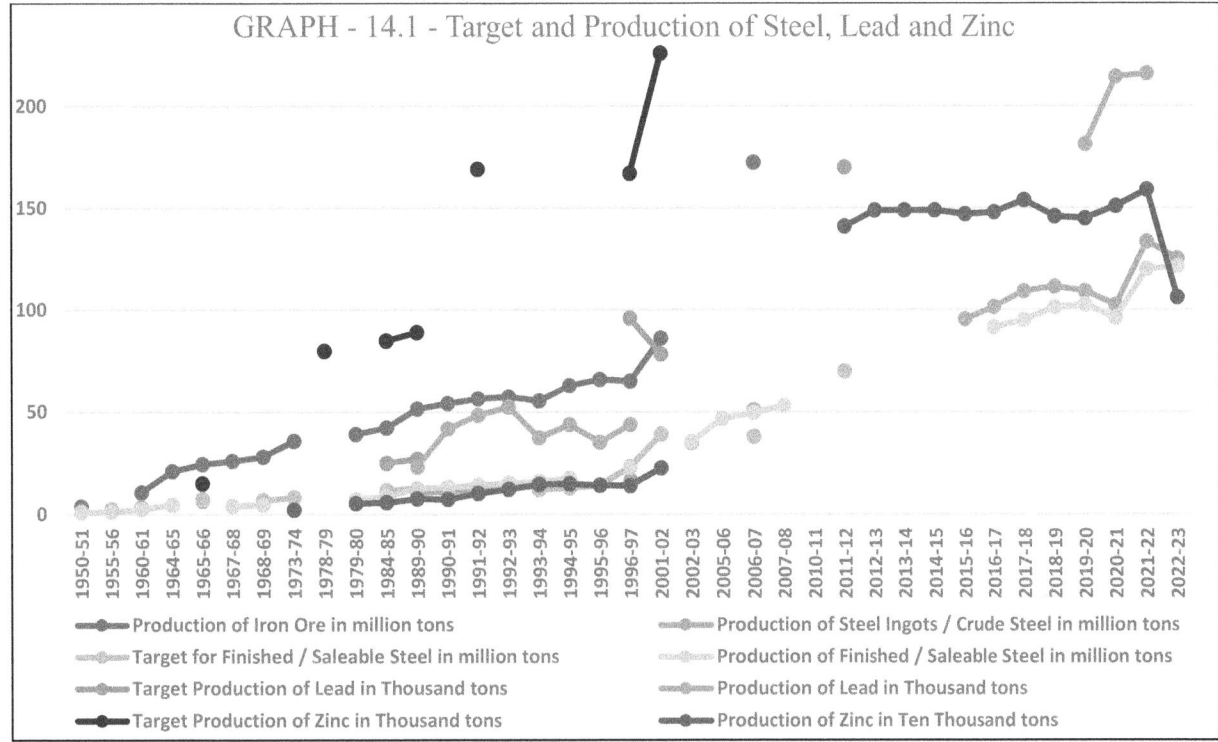

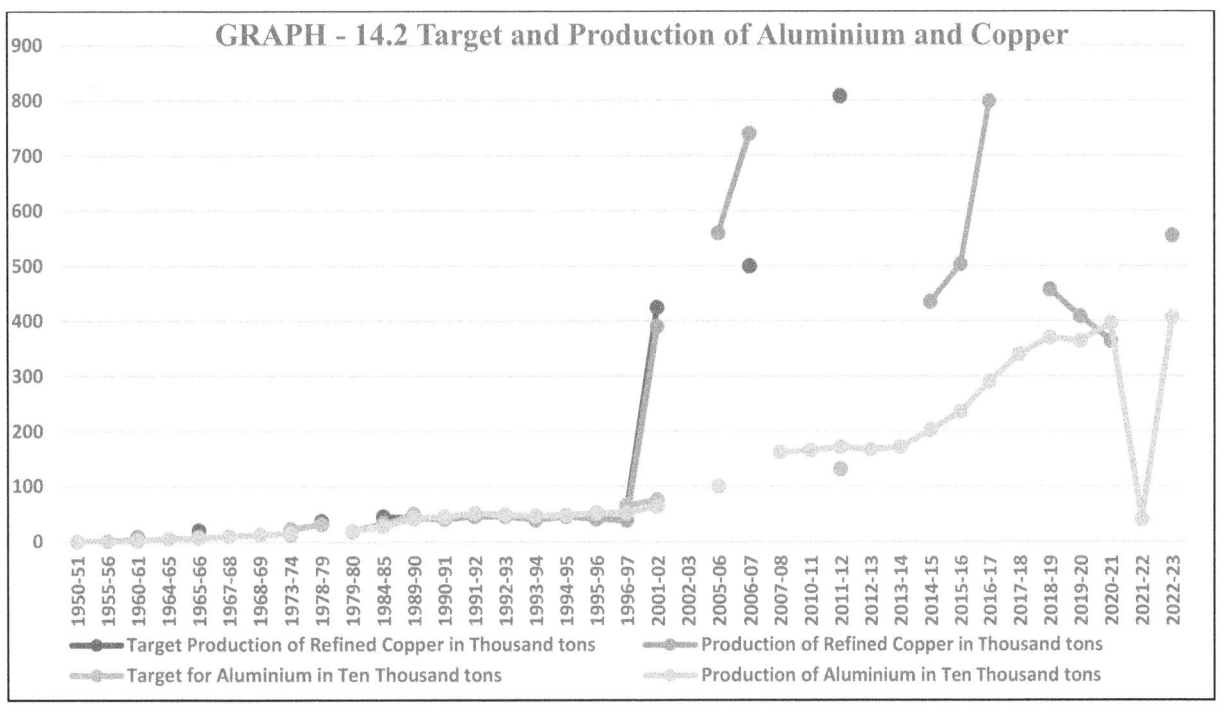

Geological Survey of India

Geological Survey of India - GSI was founded in 1851 for conducting geological surveys and studies of India and also as the prime provider of basic earth science information to government, industry, etc.
GSI started geophysical surveys in Cambay area in 1948 for petroleum deposits.
GSI undertook preliminary exploration to identify potential coal and lignite deposits.

During XI 5YP, the GSI planned to undertake the following (11.7.2.38):
(i) Survey, Mapping and Mineral Exploration (of copper, lead, zinc, iron ore, manganese ore, chromite, bauxite, and limestone; tungsten, nickel, fertilizers minerals, gold, diamond, platinum).
(ii) Special investigations on landslides, earth quakes, etc.
GSI carried out 1.14 lakh meters of regional drilling, establishing 7.07 Bt of coal and 2.95 lakh meters of promotional drilling, establishing 20.05 Bt of coal resources (12.14.106)
GSI carried out 1.32 lakh meters of regional exploration drilling during Eleventh Plan mainly by NLC, GMDC and RSMML establishing 1.85 Bt of lignite resources and 2.74 lakh meters of promotional exploration establishing 3.22 Bt of lignite resources (12.14.107)

On 8.4.2017, GSI began pilot project, with the first ever aerial survey of mineral stocks, to map the mineral stocks up to a depth of 20 km using specially-equipped aircraft.

Indian Bureau of Mines

Indian Bureau of Mines - IBM was established in 1948 to promote conservation, scientific development of mineral resources and protection of environment in mines other than coal, petroleum & natural gas.

IBM was undertaking inspection of 2500 Mines for Scientific and Systematic Mining, Mineral Conservation and Mines Environment. (11.7.2.40)

IBM also carried out (i) Mineral Beneficiation Studies - Utilization of low grade and sub-grade ores.
(ii) Analysis of environmental samples and (iii) Collection, Processing, Dissemination of data on mines and minerals through various publications.

Mineral Exploration Corporation Ltd

Mineral Exploration Corporation Ltd. – MECL was carved out of Geological Survey of India in 1972 for carrying out detailed and systematic exploration of mineral potential deposits.

MECL carries out promotional work for coal, lignite and other minerals on behalf of Government of India and Contractual Work for exploration of various minerals, CBM, geothermal and geo-technical projects on behalf of public sector, private sector and Central / State Governments.

MECL planned to improve the mineral inventory of ferrous and non-ferrous minerals, to undertake Geophysical surveys of 1535 sq km, Geophysical logging of 557462 sq m, Geological mapping of 4655 sq km, Drilling of 1066325 m and Exploratory mining of 17500 m along with IBM (11.7.2.42)

Indian Rare Earths Ltd.

Indian Rare Earths Ltd. - IREL was incorporated on 18.08.1950 as a joint venture with the then Government of Travancore, Cochin. It became a Central Government enterprise in 1963 to market beach sand minerals and value-added products thereof.

IREL is in the production of Ilmenite, Monazite, Rutile, Zircon, Garnet and Sillimanite through its units at Chavara and Udyogamandal in Kerala, Manavalakurichi in TN and Chatrapur in Orissa.

Uranium is produced from the thorium concentrate stock pile in Rare Earths Division, Aluva in Kerala. IREL is also engaged in recovering uranium from secondary sources.

IREL's share in international market for Ilmenite increased to 14.50% during 2004-05. IREL has been exporting its products to China, Japan, Korea, Germany, Norway, UAE, Malaysia, Thailand etc.

IREL produced 417275 MT ilmenite (90%), 16317 MT rutile (68%) and 23376 MT zircon (102%) during 2004-05.

Monazite Processing Plant at OSCOM was commissioned on 01.05.2015.

Installed Capacities of IREL in 2019-20 were 511222 tons for Ilmenite 24505 tons for Rutile and 40687 tons for Zircon. Capacity expansion of OSCOM Unit, REPM at Vizag and RETTP project at Bhopal were implemented in 2019-20.

IREL established facilities for production of 6N Yttrium oxide (super purity) used in defence during 2022-23. Revenue from operations was Rs. 1897.5 Cr.

National Mineral Development Corp. Ltd.

National Mineral Development Corp. Ltd. - NMDC was incorporated on 15.11.1958 for mining of iron ore, diamond and sponge iron through its units - for iron ore at Chhattisgarh and Karnataka, for diamond in Madhya Pradesh and one silica sand project at Allahabad. NMDC has one Pellet plant in Karnataka.

NMDC produced 20.743 Mt of iron ore in 2004-05 (110%). The production of diamonds at Panna unit was 78217 carats (93%).
Installed Capacity of NMDC Ltd. in 2008-09 was 27.9 Mts for iron ore.
Sponge Iron India Ltd., Telangana merged with NMDC on 01.07.2010.

NMDC has **7 Indian subsidiaries** namely J&K Mineral Development Corp. Ltd, NMDC-CMDC Ltd, NMDC Power Ltd, Jharkhand Kolhan Steel Ltd., Karnataka Vijayanagar Steel Ltd, NMDC Steel Ltd., and JNMDC Ltd and 2 wholly owned subsidiaries abroad namely NMDC-SARL in the Republic of Madagascar and NAM-India Mineral Development Corporation (Pty) Ltd. in the Republic of Namibia.

NMDC acquired 50% equity in Legacy Iron Ltd, Australia.

In 2016-17, NMDC was setting up a 15 MTPA slurry pipeline project consisting of 2 MTPA Ore Beneficiation plant at Bacheli and a 2 MTPA Pellet plant. NMDC has 1 windmill in Karnataka.

The installed capacities of NMDC in 2019-20 were 40.9 Mts for Iron ore, 1.2276 Mts for pellets and 98403 carats for diamond.

Jharkhand Kolhan Steel stands dissolved w.e.f. 17-12-2022

The blast furnace of the 3 Mt Greenfield integrated steel plant at Nagarnar in Chhattisgarh, became operational on 12.08.2023.
Gross Turnover of NMDC Ltd. in FY 2022-23 was Rs. 17667 Cr.

Madras Aluminium Company

The Madras Aluminium Company, Malco, was incorporated on 31.08.1960 in technical and financial collaboration with Montecatini of Italy as an integrated aluminium plant to manufacture aluminium ingots and alloys (from the bauxite reserves of Shevaroy Hills) and rolled products in partnership with Madras Industrial Investment Corp. Ltd, LIC and others. Malco started commercial production in 1965.
Government of Madras gave on lease mining rights for bauxite in 167.51 acres in Kolli Hills, Salem in 1967.

Achievements - Malco diversified into production of 7000 Tons of continuous sheet casting and 2000 Tons of extrusion in 1977.

Extrusion plant was commissioned and continuous casting plant was ordered on French suppliers in 1980.

Dividend of 11% was paid on preferential shares in 1980 and 13.5% in 1984.

The casting plant for manufacture of sheets over 6mm thickness was to be commissioned in September 1982 and 4-High cold rolling mill with allied facilities for the manufacture of thinner sheets was commissioned in 1985.

Lack of adequate power supply - Malco became sick only due to lack of supply of adequate power by Tamil Nadu Electricity Board and was referred to BIFR in 1987.

Inability of TNEB – Based on the scheme of revival formulated by BIFR, agreement was reached with TNEB in January 1989 for supplying 46872 KVA and 28.36 million units/ month and to increase power supply to 67 MVA subsequently. However, additional power cuts were imposed by TNEB within hardly 40 days after signing the agreement.

The production activities were suspended from 1.10.1991 due to non-availability of power and resumed from 1.2.1995. Aluminium cell house was restarted in end of March 1995. (9.5.118)

Rehabilitation Scheme – Refer Ch. 17

Sale of Malco – Refer Ch. 17

Misuse of Malco's fund – Refer Ch. 17

Selling MALCO to a company without experience in operation of Aluminium plant – Refer Ch. 17

Manganese Ore (India) Ltd.

Manganese Ore (India) Ltd. - MOIL was originally setup in 1896 as Central Provinces Syndicate, which was later taken over by the **C**entral **P**rovinces **M**anganese **O**re Company Ltd., a British Company incorporated in the UK. In 1962, following agreement between Government of India and CPMO, the assets of CPMO were taken over by the Government and MOIL was formed on 22.6.1962 to meet the requirement of high-grade manganese ore of domestic steel industries.

MOIL is mining various grades of Manganese Ore, **E**lectrolytic **M**anganese **D**i-oxide and Ferro Manganese, through its 10 mines in Maharashtra and MP and manufacturing facilities for EMD at Dongri Buzurg Mine at Bhandara and Ferro Manganese at Balaghat.

MOIL holds around 73.5 Mts of reserves of manganese ore. MOIL is the largest indigenous producer of high-grade Manganese Ore which is the raw material for manufacturing ferro alloys, an essential input for steel making and dioxide ore for manufacturing dry batteries.

MOIL was having **85% of market share** in production of manganese in 2011-12.

MOIL has two 50:50 joint ventures with RINL and SAIL.

MOIL has 8 underground mines (Kandri, Munsar, Beldongri, Gumgaon, Chikla, Balaghat and Ukwa mines) and 3 opencast mines (Dongri Buzurg, Sitapatore, and Tirodi). Balaghat mine is the largest of the mines and the deepest at 383 meters.

Various grades of the ore are used for production of manganese metal and alloys such as ferro-manganese and silicon-manganese. Refined manganese dioxide is used as a supplement in cattle feed, in fertilizers and in chemical industry.

The installed capacities of MOIL in 2019-20 were 1.4854 Mts for manganese ore, 10020 tons for ferro manganese and 1128 tons for EMD.

The production was 1.3 Mts in 2020.

Revenue from operations in 2022-23 was Rs. 1341.65 Cr.

Metal Scrap Trade Corporation Ltd.

MSTC Ltd. - MSTC was incorporated on 9.9.1964 as Metal Scrap Trade Corp. Ltd. to undertake **disposal of ferrous / non-ferrous scrap and other secondary steel** arising from integrated steel plants and obsolete / surplus stores from other PSUs and government departments.

MSTC is selling ferrous / non-ferrous scrap and marketing / importing steel melting scrap (for the use of secondary steel industry) and finished iron and steel items like HR Coils, Billets, Pig Iron, DR Pellets, Coke, Coal and other inputs and Petroleum products like Naphtha, Super Kerosene Oil, Furnace Oil etc.

It has one subsidiary namely Ferro Scrap Nigam Ltd.

MSTC set up a shredding plant for shredding of Auto / End of Life Vehicles, white goods & miscellaneous steel scrap for conversion into shredded scrap for use as raw material for induction and arc furnaces to produce steel by recycling.

MSTC acts as an e-commerce service provider to various Central / State Government Departments to ensure transparent and fair sale and purchase of Scrap, sale of Coal, Ferro manganese Ore, Iron Ore, Baryte, Chrome ore, Human Hair etc. Its e-commerce services are being utilized in Deen Dayal Upadhyay Gram Jyoti Yojana, Ude Desh Ka Aam Naagrik (UDAN) scheme, e-auction of Mining lease, etc.
MSTC has designed a platform to handle export and import of various petroproducts.

In 2019-20, MSTC launched a nationwide electronic portal eRAKAM for trading in the agriculture produces. Implemented online draw system for selection of LPG Dealership.

Around 60 Coal Mine blocks and 94 Major Mineral blocks were allotted through auction in 2022-23. Total 9000 numbers of NPAs from various banks were sold through auctions for a sale value of Rs. 7000 Cr. (approx.). Revenue from operations in 2022-23 was Rs. 324.72 Cr.

Bharat Aluminium Company Ltd.

Bharat Aluminium Company Ltd. - BALCO, incorporated in 1965, was the first public sector enterprise in India which started producing aluminium in 1974. BALCO achieved its full capacity of 0.1 Mt by 1979-80.

A new Cold Rolling Mill of 40,000 TPA capacity had been approved to be set up at the Korba Smelter of BALCO in the IX Plan. (9.5.120)

Till 2001, BALCO was a public sector enterprise owned 100% by Government of India. In 2001, Government of India divested 51% equity and management control in favor of Sterlite Industries India Ltd. Rallies and processions were carried out in the evenings to oppose the privatization and those who supported it were left in minority. Eventually, things happened as they were planned and BALCO was listed under Sterlite. There were allegations of scam involved in disinvestment of BALCO. (Wikipedia)

(Management control could have been given with disinvesting 26% stake only. Subsequently Sterlite could have invested the amount, it proposed to use to buy additional 25% shares from government, for modernization, expansion, diversification etc. Additional equity could have been issued to Sterlite for this amount. This way, government's purpose of improving the performance and profitability of BALCO could have been achieved without further disinvestment of 25%. The governments (including future governments) would have continued to receive rich dividends every year. Because of this wrong disinvestment policy, asset, created by previous governments, has been lost).

After disinvestment, 2.45 lakh tons smelter capacity was added.

Hindustan Zinc Limited

Hindustan Zinc Limited was incorporated from the erstwhile Metal Corporation of India on 10.01.1966.

The production of zinc for the first time in India was achieved by the middle of III 5YP with the commissioning of the zinc smelter of capacity 15000 tons based on zinc concentrates from the Zawar Mines in Rajasthan.

Zinc ore output of Zawar mines was increased to 2000 TPD to enable smelter at Udaipur produce 18,000 TPA of zinc in I stage and to 4000 IPD for expansion of the smelter to 36,000 TPA in II stage during IV plan. (4.14.41)

The capacity for zinc production was to increase to 95,000 tons by 1978-79 with the expansion of Debari smelter (45,000 tons) and installation of a new smelter at Vizag (30,000 tons) during V plan. (5.5.44)

During VI Plan - Installation of Leach Residue Treatment Plant at Debari for recovery of zinc, Sulphur and cadmium from the stockpile / current neutral residue and Smelter of HZL were completed. (7.7.105) The preparatory work for setting up the integrated zinc-lead mine / smelter complex (of 70,000 TPA of zinc and 35,000 TPA of lead, based upon the rich zinc-lead deposits of Rampura - Agucha was completed. (7.7.107)
The expansion of lead smelter at Vizag was completed. (7.7.105).
Rajpura - Dariba lead–zinc mine of 3000 TPD capacity, Sargipalli lead mine were completed. (7.7.106)
At Vizag Zinc Smelter, it was proposed to improve the overall metal recovery from 81.5 % to about 93 % by 1989-90 by switching over from the pyrometallurgical to hydrometallurgical process depending upon the actual results achieved by the latter process at Debari, (7.7.107)

During VII Plan
Expansion of Vizag Zinc smelters of Hindustan Zinc Ltd. was completed.
With the commissioning of Rampura - Agucha - Chanderiya integrated project of Hindustan Zinc Ltd. **in 1991-92, the country achieved near self-sufficiency in zinc.** (8.v2.5.12.1)
HZL operated zinc and lead smelters and refineries at Chanderiya (Chittorgarh), Debari (Udaipur) and Dariba (Raj Samand) in Rajasthan with total zinc and lead production capacity of 1 Mt.

During VIII Plan
Imported non-ferrous metals, particularly **copper, lead and zinc were cheaper than indigenously produced metals. The domestic companies had to resort to cut-backs in production, particularly of lead and zinc by HZL.** This led to uneconomical operation of the company, irrespective of productivity of the company and quality of the product. (9.5.115)

During IX Plan
HZL had entered into a joint venture with BHPM of Australia for exploration and development of zinc and lead resources in Rajasthan.
HZL completed expansion of the capacities of its Vizag and Debari smelters each by 10,000 TPA. (10.7.2.25)

During X Plan - After privatization, Hindustan Zinc Ltd (HZL) expanded its zinc mining and used the mineral from its captive Rampura Agucha mines to expand smelting. (11.7.2.18)

In 2001, as part of the Government's disinvestment program, HZL was put up for sale.

Improper Disinvestment - In April 2002, Sterlite Opportunities and Ventures Ltd (SOVL) made an open offer for acquisition of shares of HZL; consequent to the disinvestment of Government of India's stake of 26% including management control to SOVL, SOVL acquired additional 20% of shares from public, pursuant to the SEB Regulations 1997.

(Once SOVL obtained management control with initial 26% stake, SOVL should have invested the amount, it proposed to use to buy additional 20% shares from public and 18.92% shares from government, for modernization, expansion, diversification etc. Additional equity could have been issued to SOVL for this amount. This way, government's purpose of improving the performance and profitability of HZL could have been achieved without further disinvestment of 18.92% in second attempt. The governments (including future) would have continued to receive rich dividends every year. Because of this wrong disinvestment principle, asset created by previous governments, was lost).

5 Largest mines also sold – Refer Ch. 17

Production in 2001-02 in Mts
Total installed capacity for Zinc – 0.199.   Total installed capacity for Lead – 0.043 (11.7.2.17/18)
Total production of Zinc – 0.226   Total production of Lead – 0.071
(11.v2.7.2.29)
Consumption / Demand of / for Zinc – 0.297.   Consumption / Demand of / for Lead – 0.132

Production in 2006-07 in Mts
Total installed capacity for Zinc – 0.449   Total installed capacity for Lead – 0.085 (11.7.2.17/18)
Total production of Zinc – 0.453   Total production of Lead – 0.123 (11.v2.7.2.29)
Consumption / Demand of / for Zinc – 0.455   Consumption / Demand of / for Lead – 0.275

Productivity Loss after Privatization – Refer Ch. 17

Target for 2011-12
Total production of Lead – 0.170 Mts   Consumption / Demand of / for Lead – 0.443 Mts

HZL besides being leading producer of zinc, it is also the most important lead producer in India. HZL has production capacity of 411,000 TPA for Zinc, 85,000 TPA for Lead, and 6.2 Mt for Ore.

HZL was the world's second largest zinc producer. They are one of the world's largest integrated producers of zinc and are among leading global lead, silver and cadmium producers.

Hindustan Copper Ltd.

Hindustan Copper Ltd. - HCL was incorporated on 9.11.1967 taking over assets and liabilities of Copper Projects at Khetri, Dariba, Rakha and Agnigundala from National Mineral Development Corp. Ltd. Government of India nationalized Indian Copper Complex Ltd. at Ghatsila, Jharkhand and handed over its Management to HCL in 1972.

HCL undertakes exploration, mining, benefaction, smelting, refining and production of cathodes, CCR, wire, bar and other by-products associated with copper ore through its units Khetri Copper Complex at Khetri Nagar, Indian Copper Complex, Ghatsila, Malanjkhand Copper Project, Malanjkhand, Taloja Copper Project, Taloja and Gujarat Copper Project, Bharuch.

The market share of HCL in major copper products was **14.56% in 2002-03.**

HCL produced 30598 tons of cathode and 28003 tons of wire rod during 2003-04.

HCL, which was earlier a sick CPSE, made profits over the period 2004-07.

Cathode production (44734 tons) was the highest in the last 13 years while production of CC wire rod (58223 tons) was the highest since inception.

HCL signed an agreement for technology transfer and supply of equipment with M/s Outotec, Finland on 8.11.2007 to upgrade technology and debottleneck the ICC smelter,

Installed Capacity of HCL in 2008-09 was 0.06 Mts for wire rod and 0.0475 Mts for cathodes.

Expansion of Malanjkhand, Khetri, Kolihan, Surda and Banwas mines, reopening of Rakha and Kendadih mines and development of new Chapri-Sideshwar mines were taken up to increase production to 12.4 million TPA from existed 3.4 million TPA.

During XI 5YP, HCL planned to replace plant equipment by funding through their internal resources for maintaining the existing level of production and for enhancing production in the future. (11.7.2.4)

Work was under progress in 2016-17 to expand the production capacity of Malanjkhand mine from present 2 MTPA to 5 MTPA by developing an underground mine below the existing open cast mine.

As on 1.4.2022, copper ore reserve of HCL was 631.85 Mts with 0.99% of Cu.

Government disinvested 23.8% of its holdings in HCL after 2013-14 and was holding 66.14% in 2022-23.

The ore production capacity of Malanjkhand Mine is 2.5 Mts. HCL has planned to expand the total mining capacity to 12 Mts. Revenue from operations in 2022-23 was Rs. 1677.33 Cr.

Indian Iron & Steel Co. Ltd.

Indian Iron & Steel Co. Ltd. - IISCO was incorporated in 1918 and taken over by the Government of India on 14.07.72. IISCO became a 100% subsidiary of Steel Authority of India Ltd. w.e.f. 1.05.78. It was having its 6 units at Burdwan, Singhbhum and Dhanbad.

IISCO produced 0.357 Mt of crude steel and 0.274 Mt of saleable steel during 2004-05.
IISCO was amalgamated with SAIL on 16.02.2006 and renamed IISCO Steel Plant.

Crude steel capacity was 2.5 Mt. Crude steel production in 2017-18 was 1.80 Mts and saleable steel production was 1.69 Mts.

Steel Authority of India Ltd

Steel Authority of India Ltd - SAIL was incorporated on 24.1.1973 by merging 6 operating plants at Bhilai (established in 1955), Durgapur (1959), Rourkela (1959), Bokaro (1964), Salem (1981), Visakhapatnam (1971) and Visvesvaraya Iron & Steel Plant, Bhadravati (1923).

On 1.5.1978, iron and steel companies in the Public Sector were brought under the overall control of SAIL.

Salem plant started commercial production in 1982 with capacity of 32000 tons for stainless-steel sheets. This capacity was doubled in 1991 with the addition of another rolling mill and further to 80000 tons of saleable steel in 1995-96.

The equity structure of SAIL by the end of VIII 5YP was: Government of India - 85.82%, Financial Institutions 9.35%, GDRs - 3.5%, individuals, foreign institutional investors and domestic companies 0.63 %. (9.5.110)

SAIL was ranked 16th largest steel producer in the world during 2004.

SAIL is engaged in production of Iron and Steel and other byproducts through its **9 plants** at Bhilai, Durgapur, Burnpur (IISCO), Rourkela, Bokaro, Salem, Bhadravati (Visvesvaraya Iron & Steel), Alloy Steel Plant (Durgapur) and Chandrapur (Maharashtra Electrosmelt Ltd.).

SAIL exported 0.472 Mt of products like Billets, Wire rods, Plates, HR coils and CRNO coils during 2007-08. New export markets entered during the year were Argentina, Brazil, Malaysia and the European Union.

SAIL drew modernization & expansion plans to achieve hot metal production of over 25 Mts by 2010 from 2007-08 level of 14.6 Mts.

In 2008-09, exports of plates were made to African and Gulf countries and GP sheets to Kuwait, Uganda, South Africa, Bangladesh and Myanmar. Boiler-quality plates and GC sheets were added to the export basket.

SAIL was India's largest producer of iron ore. Installed capacity for saleable steel was 11.07 Mts in 2008-09.

5 Companies including SAIL were approved by the Government for facilitating acquisition of coking coal assets overseas to make PSUs self-reliant in the area of coking coal. A JV company International Coal Ventures Pvt Ltd was incorporated in 2008-09. SAIL was scouting for coal properties in Australia, Mozambique and other countries. (13.4.7)

SAIL was offering 50 mild, special and alloy steel products in 1000 qualities and 5000 dimensions in 2010-11.

SAIL's market share was 18% in production of crude steel and 15% in finished steel in 2011-12.

Owning India's second largest mines network provides SAIL a competitive edge in terms of captive availability of iron ore, limestone, dolomite, etc. Higher production of special grade items like API grade HR Coils / Plates / Pipes, HR Coils for cold reducers etc. enabled SAIL to achieve larger market share in value added segments.

SAIL proposed to set up a 5.6 MTPA steel plant, a 1.15 MTPA fertilizer plant in joint venture with NFL. SAIL planned to form joint ventures with RITES for manufacture & rehabilitation of railway wagons and with Arcelor Mittal for production of automotive steel and setting up of Ultra Mega Steel Plant in Bastar.

During 2019-20, SAIL became the largest crude steel producer and the largest miner of raw materials for steel in India. The installed capacity of SAIL for saleable steel was 18.5 Mts in 2019-20.

SAIL also has 4 units producing refractories.

SAIL has **5 subsidiaries** namely, IISCO-Ujjain Pipe & Foundry Co, SAIL Sindri Projects Ltd. (for the revival of Sindri unit of FCI Ltd) SAIL Jagdishpur Power Plant Ltd., SAIL Refractory Co Ltd and Chhattisgarh Mega Steel Ltd.

SAIL also has **23 Joint Ventures** in different areas ranging from power plants to e-commerce and 10 other Marketing / R&D / Training / Consultancy units.

Merger of Bharat Refractories Limited with SAIL was under implementation.

Joint venture with M/s Jaypee Associates for setting up slag-based Cement Plants at Bhilai & Bokaro and formation of JV with MOIL for setting up of Ferro-Manganese and Silico-Manganese Plant at Nandini / Bhilai were in preliminary stages.

To be a part of country's growth story, SAIL supplied steel to Dhola-Sadiya Bridge, Sardar Sarovar Project, etc.

SAIL has planned to expand the capacity to 49.6 Mts by 2030. Company profit has been reduced by 84.16% due to increase in imported coal prices. Revenue from operations in 2022-23 was Rs. 104447.36 Cr.

Mishra Dhatu Nigam Ltd.

Mishra Dhatu Nigam Ltd. - MIDHANI was incorporated on 20-11-1973 to manufacture Super-alloys, Titanium alloys and Special purpose steel required in strategic sectors like Space, Aeronautics, Defence and Atomic Energy etc.

MIDHANI is manufacturing very complex alloys, like superalloys, maraging steels, titanium & titanium alloys, special purpose steels, soft magnetic alloys, molybdenum products and welding electrodes, which only a few advanced countries in the world produce, through Hyderabad unit.

Major customers of MIDHANI are Defence, Department of Space, Defence Research & Development Organization, Nuclear, Ordnance Factories, Department of Atomic Energy, and Hindustan Aeronautics Ltd.

MIDHANI produced 1819 Tons of alloys during 2003-04 with 67% capacity utilization.
Installed Capacity of Mishra Dhatu Nigam Ltd. for Super Alloys in 2008-09 was 2729 tons
MIDHANI supplied Titan 31 satellite rings to ISRO, Titan 32 forged and machined bars for ship building and Centre and end fitting forging components for the 700 MW Pressurized Heavy Water Reactors.
Radial Axial Ring Rolling Mill was commissioned during 2013 and was contributing for the production of special alloys, super alloys and titanium alloy rings.
Market share in India during 2013-14 for Maraging steel MDN250 was 75%, for MDN350 was 100% and for Titanium alloys 65%.
6000 Tons Forge press was commissioned in November 2014.

Installed Capacity of Mishra Dhatu Nigam Ltd. for Super Alloys and special steels in 2019-20 was 6097 tons.

Considering increasing global market demand for body armour, Vehicle Armor, Bullet Proof Morcha, Bullet Resistant jackets, etc. and to cater the needs of domestic market an Armor unit of MIDHANI is being set up at Rohtak. MIDHANI is also setting up a state-of-the art Wide plate cum sheet mill.

Revenue from operations in 2022-23 was Rs. 871.94 Cr.

Maharashtra Electrosmelt Ltd.

Maharashtra Electrosmelt Ltd. - MEL was incorporated on 17.04.1974. It was promoted by State Industrial and Investment Corporation of Maharashtra to develop the Chandrapur area, which had vast deposits of good grade iron ore. MEL was taken over by SAIL w.e.f. 1.1.1986.

MEL is manufacturing Ferro Alloys such as ferro manganese, silico manganese and medium carbon ferro alloys through its Chandrapur unit. **MEL is the largest Ferro Alloys producer** in India having installed capacity of 0.1 Mt for production of Ferro Manganese Alloys.

Bharat Refractories Ltd.

Bharat Refractories Ltd. - BRL was incorporated on 22.7.1974 to run the production unit of Bhandaridah Refractories Plant, which was earlier acquired by the Government of India in 1972 and was placed under the management of Bokaro Steel Ltd.
BRL is manufacturing various kinds of refractories for integrated / mini steel plants in its 4 units at Bokaro, Hazaribagh and Bhilai.

BRL entered into technical collaboration with world leaders in refractory manufacturing like Kawasaki Refractories, Japan (for producing Magnesia Carbon bricks, slide gate refractories, gunning repair materials, cast mixes for steel Ladle, Spinel and Magnesia Spinel bricks), Shinagawa Refractories, Japan (for producing Tap Hole Clay, Silica Bricks for Coke Oven and Continuous casting Refractories) and Plibrico, France (for Ultra-low Cement Castable for BF Trough).

BRL entered into technical collaboration with SAIL - R&D Centre for Zero Cement Castable Alumina-Magnesia-Spinel Castable.

The production of bricks and masses by the BRL during 2004-05 was 65485 Tons with capacity utilization of 48%.

BRL merged with SAIL on 24.04.2008.

Kudremukh Iron Ore Co. Ltd.

Kudremukh Iron Ore Co. Ltd. - KIOCL was incorporated on 02.04.1976 to meet the long-term requirement of Iron Ore for the steel mills of Iran. However, due to political developments in Iran, KIOCL diversified into Pellets.

KIOCL is mining iron ore, benefacting iron ore into concentrate, producing and exporting iron ore concentrate and also Iron Oxide Pellets through its units at Kudremukh and Mangalore. KIOCL is mining and benefacting low-grade Magnetite iron ore & also palletizing both Magnetite & hematite iron ores.

KIOCL operated the most sophisticated mechanized Magnetite iron ore mine to produce 22.5 Mts of Run of Mine/ annum and state-of-the-art beneficiation technology to produce 7.5 Mts of iron ore concentrate. Plant was designed to produce 3.5 Mts of iron ore pellets and Pig Iron unit to produce 0.216 Mts of foundry grade Pig Iron. **KIOCL was Asia's largest iron ore mining and palletisation complex.**

KIOCL has financial joint venture with MECON and MSTC namely Kudremukh Iron and Steel Co. Ltd. to manufacture low Sulphur, low phosphorous, Pig iron and Ductile Iron Spun pipes at Mangalore. KISCO merged with the KIOCL w.e.f. 1.4.2007 and is now operating as Blast Furnace Unit of KIOCL.

KIOCL produced Iron Ore Concentrates with 65% capacity utilization and Iron Ore Pellets with 95% capacity utilization during 2004-05.

The mining lease in Kudremukh was given to KIOCL for a period of 25 years and was supposed to be closed by December 2001. Kudremukh area is a biodiversity hotspot, with Kudremukh national park nearby. The mining lease was temporarily extended. However, it was completely stopped in 2006 due to environmental reasons.

Approval was given for the diversion of 388 hectare of forest land for Mining and 13.5761 hectare for conveyor corridor, power transmission line and approach road. Mining Lease Deed executed between Govt. of Karnataka and KIOCL on 2.01.2023 for the grant of mining lease of Iron Ore and Manganese Ore over an extent of 388 ha for a period 50 years in Devadari Range.

SAIL Refractory Company Limited

SAIL Refractory Company Ltd. - In 1976, Govt of India took over Burn Standard Co. Ltd. as a subsidiary of Bharat Bhari Udyog Nigam Ltd. Soon after, BSCL underwent modernization & expansion program to meet the growing demand for high-quality basic refractories by the modern steel plants of SAIL and other private sector steel processors, non-ferrous, cement and glass industries.

Salem Refractory Unit of Burn Standard Co. Ltd. became a wholly-owned subsidiary of SAIL w.e.f. 16.12.2011 as per financial restructuring of BSCL. The unit was renamed as SAIL Refractory Co. Ltd.

SRCL range of products include Magnesite bricks, Magnesite-chrome bricks, magnesite-carbon bricks, bulk & monolithic, Dunite & Dunite fractions and ground calcined magnesite. It was endowed with 1718.30 acres of leasehold mining land with estimated magnesite reserves about 10 Mts and about 9 Mts of dunite.

SRCL products are used by SAIL steel plants, Rail Wheel Factory, Metal & Steel Factory, BHEL, HCL, etc.

Sponge Iron India Ltd.

Sponge Iron India Ltd. - SIIL was incorporated in 1978 to produce sponge iron and Ferro Alloys and to develop new technology in the field of production of coal-based sponge iron.

SIIL was manufacturing Sponge Iron with captive generation of power at its Khammam unit with a capacity utilization of 119% in 2002-03.
Installed Capacity of SIIL for Sponge Iron was 60,000 TPA in 2008-09.

SIIL merged with NMDC Ltd in July, 2010.

SIIL was planning to set up 2 kilns of 0.1 Mt capacity for sponge iron production along with 40MW power plant, Induction Furnace and Billet Cast Plant.

Ferro Scrap Nigam Ltd.

Ferro Scrap Nigam Ltd. - FSNL was incorporated on 28.3.1979 in collaboration with M/s Harsco Corporation (Inc.), USA, as a subsidiary of M/s MSTC Ltd to take over the running business of Heckett Engineering Co. in India. The main job of FSNL is to reclaim iron and steel scrap from slag in all the integrated steel plants under SAIL, RINL and IISCO through its units at Burnpur, Durgapur, Rourkela, Duburi, Bhilai, Raigarh, Bokaro, Visakhapatnam, Haridwar, Bengaluru, Bhadravati, Salem and Dolvi. It is also operating for private sector plants like NINL, IIL and JSPL.

FSNL achieved scrap recovery with a capacity utilization of 135% in 2003-04.
FSNL achieved production of 2.377 Mts of scrap and handled 4.151 Mts of slag haulage during 2007-08.
Installed Capacity of Ferro Scrap Nigam Ltd. for recovery of scrap was 1.170 Mts in 2008-09.

FSNL opened a new unit at HEC, Ranchi.
Negotiations were going on for new business at Bhadravati, KIOCL, Railway wagon factory at Bengaluru in 2010-11.

Since generation of scrap has reduced with technological development, FSNL has undertaken rendering of Custodian and Ware Housing services to customers of MSTC / STC at 27 sites.

Revenue from operations in 2022-23 was Rs, 396.25 Cr.

Cabinet Committee on Economic Affairs gave approval for strategic selling full equity of FSNL to Konoike Transport Co Ltd for Rs 320 Cr on 19-09-24. If the revenue from operations in 2022-23 was Rs. 396.25 Cr, what will be the absolute asset value of FSNL? How it can be given away for Rs. 320 Cr only?

National Aluminium Company Ltd (NALCO)

National Aluminium Co. Ltd. - NALCO was incorporated on 07.01.1981 to exploit bauxite deposits discovered in the East Coast, in technological collaboration with Aluminium Pechiney of France (now Rio Tinto - Alcan). In a major leap forward, NALCO not only addressed the need for self-sufficiency in Aluminium but also gave the country a technological edge in producing Aluminium as per world standards.

NALCO is in mining of bauxite, manufacture of Alumina, Aluminium hydrates and Aluminium metal and various types of Aluminium rolled products, alumina hydrates, calcinated alumina, special grade alumina, special grade hydrate, zeolite, Aluminium sows, standard, ingots, tee- ingots, wire rods, billets and generation of power through its 8 units (Bauxite Mines - Koraput, Alumina Refinery - Daman Jodi, Aluminium Smelter & Captive Power Plant – Angul, Wind Power Plants – Gandikota (Andhra), Jaisalmer and Sangali (Maharashtra) and Rolled Product unit at Koraput and Angul district of Orissa) and port facilities at Visakhapatnam and Paradeep ports.

NALCO produced 0.3385 Mt of aluminium metal during 2004-05. The production of calcined alumina and bauxite were 1.5667 Mts and 4.852 Mts with capacity utilization at 100% and 101% respectively. Panchpatmali bauxite mine of NALCO of capacity 4.8 Mts accounted for 40% of India's production in 2006-07.
NALCO's share in domestic market of Aluminium products was 27.28%, 29.8% and 27.1 in 2004-05, 2006-07 and 2007-08 respectively.
NALCO launched Special Products Alumina (NSPL) – 102 during 2007-08. (13.4.6)

During IX plan 12,000 tons was added by NALCO with the expansion of their smelters. (10.7.2.16)
NALCO's de-bottlenecking project of its alumina refinery and expansion of bauxite mines from 2.4 Mts to 4.8 Mts and alumina refinery from 0.8 Mt to 1.575 Mts were completed. (10.7.2.17)

NALCO had **a market share of 35% in production of aluminium.** (11.v2.7.2.43)
Its second phase expansion scheme was likely to be completed by December 2008.
In 2010-11, NALCO was undertaking expansions of Bauxite mine capacity from 4.8 Mt to 6.3 Mt; Alumina Hydrate plant's capacity from 1.575 Mt to 2.1 Mt.; Aluminium smelter capacity from 0.345 Mt to 0.46 Mt; captive power plant capacity from 960 MW to 1200 MW. (11. Annex. 7.2.9.)

NALCO appointed EIL for preparation of a detailed report for upgradation of IV stream alumina refinery from 0.525 Mt to 0.7 Mt.

NALCO set up (i) a 2 x 700 MW nuclear power plant NPCIL NALCO Power Company Ltd in Kakrapura Gujarat) in Joint Venture with Nuclear Power Corporation of India Ltd,
(ii) Angul Aluminium Park Pvt Ltd in joint venture with Orissa Industrial Infrastructure Development Corp.
(iii) 0.27 Mt caustic soda plant GACL-NALCO Alkalies & Chemicals Pvt Ltd in JV with Gujrat Alkalies & Chemical Ltd.

In 2016-17, NALCO undertook (i) addition of 1Mt capacity V steam refinery project in Alumina Refinery at Daman Jodi, (ii) establishment of 0.5 Mt brownfield smelters and (iii) 0.6 Mt Greenfield smelter in Odisha.

NALCO is the lowest cost producer of Bauxite and Alumina in the world (as per Wood Mackenzie report 2019). NALCO's export earnings accounted for 42% of the sales turnover in 2018-19.
NALCO is one of the largest integrated Bauxite-Alumina-Aluminium-Power Complex in India encompassing bauxite mining, alumina refining, aluminium smelting and casting, power generation, rail and port operations. Presently, Government of India holds a 51.5% equity in NALCO.

The installed capacity of NALCO for Aluminium in 2019-20 was 0.45975 Mts.
NALCO achieved full capacity production of 0.46 Mt and Bauxite production of 7.511 Mts in 2020-21.

Gross Turnover of NALCO in FY 2022-23 was Rs. 14255 Cr.

Rashtriya Ispat Nigam Ltd.

Rashtriya Ispat Nigam Ltd. - RINL was incorporated on 18.2.1982 for production and marketing of carbon steel products in the long category and basic grade pig iron through its Visakhapatnam unit. RINL also markets coal chemicals (Ammonium Sulphate, Benzol products etc.) and slag.

During 2007-08, RINL developed 5 new grades and 44 new products. The products of VSP include Pig Iron, rounds, structural, reinforcement bars, wire rods, blooms, billets and squares.
Installed Capacities of RINL. in 2008-09 were 3.4 Mts for Hot metal, 3.0 Mts for Liquid Steel, 0.71 Mts for Bars, 0.85 Mts for Wire rods and 2.66 Mts for Saleable steel.

In 2010-11 - 2.423 Mts of value-added steel products were produced. RINL/VSP registered capacity utilization of 113%, 114% & 116% in Hot Metal, Liquid Steel and Saleable Steel productions respectively. 25 New products were developed.
RINL along with SAIL, CIL, NMDC and NTPC formed an International Coal Ventures Ltd. for acquiring coal mines abroad with equity participation. It was contemplating a joint venture for Limestone mines in OMAN.
RINL doubled its capacity to 6.3 Mts of liquid steel by 2011-12.

RINL signed MOUs with (i) APMDC, for exploration and development of iron ore mining reserves in Kukunur area of AP (ii) NMDC to explore the possibility of laying slurry pipeline from Nagarnar to Visakhapatnam and setting up a pellet plant at Visakhapatnam (iii) KIOCL for Pellet plant at Visakhapatnam with initial capacity of 2.0 Mt. and (iv) Railways for installation of Uttarbanga RINL Rail Karkhana to produce 50,000 axles per annum for Railways at New Jalpaiguri.

A forged wheel plant of capacity 80000 special grade wheels per annum for Indian Railways was under execution in 2013-14.
RINL was the largest long products producer with market share of 8% in 2013-14.

RINL increased its capacities through revamping / up gradation of existing units to 7.3 Mts of Liquid steel by 2017-18.
Installed Capacities of RINL in 2019-20 were 1.6338 Mts for Bars, 0.09985 Mts for Pig Iron, 1.6481 Mts for Wire rods, 5.708 Mts for Saleable steel and 1.755 Mts for structural steel.
In 2019-20 RINL was setting up Forged Wheel Plant at Lalgunj, UP based on assured offtake by Railways.

RINL has one subsidiary, Eastern Investment Ltd, which in turn is having two subsidiaries namely Orissa Mineral Development Corporation and Bistra Stone Lime Company Ltd.
The company has 2 joint ventures RINMOIL and ICVL.
JV company RINL Powergrid TLT Pvt Ltd. was formed in partnership with POWERGRID for manufacture of transmission line towers.

Neelachal Ispat Nigam Ltd

Neelachal Ispat Nigam Ltd - NINL is a Joint Venture of 4 CPSEs, namely MMTC, NMDC, BHEL, MECON and 2 Odisha Government PSUs, namely Odisha Mining Corporation and Industrial Promotion & Investment Corp. of Odisha Ltd. incorporated on 27.03.1982. Basic Oxygen Furnace shop and continuous casting plant were commissioned in April 2013. The technology was supplied by SMS – Siemag and SMS – Concast, the world leader in steel melting technology. Mecon provided consultancy and project management services.

Earlier NINL commissioned 418 TPD oxygen plant supplied by Linde.
NINL became **India's largest exporter of saleable pig iron** since 2004-05.

NINL was incurring huge losses and the plant has been shut since 30.03.2020. Government approved a proposal to sell it to Tata Steel Long Products Ltd for Rs 12,100 Cr.

J&K Mineral Development Corp. Ltd.

J&K Mineral Development Corp. Ltd. - JKMDCL was incorporated on 19.5.1989 as a joint venture of NMDC and J&K Government to undertake exploration, prospecting, mining and processing of Magnesite, sapphire, marble, limestone, iron ore, coal, phosphate, manganese ore & other mineral deposits.
JKMDCL was in the mining of raw Magnesite ore at Pandhal and Udhampur.

JKMDCL is in the process of winding up. There was no production since 2001-02.
A 30000 TPA Dead Burnt Magnesite Plant was being developed at Pandhal Magnesite Project, Jammu. The work for construction of the DBM Plant was progressing as per schedule in 2013-14. Contracts for setting up the DBM plant were terminated subsequently.

FCI Aravali Gypsum & Minerals (India) Ltd.

FCI Aravali Gypsum & Minerals (India) Ltd. - FAGMIL was incorporated on 14.02.2003 (after de-merging of **J**odhpur **M**ining **O**rganization from Fertilizer Corporation of India) to take over JMO and to produce Gypsum, other Minerals and their by-products, various types of Fertilizers, all organic and inorganic chemical compounds including by-products, derivatives and mixtures thereof.

FAGMIL is involved in excavation of mineral Gypsum, processing of agriculture grade Gypsum in 16 Mines at Jaisalmer, Barmer, Bikaner and Shri Ganganagar. FAGMIL undertakes exploration & prospecting of 265 Gypsum deposits with a reserve of more than 100 Mts.
Gypsum is used mainly as a Sulphur nutrient to the soil, as a soil amendment to sodic soil and also as an input raw-material in cement manufacturing.

The domestic market share of FAGMIL was 29% during 2013-14.

The installed capacity of FAGMIL for gypsum in 2019-20 was 1.11 Mts.
FAGMIL has commenced exploration of Rock Phosphate in Jaisalmer district.
Revenue from operations in 2022-23 was Rs. 56.04 Cr.

Orissa Minerals Development Co. Ltd.

Orissa Minerals Development Co. Ltd. - OMDC was a part of Bird Groups of companies (Government managed company) and became a CPSE on 19.3.2010. OMDC is involved in mining of iron and manganese ore in Orissa.

Revenue from operations in 2022-23 was Rs. 35.53 Cr.

Bisra Stone Lime Company Ltd.

The Bisra Stone Lime Co. Ltd. - BSLC was a part of Bird Groups of companies (Government managed company) and became a CPSE on 19.3.2010.
BSLC is mining limestone and dolomite in Orissa.

BSLC in 2019-20 was having reserves of about 287 Mts of dolomite & 367 Mts of limestone.
Revenue from operations in 2022-23 was Rs. 86.19 Cr.

Khanij Bidesh India Ltd. –

Khanij Bidesh India Limited – KABIL was formed in 2019 as a joint venture of NALCO, HCL and MECL to source strategic minerals such as lithium and cobalt, etc. from abroad

KABIL has signed 3 MoUs with Argentina's state-run companies JEMSE, CAMYEN and YPF for lithium exploration and mining in 5 blocks in Argentina.

Uranium Corporation of India Ltd. – Mining and Processing Uranium – Refer Chapter 9

Minerals and Metals Trading Corp. of India – International Trading - Refer Chapter 12

Tungabhadra Steel Products – Refer to Chapter 7

CPSEs Share in Domestic Output

Domestic Production of Finished Steel in Mts							Total Output by CPSEs / Share of CPSEs to Domestic Output (%)						
1968-69	1998-99	2004-05	2005-06	2008-09	2009-10	2020-21	1968-69	1998-99	2004-05	2005-06	2008-09	2009-10	2020-21
4.58		40.64	46.82			103.545	2.55		12.32	12.59			19.515
							55.68		30.31	26.89			18.85
Aluminium in Thousand Tons													
125.3		886.26		1346.75	1524.8		Nil		338.48		718.04	699.91	
							Nil		38.19		53.32	45.9	
Primary Lead in Thousand Tons													
1.9	15.89						1.9	Nil					
							100	Nil					
Zinc in Thousand Tons													
17	212.28						13.7	Nil					
							80.59	Nil					

Market leaders in steel manufacturing in India in 2022 were JSW Steel Ltd, Tata Steel Ltd., SAIL, Hindalco Ltd., and Jindal Steel and Power Ltd. The average capacity utilizations of public and private sector steel plants were 75.25% and 71.22% respectively for 2020-21, which showed public sector steel plants were operating more efficiently. JSW Steels combined steel production was 15.53 MT in the 2020-21 fiscal. JSW Steel Ltd has overtaken long standing private player like Tata Steel.

Summary

In 1950-51, steel production was mostly by Tata Iron and Steel Co., Indian Iron and Steel Co. and Mysore Iron & Steel Works. With starting of Bhadravati. Bhilai, Durgapur, Rourkela, Bokaro and Visakhapatnam steel plants from 1955 to 1971, the capacity of the public sector integrated steel plants became 7.23 Mts in 1979-80.

i) Integrated steel Plants' capacity of saleable steel was 76.78% of total capacity for saleable steel in 1989-90, 70% in 1990-91, 64.6% in 1991-92.

ii) Finished steel production by CPSE steel plants was 26.89% of total domestic production in 2005-06 and 24.3% of Indian industry's production of 82.68 Mts in 2018-19.

The total installed capacity for Zinc in 2001-02 was 0.199 Mts. (11.7.2.17). Of this, Hindustan Zinc Ltd. Debari smelter had a capacity of 80,000 tons and Vizag smelter contributed 40,000 ton. (60.3%)

Private Sector Players –

Aluminium companies - Indal Aluminium Company Limited – 1938, Hindalco Industries Ltd. / Hindustan Aluminium Corporation Ltd. – 1958, Jindal Aluminium – 1970, Annapurna Foils Ltd – 1979, PG Foils – 1982, Hind Aluminium – 1987, Sacheta Metals – 1990,

Utkal Alumina Refinery Project Ltd – 1993, Utkal Alumina International Ltd of Hindalco – 1993, Indal – 2000, Annapurna Foils Ltd – 2002, Birla Group's Aluminium project – 2005 **(7 companies before 1991 + 5 companies before 2014).**

Copper companies - Gujarat Mineral Development Corp. – 1963, Sterlite Copper Industries – 1975, Bracco Extrusions Ltd / ABC Gas International – 1980, Bhagyanagar India Ltd. – 1985

Baroda Extrusions Ltd – 1991, Birla Copper – 1996, Indo-Gulf Copper Smelter – 1998. **(4 companies before 1991 + 3 companies before 2014).**

Kutch Copper (2021)

Steel companies - Bengal Iron and Steel Co – 1870, Tata Iron and Steel Co / Tata Steel Ltd – 1907, Tata Steel Global Wires – 1907, Hindustan Iron & Steel Products – 1936, Mukand Iron & Steel Works Limited – 1937, Indian Tube Company – 1954, Tube Products of India Ltd – 1955, Tata SSL Limited (Wire division of Tata Steel) - Wiron – 1958, Tata Refractories Limited – 1958, Usha Martin Ltd. – 1961, Mahindra Ugine Steel Co. Ltd. – 1962, Tata-Yodogawa – 1968, Jindal India Limited – 1969, Bhushan Power and Steel – 1970, Essar Steel India Ltd – 1976, Lloyds Metals & Energy Ltd. – 1977, Mahindra Intertrade Limited – 1978, Jindal Steel and Power – 1979, Tata Sponge Iron Ltd – 1982, JSW Steel Ltd – 1982, Ispat Alloys Ltd / Balasore Alloys Ltd – 1984, Ispat Industries Ltd. / Nippon Denro Ispat Ltd – 1984, Prime Gold International Ltd – 1984, Uttam Galva Steels Ltd – 1985, Ispat Profiles India Ltd – 1985, Bhushan Steel – 1987, Tata Metaliks Ltd - 1990
Kirloskar Ferrous Industries Ltd 1991, Vikram Ispat / Grasim Sponge Iron plant) – 1993, Tata Tiscon – 2000, Electrosteel Steels Ltd. / Electrosteel Integrated Ltd – 2006, Mahindra Sanyo Special Steel Pvt Ltd – 2012, Tata Steel Nest-in – 2013 **(26 companies before 1991 + 6 companies before 2014).**

Zinc companies - Ambuja Zinc Ltd – 1987, Mewat Zinc Ltd. – 1991, Sunrise Zinc Ltd – 1993.

15: GROWTH IN TRANSPORTATION INFRASTRUCTURE & SERVICES

Importance of Transportation

Indian Railways is often referred to as the lifeline of the Indian economy because of its predominance in transportation of bulk freight and long-distance passenger traffic. (11.v3.9.2.1)

Targeted Growth for Transportation by Railways

The requirements of locomotives, coaches and wagons were forecasted by government for the final year of each 5-year plan considering future growth in passenger and freight traffic and replacements required and the target locomotives, coaches and wagons production capacities, new tracks to be laid, doubling of tracks and electrification of tracks to be done, etc. for the various 5-year plans were set.

Targeted Growth for Road Transportation

The requirements commercial passenger vehicles, goods vehicles, 2 and 3 wheelers, passenger cars, etc. were forecasted by government for the final year of each 5-year plan and the target production of these vehicles, new roads including national highways to be laid, road widening to be done to 2, 4 or 6 lanes, bypass roads and bridges to be constructed during the various 5-year plans were set.

Targeted Growth in Ship Transportation

International and coastal shipping tonnage requirement was assessed and targets set for ship building to meet the ship transportation tonnage.

Targeted Growth in Port Handling Capacity

International and coastal shipping tonnage requirements were assessed and targets set for developing major and minor ports of capacity required to handle projected shipping traffic in each 5-year plan.

Targeted Growth in Civil Aviation Sector

International and domestic passenger and cargo traffic were forecasted by the government for the final year of each 5-year plan and the targets were set for new airports to be constructed, airports to be modernized, aircrafts to be procured, frequencies to be increased, new routes to be introduced, etc. during the various 5-year plans.

Rolling Stock Production by Railways

The production of Rolling Stock in 1950-51

Rolling Stock Production in 1950-51 was locomotives 293, coaches 479 and wagons 3106. (Ref. 1.31.12) The indigenous production of wagons was 3707 in 1951-52 and coaches was 673. (2.21.7)
The production of meter gauge locomotives by the **T**ata **L**ocomotive and **E**ngineering **C**o was 10 in 1951-52. (2.21.7)
Route length, electrified route length. Freight traffic, Net traffic, Passenger originating traffic and Passengers Kms in 1950-51 were 53596 kms, 388 kms, 93 Mts, 44.12 BT kms, 1284 million and 66517 Passengers Kms respectively. (10. Ann. 8.3.1)

Achievements in I 5YP -

Chittaranjan Locomotives Factory was set up in 1948/1950 with a production capacity of 120 locomotives and 50 spare boilers. Government extended financial assistance to TLEC by participating in its capital structure by Rs. 2 Cr. TLEC manufactured 50 meter-gauge locomotives in 1950-51 and 1955-56. (1.31.14) (2.21.7)

The government established **Integral Coach Factory** in 1952 / 1955 for building of coaches at Perambur with an annual single-shift production capacity of 300 to 350 all-steel integral type coaches. (1.31.16)

In 1955-56 - The production of wagons was 13,526 and coaches 1260. The Chittaranjan Locomotive Works produced 337 locomotives as against the original target of 268. (2.21.7)

Achievements in II 5YP -

In 1960-61, The railways were handling 100% more freight traffic and 27% more passenger traffic than they were handling before the commencement of the I 5YP.

Route length, electrified route length. Freight traffic, Net traffic, Passenger originating traffic and Passengers Kms in 1960-61 were 56247 kms, 748 kms, 156.2 Mts, 87.68 BT kms, 1594 million and 77665 Passengers Kms respectively.

Achievements in III 5YP

i) Chittaranjan Locomotive Works diversified into production of electric locomotives.
ii) **Heavy Electricals Ltd.**, Bhopal started manufacture of traction motors for electric locomotives. (3.26.64)
iii) A heavy structural fabrication works of capacity 10,000 tons and a plate and vessel works of capacity 18,000 - 20,000 TPA on single shift basis were expected to be established. (3.26.67)

Achievements in IV 5YP

Route length, electrified route length. Freight traffic, Net traffic, Passenger originating traffic and Passengers Kms in 1970-71 were 59790 kms, 3706 kms, 196.5 Mts, 129.36 BT kms, 2431 million and 118120 Passengers Kms respectively.

Achievements in VI 5YP –

A new wheel and axle plant was set up near Bangalore to increase availability of wheels and axles.
Railways Freight - Net Ton km with average lead of 687.9 kms in 1984-85 - 182.1 billion (7.8.1)
Route length, electrified route length. Freight traffic, Net traffic, Passenger originating traffic and Passengers Kms in 1980-81 were 61240 kms, 5345 kms, 220 Mts, 158.47 BT kms, 3613 million and 208558 Passengers Kms respectively.

Achievement in VI 5YP –

Track renewals – 9200 kms and Electrification – 1522 kms
Rail routes expanded by 8065 kms since 1950-51; 3,065 kms were converted from Meter to Broad Gauge.

Achievement in VII 5YP -

Net Ton km with average lead of 708.7 kms in 1989-90 – 236.9 billion (8.Stat. 5)
Railway Stations on 31.03.1990 were 7076.
The Indian Railways had assets worth nearly Rs. 19730.59 Cr. on 31.3.1990. (8.9.5.6)
Route length, electrified route length. Freight traffic, Net traffic, Passenger originating traffic and Passengers Kms in 1990-91 were 62367 kms, 9968 kms, 341.4 Mts, 242.7 BT kms, 3858 million and 296544 Passengers Kms respectively.

Profitability of operation - Railways declared a surplus of Rs. 533 Cr. after meeting the dividend liability and allocating Rs.6735 Cr. to Depreciation Reserve Fund and Rs.2310 Cr. to Pensions Fund (8.9.5.11)

Achievements in VIII 5YP -

(i) The Indian Railways became one of the largest railway systems in the world with 63,000 route kms., approximately 7,000 locomotives, 34,000 passenger coaches, 300,000 wagons and employing nearly 1.6 million staff. Railways carried 11 million passengers and 1.2 Mts of freight per day. (9.7.1.46)
760 km Long broad-gauge Konkan Railway Project was commissioned in January, 1998. (9.7.1.37)
(ii) The Calcutta Metro Rail System, covering a length of 16.5 kms. from Dum Dum to Tollygunge, was constructed by Ministry of Railways out of their own budgetary sources. (9.3.7.174)

Achievements in IX 5YP

Route length, electrified route length. Freight traffic, Net traffic, Passenger originating traffic and Passengers Kms in 1999-2000 were 62757 kms, 14261 kms, 456.4 Mts, 308.04 BT kms, 4585 million and 430666 Passengers Kms respectively. (10. Ann. 8.3.1)
Track length in 2001-02 was – Broad gauge 61000 km, meter gauge 15000 km, narrow gauge 3600 km (10.8.3.65)

Payment of dividend - For the first time in 17 years, in 2000-01 and 2001-02, Indian Railways was unable to pay dividend on its past investment to the Government. (10.8.3.30)

Achievements in X 5YP

Internet ticketing was introduced in August 2002 to provide tickets at the doorstep of the customer. Further, in September 2005, e-ticketing was started as a pilot project and was later extended to all trains. Booking of Tatkal tickets was also started through Internet in December 2005.
There were 127768 bridges in Indian Railways in 2006-07. (11.9.2.38)

Container Traffic in 2006-07

15 Private sector entities were licensed in January 2007 for running container trains on tracks owned by the Indian Railways. These operators were to invest in container handling facilities, such as Inland Container Depots, etc. (11.1.73)
7 New operators, excluding CONCOR, commenced operations by utilizing about 30 new rakes. (9.2.30)
Freight Operation Information System (FOIS), Rake Management System, Terminal Management System were introduced.

Achievements in XI 5YP

Dedicated Freight Corridor Corporation of India Ltd. was incorporated in 2007 to undertake construction of dedicated freight lines of 3236 route kms on two Corridors - Eastern Corridor 1767 kms, from Ludhiana to Dankuni and Western Corridor 1469 kms, from Jawahar Lal Nehru Port, Mumbai to Tughlakabad / Dadri (along with interlinking of two corridors at Dadri).

Table - 15.1 Rolling Stock Production during Tenth and Eleventh Plans

Item	Tenth Plan Achievement	Eleventh Plan Achievement
Wagons	36,222	63,481
Coaches (including EMU/MEMU/DEMU)	12,202	17,085
Diesel Loco	622	1,288
Electric Loco	524	1,218

Note: This includes acquisition, as well as, railways' own production. (TABLE 12.15.9)

A 10.5 MW capacity wind farm was commissioned to provide captive power to ICF at Chennai. (12.15.37)
Indian Railways set up a 1,000 MW power plant at Nabi Nagar through a JV with NTPC to supply power to 164 substations of Indian Railways located in Eastern and Western regions. (12.15.38)

Rail Coach Factory, being set up at Kanchrapara, for manufacturing Electric Multiple Units / Mainline EMUs and Kolkata Metro coaches was expected to be operational during XII Plan.

Rail Passenger Traffic in 2023

During the period 1.04.22 to 28.02.23, Railways earned Rs. 57,662.61 Cr from passenger services carrying 5858.39 million passengers.

Contribution of Railways for 5YPs

II 5YP - Rs. 150 crores after providing for depreciation outlays, payment of interest and dividend.
III 5YP - The estimated surplus from Railways over the III Plan was Rs. 100 crores. (3.6.17)
IV 5YP - Railway's contribution for financing the Plan was originally estimated at Rs. 415 crores. (4.4.17)
V 5YP - The contribution of railways was estimated at Rs. 575 Cr (5.4.10)
VI 5YP - Estimates of Gross Surplus of Railways for 1980-85 at 1979-80 rates was - Rs. 1698 Cr.
VII 5YP - The contribution / gross surplus of Railways was estimated at Rs. 4,225 Cr. (7.4.30)
VIII 5YP – Rs.18,827 Cr (69%) of internal resources was provided by Railways for the Plan. (9.7.1.39)
XI 5YP – Ministry of Railways made an investment of Rs. 1,92,147 Cr — comprising of GBS of Rs. 77,039 Cr, internal generation of Rs. 66,704 Cr and Extra Budgetary Resources of Rs. 48,404 Cr. (12.15.24)
XII 5YP – The estimated resources required for the Railway sector were Rs. 5,19,221 Cr including GBS of Rs. 1,94,221 Cr, IEBR of Rs. 2,25,000 Cr and private sector investment of Rs. 1,00,000 Cr. (12.15.71)

Graph– 15.1 – Passenger, Freight and Container Traffic Handled by Railways – Removed.

Public Sector Enterprises Engaged in Production of Rolling Stock

Chittaranjan Locomotives Factory

Chittaranjan Locomotives Factory was launched as Loco Building Works in **1950** to produce 120 average-sized steam locomotives and 50 spare boilers. Production of steam locomotives commenced on 26.01.1950.

A heavy steel foundry was established at CLF for meeting the requirements of railways for heavy castings.

The CLF's output of average sized locomotives was 125 per annum in 1956. (2.2.31)

Production of Electric Locomotives and 25kV AC DC loco commenced in 1961 and 16.11.1963 respectively.

Production of DC Traction Motors and Control Equipment commenced in April, 1967.

Production of Diesel Hydraulic Locomotives was taken up during 1968. After manufacturing 2351 Steam Locomotives of 5 types and 842 Diesel Hydraulic Locos of 7 types, production of steam and diesel hydraulic locos was discontinued from 1973-74 and 1993-94 respectively.

GTO Thyristor controlled 6000hp freight electric Locomotive WAG-9 (Navyug) was produced in Nov. 1998.

During 2000-01 First passenger loco WAP-5 (**Navodit**), with maximum service speed of 160 km/h and having potential up to 200 km/h, was manufactured.

It is the **largest locomotive manufacturing unit in the world**, producing 431 locomotives in 2019–20.

During the last 5 years prior to 31.03.2022, CLF increased its production from 350 to 486 Locos/ year.

Integral Coach Factory

The **I**ntegral **C**oach **F**actory was inaugurated on 2.10.**1955**. Production of all-steel all-welded unfurnished coaches started in 1955 with an installed capacity of 350 shells/ annum.
The Furnishing Division was inaugurated on 2.10.1962.

ICF produced 2,503 coaches in 2017–2018. It became the **world's largest railway coach manufacturer**, rolling out 3,262 coaches in 2018–2019, up from 1,437 coaches in 2009–2010.
ICF turns out more than 4000 coaches in more than 175 varieties every year.

In 2018-19, ICF turned out 4166 coaches, which is the **highest ever production by any coach manufacturer in the world**. ICF rolled out India's first semi high speed train set consisting of 16 coaches and designed for maximum operating speed of 160 kmph.

During October 2022, ICF achieved the distinction of having turned out 70,000+ coaches since its inception, **highest by any passenger coach manufacturer in the world.**

Production during 2022-23 includes 31 rakes of MEMU (248 coaches), 15 Vista dome tourist coaches, 2639 LHB Coaches, 4 air-conditioned new generation rakes for Kolkata Metro and 50 Diesel Electric Tower Car (Underslung) etc. In 2023-24, ICF manufactured 2829 coaches.
ICF manufactures self-propelled coaches viz. EMU, MEMU, SPART, OHE Tower car, SPIC and DEMU.

Banaras Locomotive Works

Banaras Locomotive Works (erstwhile Diesel Locomotive works) came into existence in August 1961.

First broad-gauge locomotive (WDM-2) was released in Jan 1964 and First Meter gauge locomotive (YDM-4) in Nov 1968 and 1000th locomotive in 1977,
First 2300 HP WDP-1 passenger loco and First 3100 HP WDG-2 freight loco were turned out in 1995, 4000th Locomotive in 1999, 5000th Locomotive in 2007,
First 5500 HP WDG-5 locomotive was manufactured in 2012,
Annual turnover of 334 locomotives including 317 high power and 2 electric locomotives was achieved in 2017.
Converted 2 old ALCO diesel loco (WDG3A) into Electric WAGC3 loco, which is first time in world in 2018. 100th Electric loco was turned out in 2019, first ever dual traction locomotive in 2020 and 1000th Electric loco in 2022. BLW produced 367 locomotives in 2021-22.

Rail Wheel Factory, Bangalore

Till early 1980s Indian Railways was importing about 55% of requirement of wheels and axles. Indigenous capacity was available only at TISCO and Durgapur Steel Plant. The TISCO plant was technically not capable of meeting the changing requirement of wheels and axles for the new designs of rolling stock and production was discontinued. DSP was only able to partially meet Indian Railways' needs.

Wheel and Axle Plant (now Rail Wheel Factory) was dedicated to the nation in 1980 to manufacture cast wheels, forged Axles and assemble wheelsets. The first trial wheel was cast in 1983 and first axle was forged in 1984. After successful trials, the Plant was formally inaugurated on 15.09.1984.

Starting with annual plant capacity of 56,700 cast wheels and 23,000 forged axles, RWF has grown to a capacity of 1,90,000 wheels and 70,000 axles and 48,000 wheelsets. Till 2022, RWF has manufactured more than 36 lakh wheels, 17 lakh axles and 12 lakh wheelsets.

Patiala Loco Works

To supply high precision components required for maintenance of diesel loco fleet, construction of dedicated **Diesel Component Works** started at Patiala in 1981 and production started in 1986.

DCW also started rehabilitation of Traction Machines (Traction Motors and Alternators), Engine Blocks (Crank-case) and Power Packs, giving them a new lease of life. Motorized Truck Assemblies (Bogies), Motorized Wheel Sets, etc. were manufactured.

Phase-II project of DCW for Mid Life Rebuilding work started in 1989. The unit was rechristened from DCW to **D**iesel-Loco **M**odernization **W**orks in 2003. Since inception, 2296 ALCO diesel locos were rehabilitated / modernized by DMW.

DMW also started manufacturing new WDM3D 3300HP ALCO Locomotives in 2010-11 but the activity was discontinued after 2015-16. Till then 227 new WDM3D locomotives were manufactured by DMW.

To cater to the shunting requirements, first Multi Genset loco was turned out in March 2013.
The first 3-Phase IGBT based 6000HP WAP7 Electric Loco was turned out from DMW in February 2018.
The first 8-Wheeler Diesel Electric Tower Car (DETC) was manufactured in December 2018.

DMW started manufacturing of electric freight locos and the first WAG9HC locomotive was turned out in March 2021.
DMW also took up conversion of diesel locomotives to 10000 HP twin electric loco, and the prototype WAG10 loco was turned out in March 2021.
DMW started producing 3-Phase 6FRA6068 Traction Motors required for manufacturing new loco.
During 2021-22, DMW manufactured WAP7 Electric Locos- 8 Nos, WAG9H -Electric Locos – 108 Nos, 8-Wheeler Diesel Electric Tower Cars – 81 Nos, Motorized Truck Assemblies (Bogies) – 96 Nos and Motorized Wheel Sets – 269 Nos.

Rail Coach Factory, Kapurthala

The foundation stone of Rail Coach Factory, Kapurthala was laid on 17.08.1985 to enhance the production capacity of passenger coaches. The production at RCF commenced in 1987 and the first coach was rolled out on 31.03.1988.

After transfer of technology from Linke Hofmann Busch (LHB) of Germany in 1998, it started manufacturing modern stainless steel coaches having speed potential up to 160 kmph.
The capacity of the unit was 1025 coaches/ year including varieties of coaches like 'Tejas' high-speed coach, non-AC general coach, Non-AC luggage-cum-brake van, Refrigerated parcel van, Accident relief train, etc.
This output constituted over 35% of the total population of coaches on Indian Railways. Against installed capacity of 1500 coaches, RCF produced 1701 coaches in 2013-14 including 23 different variants of coaches for Rajdhani, Shatabdi, double-decker and other trains. RCF in association with DRDE developed a highly cost-effective indigenous technology for the treatment of biowaste in coaches. Around 2096 bio-toilets were fitted in 2013–14.
RCF has manufactured more than 30000 passenger coaches of different types including self-propelled passenger vehicles which constitute over 50% of the total population of coaches on Indian Railways.

RCF was manufacturing 120 LHB coaches to be exported to Bangladesh with the first consignment of 40 set to be dispatched in March 2016. RCF exported coaches to South-East Asian and African countries which have Meter Gauge rail networks.
RCF introduced a high-capacity parcel van to carry high volumetric load at high speed and prototype of double decker of 160 kmph speed potential in 2020. RCF rolled out Indian Railway's first Air-Conditioned Economy Class coach with enhanced speed and berth capacity in 2021.

In 2022-23, ECF produced 1651 coaches including 1114 LHB coaches and 213 MEMU coaches.

Rail Wheel Plant, Bela

The Rail Wheel Plant's construction started in July 2008. Workshop Project Organization of Indian Railways awarded this project in July 2008 as EPC contract to Larsen & Toubro Ltd.

RWP started production in 2014 with a capacity of 1,00,000 wheel-discs and dispatched its first consignment of about 250 broad gauge passenger coach wheels in October 2016.

Revenue from operations as on December 2022 was Rs. 8878 Cr.

Modern Coach Factory, Raebareli

IRCON International Ltd. started construction of third railway passenger coaches factory of capacity 1000 LHB coaches in 2009. MCF was inaugurated on 7.11.2012.

These coaches were progressively to be introduced on the Shatabdi and Rajdhani trains.
The first coach was turned out in August 2014. In Dec 2015, it was named as Modern Coach Factory. Starting from 140 coaches in 2014-15, MCF produced 1920 coaches in 2019-20. A total of 8250 LHB coaches have been rolled out by MCF until 31.03.2022.
MCF was manufacturing train sets, metro coaches, aluminum body coaches, bullet train coaches, high speed coaches and LHB coaches.
MCF Raebareli is one of the most advanced coach manufacturing units of the world as it is equipped with the many state-of-the art industrial robots and machines.
MCF proposes to make aluminium coaches with potential to operate at 250 km/hr. The life of coach may go up to 40 years.

In June 2019, Mozambique Ports and Railways Authority signed an MoU with Indian railway's RITES to procure 90 coaches, including 60 loco-hauled designed on LHB coach platform and 30 DEMU coaches designed and developed by ICF and RDSO.

Electric Locomotive Factory

Electric Locomotive Factory, Madhepura is a joint venture of Alstom SA of France and Indian Railways to produce 800 high-power locomotives over 11 years designed to run on Indian tracks at 120 km/h.

In January 2014, the Union Cabinet gave approval for setting up ELF Madhepura and DLF Marhowrah. On 9.11.2015, the Ministry of Railways awarded the contracts for Madhepura project to Alstom. Manufacturing started on 11.10.2017.
The first high-speed WAG-12 12,000 HP freight electric locomotive was released in 2018. Indian Railways got its 50th locomotive delivered by December 2020 and 100th locomotive by May 2021.

As of 31.03.2022, the factory has rolled out 230 electric locomotives.

Diesel Locomotive Factory

Diesel Locomotive Factory, Marhowrah is a joint venture of GE Transportation, US and Indian Railways to produce 1000 high-power freight locomotives over 10 years.

In January 2014, the Union Cabinet gave approval for setting up ELF Madhepura and DLF Marhowrah. On 9.11.2015, the Ministry of Railways awarded the contract for Marhowrah project to General Electric.
DLF started manufacturing the locomotives from September 2018. GE Transportation will maintain the locomotives for 13 years, after which the Indian Railways will take over maintenance.

Marathwada Railway Coach Factory

Metro and rail coach manufacturing facilities were set up in Latur in Maharashtra to cater to the demands of metro coaches in cities across India along with the captive demands of Indian Railways.

Rail Vikas Nigam Ltd. commissioned Marathwada Rail Coach Factory (of initial capacity to produce 250 MEMU / EMU / LHB / train set type advanced coaches) with the production of first coach shell on 25.12.2020.

Rail Coach Factory, Sonipat

The Rail Coach Naveenikaran Karkhana, the first such unit for mid-life rehabilitation of LHB coaches in India, was expected to begin the exercise of refurbishing 12 to 14-year-old LHB coaches from July 2021.

Braithwaite and Co. Ltd. – Manufacturing Wagons, Bogies, etc. – Refer Chapter 11

Bharat Wagon & Engineering Co. Ltd. – Manufacturing Wagons – Refer Chapter 11

Burn Standard Co. Ltd. – Largest Wagon Builder – Refer Chapter 11

RITES Ltd – Supply & Operation of Rolling Stock in Other Countries – Refer Chapter 8

Public Sector Enterprises Engaged in Track Work and Electrification

Central Organization for Railway Electrification

Railway Electrification as an organization was set up in 1961. Central Organization for Railway Electrification (CORE) was set up in 1971.

It electrified 52,247 Route km (RKM) that is about 80.2% of the total Broad-Gauge network of Indian Railways (65141 RKM) by 31.03.2022. Indian railways electrified 62119 RKM till 1.03.2024 (94% 0f total broad-gauge network of 65775 RKM).

IRCON International Ltd.

Indian Railway Construction Ltd. - IRCON was incorporated on 28.4.1976 to undertake railway and other construction including turn key projects, consultancy and advisory services, laying of rail tracks, including ballast less track, rehabilitation and up-gradation of track, sidings, electrification of railway lines, construction of railways workshops, highways, bridges, tunnel, airport constructions, airport runway, metros, mass rapid transit system, signaling and telecommunication work, building electricity transmission substations etc.

The name of the Company was changed to "IRCON International Ltd" w.e.f. 17.10.1995.

IRCON IL has project offices in Afghanistan, Algeria, Bangladesh, Ethiopia, Malaysia, Mozambique, Nepal, Sri Lanka and Sharjah and financial joint ventures in Spain, Australia, Bangladesh, Malaysia, Korea and Japan.

IRCON IL had 2 joint ventures namely **C**ompanhia dos **C**aminhos de **F**erro da **B**eira, Mozambique and Ircon-Soma Tollway Pvt Ltd., India and one wholly owned subsidiary Ircon Infrastructure & Services Ltd.

During its 41 years of operation, Ircon IL had up to 2016-17 completed about **380 major infrastructure projects of National importance in India & 120 projects** across the globe **in more than 21 countries.** Ircon has completed over 1650 major infrastructure projects in India and over 900 projects across the globe in more than 31 countries as on 2022-23.

In India the company is executing several projects including rail-cum-road bridge across river Ganga, road over bridges in Rajasthan and Bihar, **New Rail Coach Factory** at Rae Bareilly, Sivok (WB) -Rangpo (Sikkim) new rail line project, J & K Rail Link Project, National building projects under Pradhan Mantri Gram Sadak Yojana, Rashtriya Sam Vikas Yojana, etc.

Revenue of IRCON for 2022-23 was Rs. 9921.2 Cr.

Konkan Railway Corp. Ltd.

Konkan Railway Corp. Ltd. - KRCL was incorporated on 19.07.1990 to construct and maintain a new broad gauge rail line between Roha (Maharashtra) and Mangalore and operate the railway traffic in this route spanning 58 stations.

KRCL undertook construction of 90 km Katra - Laole / Dharam section of Udhampur-Srinagar-Baramulla single line broad gauge project and construction of road over bridges in Jharkhand, implementation of Anti-Collision Device network in North East Frontier Railway, etc.

To improve the originating traffic, KRCL proposed to undertake construction of container freight terminus, port connectivity and hinterland rail connectivity projects.

To detect several faults in rolling stocks, Automated Train Examination Systems KRATES were developed & commissioned at Ratnagiri Station.

In 2019-20, KRCL was operating 739 km Konkan Railway system from Roha to Thokur passing 3 states with 50 passenger and 12 freight trains. Revenue from operations in 2022-23 was Rs. 5028.76 Cr.

Mumbai Railway Vikas Corp. Ltd.

Mumbai Railway Vikas Corp. Ltd. - MRVCL was incorporated on 12.7.1999 to augment transport capacity in Mumbai to match the continual growth in the number of commuters by developing coordinated plans and implementing rail infrastructure projects and integrating urban development plan of Mumbai.

MRVC undertakes commercial development of Railway land and air space to coordinate and facilitate improvements in track drainage, remove encroachments and trespassers and to coordinate with organizations operating train services and responsible for protection of Railway's right of way for Urban development. MRVC is providing services to rail infrastructure project - Mumbai Urban Transport Project.

Construction of new station at Digha under Airoli-Kalwa work of MUTP was completed in January 2023

RailTel Corporation of India Ltd

RailTel Corporation of India Ltd. - RailTel was incorporated on 26.09.2000 to modernize Railways' train control and operational safety systems by creating nationwide broadband telecom and multimedia network.

RailTel has exclusive seamless **R**ight **o**f **W**ay along 63,000 km of Railway Track passing through 7000 stations across the country. About 40873 kms of OFC have already been laid and over 37708 km of OFC Network connecting over 4200 stations were commissioned till March, 2011.

During 2010-11, RailTel laid 2910 KMs of OFC and provided STM1 connectivity to about 200 stations.

The OFC network of RailTel in 2016-17 was connecting over 600 cities & 4500 towns (covering 70% of 9 population) and was offering managed lease lines, tower colocation, MPLS based IP-VPN, Internet, telepresence, retail broadband services (Rail wire) and NGN based voice carriage services to Telecom Operators, Internet Service Providers, MSOs, enterprises, banks, government Institutions / dept., educational institutions / Universities, etc. RailTel played a major role in establishing the National Knowledge Network with multiple Giga Bit Bandwidth links to connect Knowledge Institutions across the country.

RailTel also works on various projects like implementing NIC e-office, IP based video surveillance system, hospital management information system, Wi-Fi hotspots, railway signalling, AI based solutions, Automatic Number Plate Recognition, RFID Boom Barrier based weighbridge Automation, vehicle tracking and fleet management etc. Revenue from operations in 2022-23 was Rs. 1946.52 Cr.

Rail Vikas Nigam Ltd.

Rail Vikas Nigam Ltd. - RVNL was incorporated on 24.01.2003 for creating rail infrastructure to remove capacity bottlenecks on the Golden Quadrilateral and its diagonals, providing vital linkages and augmenting capacity of existing links including the corridors connecting ports with the hinterland.

Ministry of Railways transferred 53 projects to RVNL (32 projects pertaining to strengthening of golden quadrilateral and diagonals), second bridge over river Mahanadi near Cuttack, doubling of Panvel to Jawaharlal Nehru Port track, etc. (2.2.9.1)

RVNL completed 155 Kms. of new lines, 795 Kms. of gauge conversion, 276 Kms. of doubling and 954 Kms. of railway electrification till 31.3.2008. (about 38% of total assigned length of 46 projects).

In 2010-11, RVNL was implementing 73 projects of total length 8095 kms including 36 projects for strengthening of Golden Quadrilateral and Diagonals and 29 projects for Port connectivity and corridors to hinterland and 4 projects of Kolkata Metro Railways etc. Of these 73 projects, 23 projects of length 3741km were fully completed in 2010-11.

RVNL had 5 joint ventures namely Krishnapatnam Railway Co. Ltd., Haridaspur Paradip Railway Co. Ltd., Bharuch-Dahej Railway Co. Ltd., Kutch Railway Co. Ltd. and Angul Sukinda Railway Ltd.

In 2013-14, RVNL implemented 123 projects; out of which 40 projects were completed up to March 2014, 79 projects were under implementation.

Up to 27.7.2013, RVNL completed 1385 Kms of doubling, 1590 Kms of gauge conversion, 194 Kms of new lines and 134 kms of railway electrification. RVNL was assigned Rishikesh Karanprayag new line in the Himalayas for execution. (70% completed as on March 2024 – Financial Express dated 8.03.2024)

Gross turnover of Rail Vikas Nigam Ltd. in FY 2022-23 was Rs. 20282 Cr.

Dedicated Freight Corridor Corp. of India

Dedicated Freight Corridor Corporation of India Ltd. - DFCCIL was incorporated on 30-10-2006 to undertake construction, maintenance and operation of dedicated freight lines covering about 3236 route kms on two Corridors - Eastern Corridor (1767 kms), from Ludhiana to Dankuni and Western Corridor (1469 kms), from Jawahar Lal Nehru Port, Mumbai to Tughlakabad / Dadri (along with interlinking of two corridors at Dadri).

The ports in the Western region were to be efficiently linked to the Northern hinterland. Dankuni–Sonnagar section of Eastern DFC was to be implemented through PPP. (12.15.53) The Eastern and Western Dedicated Freight Corridors were expected to be completed during the Twelfth Plan period and planning for other DFCs—North-South, East-South, East-West and South-West were to be firmed up during the Twelfth Plan period. (12.15.71)

Inauguration of the construction work of Eastern DFC was done on 10.2.2009.

Total 812 RKM of DFC network was commissioned in FY 2022-23. Cumulative of 2089 Km out of 2843 km (73.4%) of DFC has been commissioned till March 2023.

Revenue from operations in 2022-23 was Rs. 3141.48 Cr.

High Speed Rail Corporation of India Limited

High Speed Rail Corporation of India Ltd. was incorporated on 25.07.2012.

HSRC is conducting of pre-feasibility studies of dedicated high-speed Corridors for Diamond Quadrilateral to connect New Delhi-Mumbai-Chennai-Kolkata-New Delhi. Also, pre-feasibility studies of DHSC between Delhi-Chandigarh-Amritsar was assigned to HSRC by Ministry of Railways.

Chhattisgarh East Railways Ltd.

Chhattisgarh East Railways Ltd. was incorporated on 12.03.2013 to build construct, operate and maintain the East Rail Corridor (Corridor I)

Public Sector Enterprises Engaged in Setting Up and Modernization of Workshops

Central Organization for Modernization of Workshops

The Central Organization for Modernization of Workshops was established in 1979. Since its inception it has helped production units and workshops all over Indian Railways by modernization or up-gradation of their manufacturing, maintenance, training and other facilities towards enhancing the productivity.

Workshop Projects Organization

Workshop Projects Organization - WPO was established in October 2002 for setting up of Production Units and Workshops of Indian Railways on turnkey basis.

Major projects of WPO - Carriage Repair workshop, with a periodical overhauling capacity of 600 non-AC ICF design coaches per annum, was completed and handed over to East Central Railway on 12.06.2012,

Periodic overhaul facility for LHB coaches / wheelsets provided at Carriage Repair Workshop at Harnaut, maintenance Workshops at Gorakhpur, Tirupati, Pratap Nagar (Gujarat), Hazaribagh Town, maintenance facilities for MEMU rake at Bhusawal, etc.
Completion of Rail Wheel Plant, Bela, wagon repair workshop at Badnera, coach midlife rehabilitation workshop at Kurnool, Detachment free rake examination facilities at Bondamunda,
Augmentation of bogie periodical overhauling capacity at Matunga and Kharagpur, coaching infrastructure facilities at Bhagalpur, upgradation of infrastructure of Wagon Care Centre at Mughal Sarai.

Carriage Repair Workshops are located at Tirupati, Hubli, Mancheswar and Lower Parel Mumbai also.

Kanchrapara Railway Workshop

Kanchrapara Railway Workshop, located in Sealdah, caters to the major overhauling of locomotives (WAP7, WAP4, WAG9, WAG7, WAG5, WAM4), ICF Coaches, EMUs, MEMUs, DEMUs, Tower Cars, etc.

Public Sector Enterprises Engaged in Freight / Passenger Transportation Services

Container Corporation of India

Container Corporation of India – CONCOR was set up on 10.03.1988 to organize and handle multi-modal containerization for transportation of cargo. It commenced operations in 1989 with Indian Railways transferring 7 **I**nland **C**ontainer **D**epots and container related business to CONCOR.

The international and domestic container traffic handled by CONCOR increased from 96,000 and 12000 **T**wenty feet **E**quivalent **U**nits in 1991-92 to 400000 and 300000 TEUs in 1996-97 respectively. (9.7.1.45)
CONCOR owned 10,666 wagons including 9,309 high speed wagons at the end 2010-11 for inland transportation of containers. It also owned / took on lease more than 12000 containers for use in the domestic circuit. It had 55 special container handling equipment like Reach Stackers.
CONCOR expanded the network to more than 44 ICDs and 14 domestic and port side terminals and had 213 rakes of flat wagons by 2012. (12. Box 15.1)

Private sector participation

Anticipating higher container traffic at Indian ports, Railways permitted the entry of private players in the area of rail-based haulage of containers in 2005. 15 New operators procured 132 rakes and developed 9 new terminals. Competition also led to an increase in the growth of rail based intermodal traffic at 15.5% between 2007–08 and 2011–2012.

The Ministry of Railways procured 200 number, 9,000 HP electric locomotives under the JICA loan for container train operations on the Western Dedicated Freight Corridor.

CONCOR provided customs clearance, warehousing and bonded warehousing services at Container Freight Stations and moved into the Port Management through the Joint Ventures at JNPT and Cochin.
It diversified into Controlled Atmospheric Storage through its subsidiary Fresh & Healthy Enterprise Ltd.

CONCOR's share in transportation of containers in 2011-12 was 75%.

The container throughput handled by CONCOR was (i) 31,02,211 TEUs with accompanying tonnage of 38.12 Mts by rail and a network of 68 container depots in 2016-17 ii) 35,31.900 TEUs with a network of 80 container depots in 2017-18. iii) 37,47,758 TEUs with a network of 64 container depots in 2019-20 and iv) 4.36 million TEUs in 2022-23 (a total tonnage of 49 Mts by rail) with 61 container depots. (5 EXIM, 36 Combined, 17 Domestic terminals and 3 Strategic Tie-ups).

It developed many Multi Modal Logistics Parks including those at Paradip and Dahej.

On 31.03.2023, CONCOR had 108 RSTs, 37074 containers, 16731 wagons, 14 gantry cranes and 13 forklifts.

Fresh & Healthy Enterprises Ltd.

Fresh & Healthy Enterprises Ltd. - FHEL was incorporated on 1.2.2006 to set up a cold chain infrastructure for procurement, storage, transportation and marketing of fruits and vegetables to improve quality of produce, yield, storability and shelf life of variety of fruits and vegetables to enable availability for longer durations.

FHEL has set up integrated controlled atmosphere storage consisting of 3 units of 4000 MT capacity each at Rai and Sonepat and undertakes distribution of fruits and vegetables through its offices at Shimla and Sonepat.
During 2007-08, FHEL procured, stored and marketed about 12000 MT of apples.

Operations were carried out in Agri-Logistics Centre at Rai, Sonepat during 2022 23.

IRCON Infrastructure & Services Ltd

IRCON Infrastructure & Services Ltd. - IRCONISL was incorporated on 30.09.2009 as a subsidiary of IRCON international Ltd. to undertake infrastructure projects like construction 24 Multifunctional Complexes (MFCs), etc. in association with Rail Land Development Authority, in the vicinity of identified railway station premises, to provide facilities and amenities to users of Indian Railway System.

Construction of MFCs for 7 stations were completed during 2010-11. The construction of warm shells was completed at 23 stations. IRCONISL subleased operation and maintenance of 23 MFCs to third parties.
From 12.03.2012 onwards, IRCONISL carried on the business of hire purchase, leasing of all kinds of movable and immovable properties and consultancy for all kinds of engineering projects. IRCONISL supplied manpower and leased machinery for Sri Lanka & Malaysia projects of Ircon. IRCONISL

successfully executed preparation of DPR for Construction of 2 Lane Road on NH Specifications from Paletwa to Zorinpui on India-Myanmar Border.

IRCONISL is also engaged in providing Project Management Consultancy Services for Buildings, Roads, Bridges, Railways projects, etc. IRCONISL also leases out the Track Machines.

Revenue from operations in 2022-23 was Rs. 218.91 Cr.

Rites Infrastructure Services Limited

Rites Infrastructure Services Ltd - RISL was incorporated on 27.04.2010 as a wholly owned subsidiary of RITES Ltd to undertake infrastructure development at / in the vicinity of identified premises of Railway stations and on sites assigned by the ministry of railways and operation, and maintenance of Multi-Functional Complexes. The company is under voluntary liquidation and all the assets and liabilities of the company, as on 30.09.2017, were taken over by M/s RITES Ltd.

Indian Railway Stations Development Corporation Ltd

Indian Railway Stations Development Corp. Ltd. - IRSDC was incorporated on 12.04.2012 as a joint venture of Ircon International Ltd., to develop / redevelop identified Railway Stations across India for augmenting and maintaining passenger amenities at stations in a holistic manner. IRSDC was expected to undertake commercial development of the site allotted to it with Right of Way and license to the Station Development Land.

CONCOR Air Limited

CONCOR Air Limited - CAL, a 100% subsidiary of Container Corporation of India Ltd, was incorporated on 24.07.2012 to take over operation and management of Air Cargo Handling and Warehousing for International and Domestic Business.

Revenue from operations in 2022-23 was Rs. 49.99 Cr.

SIDCUL CONCOR Infra Company Ltd

SIDCUL CONCOR Infra Company Ltd - SCICL, a joint venture company between State Infrastructure and Industrial Development Corporation of Uttarakhand Ltd and Container Corporation of India Ltd, was incorporated on 21.03.2013 for providing handling and warehousing facility to the exporters, importers of Uttarakhand and domestic customers at Inland Container Depots (Dry Ports) and Container Freight Stations for Export-Import cargo for the Industries of Uttarakhand including transportation of containers by rail and road.

Revenue from operations in 2022-23 was Rs. 16.84 Cr.

Railway Energy Management Company Ltd.

Railway Energy Management Company Ltd. - REMCL was incorporated on 16.08.2013 as a joint venture of RITES Ltd. and Indian Railways to develop potential business avenues in power sector including generating and selling renewable energy for railway consumption by installing windmills and solar plants, power trading, other electrical projects etc.

REMCL completed 69.2 MW solar power projects including 65 MW Roof top Solar Power Plant (up to December 2022) on Indian Railway. REMCL concluded power procurement contracts for 1200 MW in different states.

REMCL procured 1619 MW conventional power – 819 MW from BRBCL (for MP, Maharashtra and 8 more states), 340 MW from M/s JPL (for MP and 3 more states), 210 MW from M/s DIL power for Maharashtra, etc.

Company has up to 2022-23, successfully awarded 248 MW of solar roof top projects, 52 MW of ground mounted projects and 93 MW of wind power projects including 26 MW Wind power plant at Jaisalmer, (commissioned on 16.10.2015) and 60.9 MW wind power (procured in developer mode).
Revenue from operations in 2022-23 was Rs. 114.15 Cr.

RailTel Enterprises Ltd.

RailTel Enterprises Ltd. was incorporated on 12.08.2014 as a wholly owned subsidiary of RailTel Corporation of India Ltd. to undertake the expanding activities in project execution works for telecom and signaling. Amalgamation of RailTel Enterprises with RailTel Corp. Ltd is under progress.

Revenue from operations in 2022-23 was Rs. 19.59 Cr.

Railways Contribution to GDP by Passenger and Freight Transportation Services

The gross traffic receipts of the Railways increased from Rs. 282.16 Cr in 1951-52 to Rs. 2,16,935 Cr. in 2019-20.

Road Infrastructure Development

Road work in 1950-51

About 79,363 tons of asphalt for black topping of roads was imported in 1950-51. With the establishment of petroleum refineries during I 5YP, asphaltic bitumen was expected from domestic sources from 1955-56
At the beginning of I 5YP, India had 97,500 miles of metaled roads, 151,000 miles of unmetalled roads and 22000 kms of National Highways. (2.21.36) (10. Ann. 8.3.1)   The total number of motor vehicles on the road were 294727 (goods vehicles - 81,000, passenger vehicles/ stage carriages - 34,000) at the commencement of I 5YP. (2.21.43) (3.27.4)

There were about 47,575 operators in the country of whom 25 owned a fleet exceeding 100; another 50 exceeding 50 vehicles and more than 46,000 small operators, each owning 5 vehicles or less. (1.31.82)

Achievements in I 5YP
The State Governments were expected to add 5000 vehicles to their existing fleets of State Transport Corporations. Almost all goods transport and about three-fourths of the passenger services were in the hands of private operators. (2.21.42 / 43)

Achievements in II 5YP
The production of vehicles in 1960-61 was about 30,000. Several measures were taken to liberalize the licensing policies for road transport. (3.27.43)
In 1960-61, the capacity of the road transport industry more than doubled from traffic in 1955-56. 5000 vehicles were added to the fleets of the nationalized undertakings. **The share of the nationalized undertakings in the total passenger services by road was about 30%.** (3.27.45)
Total road length, national highways, number of goods vehicles and passenger buses in 1960-61 were 525000 kms, 24000 kms, 168000 and 57000 respectively. (10. Annex, 8,3.1)

Jobs Planned in III 5YP –
Setting capacity targets for Automobiles industries - The capacity targets in respect of all transport equipment conformed to the minimum targets recommended by the Development Council for

Automobiles and Ancillary Industries with the exception of passenger cars, for which a lower figure as proposed by the ad-hoc committee on the Automobile Industry's Report of March 1960 was accepted. (3.26.70)

Increasing the indigenous content was given precedence over investment for establishing new units or expanding existing capacity. (3.26.71)

Jobs Planned in IV plan in private sector - The investment in road transport by private sector during IV 5YP was estimated at Rs 935 crores. (4.15.19)

Achievements in IV 5YP

Total road length, national highways, number of goods vehicles and passenger buses in 1970-71 were 915000 kms, 24000 kms, 343000 and 94000 respectively. (10. Annex, 8,3.1)

Delhi Transport Corporation was operating 1495 buses in 1973-74. (5.5.109)

Achievements in V 5YP –

Passenger traffic handled by the Road transport in 1978-79 - 270 billion passenger kms. (182.8 bpkms – **67.7% was handled by State Road Transport Corporations alone**)

61,661 buses (**55.5%** of mechanized passenger road transport vehicles) were in the public sector in 1978-79 (6.17.53)

Achievements in VI 5YP –

Total road length, national highways, number of goods vehicles and passenger buses in 1980-81 were 1485000 kms, 32000 kms, 554000 and 162000 respectively. (10. Annex, 8,3.1)

i) About 18,000 villages were connected with roads under Minimum Needs Program.   ii) Upgradation of National Highways taken up by widening 4224 kms for 2 lanes and 90 kms for four-lanes and completing 50 by-passes, 7 missing major bridges and 467 minor bridges.

Fleet Utilization (% of buses on road) of State Road Transport Undertakings in 1984-85 was – **84%.**
Vehicle Productivity per bus held per day in 1984-85 was – **218 km.**

Focus on improving transport services – Government's priority in first 5-year plans was improving passenger services through SRTCs rather than laying new roads and made capital investments (Rs. 8187 Cr in VIII 5YP). In VI 5YP also government gave priority for laying roads to villages than national highways.

Achievements in VII Plan

Total road length, national highways, number of goods vehicles and passenger buses in 1990-91 were 2.35 million kms, 33700 kms, 1.356 million and 331000 respectively. (10. Annex, 8,3.1)

Fleet Utilization of SRTCs in 1989-90, 1990-91 and 1991-92 were – 89%

Vehicle Productivity per bus held per day in 1989-90, 1990-91 and 1991-92 were – 257 km, 259 km and 267 kms respectively.

Achievements in VIII 5YP

The aggregate length of roads increased from 0.4 million kms in 1950-51 to 3.32 million kms in 1995-96 (9.7.1.5)

India's road network measured 3,319,644 kms. in 1995-96, comprising National Highways 34,508 kms, **State Highways** 135,187 kms. and other roads including Major District Roads, Other District Roads, **Village Roads,** Urban Roads and Project Roads having a length of 3,144,949 kms. (9.7.1.92)

Operation of SRTUs - The fleet strength of the SRTUs on 31.3.1997 was 1.13 lakhs, with a total capital investment of Rs. 8187 Cr. These SRTUs covered 1074 cr. effective kms during 1996-97 and carried 2337 Cr passengers. (9.7.1.156)

The number of registered goods motor vehicles in 1998 - 25.29 lakh (10.8.3.110)

Jobs Planned in IX 5YP
(i) A special National Highway Development Project (NHDP) of total length 11860 kms., which included the major highway linking Delhi, Calcutta, Chennai and Mumbai constituting the golden quadrangle and North-South and East-West corridors, was to be undertaken during the Ninth Five Year Plan. (9.7.1.110)
(ii) About 2700 Kms of NH in NE region was entrusted to BRDB for development. (9.7.1.115)

Achievements in IX 5YP
Total road length, national highways, number of goods vehicles and passenger buses in 1999-2000 were 2.695 million kms, 52010 kms, 3.229 million and 659000 respectively. (10. Annex, 8,3.1)

Automobile Industry in 2001-02 –
The capacity utilization in commercial vehicles, cars and multi-utility vehicles and 2 and 3-wheelers were 37%, 55% and 70% respectively. – This indicated that there was **excess capacity** and **licensing did not come in the way** of meeting consumer demands.
Automobile export increased from $ 344 million in 1991 to $ 874 million in 1995. (10.7.1.111)
Production of cars and multiutility vehicles peaked at 700,000 in 1999-2000. (10.7.1.110)
Turnover of domestic auto component industry doubled between 1997 and 2002. (10.7.1.112)

Roads in 2001-02
1159 kms of Golden Quadrilateral roads were widened to 4 lanes.
The fleet strength of 62 SRTUs on 31.03.2001 - 1.15 lakh (17.45% of total commercial passenger vehicles in 1999-2000) (10.8.3.112)
Toll - National Highways Act, 1956 was amended in June 1995. Private sector got opportunity to invest in National Highway projects, levy, collect, retain fee from users and to regulate traffic on such highways.

Achievements in X 5YP
Widening to two lanes – 4177 km (11.9.3.6)
Strengthening of weak two lanes – 8377 km
Major bridges/minor bridges including ROBs - 611
IRQP - 15326.62 + 924
Total 7627 km of roads had been four – laned as on 31.08.2007 including 5602 km of Golden Quadrilateral and 1418 km of the NS–EW corridors. (11.9.3. 9/11/16)
37487 of the total 178768 habitations had been provided with all-weather roads (11.9.3.24)
India's **road network** of 33.14 lakh km consisted of 66590 km of national highways, 137000 km of State highways, 300000 km major district roads, and Rural Roads that included other district roads and village roads. (11.9.3.2)

State Road Transport Undertakings - The share of SRTUs in total buses declined from 37% in 1985–86 to 15.8% in 2002–03. (11.9.3.64)
Of the 53 SRTUs operating in the country, 15 were operated by local bodies and 38 established by State Governments. These 38 SRTUs were estimated to have a total of 1.13 lakh buses, with a total investment of Rs 18669.19 cr. (11.9.3.65)
As on 31.03.2004, the share of private buses in passenger transport services was 85%.

Achievements in XI 5YP
As on March 2012, 30,537 km length of NHs was entrusted to NHAI, 42,483 km to State PWDs and 3,798 km to BRO. (12.15.76)
The national highways of 76,818 km comprised only 2.0% of the road network but carried 40% of the road-based traffic in 2012.

About 23% of National Highways was of 4-lane (and above standard), 54% was of 2-lane standard and 23% length was of single lane and intermediate standard. (12.15.73/76)

Pradhan Mantri Gram Sadak Yojana

New and improved **rural road network of 2,09,500 km** was completed till 2012, under PMGSY, thereby connecting 84,414 habitations with a population of 500 persons and above in plain areas and 250 persons and above in Hill States, Tribal (Schedule V) areas, the Desert Areas (as identified in Desert Development Program) and in the 82 Selected and Tribal Backward districts (under IAP). (12.15.89)

Bharat Nirman

44,089 habitations having population of 1,000 or more persons (500 or more in hilly and tribal areas) were connected by constructing **1,41,095 km of new all-weather roads**, under Rural Connectivity component of Bharat Nirman, up to 31.03.2012. (12.15.94)

Roads Under SARDP-NE

About 892 km length was completed under SARDP-NE Phase-A till end March 2012. (12.15.80)

Private Sector investment fell short of target

During XI Plan, total private-sector investment on NHDP was Rs. 62,629 Cr against a target of Rs. 86,792 Cr, which was a substantial jump over the achievement in the X Plan of Rs. 11,032 Cr. (12.15.88)

Contribution to GDP by Road and Rail Transportation in 2009-10

Road transport contributed 4.7% to India's GDP in 2009–10 which was higher than Railways that had a 1% share. (12.15.110)

Contribution by Road Transport Sector for 5YPs

VI 5YP – Estimates of Gross Surplus of SRTC for 1980-85 at 1979-80 rates were - Rs. 506 Cr. (6.5.20)
XII 5YP – The budgetary support for Central Sector Roads was Rs. 1,44,769 Cr. In addition, the sector was expected to generate an IEBR of Rs. 64,834 Cr and private-sector investment of Rs. 2,14,186 Cr. (12.15.121)

Graph 15.2 – Growth of National Highways, passenger & freight traffic by road – Removed.

Hyderabad Allwyn Ltd

Hyderabad Allwyn Ltd, a joint venture of Industrial Development Trust of the Hyderabad Government and Allwyn & Company, was established in January 1942 as Allwyn Metal Works fur manufacture of automobiles, trucks, scooters, bus coach building, refrigerators and wrist watches.

It assembled Albion CX9 buses for Hyderabad State Railways and bult buses for APSRTC including double-decker buses (in 1963). Allwyn also built the Indian Army's medium-capacity Shaktiman truck bodies. In 1969, it was taken over by the state government.

HAL started manufacture of mechanical and quartz watches in 1981 in collaboration with Seiko of Japan. In 1983 the automobile division entered into a tie-up with Nissan Motor Co, Japan to set up Hyderabad Allwyn Nissan Ltd at Zahirabad to manufacture Nissan Cab Star range of Light commercial trucks.

Andhra Pradesh Scooters Ltd manufactured Allwyn Pushpak and Vespa PL170 (of Piaggio scooters). Watch Division of HAL and Auto and Bus Body division were formed into new companies as Allwyn Watches Ltd. and Allwyn Auto Ltd. respectively.

In 1989 Allwyn Nissan was privatized and sold to Mahindra, renaming the company as Mahindra Nissan Allwyn Ltd. In 1994 MNAL was merged with Mahindra and Mahindra.

HAL's Refrigeration and Appliances division became sick and was amalgamate with Voltas Ltd. in 1994.

National Highways Authority of India

National Highways Authority of India – NHAI was set up on 10.02.1995, as an autonomous agency of Government of India, to develop, maintain and manage the national highways.

The NHAI had the mandate to implement the National Highways Development Project (NHDP) in 7 Phases - Phase I for Golden Quadrilateral portions of NS-EW Corridors, and connectivity of major ports to National Highways.

The largest highway project in India and the **fifth longest in the world** of building 5,846 km four/six lane express highways was launched in 2001 and was completed in 2012.

Phase II for NS-EW corridors - building 7,142 kms of four/six lane expressways connecting Srinagar in the north and Kanyakumari & Kochi in the south, Porbandar in the west and Silchar in the east and another 486 km of highways.

Phase III and IV for upgrade to 4-lanes of 4,035 km and 8074 kms of National Highways respectively.

Phase V for upgrade to 6-lanes for 6,500 km, (of which 5,700 km on the GQ). This phase was entirely on a Design, Build, Finance and Operate basis.

Phase VI for development of 1,000 km of expressways.

Phase VII for development of ring-roads, bypasses and flyovers to avoid traffic bottlenecks on selected stretches.

NHAI helped implementing Special Accelerated Road Development Program for North Eastern Region (SARDP-NE); aimed to upgrade National Highways connecting north-eastern state capitals to 2 or 4 lanes. NHAI is responsible for the development and maintenance of National Highways, totalling over 92,851.05 km in the total of 1,32,499 km in India.

In June 2022, the NHAI created a Guinness World record by building 75 km of highway between Amravati and Akola in Maharashtra in a span of just 5 days.

National Highways & Infrastructure Development Corp.

NHIDC was established on 18.07.2014 for Developing, building (either alone or jointly with other companies) national highways, strategic roads, pathways, expressways and other infrastructure with focus on the North East and Border areas.

NHIDC is responsible for the development, maintenance and management of over 10000 km of National Highways in hilly terrain of North-East part of India, Andaman & Nicobar Islands, Himachal Pradesh, Jammu & Kashmir, Ladakh and Uttarakhand.

NHIDC (along with Border Roads Organization) has undertaken to implement the Special Accelerated Road Development Program for North Eastern Region (SARDP-NE) covering 5224 km of National Highways and 2598 km of State roads.

The projects being implemented by NHIDC are Char Dham, Imphal-Moreh Road (connectivity between India and Myanmar), Tawang Road, Kailash Manasarovar Road, South Asia Subregional Economic Cooperation Road, Zoji-la Tunnel (all weather connectivity between Srinagar and Leh), Z-Morh Tunnel, Shinku La Tunnel, Silkyara Tunnel, Dhubri-Phulbari bridge (to become longest bridge in India), etc.

Revenue from operations in 2022-23 was Rs. 474.22 Cr.

TCIL Bina Toll Road Limited

TCIL Bina Toll Road Limited - TBTRL was incorporated on 11.07.2012 as a subsidiary of TCIL for execution Bina-Kurwai-Sironj Toll Road.

The company is engaged in operation and maintenance of Bina Kurwai Sironj Toll Road project on BOT basis under Concession Agreement with Madhya Pradesh Road Development Corporation for a period of 25 years including 2 years construction period.

The said road project has since been completed and toll collection started from the date 25.04.2014.

TCIL Lakhnadone Toll Road Ltd

TCIL Lakhnadone Toll Road Ltd was incorporated on 21.08.2013 for execution of Lakhnadone - Ghansore Toll Road project on BOOT basis. The project was completed and toll collection started in July 2016.

IRCON PB Tollway Limited

IRCON PB Tollway Ltd was incorporated on 30.09.2014 to construct Bikaner Phalodi Project Highway on NH-15, maintain and operate the toll highway over Concession Period of 26 years from the appointed date of 14.10.2015.

IRCON Shivpuri Guna Tollway Limited

IRCON Shivpuri Guna Tollway Ltd was incorporated on 12.05.2015 to construct the Highway on Shivpuri-Guna section of NH-3, maintain and operate the toll highway over the Concession period of 20 years from the appointed date of 25.01.2016.

IRCON Davanagere Haveri Highway Limited

IRCON Davanagere - Haveri Highway Ltd. was incorporated on 11.05.2017 for widening to 6 lanes of Davanagere – Haveri stretch of NH-48 of length 78.923 km.

IRCON Vadodara Kim Expressway Limited

IRCON Vadodara Kim Expressway Ltd. was incorporated on 16.05.2018 for development, maintenance and management of 8 lane Vadodara Kim Expressway in Gujarat.

Ship Building Infrastructure Development and Shipping Companies

Freight Traffic by Sea in 1950-51

In 1949, 2600 sailing vessels carried about 1 to 1.5 Mts of cargo. (1.29.41)

India had a tonnage of 0.391 million GRT in 1950-51. (2.21.47)

The total Indian registered tonnage was 417,257 GRT in 1951 including the Moghul Line tonnage. There were 73 ships with 217,202 GRT on the Indian coast and 24 Indian-owned ships of 173,505 GRT in the overseas trades. (1.29.29)

Achievements in I 5YP

Vishakhapatnam Yard was acquisitioned and developed for shipbuilding. Loans and subsidy were given to shipping companies to purchase ships built in the Yard to bridge the difference between the cost of construction and the sale price. (1.29.31)

The net increase to Indian shipping tonnage during 1951-52 was 42,000 GRT through additions of 18 ships (including 3 ships built at the Visakhapatnam shipyard) (1.29.36)

Hindustan Shipyard Ltd. was established in 1952 and berths were expanded for building ships. (1.29.21).

The total tonnage of ships was 0.6 million GRT in 1955-56. (2.4.43)

Indian Overseas and Coastal Shipping Tonnage in 1956 were 0.24 million GRT (with 36 ships) and 0.24 million GRT (with 90 ships) respectively,

Achievements in II 5YP
After the expansion of **H**industan **S**hipyard **L**td. and the construction of a drydock, the shipyard was capable of producing ships of a tonnage of 50,000—60,000 **D**ead **W**eight **T**onnage / year.
Indian Overseas and Coastal Shipping Tonnage in 1961 were 0.55 million GRT (with 75 ships) and 0.31 million GRT (with 97 ships) respectively.

Achievements in III 5YP
Ships of 216,200 GRT were to be acquired in private sector and 158,300 GRT in public sector. (3.27.51)
Indian Overseas and Coastal Shipping Tonnage in 1966 were 1.22 million GRT (with 122 ships) and 0.32 million GRT (with 99 ships) respectively.
The production capacity of HSL Visakhapatnam in 1968-69 was 2-3 ships of 12,500 DWT each

Achievements in IV 5YP
Cochin Shipyard Ltd. was incorporated on 05.04.1972.
Indian Overseas and Coastal Shipping Tonnage in 1974 were 2.83 million GRT (with 214 ships) and 0.26 million GRT (with 60 ships) respectively.

Achievements in V 5YP
Indian Overseas and Coastal Shipping Tonnage were 5.29 million GRT (with 319 ships) in 1980 and 0.25 million GRT (with 56 ships) in 1983 respectively.

Achievements in VI 5YP –
Hindustan Shipyard Ltd. started building 40,000 DWT bulk carriers in addition to their existing pioneer class vessels. In 1984-85 this yard achieved 93 % capacity utilization. (7.7.120)
Garden Reach Shipbuilders and Engineers, and **Mazagaon Dock Ltd** were engaged in the production of naval ships, commercial ships of 68,000 GRT and platforms for ONGC.
The contributions from **HSL** and **Cochin Shipyard Ltd. (CSL)** were 113,860 GRT and 161,501 GRT respectively. Thus, the total production of the Indian shipyards was 339,361 GRT. (7.7.121)
HSL had already started production of 40,000 DWT bulk carriers in addition to their existing pioneer class vessels. It also diversified into production of off-shore platforms and support vessels for ONGC. (7.7.122)
CSL, which was originally designed to produce two ships of 75,000 DWT bulk carriers/ annum, was producing 68,000 DWT bulk carriers in 1984-85. (7.7.122)
India's total shipping tonnage in 1984-85 was 6.36 million GRT and coastal tonnage from 99 vessels was 0.345 million GRT. (8.9.15.3 / 4) (8.9.16.12)
Shipping **C**orporation of **I**ndia accounted for 3.345 million GRT. (52.59% of total shipping tonnage).

Achievements in VII 5YP
Ship Building in 1991-92 - There were 40 shipyards in India. Of these, 7 were in the public sector, 2 in the State sector and the remaining in the private sector. (8.5.17.1)
India's shipping tonnage was 6 million GRT (9.7 million DWT). (8.9.15.3)
Shipping Corporation of India accounted for 2.89 million GRT (4.86 million DWT) by March 1992. (8.9.15.4)
National Ship Design and Research Centre, Vishakhapatnam became operational in May 1993. NSDRC was involved in a diversified range of activities in shipbuilding and marine industry. (10.7.1.105)

Achievements in VIII 5YP
The production in HSL was 113,895 DWT and in CSL 69,033 DWT.
CSL achieved a turnover of Rs. 390.94 crore in ship repair activity. (9.5.142)

Ship Building in 1996-97
The ship building industry had been delicensed and was open to the private sector, irrespective of the size of ships, except for construction of war-ships.
There were 80 shipping companies including Shipping Corporation of India in the country. Of these, 10 principal private companies owned a fleet of 115 ships with a tonnage of 2.245 million GRT. SCI owned 118 ships with a tonnage of 3.037 million GRT accounting for 44.2% of the total tonnage of 6.87 million GRT. (9.7.1.217)
Shipping tonnage of India's shipping companies with fleet of 484 vessels in Dec. 1997 – 7.052 million GT
Shipping tonnage of Shipping Corporation of India with 121 ships – 3.123 million GT (10.8.3.181)

Achievements in IX 5YP
Ship Building in 2001-02 –
There were 28 shipyards in the country, 19 of them in the private sector. (The number of shipyards in the private sector reduced from 31 in 1991-92 to 19 in 2001-02. Did liberalization help?) **4 Public sector shipyards were capable of building large ocean-going vessels.** (10.7.1.100)
Mazagaon Dock Ltd., Garden Reach Shipbuilders & Engineers Ltd. and Goa Shipyard Ltd. were building a variety of ships and vessels primarily for Indian Navy and Coast Guard. (10.7.1.101)
The assessed production capacity of 4 large PSUs constituted 95% of the industry turnover. The annual shipbuilding capacity in India was 0.15 million Compensated Gross Tonnage. (11.7.1.102)
Export - 6 ships (0.3 million DWT) were exported in IX 5YP

Ship Cargo Traffic in 2001-02 (as on 1.03.2002)
Shipping tonnage of 102 shipping companies with fleet of 562 vessels - 6.91 million Gross Tonnage
Shipping tonnage of SCI with 97 ships - 2.64 million GT. (40% of national tonnage) (10.8.3.181)

Achievements in X 5YP
Ship Building in 2006-07
Shipping tonnage from 787 vessels was 8.60 million GT. (11.9.4.3)
Due to the speculation regarding its disinvestment, the SCI acquired only 9 vessels of 0.79 million GT during X plan. (11.9.4.22)
With 8.42 million GT, India stood at the 20th rank among maritime nations, in terms of fleet size, with a share of 1.19% of the world fleet. (11.9.4.1)
SCI had a major share in India's shipping tonnage. Oil tankers accounted for 60.6% of the total Indian shipping fleet tonnage, bulk carriers accounted for 29.6%, with the other vessel types such as liner vessels, OSVs accounting for a mere 9.8%.
Indian shipbuilding was Centreed around 27 shipyards comprising 8 public sector (6 yards under Central Government and 2 under State Governments) and 19 private sector shipyards. (Why there was no increase in private sector shipyards in 5 years after liberalization?) The shipyards between them had 20 dry docks and 40 slipways with an estimated capacity of 281200 DWT. **A major share of this ship building capacity was held by the 8 public sector yards** and only CSL (110000 DWT) and HSL (80000 DWT) had the required infrastructure and graving dock to build large vessels. (11.7.1.265)

Private Sector Contribution - 5 Of the private sector companies were in the process of expanding or setting up new capacities, including for building Very Large Crude Carrier size ships, (11.7.1.266)
The net aggregate contribution of Shipping sector to the national economy was of the order of 2.5–3% of the national GDP. (11.9.4.6)

Coastal Shipping in 2006-07

A total of 497 vessels of 0.817 million GRT comprised the Indian coastal vessels tonnage as on 31.03.2006. Those days, coastal shipping also included activities like offshore supply and multi-purpose support for the oil and gas exploration and production, port and harbor services, and dredging.

Export Market for Ships - India's share in the world market increased from 0.1% in 2001-02 to 1.3% in 2006 with contribution from CSL, and three private sector shipyards, viz., ABG, Bharati, and Chowgule. The Indian ship-repair industry was having an average turnover of around US$ 76 million. (11.7.1.267) India emerged as a major supplier for offshore and oil industry ships such as Offshore Supply Vessels and anchor handling tugs. (11.7.1.268)

Ship Repair Industry

In India there was only one dedicated ship repair unit and all the other yards carried out ship repairs and shipbuilding side by side. There were 35 SRUs of which only 7 SRUs were registered on a permanent basis. (11.7.1.281)
During the X 5YP, the ship repair industry achieved an annual turnover of Rs 436 crore. (11.7.1.282)
Only CSL and HSL, were able to provide dry dock and repair facilities for large size vessels. There was no dry dock facility for VLCC class of vessels. Even Suez-max size vessels did not have dry docking facilities in India. (11.7.1.284)

Sethusamudram Corporation Limited

The Sethusamudram Ship Channel Project was incorporated in 2004 with the objective of creating a navigable channel from Gulf of Munnar to Bay of Bengal / Palk Bay, to save up to 424 nautical miles of navigation and up to 30 hours sailing time for ships plying between the east and west coasts. (11.9.5.8)

The dredging works in the proposed channel (at Palk Strait and Adam's bridge area) was entrusted to Dredging Corporation of India in June 2005. The dredging works at Adam's Bridge was commenced on 11.12.2006. Out of 48.05 million Cum about 9.52 million Cum of dredging was completed.
(In 2014, the government decided to implement the project by deepening the Pampan pass to save Rama Sethu from destruction. As of December 2020, the project remains unfinished.)

Achievements in XI 5YP
Shipping tonnage from 1,135 vessels was 11.03 million GT on 30.06.2012. (12.15.124)
On 31.03.12, oil tankers accounted for 63.76% of the DWT, bulk carriers accounted for 28.77% and all other vessel types such as liner vessels, Off-shore Support Vessels accounted for 7.47%. (12.15.123)

Coastal Shipping

The coastal fleet of 764 vessels accounted for 1 million GT as on 31.03.2012. (12.15.148)

Ship Building Industry in 2019-20
The maximum size of the vessels, which can be built in the public sector was 1,10,000 DWT at Cochin shipyard. Reliance Naval Engineering Ltd. had the capacity to build vessels up to 400,000 DWT and L&T Shipbuilding Ltd., Kattupalli, Chennai up to 300,000 DWT which included large LNG Carriers.
Smaller size LNG Carriers, Dredgers and other specialized vessels can be built by other shipyards also in the Private sector such as Shoft Shipyard Pvt Ltd., Chowgule & Co., Vijai Marine Shipyard, Mandovi Dry Docks, A.C. Roy & Co., Dempo Shipbuilding & Engineering Pvt Ltd etc. (Annual Report 2019-20, Min. of Shipping-5.15)

Ship Repair Industry in 2019-20
Amongst public sector shipyards, Cochin Shipyard Ltd had the highest capacity for ship repairing (125 thousand DWT). (Annual Report 2019-20, Min. of Shipping-5.20)

Ship Building Industry in 2022-23

There were 43 ship yards, 8 under central public sector (CSL, Hooghly CSL, Udupi CSL and Hooghly Dock and Port Engineers Ltd, Mazagaon Dock Ltd, GRSE, GSL and HSL), 2 under state governments (Alcock Ashdown Co. Ltd. Gujarat, Shalimar Works Ltd, WB) and 33 under private sector.
CSL is increasing its capacity to build ships from 110000 DWT to 300000 DWT.
India's share in global ship repair was less than 1% in 2022-23. (5.19 – Annual Report 2022-23)

Graph 15.3 – International & Coastal Shipping Traffic carried by Indian Vessels; Ship Building Capacity & Ships Built - Removed

Contribution by Shipping Corporation of India for 5YPs –

VII 5YP – The total internal resource generation of the Shipping Corp. of India during VII Plan was Rs.706 crores. (8.9.15.5)

XII 5YP – The outlay for the Shipping Sector included Rs. 6,960 Cr as GBS and Rs. 21,990 Cr as IEBR. (12.15.191)

Hindustan Shipyard Ltd.

Hindustan Shipyard Ltd. – HSL was set up in 1941 in the private sector and was taken over by the Government on 21.1.1952. The mission HSL was to undertake shipbuilding, ship repair and retrofitting of submarines, offshore platforms construction and structural fabrication to meet the growing requirements of Mercantile, Marine, Oil and Defence sectors.

3 ships were built at the Visakhapatnam shipyard in 1951-52.
Expansion of HSL was taken up during II 5YP to increase the rate of construction of ships to 6 of the old type or 4 of the modem type and construction of a dry dock at Visakhapatnam to produce ships of a total tonnage of 50,000—60,000 DWT/ year.
The production capacity of HSL in 1968-69 was 2-3 ships of 12,500 DWT.
HSL achieved a production of 3 ships of 21,600 DWT/ annum during V 5YP.
HSL started building 40,000 DWT bulk carriers in addition to pioneer class vessels.
The contribution from HSL was 113,860 GRT in 1984-85, achieving 93% capacity utilization. (7.7.120/121)
The shipyard diversified into production of off-shore platforms and support vessels for ONGC. (7.7.122)
During VIII 5YP, the production of HSL was 113,895 DWT. HSL was building standard (21,500 DWT) pioneer class type vessels. (9.5.140)
HSL had a ship building capacity of 0.07525 million DWT in 2008-09.

HSL was a profit-making company till 1980. Ministry of Defence nominated HSL for construction of Landing Platform Docks. The installed capacity for ship building and repair in 2019-20 was 18142 Compensated Gross Tonnage.

HSL has achieved highest ever turnover and net profit during 2022-23 and bestowed with 8 prestigious awards including Best Ship Repair Facility of the Year. Revenue from operations in 2022-23 was Rs. 1072.94 Cr.

Garden Reach Shipbuilders & Engineers Ltd.

Garden Reach Shipbuilders & Engineers Ltd. - GRSE was set up in 1884 as River Steam Navigation Co. and was subsequently converted into a limited liability company Garden Reach Workshop Ltd. in 1934. The company was taken over by Govt. of India on 12.04.1960 to make it into a lead shipyard and to strengthen the Indian Navy, Coast Guard and maritime potential by building high-tech warships and to achieve self-sufficiency in the defense requirement. The company was renamed as GRSE in 1977 due to its diversified product range as a result of taking over a number of sick engineering units.

GRSE is building modern high-tech warships to Hovercraft and support vessels viz., frigates, corvettes, LST(L)'s, fleet replacement tanker, survey vessels, Missile Corvettes, ASW Corvettes, Fast Attack Craft, Water Jet Fast Attack Craft, Fast Patrol Vessels, Interceptor Boats etc. and auxiliary vessels for the Navy and the Coast Guard and manufacturing of Bailey Bridges and ship borne machinery and systems along with value engineering items like diesel engine and pump through its 8 units at Kolkata and Ranchi.

GRSE got auxiliary / Offshore Support Vessels constructed through private shipyards. R & D developed Water Jet Fast Attack Crafts and ASW Corvettes for Indian Navy.
GRSE was also undertaking assembly of various types of MTU engines at its Engine Plant at Ranchi under license agreement with MTUF Germany.
GRSE acquired Raja Bagan Dockyard from Central Inland Water Transport Corp in 2006.
GRSE had a fabrication capacity for 3230 Tons of ship building and 2500 Tons of general engineering products and manufacturing capacity for 720 pumps and 36 diesel engines in 2008-09.
GRSE ventured into building Pollution Control and Research vessels, Air Cushion Vehicles, Dredgers, Boats for MHA, River crafts for Inland Waterways Authority of India etc.

Kamorta-Class Anti-Submarine Warfare Corvette, INS Kiltan, was built by GRSE in 2017-18.
GRSE launched Portable bridge made of carbon fibre polymer composite material for use by pedestrians and light vehicles in 2019.
The installed capacity of GRSE in 2019-20 was 75 sets of Deck machinery and pump, 88 sets of Diesel engines, 3603 tons of General engineering and 3223 tons of Ship building.

GRSE designed the most silent ship for Indian Navy for Anti-Submarine Warfare Shallow Water Craft operations in 2022-23. Revenue from operations in 2022-23 was Rs. 2561.15 Cr.

Mazagaon Dock Shipbuilders Ltd

Mazagaon Dock Ltd. - MDL was a ship repair yard incorporated on 26.2.1934 and taken over by Government of India in 1960 to cater to the needs of defense sector by building warships for Indian Navy and provide lead yard services to other defense shipyards.

MDL undertakes construction of Naval ships, submarines, Coast Guard ships, merchant vessels, fabrication of offshore platforms, repair of ship and HDW class of submarines, refitting of submarines etc. through its 3 units at Mumbai and Nhava.
MDL had a ship and submarine building capacity of 0.97 Effective Frigate Units in 2008-09.

One destroyer, 1 Frigate and 1 Multipurpose Support Vessel were launched in 2010.
MDL built 12 Frigates, 7 Destroyers, 1 Cadet Training Ship, 3 Missile Corvettes, 4 Missile Boats and 2 Submarines for the Indian Navy and 7 offshore Patrol Vessels for Coast Guard (in 2011-12). Besides, MDL had also fabricated Cargo Ships, Passenger Ships, Supply Vessels, Tugs etc. MDL's share in repair of warships in 2011-12 was 85%.
MDL was constructing 6 Missile Destroyers, 6 Submarines for Indian Navy in 2013-14.

In 2016-17, MDL was constructing 3 major warships, 7 Submarine, 4 stealth Frigate, 4 Destroyers, 4 Frigates class of ships and state of the art Scorpene submarines. INS Kalvari submarine was delivered to Indian Navy on 21.09.2017.
INS Karanj submarine was launched on 31.01.2018.
Scorpene Submarine INS Khanderi and INS Vela, Frigate INS Nilgiri and Destroyer INS Imphal were delivered in 2019.

The installed capacity for building and repairing warships and submarines was 1420 tons in 2019-20.

Destroyers, INS Mormugao and INS Surat, Scorpene Submarines INS Vagir and INS Vaghsheer, Nilgiri Class Frigate, INS Taragiri and INS Udaygiri were delivered in 2022-23.

Shipping Corporation of India

Shipping Corporation of India Ltd. - SCI was incorporated on 2.10.1961 merging 2 shipping companies Eastern Shipping Corp. and Western Shipping Corp. to serve India's overseas and costal sea born trades, offshore and other marine transport infrastructure. In 1973, the ailing Jayanti Shipping Co. was taken over by GOI and amalgamated with SCI. The Mogul Line Ltd., a Government of India enterprise, was also merged with SCI in 1986. SCI became a public limited company w.e.f. 18.09.1992. The net profit of SCI was Rs.323 Cr in 1995-96. (9.7.1.218)

The Foreign Exchange earnings of SCI were Rs.2310.06 Cr during 1996-97 out of Rs. 5008 Cr earned by Indian shipping industry. (9.7.1.220)

In 2004-05, SCI was operating 87 vessels of 2.67 million GT and also had 1 vessel of 16834 GT on lease. **SCI owned over 40.5% of Indian shipping fleet tonnage in 2004-05.**

The dividend payment was Rs 239.9 Cr in 2005–06.

The net profit of SCI increased to Rs 1042.2 Cr, the fixed assets to Rs 5729.8 Cr and net worth to Rs 4355.4 Cr in 2006-07, reflecting a rise in the level of reserves and surplus to Rs 4077.8 Cr. (11.9.4.23)

In 2007-08, the In-chartered container vessel tonnage operated by SCI comprised 5 vessels of 1,94,461 DWT and 13,556 TEU.

On 31.3.2008, overall fleet position of SCI was 79 with a total capacity of 47,60,469 DWT.

Joint ventures of SCI were SCI Forbes Ltd., Irano-Hind Shipping Co., India LNG Transport Companies (No.1 /2 /3) Ltd., India LNG Transport Company No. 4 S.A., Sethusamudram Corporation Ltd., Petronet LNG Project and SAIL SCI Shipping Pvt Ltd.

SCI also has a subsidiary 'Inland and Coastal Shipping Ltd'.

The fleet of SCI constituted **10 different types of vessels** i.e., dry cargo vessels, cellular container vessels, bulk carriers, crude carriers, product carriers, combination carriers, LPG / Ammonia carriers, phosphoric acid / chemical carriers, off shore supply vessels, anchor handling and towing ships and passenger cum-cargo vessels. In addition, SCI **managed 52 vessels on behalf of others** - 22 vessels on behalf of ONGC Ltd., 20 vessels for Andaman and Nicobar Islands, 5 for UT of Lakshadweep, 3 for Geological Survey of India and 2 for D/o Ocean Development.

SCI undertakes **coastal operations** with 2 of its owned vessels and 32 managed vessels on behalf of Government of India for Andaman & Nicobar and Lakshadweep Administrations. It also operated **Passenger-cum-cargo services** to and from main land to A & N Island and the Inter Islands.

SCI employed **10 Offshore vessels** to meet operational requirements of ONGC during 2007- 08.

In 2010-11, SCI's fleet consisted of 81 vessels. In addition, SCI was operating 20 offshore supply vessels and 5 specialized vessels of ONGC under O&M contract.

SCI held about **38% of the national tonnage of ships in 2013-14.**

With the acquisition of a second-hand Suez-max tanker on 26.04.2017, SCI's total fleet strength of 70 vessels aggregated to 6.01mn DWT.

During 2019-20, SCI commenced East Coast of India Express Service to increase inter connectivity and promote Sagarmala Project for developing Indian coastal ecosystem.

SCI as on 31.12.2019 owned 60 vessels of 5.46 million DWT/ 3.02 million GT and constituted 28% (in terms of DWT) of Indian tonnage. (Annual Report 2019-20, Ministry of Shipping – 6.57)

SCI on 1.1.2023, owned 59 vessels of 5.311 million DWT / 2.94 million GT and constituting 26% (in terms of DWT) of Indian tonnage. (13 Crude carriers, 5 VLCC, 13 Product carriers, 1 Gas carrier, 15 dry bulk carriers, 2 liner vessels and 10 Offshore supply vessels)

Inland and Coastal Shipping Ltd.

Established on 29.09.2016. ICSLs fleet caters to inland movement of variety of cargoes like iron ore, coal, coke, grain, fertilizer, steel product, etc.

Goa Shipyard Limited

Goa Shipyard Limited - GSL was established on 26.11.1957 by the Portuguese as 'Estalerios Navais De Goa', as a small barge repair facility. It was leased to Mazagaon Dock Ltd. following the liberation of Goa in 1961 till 1967. It was renamed as Goa Shipyard Ltd. in 1967.

GSL started designing and building high tech sophisticated warships since 1990 onwards.
GSL undertakes shipbuilding, ship repair and engineering services in its shipyard at Vasco Da Gama. GSL has set up facilities for GRP boats construction at Sancoale, Goa. Unit-IV was acquired to support Ship Repair and general engineering services.
The product range includes Offshore Patrol Vessels, Missile Crafts, Sail Training Ships, Tugs, Boats, Fishing and Passenger Vessels, Shore based test facilities, Damage Control Simulator, Survival at Sea Training Facility, stern gear system parts and spares for ships etc.

During 2004-05, one Survival at Sea Training Facility was delivered to ONGC.
Goa Shipyard Ltd. had a ship building capacity of 5.85 Standard Ship Units in 2008-09.
Royal Haskoning, Netherlands was appointed to modernize the yard. Modernization program comprising 6000 Ton ship lift with the ship transfer facility, etc. were commissioned in May 2011.

GSL delivered 35 Knots Fast Patrol Vessels and Advanced Offshore Patrol Vessels to Indian Coast Guard. GSL undertook construction of weapon intensive P11356 Frigates for Indian navy in collaboration with Russia in 2019-20.
The installed capacity for ship building, ship repair and general engineering in 2019-20 was 2 Standard Ship Units. (After 2013, 1 SSU = 105M Offshore Patrol Vessel).

GSL created infrastructure for Mine Counter Measure Vessels program of Indian Navy to build advanced MCMVs during 2022-23.

Cochin Shipyard Ltd.

Cochin Shipyard Ltd. - CSL was incorporated on 05.04.1972 io take over the erstwhile Cochin Shipyard Project under technical collaboration with M/s Mitsubishi, Japan.

CSL undertakes shipbuilding, ship repair and Marine Engineering training. CSL commenced shipbuilding activities in 1975 and the first vessel 'Rani Padmini', a bulk carrier built for Shipping Corporation India, was launched in 1980.
The contribution from CSL was 161,501 GRT in 1984-85. (7.7.121)
CSL, with design capacity to produce two bulk carriers of 75,000 DWT/ annum, was producing 68,000 DWT bulk carriers in 1984-85. (7.7.122)
During VIII 5YP, the production in CSL was 69,033 DWT. CSL had design capacity for building large size (86000 DWT) Panamax type vessels and oil tankers. (9.5.140)

CSL ventured into ship repair business in 1981. CSL had a share of 50% of the Indian ship repair market in 2007-08.

CSL had a ship building capacity of 0.15 million DWT in 2008-09.
CSL was the leading shipyard capable of constructing largest ships in the country. The largest and the most prestigious **aircraft carrier INS Vikrant** was built and launched on 12.08.2013 and commissioned on 2.09.2022.
CSL which was originally building 1 ship every 3 years was delivering 5 to 7 ships a year in 2010-11 and 2013-14. The clientele included foreign owners of nations like Norway, Cyprus etc.

The installed capacity for ship building in 2019-20 was 149993 DWT.
CSL undertook construction of oil rigs of both ONGC and other foreign companies.

The second 500 PAX vessel was delivered to Andaman and Nicobar Administration on 5.07.2022.

Udupi Cochin Shipyards Ltd

Established on 9.07.1984.

Consequent to takeover of Tebma Shipyards Ltd by Cochin Shipyard Ltd in September 2020 through statutory insolvency resolution process, revamping of infrastructure facilities were carried out at Malpe for commencing the operations. Out of the 3 facilities at Malpe, the revival of Babuthotta warehouse is completed and is operational. The revival of Hangakatta unit, revamping activities at Malpe Harbor Complex and restoration of main new building shop were progressing.
Udupi Cochin Shipyard Ltd mainly focuses on building fishing vessels (especially deep sea fishing vessels), tugs and specialized crafts of up to 80M length.

Revenue from operations in 2022-23 was Rs. 39.17 Cr.

Hooghly Dock & Port Engineers Ltd.

Hooghly Dock & Port Engineers Ltd. - HDPEL was incorporated in 1984 to acquire the business of Hooghly Docking and Engineering Co. Ltd., one of the oldest shipyards established in private sector for construction of fishing trawlers, barges, small passenger vessels, small crafts etc.

HDPEL was engaged in shipbuilding and ship repairing through its units at Salkia and Nazirgunge in Howrah, which had potential for construction of various ships, tugs, crafts, dredgers, floating dry docks, fire flout, mooring launches, fishing trawlers, pontoons and sophisticated vessels like offshore platform, supply-cum-support vessels, multipurpose harbor vessels, grab hopper dredger, lighthouse tender vessels, oil pollution control vessels etc.
Salkia Work had dry dock facility available along with 2 building berths. It manufactured a maximum size of vessels of 15,000 DWT. Nazirgunge Works also has 2 building berths for manufacturing maximum size of vessels of 15,000 DWT.
The yard had the capacity to build vessels of 400-500 passenger cum cargo carrying capacity and also 300 tons capacity Cargo Vessels.

HDPEL also undertook repair of vessels at KOPT Dry Docks adjacent to Kidderpore Dock complex of Kolkata Port Trust.

Govt of India approved the revival plan through formation of joint venture with private sector player on 13.10.2011.
The government brought in CSL as a strategic partner and **H**ooghly **C**ochin **S**hipyard **L**td was formed.

Nazirgunge facility was modernized and equipped for the construction of Ro-Ro vessels, river-sea cargo vessels for bulk, liquids, containers, passenger vessels and other watercraft for the inland waterways.
The Inland Water Authority of India and HCSL signed an MoU for setting up the new 'Ship Repair Facility' at Pandu.

With Cochin Shipyard Ltd. acquiring balance 26% shares of HDPEL in November 2019, Hooghly Cochin Shipyard Ltd became a wholly owned subsidiary of CSL.

HDPEL is undergoing process of closure as on 31.03.2023.

Indian Port Rail & Ropeway Corporation Ltd

Indian Port Rail & Ropeway Corporation Ltd was formed on 10.07.2015 to provide efficient rail evacuation systems to major ports and thereby enhance their handling capacity and efficiency.

Ports Infrastructure Development

Port Infrastructure in 1947
In 1947, India's foreign trade was carried on through 5 major ports of Calcutta, Bombay, Madras, Cochin and Visakhapatnam. These ports had a capacity to handle 20 Mts of cargo excluding petroleum. (1.31.49)

Kandla port project was taken up for implementation in 1949. (1.31,50).
Cargo traffic carried by major ports in 1950-51 was 19.38 Mts. (10. Ann. 8.3.1)
Port facilities were provided at Trombay for the petroleum refineries, which were being set up by Standard Vacuum Oil Co and Burmah-Shell Oil Co and expected to be commissioned before 1955. (1.31.51)

Achievements in I 5YP -
At Kandla, the bunder and the oil berth started functioning. At Bombay marine oil terminal, capability for berthing the largest oil tankers and connecting sub-marine pipelines to the mainland were provided.
During I 5YP, the capacity of the major ports increased to 25 Mts. (2.21.54)

Achievements in II 5YP
Number of major ports – 9. (7.8.1)
The 150 minor ports of India were estimated to handle 6 Mts of traffic every year. (3.27.61)
Cargo traffic carried by major ports was 33.18 million tons in 1960-61.

Minor Ports Survey Organization was created in 1962 to carry out (i) hydrographic surveys for minor ports and inland waterways, required for construction and extension of ports, harbors and inland waterways, (ii) surveys of rivers for navigation and flood control, coastal erosion etc. and (iii) general navigational surveys of harbors, creeks and approaches, including those of the Andaman and Nicobar Islands and Lakshadweep Islands. (10.8.3.171)

Achievements in III 5YP -
The **Andaman Lakshadweep Harbor Works** was set up in 1965 for planning, execution and maintenance of the port and harbor facilities in the Andaman and Nicobar Islands and Lakshadweep Islands. (10.8.3.169)
Haldia Ancillary port was completed in 1968 to provide facilities for handling bulk cargo such as coal, iron ore and food grains. (The general cargo was expected to continue to be handled at Calcutta. (3.27.56)
Intermediate ports at Paradip (to handle 5 lakh tons of iron ore), Neendakara (Kerala), Karwar, Kakinada, Masulipatnam, Cuddalore, Ratnagiri, Redi, Bhavnagar, Porbandar, Okha etc. were developed.

Port Infrastructure in 1970-71 (7.8.1)
Number of major ports – 10

Cargo traffic handled by major and minor ports were 55.58 Mts and 6.69 Mts respectively. (10.Ann. 8.3.1)

Achievements in IV 5YP -
i) Completion of Mangalore and Tuticorin port projects,
ii) Construction of a satellite port for Bombay at Nhava Sheva and
iii) **Central Dredging Organization** was set up to meet the capital dredging requirements of major and minor ports.
iv) **Minor Ports Dredging and Survey Organization** was set up for development of ports facilities in Andaman and Nicobar Islands, Laccadive, Minicoy and Amindivi Islands and a few other selected ports such as Porbandar, Mirya Bay, Cuddalore etc. (4.15.21)

Achievements in V 5YP
i)
Completion of Mormugao and Mangalore during 1976-77 (5.5.112)
ii) Development of port facilities in the Andaman and Nicobar Islands and Lakshadweep. (5.5.114)

Achievements in VI 5YP
Cargo traffic handled by major and minor ports in 1980-81 were 80.27 Mts and 6.73 Mts respectively. (10. Ann. 8.3.1)
i) Installation of container handling equipment for Bombay, Madras, Cochin, Vishakhapatnam, Kandia, Paradip, Mangalore and Tuticorin.
ii) Development of Port Blair, Chetlat and Kavaratti breakwater at Campbell Bay, deep water wharf at Port Blair, breakwater and wharf at Mus in Car Nicobar.

Achievements in VII 5YP
Jawahar Lal Nehru Port with a capacity of 5.9 Mts was commissioned in May, 1989.

Port Infrastructure in 1990-91
There were 11 major ports in 1990-91 - Calcutta and Haldia, Mumbai, Chennai, Cochin, Kandla, Visakhapatnam, Paradip, Tuticorin, New Mangalore, Mormugao and Jawahar Lal Nehru and 139 operable minor / intermediate ports.
Cargo traffic handled by major and minor ports were 151.67 Mts and 11.27 Mts respectively. (10. Ann. 8.3.1)

Achievements in VIII 5YP
(i) Development of deep-water Kakinada Port was completed with ADB loan assistance. (9.7.1.209)
(ii) Development of port and harbor facilities in Andaman and Nicobar Islands and Lakshadweep (9.7.1.210)
Cargo traffic handled by major and minor ports in 1996-97 were 227.26 Mts and 24.93 Mts respectively. (10. Ann. 8.3.1)
AP Govt. undertook development Kakinada, Machilipatnam, Vodarevu, Nizampatnam and Bhavanapadu. (9.7.1.209)

Privatization of Port Trusts
Government awarded construction, management and maintenance of 2 berths container terminal at JNPT, to augment the container handling capacity to 1 million TEUs on BOT basis to a consortium headed by an Australian firm. (9.7.1.198)

Achievements in IX 5YP
Capacity addition of 92.35 Mts was achieved by projects executed by ports and 32.5 Mts by BOT schemes of private sector.

Out of the 184 minor / intermediate ports, only 53 were well developed and provided all weather berthing facilities for cargo handling. The remaining catered to fishing boats, passenger boats etc. (10.8.3.166)
Cargo traffic handled by major and minor ports in 1999-2000 were 271.87 Mts and 62.52 Mts respectively. (10. Ann. 8.3.1)
7.2 Tons Container Terminal of JNPT was developed by NSICT, a consortium led by P&O Ports, Australia in 1999. (10. Ann. 8.3.9)

Excess Port capacity - The targeted traffic of 289.10 Mts and the anticipated capacity of 344.4 Mts at the terminal year of IX 5YP indicated that port capacity was no more a constraint. Hence, in X 5TP, there was a need only to improve productivity at the major ports and reduce the turnaround time of ships. (10.8.3.146)

Achievements in X Plan
Port Infrastructure in 2004-05
Coastal traffic at major ports - 109.80 mt, accounting for 28.6% of the total major ports traffic. (11.9.4.17)

Private Sector Participation in Ports Operation –

The government implemented a scheme for private participation in major ports mainly in container terminals, specialized cargo berths, warehousing / storage facilities, etc. on BOT basis with a concession period not exceeding 30 years.
(i) 5.5 Tons Liquid cargo berth of JNPT was completed by BPCL/IOCL.
(ii) Captive coal berths of Tuticorin, Pir Pau and New Mangalore Port, Captive berth of Paradip, Container Terminal at Chennai, multipurpose berths at Mormugao, Vizag, Haldia Dock Complex (2 contracts) and Indira Dock Mumbai were awarded to SEPC, Tata Electric Companies, Nagarjuna Power Corporation Ltd., Oswal Fertilizers Ltd, jointly to Chennai Port Trust and P&O Ports, Australia, ABG Goa Port Ltd., Gammon, consortium comprising TISCO and IQ Martrade GMBH (Germany), ISP Ltd, United Lined Agencies Ltd. respectively.
During X 5YP, 8 private sector schemes were completed adding 44.40 Mts of handling capacity. (11.9.5.7)
The total major port capacity was 504.75 Mt in 2006–07 and that of non-major and private ports was 228.31 Mt. (12.15.170)

Achievements in XI 5YP

Coastal Shipping
Out of the total traffic at major ports of 560.90 Mts, coastal traffic was 107.94 Mts with the coastal fleet of 764 vessels accounting for merely over a million GT as on 31.03. 2012. (12.15.148)
Almost 95% by volume and 70% by value of India's global merchandise trade was carried through the sea route in 2011-12. (12. 15.169)

Port Infrastructure
12 Major ports handled about 60% of the maritime cargo of the country. The balance was handled by 200 plus non-major ports. 11 Major ports are administered by the respective Port Trusts and Ennore Port, which started functioning in February 2001, is corporatized. (12.15.169)
The total major port capacity created was 689.83 MT. (12. Table 15.31) Capacity of non-major and private ports was 544.65 MT in 2011-12. (12.15.170)
Major port capacities in 2012-13 to 2016-17 were 744.91 Mts, 800.52 Mts, 871.52 Mts, 965.36 Mts, 1065.83 Mts Rerated to → 1359 Mts, 2017-18 to 2021-22 were 1451.09 Mts, 1514.09 Mt, 1534.91 Mt, 1560.61 Mt and 1597.59 Mt respectively.

Private Sector Participation

Up to 2011–12, 30 PPPs involving capacity addition of 204.65 MT were completed. (12.15.173)
The private sector was expected to invest nearly Rs. 1,70,000 Cr in the Port Sector during XII plan (12.15.191)

Container Cargo

Container cargo in India, which formed only 15.8% of total cargo handled in major ports in 2006–07, increased to 21.5% in 2011–12. (12.15.186)

Traffic Handled by Ports in 2021-22

Major and non-major ports handled a total cargo throughput of 1323.88 million Mt. Major ports handled 720.05 million Mt. (Annual Report 2022-23, Ministry of Shipping)

Contribution by Port Trusts for 5YPs

IV 5YP - The Port Trusts were expected to contribute Rs. 100 Cr from their own resources (4.15.20)

VI 5YP - The provision for VI plan included about Rs. 200 Cr to be contributed by Port Trusts from their own resources. (6.17.70)

VII 5YP – (i) The contribution of 'Other Central Enterprises' including Ports and DVC, taken together, was estimated at Rs. 31,500 Cr (7.4.32)

(ii) Rs.701.00 Cr or 52% of VII plan expenditure for ports came from the internal resources and inter-corporate loans of major ports. (8.9.19.1)

VIII 5YP – Rs.1521.42 Cr or 80% came from the internal resources and inter-corporate loans of major ports for VIII plan. (9.7.1.184)

XI 5YP – An outlay of Rs. 30,323.11 Cr (at 2006–07 prices) was approved for the port sector in XI plan, comprising Rs. 3,315 Cr as GBS and Rs. 26,574.11 Cr through IEBR. (12.15.177)

Graph 15.4 – Traffic Handling Capacity & Traffic Handled by Major and Non-Major Ports - Removed

Port Trust Board (India)

India's first Port Trust Board was established for Calcutta Port in 1870. Bombay Port Trust in 1879 and Madras Port Trust in 1905. The administration of Port Trust Boards was brought under national government in 1963.

Board members included representatives of Central government, labor employed in the port, ship owners, owners of sailing vessels, shippers, and such other interests, which in the opinion of the Central Government, ought to be locally represented.

Currently there are 13 major ports (Mumbai, Kolkata, Chennai, Kandla, Jawaharlal Nehru Port, Mormugao, New Mangalore, Cochin, V.O. Chidambaranar Port, Port Blair (Andaman and Nicobar Islands), Visakhapatnam, Paradip) and Ennore. All except Ennore Port are administered by a Port Trust Board. Ennore Port is a public co. limited by guarantee, and fully owned by the national government.

Ennore Port Ltd.

Ennore Port Ltd. - EPL was incorporated on 11.10.1999 to provide world class port and trans-shipment hubs for providing cargo handling and port services. Operation of the port commenced in June 2001. Modern unloading equipment and conveyors were installed on 2 coal berths by TNEB to handle coal needed for its Thermal Power Station.

Ennore port is the first corporate port under which most of the port services are outsourced and the port discharges only certain statutory and regulatory functions.

EPL is functioning on a Landlord Management Model. All the cargo handling facilities are being developed mainly through the private sector on BOT basis. The common facilities such as creation of necessary depths in the harbor and in the channel by dredging, aids to navigation, road / rail connectivity, etc. are funded and developed by EPL.

The cargo handling capacity of the port in 2007-08, 2010-11, 2013-14, 2016-17 and 2017-18 were 12 Mt, 15 Mt, 30 Mt, 32 Mt and Rerated 67.6 Mt respectively.

The capacity of coal handling facility was 12 MTPA in 2013-14.

EPL undertook 46 Mt Marine Liquid Terminal, Coal Terminal, Iron Ore Terminal, Container Terminal and LNG Terminal projects with private sector participation on BOT bass.

Government disinvested 66.67% stake in KPL for Rs. 2383 Cr to Chennai Port Trust in March 2020.

Indian Ports Global Ltd.

Indian Ports Global Ltd. - IPGPL, promoted jointly by Jawaharlal Nehru Port Trust and Deendayal Port Trust, was incorporated on 22.01.2015 for undertaking construction and development of ports and their common facilities, equipping and operation of terminals for port activities.

Company is currently engaged in equipping and operation of Chabahar Port. India Ports Global Chabahar Free Zone, Iran was incorporated on 03.06.2018 and operation started on 25.12.2018.

Indian Port Rail and Ropeway Corporation Ltd.

Indian Port Rail Corporation Ltd. - IPRCL was incorporated on 10.07.2015 (the company subsequently diversified into Ropeways and the name was accordingly changed to "Indian Port Rail & Ropeway Corp. Ltd") to provide rail evacuation systems to Ports in India by creating last mile connectivity of the ports, modernize the rail infrastructure at ports; create and manage internal port railway system, develop, operate & maintain ropeways and other modern transit systems.

Sagarmala Development Company Ltd.

Sagarmala Development Co. Ltd. - SDCL was incorporated on 31.08.2016 to undertake green field and brown field ports development, last mile connectivity to the ports and other relevant activities under Sagarmala Program. (Annual Report 2019-20, Ministry of Shipping – 6.80)

Dredging Corporation of India Ltd.

Dredging Corporation of India Ltd. - DCI was incorporated on 29.03.1976 to provide integrated dredging and related marine services for promoting the national and international maritime trade, beach nourishment, land reclamation, inland dredging, environmental protection, etc.

DCI undertakes ocean, maintenance and capital dredging, beach nourishment and land reclamation through its units located at Haldia, Kolkata, Paradip, Visakhapatnam, Mumbai, Chennai, Kochi, Goa, Ennore and Kandla and one overseas office at Bahrain.

DCI's customers include major ports, non-major ports, private ports, the Indian Navy and shipyards, etc.

The market share of DCI during 2003-04 was 88.90%. The domestic market share in maintenance dredging was 79% and in capital dredging 100% during 2006-07.

Disinvestment – Refer Ch. 17

DCI started commercial operations at Bangladesh and commenced capital dredging work at Mongla Port during 2017-18.

Strategic sale – Refer Ch. 17

Inland Waterways Transport (IWT) - Removed

Kaladan Multimodal Transport Project

This project was to provide connectivity from Mizoram to Haldia / Kolkata ports through River Kaladan in Myanmar. The project envisages Coastal / Maritime Shipping from Haldia to Sittwe, Inland Water Transportation from Sittwe to Paletwa (in Myanmar) and thereafter by road from Paletwa to Mizoram. Construction of port was completed in May 2023. (12.15.161)

Central Inland Water Transport Corporation (CIWTC)

Central Inland Water Transport Corporation - CIWTC was set up on 22.2.1967 by taking over sick units of Royal Steam Navigation and Company to undertake a) Lighterage operations on the Hooghly, which handled 80-85% of the total cargo carried by the corporation, b) Transportation from Kolkata to Bangladesh and to Assam (NW-2), c) Transportation from Kolkata to various destinations on NW-1, d) Construction of ships in ship building yard at Rajabagan and repair of small and medium size vessels. e) Repair of ocean-going vessels. (10.8.3.204)
CIWTC had a cargo transportation capacity of 73638 Tons in 2008-09.
Ship building and ship repairing unit Rajabagan Dockyard was handed over to Garden Reach Shipbuilders & Engineers Ltd. Deep Sea Ship Repairing unit was closed on 31.03.2002.

Union Cabinet chaired by PM gave its approval for dissolution of CIWTC on 31.08.2016. A number of assets were taken up by Inland Waterways Authority of India to provide services on Brahmaputra River (NW-4).

CIWTC was undergoing the process of closure as on 31.03.2023.

Inland Waterways Authority of India

Inland Waterways Authority of India was created on 27.10.1986 for development and regulation of inland waterways for shipping and navigation. IWAI primarily undertakes projects for development and maintenance of Inland Waterway Terminal infrastructure on National Waterways.
The Cargo movement on National Waterways achieved all time high of 108.79 Mts in 2021- 22.

Aviation Infrastructure Development

Circumstances which led to formation of Public Sector Aviation Companies in 1950s

War surplus aircrafts were available at very low prices after WW II. By the end of 1949, 9 companies were granted licenses. Soon financial condition of most of the companies was not reassuring. Air Transport Inquiry Committee, appointed by government, made recommendations for putting the air transport industry on a firm basis and for developing commercial air transport on sound lines. The report of this Committee indicated that the number of operating units was larger than that required to conduct the available volume of air transport business on an economic basis. (1.31.58)

The government decided to leave the development and operation of air transport services to private commercial organizations - 4 companies to operate main air services in India, and to give financial assistance to the operating companies in specific cases. (1.31.57)

Director-General of Civil Aviation, Ministry of Communications, held a conference with the representatives of the airline operators in January 1952 and considered the question of expansion of air fleet vis-a-vis the development of the Hindustan Aircraft. 2 new aircrafts for the **Air India International's Western Services,** 3 aircrafts for the **Bharat Airways Eastern Services** and 15 aircrafts for shorter services and major trunk routes in India were suggested to be purchased. The airline operators required loan from the Government for two-thirds of the total amount. (1.31.60)

Enquiries showed that, the existed air transport companies could not work economically under the conditions of traffic load and intensity of operations. With the introduction of the more modern, larger, faster and costlier aircrafts mentioned above, economic operations would be possible only if the existing companies merged into a single unit. A single organization in charge of internal and external operations can handle all the existing traffic with a lower number of aircraft and also save in overheads and operation cost. Under a single organization, the requirements aircraft for internal and external services were expected to be about 13, instead of 20 mentioned above. (1.31.62)

The agency proposed for operating the services, was expected to be a statutory corporation, in which the existing companies were allowed to participate pro rata as shareholders, if they wished to do so in exchange for their present holdings, the value of which could be determined on an equitable basis. The Central Government's share in the corporation was expected to be large enough to ensure control over the industry.

The Plan provided for a sum of Rs. 9.5 Cr. - (a) for the purchase of 13 aircrafts, including 3 suitable for long-distance international air services, and (b) for the payment of such compensation as may be found necessary for acquiring the assets of the existing companies, if the existing air-companies agreed to take up shares in the new corporation in exchange for their present holdings. (The amount needed was expected to be of the order of Rs. 6.5 Cr. (1.31.63)

Achievements in I 5YP –

Airports - 81 aerodromes were maintained and operated by Civil Aviation Department in 1955-56. During the I plan, 9 new aerodromes were constructed and 2 more were expected to be completed by the end of 1956. The Department took over some aerodromes from the Ministry of Defence also. (2.21.67)

Aviation Companies - The nationalization of air services was completed in the I plan period.

Air India International was set up in August 1953.

Indian Airlines Corporation came into existence in June, 1953 when 8 scheduled air transport companies were nationalized. (8.9.25.11).
IAC with a fleet of 92 aircraft linked up most of the principal Centres, and its air routes covered 32163 kms. (2.21.72)
AII provided services to 15 countries covering a total route of 37792 kms. (2.21.70)
Passenger traffic carried by airways - 0.3 billion passenger kms (1955-56).

Achievements in II 5YP –

Airports - The Civil Aviation Department maintained 85 aerodromes in 1961, including 4 added in II 5YP. 4 More aerodromes were well nearing completion.
Bombay (Santa Cruz), Calcutta (Dum Dum) and Delhi (Palam) airports were facilitated to handle jet aircraft. (3.27.65)

Aviation Companies - The capacity in ton miles offered by IAC went up from 45.84 million in 1953-54 to 69 million in 1960-61 and that offered by AII over the period from 16.91 million to 103.2 million (3.27.7 / 67)
In 1961, the operating fleet of Air India consisted of 3 Boeings and Super-Constellations.
The operating fleet of IAC in 1960-61 consisted of 69 aircrafts. The introduction of 10 Viscount aircrafts helped IAC to break-even for the first time during 1959-60. (3.27.69)

Achievements in III 5YP –

The **Indian Tourism and Development Corporation** came into existence in 1966 for providing tourism infrastructure to develop tourism in the country.

Achievements of IV 5YP -

International Airports Authority of India was constituted in 1972 to manage international airports at Bombay, Calcutta, Delhi and Madras and for creating, upgrading, maintaining, and managing civil aviation infrastructure both on the ground and air space in the country.

Achievements of V 5YP –

Airports - IAAI completed construction of Phase I of new International and Cargo Terminal Complex at Bombay. (6.17.88)

The number of Airports & Civil Enclaves in 1980-81 was 84. **(7.8.1)**

As on 31-3-1980, Indian Airlines had a fleet of 42 aircrafts and AII 19 aircrafts.

The market share of AII in the international passenger traffic was 32.8% (9.7.1.278)

Achievements in VI 5YP –

Vayudoot was established in January 1981 to serve the north-east region where the surface transport facilities were inadequate and surface routes were circuitous. Subsequently, the services of Vayudoot were extended to other regions also.

In 1984-85, Air India was operating at a loss. This position changed in the course of VII Plan (8.9.25.8)

Pawan Hans Ltd. was incorporated in 1985 to acquire and operate helicopters in the country and to provide air support services to meet the requirements of Oil Sector in their offshore operations and NTPC. (8.9.23.3)

Achievements of VII 5YP –

Indira Gandhi Rashtriya Uran Akademi was established on 7.11.1985 for providing training to students to become pilots.

National Airports Authority was set up on 1.06.1986 to manage the aerodromes, all civil enclaves and aeronautical communication systems efficiently. NAA managed 88 airports and civilian enclaves at 28 defense airports. (8.9.25.1)

Air India - The fleet of Air India consisted of 21 aircrafts, one on wet lease for freighter operation and one for passenger operations on India-USSR route. (8.9.25.7)

Air India's share of international traffic was 35% in 1985. (9.25.9)

Vayudoot - The number of stations on the operational network of Vayudoot was 48 as on 31.03.1991. (8.9.25.20)

Vayudoot also had an Agro Aviation Division which was involved in aerial spraying operations, seeding and afforestation operations. (8.9.25.21)

Aviation Infrastructure in 1991

Trivandrum became an international airport in April 1991. Number of Airports and Civil Enclaves in 1991-92 were 117.

Achievements in VIII 5YP –

Vayudoot Ltd. merged with Indian Airlines w.e.f. 25.05.1993.

Indian Airlines - IA provided air services on the domestic routes for 57 stations and 10 stations in the neighbouring countries. (8.9.25.11)

IAC fleet consisted of 56 aircrafts including Airbus, Boeing etc. During 1989-90, 15 Airbuses were acquired of which one was lost in an accident in February 1990. (8.9.25.12)

Airports - There were 20 airports in 7 States in the North-Eastern Region. Further, 2 new greenfield aerodromes were under construction at Tura in Meghalaya and Lengpui in Mizoram. (9.7.1.274)

Private Airline Companies - In 1994, 6 private operators were granted the status of scheduled airlines. During VIII Plan, 7 scheduled operators and 19 air taxi operators were given permits for operation of domestic air transport services.

Competition with new Airline Companies - The new airlines concentrated and over-expanded on trunk routes, made inroads into IA market share on these routes and in the process reduced the capacity of IA to subsidize the operation on other routes including those in backward and isolated areas.

Led by over-enthusiasm, these new entrants operated without adequately trained personnel and experience, sustained on the poached highly skilled manpower trained by the Indian Airlines and benefited by the route network developed by the national carrier during past 4 decades.

While new entrants operated old aircrafts, which were heavy on fuel, Indian Airlines, faced with shortage of skilled pilots, could not fully utilize the rated capacity of the state-of-art aircraft acquired at a heavy cost. Unhealthy business practices and the tendency to offer more frills to the passengers brought about the financial ruin of some of the new entrants; in the process, financial health of IA was also adversely affected. (9.7.1.270)

However, the main burden for providing services on routes serving remote and backward areas was borne by IA. It was felt necessary to share the financial losses of providing air services on these routes equitably by all operators to ensure that remote areas are provided with reliable air services. (9.7.1.272)

Airports Authority of India was constituted, by merging IAAI and NAAI in April 1995, for creating, upgrading, maintaining civil aviation infrastructure both on the ground and air space of the country.

AAI was responsible for the management of 92 airports, including international airports at Delhi, Mumbai, Calcutta, Chennai and Thiruvananthapuram, and 28 civil enclaves at the defense airports in 1996-97. (9.7.1.266)

Aviation Infrastructure in 1996-97

Air Traffic - In 1996-97, 0.396 million aircraft movements involving 24.3 million domestic and 12.2 million international passengers and 0.2 Mt of domestic and 0.48 Mt of international cargo were handled at 61 AAI managed airports. (9.7.1.302)

Air India - The market share of Air India in the international passenger traffic was 21.3%. (10.8.3.241). The fleet of Air India as on 31.12.1996 consisted of 28 owned Boeing and Airbus aircrafts. (9.7.1.287)

Indian Airlines - The market share of Indian Airlines in the domestic passenger traffic - 65%. (9.7.1.300) The fleet of IA at the end of VIII Plan consisted of 52 aircrafts. (9.7.1.293)

Following financial restructuring, the equity share holding of Government in IA became 49%. (9.7.1.297). Strictly speaking, IA was not a public sector company in 1996-97.

Achievements in IX 5YP

The market share of AI in the international passenger market in 1999 – 2000 was - 21.1% (10.8.3.241)
Number of Airports & Civil Enclaves in 1999-2000 was 122.
AAI managed 94 civil airports including 11 international airports at Delhi, Mumbai, Kolkata, Chennai, Thiruvananthapuram, Bangalore, Hyderabad, Ahmedabad, Goa, Amritsar and Guwahati and 28 civil enclaves at defence airfields. Only nine airports of AAI managed to make profits. (10.8.3.237)

Airports – The new airport at Nedumbassery near Kochi was constructed by Kochi International Airport Ltd., a company promoted by the Kerala government (with equity participation from a large number of non-resident Indians and financial institutions) (10.8.3.224)

Air Traffic in 2000-01

In 2000-01, 42.03 million domestic and international passengers and 0.8464 million ton of cargo were handled at various airports in the country. (10.8.3.220)

Analysis of financial performance of AI during IX Plan showed that AI's losses were only due to high non-operating expenses. If operating expenses were considered, Air India was making profit in this period.

Constraints for airline companies – ATF were subjected to sales tax varying from 20 to 36%. The high ATF cost for domestic air transport increased the cost of operation and made it unviable (10.8.3.230)

With the operationalization of subsidiary, Alliance Air, in 1996, IA was able to increase aircraft utilization. Introduction of a productivity-linked incentive scheme and the lease of 2 aircraft in 1998 contributed to an increase in the capacity in subsequent years. The market share of IA was estimated to be over 50% in 2001-02. (10.8.3.247) Indian Airlines earned a profit in the first 3 years of the IX Plan.

Hike in ATF prices, increase in landing and navigational charges and insurance premium rates and adverse impact of foreign exchange rates resulted in losses in 2000-01. (10.8.3.249)

IA was estimated to incur a net loss of Rs. 70 Cr annually on operations in the northeast (10.8.3.251)

Achievements in X plan

Airports - Development of Delhi, Mumbai, Hyderabad, and Bangalore airports by private sector entities and Modernization of Kolkata and Chennai airports and 35 non-metro and 13 other airports were underway. (11.1.82)

Air India Charters Limited, a subsidiary of AI, used to provide manpower for allied services at airports, ground handling and security, formed AI Express as first international low cost, no frill 'budget' airline from India. AI Express commenced operations on 29.04.2005. (11.9.6.40)

Air Traffic in 2006-07

Private sector's market share in the domestic traffic during 2006 reached 78.5%, which included the 29% traffic of low-cost airlines. Jet Airways emerged as the market leader with a share of 31.2%, followed by Indian Airlines (21.5%), Air Deccan (18.3%), Air Sahara (8.8%), Kingfisher (8.7%), Spice Jet (6.9%), Go Air (2.8%), Indigo (1.3%), and Paramount (0.7%).

Achievements in XI Plan

Airports Economic Regulatory Authority of India was set up in 2008 to regulate tariff and other charges for the aeronautical services rendered at airports and to monitor performance of airports. (12.15.219)

AI and Indian Airlines were merged in 2011 to optimize fleet acquisition, to leverage the asset base, to strengthen the network, and to achieve economy of scale. (12.15.195)

Airports

i) Passenger handling capacity rose from 72 million in FY 06 to over 220 million in FY 11.

ii) Cargo handling capacity rose from 0.5 Mt in FY 06 to 3.3 Mt in FY 11.

iii) AAI upgraded and modernized 26 of the planned 35 non-metro airports including those at Agra, Ahmedabad, Amritsar, Bhopal, Jaipur, Pune and Goa. (12. Box 15.12).

iv) AAI commissioned terminal T3 and associated infrastructure at Delhi international airport in 37 months.

v) Connectivity to North-Eastern region has risen from 87 to 286 flights/ week; There were 22 airports and civil enclaves in the NER, including 7 AAI airports at Agartala, Barapani, Dibrugarh, Guwahati, Imphal and Lilabari and 4 civil enclaves at Jorhat, Bagdogra, Silchar and Tezpur.

vi) Greenfield development of Hyderabad and Bengaluru international airports and modernization of Kochi, Delhi and Mumbai international airports (Box 15.12) were completed through PPP mode.

Foreign Equity Participation - Government permitted foreign equity participation up to 49% and investment by NRIs up to 100% in the domestic air transport services and 49% Foreign Direct Investment by foreign airlines in Indian airline companies. (12.15.208)

Aviation Infrastructure from 2014-15 to 2022

Air cargo traffic carried by Indian airline operators during 2013-14/ 2014-15/ 2015-16/ 2016-17/ 2019-20/ 2021/ 2022 were 2.28 Mts/ 2.528 Mts/ 2.7 Mts/ 2.98 Mts/ 3.432 Mts/ 3.137 Mts and 3.163 Mts respectively. annual_report-2017_18_en.pdf (civilaviation.gov.in)

There were 129/137/136/133 (out of total 147) airports managed by AAI including 23/23/24/23 international, 78/81/81/78 domestic, 8/10/10/10 customs and 20/23/21/22 civil enclaves / Defence airports in 2017-18/2020-21/2021/2022 respectively

Passenger carried during 2016-17/ 2019-20/ 2021 and 2022 in million were 264.97, 349.31, 182.27 and 294.14 respectively

Indira Gandhi Rashtriya Uran Akademi

Indira Gandhi Rashtriya Uran Akademi was established on 7.11.1985 for providing training to students to become pilots. IGRUA has 3 flying operation bases in Fursat Ganj, UP, Gondia, Maharashtra and Kalaburagi, Karnataka. Besides training to IGRUA'S own cadets, the campus also gives pilot training to cadets of Indian Air Force, Indian Navy, Indian Coast Guard, Border Security Force and Indian Airlines.

IGRUA signed a contract with CAE Flight Training (India) Pvt Ltd, a wholly owned subsidiary of CAE Inc, Canada in 2008 to upgrade training capacity to 100 pilots/ year including purchase of additional 14 aircrafts, setting up of MRO hub and AME school at IGRUA and extension of tarmac at Sultanpur for parking IGRUA aircraft during XII plan. (12.15.231)

In the 2021-22 academic year, IGRUA achieved flying hours of 19,110 hours, with per aircraft utilization of 1062 hours per annum, with a fleet of 18 aircraft. It has an intake capacity of 125 cadets/ annum.

Contribution by Public Sector Airline Companies for 5YPs

IV 5YP - The proposed outlay of Rs. 55 Cr for acquiring Boeing-737 jets for Indian Airlines was expected to be financed to the extent of Rs. 50 Cr from the internal resources of the Corporation. (4.15.27)

IV 5YP - The program of Air India of acquiring 4 Boeing 747 jets was expected to be financed entirely from its internal resources, except that it required Rs. 15 Cr from the government to enable it to maintain a proper debt-equity ratio. (4.15.28)

VII 5YP - IAAI was able to finance its developmental activities from out of its own resources. (8.9.25.16)

VIII 5YP - 98.76% of the expenditure of Rs. 7096.58 Cr was financed from internal and extra budgetary resources. The plan of Air India, Indian Airlines, Pawan Hans and Hotel Corporation of India were entirely financed from their IEBR. (9.7.1.268)

XI 5YP - The anticipated expenditure in Aviation sector was Rs. 44,124 Cr comprising of IEBR of Rs. 39,571.11 Cr and budgetary support of Rs. 4,552.89 Cr. (12.15.195)

XII 5YP – The projected investment from Central sector was expected to be Rs. 33,198 Cr of which Rs. 16,983 Cr was from GBS and Rs. 16,215 Cr from IEBR. Out of the GBS of Rs. 16,983 Cr, Rs. 15,096 Cr was earmarked for Air India and Rs. 1,887 Cr for all other plan schemes of the Ministry. (12.15.233)

Contribution by Public Sector Enterprises for VI 5YP –

The gross surplus of public enterprises represented their retained profits, depreciation provision and additional resource mobilization through revision of tariffs, prices, etc.

Estimates of Gross Surplus of Central and State Enterprises for 1980-85 at 1979-80 rates were - Railways - Rs. 1698 Cr, Posts and Telegraphs - Rs. 2365 Cr, other Central Enterprises - Rs. 5848 Cr, State Electricity Boards - Rs. 22 Cr, SRTCs - Rs. 506 Cr and other State enterprises - Rs. 12 Cr = Total Rs. 9395 Cr (6.5.20)

Airports Authority of India

Airports Authority of India - AAI was incorporated on 1.04.1995 by merging International Airport Authority of India and National Airports Authority to accelerate the integrated development, expansion, and modernization of the airports in India.

AAI looks after control and management of Indian air space extending beyond the territorial limits of the country as accepted by ICAO, provision of Communication, Navigation and Surveillance aids. expansion and strengthening of runways, aprons, taxiways, etc. and provision of Air Traffic Management Systems for landing and movement control aids for aircraft & vehicular traffic in operational area, design, development, operation and maintenance of passenger terminals and cargo terminals at international and domestic airports.

92 Airports, including 5 international airports and 28 civil enclaves/ defense airports were under the control of AAI in 1996-97. (9.7.1.266)
AAI participated in the development of new airports at Bangalore and Hyderabad in 2004-05.

AAI and ISRO implemented Space Based Augmentation (S-BAD) Global Navigation Satellite System (GAGAN) in 2007-08 to provide seamless navigation over Indian Air Space including oceanic region and to enable precision approaches at all Indian airports. Gagan helped achieve smooth transition to satellite-based navigation and seamless air traffic management across continents, from Africa to Australia by coordinating with systems including WAAS of USA, EGNOSS of Europe and MSAT of Japan. Gagan benefited all modes of transportation, including maritime, highways, railways, defence services, security agencies, and disaster recovery management.

Automatic Flight Inspection System was commissioned in the acquired Raytheon aircraft to facilitate calibration of navigational facilities at high altitude. The Aerodrome Visual Simulator was commissioned at CATC, Allahabad designed to simulate 3D operational airport environment as seen from control tower suitable for training Air Traffic Controllers.

AAI's share in providing airport services in 2011-12 was 100%.
In 2013-14, AAI managed 129 airports including 14 International Airports, 8 Customs airports, 26 Civil Enclaves and 81 Domestic airports. In addition, AAI also provided **Communications, Navigation and Surveillance system for Air Traffic Management facilities at 11 other airports.**

AAI had 7 JVs for airports including Delhi, Mumbai, Bengaluru & Hyderabad which were handed over to Joint Venture Companies - Delhi International Airport Pvt Ltd., Mumbai International Airport Pvt Ltd., and National Flying Training Institute Pvt Ltd. AAI also has one more JV namely MIHAN India Pvt Ltd. with Govt. of Maharashtra.

In 2016-17, AAI managed 126 airports - 107 operational airports (21 International Airports, 8 customs, 78 domestic) and 19 civil enclaves at Defense Airfields.
In 2019-20, when AAI recorded an annual loss for the first time since its inception, it paid a dividend of Rs 671.7 Cr to government. AAI News : AAI seeks waiver of annual dividend payment for 2021-22 fiscal (indiatimes.com)

Currently AAI manages **131 airports, 87 domestic airports and 26 civil enclaves.**

Gross Turnover of Airports Authority of India in FY 2022-23 was Rs. 11425 Cr (increase of 80% over turnover in 2021-22).

Air India Ltd.

Air India Ltd. - AI was incorporated on 15.10.1932 as Tata Airlines and renamed Air India in 1946. It was nationalized in 1953 and split into 2 corporations namely Air India and Indian Airlines to operate as international carrier and domestic carrier respectively.

The market share of Air India in the international passenger traffic in 1979-80, 1980-81, 1985-86, 1996-97 and 1999-2000 were - 32.8% (9.7.1.278), 42%, 35% (9.25.9), 21.3%. (9.7.1.278) and 21.1% (10.8.3.241) respectively.

National Aviation Co. of India Ltd was incorporated on 30.3.2007 to merge Air India and Indian Airlines for optimizing the operation of the combined airline company.
The name of NACIL was changed to Air India Ltd. in 2010-11.

AI comprised 6 Strategic Business Units - Passenger; Cargo; Ground Handling Services; Low-Cost Carrier; MRO (Airframes and Engines / components) and Related Business.

AI had 5 subsidiaries namely Hotel Corporation of India Ltd., Air India Charters Ltd (Air India Express), Air India Air Transport Services Ltd. Air India Engineering Services Ltd., and Airlines Allied Services Ltd.
AI also had 2 joint ventures including Air India SATS Airport Services Pvt Ltd.

In 2019-20, AI was operating in 105 stations comprising 67 domestic and 38 international stations. The company operated 4 offices abroad.

International market share in Oct-Dec 2019 - Indigo – 12.8%, Air-India – 11.5%, AI Express – 7.3%, Spicejet – 5%, GoAir – 2.6%. Indian carriers accounted for over 39% of passengers flying in and out of India.

On 8.10.2021, Air India, Air India Express and 50% shares of AISATS (ground handling company) were sold for $ 2.3 billion (Rs. 18000 Cr.) to Talace Pvt Ltd. of Tata Group. Tata Sons also got 123 aircrafts of cost price $ 21.669 Billion from Air India.

Air India's annualized domestic market share was 8.7% and 9.3% in FY2022 and FY2023 respectively. (less than 18.8% during Oct-Dec 2019). AI did not pay any dividend in FY2022 and FY 2023.

Air India Cargo

Air India Cargo was the freight carrying subsidiary of Air India. It operated freighter aircraft services off and on at different stages of its history, the latest being from 2006 to 2012. Although the company has stopped operating as an airline it continued to manage the belly cargo hold capacity of Air India's passenger fleet.

Indian Airlines Ltd.

Indian Airlines Ltd. - IA was incorporated under Air Corporations Act 1953 along with Air India as Indian Airlines. 8 Pre-independence domestic airlines – Deccan Airways, Airways India, Bharat Airways, Himalayan Aviation, Kalinga Airlines, Indian National Airways and Air Services of India and domestic wing of Air India were merged to form Indian Airlines Corporation. It started operations on 1.08.1953.

IA provided air services on the domestic routes for 57 stations and 10 stations in the neighbouring countries in 1989-90. (8.9.25.11)

In 1991 Indian Airlines Ltd. was incorporated under the Companies Act, 1956.

The market share of Indian Airlines in the domestic passenger traffic in 1996-97 and 2006-07 were - 65% and 21.5% respectively. (9.7.1.300)

IA was providing air transportation services through its 56 aircrafts. It had one subsidiary, namely Airline Allied Services Ltd., which operated as Alliance Air.

Vayudoot Ltd. continued to be a shell company of Indian Airline.

In 2007, Indian Airlines Corp. merged with Air India.

It was sold to Talace Pvt Ltd. as Air India in 2021.

Hindustan Aeronautics Ltd.

Hindustan Aeronautics Ltd. - HAL was incorporated on 1.10.1964, merging Hindustan Aircraft Ltd. with Aeronautics India Ltd. incorporated in 1940 and 16.08.1963 respectively, to manufacture and overhaul aircraft, seaplanes, helicopters, gliders, parachutes and aeroengines for civil, commercial, defence services and Coast Guards.

HAL is manufacturing and overhauling fighter, trainer, transport aircraft, helicopters, and associated aero-engines, avionics, systems / equipment for both military and civil applications, production and overhaul of marine & industrial gas turbines engines, manufacturing of integrated assemblies and structures for aerospace Launch Vehicles / satellites and Cryogenic engines through its **20 operating units** at Bangalore, Nasik, Koraput, Lucknow, Korwa, Kanpur, Hyderabad and Barrackpore. There are also 11 R&D Centres co-located with these production units.

i) Over the years, HAL produced 11 types of aircraft, including the **A**dvanced **L**ight **H**elicopter (Dhruv).

ii) Production of SU30MKI (under license from Russia) and PTA (Lakshya) commenced during 2004-05.

iii) During 2007-08, **the domestic market share of HAL was 96.05%** and HAL exported to 9 countries. HAL's Advanced Light Helicopters MRO and Composite Manufacturing Division cater to maintenance, repair and overhaul of ALH and manufacturing of composite parts of various aircraft / helicopters.

iv) HAL was engaged in development of Intermediate Jet Trainer (HJT-36), Light Combat Aircraft (Tejas) and Helicopter, Weapon System Integration on ALH, Sea Harrier upgrade, etc.

v) HAL was ranked 38th in the world in the Defense Aerospace sector in 2010-11. HAL produced 78 new aircraft and helicopters along with engines and accessories in 2010-11.

HAL's share in domestic output of Transport & Fighter Aero-planes in 2011-12 was 100%.

vi) HAL took up development of Light Utility Helicopter, Mini UVAV and Medium Thrust Engine.

vii) HAL was pursuing the selection of suitable OEM partner to manufacture a 50-80 seat commercial passenger **R**egional **T**ransport **A**ircraft and diversify into Civil Aviation Sector.

viii) Initial Operation Clearance for Light Combat Helicopter, Certificate of Airworthiness for Dornier Do228 Civil Variant aircraft and Final Operation Clearance upgrade activities of Mirage 2000 were completed successfully in 2017-18.

ix) HAL started developing Hawk aircraft under license from BAES, U.K. in 2007-08 and delivered In 2019-20. HAL diversified into Space Vehicle programs of ISRO and Industrial & Marine Gas Turbine business in 2019-20.

x) Jaguar DARIN III upgrade achieved Final Operational Clearance on 30.07.19. Light Utility Helicopter achieved Initial Operation Clearance on 7.02.20.

The installed capacity for manufacture of aircraft, helicopter and repair and overhaul in 2019-20 was 263 standard man hours.

The company has 11 joint ventures - Indo Russian Aviation Ltd., Baehal Software Ltd., Snecma HAL Aerospace Pvt Ltd. (to produce precision aero-engine components for world market), Samtel HAL Display Systems Ltd., Infotech HAL Ltd., Hatsoff Helicopter Training Pvt Ltd., HAL Edgewood Technologies Pvt Ltd., HALBIT Avionics Pvt Ltd., INCAT- HAL Aerostructures Ltd., etc.

Total assets, revenue, profit after tax and dividend paid to government by HAL for 2022-23 were Rs. 23506 Cr, Rs. 27055 Cr, Rs. 5811 Cr. and Rs. 1257 Cr respectively. (Indian Express dated 16.08.23)

Air India Charters Ltd.

Air India Charters Ltd. - AICL was incorporated on 09.09.1971 to undertake Charter operations / Flights and overcome the situation created by discounting of fares by Arab carriers and other non-scheduled operators.
However, from 1988, AICL started providing ground handling services to client airlines.
On 29.04.2005, AICL launched India's first international low cost, no frill budget airline '**Air India Express Ltd.**' from Kerala to certain points in the Gulf, which were advantageous to millions of people working in Gulf & Middle East and South-East Asia.

Airline Allied Services Ltd. – Alliance Air Aviation Ltd.

Airline Allied Services Ltd. - AASL was incorporated on 13.9.1983 to create a profit Centre under the subsidiary structure for speedy decision-making and to utilize the fleet effectively. AASL was providing services in airline business through operation of B-737 aircraft and ATR-42-320 Air Cargo.

AASL was revitalized as a scheduled airline in 1996 and named **Alliance Air Aviation Ltd**. AAAL undertook freighter charter operations with B737 freighter aircraft on lease from Air India Ltd. and other lessors.
Air India provided support services like reservations for Alliance Air flights.

In 2016-17, AAAL was operating passenger services with 10 leased aircraft to 36 stations on Category II & III route. Under the **R**egional **C**onnectivity **S**cheme "UDAAN", AAAL was allotted 15 routes in I phase. AASL planned to expand its network to neighboring countries with addition of 10 ATR 72 aircraft in September 2017. AAAL got 18 more routes under II round of bidding for RCS during 2017-18.

AAAL operated on 92 routes during 2019-20 including 61 UDAN routes. AAAL started its first international operation to Jaffna in 2019-20.

As of 31.03.2023, AAAL was operating 101 UDAN routes. Revenue from operations in 2022-23 was Rs. 1098.42 Cr.

Pawan Hans Helicopters Ltd.

Pawan Hans Helicopters Ltd. - PHHL was incorporated on 15.10.1985 to provide helicopter support services to meet the requirement of Petroleum sector, to connect remote and inaccessible areas and to operate tourist charters.

PHHL is providing helicopter support services to ONGC, GAIL, PSEs viz NHPC, etc. (for carrying ONGC men and vital supplies round the clock to drilling rings in Bombay High, undertaking pipeline surveillance, hot line insulator washing for Power grid) and state Governments of North East, Andaman & Nicobar & Lakshadweep Islands, Punjab and Bihar (for inter-island connectivity, pilgrimage services), etc. through its fleet of 46 helicopters. PHHL is also providing Helicopter services to Hardy Oil Exploration.

PHHL maintains & operates helicopters owned by other customers such as Govt. of Bihar and Gujarat, BSF and ONGC. PHHL is also in the development of heliports and helipad.

PHHL has also launched an Aircraft Maintenance Engineering (AME) training institute at Mumbai. PHHL had a fleet of 43 helicopters between 2016 to 2018.

PHHL was providing helicopter services to police, para military forces, geophysical surveys, adventure sports and tourists charters. (9.7.1.318)

Revenue from operations in 2022-23 was Rs. 415.16 Cr.

Air India Air Transport Services Ltd. / AI Airport Services Ltd.

Air India Air Transport Services Ltd.- AIATS was incorporated on 9.6.2003 to provide services at airports to any entities engaged in transporting passengers, goods, mail, and cargo by air including repairing, maintaining, servicing, refurbishing, providing engineering services of and for aircraft, flying machines, aerial conveyances, engines, auxiliary power units, etc.

AIATS is rendering ground handling services at Indian airports including passenger, ramp, security and cargo handling for Air India and associate / joint venture company i.e. AI SAT, Bangalore.

Revenue from operations during 2022-23 was Rs. 894.47 Cr.

IAL Airport Services Limited

IAL Airport Services Limited was incorporated on 27.08.2003.

Air India Engineering Services Ltd.

Air India Engineering Services Ltd. - AIESL was incorporated on 11.03.2004, as a wholly owned subsidiary of National Aviation Company of India Ltd. (erstwhile Air India Ltd.), to undertake engineering and other allied activities and provide Maintenance Repair and Overhaul (MRO) facility.

AIESL was providing services of repairing, maintaining, servicing and refurbishing aircraft and all components, flying machines, helicopters, dirigibles, balloons, aerial conveyances and their engines, auxiliary power units through its Line Maintenance (at Air India's domestic stations) and Base Maintenance facilities (at Delhi, Mumbai, Hyderabad, Trivandrum, Kolkata and Nagpur), Engine and APU Overhaul shops, Component and Avionics Overhaul shops.

AIESL was granted full MRO approval by Boeing Global Services for aftermarket work of aircraft and components for Navy P8I aircraft.

FAA approval for A320 base checks at BOM TRV and NAG received. Revenue from operations in 2022-23 was Rs. 1980.09 Cr.

National Aviation Company of India Ltd.

National Aviation Company of India Ltd.- NACIL was incorporated on 30.3.2007 to merge Air India and Indian Airlines for optimizing the operation of the combined airline company in route rationalization, fuel procurement, stores, and inventory purchase of both aircraft and non-aircraft, insurance benefits, handling of flights and employee productivity. The merger became effective on 27.8.2007.

The merged entity with the fleet of 110+ aircraft was amongst the top 30 airlines globally in size. NACIL was expected to create considerable synergy, since the 2 airlines can feed traffic to each other. Besides, it could result in redeployment of aircraft, since Air India and Indian Airlines were flying on some common routes in the Gulf and South-East Asia. During 2010-11, the name of company changed to Air India Ltd.

AAI Cargo Logistics & Allied Services Company Ltd.

AAI Cargo Logistics & Allied Services Co. Ltd.– AAICLAS, a 100% subsidiary of Airports Authority of India, was incorporated on 11.08.2016 by demerging of Cargo Department of AAI, mainly to establish, operate and management of Air Cargo Terminal.

AAICLAS commissioned International Air Cargo facility at Aurangabad, Domestic Air Cargo facility at Surat, Bhopal, Leh, Dehradun, Rajahmundry, Dimapur, Hubballi, Adampur and Udaipur airports, ILHBS at Lucknow, Jaipur, Varanasi, Trivandrum, Calicut, Srinagar, Chandigarh airports and Cold Storage facilities for Agri-Products at Varanasi Airport and Pharma products at Chennai Airport.

Revenue from operations in 2022-23 was Rs. 446.28 Cr.

Naini Aerospace Limited

Naini Aerospace Ltd - NAeL was incorporated on 29.12.2016 as a subsidiary of Hindustan Aeronautics Ltd to take-over sick Naini unit of Hindustan Cables Ltd which was closed for past 15 years. It is engaged in fabrication of looms for helicopters and aircraft and structure for helicopters.

Revenue from operations in 2022-23 was Rs. 11.53 Cr.

Adani Ports and Special Economic Zone Limited (1998)

Gujarat Adani Port Ltd., was incorporated in 1998 for setting up a captive jetty at the Port of Mundra.

Tuna Port, initially operated by Kandla Port Trust, came under Adani Kandla Bulk Terminal Private Limited from 2012 after winning contract to set up bulk terminal.

APSEZ acquired the current container port in Hazira Port, built by PSA Corporation of Singapore, in 2012, Dhamra Port in Odisha, which became operational in 2010, in June 2014, Vizhinjam port in 2015 (through signing of a 40-year agreement with the state government to build and maintain the Vizhinjam port by Adani Vizhinjam Port Pvt Ltd), Kattupalli Port from L&T in June 2018 (and renamed it as Adani Katupalli Port Private Ltd.), 75% stake in the Krishnapatnam Port Company Ltd built by Navayuga Engineering Co. Ltd in 2020, 31.5% shares of Gangavaram Port, Visakhapatnam, constructed by Gangavaram Port Ltd in 2021, Dighi Port Limited in 2021 for Rs 705 crore, an additional ICD from Navkar Corporation in Tumb, Gujarat in 2022, Karaikkal port for Rs. 1485 Cr in April 2023 (Business Standard dated 3.4.23), (at much less than the amount paid by Edelweiss Asset Reconstruction Company for taking over 97% of the port's ₹1,800 crore bank debt and turned around operations) and Gopalpur port in Odisha in 2024.

A bulk terminal in Dahej port was sub-concessioned to Adani.

APSEZ has a one-berth terminal (Berth 7) at Mormugao Port Authority.

Acquisition is a bad strategy

Acquisition of existing companies does not increase existing installed capacity or reduce shortfall in supply. (The acquiring company's inventory and operating cost reduce and profit increases additionally due to reduced competition in the market). If the same amount was invested for starting new companies, the installed capacity and generation would have increased and shortfall would have reduced. **Thus, acquisition of operating companies for profit is a bad policy and promotes monopoly.**

Summary –

1) The Indian Railways became one of the largest railway systems in the world in 1995-96 with 63,000 route kms and carried 11 million passengers and 1.20 Mts of freight per day.

2) Passenger traffic handled by the Road transport was - 270 (182.8 in SRTCs alone, i.e., 67.7%) billion passenger kms. 61,661 buses (55.5% of passenger road transport vehicles) were in the public sector in 1978-79 (6.17.53).

India had one of the largest road networks in the world of 3.314 million km in 2006-07 consisting 66590 km of national highways, 137000 km of State highways, 300000 km major district and rural Roads. (9.3.2)

3) The assessed production capacity of 4 ship building PSUs was 95% of industry turnover in 2001-02. In June 2012, Indian shipping tonnage ranked **sixteenth in the world**. (12.15.131)

4) The market share of Indian Airlines in the domestic passenger traffic in 1996-97 was - 65%. (9.7.1.300). India became the **nineth largest civil aviation market** in the world in 2011-12. (12. 15.195)

Private Sector Players –

Ship and patrol boat building companies - Scindia Steam Navigation Co – 1919, Vadyar Boats – 1969, Bharati Shipyard Ltd. – 1973, Timblo Drydocks Pvt Ltd – 1973, Dempo Shipbuilding & Engineering Pvt Ltd. – 1974, Bristol Boats Pvt Ltd – 1976, (Shalimar Works (1980) Ltd - Owned by Govt of West Bengal – 1980), L & T Shipbuilding Ltd. – 1981 / 2007, Tebma Shipyard Ltd. – 1984, ABG Shipyard Ltd – 1985, Praga Marine Pvt Ltd. – 1985, SHOFT Shipyard – 1987, Mandovi Drydocks -Shipbuilders and Ship repairers – 1988, Pipavav Shipyard Ltd – 1997, Sea Blue Marine - Engineering Pvt Ltd / Sea Blue Shipyard Ltd – 2003, Modest Infrastructure Ltd - 2006, Titagarh Marine Ltd – 2008, San Marine Shipyard – 2012.

Airline operation companies - Deccan Airways – 1946, Kalinga Airlines – 1950, Tata Air Services – 1952, East-West Airlines (India) – 1991, Jet Airways (India) Ltd. – 1992, Damania Airways Ltd. – 1993, ModiLuft – 1993, NEPC Airlines – 1993, Sahara India Airlines / Air Sahara – 1993, Simply Deccan / Air Deccan – 2003, Kingfisher Airlines – 2003, GoAir / Go First – 2005, Spicejet – 2005, InterGlobe Aviation Ltd. / Indigo – 2006, Jetlite – 2007, Air Deccan (Gujarat) – 2009, Air Asia India – 2013, Tata SIA Airlines Ltd. / Vistara – 2013, Star Air (India) – 2019, Akasa Air – 2022.

Aviation services (MRO) - Air Works India (Engineering) Pvt Ltd (1951) (Adani Defence Systems & Technologies signed agreement to buy 85.8% stake for Rs. 400 Cr in December 2024)

Civil aircraft and aircraft components companies - Dynamatic Technologies Ltd. – 1973, Raj Hamsa Ultralights Pvt Ltd. – 1980, Mahindra Aerospace – 2003, Tata Advanced Systems Ltd – 2007, Indian Rotorcraft Ltd. – 2010, Dassault Reliance Aerospace Ltd. – 2017

Bus transport operators - BEST - Brihanmumbai Electric Supply & Transport Undertaking - 1873, TVS Motor Company - 1911

Buses, commercial vehicles, Jeeps, Trucks companies - Sri Rama Vilas Service Ltd – 1938, Mahindra & Mahindra – 1947, Ashok Motors / Ashok Leyland - 1948 / 1955, TELCO – commercial vehicles in 1954 / Truck, Pickup Truck in 1988, Ford India Pvt Ltd – 1995, Mahindra Navistar / Mahindra International / Mahindra Truck & Bus Division – 2005, Pinnacle Mobility Solutions – 2019, EKA - 2022

Locomotives and wagons companies – Tata Engineering & Locomotive Co – 1945, San Engineering and Locomotive Co Ltd. – 1969, Ovis Equipment Pvt Ltd. – 1987, Titagarh Rail Systems – 1997, Texmaco Rail & Engineering Ltd / Formerly, Texmaco Machines Pvt Ltd. – 1998, Medha Traction Equipment Pvt Ltd – 2008.

Shipping companies - Essar Shipping – 1992, Adani Shipping (2006), Mahindra Marine Pvt Ltd - 2008

Hotel companies - Indian Hotels Company Ltd – 1899, Taj Mahal Hotel – 1904, Imperial Tobacco Co. of India Ltd – 1910.

Infrastructure companies - Adani Ports and Special Economic Zone Limited (1998), Adani Road Transport (2018), Adani Airport Holdings (2019),

16: GROWTH OF SERVICES SECTORS INCLUDING BANKING, INSURANCE & FINANCIAL INSTITUTIONS & INFORMATION TECHNOLOGY

Significant Role of Services Sector

The share of trade in the Indian economy stood at around 13.4% of GDP in 2001-02 and employed approximately 36 million people, a majority of whom were self-employed, engaged in the retail and wholesale trade. (10.7.8.4)

Planning Commission of India

The first and most important public sector organization, which was the soul of post-independence economic development of India, was Planning Commission, which planned and monitored implementation of the 12 Five Year Plans of India. It was established on 15.03.1950. It not only forecasted the targets for all sectors of economy, it made plan outlays to ensure balanced growth in all sectors. It coordinated with **private sector** and took their help for developments required to achieve set production capacities. After making Five Year Plans, Planning Commission consulted all state governments, economists, statisticians, others before finalization and implementation.

Financial Services Sector

Share of financial services in GDP in 2001-02 and 2006-07 were 5.7% and 6.3% respectively. The penetration of the financial sector in India remained low relative to many markets, with bank credit/GDP at under 50%, overall insurance premium/GDP at under 5%, and general insurance premium/GDP at under 1%. (11.v3.8.4.1)

Growth of Financial Institutions

Industrial Finance Corporation of India was established in 1948 as development finance institution under Ministry of Finance.

On 1.01.1949, **Reserve Bank of India** was nationalized.

During I 5YP

The State Financial Corporations Act, passed in **1951**, empowered all states and union territories to set up **State Financial Corporations** to provide financial assistance to micro, small and medium scale industries.

Central Government established **industrial finance corporations** for those States which could not start and support independent financial institutions. (1.25.27)

Until 1954, the **Industrial Finance Corporation of India** was extending loans to industries up to Rs 50 lakhs. (Ref. 2.19.5)

National Industrial Development corporation was incorporated on 20.10.**1954** for development of heavy industrial machinery including heavy foundries, forges and structural shops. (Ref. 2.19.34).

National Small Industries Corporation was established in **1955** to assist small industries.

Industrial Credit and Investment Corporation of India was established in **1955** for developing medium and small industries of the **private sector.**

During II 5YP

The Imperial Bank of India, the biggest commercial bank, was converted, in **1955**, into a public-owned and public-managed **State Bank of India** for expansion and institutionalization of rural credit. (Ref. 2.2.36)

The Reserve Bank of India discharged its regulatory functions in the sphere of currency, credit and foreign exchange and assisted in the development of cooperative credit agencies. (2.2.36)

The Reserve Bank of India provided loans to the States for participation in the share capital of cooperatives.

State Finance Corporations and the **Central Small Industries Corporation** were established for promoting and assisting small businesses. (2.2.37)

Nationalization of **Life insurance** added another public sector organization, **Life Insurance Corporation of India,** for helping to raise savings and regulate and direct the flow of funds in accordance with the requirements of the Five - Year Plans. LIC was expected to provide loans to State Governments, local bodies and State enterprises for financing the housing, water supply and power development programs. (2.2.27) (6.5.38)

State Industrial Developments Corporations were set up for promoting new schemes, participating in suitable **private sector** projects and providing financial assistance in various forms, such as special capital, the term loan, guarantees, discounting of the bills of exchange, and direct subscription to the debentures or the equity, etc.

During III 5YP

Agricultural Refinance Corporation, established by an Act of Parliament in 1963, started functioning from 1.07.**1963**.

Unit Trust of India was set up in July **1964** to channel the savings of middle- and low-income groups for investment in risk capital. (4.14.8)

Encouraged by UTI, the net household investment in corporate / cooperative shares, debentures and units of the UTI was expected to increase to Rs. 1400 Cr during 1980 - 85. (6.5.9)

Industrial Development Bank of India was set up in July **1964** to provide larger financial assistance to new industries and coordinate the activities of the existing agencies. The Refinance Corporation was amalgamated with it. (4.14.8)

During IV 5YP

Rural Electrification Corporation was set up in July **1969** to provide funds for expansion of rural electrification facilities and to help State Electricity Boards energize pump-sets across the country to boost agriculture and overcome the crippling impact of 3 successive years of deficient monsoons.

During V 5YP

State Industrial Development and Investment Corporation and State Financial Corporations extended financial assistance to small and medium entrepreneurs to undertake promotional activities in their respective States. SIDIC emphasized on provision of infrastructural facilities like development of industrial areas. (6.16.86)

During VI 5YP -

Life Insurance Corporation, **General Insurance Corporation, Rural Electrification Corporation** and **National Bank for Agriculture and Rural Development** were estimated to extend loans totaling Rs. 3,539 Cr to the States and agricultural co-operatives for various programs in the fields of housing, water supply, power, transport, etc.

Housing and Urban Development Corporation provided subsidized finance to the poorer sections of the society. **Housing Development Finance Corporation** continued to cater to the clientele belonging to fairly well-to-do sections of the society. (7.12.9)

HUDCO provided funds for rural housing. A specified proportion of **GIC**'s funds were also earmarked for rural housing. (7.12.17)

During VII 5YP -

Help to private shipping industry - Shipping Credit and Investment Co. of India (SCICI) was launched in **1987** in the place of the erstwhile Shipping Development Fund Committee (SDFC), for financing ship acquisition by private sector. The SCICI financially restructured the entire private shipping industry, who were able to reduce their debt liability and improve their viability. (8.9.15.6)

SCICI proposed to offer differential interest rate subsidy and loans to Indian entrepreneurs for acquiring deep sea fishing vessels. (8.6.16.4)

During VIII 5YP –

(i) Funds flow from Central and State Government establishments including LIC, GIC, **National Housing Bank**, HUDCO., Provident Fund, commercial banks and housing finance institutions for housing and habitation projects during the VIII Plan was about Rs.25,000 Cr. (9.3.7.59)

(ii) Under the scheme of Central Assistance for reconstruction of floods-damaged houses in Tamil Nadu, Karnataka and Kerala, HUDCO sanctioned construction of 77,969 houses till 31.12.1996, of which 20,318 houses were reconstructed. (9.3.7.69)

(iii) **Small Industries Development Bank of India** was established on 2.04.**1990** for providing credit to small-scale sector directly and through refinance to the nationalized banks and Bill Rediscounting Scheme. (9.5.283)

(iv) National Small Industries Corp. assisted small-scale entrepreneurs and artisans for hire-purchase and leasing of machinery and equipment, procurement and supply of indigenous and imported raw materials and technology transfer. (9.5.284)

During X 5YP –

i) **India Infrastructure Finance Co. Ltd** was incorporated in 2006 for providing long-term loans for financing viable infrastructure projects that typically involve long gestation periods.

ii) **Agriculture Insurance** - Under weather-based insurance schemes developed by **Agriculture Insurance Co. of India Ltd**, ICICI-Lombard General Insurance Co., and IFFCO-Tokyo General Insurance Co., coverage for deviation in rainfall index was extended and compensations for economic losses due to the less or more than normal rainfall were paid. (11.v2.1.68.)

iii) **HUDCO** gave financial assistance to State Governments and their agencies like Housing Boards, District Taluka, and Panchayat Development Boards nominated by the State Government for undertaking housing schemes. (11.v2.4.95)

Over 28 years prior to 31.03.2006, HUDCO sanctioned 2472 schemes with a loan amount of Rs 5807 Cr for construction of 86.11 lakh dwelling units in various States in the country. (11.v2.4.98)

During XI 5YP –

During XI Plan period, HUDCO's proposals envisaged sanction of Rs 74596 Cr for both its housing and urban development programs. Of this, Rs 14919 Cr was identified for housing operations. (11.11.94)

Public Sector Financial Institutions

Industrial Finance Corporation of India

Industrial Finance Corp. of India was established in **1948** as development finance institution under Ministry of Finance. IFCI has 7 subsidiaries and 1 associate.

It provided financial support for projects such as airports, roads, telecom, power, real estate, manufacturing, services sector, etc. During last 70 years, Adani Mundra Ports, GMR Goa International

Airport, Salasar Highways, NRSS Transmission and Raichur Power Corp., among others, were set up with the financial assistance of IFCI.

IFCI set up various market intermediaries like stock exchanges, entrepreneurship development organizations, consultancy organizations, educational and skill development institutes across the country.

IFCI provided interest differential subsidies to financial institutions in order to encourage the private sector to build hotels. (6.17.106)

During 2022-23, IFCI positioned itself as a preferred advisor to Government of India for Schemes launched under the aegis of Aatma Nirbhar Bharat. IFCI did not sanction any new loans or make any disbursements.

State Financial Corporations

There are 18 State Financial Corporations in India including Tamil Nadu Industrial Investment Corp. Ltd. The **State Financial Corporation of Punjab** was the first Financial Corporation to be set up in **1953.** State Financial Corporations and State Industrial Development and Investment Corporations extend financial assistance to small and medium entrepreneurs, individual trading concerns, partnership firms and private and public Ltd. companies to undertake promotional activities in their respective States. (6.16.86)

National Industrial Development Corporation –

NIDC, incorporated on 20.10.**1954,** provides consultancy services for meeting country's industrialization requirements, achieving a balanced development of Industries in the public and **private sectors**. NIDC was phenomenal in the establishment of primary producing units in the public sector. NIDC also rendered services to UNICEF, World Bank, USAID, etc. Since 1963, NIDC ceased financing private industry. National Industrial Development Corporation of India (NIDC) (yourarticlelibrary.com)

Industrial Credit and Investment Corporation of India

Industrial Credit and Investment Corp. of India - ICICI was established in **1955** as a public Ltd. Co. for developing medium and small industries of the private sector, with equity capital initially owned by companies, institutions and individuals. Later its equity capital was owned by public sector institutions like—Banks, LIC, GIC and their associate companies.
In March 2002, the ICICI merged with the ICICI Bank, creating a first universal bank in India. After this merger, ICICI ceased to exist as a development financial institution.
ICICI provided financial assistance as: (i) Long and medium-term loans both in terms of rupee and foreign currency, (ii) Participating in equity capital and debentures, (iii) Underwriting new issues of shares and debentures, (iv) Guarantee to suppliers of equipment and foreign loaners, etc.

A. Project Finance was provided to industries for establishment, modernization or expansion of manufacturing and processing activities (including purchase of equipment and machinery), for underwriting, subscription to shares and debentures in the form of rupee loans and guarantees to supply of capital equipment and foreign loaners in the form of foreign currency loans.
B. Leasing – Starting from 1983, leasing assistance was given for computerization, modernization / replacement, energy conservation, export orientation, pollution control etc.
C. Project Advisory Services were provided to Central and State Governments and public sector on policy reforms and value chain analysis and to private sector companies on strategic management.
D. ICICI offered information regarding facilities and incentives given by the Government to non-resident Indians for judiciously investing in India.

E. Foreign Currency Loans and advances were provided to Indian industrial concerns by ICICI to secure essential capital goods from foreign countries.

F. Promotion of Institutions

(a) ICICI promoted **Housing Development Finance Corporation** to provide long-term finance to individuals in middle- and lower-income groups, co-operatives, etc., for the construction and purchase of residential houses.

(b) **Credit Rating Information Services of India Ltd.** (CRISIL) was set up by ICICI in association with Unit Trust of India to provide credit rating services to the corporate sector.

(c) **Technology Development and Information Co. of India Ltd.** (TDICI) was promoted by ICICI, to finance the transfer and up gradation of technology and provide technology information.

(d) **P**rogram for the **A**dvancement of **C**ommercial **T**echnology was set up, with a grant of US $10 million from USAID, to assist market-oriented R&D activity, jointly undertaken by Indian and US companies. ICICI was entrusted with the administration and management of PACT.

(e) **P**rogram for **A**cceleration of **C**ommercial **E**nergy **R**esearch (PACER) was launched by ICICI, with a grant of US $20 million from USAID, to support selected research and technology development proposals in Indian energy sector.

National Small Industries Corporation Ltd.

National Small Industries Corporation was established in **1955** to assist Micro, Small and Medium Enterprises (MSMEs) by arranging supply of machines on hire-purchase terms, providing raw materials, organizing production by them for meeting Government orders and assisting them manufacture parts and components suitable to fit in with the products of the corresponding large units.

NSIC was providing marketing inputs for domestic production and exports, single point registration for government purchase, technical and managerial assistance, building necessary go-downs, organizing exhibitions and technology fairs, buyer-seller meets, export of projects and products, financing through syndication with banks for procurement of raw material, providing technology and credit support, bill discounting etc. NSIC helped SSI units in enterprise building, training to promote viable small industries, particularly in backward areas and in selected lines of production identified as priority areas for exports. (10.7.1.274)

NSIC made arrangements with SAIL, Rashtriya Ispat Nigam Ltd., Nalco, Hindustan Copper Ltd., CPCL, CIL and Sterlite Group for procuring raw material like steel, aluminium, copper, bitumen, coal, zinc etc., (with GAIL and IOCL for material handling arrangement with respect to LDPE/HDPE) to provide same at concessional rates to SSIs.

NSIC provided assistance to SSIs by taking orders from Government of India owned enterprises and procuring these machineries from SSI units, registering with government enterprises, providing complete assistance right from financing, training, providing raw materials for manufacturing and marketing of finished products of SSIs, which would otherwise not be able to survive in face of competition from large and big business conglomerates. It also helped SSIs by mediating with government owned banks to provide cheap finance and loans.

NSIC launched a web portal to facilitate connectivity to Indian MSMEs for global enterprises, in accessing information about the products and technologies available from MSME sector in India.

NSIC is also operating 24 go-downs at various places to make required material available at ease to small enterprises.

NSIC managed its operations in African countries through Johannesburg office, which, however, was closed in January 2018.

Credit support of Rs. 6401.16 Cr under Raw Material Assistance Scheme was given to MSMEs in 2022-23.

Unit Trust of India - Encourage savings of community for investment in development

The Unit Trust of India was set up on 1.02.**1964** (with initial capital contributed by RBI, LIC, SBI, its subsidiaries, and scheduled banks and financial institutions) to encourage and mobilize the savings of the community and channel them into productive corporate investment (4.14.8)

UTI offered small and large investors the means of acquiring shares in the properties, started for industrial growth of the country, by converting small savings into industrial financing for granting loans and advances to investors. The investors were given income tax rebate as an encouragement for investing in UTI.

UTI launched flagship scheme US-64 in 1964, Unit Linked Insurance Plan in1971, more schemes in 1986, 1992, 1993, 1995, 1997, 1999 etc.

In 1978 UTI was de-linked from the RBI and the Industrial Development Bank of India took over the regulatory and administrative control. At the end of 1988 UTI had Rs. 6700 Cr of assets under management.

The UTI Mutual Fund gained notoriety for creating a series of schemes that were suitable for all classes of Indian people. Mutual Funds were established by SBI in June 1987, Canbank in Dec 87, PNB in Aug 89, Indian Bank in Nov 89, Bank of India in Jun 90, Bank of Baroda in Oct 92, LIC in June 1989 and GIC in December 1990. At the end of 1993, the mutual fund industry had assets under management of Rs. 47,004 Cr.

UTI had in March 2000 more than Rs. 76,000 crores of assets under management

In early 2001, when the Ketan Parekh scam hit the markets leading to a huge decline in stock prices, US-64 came under severe redemption pressure. Against a face value of Rs 10, the actual value of a unit was down to Rs 6. The collapse of UTI was expected to jeopardize the savings of nearly 20 million mostly middle-class Indians, who had invested in the scheme under the mistaken impression that it was backed by the government. In September 2002, with government support, unit holders were given the option to redeem their units at par either for cash or convert them to six-year tax-free, interest-bearing bonds. When the bonds came up for redemption in May 2008, the government ended up with decent profits on the whole deal.

In end January 2003, there were 33 mutual funds with total assets of Rs. 1,21,805 Cr. The Unit Trust of India, with Rs. 44,541 Cr of assets under management, was way ahead of other mutual funds.

In February 2003, following the repeal of the Unit Trust of India Act 1963, UTI was bifurcated into two separate entities. One was Specified Undertaking of the Unit Trust of India SUUTI with assets under management of Rs. 29,835 crores (as in January 2003) including stocks of UTI Bank / Axis Bank, L&T and ITC. Second was the UTI Mutual Fund, sponsored by SBI, PNB, BOB and LIC.

UTI Mutual Fund was India's largest mutual fund, with about Rs. 35,028 Cr assets in 2006.

Government disinvested Axis Bank shares in SUUTI, fetching an amount of Rs. 5,379 Cr in 2018-19.

Total average assets under management of Axis Bank, Bank of India, IDBI, IIFCL, IL&FS, LIC, SBI and UTI Mutual Funds for the quarter Jan – Mar 2023 was **Rs. 1224050.94 Cr.** (30.21% of total Rs, 4051147.23 Cr)

Industrial Development Bank of India – Financing Industrial Investment by **Private Sector**

Industrial Development Bank of India - IDBI was constituted as a wholly owned subsidiary of the Reserve Bank of India in July **1964** to serve as the apex institution for term financing of industry, to provide larger financial assistance to new industries and coordinate the activities of the existing financing agencies. The Refinance Corporation was amalgamated with it. (4.14.8)

IDBI under its Bills Rediscounting Scheme was expected to provide Rs. 1,100 Cr for the State Plans. (7.4.40)

A network of specialized development banking institutions, with IDBI as apex, were established to help finance industrial investment in the **private sector**. These institutions, numbering over 50 in 1984-85, had become **a major source of long-term finance for the corporate sector** and had disbursed about Rs. 15,000 Cr. up to 1984-85. (7.7.4)

IDBI provided soft loan for modernization of the textile industry during VI plan period. (7.7.146)

Amalgamation of IDBI Bank Ltd., a subsidiary of IDBI Ltd., became effective w.e.f. Oct, 2004. It was empowered to finance all types of industrial concerns engaged in or to be engaged in the manufacture, processing or preservation of goods, mining, shipping, transport, hotel industry, informatics, medical and health services, generation or distribution of power, fishing or providing shore facilities for fishing, etc.

National Bank for Agriculture and Rural Development – Financing Rural Banks

NABARD was established on 12.07.**1982,** as an apex body for regulation of regional rural banks and apex cooperative banks in India, by replacing the Agricultural Credit Department and Rural Planning and Credit Cell of Reserve Bank of India and Agricultural Refinance and Development Corp.

The Department of Refinance (DOR) deals with short-term and long-term refinance functions of NABARD.
World Bank-affiliated organizations and global developmental agencies, working in the field of agriculture and rural development, help NABARD by advising and giving monetary aid for the upliftment of the people in the rural areas and optimizing the agricultural process.
NABARD implemented Self Help Group-Bank Linkage program, tree-based tribal communities' livelihoods initiative, watershed approach in soil and water conservation, increasing crop productivity initiatives through lead crop initiative and dissemination of information flow to agrarian communities through Farmer clubs.
NABARD finances institutions, providing investment for promoting developmental activities in rural areas.
NABARD refinances fund from World Bank and Asian Development Bank to State Co-operative Agriculture and Rural Development Banks, State Co-operative Banks, Regional Rural Banks, Commercial Banks and other financial institutions.
The credit flow to agriculture activities sanctioned by NABARD reached Rs 1,57,480 Cr in 2005–2006. Under Rural Infrastructure Development Fund scheme, Rs. 51,283 Cr was sanctioned for 2,44,651 projects covering irrigation, rural roads and bridges, health and education, soil conservation, water schemes etc.

Over the years, rural infrastructure funding to state governments has reached Rs. 5 Lakh Cr for 7.7 lakh projects in agriculture, rural connectivity and social sector. NABARD's Rural Infrastructure Development Fund created irrigation potential of 376 lakh hectare, laid 5.4 lakh kms of rural roads, built 13.3 lakh meters of rural bridges and generated 3029.2 Cr person days of non-recurring employment. annual-report-2022-23-full-report.pdf (nabard.org)

Infrastructure Leasing & Financial Services Ltd.

Infrastructure Leasing & Financial Services Ltd. - IL&FS, a state-funded infrastructure development and finance Co., was formed in **1987** by the Central Bank of India, Unit Trust of India and Housing

Development Finance Corp., to provide finance and loans for major infrastructure projects. Subsequently Orix Corp. of Japan, Abu Dhabi Investment Authority, LIC, SBI also invested in IL&FS.

In 2012, A2Z Group acquired IL&FS Property Management & Services Ltd in a cash and stock deal.
IL&FS had 256 group companies as of 2018, including subsidiaries, joint venture companies and associate entities. Though on the surface, the Co. appears to have 23 direct subsidiaries, 141 indirect subsidiaries (including special purpose vehicles for different projects), 6 joint ventures and 4 associate companies, each of them is further subdivided into additional legal entities, with much cross ownership as well as ownership by investment vehicles of various governments.

Infrastructure Services
a) IL&FS Energy Development Co. Ltd. - involved in development of power generation and transmission projects
b) IL&FS Infrastructure Development Corp. Ltd. - advisory and project development
c) IL&FS Transportation Networks Ltd. - involved in development projects related to surface transport (roads, highways, flyovers and bridges).
d) IL&FS Environmental Infrastructure & Services Ltd.
e) IL&FS Education and Technology Services Ltd.
f) New Tirupur Area Development Corp. Ltd. – implementation of Tirupur Area Development Program.
g) Noida Toll Bridge Co. Ltd – operation and maintenance of DND Flyway connecting Delhi with Noida.

Financial Services
a) IL&FS Financial Services Ltd - Investment Banking Arm of IL&FS
b) IL&FS Investment Managers Ltd. - domestic private equity fund management
c) ORIX Auto Infrastructure Services Ltd. - transport finance and transport infrastructure development
d) IL&FS Trust Co. Ltd. - ITCL – Debenture and bond trusteeship, trusteeship and investor representative for securitized paper, services as security trustee and facility agent, secure document management, and paralegal services.

IL&FS has several projects in different sectors including Transportation, Area Development, e-Governance, Health Initiatives, Cluster Development, Finance, Power, Ports, Water and Waste Water, Urban Infrastructure, Environment, Education, and Tourism.

In 2009, IL&FS promoted Maytas Infra Ltd. in 2009, and took it over in January 2011 and renamed as IL&FS Engineering and Construction Co. Ltd.
IL&FS was the principal lender for the construction of the 9.28 km long Dr. Syama Prasad Mookerjee Tunnel, located on the route of NH44 in Jammu & Kashmir. Its work was started in July 2011 and the tunnel was opened for traffic on 2.04.2017.

IL&FS reported defaults on its borrowing obligations during 2018-19. IL&FS has initiated the divestment processes in relation to various group entities. Of the recovery of Rs. 99355 Cr, Rs. 29030 Cr has already been addressed through resolution and cash recovery as on 14.07.21.

Small Industries Development Bank of India – Financing Small-scale Sector

Small Industries Development Bank of India - SIDBI was established on 2.04.**1990**, as a subsidiary of Industrial Development Bank of India, for promotion, financing and development of the small-scale industry by providing credit directly and through refinance to the nationalized banks and Bill Rediscounting Scheme. (9.5.283)

SIDBI was de-linked from IDBI with effect from 27.3.2000.

SIDBI and Scheduled Commercial Banks were asked to stimulate priority sector lending and expand direct lending to Small-scale units including MSMEs. (11.1.63).

The Credit Guarantee Cover Fund Scheme for Small Industries was launched jointly by the Govt of India and SIDBI (on a 4:1 contribution basis) in August 2000, to ensure greater flow of credit to the MSE sector without collateral security. Till the end of March 2007, 68062 proposals were approved and guarantee covers for Rs 1705 Cr were issued. (7.1.364)

Wholly owned subsidiaries of SIDBI are Micro Units Development & Refinance Agency Limited (MUDRA), SIDBI Venture Capital Ltd, SIDBI Trustee Company Ltd.

Outstanding loans & advances of SIDBI were Rs. 3,36,488 Cr in FY 2023, enabling higher MSE credit at competitive interest rates.

Irrigation and Water Resources Finance Corporation Ltd.

Irrigation and Water Resources Finance Corporation Ltd. - IWRFC was established on 29.03.**2008** to focus on Wastewater management and reuse including sanitation and waste management, Micro-irrigation and contract farming.

BANKING SECTOR

The Government of India took control of the Imperial Bank of India in 1955, with Reserve Bank of India taking a 60% stake, renaming it **State Bank of India**.

Indira Gandhi announced nationalization of 14 commercial Indian banks (Allahabad Bank, Canara Bank, United Bank of India, UCO Bank, Syndicate Bank, Indian Overseas Bank, Bank of Baroda, Punjab National Bank, Bank of India, Bank of Maharashtra, Central Bank of India, Indian Bank, Dena Bank and Union Bank) with deposits of over Rs 50 crores on 19.07.1969. These banks had **85% of bank deposits** in the country.

In 1980, six more banks with deposits over Rs. 200 Cr (Punjab and Sind bank, Oriental Bank of Commerce, Corporation Bank, Andhra Bank, New Bank of India and Vijaya Bank) were nationalized. With the second round of nationalization, government controlled approx. **91% of the banking business** of the country.

State Bank of India

Bank of Madras, Bank of Calcutta (oldest commercial bank in the Indian subcontinent, founded in 1806) and Bank of Bombay merged on 27.01.1921 to form the Imperial Bank of India.

On 1.07.**1955**, the Imperial Bank of India became the State Bank of India with RBI acquiring 60% stake. In 2008, the Government acquired the Reserve Bank of India's stake in SBI.
8 Banks that had belonged to princely states – State Bank of Bikaner and Jaipur, State Bank of Hyderabad, State Bank of Indore, State Bank of Mysore, State Bank of Patiala, State Bank of Saurashtra and State Bank of Travancore - were made subsidiaries of SBI in **1959**.

Banks merged with SBI - State Bank of Jaipur (est. 1943) and State Bank of Bikaner (est.1944) in 1963, State Bank of Saurashtra on 13.08.**2008**, State Bank of Indore with 470 branches on 19.06.**2009** and 5 remaining subsidiary banks (State Bank of Hyderabad, State Bank of Indore, State Bank of Mysore, State Bank of Patiala and State Bank of Travancore) on 1.04.2017.

Banks rescued by SBI - Bank of Bihar (est. 1911) with 28 branches in **1969**, National Bank of Lahore (est. 1942) with 24 branches in **1970** and Krishnaram Baldeo Bank, (established in 1916 in Gwalior State), in **1975**.

State Bank of India acquired 48.2% of the shares of Yes Bank as part of RBI directed **rescue** deal in March **2020**.

In **1985**, SBI acquired the Bank of Cochin, with 120 branches. SBI's affiliate, the State Bank of Travancore, already had an extensive network in Kerala.

SBI had over 24,000 branches in India. In **2012–13,** its revenue was Rs. 2.005 trillion (US$25 billion) As of **2014–15**, the bank had 191 overseas offices spread over 36 countries

SBI's non-banking subsidiaries include SBI Capital Markets Ltd, SBI Cards & Payments Services Pvt Ltd., SBI Life Insurance Co. Ltd., (formed In March 2001, with 74% of the total capital by SBI) and SBI Mutual Fund.

SBI is the 48th largest bank in the world by total assets and ranked 221st in the Fortune Global 500 list in 2020. It is **the largest bank in India** with a 23% market share by assets and **a 25% share of the total loan and deposits market.**

As on Dec 2023, Government of India held around 57.49% equity shares in SBI.
Revenue Rs. 504000 Cr (US$ 63 billion) in 2023.

Bank of Baroda –

Bank of Baroda was established in 1908 and was nationalized in 1969.

Banks acquired by BOB - Bareilly Corporation Bank (est. 1954) and Nainital Bank (est. in 1922) in 1975, Traders Bank in Delhi with 34 branches in 1988 and Mumbai-based Memon Cooperative Bank with 15 branches in Maharashtra and 3 in Gujarat in 2011.

Banks rescued by BOB - Punjab Cooperative Bank in 1997, Bareilly Corporation Bank with 64 branches in 1999, Benares State Bank with 105 branches (at the Reserve Bank of India's request) in 2002 and failed South Gujarat Local Area Bank in 2004.

Financial institutions established by BOB - IUB International Finance, a licensed deposit taker, in Hong Kong jointly with Union Bank of India and Indian Bank in 1980, Indo-Zambia in Lusaka jointly with Bank of India, Central Bank of India and ZIMCO (Zambian government) in 1985, Bank of Baroda (Botswana) in 2000, IndiaFirst Life Insurance Co. as a joint venture with Andhra Bank and Legal & General (UK) in 2008 and India International Bank Malaysia by a consortium with Indian Overseas Bank and Andhra Bank in 2010,

After IPO in 1996, the government of India owns 66% of the bank's equity.

In 2007, BOB's branches crossed 2000, and its global customer base 29 million people.

Dena Bank and Vijaya Bank merged with the Bank of Baroda w.e.f. 1.04.2019. Post-merger, the consolidated entity, with over 9,500 branches, 13,400 ATMs, 85,000 employees, 120 million customers and a combined business of Rs14.82 trillion, became the **third largest bank** after SBI and ICICI Banks

The bank has 107 branches/offices in 24 countries (excluding India) including 61 branches/offices of the bank, 38 branches of its 8 subsidiaries and 1 representative office in Thailand.
It is the **third largest public sector bank** in terms of revenue, with a total business of US$218 billion. Based on 2019 data, it is ranked 1145 on Forbes Global 2000 list.
Revenue of BOB was Rs. 110778 Cr (US $ 14 Billion) in 2023.

Punjab National Bank

Punjab National Bank was established on 19.05.1894.

Banks rescued by PNB - Hindustan Commercial Bank (est. in 1943) with 142 branches in 1986.

Banks acquired by PNB - New Bank of India in 1993 and Nedungadi Bank, the oldest private sector bank in Kerala, in 2003.

PNB acquired 30% stake in US based life insurance Co. MetLife's Indian affiliate MetLife India Ltd. and renamed as PNB MetLife India Ltd.

The Oriental Bank of Commerce and United Bank of India merged with Punjab National Bank w.e.f. 1.04.2020. After merger, Punjab National Bank became the second largest public sector bank in the country with assets of Rs.17.95 lakh Cr (US $ 220 billion) and 11,437 branches.

Subsidiaries of PNB - PNB Housing Finance Ltd., PNB MetLife India Insurance Co., Canara HSBC OBC Life Insurance Co. Ltd, India SME Asset Reconstruction Co. Ltd., PNB Cards and Services Ltd, PNB Insurance Broking Services Ltd (under winding up), PNB Investment Services Ltd, PNB Gilts Ltd, PNB International Ltd UK, Druk PNB Bank Ltd Bhutan, JSC (SB) PNB Bank Kazakhstan, Everest Bank Ltd Nepal, Sarva Haryana Gramin Bank, Himachal Gramin Bank, Punjab Gramin Bank, Prathama UP Gramin Bank, Dakshin Bihar Gramin Bank, Bangiya Gramin Vikash Bank, Assam Gramin Vikas Bank, Tripura Gramin Bank and Manipur Rural Bank.

Punjab National Bank is the fourth largest government-owned bank in terms of revenue. The bank has over 180 million customers, 12,248 branches, and 13,000+ ATMs.

Revenue of the bank was Rs. 99085 Cr (US$ 12 billion) in 2023.

Canara Bank

Canara Bank was established on 1.07.1906.

In 1976, Canara Bank inaugurated its 1000th branch.
In 1985, Canara Bank acquired Lakshmi Commercial Bank in a **rescue**.

Subsidiary companies: Canfin Homes Ltd. (with 110 branches), Canbank Factors Ltd., Canbank Venture Capital Fund Ltd., Canbank Computer Services Ltd., Canara Bank Securities Ltd., Canara Robeco Asset Management Co. Ltd., Canbank Financial Services Ltd., Canara HSBC Life Insurance Co. Ltd.

Canara Bank sponsored 4 Regional Rural Banks: Andhra Pragathi Grameena Bank, Kerala Gramin Bank, Karnataka Gramin Bank (with 1119 branches) and Karnataka Vikas Grameena Bank, (constituted on 12.09.2005 after amalgamation of 4 Regional Rural Banks – Malaprabha Grameena Bank, Bijapur Grameena Bank, Varada Grameena Bank and Netravathi Grameena Bank).

Syndicate Bank merged with Canara Bank with effect from 1.04.2020 creating the **Second largest public sector bank** in terms of revenue with total business of Rs. 15.20 lakh Cr (US$190 billion) and 10,324 branches. **Canara Bank's Revenue was Rs. 111210 Cr (US $ 14 Billion) in 2023. Government owns 62.93%.**

AXIS Bank / UTI Bank

Axis bank was founded on 3.12.1993 as **UTI Bank**, promoted jointly by Unit Trust of India, LIC, GIC, National Insurance Co., New India Assurance Co., The Oriental Insurance Corp. and United India Insurance Co. The first branch was inaugurated on 2.04.1994.

UTI Bank opened overseas branches in Singapore and Shanghai, China in 2006, Dubai and Hongkong in 2007.
On 30.07.2007, UTI Bank changed its name to Axis Bank.

In 2013, Axis Bank's subsidiary, Axis Bank UK commenced banking operations.

As of 31.03.2023, the bank had a network of 4,903 branches and extension counters, 9 international offices, 15,953 ATMs and cash recyclers. It operates an ATM at one of the world's highest sites at Thegu, Sikkim at a height of 4,023 m.

Axis Bank has subsidiaries – Axis Capital Ltd., Axis Securities Ltd., Axis Private Equity Ltd. and Axis Mutual Fund.

Revenue of Axis Bank was Rs. 137989 Cr. (US $ 17 billion) in 2024.

Union Bank of India

Union Bank of India was established on 11.11.1919 in Bombay.

When the Indian government nationalized Union Bank of India in 1969, it had 240 branches.
In 1975, UBI acquired private sector Belgaum Bank in 1975, Miraj State Bank, with 26 branches, in 1985 and Sikkim Bank with 8 branches in 1999.

Subsidiaries of Union Bank of India are – Union Bank of India (UK) Ltd., Union Asset Management Co. Pvt Ltd., Union Trustee Co. Pvt Ltd, Star Union Daichi Life Insurance Co. Ltd., Chaitanya Godavari Grameen Bank, Corpbank Securities Ltd. and UBI Services Ltd.

After amalgamation with Corporation Bank and Andhra Bank on 1.04.2020, Union Bank became the **fifth largest public sector bank** in the country with assets of ₹14.59 lakh Cr (US$180 billion) and 9,609 branches, 11100+ ATMs, 15300+ Business Correspondent Points serving over 120 million customers.

Union Bank of India, has a total business of US$106 billion.

Revenue of the bank was Rs. 97078.5 Cr (US $ 12 billion) in FY 23. Government holds 83.49%.

Bank of India

Bank of India was established in 1906.

In 1986, Bank of India acquired Parur Central Bank in Ernakulam, Kerala (founded in 1930) with 51 branches in a **rescue** and amalgamated in 1990
BOI took over 3 UK branches of Central Bank of India in 1987.
In 2007, BOI acquired 76% of Indonesia-based PT Bank Swadesi.

Subsidiaries established by BOI - Bank of India (New Zealand) Ltd. in Auckland on 6.10.2011, Bank of India (Uganda) Ltd. on 18.06.2012 and Bank of India (Botswana) Ltd. on 9.08.2013.

As on 31.12.2023, Bank of India's total business stood at Rs. 12,72,887 Cr. (US$160 billion), had 5139 branches and 8166 ATMs around the world (including 22 overseas branches). There were 60 branches, 5 subsidiaries, and 1 joint venture abroad.

Revenue of the bank was Rs. 55143 Cr. (US $ 6.9 Billion) in 2023

Indian Bank

Indian Bank was established in 1907.

Indian Bank founded the first regional rural bank, Sri Venkateswara Grameena Bank, in 1981.
In 1990, Indian Bank **rescued** Bank of Tanjore (established in 1901), with its 157 branches.

Subsidiaries established by Indian Bank - Indbank Merchant Banking Services in 1989 and Ind Bank Housing Ltd. in 1991.

Indfund Management Ltd was established in 1994 to manage the operations of Indian Bank Mutual Fund and was amalgamated with Indian Bank in 2012.

In June 2015, business of the bank crossed the milestone target of Rs. 3 lakh Cr (US$38 billion).

Allahabad Bank merged with Indian Bank on 1.4.2020, making Indian Bank the **seventh largest public sector bank** in the country with assets of Rs. 8.08 lakh crore (US$100 billion).

Indian Bank serves over 100 million customers with 5,814 branches, 4929 ATMs and Cash deposit machines. It has 227 overseas correspondent banks in 75 countries.
Total business of the bank touched Rs. 10,94,752 Cr. (US$130 billion) as on 31.03.2023.
Revenue of Indian Bank was Rs. 52085 Cr (US$ 6.5 billion) in 2023. Government owns 79.86%.

Syndicate Bank

Syndicate Bank was founded in 1925 as Canara Industrial and Banking Syndicate Ltd.

In December 1969, Syndicate Bank had 350 branches and by December 1974, it had 700 branches. Syndicate bank established the first Regional Rural Bank of India, Prathama Bank, in Moradabad, UP in 1975 and Netravati Grameena Bank in Mangalore and Varada Grameena Bank in Kumta in 1984, sponsored establishment of Malaprabha Grameena Bank in Dharwad, Karnataka in 1976 and Bijapur Grameena Bank in 1983
By December 1986, it had 1456 branches.
In1999, Syndicate Bank held its first IPO, which diluted the **stake of Government of India to 76%.**

By March 2015, the bank had 3552 branches.

Revenue of the bank was Rs. 23949.22 Cr (US $ 3.0 billion) in 2019.

Syndicate Bank merged with Canara Bank with effect from 1.04.2020.

Indian Overseas Bank

Indian Overseas Bank was founded in February 1937 for specializing in foreign exchange business and overseas banking.

Banks acquired by IOB - Bank of Tamil Nadu, with 99 branches, in a **rescue** in 1988-89, Mumbai-based Adarsh Janata Sahakari Bank in 2001, (took over) Bharat Overseas Bank in 2007 and Shree Suvarna Sahakari Bank, with 12 branches in 2009

Financial institutions established by IOB - United Asian Bank Berhad in Malaysia with Indian Bank and United Commercial Bank in 1973 and Bharat Overseas Bank with 6 Indian private banks (as a Chennai-based private bank) to take over IOB's Bangkok branch.

In 1984, 1000th branch of IOB was opened.
Initial Purchase Offering in 2000 brought the **government's share in the bank's equity down to 75%.**
In 2010, Yamuna Vihar, New Delhi branch was opened as 2000th branch.
As on 31.3.2013, total deposits reached Rs. 202,135 cr. (US$37,236Mn.), total advances reached Rs. 164,366cr. (US$30,278 Mn.) and total Business Mix was at Rs. 366,501 cr. (US$67,514Mn.), Total No. of Branches 2908.
Bank surpassed the landmark of 3000 ATMs on 31.07.2014

IOB entered into Non-Life Insurance Business with Universal Sompo General Insurance Co. Ltd with equity participation of 19% along with Indian Bank, Karnataka Bank, and Dabur Investments.

As on 31 March 2022, IOB's total business stood at ₹417,960 crore (US$52 billion).

Revenue of the bank was Rs. 23509.07 Cr. in 2023.
As of June 2023, IOB had 3,222 domestic branches and 3495 ATMs.

Central Bank of India

The Central Bank of India, established on 21.12.1911, was the first commercial Indian bank completely owned and managed by Indians.

Before World War II, CBI established a branch in Rangoon to carry on business between Burma and India, especially telegraphic transfer.

In 1963, the revolutionary government in Burma nationalized CBI's operations there, making it People's Bank No. 1.

Indian Government nationalized CBI on 19.07.1969.

CBI was one of the first banks to issue credit cards in 1980 in collaboration with Mastercard.

On its 108th Foundation Day (2019), CBI launched banking robot named "MEDHA"

As on 31.03.2021, the bank had a network of 4,608 branches, 3,644 ATMs, with a **revenue of Rs. 29626 Cr. in 2023.**

Andhra Bank

Andhra Bank was established on 28.11.1923.

IndiaFirst Life Insurance Co. was incorporated in 2009 as a joint venture with Bank of Baroda and UK's financial and investment Co. Legal & General.

India International Bank (Malaysia) was formed jointly with Bank of Baroda and Indian Overseas Bank in 2010.

The bank did a total business of Rs. 3,106 billion (US$39 billion) in 2015–16.

Andhra Bank had a network of 2885 branches, 4 extension counters, 38 satellite offices and 3798 ATMs as of 31.03.2019.

The **government of India owned 90.85% of its share capital** as on 31.03.2019.

Revenue of Andhra bank was Rs. 20977.26 Cr (US $ 2.6 billion) in 2018-19.

Andhra Bank and Corporation Bank merged into Union Bank of India on 1.04.2020.

Vijaya Bank

Vijaya Bank was established by a group of farmers on 23.10.1931.

The bank became a scheduled bank in 1958.
Vijaya Bank grew into a large All India Bank with 9 smaller banks merging with it during 1963–1968.
At the time of nationalization in 1980, Vijaya Bank had 571 branches, with a total business of ₹605.95 Cr.

The bank had a network of 2031 branches (as of March 2017) throughout the country and over 4000 customer touch points including 2001 ATMs.
The bank's total business was Rs. 2,29,000 Cr as at 31.3.2017. **Its revenue was Rs. 14190 Cr in 2018.**

Vijaya Bank merged with Bank of Baroda on 1.04.2019

Allahabad Bank –

Allahabad Bank was founded in 1865.

In 1989, Allahabad Bank acquired United Industrial Bank, established in 1940, with its 145 branches.
In 1991, Allahabad Bank established AllBank Finance Ltd. as a wholly owned merchant banking subsidiary.

The IPO of Oct 2002 and second public offering of Apr 2005, reduced the **Government's shareholding to** 71.16% and **55.23%.**

As of 31.03.2018, Allahabad Bank had over 3245 branches across India. The bank did a total business of Rs. 3.8 trillion during 2017–18. The bank's market capitalization in June 2018 was US$ 573 million and ranked number 1,882 on the Forbes Global 2000 list.

Revenue of the bank was Rs. 18564.50 Cr. (US $ 2.3 Billion) in 2019.

Allahabad Bank was merged with Indian Bank in 2020.

Oriental Bank of Commerce

Oriental Bank of Commerce was established on 19.02.1943.

In 1997, OBC acquired Bari Doab Bank and Punjab Cooperative Bank.
On 14.08.2004, OBC amalgamated Global Trust Bank with its 103 branches.
The bank crossed the Business Mix mark of Rs. 2,37,000 Cr on 31.03.2010 making it the seventh-largest Public Sector Bank in India.

OBC had 2390 branches and 2625 ATM's in 2018-19.

Revenue of the OBC was Rs. 17867.69 Cr (US$ 2.2 billion) in 2019.

In April 2020, OBC bank along with United Bank of India merged with Punjab National Bank.

Bank of Maharashtra

Bank of Maharashtra was registered on 16.09.1935 and became operational on 8.02.1936.

The total business of the bank crossed Rs. 3,15,620 Cr as on 31.12.2021.

The bank had 29 million customers across the country with 2022 branches as of March 2022.

Revenue of Bank of Maharashtra in 2023 was **Rs. 18178.73 Cr (US $ 2.3 Billion).**

United Commercial Bank (UCO Bank)

United Commercial Bank was established in 1943.

United Commercial Bank, Indian Overseas Bank, and Indian Bank formed a new joint-venture bank "United Asian Bank" in Malaysia. At the time, Indian Bank had 3 branches, and Indian Overseas Bank and United Commercial Bank had 8 between them.

UCO Bank ranked 1948 in Forbes Global 2000 list of year 2018.
Based on 2020 data, UCO Bank ranked 80 on the Fortune India 500 list.
UCO Bank had 3,205 branches, 2,564 ATMs. 4 overseas branches in Singapore and Hongkong.

Revenue of the bank was Rs. 20158.97 Cr. (US $ 2.5 Billion) in 2023.
In FY 2022–23, its total business was Rs. 4.1 lakh Cr. As on 31.3.2021, **government share-holding in the bank was 95.39%.**

United Bank of India

When Comilla Banking Corporation, Bengal Central Bank, Comilla Union Bank and Hooghly Bank were in financial crunch, **Reserve Bank of India assisted these banks** in amalgamation to form United Bank of India in 1950.

At the time of nationalization in 1969, UBI had 174 branches.
UBI acquired Hindustan Mercantile Bank (est. in 1944) in 1973 and Narang Bank of India, (est. in 1943) in 1976.

Revenue of the bank was Rs. 10945.00 Cr. (US $ 1.4 billion) in 2019.

United Bank and Oriental Bank of Commerce merged with Punjab National Bank on 1.04.2020.

Dena Bank

Dena Bank was founded on 26.05.1938 under the name Devkaran Nanjee Banking Co.

Dena Bank had 1872 branches and **revenue of Rs. 8932.23 Cr (US $ 1.1 Billion) in 2018.**
Dena Bank merged with Bank of Baroda with effect from 1.04.2019 along with Vijaya Bank.

IDBI Bank Ltd.

IDBI Bank Ltd., a subsidiary of Life Insurance Corporation, was established in 1964 as Industrial Development Bank of India to function as a development finance institution and to provide financial and banking services to industrial sector

In 2005, IDBI was merged with its commercial division, IDBI Bank, forming the present-day banking entity and was categorized in "other public sector banks" category.

Later in March 2019, RBI recategorized it as a private bank and government asked LIC to infuse capital in the bank due to high NPA and capital adequacy issues and also asked LIC to manage the bank to meet the regulatory norms.
Many national institutes find their roots in IDBI like SIDBI, India Exim Bank, National Stock Exchange of India, SEBI and National Securities Depository Ltd.
As of September 2021, Life Insurance Corporation held 49.24% shareholding and the Union government held 45.48%, with LIC being in control of the management of the bank.
IDBI provided financial assistance, both in rupee and foreign currencies, for green-field projects and also for expansion, modernization, and diversification purposes.
IDBI has 2,005 Retail Banking Branches and 3,353 ATMs including one overseas branch in Dubai.

Revenue of the bank was Rs. 25166.91 Cr (US $ 3.2 Billion) in 2023.

Punjab and Sind Bank

Punjab and Sind Bank was established on 24.06.1908.

As of 18.04.2023, the Punjab and Sind Bank had 1553 branches.
In FY 2020-21, total business of the bank stood at Rs. 1,63,919.18 Cr.
Revenue of the bank was Rs. 8826.92 Cr (US$ 1.1 billion) in 2020.

Corporation Bank

Corporation Bank was founded on 12.03.1906.

Corporation Bank had a network of 2,432 fully automated CBS branches, 3,040 ATMs, and 4,724 branchless banking units across the country.
Revenue of the bank was Rs. 17494.70 Cr. (US $ 2.2 Billion) in 2019.

Corporation Bank and Andhra Bank merged into Union Bank of India on 1.04.2020.

New Bank of India

New Bank of India was established in 1936.

Punjab National Bank acquired New Bank of India in 1993.

Yes Bank

Yes Bank was founded in 2004 by rebranding a non-banking financial enterprise started in 1999.

Yes Bank's inability to raise capital over several years led to a steady deterioration in its financial position in 2020, leading to potential loan losses, and to downgrades, which prompted investors to invoke bond covenants, and withdrawal of deposits.

On 5.03.2020, the RBI announced suspension of Yes Bank's board and imposed a 30-day moratorium on its operations, during which period, Yes Bank customers were allowed to withdraw only up to Rs. 50,000 from their accounts for the following month, except in certain situations, subject to RBI's approval.

A consortium of 8 public and private banks (State Bank of India, ICICI Bank, HDFC Bank, Axis Bank, Kotak Mahindra Bank) and other private parties agreed to infuse capital of Rs. 12,000 Cr. into Yes Bank. The bank came out of the moratorium and resumed full-fledged banking operations from 18.03.2020. In March 2020, SBI invested Rs. 7,250 Cr (US$910 million) in Yes Bank and held 30% stake as of 28.7.2020.

Revenue of the bank was Rs. 32961 Cr (US $ 4.1 Billion) in 2024

Bharatiya Mahila Bank

Bharatiya Mahila Bank is a fully owned subsidiary of State Bank of India and was inaugurated on 19.11.2013.

The bank merged with State Bank of India on 1.04.2017. As on date of merger, it had 103 Branches. The merger of this bank with SBI added business of Rs. 1,600 crores to SBI.

India Post Payment Bank Ltd

India Post Payment Bank Ltd was set up on 27.08.2016 to provide easy access to formal financial services by removing the barriers for the unbanked.

The Bank offers savings and current accounts up to a balance of Rs 1 Lac, digitally enabled payments and remittance services of all kinds between entities and individuals and also provides access to insurance, mutual funds, pension, credit products, forex, and more, in partnership with insurance companies, mutual fund houses, pension providers, banks, international money transfer organizations etc.

As of January 2024, the bank had more than 8 crore customers.

Repco Bank

Repco Bank (Repatriates Cooperative and Finance and Development Bank) is a cooperative bank established by the Government of India in **1969** to meet the financial needs of repatriates from neighbouring countries mainly from Sri Lanka and Burma. The total business of Repco Bank grew to Rs. 17746 Cr as of 31.03.23.

Repco Bank has 2 subsidiaries namely, Repco Home Finance Ltd and Repco Micro Finance Ltd.

Security Printing and Minting Corporation of India Ltd.

Security Printing and Minting Corporation of India Ltd. – The Government of India Mint at Alipore was opened on 19.03.1952. The full operation for the coinage and preparation of medals, decorations and badges started from this date. In addition to production of coins for domestic use, this mint also produced coins for other nations.

A security paper mill was to be set up for achieving self-sufficiency in the supply of security and bond paper. (2.19.38)

SPMCIL was incorporated on 13.1.2006 after corporatization of 9 Mints / Presses / Mills which were working earlier under the Ministry of Finance as industrial departmental organizations, to produce high quality security products of international standards and to fully meet the requirements of Central Government and State Governments regarding security products and currency and coin indents of RBI.

SPMCIL is engaged in providing services in the field of manufacture of security paper, minting of coins, printing of currency, non-judicial Stamp papers, postal stationery, stamps, cheques for Government of India departments, passport, visa stickers, identity cards, commemorative coins, MICR and Non-MICR cheques, bonds, warrants, security inks, medallions, refining of gold, silver and assay of precious metals, etc. through its 9 operating units (2 security Presses - Nashik and Hyderabad, 2 currency presses at Dewas and Nashik, 4 Mints - Mumbai, Hyderabad, Kolkata and Noida and one paper mill – Hoshangabad).

The installed capacities of SPMCIL in 2019-20 were 8100 million pieces for bank notes, 7750 million pieces for Circulating coins, 420 million pieces for non-judicial stamp paper and 15 million pieces for passports and allied booklets.

Central Registry of Securitization Asset Reconstruction and Security Interest of India

Central Registry of Securitization Asset Reconstruction and Security Interest of India was incorporated on 05.03.2011 for maintaining and operating Central KYC Records Registry, Security Interest and Factoring transactions Registry.

Repository of 532 million KYC information of individuals and 1.5 million KYC information of legal Entities completed during 2022-23. Gross turnover in 2022-23 was Rs. 142.59 Cr.

INSURANCE COMPANIES

Life Insurance Corporation of India was established in the year 1956 with a view to reach all insurable persons and provide them with adequate financial cover at a reasonable cost.

Since the opening up of the insurance sector in 1999, the number of participants in the sector went up from six insurers in 2000 to 42 insurers operating in life, non-life and reinsurance segments (as in October, 2008).

As many as 8 insurance companies (life and non-life insurance) are functioning in the public sector. These enterprises are LIC, National Insurance Co. Ltd., New India Assurance Co. Ltd., Oriental Insurance Co. Ltd., United India Insurance Co. Ltd., General Insurance Corp. of India, Agriculture Insurance Co. of India Ltd. and Export Credit Guarantee Corp. of India.

Private life insurance companies - Allianz Bajaj Life Insurance Co. Ltd., Birla Sun-Life Insurance Co. Ltd., HDFC Standard Life Insurance Co. Ltd., ICICI Prudential Life Insurance Co. Ltd., ING Vysya Life Insurance Co. Ltd., Max New York Life Insurance Co. Ltd., MetLife Insurance Co. Ltd., Om Kotak Mahindra Life Insurance Co. Ltd., SBI Life Insurance Co. Ltd., TATA AIG Life Insurance Co. Ltd.

Private General Insurance Companies - Bajaj Allianz General Insurance Co. Ltd., ICICI Lombard General Insurance Co. Ltd., IFFCO-Tokio General Insurance Co. Ltd., Reliance General Insurance Co. Ltd., Royal Sundaram Alliance Insurance Co. Ltd., TATA AIG General Insurance Co. Ltd.,

The **Insurance Regulatory and Development Authority** (IRDA) was constituted on 19.04.2000 to regulate and develop the business of insurance and re-insurance in the country.

Life insurance penetration increased to 2.82% in 2019.

Life Insurance Corporation of India

Life Insurance Corporation of India (LIC) was established in 1956 to reach all insurable persons in the country and provide them with adequate financial cover at a reasonable cost.

In 2007-08 - LIC covered 63,546 policies and generated total premium income of Rs.550 Cr. Number of agents were 11,93,744.
At the end of 2012-13, LIC had 53 individual products and 10 group products for sale.

LIC had 8 Zonal Offices, 113 Divisional Offices, 2048 Branch Offices, 1401 Satellite offices and 1240 Mini Offices on 31.03.2016.
LIC has branch Offices (in U.K., Mauritius and Fiji), joint venture companies and wholly owned subsidiary in 14 countries.

It has Joint Venture Companies – (i) Life Insurance Corp. (International), Bahrain, (covering Qatar, Kuwait, Oman, Dubai and Abu Dhabi), (ii) Kenindia Assurance Co. Ltd., Nairobi, (iii) Life Insurance Corp. (Nepal) Ltd, (iv) Life Insurance Corp. (Lanka) Ltd. (v) Life Insurance Corp. (Mauritius) Offshore Ltd. regd. in Nairobi - a Joint Venture of LIC and GIC with focus on non-life reinsurance business, (vi) Saudi Indian Co. (joint venture with New India Assurance Co. Ltd. and others) for Co-operative Insurance in the Kingdom of Saudi Arabia to transact both Life and Non-Life Insurance business, (vii) a Wholly Owned Subsidiary in Singapore in 2015-16.(viii) LIC Bangladesh Ltd.

LIC's asset base crossed Rs 38 Lakh Cr on 6.9.2021, which was more than **15 times the AUM of top private life companies like HDFC Life or ICICI Prudential.**

As of March 2021, LIC's total investments were Rs. 36,76,110 Cr with a life fund of Rs. 34,36,686 Cr (the life fund grew from Rs.6,86,616.45 Cr. on 31.3.2008)

LIC became India's **Fifth** most valuable Co. with a market capitalization of Rs. 5.54 lakh Cr. on 17.05.22.

Share in premium - LIC's **total premium** up to February 2023 was Rs. 11,879 Cr against total premium of Rs. 10,968 Cr of private life insurers. LIC sold 16 lakh policies (**70%**) up to February 2023, out of total 22.86 lakh policies issued in life insurance segment. (Indian Express dt 9.03.23).

LIC's **first year premium income** in FY23 was Rs. 2.3 Lakh Cr. (**62.6%** of total first year premium income of insurance industry of Rs. 3.7 lakh Cr). The balance was shared by 22 private insurers. (Indian Express dt 26.05.23)

LIC Supports industrial development – As on 31.03.2022, LIC managed Reliance Industries Ltd. stocks of Rs 1,01,211 Cr, ITC stocks of Rs. 72,745 Cr, TCS stocks of Rs. 52393 Cr, Infosys stocks of Rs 42,588 Cr., etc.
SBI (Rs 33,855 Cr), L&T (Rs 31,960 Cr), ICICI Bank (Rs 31,948 Cr) and Hindustan Unilever (Rs 24,747 Cr) were among LIC's biggest holdings as of 31.12.2021 in value terms.
LIC owned more than a 1% stake in 278 NSE-listed companies as of 31.12.2021.

ITC (16.21%), Hindustan Copper (14.22%), NMDC (14.16%), MTNL (13.12%), Larsen & Toubro (12%) and Oil India (11.85%), Castrol India Ltd (11.34%) were some of the companies where LIC had the highest shareholdings in percentage terms.

LIC had exposure to 15 private companies, which were facing insolvency during 2015-16 including DHFL, Reliance Communications, Reliance Capital, Jaiprakash Associates, Amtek Auto, IL&FS and Sintex.

LIC stocks: LIC owns stocks worth Rs 9.5 lakh crore! Check out its biggest holdings - The Economic Times (indiatimes.com)

LIC's total assets were Rs. 49,24,495.5 Cr and revenue was Rs, 7,84,889 Cr in 2023.

National Insurance Co.:

National Insurance Co. Ltd. was formed by nationalizing and amalgamating 21 Foreign & 11 Indian non-life insurance companies in 1972.

NIC transacts fire, marine, general, vehicle, health, property, crop, aviation insurances
Starting off with a premium base of Rs. 50 Cr in 1974, the gross premiums from underwriting by NIC grew from Rs. 61 billion in 2010-11 to Rs. 100 billion in 2013–14 and Rs. 160 billion in 2017–18.
NIC ranked **second among general insurance companies**, behind New India Assurance 0n 31.03.2014. NIC had 1,995 offices including Micro offices in 2014-15.

On 2.02.2018, Government of India merged NIC with United India Insurance Co and Oriental Insurance.

Total Assets – Rs. 38896 Cr and Revenue – Rs. 17385 Cr. (2023), Owner – GoI 100%.

New India Assurance Co.

The New India Assurance Co. Ltd. was formed by nationalizing and amalgamating 32 Foreign & Indian non-life insurance companies in 1972. NIA undertakes general, vehicle, health, marine, property, crop, aviation insurances.

NIAC had 2221 offices in 2014-15.
NIAC operates through a network of 19 Branches, 7 Agencies, 3 Subsidiary Companies and 4 Associate Companies in 20 countries in 2014-15.
NIAC, which collected direct premium of Rs. 26,813 Cr. in 2019-20, remained as the **largest general insurance Co.** in India.

Total assets Rs. 98223 Cr. and revenue Rs. 41073 Cr in 2023. Government of India owns 85.44%.

Oriental Insurance Co.

The Oriental Insurance Co. Ltd. was formed by nationalizing and amalgamating 10 Foreign & 12 Indian non-life insurance companies in 1972.

OIC has more than 2000 offices with foreign operations in Nepal, Dubai & Kuwait.
OIC offers more than 170 products in General insurance and health insurance.

It recorded a gross premium of ₹15,993 crore (US$2.0 billion) in 2022–23.
OIC had total assets of Rs 35167 Cr. in 2023. **Government of India owns 100%.**

United India Insurance Co.

United India Insurance Co. Ltd. was formed by nationalizing and amalgamating 12 Indian companies, 4 cooperative societies & Indian operations of 5 foreign companies

UIIC had 1,941 offices including 30 regional offices and 511 micro-offices on 31.03.2023.
UIIC products included General Insurance, Vehicle insurance, Health Insurance, Marine insurance, property insurance, Crop insurance, Aviation insurance, Fidelity bond, etc.
It gave complicated insurance covers to ONGC, GMR – Hyderabad International Airport, Mumbai International Airport, Tirumala – Tirupati Devasthanam, Kochi Metro Rail Corp. etc.
On 2.02.2018, govt of India announced merger of UIIC with Oriental Insurance and National Insurance Co Ltd.

The gross direct premium for 2022-23 was Rs. 17644 Cr.
Revenue Rs. 17644 Cr (2022-23), Total Assets – Rs. 44253.5 Cr. Owner – 100% GOI.

General Insurance Corporation of India (GIC)

General Insurance Corporation of India (GIC) was set up on 22.11.1972 for the purpose of superintending, controlling and carrying on the business of 'General Insurance' through its 4 subsidiaries viz. NIC, NIAC, OIC. and UIIC. The GIC was designated as the 'Indian Reinsurer' on 3.11.2000 and its supervisory role over its subsidiaries ended. GIC Re provides reinsurance support for all the non-life general insurance companies in India.

GIC also holds 35% share in Agriculture Insurance Co. of India Ltd.

GIC undertakes foreign reinsurance business through its branch offices in Dubai, Kuala Lumpur and London, and a Representative Office in Moscow. GIC Re leads the reinsurance programmers of insurance companies in SAARC region, African countries and in the Middle East.

GIC Re participates in the share capital of Kenindia Assurance Co. Ltd. (Kenya), India International Insurance Pte Ltd., Singapore, LIC (Mauritius) Offshore Ltd., GIC Bhutan Re Ltd (Bhutan), Asian Reinsurance Corp., Bangkok and East Africa Re and East Africa Reinsurance Co. Ltd., in Kenya.

GIC diversified into life reinsurance, off-shore energy and liability business. GIC Re has an 'Eventual Reinsurer' status in Brazil.

The insurance market was opened to foreign reinsurance players by late 2016 including companies from Germany, Switzerland and France.

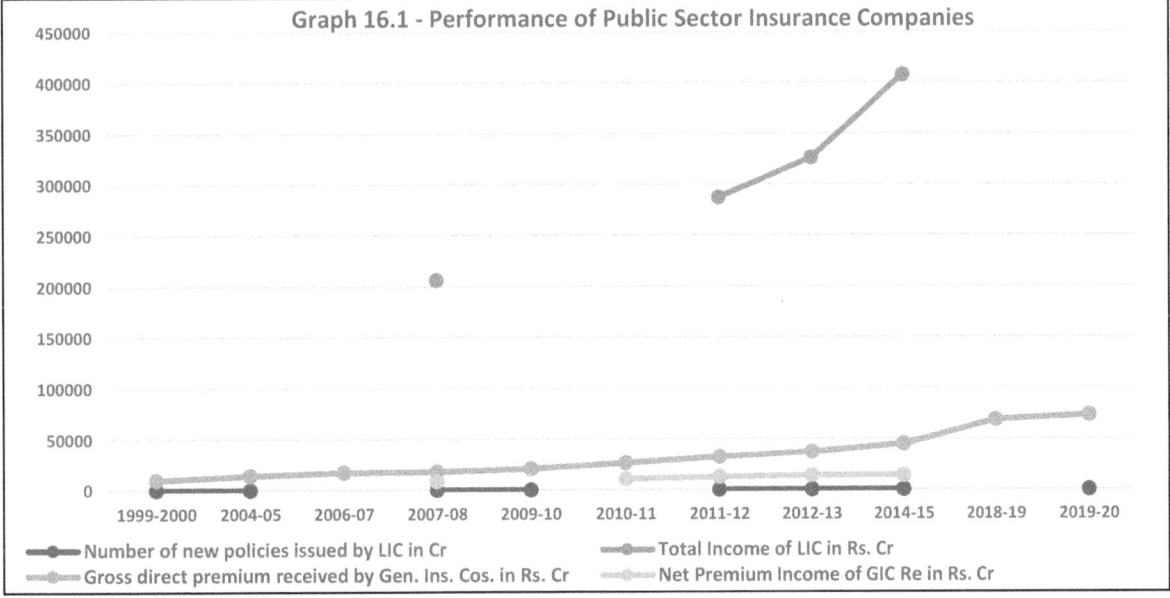

Graph 16.1 - Performance of Public Sector Insurance Companies

*GIC was mainly underwriting Aviation Insurance Business of Air India and Indian Airlines, besides administering the Crop Insurance initially. **GIC Re was also the 5th largest aviation reinsurer globally.**

*In 2022, GIC was the 15th largest Global Reinsurer, a USD 7 billion net worth Co.
Revenue – Rs. 47751 Cr. and Net Assets – Rs. 162731 Cr. in 2023. Government holds 85.78%.

Contribution to GDP - Banking and insurance services add about 7% to India's GDP

Insurance Regulatory and Development Authority

The Insurance Regulatory and Development Authority - IRDA was constituted on 19.04.2000 to regulate and develop the business of insurance and re-insurance by promoting competition to enhance customer satisfaction with increased consumer choice and lower premiums while ensuring the financial security of the insurance market.

IRDA opened up the market in August 2000 with an invitation for registration of applications; foreign companies were allowed ownership up to 26%. IRDA framed regulations ranging from company registrations to the protection of policyholder interests since 2000. The FDI limit in the insurance sector has been raised to 74% according to the 2021 union budget.

Agriculture Insurance Company of India Ltd. (AICIL)

The Agriculture Insurance Co. of India Ltd. - AICIL was set up to implement various Crop Insurance Schemes of Government of India likely to be introduced from time to time and other insurance products relating to agriculture with equity participation from GIC, NABARD, and 4 public sector general insurance companies (i.e., NIC, NIAC, OIC & UIIC).

AICIL commenced its business w.e.f. 1.4.2003 with transfer of Crop Insurance Business from GIC and assets and liabilities of Central Crop Insurance Department, Delhi.

National Agricultural Insurance Scheme was implemented by 24 States and 2 Union Territories. Since introduction in Rabi 1999-2000 to Rabi 2014-15, NAIS covered about 24.02 Cr farmers covering 35.76 Cr hectare area for sum insured of Rs. 386285.73 Cr against premium of Rs. 11563.26 Cr.

AICL launched **Weather Based Crop Insurance Scheme** during Kharif 2007 season in Karnataka insuring 50,000 hectares of crops for a risk value of Rs. 53 Cr with a premium of Rs. 7.03 Cr (farmers' share of premium was Rs. 1.42 Cr).

For Rabi 2007-08, AICL implemented WBCIS in Bihar, Chhattisgarh, Madhya Pradesh and Rajasthan covering 6.27 lakh farmers growing crops in over 9.84 lakh hectares against a sum insured of Rs. 1,705 Cr, with a gross premium of Rs. 139 Cr, of which the farmers' share of premium was Rs. 43 Cr. Total claims for this season were Rs. 101 crores. The Gross Direct Premium of the Co. was Rs. 835.00 crore. (12.14.6.1)

Since introduction in Kharif 2007 to Rabi 2014-15, under WBCIS, AICIL covered about 3.45 Cr farmers insuring 4.63 Cr hectare area for sum insured of Rs. 63494.68 Cr. against premium of Rs. 6021.72 Cr.

The Co. enjoys the distinction of being **the largest crop insurance provider in the world** in terms of the number of farmers insured annually.

Monopolies and Restrictive Trade Practices Commission

Monopolies and Restrictive Trade Practices Commission was set up under Monopolies and Restrictive Trade Practices Act 1969 under Ministry of Company Affairs to prevent practices of companies, wielding monopolistic power, to abuse the market in terms of production and sales of goods and services.

In terms of the behavioural doctrine, the conduct of the entities, which indulge in trade practices detrimental to the public interest is examined whether said practices constitute any monopolistic, restrictive or unfair trade practice.

In terms of the reformist doctrine, when MRTP Commission finds that errant undertaking indulged in restrictive or unfair trade practice, it can direct the undertaking to discontinue or not to repeat the undesirable trade practice, can accept assurance of errant undertaking that it took steps to ensure that the prejudicial effect of trade practice no longer exist.

The commission disposed of nearly 4700 cases in 1999 and only 2404 cases were pending at the end of 1999. The number of cases declined sharply between 1997 and 1999. The end of 2004 saw the pendency of cases reduced to little less than 500. There were very few cases relating to MTP.
https://www.cuts-ccier.org/pdf/Why_India_Adopted_a_new_Competition_Law.pdf

In 1998, the All-India Float Glass Manufacturers' Association filed a complaint on Indonesian float glass manufacturers of selling their products at predatory prices. The MRTP Commission issued an injunction against the Indonesian companies from exporting float glass to India. The Supreme Court ruled that MRTP Commission had no extra-territorial jurisdiction in the float glass case.

Competition Commission of India

Competition Commission of India was set up on 14-10-2003 under Competition Act 2002 under Ministry of Corporate Affairs to prevent practices that have an appreciable adverse effect on competition in India. CCI also approves combination under the act so that two merging entities do not overtake the market. CCI became fully functional in May 2009.

The Act prohibits anti-competitive agreements, abuse of dominant position by enterprises and regulates combinations (acquisition, acquiring of control and merger and acquisition), which may have appreciable adverse effect on competition within India.

CCI has power to take extra-territorial action by restraining imports, if imports (after effectuating) contravene the substantive provisions of the law.

In 2012, CCI imposed a fine of US$790 million on 11 cement companies for cartelization, fixing prices by meeting regularly, controlling market share and holding back supply to earn illegal profits.

In 2013, CCI imposed a penalty of US$6.5 million on Board of Control for Cricket in India for misusing its dominant position and for framing IPL team ownership agreements in unfair and discriminatory manner.

In 2014, CCI imposed a fine of Rs. 2544 Cr on 14 Indian car manufacturers (Maruti Suzuki, Mahindra & Mahindra, Tata Motors, Toyota, Honda, Volkswagen, Fiat, Ford, General Motors, Nissan, Hindustan Motors, Mercedes Benz and Skoda) for failure to provide branded spare parts and diagnostic tools to independent repairers.

In 2015, CCI imposed a fine of Rs. 258 Cr on 3 airlines (Jet Airways, Indigo and SpiceJet) for cartelization in determining the fuel surcharge on air cargo.

In 2018, CCI fined Google's parent Co., Alphabet Inc. for Rs. 135.86 Cr. for search bias.

In 2019, CCI ordered an **antitrust probe against Google** for abusing its dominant position with Android to block market rivals. Mandatory Pre-installation of entire Google Mobile Services suite under Mobile Application Distribution Agreements amounted to imposition of unfair condition on the device manufacturers. Leveraging of Google's dominance in Google Play Store to protect relevant markets such as online general search in contravention of Competition Act 2002.

In October 2022, CCI imposed US$170 million penalty on **Google for abusing its dominance** in the licensing of Android OS for smartphones, app store market for Android, general web search services, non-OS specific mobile web browsers and online video hosting platforms in India. A week later, CCI levied a separate US$120 million penalty for abusing its Play Store policies.

National Payments Corporation of India

National Payments Corporation of India was established by the RBI and Indian Banks' Association in December 2008 for creating and operating a robust Payment & Settlement Infrastructure in India.

Initially, there were 10 promoter banks viz. SBI, PNB, Canara Bank, BOB, Union Bank of India, BOI, ICICI Bank, HDFC Bank, City Bank and HSBC. In 2016, the shareholding was diluted to additionally include 13 public sector banks, 15 private sector banks, 1 foreign bank, 10 multi-state co-operative banks and 7 regional rural banks.
NPCI created a subsidiary NPCI International Payments Ltd. to take its products like RuPay and Universal Payments Interface to global market.
In April 2021, NPCI created another subsidiary NPCI Bharat BillPay Ltd. to increase growth in business to consumer segment for small businesses.

The Bharat Bill Payment System, conceptualized by RBI and driven by the NPC, offers myriad bill collection categories like electricity, telecom, DTH, gas, water bills etc. through multiple payment channels like Internet, Internet Banking, Mobile, Mobile-Banking, Point of Sale terminal, Mobile Wallets, Mobile Point of Sale terminal, Kiosk, ATM, Bank Branch, Agents and Business Correspondents. Bharat BillPay supports multiple payment modes including Credit, Debit and Prepaid cards, NEFT Internet Banking, UPI, Wallets, Aadhaar based payments and cash. More categories like insurance premium, mutual funds, school fees, institution fees, credit cards, local taxes, invoice payments, etc. may be added in the future.

NPCI developed BharatQR in collaboration with American Express, Mastercard and Visa for ease of payments and interoperability

Securities and Exchange Board of India

Securities and Exchange Board of India - SEBI was established on 12.04.1988 as a regulatory body for securities and commodity market in India under Ministry of Finance. It was given statutory powers on 30.01.1992. Controller of Capital Issues was the regulatory authority before SEBI came into existence; He derived authority from the Capital Issues (Control) Act, 1947.

SEBI did away with physical certificates by passing Depositories Act, 1996.
After the amendment of 1999, collective investment schemes were brought under SEBI except Nidhis, chit funds and cooperatives.
The basic functions of SEBI are to protect the interests of investors in securities and to promote the development of, and to regulate the securities market.
SEBI made the markets electronic and paperless by introducing T+5 rolling cycle from July 2001 and progressed to T+2 in April 2003.

INFORMATION TECHNOLOGY & SOFTWARE DEVELOPMENT SERVICES

Status in 2001-02
The potential for Business Process Outsourcing in India in 2001-02 was - $1.49 billion (10.7.4.39)
The global online education and e-learning market was projected at $ 11.4 billion in 2003. More than 1,600 companies, including nearly half the Fortune 500 firms, had built corporate universities. (10.7.4.44)
From US$ 3 billion in 2002–03, the domestic software market grew to nearly US$ 5 billion in 2004–05. (11.13.36)
35 Government and 25 private software technology parks made significant contributions to national software exports. (10.7.4.23)

India accounted for 69 of the 122 IT companies in the world having the prestigious CMM 4 and 5 level quality certification. India was expected to soon have the highest number of ISO certified companies in the world. (10.7.4.35)

Achievements during X 5YP

The number of professionals employed in this sector had grown to 1.28 million by 2005–06. (11.12.2.6)
The domestic IT market in India was valued at approximately Rs 54000 crore in 2006. (11.12.2.2)
India had an estimated share of 65% of global off-shore IT and 46% of global BPO. The addressable market for offshore BPO globally stood at US$ 300 billion. The IT sector was estimated to provide direct employment in IT sector (both software and hardware) to over 3.08 million people in 2006-07. The indirect employment generated by the sector, was about 3 times the direct employment. (11.1.87)

Strength of Indian IT Companies - As of December 2006, over 440 Indian companies had acquired quality certifications, with 90 companies certified at Software Engineering Institute–Capacity Maturity Model (SEI– CMM) Level 5—higher than any other country in the world. (11.8.3.4)

Employment in IT sector - The exports segment of the Indian IT-ITES sector directly employed over 920000 people in 2005–06 (8.3.5)
Total IT-ITES Professionals (not including employee in the hardware sector) – 284000 in 1999–2000 / 430114 in 2000–01 / 522250 in 2001–02 and 1287000 in 2005-06 (11.v3.8.3.9)

The Indian IT-ITES industry, with revenues of US$ 39.6 billion, had emerged as the largest private sector employer in the country in 2006-07 with direct employment of 1.6 million professionals, and indirect employment for over 6 million people in different sectors. (11.v3.8.3.24)

In a study conducted by NASSCOM in 2006, 76% of software professionals in IT companies were men, 24% women. The ratio of men to women was 31:69 in the ITES-BPO sector.

Health care BPO operations - Health care majors in the developed world, especially the US, were outsourcing back-end health care services to Indian BPO firms. The major health care BPO operations in the country were Hinduja TMT (claims adjudication), Apollo Health Street (claims adjudication, billing and coding), Comat Technologies (transcription), Datamatics (transcription and forms processing) and Lapiz (medical billing). (11.13.50)

Refer to Annexure for Graph – 16.2 for Software and Hardware Production and Export 1989 to 2012

IT Companies

Infosys Technologies Ltd. was started by N R Narayana Murthy along with 6 others in 1981.

Infosys had a valuation of $100 million in 1994, $10 Billion on 6-1-2000 and $50 Billion on 16-7-2020. It earned a **revenue of Rs. 1900.60 Cr in 2000-01.** Infosys had marketing channels in the USA, UK, Australia, Belgium, Canada, France, Germany, Singapore, Japan etc. (10.7.4.18) Infosys joined the elite club of companies with $100 Billion or more market capitalization on 24-8-21.

Wipro Technologies (started in 1945 as Wipro Ltd.) **earned revenue of Rs.2642.92 Cr in 2000-01.**

Tata Consultancy Services (started in 1968) employed more than 16,000 consultants across 50 countries and its solutions were backed by 60,000 person-years of experience. 7 Out of the US Fortune Top 10 companies were TCS clients. **TCS earned a revenue of Rs. 3,142 Cr in 2000-01.**

Satyam Computer Services Ltd. (started in 1987) operated in 35 countries and had over 300 global clients, including 40 Fortune 500 corporations. Satyam and its associated companies provided customized IT solutions from development Centres in India, USA, UK, West Asia, Japan and Singapore. The Co.

earned a **revenue of Rs. 1,220 Cr in 2000-01. Tech Mahindra** (started in 1986) took over Satyam Computer Services in June 2009.

HCL Technologies Ltd (started in 1991) was doing business in the USA, UK, Japan, Germany, Sweden, France, Netherlands, Italy, Australia, Hong Kong etc. It had 5 major international collaborations, and earned a **revenue of Rs. 1,405.10 Cr in 2000-01.**

I-flex Solutions Ltd (started in 1992) was among the top 2 companies selling solutions worldwide for two consecutive years — 1999 and 2001. Its flagship product was 'FLEXCUBE', a universal banking solution. Apart from India, I-flex had representative offices in the USA, UK, Argentina, the Netherlands, Kenya, Nigeria, Singapore and earned **Rs.308.58 Cr revenue in 2000-01.**

Mahindra – British Telecom Ltd. - MBT offered services to telecom operators, mobile operators, telecom equipment manufacturers and technology suppliers. MBT had 21 marketing offices and development centres worldwide and earned a revenue of **Rs.387.39 Cr** in 2000-01.

NIIT Ltd.: NIIT (established in 1981), a global IT solutions and training Co., operated in 38 countries with regional headquarters in the USA, Japan and several other countries in Europe and Southeast Asia. It earned **revenue of Rs. 682.80 Cr in 2000-01**

Patni Computer Systems Ltd., established in 1978, earned **a revenue of Rs. 518 Cr in 2000-01**.

Pentamedia Graphics Ltd.: Pentamedia Graphics (established in 1976) was one of the world's biggest entertainment graphics players, focusing on animation and special effects for big, small and personal screens. The Co. extended its expertise into core areas of films / broadcasting, video, compact disks / digital versatile disks entertainment, including studio, media, web, and sports entertainment. The Co. had markets in USA, UK, Singapore, Japan, Malaysia, Australia, West Asia etc., and had alliances with IBM, Silicon Graphics, Softimage and Eastman Kodak. It earned **a revenue of Rs. 552.38 Cr in 2000-01.**

Silverline Technologies Ltd. (established in 1992) earned a **revenue of Rs. 707 Cr in 2000-01.**

Public Sector IT Organizations

National Informatics Centre

The National Informatics Centre - NIC was established in **1976** by Late N Seshagiri, Additional Secretary, Electronics Commission of India, who was the first to introduce a network system in India called NICNET.

NIC, as technology partner of Government of India, helped the Indian government embrace IT in the 1990s. NIC provided infrastructure, IT Consultancy, IT Services including architecting, design, development and implementation of IT Systems in Central and State Government departments, thus enabling delivery of government services to citizens and pioneering the initiatives of Digital India.

NIC provided e-governance network and technical support to Central and State Governments, UTs, and about 600 district administrations in the country. It had been facilitating the process of e-governance in the country for the last 30 years. (12.2.4)

Computerization of Government Departments - Computerization of the Registration and Transport Departments, Treasuries, district administration and Citizen Centric Services, e-gram, e-Panchayat, e-Municipality, Land Records, Online Monitoring of NREGS, e-Courts, Passport System, VAT computerization, AGMARKNET, National Panchayat Portal, Rural Water Supply & Sanitation / PHED Computerization, Integrated Information System for food grains management – were implemented in many states.

The portal AGMARKNET, which provides daily market information on commodity prices in respect of 300 commodities and 2000 varieties from over 2700 markets, is a Sunshine Portal for farmers to bargain better prices for their produce. Similarly, the 'Gyandoot' portal of Madhya Pradesh provides information on rates of grains and vegetables, dispenses land records and issues income, domicile, and caste certificates. (11.8.3.29)

The Digital Library of India, hosted by the Indian Institute of Science, Bangalore, provides free access to many books in English and Indian languages and has digitized more than 2.97 lakh books containing a total of approximately 80.7 million pages till September 2007. (11.12.2.18)

Centre for Development of Advanced Computing

Centre for Development of Advanced Computing - C-DAC was created in November 1987. In 1988, when the US Government refused to sell India a Cray supercomputer, India started development of its own supercomputer.

A prototype computer was benchmarked at the 1990 Zurich Super-computing Show. It demonstrated that India had the second most powerful, publicly demonstrated, supercomputer in the world after the United States. The final result of the effort was the PARAM 8000, released in 1991. It is considered to be India's first supercomputer.

The National Centre for Software Technology, Electronic Research and Development Centre and CEDTI were merged into C-DAC in 2003.

C-DAC developed VEGA Microprocessors – (India's first indigenous 64-bit Multi-core Superscalar Out-of-Order RISC-V Processor), M-Kavach 2 – (a mobile device security solution addressing emerging threats), Bharat Operating System Solutions – (a Linux-based general purpose operating system), Anvaya – (a workflow environment for automated genome analysis), Namescape – (the search engine for the Aadhaar unique-ID project), GARUDA – (India's National Grid Computing Initiative), TaxoGrid – (a grid-based molecular phylogenetics and drug discovery system, GIST –(Graphics and Intelligence based Script Technology), OLabs – (an internet based platform for conduct of school laboratory experiments and assessment), QSim – (India's first Quantum Computer Simulator Toolkit) and CerviSCAN – (a Cervical Cancer screening device suite)

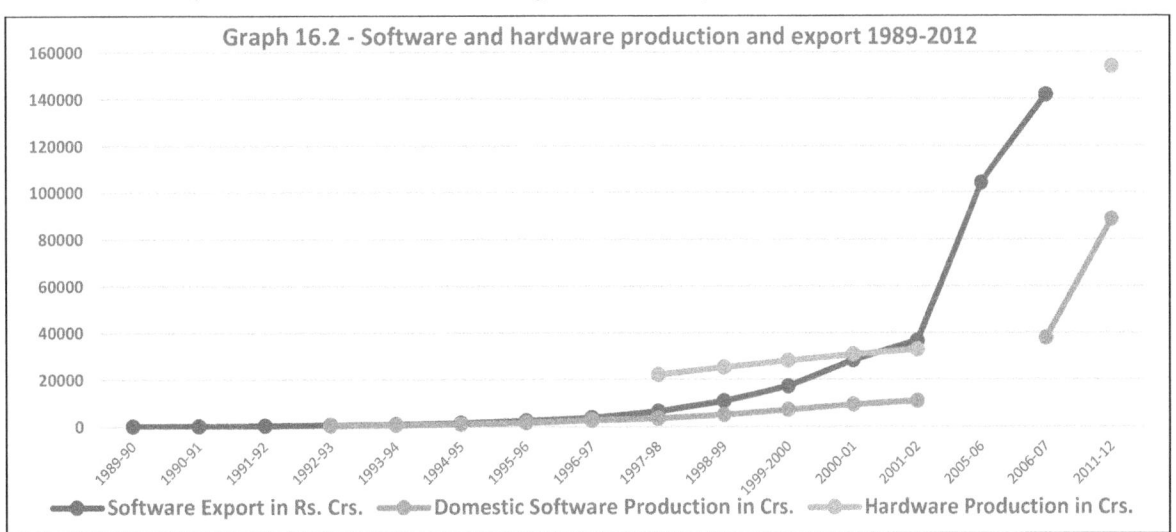

Graph 16.2 - Software and hardware production and export 1989-2012

National Informatics Centre Services Incorporated

National Informatics Centre Services Incorporated - NICSI was incorporated on 28.08.**1995** for providing total IT solutions to the Government organizations and operational support for National Informatics Centre's mega-projects.

NICSI is engaged in promoting application of - IT and computer communication networks, informatics, digital automation and computer aided modernization - in various facets of Government and Society including local governments, educational, financial and research institutions, etc. in public, private and cooperative sectors - through non-commercial and commercial applications of software, hardware, database, information base, Value Added Telecom services, and other services developed by the NIC. - including its computer communication network (NICNET) and associated infrastructure and services etc.

NICSI procures hardware, software and support services for Government organizations from leading Information and Communication Technology and management organizations.
Gross turnover for 2022-23 was Rs. 1604.18 Cr.

Public Sector Enterprises Which Provide Financial Services

Export Credit Guarantee Corp. of India Ltd.

Export Credit Guarantee Corp. of India Ltd.- ECGC was incorporated on 30.7.**1957** as Export Risk Insurance Corporation of India Ltd., to support and strengthen the export promotion efforts of Indian companies by issuing credit insurance covers to protect the exporters against non-realization on account of commercial and political risk.

Insurance covers are provided to banks in India to protect them from losses that may be incurred in extending packing credit and post-shipment loans/advance to exports due to protracted default or insolvency of the exporter.

ECGC is providing insurance and trade related services and extending financial guarantees to the exporters and banks respectively, through its 57 branch offices. On 31.03.2008, there were 12,533 policies including transfer guarantees in force.

ECGC further provides overseas investment insurance to Indian Companies investing in joint ventures abroad in the form of equity or loan. **ECGC has almost 100% market share in the credit insurance business since inception.**

ECGC was the **seventh largest credit insurer of the world** in terms of coverage of national exports in 2013-14.
ECGC signed Memorandum of Understanding with Agri Re (Mongolia) and Credit Oman (Oman)

Gross turnover for 2022-23 was Rs. 1509.93 Cr.

Agriculture Refinance Corporation

RBI set up Agricultural Refinance Corporation in **1963** to work as a refinancing agency in providing medium and long-term agricultural credit to support investment credit needs for agricultural development. In 1975, ARC was renamed as Agriculture Refinance and Development Corporation to give focused attention to credit offtake, development and promotion of the agricultural sector.

Rural Electrification Corp. Ltd.- Financial Assistance for Rural Electrification - Refer Chapter 10.

Housing & Urban Development Corp. Ltd. – Finance for Housing & Urban Development – Refer Ch. 10

Indian Railway Finance Corporation Ltd. – Financing Funding Needs of Railways

Indian Railway Finance Corp. Ltd. - IRFC was incorporated on 12.12.**1986** to raise financial resources to part finance the annual funding needs of the railways. IRFC is borrowing from the commercial markets, domestic as well as overseas, to finance the acquisition of rolling stock assets including wagons, coaches and locomotives which are leased out to Railways through a 30 years financial lease agreement.

IRFC created Rolling Stock assets worth Rs 69,843 Cr. for Indian Railways up to 2010-11.

IRFC raised funds through structured term loan for tenor of 20 Years for Rs. 4,000 crores from National Bank for Financing of Infrastructural Development during 2022-23.
Gross Turnover of Indian Railway Finance Corporation Ltd. in FY 2022-23 was Rs. 23891 Cr.

Balmer Lawrie Investments Ltd.

Balmer Lawrie Investments Ltd. - BLIL was incorporated on 20.9.**2001** to facilitate disinvestment of IBP Co. Ltd. The shareholding of IBP Co. in Balmer Lawrie and Co. Ltd. was de-merged in favor of BLIL w.e.f. 15.10.2001. BLIL is holding the equity shares of its subsidiary Balmer Lawrie and Co. Ltd. BLIL is registered with RBI as a Non-Banking Finance Co. **Gross turnover** in 2022-23 was Rs. 76.08 Cr.

Jammu & Kashmir Development Finance Corporation

Jammu & Kashmir Development Finance Corporation - JKDFC was set up on 30.05.**2005** for providing credit facilities & other infrastructural support to (i) industrial enterprises, (ii) tourism industry (iii) small road transport operators for passenger & cargo transportation (iv) construction companies, etc.

JKDFC was providing fund for (i) equipment financing to industrial enterprises (ii) for setting up of Mini & Small Hydro projects, etc. in order to accelerate industrial & tourism development, employment generation & faster economic growth in the State of Jammu & Kashmir. **Revenue was Rs. 5.24 Cr in 2022-23.**

India Infrastructure Finance Company Ltd.

India Infrastructure Finance Company Ltd. - IIFCL was incorporated on 05.01.**2006** for providing financial assistance for development of infrastructure projects including roads and bridges, railway, seaport, airports & other transport projects, power, urban transport, water supply, sewerage, solid waste management, gas pipeline, projects in special economic zones etc.

IIFCL provided financial assistance up to 20% of the project cost both through direct lending to project companies and by refinancing banks and financial institutions. IIFCL raised funds from both domestic and overseas markets on the strength of government guarantees. (11.12.29)

The lead Bank was made responsible for regular monitoring and periodic evaluation of compliance of the project with agreed milestones and performance levels, particularly for purpose of disbursement of IIFCL funds.
During 2006-07, loan was sanctioned for 32 road, 11 power, 1 airport and 2 seaport projects of total projects value Rs. 56231 Cr.
During 2007-08, loan was sanctioned for 9 road, 9 power, 1 airport, 1 urban infrastructure and 2 seaport projects, etc. of total projects cost Rs. 62472 Cr.
For the 78 projects financed by IIFCL up to 2008, total loan of Rs. 14424 Cr was sanctioned.
On cumulative basis, gross sanctions as on 31.3.2011 were Rs. 31,778 Cr to 176 projects involving project cost of Rs. 2,70,920 Cr.

IIFCL has 2 wholly owned subsidiaries namely IFCL Projects Ltd. and IFCL Asset Management Co. Ltd.

IIFC (UK) Ltd. was incorporated at London as subsidiary on 7.2.2008 for borrowing funds from the RBI and providing foreign currency loans to Indian infrastructure companies for meeting their capital expenditure for import solely outside India.

IIFC has a joint venture Co. India Infrastructure Fund with participation from IDFC and Citi Bank.

Gross turnover in 2022-23 was Rs. 4074.92 Cr.

Eastern Investment Ltd.

Eastern Investment Ltd. - EIL was a part of Government managed Bird Groups of companies and became a CPSE on 19.3.**2010**.

EIL had acquired shares of Orissa Minerals Development Co. Ltd. and Bisra Stone Lime Co. Ltd. with a view to convert these two mining companies to its subsidiaries.
During 2010-11, the BIRD Group of Companies were made subsidiaries of Rashtriya Ispat Nigam Ltd.

IIFCL Projects Ltd.

IIFCL Projects Ltd. - IPL was established on 14.02.**2012**, as a wholly owned subsidiary of Indian Infrastructure Finance Co. Ltd., to function as project advisory Co. involved in project appraisal, syndication, transaction advisory, and infrastructure consultancy services.

IPL caters to the demand for advisory services from infrastructure sectors including roads, highways, ports, airports, power including renewable, tourism, urban infrastructure like water supply & sewerage projects, solid waste management etc.

Gross turnover in 2022-23 was Rs. 13.25 Cr.

IIFCL Assets Management Co. Ltd.

IIFCL Assets Management Co. Ltd. - IAMCL was incorporated on 24.03.**2012** as a subsidiary of IIFCL to manage and support various schemes issued by the IIFCL Mutual Fund (IDF). (which was registered by SEBI in January, 2013).

Revenue from operation in 2022-23 was Rs. 5.67 Cr.

Power Finance Corp. Ltd. – Financing Power Generation, Transmission, Distribution Projects – Refer Chapter 10.

Indian Renewable Energy Development Agency Ltd. – Promote investment in Renewable Energy – Refer Chapter 10

National Film Development Corp. Ltd. – Refer Chapter 5

Public Sector Enterprises Engaged in Trading and Marketing Services

State Trading Corp. of India Ltd.

State Trading Corp. of India Ltd. – STC was incorporated on 18.05.**1956** to trade with East European countries and to develop exports of private trade and industry. STC was providing services for exports, imports and domestic trading in a large basket of items.

The items exported by STC included wheat, rice, tea, coffee, cashew, extractions, castor oil, sugar, maize, chemicals, pharmaceuticals, light engineering goods, construction materials, industrial lubricants, consumer goods, sports goods, processed foods, marine products, spices, textiles, garments, jute goods, leatherware, steel raw materials, steel plates / Coils, iron ore, gold jewellery, etc.

Major items of imports by STC included bullion, wheat, hydrocarbons, minerals, metals, manganese, steam coal, fertilizers, petrochemicals, edible oils, pulses, dry fruits, etc. STC arranged import of crucial raw materials as and when needed by the Indian Industry. It also undertook import of technical and security equipment on behalf of State Police and Intelligence Departments and Paramilitary Organizations.

It also arranged imports of essential items of mass consumption such as wheat, pulses and edible oils to meet domestic shortages when asked by the Govt. of India. STC imported about 1.3 Mts of wheat in 2007-08 on behalf of the Govt. of India to meet domestic shortages.

STC also undertook domestic sales of hydrocarbons, metals, tea, pulses, jute, cardamom, fertilizers, coal / coke, etc. The import turnover of hydrocarbons, minerals and metals during 2007-08 was Rs. 1438 Cr. Bullion was the single largest item of import valuing about Rs. 5710 Cr, followed by petrochemicals valuing Rs. 3300 crores and fertilizer - Rs 1615 Cr in 2008-09.

STC signed offset agreements with Boeing and GE for monitoring offset obligation worth Rs. 5676 crores arising out of purchase of civilian aircrafts by Indian Airlines / Air India (NACIL). (13.4.8)

It had one subsidiary namely Spices Trading Corp. Ltd. (STCL).

STC also formed a joint venture namely NSS Satpura Agro Development Co. with NAFED and STCL.

Recently, STC has stopped undertaking any new business activity and is currently continuing as a non-operative company for the time being. Present Activities | THE STATE TRADING CORPORATION OF INDIA LTD. (stclimited.co.in)

MSTC Ltd – Refer Chapter 14

Cotton Corporation of India Ltd. – Refer Chapter 4

Central Cottage Industries Corp. of India - Refer Chapter 4

Handicrafts & Handlooms Export Corp. India Ltd. - Refer Chapter 4

Jute Corporation of India Ltd. - Refer Chapter 4

North Eastern Handicrafts & Handloom Development Corp. Ltd. - Refer Chapter 4

Food Corporation of India Ltd. - Refer Chapter 4

Central Warehousing Corp.

Central Warehousing Corp. - CWC was incorporated on 02.03.**1957** to provide scientific storage facilities for agricultural inputs and produce and other notified commodities at Container Freight Stations / Inland Container Depots, Land Customs Stations, Air Cargo Complexes (for import-export cargo), etc.

The CWC offers a rebate of 30% in its storage charges for the farmers' stocks.

CWC has been providing Pest Control services from 1968 to prevent the loss caused by various insects and pests by undertaking pest control operation in railway coaches, pantry cars, aircrafts, hospitals, hotels and restaurants as well as export / import containers and ship fumigation.

During 2004-05, 34 new warehousing units were opened and 14 closed down.

CWC started container train operations in 2007-08 and started operating a Truck terminal at Petrapole (West Bengal) on Indo Bangladesh border for import-export trade.

CWC has **19 State Warehousing Corporations** as subsidiaries. These SWCs, as on 31.3.2011, were operating a network of 1689 warehouses with an aggregate storage capacity of 26.696 Mts. During 2010-11, 0.145 Mt capacity covered go-downs were added while about 0.115 Mts capacity go-downs / warehouses were specifically hired for various commodities and 0.116 Mt of open storage capacity were de-hired consequent upon release of stocks or termination of management contract.

As on 31.03.2014, CWC was providing storage facilities through its 501 warehouses with a total storage capacity of 10.494 Mts including 95 custom bonded warehouses, 4 Air Cargo complexes, 34 Container Freight Stations / Inland Clearance Depots and 3 temperature-controlled warehouses. (PE Survey 2013-14) 1-Vol2_trading_17_0.pdf (dpe.gov.in)

CWC set up one subsidiary namely Central Railside Warehouse Co. Ltd.
CWC formed a joint venture namely National Multi Commodity Exchange of India Ltd. (NMCE).

CWC is the largest public warehousing logistics organization in the world.

CWC operates its Farmers Extension Service Scheme to train the farmers on post-harvest technology through 304 rural based warehouses.

The domestic market share of CWC in warehousing of foodgrains, agriculture produce, agriculture inputs and other notified commodities was 33% in 2011-12.

CWC achieved turnover of Rs 2104 Cr. during 2022 23.

Minerals and Metals Trading Corporation of India Ltd

MMTC Ltd., till 1993 known as Minerals and Metals Trading Corporation of India Ltd., was incorporated on 26.09.**1963** to render services in international trading of minerals and metals, coal, fertilizers, hydrocarbons, precious metals, diamonds, gems, jewelry, Agro-products and other general commodities. MMTC provides market coverage in over 65 countries in Asia, Europe, Africa, Oceania and America etc.

It has one wholly owned subsidiary, namely MMTC Transnational Pte. Ltd., registered at Singapore. During 2008-09, MTPL achieved business turnover of US$ 686 million. (13.4.4) 72_MMTC ENGLISH Annual Report 2008-09.pdf (mmtclimited.gov.in)

During 2016-17, MTPL achieved sales turnover of USD$113.17 million. (13.4.4)

MMTC promoted an iron and steel plant namely Neelachal Ispat Nigam Ltd. of 1.1 Mts capacity, 0.8 Mt coke ovens jointly with the Government of Orissa.

MMTC has 5 more joint ventures:

(i) MMTC put up a Gold / Silver Medallion manufacturing unit with a gold refinery, MMTC-PAMP, in collaboration with PAMP of Switzerland with a capacity to refine 200 tons of Dore or impure gold annually. MMTC has, through a joint venture, set up a chain of retail stores at various cities for sale of medallions, jewellery and finished products from this unit.
(ii) MMTC set up a 15MW Wind Energy Farm in Karnataka.
(iii) MMTC set up a Commodity Exchange in November 2009 and Currency Exchange in September 2010.
(iv) MMTC undertakes mining of coal in Jharkhand coalfields having estimated reserves of 800 Mts of coking and thermal coal.
(v) As a member of consortiums, MMTC constructed permanent Iron Ore loading berth at Ennore port, a deep draft iron ore berth at Paradip port and free trade and warehousing zones at Haldia and Kandla.

Revenue from operations in 2021-22 was Rs, 8393.29 Cr. Government was holding 89.93% stake in MMTC as on 9.08.2023.

Project and Equipment Corporation of India Ltd.

PEC Ltd., formerly Project and Equipment Corporation of India Ltd., was incorporated on 21.04.**1971**, as a subsidiary of State Trading Corp. of India, to export railway and engineering equipment & turn key projects, projects and equipment of small and medium enterprises and to trade internationally in commodities such as agricultural products, industrial raw materials, chemicals and bullion and installation of roof-top Solar Power Plant.

PEC executed cement, textile and sugar plants, warehouses, flats, prefabricated shelters, offices, substations, transmission lines, tea. Potato chips, etc.

From 27.03.1991, PEC Ltd. became an independent Co. directly owned by the Government of India.
The name was changed to PEC Limited in 1997. PEC diversified into Agro Commodities, Industrial Raw Material, Manufactured Goods and Bullion.   PEC (peclimited.com)

PEC was providing services in export and import of agricultural commodities, import of industrial raw materials and bullion. PEC undertook structuring of Special Trading Arrangements, counter trade transactions, third country trading and domestic marketing.

PEC Ltd. also had a subsidiary Tea Trading Corporation Ltd which was under liquidation.

PEC Ltd was incurring losses since 2014-15 and stopped all business activities since September, 2019.

HMT (International) Ltd.

HMT (International) Ltd. - HMT(I) was incorporated on 13.12.**1974** to function as exporters, importers and consultants of HMT products and other engineering products.

HMT(I) is providing services for setting up projects abroad for machines / watches of group companies, export of HMT and Non-HMT products and import of components and other parts required for holding Co. units.

HMT(I) has one financial joint venture namely Gulf Metal Foundry, Dubai. HMT(I) was implementing Small and Medium Enterprises Development Project in Zimbabwe, Information Technology Project in Kyrgyzstan and Indo-Mozambique Cashew-nut Processing Centre Project in Mozambique.

Revenue from operations in 2022-23 was Rs. 14.15 Cr.

India Trade Promotion Organization

India Trade Promotion Organization - ITPO was incorporated on 30.12.**1976** as Trade Fair Authority of India (TFAI), amalgamating 3 organizations of the Government viz., India International Trade Fair Organization, Directorate of Exhibition and Commercial Publicity and Indian Council of Trade Fair and Exhibitions. Subsequently, Trade Development Authority, a society under M/o Commerce and Industry, was also merged with TFAI on 1.1.1992 and ITPO was formed with effect from 16.4.1992.

ITPO is providing services through organizing / participating in trade fairs in India and abroad and by providing trade information. ITPO serves by (i) letting out the exhibition halls and convention centre, to organize exhibitions, trade fairs, (ii) trade development and promotion through specialized programs such as Buyer-Seller Meets and (iii) coordination of business delegations etc.

During 2007-08, ITPO organized 10 trade fairs in Europe, 7 in Africa & Middle East region, 4 in Latin America, 11 in South East Asia including Far-East, 4 in USA and one in CIS region. In addition, ITPO organized 19 fairs both national and international in India.

ITPO is a founder member of Asia Trade Promotion Forum. ITPO is operating a trade portal having all trade related information for many countries.

It has 3 subsidiaries namely Karnataka Trade Promotion Organization, Tamil Nadu Trade Promotion Organization and West Bengal Trade Promotion Organization and one financial joint venture namely National Centre for Trade Information with equity participation with National Informatics Centre.

ITPO undertook mega redevelopment project of International Exhibition-cum-Convention Centre (IECC) at Pragati Maidan in 2019-20. **Revenue from operation in 2022-23 was Rs. 403.29 Cr**

Bharat Leather Corporation Ltd.

Bharat Leather Corporation Ltd. - BLC was incorporated in **1977** to act as apex body for the promotion and development of leather and leather products.
The Company operation closed in the month of September 2001 and the winding up process was going on.

Spices Trading Corp. of India Ltd.

STCL Ltd. was incorporated on 23.10.**1982** as 'Cardamon Trading Corp. Ltd.' to process and cure spices, to manufacture spice products and agricultural products of international standards and to carry on domestic and international trade (in industrial goods, iron ore, bullion, precious metals, limestone, met-coke, other minerals, polymer, polyester yarn, cotton yarn, other textile products, PVC resins, HMS Scraps and other metal scrap). It was renamed as Spices Trading Corp. of India Ltd. in 1987 (again renamed as STCL Ltd. in 2004).

STCL was conducting Cardamom auctions.
STCL had one joint venture namely NSS Satpura Agro Development Corp. Ltd. with STC (holding Co.) and NAFED. The Union Cabinet approved winding up of STCL Ltd. on 13.08.2013 as STCL suffered liability of Rs 1,208 crore on account of fraud and could not be revived. The scam involved passing off iron-ore scrap as nickel and copper scrap in 2008.

STCL is undergoing process of closure as on 31.03.2023.

Tamil Nadu Trade Promotion Organization

Tamil Nadu Trade Promotion Organization - TNTPO was incorporated on 17.11.**2000** as a joint venture between ITPO and Tamil Nadu Industrial Development Corp., to promote, organize and participate in industrial trade fairs or exhibitions in India and abroad and to take measures for promotion of Indian industry trade and enhance its global competitiveness.

TNTPO is letting out the exhibition halls and convention Centres for industrial exhibitions, trade fairs, product launch, seminars, conferences and other business functions etc. TNTPO organizes trade fairs and exhibitions in India and abroad and Buyer-Seller meets;
The Convention Centre at Chennai with 10560 sq. mt of air-conditioned space offers conferencing and banquet rooms for 250 to 1500 delegates. It offers facilities like infrared digital interpretation system, theatrical lighting system, digital audio-video system, etc. TNTPO is planning for Expansion of Chennai Trade Centre for rentable area 20,322 sq. mt with parking of 2,320 cars during the year 2019-20.

Karnataka Trade Promotion Organization

Karnataka Trade Promotion Organization - KTPO was incorporated on 6.12.**2000** as a joint venture between ITPO and Karnataka Industrial Area Development Board to set up an exhibition complex at Bangalore, to promote, organize and participate in industrial trade fairs and exhibitions in India and abroad and to take measures for promoting Indian trade and enhance its global competitiveness. KTPO came into operation on 23.9.2004.

Central Railside Warehouse Co. Ltd.

Central Railside Warehouse Co. Ltd. - CRWCL was incorporated on 10.7.**2007** for providing quality storage facility at transit nodes (by developing **R**ailside **W**arehousing **C**omplexes on land leased from

Railways or acquired otherwise or by better utilization of existing good-sheds of Railways) and state-of-the-art warehouse handling facility,

The Railways identified 22 Railway Terminals for development of RWCs. 18 RWCs became operational as on 31.03.2014. CRWCL had 19 RWCs as on 31.03.2017. Construction of RWC Fatuha, Bihar was in progress.
IFFCO CRWC Logistics Ltd., a Joint Venture of CRWCL with IFFCO KISAN SEZ and Indian Potash Ltd., was incorporated on 03.06.2016 for the development of Freight Terminals at IFFCO Kisan SEZ, Nellore.
CRWCL is acting as a Marketing and Logistic partner for the new Web Portal - e-RAKAM (Rashtriya Kisan Agri Mandi), for which technical platform was provided by MSTC.

CRWCL merged with Central Warehousing Corporation in 2021.

Land Port Authority of India

Land Port Authority of India – LPAI was established on 1.03.**2012** for facilitating cross-border trade and passenger movement across India's land borders by setting up of Integrated Check Posts, at designated locations along India's international border, to house all regulatory agencies in a single sanitized complex and provide complete state of the art infrastructure facilities such as warehouses, examination sheds, parking bays, weighbridges etc.

There are currently 11 Land ports operational in India at Attari, Agartala, Dawki, Petrapole, Raxaul, Rupaidiha, Jogbani, Moreh, Sutarkandi, Srimantapur and PTB at Dera Baba Nanak. In 2023-24, Land Ports in India facilitated trade worth Rs.29,352.61 Cr. till August, 2023. https://lpai.gov.in/en

Public Sector Enterprises Engaged in Tourist Services

India Tourism Development Corp. Ltd.

India Tourism Dev. Corp. Ltd. - ITDC was incorporated in **1966** to construct and manage hotels, motels and cottages, duty-free shops, beach resorts, travelers' lodges / restaurants, to renovate and expand tourist bungalows, to set up of transport units, and to provide transport, entertainment, duty free trade and consultancy services. It also produces tourist publicity literature.

It provided loans to hotel industry in the private sector for integrated development of tourist resorts at Kovalam, Gulmarg, Goa and Kulu - Manali and for construction of a number of youth hostels, tourists bungalows and forest lodges.
ITDC had 31 hotels / traveller lodges with 3762 rooms. The turnover increased from Rs.72.11 crores in 1985-86 to Rs. 121.92 crores in 1990-91. (8.9.30.3)
ITDC owned over 17 properties under the Ashok Group of Hotels brand, across India. ITDC is in the field of hotel management having a network of 8 Ashok Group of Hotels, 6 restaurants, including airport restaurants, 12 Ashok Travel and Tour Units, 36 Duty free shops and two sound and light divisions. ITDC is also managing a Hotel at Bharatpur and a Tourist Complex at Kosi.
It has 7 joint venture subsidiaries to manage hotels at Guwahati, Ranchi, Puri, Pondicherry, Bhopal Chandigarh and Itanagar. The other joint venture is ITDC Aldeasa India Private Ltd.

Revenue from operation in 2022-23 was Rs. 458.08 Cr. Government owns 87.02%

Hotel Corporation of India Ltd.

Hotel Corporation of India Ltd. was incorporated on 08-07-**1971** as a subsidiary of Air India Ltd. to carry on the business of Hotels and Flight Catering Services through its 2 Hotels at Delhi and Srinagar. It also had hotels in Bombay and Rajgir. The Co. is also running two flight catering units at Delhi and Mumbai by the name of Chefair.

Assam Ashok Hotel Corporation Ltd. – Removed.

Ranchi Ashok Bihar Hotel Corporation Ltd. - Removed

Utkal Ashok Hotel Corporation Ltd. – Removed.

M.P. Ashok Hotel Corporation Ltd. – Removed.

Pondicherry Ashok Hotel Corporation Ltd. – Removed.

Donyi Polo Ashok Hotel Ltd. – Removed.

Punjab Ashok Hotel Company Ltd. – Removed.

Indian Railway Catering and Tourism Corporation Ltd.

Indian Railway Catering and Tourism Corp. Ltd. - IRCTC was incorporated on 27.9.**1999** to strengthen railway's marketing and service capabilities in rail catering, tourism and passenger amenities.

IRCTC is providing on-board catering in Indian Railway along with hospitality services at stations, internet-based ticketing and reservation and producing / distributing packaged drinking water. IRCTC is managing the departmental catering business of 17 divisions of Indian Railways.
IRCTC is also involved in promotion of value-added Package tours.
It has also formed a joint venture with Cox & King (India) Ltd.
It also provides Catering services at various offices & institutions and also events and function such as commonwealth games Delhi 2010.
Apart from this IRCTC has opened fully automated food factory at Noida with a capacity of about 25000 meals/day.
Packaged drinking water plant is being set up at Ambernath (Mumbai). IRCTC operates through its 6 Rail Neer bottling plants at Nangloi (Delhi), Danapur (Patna), Palur (Chennai), Ambarnath (Maharashtra), Parassala (Kerala) and Amethi (Uttar Pradesh), one central kitchen at Noida and 4 base kitchens at New Delhi, Howrah, Ahmedabad and Patna.

Revenue from operations in 2022-23 was 3541.47 Cr.

Kumarakruppa Frontier Hotels Ltd. – Removed.

Performance of State Level Public Enterprises (SLPEs)

Detailed performance analysis could not be made as no regular survey was carried out for SLPEs.

SLPEs in 1994 - There were 885 SLPEs as on 31.3.1994, with an estimated investment of about Rs.31,848 Cr. Number-wise SLPEs in Kerala – 104, U.P. - 74, Karnataka and TN - 68 each, Andhra - 59, Bihar - 50, Gujarat - 45, Maharashtra, Orissa and Rajasthan – 43 each and Tripura - 2. (9.5.34)

There were 137 continuously profit-making SLPEs in Gujarat and U.P. - 13 each, Maharashtra - 11, Haryana, Karnataka and Punjab - 9 each, Rajasthan – 8, J&K - 1, Meghalaya - 2 and Bihar - 3. (9.5.36)
There were 41 continuously loss-making SLPEs with Kerala heading the list (8 units). (9.5.37)
Most of the sick enterprises were in the commercial sector and were engaged in the manufacture of scooters, textiles, electronics, power generating devices, detergents and chemicals, plywood products, rubber products, engineering goods, drugs and pharmaceuticals, etc. (9.5.39)
As many as 159 enterprises were showing mixed performance. (9.5.38)

SLPEs in 2005 - As on 31.03.2005, 1129 SLPEs were in operation. A total of 579 SLPEs (51%) were in manufacturing, followed by utilities, promotional, and welfare enterprises.

Manufacturing SLPEs constituted a major share in Assam, Gujarat, Kerala, Maharashtra, Rajasthan, TN, UP, and WB. A considerable number of these enterprises were taken over sick units. (11.v3.7.1.79)

The total investment in SLPEs increased every year in the post- reform period reaching Rs 285564 Cr in 2002–03 before going down and ending up with Rs 259124 cr. in 2004–05.

The turnover of these SLPEs increased from Rs. 42986 Cr in 1991-92 to Rs. 86681 Cr. in 1996-97, remained stagnated up to 2002-03 (Rs. 86284 Cr) and then increased to Rs. 113208 Cr. in 2003-04 and to **Rs. 127150 Cr in 2004-05.** Accumulated losses of SLPEs gradually increased to Rs 60517 crore in 2004–05, with consequential adverse fiscal impact on the States.

Restructuring of SLPEs - According to data collected up to 2004-05 by Institute of Public Enterprises, Hyderabad, 30 units including co-operatives were privatized in Andhra, 3 in Gujarat, and 1 each in Haryana, Orissa, Punjab, and Rajasthan.

Out of 82 PSEs in WB, 18 were profit making, and 63 were loss making at the end of 2004– 05. Of the 34 units restructured by WB government in I phase, 4 were successfully restructured under government ownership, 3 were converted into joint ventures, and 21 units were closed. (11.v3.7.1.80)

Contribution to XI 5YP by CPSEs

In 2004–05, the share of CPSEs in the GDP was 6.82% out of 11.85% contributed by Non-Departmental Enterprises. (11.7.1.70).

The Internal and Extra Budgetary Resources (IEBR) of the CPSEs were projected to provide Rs. 10,59,711 Cr, but the actual realization was only Rs. 6,84,272 Cr (64.57 % of the projected amount). (Ref 12-3-16).

The investment by CPSEs is financed through budgetary support provided by the Central Government, which is a part of GBS and IEBR raised by CPSEs on their own. IEBR comprises of Internal Resources (IR) and Extra-Budgetary Resources (EBR). IR comprise retained profits—net of dividend paid to Government, depreciation provision, carried forward reserves and surpluses. EBR consist of receipts from the issue of bonds, debentures, External Commercial Borrowings (ECB), suppliers' credit, deposit receipts and term loans from financial institutions. (Ref. 12.3.17).

IEBR contributed 64.3% of the Plan outlay of CPSEs during the Eleventh Plan, the rest being budgetary support. Of this, IR contributed 55.28% and EBR 44.72%. (Ref. 12-3-18).

Assets Created by Establishing CPSEs - Graph – 16.3 – Investment done, Capital employed, Gross Revenue, Net Worth and Market Capitalization – Removed (Refer to Table 17.4)

Increase in market capitalization of CPSEs in 2023 – The combined market capitalization of 65 odd CPSEs jumped by Rs. 15.8 lakh Cr (45%) in 2023 to Rs. 50.5 lakh Cr. (Mid-caps of NTPC, LIC, CIL, Indian Railway Finance Corp., REC, IOCL and SBI increased by 87%, 22%, 67%, 205%, 254%, 70% and 5%.

Market capitalization of Aditya Birla, Tata and Bajaj groups and Reliance Industries increased by 38%, 32%, 23% and 1.6% respectively, where as that of Adani group fell by 29%.

PSU: PSU Companies' Market Cap Surges 45% to ₹51 Lakh Crore in 2023 | Mumbai News - Times of India (indiatimes.com)

The combined market capitalization of 56 PSU stocks jumped to Rs. 6803059 Cr on 19-06-2024. (Economic Times dated 21-06-2024)

These data show comparatively **better performance of public sector units over private sector companies** and the increasing loss of dividends to government on account of disinvestment.

Dividends Paid by Public Sector Banks to Central Government

State-owned banks gave the government Rs. 8718.48 Cr as dividends in 2021-22. SBI paid Rs. 3,606.64 Cr (As of 31.03.2017, government held 61.23% equity shares in SBI), Union Bank of India – Rs. 1,084.26 Cr. (Government holds 83.49%), Bank of Baroda – Rs. 942.83 Cr (government owns 66% of the bank's equity), Canara Bank – Rs. 742.11 Cr (government owns 62.93%), Bank of India – Rs. 668.17 Cr, Indian Bank – Rs. 646.45 Cr. (Government owns 79.86%), Punjab National Bank – Rs. 515.46 Cr, Bank of Maharashtra – Rs. 306.13 Cr and Punjab & Sind Bank – Rs. 206.43 Cr. (**The loss in dividends on account of disinvestments in banks was Rs. 2301 Cr – 26.39% of dividends received**)

The Government expected to receive dividend income aggregating Rs. 13,804 Cr from public sector banks in 2022-23. (58% higher than the Rs. 8,718 Cr paid out in 2021-22). State Bank of India - Rs. 5740.14 Cr, Union Bank of India – Rs. 1712 Cr., Bank of Baroda – Rs. 1819.5 Cr, Canara Bank – Rs. 1370.05 Cr, Bank of India – Rs. 668.17 Cr, Indian Bank – Rs. 855.31 Cr, Punjab National Bank – Rs. 523.51 Cr, Bank of Maharashtra – Rs. 796 Cr and Punjab & Sind Bank – Rs. 319.63 Cr. (**The loss in dividends on account of disinvestments in banks was Rs. 3806.87 Cr – 27.58% of dividends received**)

Central Bank of India, which was brought out of Prompt Corrective Action Framework (PCAF) by RBI in September 2022, Indian Overseas Bank and UCO Bank (both of which were brought out of PCAF in September 2021), did not declare dividend.
Govt rakes in the moolah from handsome dividend by public sector banks - The Hindu BusinessLine

Dividends Paid by Public Sector Insurance Companies to Central Government

In the 2019-20 fiscal, LIC paid Rs 2,610.75 crore as dividend to the government from profits pertaining to FY 2018-19.

Life Insurance Corporation did not pay any dividend to the government in 2020-21 and used the free reserves to increase its paid-up capital, which rose to Rs 6,325 crore on 31 December 2021.
LIC didn't pay dividend to govt in FY21; used free reserves to raise paid-up capital - BusinessToday
LIC on 14.09.2023 paid a dividend of Rs. 1,831.09 Cr to the Centre for 2022-23.
LIC hands over ₹1,831.09 cr. dividend cheque to Finance Minister - The Hindu

Dividends Paid by CPSEs to Central Government – Graph – 16.4

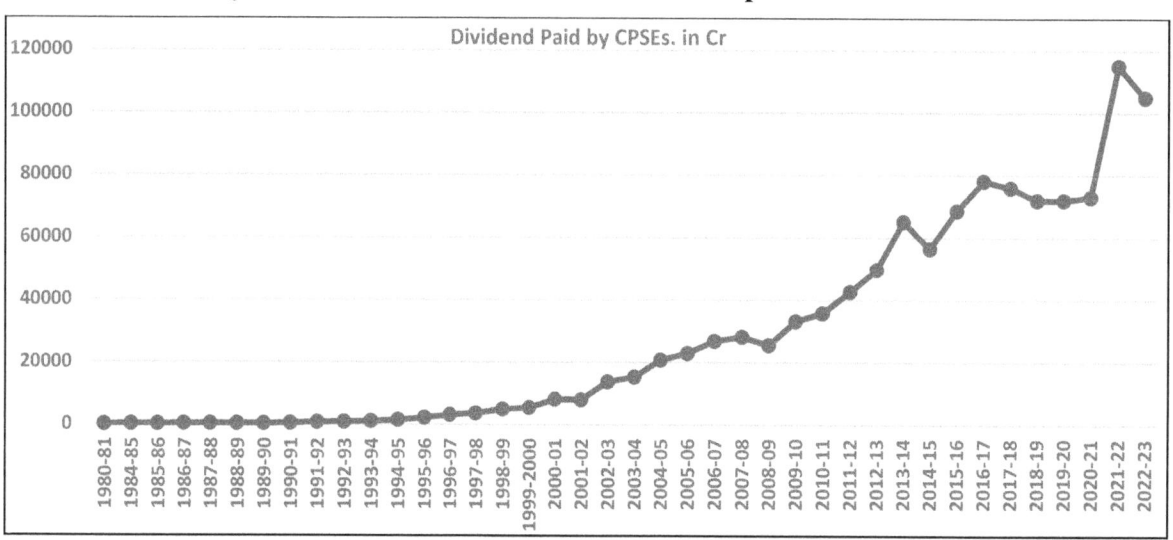

Contribution to Capital Expenditures of Central Government in Financial Year 2022-23

Central government was planning to spend Rs. 11.3 lakh Cr for creating new assets and infrastructure in 2022-23. CPSEs had spent Rs. 5.06 lakh Cr. in capital expenditure as of January 2023 against their full financial year target of Rs. 6.62 lakh Cr, which was 58.58% of government's target. The expected capital expenditure by CPSEs for whole financial year (at the current rate) of Rs. 6.072 lakh Cr, together with Rs. 50,300 Cr dividends already paid by CPSEs up to January 2023 constituted 58.19% of total planned Central government's capital expenditure of Rs. 11.3 lakh Cr. (Indian Express dt 9.3.23)

CPSE capex in April-Jan period tops Rs 5 lakh crore (newindianexpress.com)

Extra-Budgetary-Resources for 2020-21

Government seemed to have paid (i) dues for PDS food grains to Food Corporation of India through National Small Savings Fund and (ii) dues to NHAI infrastructure development programs by letting NHAI issue bonds instead of actually covering from budget (as these provisions have not been reflected in the Union government's budget)

Study: States may have breached debt ceilings - Times of India (indiatimes.com)

Indirect Contribution of CPSE's to Private Sector

Many, if not most, private sector companies were formed by taking employees, including technicians, engineers, senior executives and directors from many public sector establishments, thereby absorbing creamy layer and saving on training, these people got in parent public sector establishments.

Summary –

Share of Public Sector and CPSEs in GDP on Current Prices at Factor Cost

The contribution of public sector including CPSEs and CPSEs independently to GDP increased from 19 % and 12.4% in 1980-81 to 27.6% and 18.7% in 1993-94 respectively.

The contribution of public sector to GDP was 25% in 2004-05.

The share of public sector was 23% in 2005-06.

The reduction in contribution from CPSEs was because many industries, earlier reserved for public sector were opened for private investment in the post-reform period. The reduction in contribution from CPSEs to GDP was negligible which suggested that these enterprises adjusted themselves in the changing scenario. The share of CPSEs in Gross Domestic Capital Formation (GDCF) reduced faster than the corresponding deduction in the share of CPSEs in GDP. It showed that productivity of public enterprises improved in the post-liberalization period. (Ref - The IUP Journal of Managerial Economics, Vol. IX, No. 3, 2011)

Contribution of Public Sector Units to GDP in 2019-20

I - a) Total Gross Revenue from Operations of 256 operating CPSEs during 2019-20 was **Rs. 24,61,712 Cr.** (67.4% from Manufacturing, processing and generation units, 22.4% from services). (PE Survey 2019-20, Box 1.1)

b) The total revenues of public sector banks in Rs. Cr = 406973 (SBI in 2022) + 82859.5 (BOB in 2021) + 84525 (Canara in 2021) + 88339 (PNB in 2022) + 86114 (Axis in 2022) + 80104.19 (UBI in 2021) + 45955 (BOI in 2022) + 45771 (IB in 2022) + 22422.91 (IOB in 2021) + 25897.44 (CBI in 2021) + 13144.67 (BOM in 2020) + 18166.42 (UCB in 2021) + 25166 (IDBI in 2023) + 8826.92 (PSB in 2020) = **Rs. 1034265.15 Cr.**

c) Total income of Life Insurance Corporation of India in 2014-15 was Rs. 407546.36 Cr.

Gross direct premium of General Insurance Corp of India in 2014-15 was Rs. 84732.08 Cr.

Gross direct premium received by Public Sector General Insurance Companies in 2019-20 was Rs. 73263.08 Cr. Total income of public sector insurance Companies was **Rs. 565541.52 Cr.**

d) The turnover of 1129 State-Level Public Enterprises during 2004-05 was **Rs. 127150 Cr**.

e) Indian Ordnance Factories total sales were at US$3 billion (**Rs. 22,389.22 Cr.**) in the year 2020–'21.

f) Total revenues of public sector banks' mutual funds - Rs. 36.73 Cr (Axis Bank MF in 2022) + Rs. 22.45 Cr (Bank of India MF in 2019-20) + Rs. 29.91 Cr (IDBI MF in 2019-20) + (IIFCL MF) + 44.18 Cr (IL & FS MF in 20017-18) + 56.79 Cr (LIC MF in 2021-22) + 1316.86 Cr (SBI MF in 2019-20) + 1173 Cr (UTI MF in 2020-21) was **Rs. 2679.92 Cr.**

g) Railways' revenue for 2019-20 was estimated at **Rs. 216935 Cr** including revenue from traffic of Rs. 216675 Cr.

h) Contribution by Reserve Bank of India – Income for 2019-20 was **Rs. 149672 Cr** as per RBI Annual Report 2019-20.

i) Contribution from Port Trust Boards in 2019-20 was **Rs. 14759.94 Cr** (Paradip Port Trust - Rs. 1563.26 Cr, Chennai Port Trust - Rs. 787.55 Cr., Mumbai Port Trust Rs. 1662.64 Cr, Cochin Port Trust - Rs. 649.03 Cr, Mormugao Port Trust - Rs. 431.17 Cr, Visakhapatnam Port Trust – Rs. 1404.18 Cr, V O. Chidambaranar Port Trust - Rs. 636.54 Cr, New Mangalore Port Trust - Rs. 662.47 Cr, Jawaharlal Nehru Port Trust - Rs. 1899.61 Cr, Kamarajar Port Trust - Rs. 733.68 Cr, Kolkata Port Trust - Rs. 2601.65 Cr and Kandla / Deendayal Port Trust - Rs. 1728.16 Cr.)

j) Contribution from Co-operative Sector major companies – **Rs. 84201.13 Cr.** (IFFCO, Amul, Mother Diary, etc. IFFCO's turnover was Rs 29,412 crore in the 2019-20 fiscal. The group turnover of IFFCO, including its joint ventures, subsidiaries and associate companies, rose to Rs 57,778 crore in the same period. GCMMF had registered a sales turnover of Rs 38,542 crore in 2019-20. Total revenue of Mother Diary was Rs.10,447.13 crore in FY 2019-20. Aavin reported the annual turnover of ₹5800 crore for 2019-20).

k) The total turnover of disinvested CPSEs – Maruti Udyog Ltd – **Rs. 119712 Cr** in 2023 + Hindustan Zinc Ltd – **Rs. 34098 Cr** in 2023 + Hindustan Teleprinters Ltd – **Rs. 474.22 Cr** in 2018-19 / $ 5 million in 2021 + Modern Food Industries (turnover of Grupo Bimbo in India) – **Rs. 400 Cr** in 2020 + Computer Maintenance Corporation Ltd – **Rs. 2513.5 Cr** in 2014-15 + Indian Petrochemicals Corporation Ltd. - **Rs. 12372.52 Cr** in 2005-06 + Videsh Sanchar Nigam Ltd. – **Rs. 18201.41 Cr** in 2023 + Bharat Aluminium Co. Ltd – **Rs 13607 Cr** in 2021-22 + Lagan Jute Machinery Co. Ltd. + Jessop and Co. Ltd. **Rs. 79.34 Cr** in 2004-05 + Paradeep Phosphates Ltd - **Rs. 7858.72 Cr** in 2021-22 = **Rs. 209316.71.** (As these companies were initiated, constructed, commissioned, personnel trained, production stabilized, teething problems overcome as public sector companies and many of these companies performing well at the time of privatization, considering them as given on lease, the contribution of these companies has been included with public sector establishments.)

Thus, the turnover of public sector units (sum of a to k) in 2019-20 was arrived at **Rs. 48,88,622.59 Cr.**

II - The **GDP (PPP) of 2019 was Rs. 128,08,778 Cr.** The contribution to GDP by agriculture sector was 14.39%.

The contribution to GDP by industry and services sectors was 85.61% amounting to Rs. 109,65,594.85 Cr. **The contribution by public sector units of Rs. 48,88,622.59 Cr amounted to 44.58%** of total contribution to GDP by industry and services sectors.

As per Indian Express Editorial dated 6-10-2024, 60 million MSMEs (29.7 million registered in Udaya portal) account for 30% GDP, 45% of manufacturing output and 48% of exports.

The balance 25.42% includes contribution of retail trading community, small / individual business people, professionals like accountants, lawyers, personnel employed in Central and State government departments, police and armed services, education, health care sectors, **who are like public**, besides big companies and corporates. The contribution by **corporate houses** could not be assessed separately.

2022-23 - Out of 402 CPSEs covered in PE Survey 2022-23, 254 CPSEs were operating with a total operating income (Gross Turnover) of Rs. 37.90 lakh crore.

As per National Accounts Statistics 2023, the GDP estimated at current prices was Rs. 272.41 lakh crore in FY 2022-23, as against Rs. 234.71 lakh crore in FY 2021-22.

Private Sector Players

Banks - South Indian Bank – 1929, Federal Bank – 1931, J & K Bank – 1938, RBL Bank – 1943, Kotak Mahindra Bank – 1985,
Axis Bank – 1993, HDFC Bank – 1994, ICICI Bank – 1994, IndusInd Bank – 1994, Yes Bank – 2004.

IT Solution companies - Wipro Ltd – 1945, Tata Consultancy Services – 1968, Infosys – 1981, Tech Mahindra – 1986, Satyam Computer Services – 1987, Oracle Fin Serve – 1990, Persistent – 1990, Forbes Technosys Ltd – 1991, HCL Technologies – 1991
ITC Infotech India Ltd – 1996, L&T Infotech Ltd – 1996, LTIMindtree Ltd – 1996, Mphasis Ltd.- 1998, Robert Bosch Engineering & Business Solutions Ltd. – 1998, Birla Technologies – 2001, Aditya Birla Minacs / Transworks Information Services Pvt Ltd. – 2002, PSI Data Systems – 2002, L&T Technology Services – 2012, AdaniConneX (2021)

Life Insurance companies - Birla Sunlife Insurance – 2000, HDFC Life Insurance – 2000, ICICI Prudential Life Insurance – 2000, Max Life Insurance Co. – 2000, Bajaj Allianz Life Insurance Co. – 2001, Reliance Nippon Life Insurance Co. – 2001, SBI Life Insurance Co. – 2001, TATA AIA Life Insurance Co. – 2001, Bharti AXA Life Insurance Co. – 2006

General Insurance companies - Bajaj Allianz General Insurance Co. – 2001, Cholamandalam MS General Insurance Co Ltd – 2001, PNB MetLife India Insurance Co. Ltd – 2001, Tata AIG General Insurance Co. Ltd – 2001, Bharti AXA General Insurance Co. – 2008, Kotak Mahindra General Insurance – 2015.

Housing loan Co. - HDFC Ltd – 1977

Investment service providers - Cholamandalam Financial Holdings Ltd – 1949, Cholamandalam Investment & Finance Co Ltd – 1978

Shipping agencies - Forbes & Co. Ltd formerly Forbes Gokak Ltd. – 1767, Volkart Fleming Shipping & Services Ltd – 1920

Export Co. - Adani Enterprises Ltd / Adani Exports Ltd (1993), Meloden Exports Ltd – 1994.

Farm advisory service - Krish-E - 2020

Utility operation Co. - Mahindra Water Utilities – 1999.

17: SOCIAL DEVELOPMENT – ACHIEVEMENTS AND THREATS

Development of Scheduled Castes, Tribes and Other Backward Castes

Section of the population, in and around mountains, forests and such remote areas, lived in isolation from civilizations for several centuries and hence remained un-educated and did not seek employment in cities and villages. The Scheduled Castes population constituted 16.23% of India's population in 2007. (11.6.3)

The Scheduled Tribes population in India was 84.33 million as per Census of 2001. STs constituted 8.2% of the total population of the country. (11.6.54)

Communities which remained poor, less educated and were doing lesser paid jobs for generations formed Other Backward Communities. Based on the Census of 1931, it was estimated that OBCs constituted 52% of the population. (11.6.111)

In 1954, the Ministry of Education suggested that 20% of places should be reserved for the SCs and STs in educational institutions with a provision to relax minimum qualifying marks for admission by 5% of wherever required.

In 1980, the Mandal commission recommended that a reserved quota for OBCs of 27% should be allotted in services and public sector bodies operated by the Union Government.
*In 1982, it was specified that 15% and 7.5% of vacancies in public sector organizations and government-aided educational institutes should be reserved for the SC and ST candidates respectively.

No such reservations are offered by private companies and hence very little people from these classes get employment opportunities in private sector.

Table – 17.1 - Employment Opportunities for SC, ST and OBCs in CPSE Companies

Year	Companies	Employees						
		Total	S. Caste	S. Caste %	S. Tribe	S. Tribe %	OBC	OBC %
1-1-1971	85	553,180	45,187	8.17	12,386	2.24		
1-1-1980	177	1,856,332	340,170	18.35	139,856	7.53		
31-3-1991	236	2,301,000						*
1994		3,567,112	602,670	16.9	195,802	5.49		
1999		3,544,262	591,740	16.7	218,653	6.17		
1-1-2004		3,058,56	521,423	17.05	199,991	6.54	138,680	4.53
1-1-2005		1,227,053	225,430	18.37	115,602	9.42	191,663	15.61
1-1-2006	201	1,254,071	238,189	18.99	110,230	8.78	182,008	14.51
1-1-2007	210	1,272,679	237,921	18.69	120,384	9.49	186,713	14.672
1-1-2008	206	1,540,672	290,212	18.83	129,190	8.38	214,432	13.91
31-3-2014	234	1,349,493	238,845	17.7	115,438	8.55	206,083	15.27
31-3-2016	244	1,232,161	214,132	17.38	104,888	8.51	205,385	16.67
31-3-2017	257	1,129,261	211,345	18.72	104,848	9.28	211,620	18.74
31-3-2018	257	1,086,728*	189,193	17.41	104,649	9.63	209,318	19.26
31-3-2019	249	1,031,049*	180,780	17.53	101,628	9.86	197,428	19.15
31-3-2020	270	9,19,648	160,384		99,693		198,581	
31-3-2021	255	8,60,165	148,604		89,945		192,667	
31-3-2022	248	8,38,745	145,780	17.38	85,450	10.19	189,769	22.63
31-3-2023	254	8,42,880	144,442	17.17	82,935	9.86	199,899	23.77

For 31.03.2019 - PE_seurvey_ENG_VOL_1.pdf (dpe.gov.in) and similar for other years.

*- Ref. 8.5.1.10 - Total employees on 31.03.2018, 2019, 2022 and 2023 including contract and casual employees were 1,554,967, 1,514,064, 14,55,446 and 14,90,490 respectively. (PE Survey 2022-23)

Thus, on an average, 262580 SC employees, 118420 ST employees and 194589 OBC employees got employment in 226 CPSEs.

Employment in other public sector units – Besides CPSEs, Railways, Banks, Insurance Companies, Post & Telegraph, Telephones, All India Radio, TV Broadcasting, government hospitals, public educational institutions, Central and State government offices, State Electricity Boards, State Transports, armed forces, police, courts, etc. also had reservation for these 3 categories.

The Indian Railways had a regular work force of over 16 lakh employees in 1997. It was the single largest employer in the country. (9.7.1.90)

Employment in government service - SC Representation in Central Government Services in 1994, 1999, and 2004 (as on 1.1.2004) were 602670 (16.9% of Total 3567112 employees), 591740 (16.7% total 3544262) and 521423 (17.05% of total 3058506) respectively. (11. Table 6.6)

ST Representation in Central Government Services in 1994, 1999, and 2004 (as on 1.1.2004) were 195802 (5.49%), 218653 (6.17%) and 199991 (6.54%) respectively. (11. Table 6.11)

Despite 27% posts being reserved for OBCs from 1993, the overall representation of OBCs in government service on 1-1-2004 was abysmally low 138680, just 4.53% of total employees. (11. Table 6.13)

Scheme to Encourage SC Entrepreneurs by Industrial Finance Corporation of India

The Government of India placed a Venture Capital Fund of Rs. 200 Cr for the "Scheme of Credit Enhancement Guarantee for Scheduled Caste Entrepreneurs" in March, 2015 to encourage entrepreneurs in the lower strata of society and to provide concessional finance.

Industrial Finance Corporation of India contributed Rs.50 Cr as lead investor and Sponsor of the Fund. IFCI Venture Capital Funds Ltd., a subsidiary of IFCI Ltd., was the Investment Manager of the Fund. The Fund was operationalized during FY 2014-15. Under the scheme, IFCI provided guarantees to banks against loans to young and start-up entrepreneurs belonging to SCs.

Artificial Limbs Manufacturing Corp. of India – Services for Disabled

Artificial Limbs Manufacturing Corp. of India - ALIMCO was incorporated on 30.11.1972 for manufacturing quality rehabilitation aids and appliances to benefit the disabled persons to the maximum extent possible. It started manufacturing activities from 1976.

ALIMCO is engaged in the manufacturing of artificial limbs, rehabilitation aids and appliances for disabled persons through Kanpur unit and 4 auxiliary production centers at Bhubaneshwar, Jabalpur, Chanalon (Punjab) and Bangalore. ALIMCO obtained license by BIS for IS marking on 355 products in 17 categories.

*During 2004-05, Light Weight Foldable Stretcher, Wheel Chair Tubular Folding, Electrical Hand, Myo-Electric Hand, Solar Battery Charger for Hearing Aid, Size-II and Body Level Hearing Aid with Tele-Coil facility were taken up for development.

*During 2007-08, ALIMCO developed Active Prosthetic Leg, Tetron Cloth Canopy in Multi Utility Tricycle, Hand Propelled Tricycle (Child Size), Plastic Molded Foot rest for Wheel Chair, and Wheel Chair Tubular Folding.

*ALIMCO's share in domestic production of Artificial Limbs & Rehabilitation Parts was 60%

Export and recognitions - ALIMCO exported its products to Bangladesh, Sri Lanka, Bhutan, Afghanistan, Cambodia, UAE, Angola, Ghana, Uzbekistan, Tanzania, Nepal, Israel etc. It was conferred with Defence Technology Spinoff Award for 2004 for production of Standard Modular Floor Reaction Orthosis. International Red Cross Society, UNICEF and WHO have been patronizing ALIMCO products and placing orders for supply to their programs undertaken in developing countries. ALIMCO also functions as an implementing agency under Assistance to Disabled Person Scheme and Sarva Siksha Abhiyan.

Installed Capacity - ALIMCO had product installed capacity of Mech. Hand 6300 nos., Axilla Crutch 62400 nos., Wheel Chair 30000 nos., Tricycle 78000 nos. and Hearing Aid 25200 nos. in 2008-09.
*The installed capacities in 2019-20 were 62399 numbers for Crutches, 150004 numbers for hearing aids and 146995 numbers tricycle and wheel chairs.
*During 2022-23, a Design Studio has been set up at Faridabad for 3D Printing of Prosthesis and Orthosis. ALIMCO is setting up Pradhan Mantri Divyasha Kendra in all the States of the country. Revenue from operations in 2022-23 was Rs. 458.67 Cr.

National Schedule Castes Finance & Development Corp.

National Schedule Castes Finance & Development Corp. - NSCFDC was incorporated on 8.2.1989 as National SC and ST Finance and Development Corp., which was later bifurcated into 2 corporations one for SCs and another for STs with an objective to exclusively work for the economic development of the people belonging to SC (and ST categories) living below double the poverty line limit (i.e., Rs. 98,000/- in Rural Areas & Rs.120000/- in Urban Areas) with effect from 10.04.2001, through income generating schemes, micro credit finance at concessional interest rates, grants for skill development programs etc. through 37 State / UT Channelizing Agencies (SCAs) and other recognized institutions nominated by the respective State / UT Government.

NSCFDC provides advisory services to the target group and arranges Exhibition-cum-Fairs for marketing the products of beneficiaries.
*As on 31.3.2005, NSCFDC had sanctioned 3676 schemes costing Rs.2154.34 Cr to SCAs for covering 512053 SC beneficiaries and disbursed Rs.1238.55 Cr to the implementing agencies for implementing the schemes.
*Number of SC persons who received assistance during X 5YP (up to December 2006) was 257901. (11.6.9)
*NSCFDC introduced an Education Loan Scheme in December 2009. As on 31.3.2012, NSCFDC had disbursed Rs. 2,302.91 Cr. benefitting 7.95 lakh SCs. (12.24.18.)

Revenue from operations in 2022-23 was Rs. 63.23 Cr.

National Backward Classes Finance and Development Corp.

National Backward Classes Finance and Development Corp. - NBCFDC was incorporated on 13.1.1992 to promote economic development activities for the benefit of members of backward classes (OBCs) living below double the poverty line. (11.6.113.)

NBCFDC disburses concessional loans (term loans, margin money loans and micro finance schemes) to members of backward classes under self-employment generation schemes through SCAs (at Kolkata, Mumbai, Chennai, Kanpur and Hyderabad) and State Backward Classes Finance & Development Corps.
*NBCFDC is assisting eligible artisans and people engaged in traditional occupations, technical trades, small-scale and tiny industry, small business, transport services, etc. with a wide range of income

generating activities including agricultural and allied activities. NBCFDC disbursed Rs 1150.89 Cr, covering 750432 beneficiaries up to December 2006. (11.6.116.)

*During 2006-07, the NBCFDC invited the artisans of the target group to participate in 14 exhibitions in India and 2 exhibitions abroad and showcase their inherent skill to the market, provided adequate space free of cost and also bore their traveling cost.

*Up to 31.3.2011, the cumulative disbursement of funds by NBCFDC was Rs. 1850.11 Cr.

NBCFDC arranged income generation scheme for assisting 140343 people and skill development schemes to 13375 trainees belonging to backward classes during 2022-23. Revenue from operations was Rs. 53.13 Cr.

National Minorities Development and Finance Corp.

National Minorities Development and Finance Corp. - NMDFC was incorporated on 30.9.1994 to help economic development of backward sections amongst minorities defined under National Commission for Minorities Act 1992.

NMDFC is providing financial assistance (including Term Loan, Margin Money, Micro Credit, Interest Fee Loan, Revolving fund scheme under Micro Financing, Educational Loan, Vocational Training, Grant for skill development / Marketing assistance scheme, etc.) at concessional rate of interest to the eligible minorities living below double the poverty line for self-employment ventures and technical and professional education, with preference to women and occupational groups, through 36 SCAs (in 26 States and 2 UTs) and a network of 144 NGOs across the country.

*Loans amounting to more than Rs. 700 Cr were disbursed to about 3 lakh beneficiaries up to 31.3.2005.

Revenue from operations in 2022-23 was Rs. 80.11 Cr.

National Handicapped Finance & Development Corp.

National Handicapped Finance & Development Corp. - NHFDC was incorporated on 24.1.1997 for economic empowerment and social development of persons with disability.

NHFDC is providing financial assistance (loans for setting up small business in service / trading sector; purchase of vehicles for commercial hiring, setting up small industrial unit; promoting agriculture activities; self-employment amongst persons with mental retardation, cerebral palsy and autism; arranging professional / educational / training courses; financial assistance for skills and entrepreneurial development; Micro Credit Finance; and Parents' Association of mentally retarded persons) to disabled persons through SCAs.

Name of NHFDC was changed to National Divyangjan Finance and Development Corporation w.e.f. 9.08.2023.

National Safai Karam Charis Finance & Development Corp.

National Safai Karam Charis Finance & Development Corp. - NSKFDC was incorporated on 24.1.1997 to promote socio-economic up-lifting of Scavengers, whose income is below double the poverty line, by promoting self-employment in alternative occupations and encouraging skill development by providing concessional financial assistance including term loan, micro credit finance, Mahila Samrddhi yojana, educational loan etc. to Safai Karam Charis and their dependents through income generating viable projects, by arranging technical and professional training, quality control, technology up-gradation, and common facility centers for carrying out sanitation works through SCAs nominated by 26 State Govts. / UTs.

The SCAs for identification of beneficiaries and disbursement of loans are the State Scheduled Caste Development Corporations. No income ceiling is fixed for availing financial assistance. Priority is, however, accorded to economic development and rehabilitation of scavengers, whose income is below double the poverty line besides women and persons with disabilities among the target group. (12.24.21)

During the X 5YP, NSKFDC introduced the Micro Credit Finance Scheme and the Mahila Samridhi Yojana, benefitting 102187 persons. During 2006–07, it disbursed loans to 16545 beneficiaries (up to December 2006) for various income generating activities in 23 States and 2 UTs. (11.6.10.)

Cumulative disbursements till 31.3.2012 were Rs. 724.24 Cr, which benefitted 2.31 lakh beneficiaries.

Revenue from operations in 2022-23 was Rs, 12.08 Cr.

National Scheduled Tribes Finance & Development Corp.

National Scheduled Tribes Finance & Development Corp. - NSTFDC was incorporated on 10.4.2001 by bifurcating erstwhile National SCs and STs Finance and Development Corporation to work for the economic development of Scheduled Tribes.

NSTFDC is providing concessional financial assistance and grants for viable income generating schemes and skill development programs through SCAs for the economic development of ST persons having annual family income below double the poverty line income limit. (i.e., Rs. 81,000 in Rural Areas & Rs.1,03,000 in urban areas). It also extends financial assistance for undertaking procurement and marketing of agricultural / minor forest produce and undertaking training programs for skill and entrepreneurial development of target group.

In 2010-11, NSTFDC covered 95632 beneficiaries under income generating activities since inception. *About 0.388 million STs were benefitted through NSTFDC during XI plan. (12.24.58)

Revenue from operations in 2022-23 was Rs. 41.27 Cr.

Summary for Social Service Organizations –

The contribution of these social service organizations is not reflected directly in computation of GDP, though they provide invaluable service to deprived section of society.

Uniform Wealth Distribution Obtained Through Public Sector Units

Welfare of Scheduled Castes etc. - The 24.43% of population constituted by Scheduled Caste and Scheduled tribe benefited to a very great extent by getting employment in public sector units with more ease than obtaining employment in private sector. They were living in poverty for many generations and centuries. With one person getting employment, the living standard of his entire family (parents, siblings and children) improved, they got educated and became qualified for employment.

The 52% of population constituted by Other Backward Castes also got benefited significantly by getting employment under quota with relative ease than candidates of same qualification belonging to general category. Their living standard also improved significantly.

Employees in Government Services - People employed in government services got their salaries raised regularly through Pay Commission recommendations.

i) The recommendations of second pay commission set up in 1957 had a financial impact of Rs. 39.6 crore.
ii) The implementation of Third Pay Commission's proposals cost the government Rs 144 crore in March 1973 and that of Fourth Pay Commission set up in 1983 cost Rs. 1282 Cr.

iii) The Sixth Central Pay Commission report, submitted in March 2008, estimated the financial implication of its recommendations to be Rs. 7975 Cr for 2008 – 2009, and an additional, one-time burden of Rs. 18060 Cr on payment of arrears. (The cost of hikes in salaries was anticipated to be about Rs. 20,000 Cr for a total of 5.5 million government employees).

iv) On 19.11.2015, the Seventh Central Pay Commission recommended 23.55% hike in pay and allowances which were to be implemented from 1.1.2016.

Vajpayee Government didn't implement Fifth Pay Commission Reports - The recommendations of the Fifth Pay Commission, released in January 1997 were, however, mostly ignored by the Janata Dal (United Front), and BJP Government of Vajpayee that followed. Mulayam Singh Yadav, Defence Minister (1.06.1996 – 19.3.1998), Indrajit Gupta, Home Minister (29.6.1996 – 19.3.1998), and L.K. Advani, Home Minister (19.3.1998 – 22.5.2004) did little to implement these recommendations.

Modi Government Paid Less Than Recommendations - On 29.06.2016, Government accepted the recommendation of 7th Pay Commission Report with meagre increase in salary of 14% after six months of intense evaluation and successive discussions.

*The representations by former Chiefs and the Chiefs of Staff to the Ministry of Defence, the PM and other bureaucratic bodies reviewing the 7CPC recommendations were in vain. On 25.07.2016, without addressing or taking into account the key concerns of the armed forces, the Government issued instructions implementing 7CPC's "general recommendations on pay without any material alteration" including separate "Pay Matrices" (for civilians) and the armed forces.

Better Salary for Lower-Level Employees - Subsequent to these revisions, the people in government service started getting very good salary comparable to their counterparts in good private sector companies. (Previously private sector jobs were considered more remunerative). The people in lower cadres of government service got higher salary than their private sector counter parts. (Refer to following analysis and graph)

Emoluments of CPSE Employees

The standard of living of those, who got employment in CPSEs, improved to a great extent in accordance with Per Capita Emoluments indicated in the table. **Table - 17.2**

Year	Employees in Lakh	Per Capita Emoluments in Rs.	Population in million	Per capita Net National Income at factor cost at constant prices in Rs.
1950-51			361	7114
1960-61			439.2	8889
1970-71			548.2	10016
1980-81			683.3	10712
1990-91			846.4	14330
1991-92	21.79	56508		
1992-93	21.52	64983		
1993-94	20.70	72043		
1994-95	20.62	82517		
1995-96	20.52	106876		
1996-97	20.08	110662		
1997-98	19.59	129582		
1998-99	19.00	138179		
1999-2000	18.06	168339		
2000-01	17.40	219672	1028.7	20362
2001-02	19.92	193554		
2002-03	18.66	225986		
2003-04	17.62	248481		
2004-05	17.00	286112		24143

Year	Employees in Lakh	Per Capita Emoluments in Rs.	Population in million	Per capita Net National Income at factor cost at constant prices in Rs.
2005-06	16.49	284123		27131
2006-07	16.14	325869		31206
2007-08	15.65	410898		35825
2008-09	15.33	541716		40775
2009-10	14.90	589210	1177	46249
2010-11	14.40	683347	1210.57	54151
2011-12	14.50	728606		61564
2012-13	14.02	830263		68757
2013-14	13.49	906665		
2014-15	12.91	986598		
2015-16	11.85	1072920		
2016-17	11.35	1241165		
2017-18	10.88	1415556		
2018-19	10.33	1478280		

Ref. for Per Capita Income – Statement 2.6b of Annual Report for 2013-14

Third Pay Revision Committee recommended revised pay-scales for below board level employees for Schedule A/B/C/D CPSEs effective from 1.1.2017. E0 and E1 level employees pay scale increased from 12600-32500 and 16400-40500 to 30000-120000 and 40000-140000 respectively.

Min. / Max. pay of Director and CMD were Rs. 180000 / 340000 and Rs. 200000 / Rs. 370000 in Schedule A CPSE, Rs. 160000/290000 and 180000/ 320000 in Schedule B CPSE, Rs. 120000 / 280000 and Rs. 160000/ 290000 in Schedule C CPSE and Rs. 100000 / 260000 and Rs. 120000 / 280000 in Schedule D CPSE.

Employees of Public Sector Banks

Junior level employees of public sector banks get higher salaries than their counterparts in private sector banks. This is evident from high attrition levels of 34% in HDFC Bank, 35% in Axis Bank, 43% in Yes Bank and 46% in Kotak Mahindra Bank in 2022-23 at their entry level staff. (TOI dated 27-7-23)

Indirect Employment

When one public sector company is started, number of construction companies and casual / contract labors get temporary job opportunities during construction stage. When the company starts functioning, a large number of people get employment in shops, restaurants, hotels, schools, hospitals, transporters for raw material and finished goods, dealer and distribution network, banks, etc. for serving direct employees. More townships formed around CPSEs than around private companies.

Extended Employment

A large proportion of people retired from government services, public sector banks, insurance companies and public sector units get pension. Consequently, the number of people receiving income is much higher than people actually in service in these units.

Remuneration in Private Sector Companies

Remuneration paid to different levels of employees in 10 big private sector companies in 2022-23 are given below:

Table – 17.3

Name of Companies		Junior	Middle Management	Senior Management	BOD / Directors	Chairman / MD / CEO / CFO	Promotors
Tata Consultancy Services (Tata Group)	No. of Employees	288307	213404	22127	BOD - 9; KMP - 4;	CEO & MD - 1; COO & ED - 1	
	Median Remuneration	382063	1341136	3573247	28322308	263810000	304096000000
	Distribution - as % of Chairman / MD / CEO /CFO	0.145	0.508	1.354	10.736	100.000	115270.839
Reliance Industries Ltd. (Consolidated / Group)	No. of Employees	Employees – 389414			Non - Executive Directors -10	Executive Directors - 5	
	Median Remuneration*	544716			17220000	169750000	29904732432
	Distribution - as % of Chairman / MD / CEO /CFO	0.321			10.144	100.000	17616.926
Larsen & Toubro Ltd. (Consolidated / Group)	No. of Employees	Workers - 2104	Employees – 53089		Ex. Directors - 7; Non-Ex. Dirs- 8; Comp. Sec. -1	Chairman; CEO & MD; CFO	
	Median Remuneration	960485	980407		73425000	204033333	0
	Distribution - as % of Chairman / MD / CEO /CFO	0.471	0.481		35.987	100.000	0.000
Hindalco Industries Ltd. (Birla Group)	No. of Employees	Workers - 13474	Employees – 9186		BO Directors- 11; KMP - 4;	CEO & MD; CFO	
	Median Remuneration	593616	918299		181474933	224450000	2291766564
	Distribution - as % of Chairman / MD / CEO /CFO	0.264	0.409		80.853	100.000	1021.059
Mahindra and Mahindra Ltd. (Mahindra Group)	No. of Employees	Workers - 11249	Employees – 12246		BOD-12; Ind. Dir. 8; KMP -4 Comp. Sec.-1	Chairman; CEO & MD; CEO & ED; CFO	
	Median Remuneration	599004	1680965		20348000	99975000	3815983405
	Distribution - as % of Chairman / MD / CEO /CFO	0.599	1.681		20.353	100.000	3816.938
Hindustan Unilever Ltd.	No. of Employees	Workers - 11251	Employees – 7716		BOD- 10; Ind. Dir. 6; KMP - 3 Comp.Sec. - 1	CEO & MD; ED; CFO	
	Median Remuneration	561398	1274158		21380238	122966667	56722101462
	Distribution - as % of Chairman / MD / CEO /CFO	0.457	1.036		17.387	100.000	46128.030

Name of Companies		Junior	Middle Management	Senior Management	BOD / Directors	Chairman / MD / CEO / CFO	Promotors
HDFC Bank Ltd	No. of Employees	Workers - NA	Employees – 173222		BOD- 10; Ind. Dir. 7; KMP - 4; Non-Ex. Dir - 1;	Chairman; CEO & MD; ED;	
	Median Remuneration	NA	482917		14443455	71583665	22127890846
	Distribution - as % of Chairman / MD / CEO /CFO	NA	0.675		20.177	100.000	30911.928
Bajaj Finance Ltd	No. of Employees	Workers - NA	Employees – 45498		KMP - 2; Non Ex. Dir - 7;	Chairman; CEO & MD; ED;	
	Median Remuneration	NA	709420		11155556	63533333	10155738690
	Distribution - as % of Chairman / MD / CEO /CFO	NA	1.117		17.559	100.000	15984.898
Vedanta Ltd. (Annual Report 2021-22)	No. of Employees	Workers # - 68056	Employees - 8129 Note $		Non-Ex. Dir - 1;	Chairman; Vice Chairman; CEO; CFO;	
	Median Remuneration	#	811908		11300000	82179096	116566000000
	Distribution - as % of Chairman / MD / CEO /CFO	#	0.988		13.750	100.000	141843.857
Adani Enterprises Ltd. (Annual Report 2021-22	No. of Employees	Workers - 14911	Employees – 1149		BOD- 8; KMP - 6;	Chairman; MD; ED - 2;	
	Median Remuneration	NA	1376501		31707143	119175000	823963481
	Distribution - as % of Chairman / MD / CEO /CFO	NA	1.155		26.606	100.000	691.390
Average of 10 above Private Sector Companies	No. of Employees	Workers -	Employees		BOD; KMP;	Chairman; MD; ED	
	Median Remuneration	NA					
	Distribution - as % of Chairman / MD / CEO /CFO	0.387	0.941		19.189	100.000	
World Inequality Report 2022 for India	Indian Population	Bottom 50%	Middle 40%		Top 10%	Top 1%	
	Pre-tax national income | share | adults | equal split in $	1952	5527		42472	161546	
	Distribution - as % of Top 1%	1.208	3.422		26.291	100.000	0.000

Name of Companies		Junior	Middle Management	Senior Management	BOD / Directors	Chairman / MD / CEO / CFO	Promotors
Indian Oil Corporation	No. of Employees	Non-Executives / Workers - 12610	Executives - Asst. Officer - Managers – 12626		Executives - Sr. Manager - Ex. Director - 5799	Chairman; Directors Func - 7; CFO; Comp. Sec.	Government
	Median Remuneration	524226	1237571		1917960	8325090	21816599301
	Distribution - as % of Chairman / MD / CEO /CFO	6.297	14.866		23.038	100.000	262058.420
Chennai Petroleum Corp. Ltd.	No. of Employees	Workmen / Clerical Level - 745	Supervisory Level - 224		Managerial Level - 497	MD; Directors Func - 3; Comp. Sec.	Indian Oil Corp. (Holding Co.)
	Median Remuneration	549206	1089519		1577560	8770000	2086160400
	Distribution - as % of Chairman / MD / CEO /CFO	6.262	12.423		17.988	100.000	23787.462
HSCC (India) Ltd.	No. of Employees	Workmen / Clerical Level - 8	Supervisory Level - 78		Managerial / Executive Level - 73	MD; Director Engg.; CFO; Comp. Sec.	NBCC (India) Ltd. (Holding Co.)
	Median Remuneration					2609250	81186314
	Distribution - as % of Chairman / MD / CEO /CFO	0	0		0	100	3111
Indian Medicines & Pharmaceutical Corp. (2020-21)	No. of Employees	Non-Officers - 79	Officers - 13		Managerial Level -	MD; KMP; Comp. Sec.	Indian Oil Corp. (Holding Co.)
	Median Remuneration					2546180	62900000
	Distribution - as % of Chairman / MD / CEO /CFO	0	0		0	100	2470

RIL-Integrated-Annual-Report-2022-23.pdf (rilstaticasset.akamaized.net) AnnualReport_2022-23.aspx (ril.com), annual-report-2022-2023.pdf (tcs.com), L&T Integrated Annual Report 2022-2023 (larsentoubro.com), hindalco-annual-report-2022-23.pdf, MM-Annual-Report-2022-23.pdf (mahindra.com), Annual Report – 2022-23 (hul.co.in), 723fb80a-2dde-42a3-9793-7ae1be57c87f.pdf (hdfcbank.com), bajaj-finance-limited-ar-2022-23.pdf (bajajfinserv.in), VedantaIR2022-040822.pdf (vedantalimited.com), AEL-04-07-22_F.pdf (adanienterprises.com), IndianOil AR 2022-23.pdf, High Res_Final_CPCL_IAR_FY 22-23 Consolidated.PDF, HSCC_English_Annual_Report-2022-23.pdf (hsccltd.co.in), finalenglish booklet print duo paper 10 pcs with binding..cdr (impclmohan.nic.in)

Note 1 - **Reliance Industries Ltd.** - Median remuneration has not been given for employees. It was calculated as = (Salary and wages of Rs. 21212 Cr) / 389414.

Note 2 – **Vedanta Ltd.** - # - There were 8,129 employees on 31.03.2022. Employees including contactors 76,185;

$ - As per Standalone Balance Sheet, Employee benefits expense was only Rs. 1423 Cr against total income of Rs. 71624 Cr in 2021-22 including salaries and wages of Vedanta Rs. 660 Cr and of its joint ventures Rs. 556 Cr.

*As per Consolidated Balance Sheet, Employee benefits expense was only Rs. 2811 Cr against total income of Rs. 135332 Cr in 2021-22 including salaries and wages of Vedanta Rs. 2220 Cr and of its joint ventures Rs. 556 Cr. If entire Rs. 660 Cr of salary is considered for 8129 employees only (without any workers), median remuneration comes to Rs. 811908.

*Remuneration by way of commission and sitting fees paid to Non-EDs (Independent) of Rs. 42010959 was not included in directors' payment.

Adani Enterprises Ltd. - AEL has 790 permanent and 14121 other than permanent workers, who are paid more than minimum wage. AEL has 4261 permanent and 247 other than permanent employees in the complete group. Besides commission, Non-EDs are paid sitting fees of Rs. 50,000/- for attending Board and Audit Committee meetings and Rs. 25,000/- for attending other Committee meetings. The total sitting fees came to Rs. 10150000.

Remuneration of CPSE employees - Remuneration of workers and executive employees have not been given in the annual reports of Indian Oil Corp., Chennai Petroleum Corp., HSCC (India) Ltd. and Indian Medicines Pharmaceutical Corp. Remuneration of workers and executives have been calculated **considering only starting basic pay of the respective scale** and **allowances other** than Dearness Allowance and House Rent Allowance **have not been taken into consideration.**

Indian Oil Corporation - Sitting fees of Independent Directors of Rs. (600000+880000+920000+840000 + 920000+920000+400000+680000) = Rs. 6160000 is not included in directors' payment as they are not full-time directors.

*Besides government, ONGC, LIC and Oil India received a dividend of Rs. 11770287336.

Chennai Petroleum Corp. - Sitting fees of Independent Directors of Rs. (470000+530000+ 280000+290000+ 250000) = Rs. 1820000 is not included in Directors' payment as they are not full-time directors.

HSCC (India) Ltd. - Sitting fees of Independent Directors of Rs. (90000+100000+220000) = Rs. 410000 is not included in Directors' payment as they are not full-time directors.

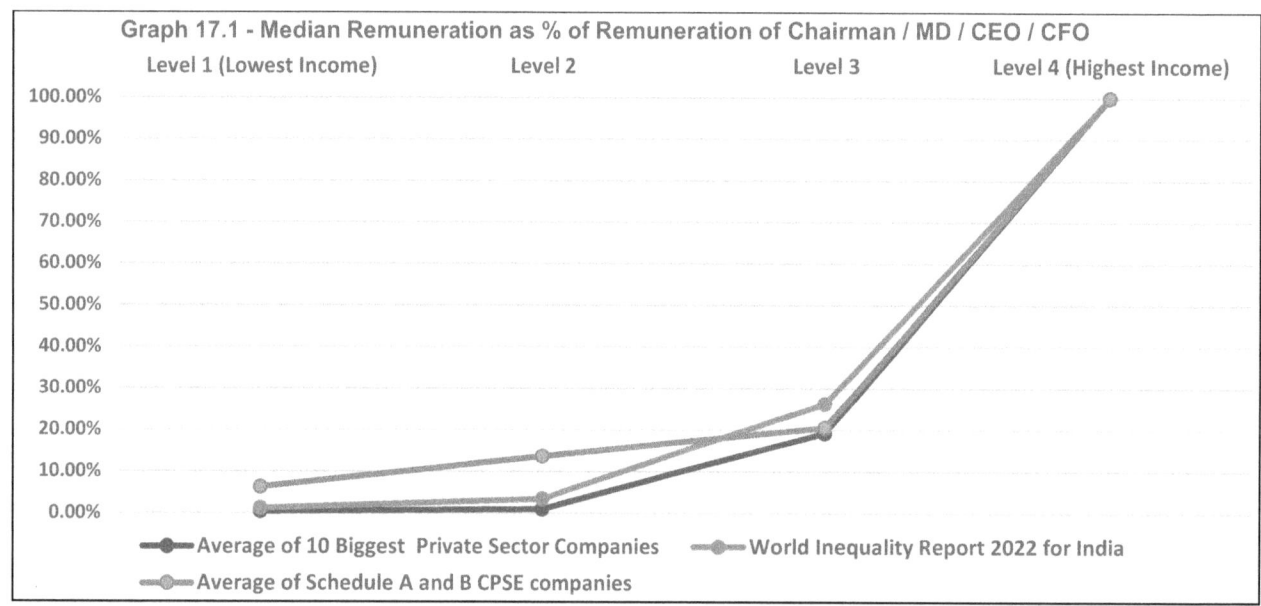

Outcomes of Remuneration Analysis - The analysis shows the impact of the salary structure of private sector companies on increasing the inequality in income distribution among the lower, middle, upper middle, rich and richest strata of society. The analysis of salary structure of 4 (different categories of) public sector companies shows the comparatively even income distribution among the same 5 classes of society with emphasis on **much higher income for the lower classes** compared to private sector companies.

*This analysis quantitatively illustrates the fruitful results of the Economic Development Model highlighted in the book.

*This analysis poses challenge to all advanced Western countries of private sector-based economies as why public sector companies should not be preferred over private sector companies as both give same output / production for same capacities with additional contribution for decreasing inequality and giving dividends to government.

Housing was provided to Employees of many CPSEs across the Country (Above 26 States)

CPSE employees were provided with 5,89,234 houses by setting up 14 Super Mega townships with houses above 10000 houses each (AP – 1, Assam – 3, Bihar – 1, Chhattisgarh – 1, Gujarat – 2, Haryana – 2, J & K – 1, Jharkhand – 4, Karnataka – 3, Kerala – 1, MP – 9, Maharashtra – 4, Manipur – 1, Odisha – 3, Rajasthan – 4, Sikkim – 1, TN – 8, Uttarakhand – 1, UP – 8, WB – 4) , 6 Mega Townships of houses 5000 – 10000 each (Arunachal -1, Assam – 4, Chhattisgarh – 2, Delhi – 1, Haryana – 2, Himachal – 3, J&K – 1, Karnataka – 2, Kerala – 1, MP – 2, Maharashtra – 3, Mizoram – 1, Odisha – 2, Punjab – 1, Raj – 1, TN – 2, Telangana – 1, UP – 3) , 26 Townships of 1000 – 5000 houses each, 6 Townships of houses 500 – 1000 each and 12 Mini-townships of houses 100 – 500 each, etc.

- https://dpe.gov.in/sites/default/files/E1Statement21.xls

Poverty Reduction

The incidence of poverty in India in **1947** was 80% (25 Cr people were poor)

People Below Poverty Line in India were 32.1336 Cr (54.9%) in **1973**, 48.44% in **1979-80** (6. Table 2.1), 32.2897 Cr. (44.5%) in **1983**, 32.0368 Cr (36%) in **1993** and 30.172 Cr (27.5%) in **2004**. (11. Table 4.2)

Around 36 million people crossed the poverty line between 1977-78 and 1983-84. (7.3.27)

The percentage of population with a consumption standard below the poverty line was expected to come down from an estimated 36.9 % in 1984-85 to 25.8 % in 1989-90. In absolute terms, the number of poor persons was expected to fall from 273 million in 1984-85 to 211 million in 1989-90, the bulk of this improvement was in the rural areas. (7.3.28)

The percentage of the population below the poverty line declined at the rate of 1.5 percentage points per year in the period 2004–05 to **2009–10**, twice the rate at which it declined during the period 1993–94 to 2004–05.

The research "The Great Indian Middle Class: Results from the NCAER Market Survey of Households" (by the National Council for Applied Economic Research in association with Business Standards in 2004) and report "The 'Bird of Gold': the Rise of India's Consumer Market", (by McKinsey & Company in 2007) brought out that the number of households with an income above Rs 2 lakh were expected to rise from 14.4 million households in 2005 to 63.9 million in 2015 and 137.5 million in 2025. The aggregate disposable income in the hands of this class was expected to rise by four-fold by 2015 and more than 10-fold by 2025. **By 2025, India was expected to become the fifth largest market in the world, overtaking Germany's consumer market.** 'Rising incomes will lift 291 million out of poverty and create a 583 million-strong middle class" (McKinsey). (11.v2.7.1.29)

(India, with nominal GDP of $ 2.94 Trillion, became the fifth-largest economy in 2019, overtaking the United Kingdom and France).

Population Below Poverty Line in **2011-12** was 21.9%. (According to UN Millennium Development Goals program, 21.9% of India's population lived below poverty line of $ 1.25 per day in 2011-12).

India saw a spectacular average GDP growth rate of 7.8% during **2004-14** (the period globally witnessed the Great Recession and sky rocketing oil prices) and concomitantly lifted 270 million people above the poverty line, **it was because its model of growth with equity worked magically.**

The 2019 Multidimensional Poverty Index report released by United Nations Development Program said that people in India, who were in multidimensional poverty, reduced from 640 million in 2005-06 to 365.55 million by **2016-17**, an impressive reduction of 271 million. **Total wealth at end of 2019 was 15309 Bn USD.**

The global Multidimensional Poverty Index released by the United Nations Development Program and Oxford Poverty and Human Development Initiative indicated that India saw a remarkable reduction in poverty, with 415 million people exiting poverty within a span of just 15 years (2005/6 – **2019/21**)

Increase in Food Insecurity from 2014

Data from State of Food Security and Nutrition in the World (SOFI) report show that prevalence of food insecurity increased by 3.8% in India between 2014 and 2019. By 2019, 6.2 Cr more people were living with food insecurity than the number in 2014. (The Hindu dated 24-08-2020)

Between 2019 and 2021, approximately 307 million Indians experienced severe food insecurity, while 224 million individuals were affected by chronic hunger. The stark divide in socio-economic structures, among other social determinants, was a major contributor to food insecurity in the country. There was a consistent increase among Indians that went hungry in recent years. (Statista Daily Data dt 28-5-24).

Growth of Inequality in India from 2000 to 2021

India among the most unequal countries with an affluent elite – Report dt 8.12.2021
While the top 10% and top 1% hold respectively 57 per cent and 22 per cent of total national income, the bottom 50 per cent share has gone down to 13 per cent "India stands out as a poor and very unequal country, with an affluent elite."
India among most unequal nations; top 1% of population holds 22% of national income: Report, India News News | wionews.com

Next to Russia and Brazil, wealth inequality was highest in the World in India in 2021. Wealthiest 1% of the population held 40.6% of country's wealth in 2021, compared to some 33% in 2000. Japan, Great Britain, France and Canada had least inequalities and the wealth held by wealthiest 1% reduced from 2000. (Credit Suisse Global Wealth Report 2022 – Statista Daily Data dated 1-10-24)

Wealth Distribution in 2022

As per World Inequality Report 2022, Income and wealth inequalities have been on the rise nearly everywhere since the 1980s, following a series of deregulation and liberalization programs which took different forms in different countries. The rise has not been uniform. Certain countries have experienced spectacular increases in inequality (including the US, Russia and India).

According to this report, Pre-tax national income of wealthy Top 10% of population of $ 39123 was 22 times the Pre-tax national income of Bottom 50% wealthy people of India of $ 1798. This was worse than corresponding USA's figure of 17.

As per report published by Statista Research department on 14-05-2024, the top 10% Indian population group was estimated to hold over 57% of total income in India in 2022, whereas the bottom 50% group only made up just over 15% of total income.

Uneven wealth distribution in India skews progress in per capita metrics

According to Oxfam's "**Survival of the Richest**" report published in 2023 World Economic Forum at Davos, the top 1% in India owned more than 40.5% of total wealth in 2021 while the bottom 50% of the population (700 million) had around 3% of total wealth.

From the start of the pandemic to November 2022, Oxfam noted that billionaires in India witnessed a 121% growth in their wealth – INR 36.08 billion/day in real terms, as the number of impoverished ["hungry Indians"] grew from 190 million to 350 million. India's Per Capita Income in 2022-23 (india-briefing.com)

Wealth Distribution in 2024

The Global Wealth Report 2024 released on 10-07-2024 by Swiss Bank UBS indicates that inequality has increased (to Wealth inequality / Gini index of 73, fourth highest in the world) in India by 16.2% since 2008. (Statista Daily Data e-Letter dated 10-07-2024).

Increase in wealth of Billionaires in India in 2024

The UBS Billionaire Ambitions Report (TOI dated 9.12.2024) said during last 10 years, the number of Indian billionaires more than doubled to 185 and their combined wealth increased by 263% to reach $ 905 billion.

Factors Which Led to Increased Inequality

Less and Reduction in Employment Opportunities offered by CPSEs - Though, this economic development model, centred on public sector units, restricted industry becoming monopolistic in most sectors to a large extent, and improved production in all sectors, it could not achieve the desired uniform wealth distribution, mainly because only a small portion of population could find employment in these sectors.

Total employment in manufacturing in 1979-80 was 2,20,12,000 (6.13.1). Of which only 18,56,332 were employed in 177 CPSEs, which was just 8.43%.

As indicated in Table 17.1, the employment opportunities increased to 2.301 million in 1990-91 and thereafter decreased as the units started reducing man power in their effort to reduce overheads and expenses to become competitive with private sector companies after liberalization. Though, the number of CPSEs increased from 236 in 1990-91 to 257 in 2017 and 270 in 2020, employment opportunities reduced to 36.45% in 2021-22 for same reason.

Table – 17.4 Assets Built by Starting CPSEs from 1950

Year	Investment In Cr	Capital Employed in Rs. Cr	Net Worth in Rs. Cr.	Market Capitalization in Rs. Cr.	Gross Revenue in Rs. Cr
1950-51	29				
1955-56	81				
1960-61	948				
1965-66	2410				
1968-69	3897				
1973-74	6237				
1978-79	15534				
1979-80	18150				

Year	Investment In Cr	Capital Employed in Rs. Cr	Net Worth in Rs. Cr.	Market Capitalization in Rs. Cr.	Gross Revenue in Rs. Cr
1980-81		18207			
1984-85	42673	36382			
1985-86		42965			
1986-87		51835			
1987-88		55617			
1988-89		67629			
1989-90	99329	84760			
1990-91		102084			
1991-92	135445	117991			
1992-93		140110			
1993-94		159836			
1994-95		162451			
1995-96		173874			
1996-97	213610	202021			
1997-98	231024	249855			
1998-99	239167	265093			
1999-2000	252745	302867			
2000-01	274198	331372			
2001-02	324614	389934			
2002-03	335647	417160			630704
2003-04	349994	452336	291828		630704
2004-05	357849	504407	341595		744307
2005-06	403706	585484	397275	653924	837295
2006-07	420771	661338	454134	679089	964890
2007-08	455367	724009	518485	1120752	1096308
2008-09	513522	792232	583144	813530	1271536
2009-10	580784	908007	652993	1426212	1244805
2010-11	666848	1153833	709505	1506698	1498018
2011-12	729298	1337821	776161	1257792	1822049
2012-13	850599	1508177	850921	1116817	1945814
2013-14	992096	1710453	926663	1102730	20,66,057
2014-15	1095554	1833274	962518	1327394	1995176
2015-16	1161019	20,37,318	10,79,953	1294245	18,34,635
2016-17	1245819	21,38,069	10,66,885	15,18,920	19,55,675
2017-18	1431008	23,57,913	11,15,552	15,20,412	21,54,774
2018-19	1782878	27,80,247	12,11,311	13,71,116	25,45,697
2019-20	21,28,000	30,97,000	12,47,000	8,20,000	24,58,000
2020-21	21,58,000	32,93,000	13,81,000	12,20,000	24,08,000
2021-22	22,89,000	34,78,000	14,97,000	15,46,000	31,36,000
2022-23	25,35,000	38,16,000	17,33,000	16,69,000	37,90,000

Indian governments invested heavily for starting CPSEs for the purpose of increasing production in various sectors to achieve self-sufficiency and provide employment to people simultaneously preventing development of monopoly of private sector companies in crucial sectors.

Change in Government Policies

As per World Inequality Report 2022, when state control was loosened in countries like China and India to allow private sector-led growth, the ideology "that the institutions that kept inequality low were to blame, and that what we needed was to unleash an entrepreneurial culture that celebrates the unabashed accumulation of private wealth" got trotted out to justify not worrying about inequality, with the consequence that India is now among the most unequal countries in the world.

Vajpayee government handed over a portfolio of assets including mines of zinc, silver, lead, aluminium, chromium, copper, nickel, oil and gas and processing facilities, created through tax payers' money at throw away price to Sterlite Technologies, in which Anil Agarwal and his family owned 54%. Thus, one public (sector) asset was handed over an individual billionaire in 2001. Thus year 2001 is the (downward) turning point in growth in asset creation / uniform wealth creation.

Disinvestment and Privatization of Public Sector Units

Privatization of public sector units started when Vajpayee government adopted a three-fold objective: i) revival of potentially viable enterprises; ii) closing down of those PSUs that cannot be revived; iii) and bringing down government equity in non-strategic PSUs to 26% or lower.

Closing down non-viable PSUs

The prime aim of starting any company is to produce targeted quantity of a product - aluminium, zinc, lead, etc or so many numbers of vehicles per year - and not to maintain a particular net worth or to give a specified profit.
Hence considering loss or less dividend as criteria for disinvestment without considering productivity and capacity utilization by these CPSEs and contribution to national GDP is a wrong concept.

Aid given earlier for restructuring of sick CPSEs and reduction of number of sick CPSEs

Aid given for restructuring till 2007 - Till 31.10.2007, Board for Reconstruction of Public Sector Enterprises made recommendations for restructuring in respect of 47 CPSEs, and government approved the proposals for restructuring of 28 CPSEs with an aid of Rs. 8285 Cr including **cash assistance of Rs. 1955 Cr** (Rs. 70 Cr one time aid per CPSE may be less compared to turnover of these companies)

Reduction in number of sick CPSEs - The number of sick CPSEs came down from 105 in March, 2003 to 64 in March 2011.

Status in 2011-12 of sick CPSEs referred to BPRSE – Of the Government approved revival proposals in respect of 43 CPSEs, 24 CPSEs posted profits. Out of these 24 CPSEs, 13 were declared as turnaround companies as they were in profits (before tax) continuously for 3 years and more.

Improvement in performance of sick CPSEs –
Number of sick CPSEs came down from 90 in 2004-05 to 66 in March 2012.
19 Companies made net profit for more than 3 years and were declared Turnaround CPSEs in 2012-13

Aid given for restructuring sick CPSEs till 2012-13 –
Cash and non-cash assistance approved by the government in respect of BRPSE recommended proposals for 67 sick CPSEs up to 31.10.2012 were Rs. 4739.44 Cr (Rs. 105 Cr one time aid per CPSE may be less compared to turnover of these companies) and Rs. 22237.83 Cr. (average Rs. 494 Cr) respectively.

Improvement in performance of sick CPSEs –
Of the 44 operating CPSEs registered with BIFR as on 31.3.2013, a) 3 CPSEs were declared 'No Longer Sick'; b) 6 CPSEs were dropped from the list of 'sick industrial CPSEs' on their net worth becoming positive; c) 4 CPSEs had been declared as 'nonmaintainable' on account of the net worth of the CPSE becoming positive

Reduction in number of sick CPSEs –
Sick CPSEs came down from 81 in 2004-05, to 58 in March 2014.

Improvement in performance of sick CPSEs –
Out of 40 CPSEs registered with BIFR as on 31.03.2016, Andrew Yule & Company Ltd., Hindustan Insecticides Ltd, Projects & Development India Ltd, Scooters India Ltd, and Vignyan Industries Ltd did not have accumulated losses on 31.03.2016. (PES 2014-15.12.10)

Shutting Down Unviable / 'Under Performed' CPSEs

Modi government liquidated 31 CPSEs and Tamil Nadu Goods Transport Corp. Ltd., without trying to improve their performance or diversify to keep them continue to operate utilizing existing plant, machineries and experienced men, without trying to compensate for production loss leading to price increase in the market segment and without consideration of how to satisfy the purpose for which these companies were started. (Each of these companies were established with specific purposes besides backward area/ regional development, import substitution by development of indigenous technology and to become self-dependent in different fields and earning profit was not primary motive).

1) **Tungabhadra Steel Products Ltd.** was fabricating hydro mechanical equipment like radial gates, stop-log gates, penstock pipes, EOT cranes, dome walls, skid assembly, diffuser assembly and other products for irrigation, power and other core sectors. It was liquidated in December 2015.

2) **HMT Chinar Watches Ltd** was closed on 6.01.2016 without trying for diversification.

3) **HMT Watches Ltd.** was closed on 6.01.2016 without trying for diversification.

4) **HMT Bearings Ltd.** was set up to produce Taper Roller Bearings, Cylindrical Roller Bearings and Ball Bearings.
The business revival plan submitted by Government appointed consultant Price Waterhouse Coopers, was approved by the BRPSE on 30.05.2013.
HBL was shut down in January 2016 in a hurry without implementing BRPSE approved revival plan.

5) **HMT Tractor division** was started to manufacture agricultural machineries like Tractors. The company achieved market leadership in tractors by enlarging its range to cover most of the applications. HMT produced and marketed over 400,000 tractors since inception in India and abroad. Since poor farmers could not repay loans taken for purchase of tractors, banks refused to give further loans to farmers and order book became depleted. Tractor division was closed down in 2016.

6) **Hindustan Cables Ltd.** was incorporated to make the country self-reliant in the manufacturing various types of telecommunication wires and cables.

HCL plant was modern – Refer Ch. 6.

Diversification not encouraged by government - Various projects like FRLS cables, instrumentation and control cables, high count optical fibre cables, power cables using XLPE technology, HDPE tarpaulin and HDPE pipe were planned to be taken up by company as diversification on receipt of external fund support.

Take over by another public sector unit was not encouraged - Department of Defence Production informed BIFR on 13.02.13 that it had obtained "in principle" approval for takeover of HCL by Ordinance Factories Board and the letter in this regard had been received by Department of Heavy Industries. Consequently, all necessary procedural formalities of taking over had been progressing.

The Union Cabinet in its meeting held on 28.09.2016, inter alia, approved closure of the company. Why the company was closed without giving fund for diversification or allowing OFB to take over is a mystery.

7) **Hindustan Photo Films Mfg. Co. Ltd.** was incorporated to make India self-reliant in the field of photosensitized goods to cater to health care, education, defense and entertainment needs of the country. It was liquidated in August 2016 without trying for diversification using existing plant and machineries.

*While Hindustan Photo Films was shut down for reduction in demand for its products, Garware Motors & Engineers Pvt Ltd / Garware Hi-Tech Films Ltd is still doing business in polyester film, metalized and coated polyester film, sun control polyester film, X-Ray film and graphic art films, etc.
Is Garware Hi-Tech Films Ltd. doing better because its competitor HPF was closed down?

8) **Central Inland Water Transport Corporation** was set up to undertake a) Lighterage operations on the Hooghly, which handled 80-85% of the total cargo carried by the corporation, b) Transportation from Kolkata to Bangladesh and to Assam on NW-1 and 2, c) Construction of ships in ship building yard at Rajabagan and repair of small and medium size vessels and d) Repair of ocean-going vessels.
The Union Cabinet gave its approval for dissolution of CIWTC on 31.08.2016 without effectively using cheap mode of transportation.

9) **Instrumentation Ltd.** was incorporated for providing instrumentation and control systems to thermal power, steel, fertilizer, refineries & other process industries, nuclear application, service sectors of offshore projects like Oil & Natural Gas and Defence.

Diversification was not pursued properly – Refer Ch. 13

In spite of **increase in turnover,** net loss increased in 2004-05 due to higher interest burden. The cabinet, on 30.11.2016, decided to close Kota unit without giving any relief from tax burden and in principle approval was given for transfer of Palakkad unit to Government of Kerala in a time bound manner.

10) **Tyre Corporation of India Ltd.** was incorporated to supply automotive tires to different State Transport Units, government departments and defence. It was closed in 2016.

11) **Hindustan Organic Chemicals Ltd.** was started for manufacturing basic organic chemicals, which were important intermediates in the manufacture of drugs and pharmaceuticals, dyes, dye intermediates, plastics, rubber chemicals, pesticides and laminates.
*The market share of HOCL was 47% for Phenol and 42% in Acetone in 2007-08.
*HOCL planned to change the feed stock of Hydrogen from Naphtha to Natural Gas and to use natural gas in place of furnace oil to reduce operational cost. The unit located at Rasayani (9 of the 14 factories) was closed down in 2017 (Whether it was tried to reduce operational cost?)

12) **Andaman & Nicobar Islands Forest and Plantation Dev. Corp. Ltd.** was engaged in forestry operation, cultivation and marketing of Red Oil Palm and Rubber Plantation. ANIFPDC had capacity to process 4 MT fresh fruit bunches/ hour. The production capacity of Crude Palm Oil was 1400 TPA. ANIFPDC was generating 75% of turnover through harvesting of timber. It was liquidated in August 2017 without considering about regional development, when people of Andaman and Nicobar Islands did not have many avenues of income.

13) **Bharat Wagon & Engineering Co** was engaged in production of rolling stock - open / covered wagons of all types and special purpose wagons for Railways, sugar mill machinery, fuel storage tanks, miscellaneous project equipment, turnkey projects and steel fabrication. It was liquidated on 5.07.2022 in spite of its wide product range.

14) **Hindustan Vegetable Oils Corp. Ltd**. was incorporated to promote the edible oil supply to the consumers at competitive price and breakfast foods including corn flake. It was liquidated in November 2017.

15) **Creda-HPCL Biofuel Ltd.** was incorporated for promoting alternate fuels by undertaking cultivation of jatropha plants on 15,000 hectares of land. It was closed in 2017-18.

16) **Indian Oil Creda Biofuels Ltd.** was incorporated to produce biodiesel from variety of tree borne oil seed crops by undertaking plantation activities for Jatropha plants in 5889 hectares in Chhattisgarh. It was closed in 2017-18 without taking it as alternative fuel development.

17) **Burn Standard Co Ltd** was engaged in the production of freight wagons and basic Magnesia Carbon Bricks and Bulk Refractories for steel plant convertor operations.
*The loss was mainly on account of high interest burden of about Rs. 161.87 Cr.
*BSCL had a product installed capacity of 2100 vehicle units of wagons, 2400 numbers of bogies, 2400 numbers of couplers and 61292 MT of refractories in 2008-09. Bulk production of stainless-steel wagon started in 2010-11. During the year 2013-14, the company, maintained leadership position as **largest wagons builder in the country**.
*BSCL was closed on 4.04.2018 without considering for production loss or exporting.

18) **National Jute Manufacturers Corp. Ltd.** was incorporated to take over 6 jute mills. NJMC was producing 0.16 Mts of jute goods in 1984-85. Due to disconnection of power supply by CESC / BSEB to all units of NJMC, there was no production for more than 8 years since 2003-04. Regular production of the company started in Khardah and Kinnison mills in West Bengal and RBHM Mill in Bihar units during 2012-13. It was liquidated in October 2018 without helping small scale industries to overcome power shortage.

19) **Birds Jute & Exports Ltd.** was a processing factory for bleaching, blending, dyeing and printing of jute cotton and blended fabrics / curtain, etc. It was liquidated in October 2018.

20) **Biecco Lawrie Ltd** was manufacturing medium voltage switchgear & spares, under taking execution of electrical turnkey projects, repair of motors / alternators and lube oil blending and filling. BLL was engaged in the execution of 33/66 KV sub-stations, switchyards, micro/small hydel projects etc.
***Installed capacity** of BLL. was 1375 Nos. of Control & Switchgear, 10000 KL of Lube oil blending in 2008-09. BLL entered un-manned substations projects in 2013-14.
*BLL also provided security solutions through Wi-Max-based Wireless Video Surveillance System. It was liquidated in October 2018 without adequately trying to improve its marketing activities.

21) **Handicrafts & Handlooms Export Corp. India Ltd.** was incorporated to undertake exports of handicrafts, handlooms, khadi products of village industries, readymade garments, hand-knitted carpets, fashion garments, gold and silver jewellery and import of bullion, silk, timber and cotton. It was liquidated in March 2018. Clearly, HHECIL was not operating with profit motive. By liquidating HHECIL government has harmed the welfare of craftsman, village industries, etc.

22) **Hindustan Paper Corp. Ltd.** was incorporated to establish pulp, paper and newsprint mills to make paper available for mass consumption. HPC was manufacturing writing and printing paper, caustic and chlorine in Nagaon Paper Mill and Cachar Paper Mill, of capacity 100000 Tons each. The byproducts produced by HPCL were Liquified Chlorine Gas (of capacity 18150 MT), Caustic Soda (capacity 36300 MT), Calcium Hypochlorite (capacity 14310 MT), Hydrochloric Acid (capacity 6600 MT) and Chlorine Dioxide (capacity 1090 MT). It was liquidated in May 2019 without using its potential fully.

23) **Hindustan Prefab Ltd.** was incorporated to develop and supply cost-effective pre-fabricated building components for the building industry and Indian Railways. HPL introduced PRC railway sleepers, a substitute to wood and steel railway sleepers. HPL was credited with building a large number of residential, industrial, and institutional structures using pre-cast concrete and prefabrication techniques. It was liquidated in September 2019 without using its potential.

24) **Hindustan Fluorocarbons Ltd** was engaged in the production of PTFE (a versatile engineering plastic), TFE and (Chloro-Fluro Methane Gas) CFM-22, refrigerant gas. The installed capacity for Chloro-Di-Fluoro Methane was 1262 tons in 2019-20. It was liquidated in January 2020 in spite of demand for its products.

25) **Scooters India Ltd** was established for the manufacture of scooters, mopeds, motorcycles, 3 wheelers and their components to provide economical and safe means of transportation for movement of cargo and people. SIL manufactured ten-seater electric trolley bus in 2002-03 and 1000 cc CNG vehicles in 2008-09. During 2009-10, SIL had a market share of 83.82% in passenger carrier (6+1) segment. It was liquidated in January 2021.

26) **Bharat Pumps and Compressors Ltd** was incorporated to supply pumps and compressors to Oil and Natural Gas, Petrochemicals, Refineries, Nuclear and Thermal Power Plants, Fertilizers, other process downstream industries. Installed capacity was 283 nos. Pumps, 23 nos. Compressors and 48000 Nos. Gas Cylinders in 2008-09. BPCL had a domestic market share of 90% for centrifugal pumps in 2011-12. It was liquidated in January 2021 without considering how the requirement of pumps and compressors would be met for future projects like refineries, oil exploration, etc. or trying to find export market for its products.

27) **Indian Drugs and Pharmaceuticals Ltd.** was incorporated to create self-sufficiency in respect of essential life-saving medicines and to provide medicines at affordable prices. IDPL had installed capacity of 1641 million nos. for Tablets, 430 million nos. for Capsules, 600 Kilo liters for Liquid Orals and 2 million bottles for Dry Syrup in 2008-09. It was liquidated in February 2021.

28) **Rajasthan Drugs and Pharmaceuticals Ltd.** was incorporated to supply life-saving and other essential drugs to the state Government Medical Health Department, Central government Institutes, viz ESIC, Defence, Railways, other PSUs and also to other state Government institutions. RDPL was a prime partner in the implementation of "Jana Aushadhi" program, which supplied generic medicines to the public at affordable price.
In 2013-14, the company was diversifying into pharma prescription markets, veterinary markets, marketing of Ayurvedic and other Indian system of medicines. RDPL was liquidated in February 2021 without considering its service to the community.

29) **Spices Trading Corporation** was incorporated to process and cure spices, to manufacture spice products and agricultural products and to carry on domestic and international trade (in industrial goods, iron ore, bullion, precious metals, limestone, met-coke, other minerals, polymer, polyester yarn, cotton yarn and other textile products, PVC resins, HMS and other metal scraps). It was liquidated in September 2022.

30) **Project and Equipment Corp. of India Ltd.** was incorporated to export railway and engineering equipment & turn key projects, projects and equipment of small and medium enterprises and to trade internationally in agricultural products, industrial raw materials, chemicals and bullion and installation of roof-top Solar Power Plant.
PEC executed cement, textile and sugar plants, warehouses, flats, prefabricated shelters, offices, substations, transmission lines, etc. It was liquidated in September 2019.

31) **Triveni Structurals Ltd.** was incorporated to meet the demand for fabricated structures and infra-structure requirement of Power Plants, Steel Plants, Nuclear, Defence, Fertilizers, Petrochemicals & Chemical Industries. TSL was engaged in design, fabrication and erection of hydraulic gates, pressure vessels, pipes & penstocks, building structures, T.V. towers, Microwave towers and transmission towers,

satellite launching platforms, VLF antenna system for Indian Navy, Defence projects, Skylark, passenger ropeways at Nainital & Joshimath, railway wagons and parts for diesel engines for Diesel Loco Works, Varanasi.

TSL had an **installed capacity** for building 13600 Tons of structures in 2008-09.

TSL is under liquidation subsequent to High Court of Allahabad order dated 08.10.2013.

32) **Mining and Allied Machinery Corp. Ltd.** was incorporated to manufacture mining equipment like scrapper chain conveyors. It was closed on January 2002 by Vajpayee government.

33) **Pyrites, Phosphates and Chemicals Limited** was set up on 27.3.**1960**, for exploring and mining of pyrites and rock phosphate deposits.

PPCL's production of SSP and Sulphuric Acid were 230,000 Tons and 79,000 Tons in 1996-97 respectively and of phosphatic fertilizers during 1997-98 was 110101 Tons.

Mining operations In Dehradun Unit were suspended from 1.09.1998 as withdrawal of import substitution incentive resulted in mounting losses. Government approved closure of all units situated at Amjhore, Dehradun and Saladipura w.e.f. 2002-2003.

Table 17.5 - Loss of production and contribution to GDP due to closing down of CPSEs

S. No	Name of CPSE	Product – Installed Capacity	Production Lost Years
1	Tungabhadra Steel Products Ltd.	Hydro Mechanical Equipment structural - 8213 MT and Hydel Power generation 50.09 Lakh MW.	from 2015
2.	HMT Bearings Ltd.	Ball Bearing, Taper and Cylindrical Roller Bearing - 3.1 million	from 2016
3	HMT Tractor division	Tractors - 8800 nos.	from 2016
4	HMT Chinar Watches Ltd	Gents' watches - 0.5 million	from 2016
5	HMT Watches Ltd.	Watches & components - 7.5 million nos.	from 2016
6	Hindustan Cables Ltd.	Polythene insulated jelly filled Cables and Aerial cables – 63 LCKM (Lakh Conductor kms) Telephone coiled cords - 1 million pairs Computer cords - 1.5 million pieces PIJF Cables of range up to 3600 pairs - 44 LCKM. Manufacture of cable making equipment and a wide range of special purpose machine tools and spares. Installation of Microwave Tower Antenna inclusive of Microwave connection.	from 2016
7	Hindustan Photo Films Mfg. Co. Ltd.	Cine Products - 5.06 million Sq. M X-Ray Films - 12.33 million Sq. M Graphic arts films - 2.25 million Sq. M	from 2016
8	Central Inland Water Transport Corporation	Cargo transportation capacity was 73638 metric tons in 2008-09.	from 2016
9	Instrumentation Ltd.	Telecom equipment, Instruments and Automation products, Panels/Cabinets, Gas analyzers, Control valves, Butterfly valves, Safety Relief Valves, Bellow Sealed Valves, Pneumatic / Electric Actuators, Custom-built special products like Valve stand	from 2016
10	Tyre Corporation of India Ltd.	Automotive tires to different State Transport Undertakings, government departments and defense.	from 2016
11	Hindustan Organic Chemicals Ltd.	Acetone - 24541 tons, H2O2 - 10454 tons and Phenol - 39979 tons.	from 2017

S. No	Name of CPSE	Product – Installed Capacity	Production Lost Years
12	Andaman & Nicobar Islands Forest & Plantation Dev. Corp. Ltd.	Red Palm Oil processing capacity - 4 MT Fresh Fruit Bunches / hour. Crude Palm Oil capacity - 1400 MT per annum.	from 2017
13	Bharat Wagon & Engineering Co	Wagons - 880 vehicle units	from 2017
14	Hindustan Vegetable Oils Corp. Ltd.	Edible oil Breakfast foods including corn flake.	from 2017
15	Creda - HPCL Biofuel Ltd.	Alternate fuel	from 2017
16	Indian Oil Creda Biofuels Ltd.	Biodiesel	from 2017
17	Burn Standard Co Ltd	Wagons - 2100 vehicle units, Bogies - 2400 numbers, Couplers - 2400 numbers and Refractories - 61292 MT.	from 2018
18	National Jute Manufacturers Corp. Ltd.	Jute products – 0.16 million tons	from 2018
19	Birds Jute & Exports Ltd.	Jute cotton and blended fabrics / curtain, etc.	from 2018
20	Biecco Lawrie Ltd	Control & Switchgear – 1375 Nos., Lube oil blending - 10000 KL	from 2018
21	Handicrafts & Handlooms Export Corp. India Ltd.	Export of handicrafts, handlooms, khadi products of village industries, hand-knitted carpets, garments, etc.	from 2018
22	Hindustan Paper Corp. Ltd.	Paper – 3.33 Lakh Tons, Chlorine Gas (Liquified) - 18150 MT, Caustic Soda - 36300 MT, Calcium Hypochlorite - 14310 MT, Hydrochloric Acid - 6600 MT and Chlorine Dioxide - 1090 MT.	from 2019
23	Hindustan Prefab Ltd.	Buildings like Palam Airport terminal building, East and West Block in R.K. Puram, etc.	from 2019
24	Hindustan Fluorocarbons Ltd	Chloro Di Fluoro Methane - 1262 tons	from 2020
25	Scooters India Ltd	scooters, mopeds, motorcycles, 3 wheelers, etc.	from 2021
26	Bharat Pumps & Compressors Ltd	Heavy duty Pumps – 283 Nos, 23 nos. Compressors – 23 Nos and Gas Cylinders - 48000 nos.	from 2021
27	Indian Drugs & Pharmaceuticals Ltd.	Tablets - 1641 million Nos, Capsules - 430 million Nos., Liquid Orals - 600 Kilo liters and Dry Syrup - 2 million bottles	from 2021
28	Rajasthan Drugs & Pharmaceuticals Ltd.	Life-saving and other essential drugs to state Government Medical Health Department, Central government Institutes, viz ESIC, Defence, Railways, other PSUs and also to state Government institutes.	from 2021
29	Spices Trading Corporation	Trading of spices, agricultural commodities and agricultural inputs and conducting Cardamom auctions.	from 2022
30	Project & Equipment Corporation of India Ltd.	Export of railway and engineering equipment	from 2022
31	Triveni Structurals Ltd.	Building of structures - 13600 MT	
32	Mining & Allied Machinery Corp.	Scrapper chain conveyors.	from 2022
33	Pyrites, Phosphates and Chemicals Ltd.	Single Super Phosphate – 230000 Tons, Sulphuric Acid - 79,000 Tons, phosphatic fertilizers - 110101 Tons	From 2003

Selling of CPSEs / Selling Public Sector Assets Created

Sick industrial company, as per Sick Industrial Companies Act 1985, is defined as "an industrial company which has at the end of any financial year accumulated losses equal to or exceeding its entire net worth."

As per BRPSE, (set up by the government in December, 2004), a company is considered 'sick' if it has accumulated losses in any financial year equal to 50% or more of its average net worth during 4 years immediately preceding such financial year (enabling more CPSEs to be declared sick and closed eventually)

The common reason given for strategic selling was that because of accumulated losses, the net-worth of the company got eroded by more than 50% of its peak net-worth. This is net worth of the company **for the owner / promotor / investors** (in this case, the government).

The **absolute net worth** of the company does not depend on loans and other liabilities of the owner and should be fixed considering i) the land value ii) the total cost of installation of new plant of same capacity with buildings and offices, iii) interest for the period, a new plant would have taken to reach capacity production from start of construction, iv) cost of recruiting and training employees, v) cost of setting up marketing network, etc. and **base price for selling the company** should be fixed accordingly. The old owner would have to settle loans and liabilities from sale proceeds and owner's realization would reduce accordingly. The purchaser must pay as per absolute net worth price of the company.

Vajpayee and Modi governments sold 15 CPSEs.

1) Modern Food Industries (India) Ltd

MFIL was set up as the first branded bread manufacturer.

Achievements – Refer Ch. 4. Modern Foods had over 40% of the bread market in India.

MFIL was divested by the Government to Hindustan Unilever Ltd. (the sole bidder) in January 2000 for Rs 105.45 Cr, for 74% of the shares. Later the government sold 26% shares also to HUL for Rs 44.07 Cr in November 2002.

Discrepancies - In July 2001, the CAG raised several issues like valuation of plant and machinery, land and buildings, valuation considering nil value for 24 franchisees.

Bad performance after privatization – HUL was paid Post Closure Adjustments of Rs. 17.48 Cr, reducing realization to Rs. 88 Cr.
*Senior HUL officials said the acquisition was a complete misfit with the HUL culture and systems and that the acquisition was a mistake on account of improper due diligence.
*In 2001, HUL referred MFIL to BIFR. In 2006, HUL merged MFIL with itself.
*Subsequently HUL sold MFIL to Everstone Capital of Singapore in April 2016.
*In February 2021, it was acquired by Mexican bakery company Grupo Bimbo.
A bread which had 40% all India market share in 2000 has largely disappeared from the market now as these private companies could not run the company successfully.

2) Hindustan Teleprinters Ltd.

Hindustan Teleprinters Ltd. was incorporated to manufacture teleprinters for the national telecom network.

Original manufacturing capacity – 5010 Teleprinters in 1968-69. HTL was modernized to start manufacturing Electric Typewriter and the Electronic Teleprinter.
Achievements during 1992-97 – Refer Ch. 6
Diversification on teleprinters becoming obsolete – Refer Ch. 6
Diverse manufacturing facilities – Refer Ch. 6

The government sold 74% equity share of the company to Himachal Futuristic Communications Ltd. for Rs 55 crore in May 2000, which appears to be very less considering wide product range and plant capabilities and Govt of India still retains 26% equity stake in the Company.

Overall loss for the government - In September 2002, the buyer submitted a post-closing adjustment claim of Rs. 56.49 Cr which was accepted by the arbitral tribunal in 2007 and Delhi High Court in 2012, wiping off almost the entire realization from disinvestment (INR 55 crore) of HTL. That meant, HTL was given not only free, but also with a cash bonus of Rs. 1.49 Cr.

3) Lagan Jute Machinery Company

Lagan Jute Machinery Company was set up for manufacturing jute machinery.
Achievements – Refer Ch. 11
In July 2000, the government sold 74% equity shares at Rs 2.53 crore. The absolute net worth of the company, as indicated above must be very much higher than Rs. 2.53 Cr.
Difficulties after privatization - As government subsidized jute machineries were not available, jute manufacturers started using imported second-hand machinery.

4) Bharat Aluminium Company Ltd.

BALCO was the first public sector enterprise in India which started producing aluminium in 1974.

Production increase in Aluminium planned during IX plan - The demand for aluminium was anticipated to grow at an average annual compound growth rate of 8% during IX Plan period.
The installed capacity for aluminium was expected to increase from 0.67 million tons in 1996-97 to 0.714 Mts in 2001-02, including by setting up a new Cold Rolling Mill of 40,000 TPA capacity by BALCO during IX Plan. (9.5.119)

Actual increase during IX plan - Total installed capacity for aluminium in 2001-02 was – 0.697 Mts. (11.7.2.13)
Production of aluminium – 0.634661 million tons. (Capacity utilization of 91%) (10.7.2.57) Consumption of / Demand for Aluminium in 2001-02 – 0.7 million tons (11.v2.7.2.29)

Capacity of BALCO to undertake modernization – With projected public sector plan outlay for the IX Plan of Rs.859200 crore at 1996-97 prices, aggregate budgetary support by the Centre including the provisions to Special Action Plans of Rs. 374000 crore and **cash reserve accumulated by BALCO of Rs. 437 Cr**, BALCO could have completed its modernization without need (for privatization) private sector investment in BALCO. (9.3.1)

Financial strength of BALCO - Annual turnover of BALCO was Rs 898 Cr in 2000, with a profit of Rs 56 Cr.

At the time of disinvestment BALCO had one unit in Korba and another in Bidhanbag, West Bengal.

Privatization - In 2001, Government divested 51% equity and management control in favor of Sterlite Industries India Ltd. of Vedanta group for Rs. 826.5 Cr (Rs. 551.5 Cr for 51% equity + Rs. 244 Cr for capital restructuring + Rs. 31 Cr towards Tax) along with Gandhamardan bauxite mine, other captive mines and 270 MW capacity captive power plant.

In-experienced Buyer - Sterlite Industries Ltd had hardly 5 years' experience in operation of aluminium plant (MALCO) and was investigated by Income Tax Department on 8.12.99 and Enforcement Directorate on 26.05.2002 **for foreign exchange violations of Rs. 2.08 billion** between 1993 and 1999.
Discrepancies pointed out by CAG - Comptroller and Auditor General of India in 2006, made several adverse findings like, asset replacement cost obtained based on verbal inquiry instead of obtaining price by sending written enquiries, **non-consideration of new commissioned capacity, skipping valuation of land** and non-core assets, etc.

Bad performance after privatization –
The installed capacities of BALCO was 0.1 Mt in February 2003.
*The production of BALCO in 2006-07 to 2009-10 were 313189 Tons, 358671 Tons, 356781 Tons and 268425 Tons and there was no production between 2010-11 to 2012-13, as it had closed its old smelter of 0.1 Mt capacity due to its non-viability. 9.4.pdf (teri.res.in). (Ministry of Mines. Annual Report 2012/13)
***BALCO Stopped Production from 2009-10** – If a plant, which was operating for over 20 years as a public sector company, had to be closed down within 10 years after privatization, it was a **clear case of failure of privatization, second failure for Sterlite Industries after MALCO in aluminium sector.**
*Revenue from operations on 31.03.2019 was Rs. 10049.12 Cr., profit for the year was Rs. 573.08 Cr, with a profit ratio of 5.7% (much less than 6.24% in 2000)
*BALCO did not pay any dividend for 2019-20, while 105 CPSEs including NALCO paid dividend. Where are improvements after privatization?

5) Computer Maintenance Corporation Ltd

Achievements - CMC was carrying out maintenance of IBM installations at over 800 locations around India from 1978 and subsequently computers supplied by other foreign players and provided support services in India and 20 other countries for Photogrammetry equipment supplied by Swiss multinational Leica
*CMC Limited introduced computer applications at a mass scale with its design and deployment of Indian Railways Reservation System on 15.10.1985. in 1991, CMC acquired Baton Rouge International Inc, USA. (renamed CMC Americas, Inc, in 2003).
***Software package clients -** CMC undertook development of different software packages for more than 40 companies
***International contracts** - CMC executed various international contracts for more than 10 companies.
*Sun Microsystems engaged CMC for setting up Competency center for development of Sun's Java technologies in association with Department of Electronics and NASSCOM.
***Packages developed** – Foreign exchange and Trade finance package, Integrated Retail Banking package, Screen based Stock Trading system, AMIGAS system for weather forecasting, Monitoring packages for various generating stations, Front office banking operations package, software for Electronic Air Warfare, Materials and Maintenance Management package, India's first insurance application software package Genesis, etc.

In 1992, the Indian government divested 16.69% of CMC's equity to the General Insurance Corporation of India and its subsidiaries who, in turn, sold part of their stake to the public in 1996.

Privatization – In October 2001, the government divested 51% equity of CMC to Tata Sons Ltd, through a sale for Rs. 152 Cr **to make TCS a market leader by sacrificing a public sector player at a very low price compared to the business CMC was doing.**
*In 2002-03, government received Rs. 6.07 Cr in 2002-03 through OFS to Employees
*In 2004, the government disinvested its remaining 26.5% stake in CMC to the public to get Rs. 190.44 Cr.

Improprieties pointed out by CAG - In 2006, the CAG report flagged **lower projection of future revenues** than the firm's business plan,

On 16.10.2014, CMC merged with Tata Consultancy Services Ltd.

6) Indian Petrochemical Corporation Limited (IPCL)

IPCL was established on 22.03.1969, as a Government of India undertaking, for promoting the development of the petrochemical industry in India.

In August 1992, the Company's shares were listed on all major stock exchanges in India.

Disinvestment to Public Institutions - The Government of India held 100% of the equity of IPCL till 1992 when it disinvested 20.35% of its share in the markets. Subsequently, IPCL raised capital by making a public issue in November 1992, GDR issue in December 1994, issuing 14.4% to Financial Institutions, 2.91% to Domestic Companies, 2.39% to Foreign Institutional Investors and reducing GOI's stake to 59.95%.

Large Production Matrix - Vadodara Complex, comprising a Naphtha Cracker of 0.13 Mt capacity, Xylene Plant, Propylene Separation Plant and 15 Downstream Plants, produced LDPE, PPCP, PP, PVC, PBR Fibre & Fibre Intermediates - Acrylic Fibre, Dry Spun Acrylic Fibre & Mono-ethylene Glycol Chemicals - Linear Alkyl Benzene, Ethylene Oxide, & Acrylates.
*Nagothane complex, comprising Ethane / Propane Cracker of 0.4 Mt capacity and Downstream Plants produced LLDPE, LDPE, HDPE, PP, Wire & Cable, Mono-ethylene Glycol, Ethylene Oxide.
*Gandhar complex, comprising a Gas Cracker of 0.3 Mt capacity and Downstream Plants, produced PVC, HDPE, Mono-ethylene Glycol, Caustic Soda, Ethylene Oxide, etc

Captive Power Plants - The Vadodara, Nagothane and Gandhar complexes had 65 MW, 64 MW and 160 MW power plants respectively and Vadodara unit had 25 MW diesel generator sets also.

Infrastructure – Port - IPCL had a 37% equity stake in Gujarat Chemical Port Terminal Co. Ltd., which operated liquid chemical handling port at Dahej, which enabled IPCL to handle export consignments and access feedstock.

Storage and Pipeline Connectivity - IPCL had storage terminal for receiving propane at Pirpau Jetty and connected it with the Nagothane Complex by a pipeline to augment the feedstock. IPCL had product pipelines connecting manufacturing facilities at Gandhar and Vadodara Complexes.

High-Capacity Utilization - IPCL was consistently working at capacity utilization levels of over 80% in its Vadodara Complex in Gujarat for the past 20 years. Nagothane and Gandhar Complexes were operating at capacity utilization of 95% and 75% respectively.

Special / Monopolistic Production - IPCL expanded into production of sophisticated catalysts & absorbents and was the sole domestic producer of products like molecular sieves, activated alumina and dehydrogenated paraffin catalyst.

Expansion Plans - IPCL was proposing to selectively expand production capacity for PVC, ACN, PBR, ethylene and polyethylene, domestic demand for which was unlikely to have been fully met by domestic supply.

Market Leader - IPCL was the II largest integrated manufacturer of polymer and chemical products from hydrocarbon feed stocks. It ranked second in the production of basic chemicals, first in polyethylene (LDPE, LLDPE, HDPE), second in fibre and fibre intermediates (DMT, acrylic fiber) and was a major player in chemicals (LAB, Chlorine, OX) production. IPCL's production capacity for most of its products enabled it to derive significant economies of scale from its operations, resulting in lower production costs and increased competitiveness.

Financial Strength - IPCL's operating income and profit showed steady rise from FY 93 to FY 97 due to improved sales volume and realization. Operating income increased from INR 1697 crore to INR 2773.5 crore, whereas operating profit increased from INR 36.9 crore to INR 516.6 crore. Total revenue and profit before and after tax for the year 2000-01 were Rs. 5173.7 Cr, 273.9 Cr and 248.9 Cr. (4172.1 Cr / 3194.3 Cr, 199.2 Cr. / 39.8 Cr, 188.8 Cr. / 29.4 Cr for 1999-2000 / 1998-99) and **total assets on 31-03-2001 were Rs. 8785.6 Cr** (Rs. 9220.5 Cr / 8951.2 Cr).

Governments Assurance - The acquisition of a strategic stake in IPCL was expected to enable the Strategic Investor to instantly gain a dominant and reliable foothold in one of Asia's most promising markets through an investment in an established leader in the industry.

Preliminary Information Memorandum (PIM) for Bidders - INDIAN PETROCHEMICALS CORP.LTD. | Department of Investment and Public Asset Management | Ministry of Finance | Government of India (archive.org)

Sale of IPCL - In June 2002, the Government of India, divested 26% of its equity shares in favor of Reliance Petro Investments Ltd, a Reliance group company **for Rs. 1490.84 Cr** and **transferred management control to RIL.** It also assured to sell additional 25% minimum equity within specified time, with first right of refusal to successful bidder. RPIL acquired an additional 20% equity shares through a cash offer of Rs. 1202.85 Cr in terms of SEBI (Takeover Regulations) and held 46% of Company's equity shares.

*In February 2004, government sold 28.95% stake through offer for sale and remaining 4.58% were allotted to the employees between 2004 and 2005.

*On 1.04.2005, polyester companies namely Apollo Fibres Ltd., Central India Polyesters Ltd., India Polyfibres Ltd, Orissa Polyfibres Ltd., Recron Synthetics Ltd. and Silvassa Industries Pvt. Ltd were amalgamated with IPCL making Reliance a monopolistic company.

*IPCL merged with Reliance Industries Ltd. in 2007

RIL becomes a monopolistic company in petrochemical industries with governments help - The acquisition of a strategic stake in IPCL enabled, as forecasted by the government, RIL to **instantly gain a dominant** and reliable foothold in one of Asia's most promising markets through an **investment in an established leader in the industry.**

Thus, the sale of 26% equities of such high-ranking company with such revenue, profit and asset value of Rs. 8786 Cr for Rs. 1491 Cr, **corresponding to only 17% of asset value,** with assured dominant position for the purchaser in the market appeared to be fishy and against the principles of avoiding monopoly in any sector.

Improprieties pointed out by CAG - CAG's audit report highlighted several irregularities in the deal like, under valuation of non-core assets, wrong determination of capital gain tax and contingent liability, non-consideration of intangible assets (IPCL had 12 granted patents), discrepancies in the valuation of Gandhar plant and application of higher discounting rate which depressed the value of the firm.

After sale claim - Reliance had raised a claim of Rs 927.41 crore on account of non-disclosure of financial information during the due-diligence process which reflected a serious flaw in the disinvestment process.

7) **Hindustan Zinc Ltd.**

India becoming Self-sufficient in 1991-92 and fall in demand for zinc during 1992-97 – Refer Ch. 14

Achievement of capacity target set for VIII Plan (1992-97) – The zinc capacity creation target for VIII plan of 0.179 Mts was achieved with **B**inani **Z**inc **L**td., in private sector, completing expansion of its smelter in Alwaye.

HZL deferred major investments planned to be taken up in the VIII Plan on commercial considerations. (9.5.125)

HZL was market leader - HZL was almost a monopoly producer of zinc and lead with **55-60% market share.** It was the only integrated producer of these metals. Other companies did not start zinc production from mining stage.

HZL completed expansion during 1997-2002 - Taking into account the expansion plans of 20,000 and 30,000 tons by HZL and BZL respectively and the availability from the secondary sources, the demand-supply gap was expected to be 50,000 tons in 2001-02. However, this was expected to increase to 70,000 tons if the production from secondary sources failed to materialize, consequent to the ban on international movement of hazardous waste and scrap, including zinc ash under Basal Convention. (9.5.126).
*HZL completed expansion of its Vizag and Debari (Rajasthan) smelters each by 10,000 TPA (10.7.2.25)
*HZL had entered into a joint venture with Broken Hill Propriety Co. of Australia for exploration and development of zinc and lead resources in Rajasthan. (9.5.126)

Disinvestment I phase - After auction of 20% equity to financial institutions in January 1992, IPO in November 1992, conversion of rights partly convertible debentures in July 94 and GDR in December 1994, in August 1996, government shareholding stood at 75.92%.

Disinvestment Commission did not recommend disinvestment beyond 49% due to HZL's dominant market share and ownership of **considerable ore reserves,** as this could convert public monopoly into a private monopoly.

Disinvestment to a Company without any prior experience in Zinc or Lead industry – Government disinvested 26% of equity to Sterlite Opportunities and Ventures Ltd for Rs. 445 Cr. on 11.04.2002. The mandatory open offer by the buyer for 20% shares was completed in July 2002 at the disinvestment price. Government received Rs. 6.19 Cr from Employee OFS in 2002-03.

Sterlite used call option part of the deal to acquire additional 18.92% at the same price in November 2003 in exercise of call option clause in the shareholder's agreement between GOI and SOVL and paid Rs. 323.88 Cr. SOVL's stake in HZL went up to 64.92%. Thus, GOI's stake in the company stood at 29.54%.
*Thus, government **disinvested 64.92% exceeding Disinvestment Commission's recommended limit** of 49%.

Discrepancies - Sterlite group did not have experience in operation of Zinc or lead plants in 2002. It was investigated by Income Tax Department on 8.12.99 and Enforcement Directorate on 26.05.2002 for foreign exchange violations of Rs. 2.08 billion between 1993 and 1999.

Improprieties pointed out by CAG - CAG's audit in 2006, pointed out that HZL's business plans, which were a fundamental document for any valuation exercise based on future projections, were not projected. In the absence of this document, the valuation done by the Government Auditor was questionable. Audit examination revealed that both the Finance Ministry and the GA had not maintained past records of assumptions and rationale behind deviations from set accounting norms related to the valuation exercise. Further, in the opinion of CAG higher discounting rate was applied which depressed the enterprise value of HZL.

5 Largest mines also gifted – Rampura Agucha mine, India's largest zinc mine producing about 0.3956 Mts of zinc and an estimated 3.9 Mts of Run-of-Mine (in 2021), Sindesar Khurd mine (II largest producing 0.104 Mts of zinc and 2.96 Mts of ROM), Zawar (III largest producing 0.0596 Mts zinc), Kayad (IV largest producing 0.0575 Mts of zinc) and Rajpura Dariba (V largest, producing 0.0399 Mts zinc) were all sold to Vedanta Resources with HZL **without any additional cost.** Nation's zinc assets sold for just Rs. 445 Cr.

Vajpayee government handed over a portfolio of assets including mines of zinc, silver and lead, created through tax payers' money at throw away price to Sterlite Technologies, in which Anil Agarwal and his family owned 54%. Thus public (sector) asset was handed over to an individual billionaire. This (2001) is the (downward) turning point in growth in asset creation / uniform wealth creation.

SOVL was merged with Sterlite Industries India Ltd in April 2011. Sterlite Industries merged with Sesa Goa Ltd. to form Sesa Sterlite Limited in August 2013. Sesa Sterlite was renamed as Vedanta Ltd in April 2015. Hindustan Zinc is now a direct subsidiary of Vedanta Ltd.

Cabinet Committee for Economic Affairs directed that the residual equity, i.e. 29.54%, be disposed of in the open market during 2014-15.

Manipulation of national assets - Vedanta **merged** Sesa Goa Ltd and **Sterlite Industries (India) Ltd.** in 2013 to create more value to shareholders. Cairn India Ltd. merged into Vedanta Ltd. in 2017.
*Vedanta, on 30.09.23, proposed to **split Vedanta Ltd**. into 5 companies to enable its parent co. Vedanta Resources Ltd. repay bonds worth $2 billion maturing in 2024. This is manipulation of national assets by an individual.
Vedanta plans to spin off, list 5 entities as $2bn debt looms - Times of India (indiatimes.com)

Sterling group should have invested in a new plant to bridge the gap between demand and supply - From the above it was clear that Indian Zinc companies were producing zinc with capacity utilization of 114% and all domestic companies were equally under financial stress. There was a shortfall in domestic supply by 71000 tons with respect to demand / consumption in 2001-02. How selling an efficient HZL (capacity utilization 114%) to an inexperienced investor with dubious financial track record will increase the productivity by 71000 tons? Instead of buying a plant in production, Sterling group could have invested the amount spent for buying 64.92% equities of HZL in starting a new plant of capacity 71000 Tons or more.

Productivity Loss after Privatization – The capacity utilization was 114% for zinc in 2001-02 and 76.1% of demand was met. (11.v2.7.2.29) After privatization, the capacity utilization was 101% for zinc in 2006-07 and 100% of demand was met. (11.v2.7.2.29)
*The capacity utilization was 165% for lead in 2001-02 and 54% of demand was met. After privatization, the capacity utilization was 145% for lead in 2001-02 and 44.7% of demand was met. (11.v2.7.2.29)
*Productivity loss results in loss to the country. Profitability leads to owners of private companies becoming rich at the cost to government and public.

Government bypassed environment laws to help mining operations of Vedanta – In early 2022, India's environment ministry allowed mining companies (at the request of Vedanta's letter dated 15.01.2021) to increase production by up to 50% without needing to hold public hearings, which many in the industry considered most onerous requirement of environment clearance process. Though production increased in Gandhamardan bauxite mine, other captive mines of BALCO and Rampura Agucha, Sindesar Khurd, Zawar, Kayad and Rajpura Dariba mines of HZL, they did not pay dividend to investors.
Inside Indian Energy and Mining Giant Vedanta's Campaign to Weaken Key Environmental Regulations - OCCRP

Vedanta pledged HZL as collateral - Vedanta pledged its holdings of 64.51% of total 64.92% on 23.05.2023 as collateral for loans taken by the group, which shows improper handling of nation's assets.
Extracting funds of HZL - In a related party transaction, Vedanta tried to sell its 29.54% holdings in THL Zinc Ltd, Mauritius, which deals with Africa based zinc assets, to HZL for $2.98 billion in January 2023. The Rajasthan-based company has long been a cash cow for Vedanta group squeezing out rich

dividends. This transaction of $2.98 billion is **seen by government as another way of extracting more funds out of HZL.**

Government opposes Vedanta move to sell zinc assets for $2.98 bn, ET EnergyWorld (indiatimes.com)

Vedanta exhibits monopolistic attitude – Vedanta, in its advertisement dated 3.10.2023, claimed that, being a sector-leading group in commodities, with unique portfolio of natural resource assets – zinc, silver, lead, aluminium, chromium, copper, nickel etc., "10% increase in prices of zinc, aluminium and oil would drive a 20% increase in Group EBITDA"

*Price is to be increased only to compensate for increase in cost of ore, mining, smelting, refining and processing cost, etc. and not arbitrarily for earning profit.

*The advertisement also said "Demand for commodities is expected to rise exponentially as the country continues to build infrastructure and strives to achieve aggressive targets for the energy transition, which is highly mineral intensive (**which are mostly under the control of Vedanta**)"

8) Maruti Udyog Limited

Maruti Udyog Limited (MUL) was founded by the Government of India on 24.02.1981, with Suzuki Motor Corporation as a 26% minor partner, to manufacture cars for middle-class Indians. The installed capacity of the Gurgaon plant was 40,000 units in 1984. Maruti was a new public sector entrant in 1981 when the car market was dominated by private manufacturers like Hindustan Motors, Premier Automobiles, Standard Herald, etc.

As per terms of the agreement, Suzuki used the option to increase its equity from 26% to 40% in 1987. Suzuki increased its stake in Maruti to 50% in 1992, making the company a 50-50 joint venture.

In 1998, the NDA government announced its intention to exit MUL.

Financial status prior to disinvestment - Total income in 2001-02 was Rs. 7397.1 Cr; Profit before Tax = Operating profit – Interest – Depreciation = 537.9 – 76.4 – 342.9 = 118.6 Cr.

Disinvestment Stage I - In May 2002, government and Suzuki made a revised Joint Venture Agreement whereby the government decided to disinvest its stake in MUL. Suzuki agreed to pay Rs. 1000 Cr to the government as share premium for the shares allotted in 1987 and 1992 and agreed to underwrite the public issue of MUL at Rs. 2300 per share.

*The government sold 49.74% stake of MUL in 2002 to Suzuki for Rs. 2,424 Cr. Government got Rs. 400 Cr for renouncing its rights share to Suzuki and Rs. 1000 Cr to give management control to Suzuki.

*Suzuki Motor Corporation increased its stake in Maruti to 54.2% in May 2002.

Maruti was a market leader at the time of disinvestment - MUL had a 55% market share in the largest selling A & B segments, which accounted for 85% of cars sold in the Indian market in 2003.

Maruti was most efficient - In 2002-03, the capacity utilization was 102% while capacity was 350000, whereas Hyundai capacity utilization was only 78% (even lesser for other companies) during same period.

MUL Overall Market share in 1999-2000, 2000-01, 2001-02 and 2002-03 were 62%, 58%, 59%, and 57% respectively.

MUL had higher potential capacity - As per IPO document dated 12.06.2003, MUL's Gurgaon plant had an installed capacity of 350,000 vehicles. However, MUL, through productivity improvement initiatives, was **expected to produce 500,000 vehicles with its existing facilities**.

Disinvestment Stage II - Government held an IPO of 25% of MUL in June 2003 and received Rs. 993.34 Cr.

Disinvestment Stage III - Selling equities to the public sector institutions - The Government sold 8% equity in January 2006 out of its residual shareholding of 18.28% to public sector financial institutions and public sector banks and realized Rs.1567.60 Cr.

*In March 2006, 0.01% equity of MUL was sold to the employees and the Government realized Rs.2.08 Cr.

Disinvestment Stage IV - Government realized Rs. 2366.94 Cr. from disinvestment of its entire residual shareholding of 10.27% in May 2007 to public sector FIs, banks and Mutual Funds completely exiting the company.

Cost of foreign collaboration - MUL was paying a royalty of Rs. 750 - 800 million up to FY2004 on its older models such as M800, Omni, Gypsy, Zen and Esteem till technological changes were made in these models.

In July 2014 it had a market share of more than 45%.

Disinvestment Led to Loss of Dividend – MUL, through productivity improvement initiatives, was capable of producing 500,000 vehicles with facilities existed in 2001-02.

MUL had a **market share of 59% in FY 2001-02.**

*The total income in 2001-02 was Rs. 7397.1 Cr and Operating profit was Rs. 537.9 Cr.

*Hence there was no need to sell (49.74% in 2002 + 25% in 2003 + 8.01% in 2006 + 10.27% in 2007) of the government's equities.

*After disinvestment, **market share of Maruti fell to 45% in 2014 from 62% in 1999-2000** and labor unrest increased from 2012.

*The total income in 2021-22 was Rs. 88295.6 Cr and Operating profit was Rs. 3766.3 Cr. The profit was 4.27% of the total income (compared to 7.27% in 2001-02). **Hence increase in profit is not perceivable after 20 years of privatization.**

Published_financial_results_for_period_ended_31-March-2022.pdf (windows.net)

*The dividends paid by Maruti Suzuki were Rs. 1.5 on 17.05.2004, Rs. 2 on 6.05.2005, Rs. 3.5 on 31.07.2006, Rs. 4.5 on 24.04.2007, Rs. 5 on 24.4.2008, Rs. 3.5 on 24.04.2009, Rs. 6 on 26.04.2010, etc. Maruti Suzuki India | Dividends > Auto - Cars & Jeeps > Dividends declared by Maruti Suzuki India - BSE: 532500, NSE: MARUTI (moneycontrol.com)

*For the year ending March 2023, Maruti Suzuki declared an equity dividend of 1800.00% amounting to Rs 90 per share. At the current share price of Rs 9443.05, this resulted in a dividend yield of 0.95%.

*The justification given for selling was "The dividend received by GOI in the past several years was about **Rs.13-20 crore** per annum". But Maruti Suzuki, after privatization, paid dividends of Rs. 1.8 Cr in 2004, 2.4 Cr in 2005, Rs. 4.2 Cr in 2006, Rs. 5.4 Cr in 2007 and Rs. 6 Cr in 2008 and Rs. 4.2 Cr in 2009 on 1,20,06,278 shares of GOI.

Maruti Suzuki paid less dividends to investors to accumulate cash reserve of Rs. 46000 Cr. – Maruti Suzuki had a cash reserve of Rs. 46000 Cr at the end of June 2023 quarter, besides provision for depreciation. This clearly meant investors were not given dividends at the same norm practiced before privatization; this also meant investors profited less after privatization. Then how can it be said that investors will get more profit after privatization? Maruti for preferential share issue to buy Suzuki's Gujarat unit - Times of India (indiatimes.com)

Utilization of gross surplus to fund projects - In contrast, the gross surplus of public enterprises, represented by their retained profits, depreciation provision and additional resource mobilization through revision of tariffs, prices, etc., was given to government to fund the projects taken in these CPSEs during various 5YPs.

Estimates of Gross Surplus of Central and State Enterprises for 1980-85 at 1979-80 rates were - Railways - Rs. 1698 Cr, Posts and Telegraphs - Rs. 2365 Cr, other Central Enterprises - Rs. 5848 Cr, State Electricity Boards - Rs. 22 Cr, SRTCs - Rs. 506 Cr and other State enterprises - Rs. 12 Cr = Total Rs. 9395 Cr (6.5.20)

9) **Videsh Sanchar Nigam Ltd.**

Videsh Sanchar Nigam Ltd. was established on 19.3.1986 to offer telephony, telex, telegraph, Internet access, packet switched data transmission, video conferencing, television relay and other value-added services.

Achievements during 1994-97 – Refer Ch. 6
VSNL's Communication network – Refer Ch. 6

WTO's pressure on VSNL - Following the World Trade Organization agreement in February 1997, the Indian Government committed to opening domestic long-distance and international telecom services to private and foreign companies by 2004.
*VSNL encountered difficulty in reducing its tariffs immediately to bring them close to that of foreign carriers because it had incurred heavy capital costs in infrastructure projects in the recent past. AT&T, MCI and Sprint were "instructed" by the FCC to pressure VSNL to reduce the "basic cost" of a U.S-to-India call from 79 cents to 23 cents.

Competitiveness of VSNL - New projects undertaken during the period 1992-97 enabled VSNL to strengthen itself before the impending entry of foreign companies into the field.

VSNL's expansion plans - In 1997, VSNL chose British Telecom as its partner for Jalmala project to develop the South Asian regional hub with 23 landing projects, connecting dense traffic points.
*VSNL planned to invest Rs.5,200 Cr between 1998 and 2003 to establish a regional hub, provide direct-to-home services for internet, data and entertainment and install optic fibre cables. VSNL was interested in working with the DoT to develop an Internet backbone.

VSNL was a profit-making company - In 1996-97, VSNL generated revenue of Rs.4,996 Cr and made a net profit of Rs.505 Cr in 1996-97 and Rs. 415 Cr in the 6 months ending 30.09.1997.

Disinvestment Stage I - Instead of offering support to VSNL, the Government chose to divest its holding in the profitable company. After several rounds of divestment since 1992 - including a $526-million Global Depository Receipts issue in 1996-97 (by issuing 1.2 crore fresh shares and 4.23% (39 lakh shares) of government's total stake. (Rs. 379.67 Cr.), US$ 185 million GDR in February 1999 (by issuing 28 lakh new shares and 10 million shares of the government, together constituting 10.53% equity of the total stake), domestic offer of VSNL in 1999-2000, which yielded Rs. 75 Cr - the Government's holdings in VSNL came down to 65%.

Pressure from WTO - WTO, under the General Agreement on Trade of Services, stipulated that internet providers and long-distance telephony should not be under the control of state-run monopolies. Can they be under the control of private monopoly? Why? There was no limitation for private companies to start afresh, grow and compete with VSNL so that control of state-run monopoly is nullified.

Government grabbed cash reserve of VSNL - VSNL, as a monopoly overseas telecommunications carrier and India's biggest internet service provider, was sitting on a cash pile worth Rs 4,000-4,500 crore. Government asked VSNL to distribute this cash as special dividend to shareholders before intended sale. Government planned to sell 25% stake along with management control to a strategic partner and 1.97% to the company's employees from 52.97% stake in VSNL.

https://economictimes.indiatimes.com/stocks/vsnl-sets-750-special-dividend/articleshow/310805182.cms?utm_source=contentofinterest&utm_medium=text&utm_campaign=cppst

VSNL planned to invest Rs.5,200 Cr between 1998 and 2003 to. This Rs. 4000 to 4500 Cr was perhaps proposed to be used for establishing a regional hub, provide direct-to-home services for Internet, data and entertainment and install optic fibre cables. It was good that VSNL had required fund for the project. But the government wanted special dividend from this money instead of allowing VSNL to complete the project.

Disinvestment Stage II - Government received Rs. 1439 Cr from Tata group company through strategic sale of 25%, Rs. 1887 Cr as special dividend from VSNL, Rs. 363 Cr as dividend tax and sale of shares to VSNL employees in 2001-02. (Government neglected the fact that VSNL shares traded at Rs. 750 per share - As per Disinvestment Policy Procedures and Progress Report - February 2003 - Page 52)
*In addition, 1.97% of VSNL equity capital was given to employees in February 2002. Panatone Finvest Ltd. made an open offer for acquiring up to 20% of equity shares from general public.

Improprieties pointed out by CAG - VSNL had 773.13 acres of surplus land which was not separated / demerged before carrying out disinvestment. Since the ministry instructed not to value the surplus land, it was not included in the valuation of VSNL.

Under valuation of VSNL - Government sold 71.25% equity between 1999-2000 and 30.11.2002 and received Rs. 3689 Cr, whereas, VSNL had spent Rs. 2211 Cr. and Rs. 1600 Cr. just for 2 of its many projects. Thus, the sale proceeds did not even cover the cost of even two of the many projects VSNL executed.

Later, Tata Group acquired a 45% stake in VSNL and renamed it as Tata Communications on 13.2.2008. The government was holding 36% equity share in the company in 2017-18.

Creation of Private Sector Monopoly - If VSNL operating as a monopoly was harmful, Tata group or **any private company could have started a new company and competed with VSNL** by providing better services. Why sell an established and efficient company to a private company at lower cost (than establishing a new green field company of same capacity) and make the private company a monopoly, which is definitely more harmful?
*In July 2000, when the DOT informed Tata Group that VSNL would be de-monopolized by March 2002, the Tatas contended that the monopoly status up to 2004 was a promise made to them as part of the strategic sale and therefore, took the matter to the Bombay High Court. While the government offered compensation in lieu of the potential losses caused to the Tata Group, the Tata Group sought additional compensation. The issue remained to be settled in 2020. **It is strange that while WTO stipulated elimination of state - run monopoly, government promised continuation of private controlled monopoly for 3 years.**

Private monopoly is continuing even today - Even today, Tata Communications is the only Indian company working in the fields of overseas communication, internet, web connectivity, etc. Earlier it was VSNL's monopoly and profit was going to government. Now, it is private sector monopoly and profit is going to private entrepreneurs. Now, the competitors are Avaya, Cisco, Microsoft, Huawei, Alcatel Lucent and Mitel. Did WTO think that these foreign companies could not compete with a public sector company?

10) Paradeep Phosphates Ltd.

Paradeep Phosphates Ltd. was incorporated in 1981 as a joint venture between Government of India and the Republic of Nauru to set up phosphatic fertilizers manufacturing unit at Paradeep, Orissa. In August 1986, the second largest integrated Di-Ammonium Phosphate plant was commissioned with an annual capacity of 0.72 Mts.
*0.66 Mt Sulphuric acid plant and 0.225 Mt Phosphoric Acid plant were commissioned in June 1992.

Fall in demand for phosphatic fertilizers - PPL, which produced only phosphatic fertilizers, suffered due to shrinkage of demand for phosphatic fertilizers following decontrol in August, 1992. (9.5.163)
Also, PPL was at a disadvantageous position **compared to its competitors because the prices of DAP output was controlled by the government** which led to higher cost of production and poor margins.

Production in 1997-98 was 110101 Tons. It produced 0.23 Mt of DAP in pre-privatization year 2001-02.

Disinvestment - PPL had accumulated loss of Rs 649.93 Cr as on 28.02.2002, with a negative net worth of Rs 217.28 Cr.
*In February 2002, Government divested 74% of their stake in PPL to selected partner **Z**uari **M**aroc **P**hosphates Pvt **L**td for Rs. 151.7 Cr.

Probability of losing entire sale proceeds - In December 2002, the buyer raised a post closure adjustment claim of Rs. 151.55 Cr. which remained unsettled till 2007. (Mediating auditing firm suggesting Rs 141.32 crore as decrease in net assets for the 74% share.)

Rights issue in 2003 was entirely subscribed by ZMPPL, increasing its stake to 80.45% of the paid-up equity share capital.

Improper valuation – If a plant operating at 32% capacity utilization in 2001-02, can be made to run at 175% capacity utilization and produce 1.25 Mt in 2005-06 with same staff and machinery, by just spending Rs. 142.8 Cr for debottlenecking, modernization, repairs and maintenance of critical items, then selling the plant considering negative net worth as 217.28 Cr is a **wrong concept.**
*It should have been sold at **absolute Asset value of 0.72 Mt DAP plant** with all by-products, land and other assets **less Rs. 142.8 Cr** and not at Rs. 151.7 Cr.
*PPL was sold at Rs 151.70 crore, below the reserve price of Rs 176.09 crore.

Poor performance after disinvestment - Post disinvestment, PPL was referred to BIFR and in July 2005, it was formally **declared as sick company.**

In March 2007, the Government of India was holding remaining 19.55% stake in the company.

No capacity addition or expansion was done after privatization other than debottlenecking and modernization. Paradeep and Goa plants of Zuari have an NPK / **DAP production capacity** of 1.8 million TPA and **0.8 million TPA** respectively,
*PPL's sales and operating revenue including subsidy and other income for the year 2010-11 was Rs. 3630.64 Cr. from the sale of own fertilizers and traded fertilizers of 11,68,592 MT and 2,77,492 MT respectively. (Not just from the production of DAP, Sulphuric and Phosphoric acids from PPL plant at Paradeep) **There seems to be not much value addition done**

Mis-use of PPL's funds - PPL acquired the Goa fertilizer facility of Zuari Agro Chemicals Ltd. for USD 280 million in June 2022. Is it a related party transaction to drain money from PPL? Why Paradeep Phosphates disinvestment was good - The Economic Times (indiatimes.com)

11) Jessop and Company

The management of Jessop and company was taken over by Government in 1958 (and subsequently in 1973, it was wholly taken over by Government of India) to undertake various engineering activities.

Achievements – Refer Ch. 8

Disinvestment - On 29.08.2003, the Government sold 72% stake in Jessop under privatization program to M/s Indo Wagon Engineering Ltd. of Ruia group owned by Pawan Kumar Ruia for Rs. 18.18 Cr.

12) Madras Aluminium Company

The Madras Aluminium Company, Malco, was incorporated on 31.08.1960 to manufacture aluminium ingots and alloys from the bauxite reserves and rolled products. Malco started commercial production in 1965.

Government of Madras gave on lease mining rights for bauxite in 167.51 acres in Kolli Hills area in Salem in 1967.

Achievements – Refer Ch. 14.

Dividend of 11% was paid on preferential shares in 1980 and 13.5% in 1984.

Lack of adequate power supply – Refer Ch. 14
Inability of TNEB – Refer Ch. 14
*The production activities were suspended from 1.10.1991 due to non-availability of power and resumed from 1.2.1995. Aluminium cell house was restarted in end of March 1995. (9.5.118)

Rehabilitation Scheme - The BIFR rehabilitation scheme, sanctioned on 23.12.1994, envisaged change of management with one time settlement of dues of banks and financial institutions inter-alia to augment alumina refining capacity from 40000 to 80000 TPA, change of design of smelter and continuation of package of reliefs agreed by Government of Tamil Nadu.

Sale of Malco - Malco issued 12.76 lakh equities to Agarwal Associates of Sterlite group and 5.24 lakhs equities for conversion of unsecured loans to equity share capital in 1994-95.

In 1996, Malco undertook setting up a 75 MW captive power plant for assured power supply throughout the year for smelter.

Misuse of Malco's fund - Malco subscribed to 1.1 Cr equity shares and 1 Cr. equity warrants of India Foils Ltd in 2000. Vedanta used this money to purchase India Foils Ltd from B.M. Khaitan group in 2000. This is misuse of Malco's fund.

Selling MALCO to a company without experience in operation of Aluminium plant - Sterlite group did not have any experience in operation of Aluminium smelting plants in 1995. Also, it was investigated by Income Tax Department on 8.12.99 and Enforcement Directorate on 26.05.2002 for foreign exchange violations of Rs. 2.08 billion between 1993 and 1999.

Production as a Private Enterprise - The installed capacity of MALCO was 25000 tons in February 2003. The production of MALCO in 2006-07 and 2007-08 were 37652 and 37635 Tons respectively at capacity utilization of 151%.

MALCO Stopped Production from 2008-09 – MALCO's production in 2008-09 was 23224 Tons only as MALCO had closed its smelter since December, 2008, even though the capacity utilization was 93%. There was no production from 2009-10 to 2012-13. Ref: Ministry of Mines Annual Report 2012/13. 9.4.pdf (teri.res.in)

If a plant, which was operating for over 30 years as a public sector company, had to be closed down within 13 years after privatization, it is a **clear case of failure of privatization.** Madras Aluminium Company > Company History > Aluminium > Company History of Madras Aluminium Company - BSE: , NSE: (moneycontrol.com)

13) Dredging Corporation of India Ltd.

Dredging Corporation of India Ltd. - DCI was incorporated on 29.03.1976 to provide integrated dredging and related marine services for promoting the national and international maritime trade, beach nourishment, land reclamation, inland dredging, environmental protection, etc.

Achievements - DCI was providing services in the field of ocean dredging, maintenance dredging, capital dredging, beach nourishment and land reclamation.
*DCI's customers include major ports under M/o Shipping, non-major ports under Government of India and State Governments, private ports, the Indian Navy and shipyards.
*The market share of DCI came down to 66.13% during 2004-05 as compared to 88.90% during previous years. The domestic market share in maintenance dredging was 58% and in capital dredging 84% during 2007-08.

Disinvestment - The Government received an amount of Rs. 53.33 crore through disinvestment of its 5% paid up equity capital in DCIL through an OFS transaction on 21.08.2015 and had 73.56% equity to its account.
*The Government received an amount of Rs.0.93 crore through disinvestment of its 0.09% paid up equity capital in DCI through Employees OFS transaction in October - November, 2016 with 73.47% remaining.

DCI started commercial operations at Bangladesh with capital dredging work at Mongla Port during 2017-18.

Strategic sale - Government concluded the Strategic disinvestment of DCIL on 8.03.2019 by transferring management control and selling whole 73.47% equity share capital of DCIL it held to the 4 ports – Visakhapatnam Port Trust, Paradip Port Trust, Deendayal Port Trust and Jawaharlal Nehru Port Trust at Rs. 1049.17 Cr.

14) Air India

Air India Ltd. - AI was incorporated on 15.10.1932 as Tata Airlines and renamed Air India in 1946. AI was nationalized in 1953 and split into 2 corporations namely Air India and Indian Airlines to operate as international carrier and domestic carrier respectively.

Achievements - In 2019-20, AI was operating in 105 stations comprising 67 domestic and 38 international stations. The company operated 4 offices abroad.
*International market share in Oct-Dec 2019 - Indigo – 12.8%, Air-India – 11.5%, AI Express – 7.3%, SpiceJet – 5%, GoAir – 2.6%. Indian carriers accounted for over 39% of passengers flying in and out of India.

Strategic sale - On 8.10.2021, Air India, Air India Express and 50% shares of AISATS (ground handling company) were sold for $ 2.3 billion (Rs. 18000 Cr.) to Talace Pvt. Ltd. of Tata Group. Tata Sons also got 123 aircrafts of **cost price $ 21.669 Billion** from Air India.

Deterioration in performance - The loss after tax attributable to shareholders for FY 2022 was Rs.9591.56 Cr registering a growth of 35.4% over the loss of Rs.7083.91 Cr. for FY 2021.
Air India's annualized domestic market share was 8.7% in 2022. (Less than 18.8% during Oct-Dec 2019)

In its first full fiscal year under Tata ownership, FY23, the airline reported a loss of Rs.11,381 Cr, up 18.6% from FY22, which had a loss of Rs. 9,591 Cr after accounting for write-offs and exceptional items. Air India's losses up by 18 per cent in FY23; revenues double - The Hindu BusinessLine

15) Neelanchal Ipsat Nigam Ltd – Govt began privatization proceedings in March 2020 and stopped production.

Disinvestment Adopted Only to Cover Fiscal Deficit

While discussing the issue of privatization of Bharat Aluminium Co., government admitted in Parliament that the earlier governments from 1991-1997 adopted an erroneous policy of selling minority shares of the blue-chip companies to cover up the fiscal deficit, which neither changed the performance of the firms nor served **the objective of disinvestment** (Lok Sabha, 2001b). (Page 143, History of disinvestment in India 1991-2020)

Listing of CPSEs and Different Purposes of Disinvestment

Disinvestment to cover current Fiscal Deficit led to Perennial Loss of Dividend

Till 1999-2000, disinvestment was primarily through sale of minority shares in small lots. From 1999-2000 till 2003-04, the emphasis of disinvestment changed in favour of strategic sale.

Types of disinvestments done

Public offer (excluding fresh capital rising), offer of 1 CPSE to another CPSE, auction to Financial Investor like public sector financial institutions, auction to Private Entity, Sale to Employees, Institutional placement Program in CPSEs, buy back by CPSE from govt, block deal/Market sales and through ETF.

Disinvestment steps of Manmohan Singh government

List large, profitable CPSEs, list CPSEs with net worth in excess of Rs. 200 Cr through IPO, listing of CPSEs which earned net profit in 3 preceding consecutive years, enter capital market to raise resources, develop people's ownership of CPSEs by encouraging investment, Offer For Sale to list profitable CPSEs not meeting the mandatory shareholding of 10% by public through issue of fresh shares, Follow-on public offer to meet needs for capital investment, Buy-back of shares by using surplus cash, etc.

Disinvestment principles of Modi government (till 2015-16) –

Offer for Sale to meet revised mandatory shareholding of 25%, Buy back of shares, buy back of shares by CPSE having net-worth of at least Rs. 2000 Cr and cash and bank balance of over Rs. 1000 Cr, CPSE to issue bonus shares if their defined reserves and surplus is equal to or more than 10 times of its paid-up equity share capital, CPSE to split-off its shares when market price or book value of its share exceeds 50 times of its face value, etc.

Drastic disinvestment drive - In 2015-16, Modi government decided to go for Strategic disinvestment by way of sale of substantial portion of Government shareholding **in identified CPSEs up to 50% or more,** along with transfer of management control. (P E Survey 2015-16, Page 246)

Table 17.6 - Disinvestments lead by Vajpayee and Modi governments.

S. No	NAME OF CPSE	Residual share of Govt in %	Shares at the time of SALE / Disinvestment	S. No	NAME OF CPSE	Residual share of Govt in %	Shares at the time of SALE / Disinvestment
1	Air India	0%	626.1 Cr Shares of Rs. 10 Each	73	Karnataka Antibiotics & Pharmaceuticals Ltd.	59.15%	
2	Andrew Yule and Co. Ltd.	89.25%		74	Karnataka Trade Promotion Organization	51.00%	Held by India Trade PO
3	Antrix Corporation Ltd.	100%		75	KIOCL Ltd.	99.03%	

S.No	NAME OF CPSE	Residual share of Govt in %	Shares at the time of SALE / Disinvestment	S.No	NAME OF CPSE	Residual share of Govt in %	Shares at the time of SALE / Disinvestment
4	Balmer Lawrie & Co Ltd	61.8%	Held by BLIL	76	Kochi Refineries Ltd	0%	51% Sold to BPCL
5	Balmer Lawrie Investments Ltd	59.68%		77	Konkan LNG Ltd.	93.5	Held by GAIL
6	BEL-Thales Systems Ltd	74%	74% to BEL	78	Konkan Railway Corp. Ltd.	85.23	
7	Bharat Aluminium Co Ltd.		22,08,23,473	79	Kumarakruppa Frontier Hotels Pvt Ltd.	89.8	
8	Bharat Dynamics Ltd.	74.93%		80	Life Insurance Corporation of India	96.50%	
9	Bharat Earth Movers Ltd.	53.87%		81	Loktak Downstream Hydro-Electric Corp	74.92%	NHPC
10	Bharat Electronics Ltd.	51.14%		82	M S T C LTD.	64.74%	
11	Bharat Heavy Electricals Ltd.	63.17%		83	Madras Fertilizers Ltd	59.12%	Original 51%
12	Bharat Immunological & Biologicals Corp.	59.26%		84	Madras Refineries Ltd	51%	51% Sold to IOCL
13	Bharat Petroleum Co. Ltd.	52.98		85	Mahanagar Telephone Nigam Ltd.	56.25%	
14	Bhartiya Rail Bijlee Co Ltd	74.00%	NTPC	86	Maharashtra Antibiotics & Pharmaceuticals Ltd	96.77%	Hindustan Antibiotics Ltd.
15	BHEL Electrical Machines Ltd	50.95%	BHEL	87	Mangalore Refinery & Petrochemicals Ltd	71.63%	ONGC
16	Bihar Drugs & Organic Chemicals Ltd	100.00%	IDPL	88	Manipur State Drugs & Pharmaceuticals Ltd	50.59%	Hindustan Antibiotics Ltd.
17	Biotechnology Industry Research Assistance Council	99.00%		89	Maruti Udyog Ltd.		1,20,06,278
18	Bisra Stone Lime Company Ltd.	50.01	Held by Eastern Investments Ltd	90	Mazagaon Dock Shipbuilders LTD.	84.83%	
19	Bongaigaon Refinery and Petrochemicals Ltd.	0	74.46% sold to IOCL	91	Minerals and Metals Trading Corp. Ltd.	89.93%	
20	BPCL KIAL Fuel Farm Pvt Ltd	74%	Held by BPCL	92	Mishra Dhatu Nigam Ltd.	74%	
21	Brahmaputra Crackers & Polymer Ltd.	70%	GAIL	93	MOIL Ltd.	53.35%	
22	Bridge & Roof Co. India	99.35		94	Mumbai Railways Vikas Corp.	51.00%	
23	Bundelkhand Saur Urja Ltd	86.94	NHPC	95	Narmada Hydroelectric Dev. Corp. Ltd	51.08%	NHPC
24	Central Registry of Securitization Asset Reconstruction and Security Interest of India	51.02		96	National Aluminium Company Ltd.	51.28%	
25	Central Warehousing Corp.	55.01%		97	National Fertilizers Ltd.	74.71%	
26	Chandigarh International Airport Ltd.	51.00%	Held by AAI	98	National Minorities Dev. & Finance Corp	83.98%	
27	Chennai Petroleum Corp. Ltd	51.89%	IOCL	99	National Projects Construction Corp.	98.89%	Held by Wapcos
28	Chhattisgarh East Railway	63.97	Held by SE Coalfields	100	National Textile Corp	99.76	
29	CMC Ltd.		1,51,28,894	101	NBCC (India) LTD.	61.76%	
30	Coal India Ltd.	66.13%		102	NEPA Ltd	97.74	
31	Cochin Shipyard Ltd..	72.86%		103	New India Assurance	85.44%	

S.No	NAME OF CPSE	Residual share of Govt in %	Shares at the time of SALE / Disinvestment	S.No	NAME OF CPSE	Residual share of Govt in %	Shares at the time of SALE / Disinvestment
32	Container Corporation of India Ltd.	54.80%		104	Neyveli Lignite Corp. Ltd.	79.20%	
33	Dredging Corporation of India Ltd.	0	73.44% Sold to Consortium of 4 Ports	105	NHPC Ltd.	70.95%	
34	Eastern Investments Ltd	15.97 %	50.69% by RINI	106	NLC Tamil Nadu Power Ltd	89.00%	NLC
35	Engineers India Ltd.	51.32%		107	NINL	0	
36	Fertilizers and Chemicals (Travancore) Ltd.	90%		108	NMDC Ltd.	60.79	
37	GAIL (India) Ltd.	51.52%	Sold to ONGC	109	North Eastern Electric Power Corporation Ltd.	0	100% Hold by NTPC
38	Garden Reach Shipbuilders & Engineers Ltd.	74.50%		110	NTPC Ltd.	51.10%	
39	General Insurance Corporation	85.78%		111	Numaligarh Refinery Ltd.	69.63	Oil India Ltd
40	Goa Antibiotics & Pharmaceuticals Ltd.	73.97%	HLL	112	Oil & Natural Gas Corporation Ltd.	58.89	
41	Goa Shipyard Ltd	51.08%		113	Oil India Ltd.	56.66%	
42	H.M.T Ltd	78.62%		114	ONGC Mangalore Petrochemicals Ltd.	51.01%	MRPL
43	Hemisphere Properties India Ltd	51.12		115	Orissa Mineral Devel. Company Ltd.	50.01%	Held by Eastern Investments
44	Hindustan Aeronautics Ltd.	71.65		116	Paradeep Phosphates Ltd	0	43,34,038
45	Hindustan Cables Ltd.			117	Patratu Vidyut Utpadan Ltd.	74%	NTPC
46	Hindustan Copper Ltd.	66.14%		118	Pawan Hans Helicopter Ltd.	51%	
47	Hindustan Fluorocarbons Ltd	56.43%	HOCL	119	Pondicherry Ashok Hotel Corp. Ltd.	51.25	Held by ITDC
48	Hindustan Organic and Chemicals Ltd	58.69%		120	Power Finance Corporation Ltd.	55.99%	
49	Hindustan Petroleum Corporation Ltd.	54.89	Hold by ONGC	121	Power Grid Corp	51.34%	
50	Hindustan Photofilms Mfg. Co. Ltd			122	Punjab Logistic Infrastructure Ltd	51.38%	Held by CONCOR
51	Hindustan Steel Works Construction Ltd.	49%	51% Held by NBCC	123	Rail Vikas Nigam Ltd.	78.2	
52	Hindustan Teleprinters Ltd		14,99,986	124	RailTel Corporation India Ltd.	72.85%	
53	Hindustan Zinc Ltd.	0	42,26,02,089	125	Railway Energy Management Co. Ltd.	49.00%	51% to RITES
54	Hospital Services Consultancy Cor (Ind) Ltd.	0	100% Sold to NBCC	126	Rajasthan Electronics and Instruments Ltd	51.02%	
55	Hotel Corp. of India	80.38	Held by Air India Assets Holding	127	Rashtriya Chemicals and Fertilizers Ltd.	75%	
56	Housing & Urban Dev. Corporation. Ltd.	81.81%		128	Ratnagiri Gas & Power Ltd.	86.49	Held by NTPC
57	IBP Ltd	Sold to IOCL	2,22,83,696	129	Richardson & Cruddas	85.15	
58	Indian Medicines & Pharmaceutical Corp. Ltd	98.11%		130	RITES Ltd.	72.20%	

S.No	NAME OF CPSE	Residual share of Govt in %	Shares at the time of SALE / Disinvestment	S.No	NAME OF CPSE	Residual share of Govt in %	Shares at the time of SALE / Disinvestment
59	Indian Oil Corporation Ltd.	51.5		131	Rural Electrification Corporation Ltd.	52.63%	Held by Power Finance Corp
60	Indian Petro Chemical Corp. Ltd (now RIL)	0	24,82,51,748	132	Sambhar Salts Ltd	60%	Hindustan Salts Ltd.
61	Indian Railway Catering and Tourism Corp. Ltd.	62.40%		133	Steel Authority of India Ltd.	65%	
62	Indian Railway Finance Corporation Ltd.	86.36%		134	Security Printing & Minting Corp. India Ltd.	100%	
63	Indian Renewable Energy Develop Agency	100%		135	Shipping Corp. of India Ltd.	63.75%	
64	Indian Telephone Industries Ltd.	97.84%		136	SIDCUL CONCOR Infra Company Ltd.	73.99%	Held by CONCOR
65	Indian Vaccine Corporation Ltd	66.68%		137	SJVN Ltd.	59.92%	
66	IRCON	85%		138	State Trading Corp. of India Ltd.	90%	
67	IRCON International Ltd.	73.18		139	SUUTI (Remittance from SUUTI)	0	Rs. 23937.45 Cr
68	India Tourism Development Corp.	87.02%		140	Tamil Nadu Trade Promotion Org.	51%	Indiia Trade PO
69	J & K Mineral Development Corp. Ltd.	95.86%		141	THDC India Ltd.	74.5%	Held by NTPC
70	J & K Development Finance Corp. Ltd.	62.50%		142	Videsh Sanchar Nigam Ltd.		28,49,50,495
71	Jessop Company Ltd		94569288.00	143	Vignyan Industries Ltd	96.42%	Held by BEML
72	Kamarajar Port Ltd.	0	Sold to Chennai Port Trust	144	Visakhapatnam Port Logistics Park Ltd	60.00%	BLCL

Loss of Dividend in 2019-20 on account of disinvestment & Strategic Sale –

Government received a dividend of Rs. 72135.6 Cr in the year 2019-20.
*But lost dividend amounting to Rs. 42561.49 Cr on account of disinvestment and Rs. 11262.91 Cr. on account of selling of CPSEs during 2019-20.
*In this year Bharat Aluminium Co., Madras Aluminium Co., Hindustan Zinc Ltd., HFCL Ltd and Modern Food Industries did not pay any dividend, though the effect of Covid 19 was minimal up to March 2020 in India and 105 CPSEs paid dividends (including National Aluminium Co. which paid dividend of Rs. 513.04 Cr.) for the same Covid 19 affected period. *When **CPSE National Aluminium Co paid dividend and privatized BALCO in the same sector did not pay any dividend**, how can it be said that privatization will make CPSEs efficient or profitable?
*Thus, the loss of dividend on account of disinvestment and sale would have been more than **Rs. 53824.4 Cr,** had these 3 private sector giants also paid dividend for 2019-20.

Governments wants more dividends from CPSEs

New Mandate for Investment Management in CPSEs 2015-16, stipulated that every CPSE would pay a minimum annual dividend of 30% of profit after tax or 5 % of the net worth, whichever was higher. This enabled government to receive higher dividends from CPSEs. Had this mandate been extended to private companies as well, Maruti Suzuki could not have accumulated a cash reserve of Rs. 46000 Cr at the end of June 2023 quarter.
*If government understands that CPSEs are sources of dividends, why does it disinvest or sell CPSE at all and loose dividends?

Table – 17. 7 - Loss of dividend in 2019-20 on account of Disinvestment in 144 CPSEs – Removed.

Table – 17. 8 - Loss of dividend in 2019-20 on account of Strategic Sale – Removed.

Loss of Dividend in 2021-22 on account of Disinvestment & Strategic Sale

Government received a dividend of Rs. 115170 Cr in the year 2021-22.

But lost dividend amounting to Rs. 80123.88 Cr on account of disinvestment and Rs. 11682.84 Cr. on account of selling of CPSEs during 2021-22. Thus, the loss of dividend on account of disinvestment and sale was Rs. 91806.72 Cr. If disinvestment was not done or CPSEs not sold, government would have received Rs. 206976.72 Cr, but received only 55.64%.

Table – 17. 9 - Loss of dividend in 2021-22 on account of Disinvestment in 144 CPSEs – Removed.

Table – 17. 10 - Loss of dividend in 2021-22 on account of Strategic Sale – Removed.

Loss of Dividend in 2022-23 on account of Disinvestment & Strategic Sale

Government received a dividend of Rs. 105385 Cr in the year 2022-23.

But lost dividend amounting to Rs. 86252.64 Cr on account of disinvestment and Rs. 27590.08 Cr. on account of selling of CPSEs during 2022-23. Thus, the loss of dividend on account of disinvestment and sale was Rs. 113842.72 Cr. If disinvestment was not done or CPSEs not sold, government would have received Rs. 219227.72 Cr, but received only **48.07%. This loss has been increasing year after year.** (From Rs. 53824.4 Cr in 2019-20 to Rs. 91806.72 Cr. in 2021-22 and Rs. 113842.72 Cr in 2022-23.)

Table – 17. 11 - Loss of dividend in 2022-23 on account of Disinvestment

S. No	CPSEs Name	Dividend paid (Rs. Cr.)	Total Disinvestment in CPSE %	Loss of Dividend in 2022-23 in Rs. Cr.
1	Oil & Natural Gas Corporation Ltd.	17612	41.11	12294.61
2	Coal India Ltd.	14328	33.87	7338.41
3	Mahanadi Coalfields Ltd.	8425	0	0.00
4	Northern Coalfields Ltd.	3659	0	0.00
5	Oil India Ltd.	2115	43.34	1617.79
6	NMDC Ltd.	1099	39.21	708.86
7	South Eastern Coalfields Ltd.	1064	0	0.00
8	Central Coalfields Ltd.	1024	0	0.00
9	National Aluminium Company Ltd.	918	48.72	872.17
10	ONGC Videsh Ltd.	480	0	0.00
	Top 10 CPSEs of Mining & Exploration Sector	50724		22831.85
11 to 23	Other 13 CPSEs	843		379.45
	Grand Total of 23 CPSEs of Mining & Exploration Sector	51567		**23211.30**
24	Power Grid Corporation of India Ltd.	8545	48.66	8098.94
25	REC Ltd.	3120	44.01	2452.42
26	GAIL (India) Ltd.	3068	48.48	2886.97
27	Power Finance Corporation Ltd.	2640	44.01	2075.13
28	Indian Railway Finance Corp. Ltd.	1869	13.64	295.20
29	Airports Authority Of India	892	0	0
30	Container Corporation Of India Ltd.	731	45.2	602.94
31	Housing & Urban Dev. Corpn. Ltd.	701	18.19	155.86

S. No	CPSEs Name	Dividend paid (Rs. Cr.)	Total Disinvestment in CPSE %	Loss of Dividend in 2022-23 in Rs. Cr.
32	E. C. G. C. Ltd. Financial Services	434	0	0
33	RITES Ltd.	433	27.8	166.72
	Top 10 CPSEs of (Services) Sector	22433		16734.19
34 to 167	Other 134 CPSEs	2926		2182.68
	Grand Total 144 CPSEs of Services Sector	25360		**18916.87**
	Manufacturing, Processing and Generation			
168	Bharat Petroleum Corp. Ltd.	1302	47.02	13091.58
169	Indian Oil Corporation Ltd.	3305	48.5	9079.39
170	NTPC Ltd.	7030	48.9	6634.51
171	Steel Authority of India Ltd.	1342	35	1845.85
172	Hindustan Petroleum Corp. Ltd.	1986	45.11	2652.03
173	NHPC Ltd.	1909	29.05	682.54
174	Nuclear Power Corp. Of India Ltd.	2058	0	0.00
175	Hindustan Aeronautics Ltd.	1672	28.35	529.41
176	Bharat Electronics Ltd.	1243	48.86	977.39
177	Numaligarh Refinery Ltd.	1251	30.37	321.02
	top 10 CPSEs of (M, P & G) Sector	23098		35813.72
178-252	Other (75 CPSEs) of (M, P & G) Sector	5360		8310.74
	Grand Total 85 CPSEs of (M, P & G) Sector	28458		**44124.47**
	Grand Total of 252 CPSEs	105385		**86252.64**

Table – 17. 12 - Loss of dividend in 2022-23 on account of Strategic Sale

S. No	YEAR	NAME OF CPSE	Shares at the time of SALE / Disinvestment	Earning per Share in Rs.	Loss of Dividend in 2022-23 in Rs. Cr.	Loss of Dividend based on EPS) in 2022-23 in Rs. Cr.
1	2021-22	Air India	6,261,000,000	5.66	0.00	3543.73
2	2014-15	Bharat Aluminium Co Ltd.	220,823,473	1.92	0.00	42.40
3	1991-92	CMC Ltd.	15,128,894	115.19	17398.23	17398.23
4		Hindustan Teleprinters Ltd	1,499,986	2.18	3.00	32.70
5	2014-15	Hindustan Zinc Ltd.	422,602,089	24.88	9437.50	3110.00
6	2001	IBP Ltd	22,283,696			
7	1991-92	Indian Petro Chemical Corp. Ltd (now RIL)	248251748 (4,96,50,350 RIL Shares)	98	44.69	476.64
8		Jessop Company Ltd	94569288			
9		Maruti Udyog Ltd	12,006,278	266.46	108.06	319.92
10	2022-23	Paradeep Phosphates Ltd	4,334,038		0.22	
11	1991-92	Videsh Sanchar Nigam Ltd. 15	284,950,495	63.02	598.40	1795.76
12		Modern Food Industries Ltd		149.07	0.00	
		Total Loss			**27590.08**	**26719.37**

Air India and Bharat Aluminium Co. Ltd. did not pay any dividend in 2022-23

Selling National Assets

Finance Minister, on 23-8-21, launched a 4-year roadmap for getting Rs 6 Lakh Cr from selling following national assets through Asset Monetization Plan:
Roads and highways – Rs. 160,200 Cr,

Railway station redevelopment, private trains, tracks, goods sheds, dedicated freight corridor, 15 Railway stadiums – Rs. 1,52,496 Cr,
Power Transmission towers and transmission lines – Rs. 45,200 Cr,
Power Generation – Rs. 39832 Cr,
Telecom towers, etc. – Rs. 35100 Cr,
Warehousing – Rs. 28,900 Cr,
Mining including 160 projects in coal mining, 761 Mineral mining blocks – Rs. 28,747 Cr,
Natural Gas Pipeline – Rs. 24462 Cr,
Product Pipeline – Rs. 22504 Cr,
Aviation with 25 airports – Rs. 20,782 Cr,
Urban Real Estate including redevelopment of colonies & hospitality assets – Rs. 15000 Cr,
Ports with 31 projects in 9 major ports – Rs. 12,828 Cr,
Stadiums with 2 national stadiums – Rs. 11,450 Cr.
(Ref: - FM unveils Rs 6 Lakh Cr national asset monetization plan – TOI dated 24-8-21)

Selling telecom assets –

Power Transmission Towers - BSNL and MTNL jointly owned 69047 mobile towers. National Monetization Pipeline had valued 13567 mobile tower assets of BSNL and 1350 of MTNL at Rs. 8800 Cr for monetization by FY24. At the rate of Rs. 8800 Cr for 14917 mobile towers, **asset value of 69047 towers comes to Rs. 40733 Cr. Why Rs. 35100 Cr only is indicated to be received**?

Optic Fibre Cables - Total approved cost of Bharat-net project was Rs. 61109 Cr, including Rs. 42068 Cr for Bharat-net (phases -1 and 2) and a maximum of Rs. 19041 Cr on viability gap funding for implementation of the PPP model of Bharat-Net in 16 states. As on 31.03.2021, the govt had utilized Rs. 24,201 Cr for the project.
*According to NMP, 525706 km of optical fibre had been laid under Bharat-Net project, for connecting all villages in India with a high-speed broadband network. Earlier, the scope of the project was limited to 2.5 Lakh gram panchayats, which was extended to village level.
*Of this 5,25,706 km of optical fibre, Niti Aayog has valued over 2.86 lakh kms of optical fibre assets at Rs. 26300 Cr. (Ref: - NITI Aayog expects Rs. 35100 Cr from telecom assets by FY24 – Economic Times dated 23-8-21)
*At the rate of Rs. 26300 Cr for 2.86 lakh kms, **Niti estimated cost** of 5.25706 lakh kms of optical fibre **comes to Rs. 48343 Cr only against project cost of Rs. 61109 Cr. Only Rs. 35100 Cr is proposed to be received** through monetization of 69047 **towers of Rs, 40733 Cr and** 525706 kms of **optical fibre of Rs. 61109 Cr.** Is it not **handing over public assets to private sector at throw away cost**?

Asset Monetization of Highway Projects

During past 5 years, NHAI had monetized 1614 kms of operational national highway projects for Rs. 26366 Cr. for 20 years concession period under Toll, Operate and Transfer model. Purchaser was allowed to collect toll as notified by the government. (TOI dated 30-10-23)
*NHAI, up to 15-12-23 (in 2023-24), had auctioned out 4 bundles of completed highway projects to raise around Rs. 16000 Cr under monetization drive. Cube Highways had quoted Rs. 7707 Cr (15% more than estimated price) for 1 project and IRB Infrastructure quoted Rs. 1683 Cr. (about 1% more than estimated price). This implied in the remaining cases, the offers were less than estimated price. (TOI dated 15-12-23)

It is unclear whether **Minimum Auction prize** was fixed considering (1) actual building cost and interest for the construction period or (2) building cost in 2023 and interest on this cost for the standard construction period, whichever is higher with compensation for lost toll income.

*India's road network benefited greatly from the **National Highway Development Program** which envisaged an investment of about Rs. 2,36,247 Cr during the period 2005–12. It is not clear why government proposes to sell roads and highways for just Rs. 160200 Cr, when only a part of road network costed Rs. 236247 Cr. (12.15.78).

Handing over oil exploration and production rights to private sector

In a move that will turn ONGC into lame duck, the Oil ministry drew up plans to carve up the country's largest explorer into smaller entities, sell stakes in its major producing and upcoming fields to private companies and privatize smaller discoveries.

*It identified Ratna-R and **Pana-Mukta** offshore fields as well as Gandhar on-land in Gujarat for inducting private partners. In the eastern offshore, the $5 Billion KGDWN-98/2 gas project, slated to be the crown jewel, Deendayal west block, acquired from GSPC for $ 995 million in 2017 and Ashok Nagar on-land discovery near Kolkata were flagged for inducting global majors as partners. (Oil Min plans to carve up ONGC - TOI dated 26-4-21)

*This was an attempt to enable private companies pick up part of the profits of ONGC, which did not need external funding from these operations.

*Vedanta was the top benefactor of government push to boost domestic oil exploration, scooping up 62 of the 220 blocks put up for sale across the country between 2018 and 2022.

Government got its fingers burnt by giving oil exploration to private companies –

(i) It got into case against Cairn Energy involving dispute of $ 1.23 billion plus interest and $22.38 million toward arbitration and legal costs. (Cairn Energy moves to settle $ 1 billion tax dispute with India Explained: Issues in the Cairn Energy-govt dispute | Explained News, The Indian Express

(ii) It got into case against Reliance Industries Ltd and BG Exploration & Production India Ltd in a cost recovery dispute of $ 111 million in Panna-Mukta and Tapti oil and gas fields. They wanted to raise the limit of cost that could be recovered from the sale of oil and gas before profits are shared with the government. (Indian Express dt 14.6.22)

(iii) Vedanta recovered, government disputed cost of Rs. 9545 Cr. (about $ 1.2 billion) incurred by it in its Rajasthan Oil and Gas fields before splitting profit in a pre-determined ratio with the government. (Vedanta wins arbitration against government in Rs. 9.5k Cr. case – TOI dated 28.08.23)

*What are the charges per Ton incurred by ONGC and Oil India on these heads? Why norms were not fixed while signing the contracts?

*In spite of disputes like these cases, why government wants to hive off projects from ONGC and give them to private companies?

Relaxation in Environment Regulations to Private Oil Exploration Company - In March 2019, Cairn asked approval to start exploration in Rajasthan blocks without conducting public hearings pleading the exploration projects were only short term and temporary. The government exempted oil exploration from conducting public hearings in 2020 and Cairn got exemptions for 6 blocks in Rajasthan and Cairn went on to recover more cost than allowed by contract later.

Privatization of Airports –

The National Monetization Pipeline envisaged privatization of 25 airports with estimated monetization value of Rs. 20782 Cr over FY 22-25. Airports Authority of India approved the privatization of 13 more airports by early 2022 (6 major airports – Varanasi, Amritsar, Bhubaneswar, Raipur, Indore and Trichy and 7 smaller ones Kushinagar, Gaya, Kangra, Tirupati, Aurangabad, Jabalpur and Hubli. (Privatization of 13 more airports Ayed – TOI dated 10-9-21)

Airports given under the control of private sector

Government decided to modernize the non-metro airports through the Airports Authority of India and the **city side development at these airports** through Public Private Partnership.

*The modernization of airport terminal buildings is nothing but building shopping complexes or malls, which house large number of shops and restaurants, where common man hesitates to purchase even water or coffee because of their high cost. These buildings just accommodate check in counters and security check, but earn profit by selling these shops, by assuring foot fall of air travelers. While AAI handles the technical part of the airport by constructing runways and air traffic control including landing and take-off requirements, these private companies only handle real estate business.

* International Airport is operated by Cochin International Airport Ltd., an entity founded in 1994 with Government of Kerala, Bharat Petroleum, Air India, financial institutions, NRIs, airport service providers and around 18,000 shareholders from more than 25 countries.

*Delhi International Airport Ltd., a consortium of GMR Group (64%), AAI (26%) and Fraport AG (10%), was given operation and development contract for Delhi airport in 2006. It oversaw the construction of Delhi International Airport's terminal and runway buildings. DIAL opened integrated passenger terminal T3 with capacity to handle 37 million passengers/ annum in June 2010.

*Hyderabad International Airport Ltd., a consortium of GMR Group (63%), Government of India (13%), Government of Telangana (13%) and Malaysia Airports Holding Bhd. (11%), was given the contract to develop and operate Hyderabad Rajiv Gandhi International Airport of capacity 40 million passengers in December 2004 on BOOT basis. The airport was inaugurated in March 2008.

*Kazi Nazrul Islam International Airport, Durgapur built by Bengal Aerotropolis Projects Ltd. (32.2%), IL&FS Airports Ltd. (12.7%) WB Industrial Development Corp. (1.2%) and other private companies (53.9%)] started operation from May 2015.

*Bangalore International Airport Ltd., a consortium of GVK Group India (43%), Siemens Project Ventures GmbH (26%), Flughafen Zurich AG Ltd. (5%), AAI (13%) and Karnataka State Industrial Investment & Development Corp. Ltd (13%) built the Kempe Gowda International Airport, Bangalore. It became operational in May 2008.

*In 2006, Mumbai International Airport Pvt Ltd., a joint venture of consortium of GVK Group India, Airports Company South Africa, and Bidvest (74%) and Airports Authority of India (26%), was awarded the contract for refurbishment of domestic terminals 1A & 1B, the international terminals 2B & 2C, opening new terminals 1C and 2, commissioning of new taxiways, aprons, reconstruction of the runway intersection, main runway 09/27 and the secondary runway 14/32 and a new ATC tower.

Operation of airports by Adani group –

Adani Airports had entered the airport business in 2019, bagging a project to modernize and operate the six airports of Lucknow, Ahmedabad, Thiruvananthapuram, Mangaluru, Jaipur and Guwahati.

*Because of his perceived closeness to Narendra Modi, critics say, the government eased bidding rules to help Adani Group bag those airport projects despite the group's glaring lack of aviation credentials. The case was still being heard by the Supreme Court.

*Adani took controls of Mumbai airport, India's second busiest airport, built by GVK group, from July 2021.

*This new business of Adani group has become the top airport platform in the country in a very short time. Adani tweaks his airport playbook, sets in motion next big plan - The Economic Times (indiatimes.com) (11-6-21)

Resistance of government arms to privatization of Nagpur Airport -

MIHAN India Ltd., a joint venture of Maharashtra Airport Development Co. and Airports Authority of India, awarded the contract for upgradation and operation of Nagpur Airport to GMR in March 2019.
*Earlier, GMR had offered a 5.76% share on revenue, which was later increased to 14.49%. MIL, however, cancelled the allotment as MAL already got a higher revenue by running the airport on its own, as against what was offered by GMR. Even **Union ministry of Aviation** in 2019 had questioned the need for privatization, if the revenue offered by GMR was so low. **Govt of Maharashtra** decided to cancel the tender process in March 2020 and MIL issued a letter annulling the bid process.
*Bombay High Court quashed the communication of MIL and Supreme Court upheld Bombay High Court order placing faith on latter without going into the case. (After court verdict, GMR plans city airport takeover – TOI dated 21-8-21)

Privatization of Port operations

Ennore port was the first corporate port under which most of the port services were outsourced and the port discharged only certain statutory and regulatory functions.
*EPL is functioning on a Landlord Management Model. All the cargo handling facilities are being developed (on berths constructed by Ministry of Shipping / public sector) mainly through the private sector on BOT basis.
*The common facilities such as creation of necessary depths in the harbor and in the channel by dredging, aids to navigation, road / rail connectivity, etc. are funded and developed by EPL. Thus, main functions of building the infrastructure were undertaken by Port Trust, and only operation, loading and unloading are done by private sector.

Debt helped Adani group to build and buy projects

Adani group's total debt increased from Rs 2,27,248 crore in March 2023 to Rs 2,58,276 crore in Sept 2024. The exposure of domestic banks and financial institutions rose to Rs 1,07,985 crore by Sept 2024, up from Rs 70,213 crore in March 2024. Public sector bank exposure grew from Rs 31,609 crore to Rs 47,435 crore in Sep 2024.

The group's total assets reached Rs 5.5 lakh crore in H1FY25,

In March 2023, Total debt was Rs 227248 Cr, debt to global institutions was Rs. 63629.44 (28%), capital market borrowing was Rs. 84309 Cr (37.1%) and debt to domestic bank was Rs. 70446.88 Cr (31%)

In Sep 2024, Total debt was Rs 258276 Cr, debt to global institutions was Rs. 69734.52 (27%), capital market borrowing was Rs. 74900.04 Cr (29%) and debt to domestic bank was Rs. 107985 Cr (42%).

Adani group used this fund mostly to acquire existing companies, which did not help to increase country's total installed capacities in various sectors, as explained in Chapters 2, 10, 15 and 17, but only helped Adani group to increase its market control (nearing monopoly) to increase profit to the company.

Whether Adani got any preferential treatment in allotment of loans by domestic banks or concessional rate of interest, in view of his relations with governing party, needs to be investigated

Privatization of State Level Public Enterprises –

Auto Division of Allwyn Ltd. was hived off and handed over to Mahindra and Mahindra Ltd. and the Refrigerator Division was privatized with the sale of its assets to Voltas in 1994.

Gujarat State Finance Commission recommended privatization of Gujarat Insecticides Ltd., Gujarat State Seeds Corporation, Gujarat State Handicrafts Corporation, Gujarat Maritime Board, Gujarat Agro Industries Corporation, Gujarat Industrial Development Corporation, Gujarat Small Industries Development Corporation, etc. (9.5.41)

*Two large public enterprises Haryana Concast Ltd. and Haryana Breweries were privatized in Haryana. (9.5.42). The Charge Chrome Division of Orissa Mining Corporation was sold to Tata Iron and Steel Co. in 1991. Badamba Cooperative Sugar Mills and Bargarh Cooperative were handed over to Shakti Sugar Management Corporation of Tamil Nadu and Ponni Sugar Management Industry respectively on management contracts in 1991. The East Coast Breweries was leased to United Breweries in 1993.

*Privatizations were completed in Punjab (3 units), Rajasthan (2 units privatized and 2 units closed down), Tamil Nadu (4 units under restructuring), U.P. (15 sugar mills, 1 electronics unit and several textile mills were listed for sale), West Bengal (13 electronic units partly/wholly privatized and 3 units listed for outright sale), Assam (5 units listed for privatization and Ashok Paper Mills leased out to Sanghi Industries).

*Karnataka Telecom Ltd., Karnataka State Electronics Development Corp. Ltd., Kerala Minerals and Metals Ltd., Trivandrum Rubber Works Ltd., Scooters Kerala Ltd., Kerala State Salicylates and Chemicals Ltd., etc. State Industrial Corporation of Maharashtra (SICOM), Maharashtra Tourism Development Corporation, etc. were listed for privatization by respected state governments. (9.5.43 / 44)

Failure of Disinvestment in LIC

Within 1 year of listing, about 6.87 lakh retail stockholders exited from LIC till 17.05.2023. After IPO in May 2022, the market capitalization value of LIC fell to 3.86 Lakh Cr on 16.11.2023 and then recovered to Rs. 5.6 Lakh Cr to become tenth most valued company in India on 16.01.2024. (TOI dated 17.01.2024) One year of IPO - Will LIC revive investors' confidence? - The Hindu BusinessLine
Government holds 96.5% in LIC.

Only Annual Budgets are made by Modi Government instead of Long-Term Budgets / 5 Year Plans

Example – In the 2023-24 budget, Rs. 3502136 Cr was for revenue expenditure and Rs. 1000961 Cr only for capital expenditure (investment) out of total budget of Rs. 4503097 Cr.

Major capital expenditures planned were Rs. 258606 Cr for Road Transport and Highways, Rs. 240000 Cr for Railways, Rs. 162600 Cr for Defence services, Rs. 61692 Cr for Communication, Rs. 35509 Cr for Petroleum and Natural Gas, Rs. 25997 Cr for housing and urban affairs, Rs. 15982 Cr for Atomic Energy, Rs. 11810 Cr. for Police, Rs. 6357 Cr. for Space Research, Rs. 5300 Cr for Health and Family Welfare, etc.

*From this, it is clear that government or Niti Ayog **does not undertake forecasting of demands** for all products like cement, coal, drugs, fertilizers, power generation, transmission, power generation equipment, renewable power equipment, petroleum and petrochemicals, electronic equipment like mobiles, laptop, CCTV, etc., steel, aluminium, copper, zinc, lead, silver, etc., ship building, cargo traffic to be handled by ports, passenger traffic to be handled by airports, etc. and **arrange coordinated investment** by different private sector and public sector companies required for **achieving forecasted production capacities** for all above products.

Mr. Vajpayee made IX and X 5YPs as Chairman of respective Planning Commissions. Mr. Vajpayee, on 21-12-2002, said "Planning has been one of the pillars of our approach to economic development since independence, and has stood us in good stead. There is substantial excess capacity in some sectors of the economy and it should be possible to increase output without a commensurate increase in investment". In X 5YP, Vajpayee said the economy performed better than the target in 5 of the 9 previous plans and explained the reason for shortfall in other plans. (10.2.4)

No co-ordinated planning with States / Union Territories and CPSEs - The Public Sector Plan Outlay during IX 5YP was placed at Rs.8,59,200 Cr at 1996-97 prices (57% by Centre and 43% by States and Union Territories). The Centre's Plan Outlay of Rs.4,89,361 Cr was to be financed to the extent of 44 % and 56 % by way of Gross Budget Support and Internal and Extra Budgetary Resources of the CPSEs respectively. The CPSEs were expected to finance 90 % of their Plan Outlay through IEBR. (9.3.23)

With dropping of 5 Year plans, there is no co-ordination or involvement of States / Union Territories, CPSEs and private sector in long-term development planning.

(Long term) Development planning of States and Union Territories drastically reduced

National Development Council, which approved and reviewed 5YPs, was chaired by PM and included Union Ministers and CMs of all States. All the 5 Year plans were made in consultation with States, included projects in States and were executed with the contribution of States and Union Territories.

Five Year Plan	Contribution of Central Govt in Rs. Cr	Contribution of State & Union Territories in Rs. Cr.	Contribution of Corporate Sector in Rs. Cr.	Contribution of Household Sector in Rs. Cr	Reference
III - Actual	4412	4165			4.4.7
IV - Planned	8871	7031	1950	7030	4.3.12 / 4.4.34
V - Planned	20404	18899	27048		5.5.6 / 5.4.41
VI - Planned	33750	50250	19582	55128	6.4. Annex, 6.3.11/31
VII - Planned	69752 / 95534 (A)	84466 / 89466 (A)	168148		7.3.22/23/26 / 8.Preface.10
VIII - Actual	460300		938400		9. Table 2-5
IX - Planned	681761	369839	1119000		9. Tab 2.25/3.2
X - Planned	1380490	588325			10.2.47
X - Actual	387477	326748	201951		12. Tab 3.15
XI - Planned	2156571	1488147			11.1.154
XI - Actual	2025130	1725848	887504		12. Table 3.9/16
XII - Planned	4333739	3716385	2683840		12.3.32/35/68

With the dropping of 5 Year planning by Modi government, the States are spending money giving freebies in the form of Power subsidies, free travel on state buses for women, free electricity, farm loan waivers, free laptops, free gas cylinders and financial aid for women, unemployed youth, farmers and labourers, etc - instead of investment in projects to improve productivity and create employment. (Maharashtra – Rs. 96000 Cr, Karnataka – Rs. 53700 Cr, Telangana – Rs. 35200 Cr, Rajasthan – Rs. 30700 Cr, Andhra Pradesh – Rs. 27300 Cr, Madhya Pradesh – 23400 Cr, Odisha – Rs. 16900 Cr, Haryana – Rs. 13700 Cr, Chhattisgarh – Rs. 8300 Cr, Jharkhand – Rs. 5500 Cr, etc). Out of 12 top states with largest state GDP, the capital expenditures of 8 states are less than 2% of GSDP. How states pay an exorbitant price for freebies announced during elections - India Today

Modi government, not only closed Planning Commission, it made all the 12 5YPs unavailable to public by removing https://niti.gov.in/planningcommission.gov.in/docs/plans/planrel/fiveyr/welcome.html so that people cannot get any information about how targets were fixed for increasing capacities and productions, how investments were done to achieve targeted GDP growth, what were the growth in various sectors, etc.

Reduction in compound annual wealth growth (after 2010)

The compound annual wealth growth in India between 2000-2010 was about 14%, which more than halved during the period 2010-2023 (about 7%) (Global Wealth Report 2024 released by Swiss Bank UBS dated 10-7-2024)

Reduction in manufacturing sector growth during 2013-2023

Manufacturing sector growth during 2006-2012 - India was not among the top 10 World's Manufacturing Superpowers before 2006 in terms of value addition in manufacturing sectors in Constant 2015 US Dollars. In 2006, it overtook Mexico with 184.303 Bn, Brazil with 222.448 Bn in 2008, UK with 250.41 Bn in 2011, France (and UK) with 260.768 Bn in 2011 and Italy with 269.978 Bn in 2012.

Unable to improve rank from 2012 - 2023
South Korea was above India with 368.089 Bn in 2012 at fifth position. India's value addition in manufacturing sector grew to 295.63 Bn, 317.312 Bn, 360.076 Bn, 385.190 Bn, 406.778 Bn, 401.068 Bn, 417.024 Bn, 423.797 Bn, 443.9 Bn during the period 2013 – 2021 and 455.77 Bn in 2023.
South Korea maintained its fifth rank with 428.454 Bn in 2020 and 461.1 Bn in 2021.
https://m.youtube.com/watch?v=HGbdPmdW-6A&pp=ygUqbGFyZ2VzdCBtYW51ZmFjdHVyaW5nIGNvdW50cnkgaW4gdGhlIHdvcmxk

India attained fifth position in 2023 when total manufacturing value added became $455.77 Bn and that of South Korea dropped to $416.39 Bn as per www.insidermonkey.com report 'Top 25 manufacturing countries in the world' dated 10-7-2024. https://finance.yahoo.com/news/top-manufacturing-country-world-2024-231816018.html

The share of value addition by manufacturing sector in 2023-24 was 15.9% compared to 16.7% of GDP (in constant price) in 2013-14 as per Indian Express Editorial dated 30-09-2024. India became fifth highest economy in the world with GDP of $ 2940 Bn in 2019 helped by higher growth in Service and Software sector only.

It can be concluded that manufacturing sector growth was less during the period 2013-2020 compared to 2006-2012.

Inability to achieve self sufficiency - India not only became a net importer of special (finished) steels due to giving up long term planning, it had to meet 57% of edible oil requirements through import of 16.5 Mts in 2022-23. Press Release:Press Information Bureau

The actual production of oil seeds in 2006-07 and 2011-12 (fourth advance estimate) were 24 and 30 Mts and projected demand for 2016-17 and 2020-21 were 59 and 71 Mts. (12.12.49 – Table 12.9)

The production of oil seeds in 2013-14 was 32.7 Mts (domestic availability of edible oil 10.19 Mts). It decreased to 31.3 Mts in 2016-17 against forecasted demand of 59 Mts and increased to 35.9 Mts in 2020-21 against projected demand of 71 Mts. The domestic availability of edible oil in 2020-21 was 11.15 Mt, which was 45.3% of consumption (just about 1 Mt increase in production from 2013-14 against projected increase in demand of about 38 Mt over 7 years).

Edible Oil Scenario | Welcome to Department of Food and Public Distribution

Deterioration in financial performance of some big private sector companies from 2017

Many big companies, which were operating profitably, became sick and faced insolvency proceedings.

Before Feb 2018, Insolvency proceedings were initiated against 40 companies with a total debt of Rs. 4 Lakh Cr.

After Feb 2018, Insolvency and Bankruptcy Code proceedings were enforced on about 75 companies in Power, Sugar, Infrastructure, Steel and Telecom sectors as they had defaulted on repaying loans totalling Rs. 2.24 Lakh Cr.   Table – 17.13

Name of Company	Start of Insolvency Proceedings	Default debt in Rs. Cr.	Taken over by	Acquired at Rs. Cr.
King Fisher Airlines	2012	9000	Case pending due to escape of Vijay Mallya to UK in 2016	
Rotomac	2012	3695	Liquidated in March 2018	
Zenith Computers	March 2017	92	Liquidated in May 2018	
Era Infra Engineering	April 2017	22200	SA Infrastructure Consultants Pvt Ltd	525
Lohia Machines Ltd	June 2017	500	Liquidated in March 2018	
Bhushan Steel	July 2017	44478	Tata Steel	35200
Monnet Ispat & Energy Ltd	July 2017	11478	JSW Steel – AION Investments Pvt Ltd	2875
Jyoti Structure	July 2017	7011	Group of High-Net-Worth Individuals led by Sharad Sanghi	3965
Alok Industries	July 2017	29500	Reliance Industries – JM Financial Asset Reconstruction Co	5052
Lanco Infratech	July 2017	44364	Liquidated in August 2018	
Bhushan Power & Steel Ltd	July 2017	47000	JSW Steel	19350
Amtek Auto Ltd	July 2017	12300	Deccan Value Investors LP	2700
Essar Steel	August 2017	54000	Arcelor Mittal Nippon Steel India Ltd	42000
Jaypee Infratech Ltd	August 2017	22000	Suraksha Group	2500 Acres + 2634 Cr
ABG Shipyard	August 2017	22842	Welspun Corp	659
Moser Baer	Nov 2017	4400	Liquidated in Sept 2018	
Electro Steel	2017	11000	Vedanta Ltd	5320
Jaiprakash Associates Ltd	2017	52074	National Asset Reconstruction Co Ltd has offered Rs 12000 Cr	
Reid & Taylor India	April 2018	9000	Liquidated in December 2018	
Reliance Communications	May 2018	47251	UV Asset Reconstruction Co. Ltd.	455.9
Videocon Group	June 2018	64838	Buyer could not be found till December 2022	
Sterling Biotech	June 2018	8100	Perfect Day	638
Reliance Home Finance Ltd	May 2019	11540	Authum Investments	3351
Jet Airways	June 2019	7800	Liquidated in November 2024	
Reliance Infratel	Sept 2019	41055	Reliance Project & Property Management Services Ltd	3720
Reliance Commercial Finance	Oct 2019	9000	Authum Investment & Infrastructure Ltd	1629
Dewan Housing Finance Ltd	Nov 2019	90000	Piramal Group	34250
Reliance Capital	Nov 2019	40000	IndusInd International Holdings Ltd (Hinduja group)	9861
Go Air	May 2023			
Infrastructure Leasing & Financial Services (Govt. Company)		61000	As of September 2024, IL&FS had resolved a debt of Rs. 55000 Cr	

Table – 17.14 - Rise in Insolvency Cases – TOI dated 18-8-21

	Mar 19	June 19	Sep 19	Dec 19	Mar 20	Jun 20	Sep 20	Dec 20	Mar 21
No of active cases for over 180 days	548	666	859	882	1232	1633	1791	1550	1425
No of Total active cases	1142	1281	1507	1960	2161	2121	1947	1722	1717

Days on average from insolvency commencement date to Adjudicating Authority approval of plan = 459 instead of intended 180 days

PLI Schemes –

Modi government promoted Production Linked Incentive schemes for encouraging investment by private sector for various sectors like Food Processing, telecommunication, automobile (electric vehicles) Industries, etc. However, these schemes are **not targeting to increase production capacity**, but give incentive based on threshold sales, with thresholds increasing according to investment. Incentives are given only if threshold sales are exceeded and paid only on the increased sales above threshold sales.

Example - PLI Scheme for food processing sector - Government of India passed PLI Scheme for food processing sector on 9-4-21, with budgeted incentive outlay of Rs 10900 Cr over a period of 6 years starting from FY 21-22.

*Minimum threshold investment to qualify for the scheme ranged from Rs 23 Cr to 100 Cr, with threshold sale ranging from Rs. 150 Cr to Rs. 500 Cr. Once eligible, incentive will be granted in the range of 4 to 10% depending upon the approved sub sectors.
*Suppose, if a company invests Rs 100 Cr in additional machinery to expand its operations. Incremental sales will be difference between the eligible sales for the year of incentive claim and the threshold sales for the base year 2019-20. If suppose the sales in FY 2019-20 was Rs 500 Cr, FY21-22 was 550 Cr, FY 22-23 was 605, FY 23-24 was 665.5, FY 24-25 was 732.05, FY 25-26 was 805.26, and FY 26-27 was 885.79 Cr, the company will be eligible for total incentive of Rs 100.68 Cr over 6 years.

Ineffectiveness of PLI Scheme – This scheme does not forecast demand for processed food at the end of 6 years, additional capacity to be created over the existing production capacity to meet the demand and give incentive proportional to additional production made above the existing / threshold production (except schemes like Storage Batteries).
*Sales value depends on cost of raw material, cost of production, demand - supply gap, etc. and not just on production volume. So, the incremental sales do not depend only on increase in production volume.

PLI Scheme for Storage Batteries –

Union Cabinet on 12.05.2021 approved a PLI Scheme for setting up manufacturing facilities for Advance Chemistry Cell, Battery Storage in India, with a total manufacturing capacity of 50 Giga Watt Hour (GWh) for 5 years. The production-linked subsidy is based on applicable subsidy per kWh and percentage of value addition achieved on actual sale for manufacturers who set up production units with a capacity of at least 5 GWh up to a maximum of 20GWh. Against Request for Proposal dated 22.10.2021, 10 domestic/international manufacturers submitted their proposal for about 130 GWh as per technical bids opened on 15.01.2022.

PLI Scheme for Special Steels –

Government has approved inclusion of 'Specialty Steel' under the Production Linked Incentive (PLI) Scheme with a 5-year financial outlay of Rs. 6322 Cr. to promote the manufacturing of 'Specialty Steel' within the country by attracting capital investment.

Ineffectiveness of PLI Schemes - The World's second biggest crude steel producer India became a net importer of alloy in 2023-24. Finished steel imports from China hit a 7 year high, while overall finished steel imports hit a 6 year high of 3.7 Mts. This means target was not set for 2021-22 (XIII 5YP) and 2026-27 (XIV 5YP) through 5 year plans and target was not achieved for finished steel. This is entirely due to dropping of long-term planning for installed capacity and production.

Steelmakers seek higher tariffs amid Chinese supply surge – The Hindu dated 27-9-2024

PLI Scheme (for drones) is not permanent subsidy –

Minister Piyush Goyal said that purpose of PLI is (only) to kick start, it is not a permanent subsidy and hence industry shouldn't become dependent on it. (Economic Times ePaper dated 5-07-2024).
*It is not clear how long benefits can be claimed from other PLI Schemes also.

Uniform Wealth Distribution Desired

The desired uniform wealth distribution may, therefore be, obtained by
i) Stopping further disinvestments and strategic sales
ii) Stopping selling of national assets under National Asset Monetization Plan and taking back assets already given under this plan
ii) Going in for another wave of nationalization of private sector giants, which have significant hold on economy, (nationalization of banks in 1969 and insurance businesses in 1972 was successful) and
iii) by government investing in these companies to get equity up to 49%, with existing corporates holding on to management control of these companies.
*With present government not investing for starting new public sector companies and almost all infrastructure having been developed already or being developed by private sector companies presently,
{As per Indian Express dated 18.5.2019, government's project investment announcements reduced from Rs. 11.62 Tn in 2015 to Rs. 3.3 Tn in 2019 and total investment announcements, including those of private sector, reduced from Rs. 20.86 Tn in 2015 to Rs. 9.76 Tn in 2019 – with average government announcements for 5 years being Rs. 7.756 Tn and the average private sector investment announcements for the same period was Rs. 7.954 Tn},
government should invest about 20% of GDP

{as was done in five-year plans in the past –
Example 1 - The growth of 5.3% per annum in the period (1985-86 to 1991-92) was supported by an investment rate of 23.1 % of GDP. (8.3.2.1)
Example 2 - A planned investment of Rs. 798000 Cr. during VIII 5YP implied an investment rate of 23.2 % of GDP. The investment rates in the Sixth and the Seventh Plans were 21.1 % and 22.7 % respectively. (8,3.2.8)
The public investment in VIII plan was 8.3% of GDP, total investment was 25% of GDP. (9. Table 2-3)
Example 3 - The rate of investment in the economy during IX Plan was 24.2% of GDP at market prices. Public investment accounted for nearly 29.5% of total investment, the balance 70.5% being accounted for by private investment. (10.2.7)
The average investment required in Tenth Plan was 28.4% of GDP (10.2.30)}

to purchase equities in big private sector companies, (for example government can make an open offer for acquisition of shares of HZL as Sterlite made in April 2002), so the government can get dividends.
Thus, private sector profit will get distributed among the public and wealth addition to the rich also will get reduced correspondingly.